Prentice Hall

The Reader's Journey

STUDENT EDITION

GRADE SIX

PEARSON

Boston, Massachusetts • Glenview, Illinois • Parsippany, New Jersey • Shoreview, Minnesota • Upper Saddle River, New Jersey

Acknowledgments appear on page 533, which constitutes an extension of this copyright page.

Cover Design: Judith Krimski, Judith Krimski Design, Inc.

PEARSON

978-0-13-363597-3
0-13-363597-X
1 2 3 4 5 6 7 8 9 10   13 12 11 10 09

Program Advisory Board

The following educators helped shape the program from the very beginning. As classroom practitioners and advocates of a novel-based approach to the teaching of the language arts, they helped to conceptualize the program, lending their advice to the student Work Text, the Teacher's Guide, and the Anchor Book library alike.

Linda Banas
Department of Learning
and Instruction at SUNY Buffalo
Buffalo, NY

Diane Boni
Director of Language Arts
Greece Central School District
Rochester, New York

Heidi Driscoll
English Language Arts
Curriculum Supervisor, 7-12
Taunton Public Schools
Taunton, Massachusetts

Laurie Herriges
Language Arts Instructor
Morgan Butler Middle School
Waukesha, Wisconsin

Sharon Hiller, Ph.D.
Director of Curriculum and
Educational Services
Richmond Community Schools
Richmond, Michigan

Darlene Groves Musso
English Department Chairperson
Broward County School District
Plantation, Florida

Deborah Nevill
Language Arts Instructor
Granite Valley Middle School
Monson, Massachusetts

Helen Shiffer
English Department chairperson
Carmel School District
Carmel, Indiana

Ginny White
Language Arts Instructor
Fernandina Beach Middle School
Fernandina Beach, Florida

Teacher Reviewers

The program reviewers provided ongoing input throughout the development of *The Reader's Journey*. Their valuable insights ensure that the perspectives of the teachers throughout the country are represented within this language arts series.

Ella Briand
Humanities Coordinator
Syracuse City Schools
Syracuse, New York

Julia Delahunty
English Department Head
Township Public Schools
Edison, New Jersey

Sharon Hoff
Language Arts Instructor
Grand Terrace School District
Grand Terrace, California

Marilyn Kline
Language Arts Instructor
Bradenton School District
Bradenton, Florida

Kathleen Orapollo, Ph.D.
National Educational Consultant
Zephyrhills, Florida

Elizabeth Primas, Ph.D.
Director of Literacy
District of Columbia Public Schools
Washington, D.C.

Ellin Rossberg
Language Arts Instructor
Bronx School District
Bronx, New York

Helen Turner
Language Arts Instructor
Pleasant Hill School District
Pleasant Hill, California

Charles Youngs
Language Arts Curriculum Facilitator
Bethel Park High School
Bethel Park, Pennsylvania

Welcome to a New Journey

Setting the Destination

Have you and your friends ever been eager to go somewhere but you couldn't agree on where? If you are going on a journey, you have to know your destination. *The Reader's Journey* provides a new destination for each of its six units. It comes in the form of a Big Question for you to answer as you travel through the unit.

At the beginning of the unit you and your classmates will share what you know. Some questions seem easy to answer from the start. But once you travel through the unit you will see that there is so much to think and talk about.

Along the way—Everything you read and do in your journey through the unit will help you think more deeply into the question. Be prepared for lots of critical thinking.

At the end of the unit you will reflect back on the Big Question. Will your thoughts change from beginning to end? You'll see.

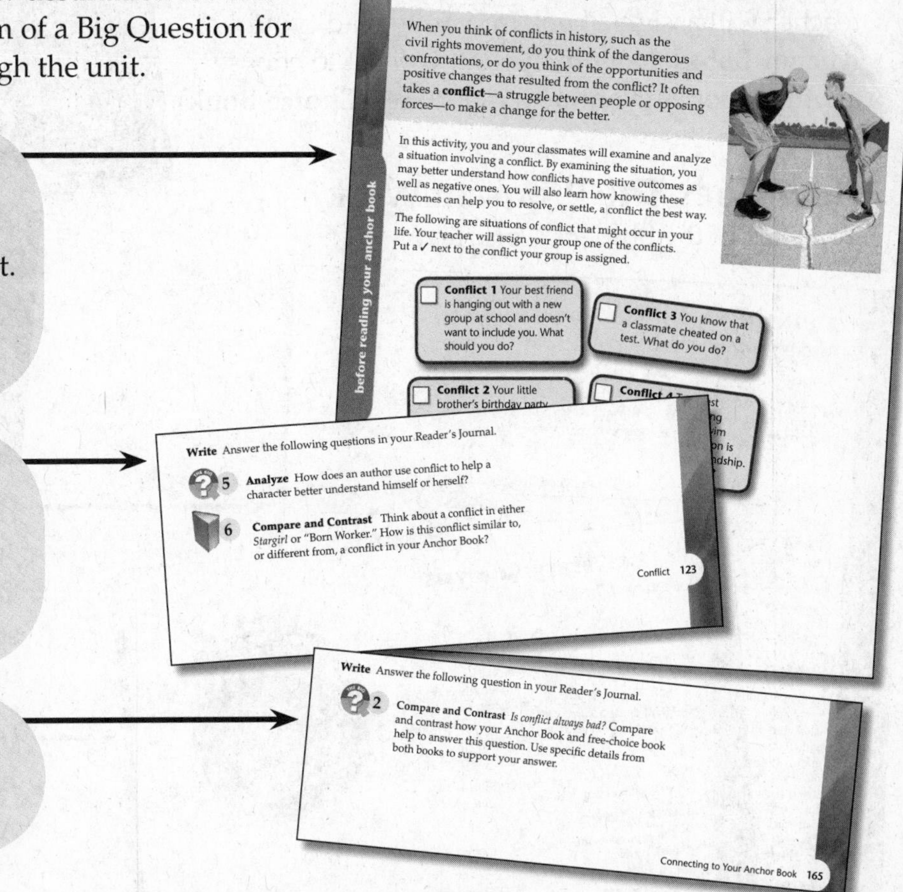

THE BIG ?

2-1 Understanding the Big Question
Is Conflict Always Bad?

When you think of conflicts in history, such as the civil rights movement, do you think of the dangerous confrontations, or do you think of the opportunities and positive changes that resulted from the conflict? It often takes a **conflict**—a struggle between people or opposing forces—to make a change for the better.

In this activity, you and your classmates will examine and analyze a situation involving a conflict. By examining the situation, you may better understand how conflicts have positive outcomes as well as negative ones. You will also learn how knowing these outcomes can help you to resolve, or settle, a conflict the best way.

The following are situations of conflict that might occur in your life. Your teacher will assign your group one of the conflicts. Put a ✓ next to the conflict your group is assigned.

☐ **Conflict 1** Your best friend is hanging out with a new group at school and doesn't want to include you. What should you do?

☐ **Conflict 3** You know that a classmate cheated on a test. What do you do?

☐ **Conflict 2** Your little brother's birthday party

☐ **Conflict 4**

before reading your anchor book

Write Answer the following questions in your Reader's Journal.

5 **Analyze** How does an author use conflict to help a character better understand himself or herself?

6 **Compare and Contrast** Think about a conflict in either *Stargirl* or "Born Worker." How is this conflict similar to, or different from, a conflict in your Anchor Book?

Conflict 123

Write Answer the following question in your Reader's Journal.

2 **Compare and Contrast** *Is conflict always bad?* Compare and contrast how your Anchor Book and free-choice book help to answer this question. Use specific details from both books to support your answer.

Connecting to Your Anchor Book 165

Here are the Big Questions you are about to explore.

UNIT 1 How do we decide what is TRUE?
UNIT 2 Is CONFLICT always bad?
UNIT 3 What is important to KNOW?
UNIT 4 Do we need words to COMMUNICATE?
UNIT 5 How do we decide WHO we are?
UNIT 6 How much should our COMMUNITIES shape us?

Enjoy the journey!

A Novel Way to Learn!

Learning Through Reading Books

This program is like no other you have studied from. You will get to read lots of interesting books of all sorts, from novels to nonfiction. In each unit, your teacher will assign a book for you to read (your **Anchor Book**). Later in the unit you get to choose another book on your own (your **Free-Choice Book**).

How Does The Program Work?

You start in the Student Work Text.

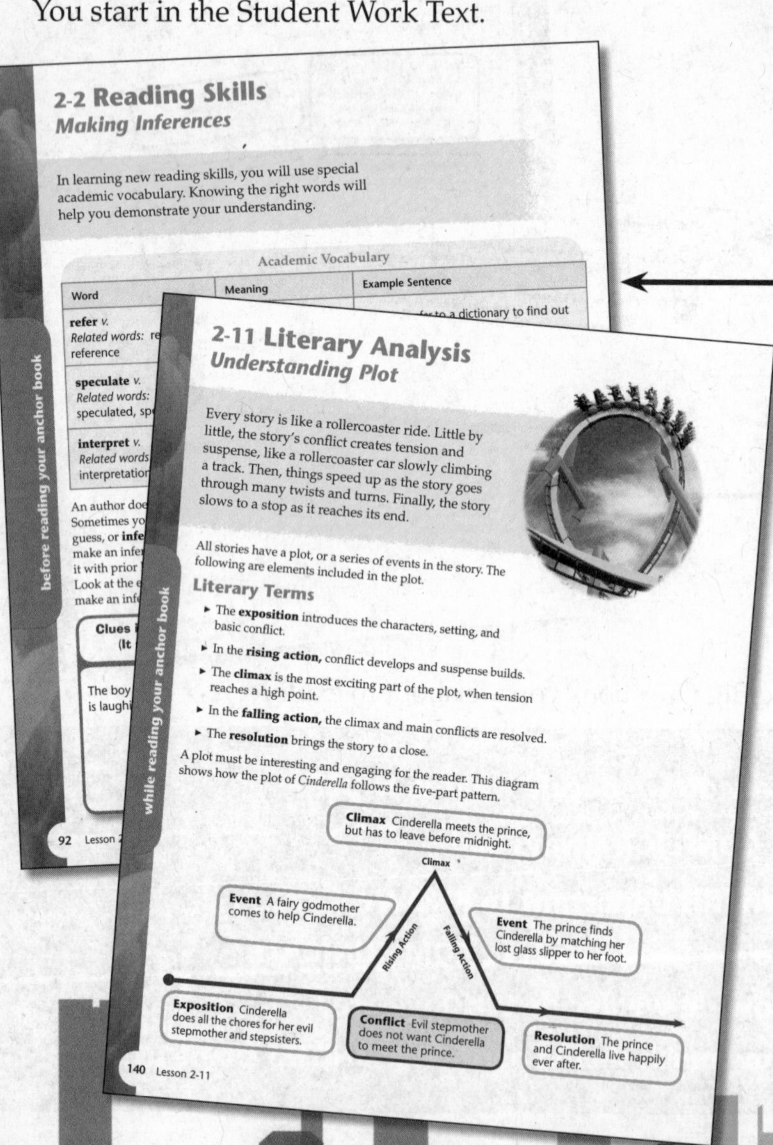

2-2 Reading Skills
Making Inferences

In learning new reading skills, you will use special academic vocabulary. Knowing the right words will help you demonstrate your understanding.

Academic Vocabulary

Word	Meaning	Example Sentence
refer *v.* *Related words:* re... reference		...fer to a dictionary to find out
speculate *v.* *Related words:* speculated, sp...		
interpret *v.* *Related words:* interpretation...		

An author doe... Sometimes yo... guess, or **infe**... make an infer... it with prior... Look at the e... make an infe...

Clues (It...

The boy... is laughi...

before reading your anchor book

92 Lesson 2...

2-11 Literary Analysis
Understanding Plot

Every story is like a rollercoaster ride. Little by little, the story's conflict creates tension and suspense, like a rollercoaster car slowly climbing a track. Then, things speed up as the story goes through many twists and turns. Finally, the story slows to a stop as it reaches its end.

All stories have a plot, or a series of events in the story. The following are elements included in the plot.

Literary Terms

- The **exposition** introduces the characters, setting, and basic conflict.
- In the **rising action,** conflict develops and suspense builds.
- The **climax** is the most exciting part of the plot, when tension reaches a high point.
- In the **falling action,** the climax and main conflicts are resolved.
- The **resolution** brings the story to a close.

A plot must be interesting and engaging for the reader. This diagram shows how the plot of *Cinderella* follows the five-part pattern.

Climax Cinderella meets the prince, but has to leave before midnight.
Climax
Event A fairy godmother comes to help Cinderella.
Event The prince finds Cinderella by matching her lost glass slipper to her foot.
Rising Action
Falling Action
Exposition Cinderella does all the chores for her evil stepmother and stepsisters.
Conflict Evil stepmother does not want Cinderella to meet the prince.
Resolution The prince and Cinderella live happily ever after.

while reading your anchor book

140 Lesson 2-11

Before Reading Your Anchor Book

You will learn reading strategies and how to set up your **Reader's Journal**.

While Reading Your Anchor Book

Along the way you will learn lots of other skills that will help you too.

From time to time you will get to talk about your Anchor Book and your ideas in special **Literature Circles**.

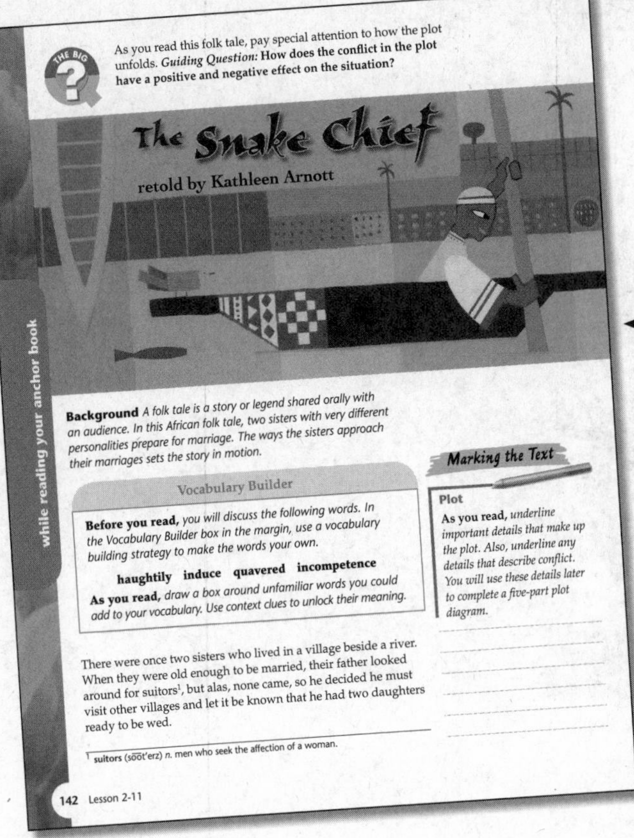
THE BIG ? As you read this folk tale, pay special attention to how the plot unfolds. *Guiding Question:* **How does the conflict in the plot have a positive and negative effect on the situation?**

The Snake Chief

retold by Kathleen Arnott

while reading your anchor book

Background *A folk tale is a story or legend shared orally with an audience. In this African folk tale, two sisters with very different personalities prepare for marriage. The ways the sisters approach their marriages sets the story in motion.*

Vocabulary Builder

Before you read, *you will discuss the following words. In the Vocabulary Builder box in the margin, use a vocabulary building strategy to make the words your own.*

haughtily induce quavered incompetence

As you read, *draw a box around unfamiliar words you could add to your vocabulary. Use context clues to unlock their meaning.*

Marking the Text

Plot

As you read, *underline important details that make up the plot. Also, underline any details that describe conflict. You will use these details later to complete a five-part plot diagram.*

There were once two sisters who lived in a village beside a river. When they were old enough to be married, their father looked around for suitors[1], but alas, none came, so he decided he must visit other villages and let it be known that he had two daughters ready to be wed.

[1] **suitors** (sōōt'ərz) *n.* men who seek the affection of a woman.

142 Lesson 2-11

Learn to Mark Texts Too!

Here is what is really cool about this Work Text. It's *yours*. You will get to interact with the text by marking passages while you read—underlining important phrases, marking vocabulary words, and making notes in the margins.

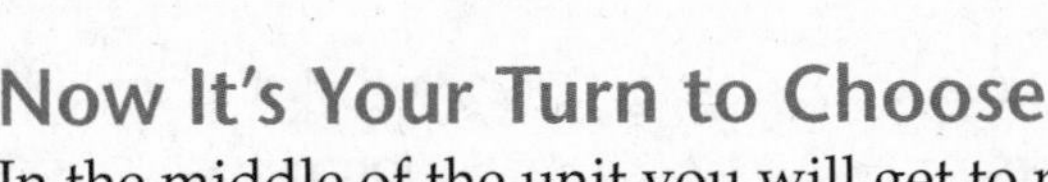

Now It's Your Turn to Choose

In the middle of the unit you will get to pick a Free-Choice Book. How does it compare to your Anchor Book?

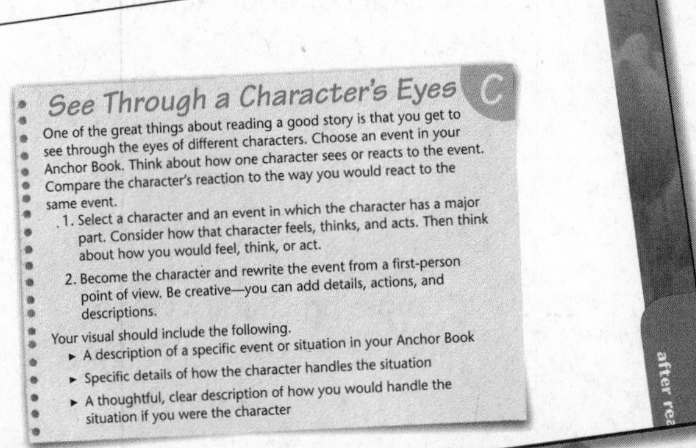
See Through a Character's Eyes C

One of the great things about reading a good story is that you get to see through the eyes of different characters. Choose an event in your Anchor Book. Think about how one character sees or reacts to the event. Compare the character's reaction to the way you would react to the same event.

1. Select a character and an event in which the character has a major part. Consider how that character feels, thinks, and acts. Then think about how you would feel, think, or act.
2. Become the character and rewrite the event from a first-person point of view. Be creative—you can add details, actions, and descriptions.

Your visual should include the following.

- A description of a specific event or situation in your Anchor Book
- Specific details of how the character handles the situation
- A thoughtful, clear description of how you would handle the situation if you were the character

after rea

After Reading Your Anchor Book

You will get to do some fun projects based on your Anchor Book. Which project you choose is up to you.

So are you ready for The Reader's Journey?

Unit 1 How do we decide what is *true*?

Genre Focus: Fiction and Nonfiction

Unit Book Choices

With this unit you will read a book (your Anchor Book) as you learn unit skills. Here are six books that complement the unit well.

- Going Home
- Behind the Blue and Gray
- Edgar Allan
- Racing the Past
- Jim Thorpe: Original All-American
- Leon's Story

Free-Choice Book

Enrich and extend your learning with a free-choice book.

Before Reading Your Anchor Book

While Reading Your Anchor Book

After Reading Your Anchor Book

Unit 2

Is *conflict* always bad?

Genre Focus: The Novel

Unit Book Choices

With this unit you will read a book (your Anchor Book) as you learn unit skills. Here are six books that complement the unit well.

- Miracle's Boys
- Tangerine
- Bearstone
- Redwall
- Maniac Magee
- The Clay Marble

Free-Choice Book

Enrich and extend your learning with a free-choice book.

Before Reading Your Anchor Book

While Reading Your Anchor Book

After Reading Your Anchor Book

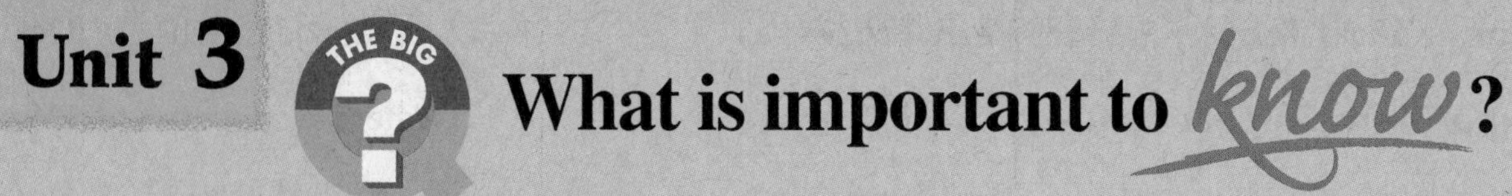

Unit 3 What is important to know?

Genre Focus: Nonfiction

Unit Book Choices

With this unit you will read a book (your Anchor Book) as you learn unit skills. Here are six books that complement the unit well.

- Amistad: The Story of a Slave Ship
- The Tarantula in My Purse: And 172 Other Wild Pets
- A Strong Right Arm
- You Want Women to Vote, Lizzie Stanton
- Thura's Diary: My Life in Wartime Iraq
- Under the Royal Palms

Free-Choice Book

Enrich and extend your learning with a free-choice book.

Before Reading Your Anchor Book

While Reading Your Anchor Book

Unit 4

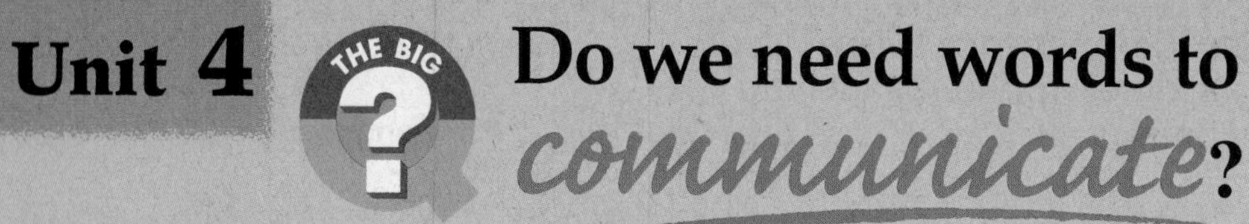

Do we need words to communicate?

Genre Focus: Poetry and Prose

Unit Book Choices

With this unit you will read a book (your Anchor Book) as you learn unit skills. Here are six books that complement the unit well.

- Number the Stars
- The Westing Game
- Fearless Fernie: Hanging Out with Fernie and Me
- The Liberation of Gabriel King
- Cheaper by the Dozen
- The Hero's Trail: A Guide for a Heroic Life

Free-Choice Book

Enrich and extend your learning with a free-choice book.

Before Reading Your Anchor Book

While Reading Your Anchor Book

Unit 5 How do we decide *who* we are?

Genre Focus: Drama

Unit Book Choices

With this unit you will read a book (your Anchor Book) as you learn unit skills. Here are six books that complement the unit well.

- Pushing Up the Sky
- Escape to Freedom
- Mother Hicks
- The Mousetrap and Other Plays
- Play to Win
- I Never Saw Another Butterfly

Free-Choice Book

Enrich and extend your learning with a free-choice book.

Before Reading Your Anchor Book

While Reading Your Anchor Book

After Reading Your Anchor Book

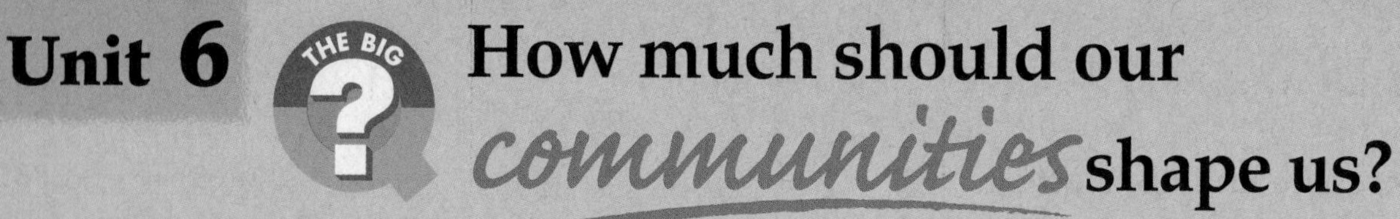

Unit 6 How much should our communities shape us?

Genre Focus: The Research Process

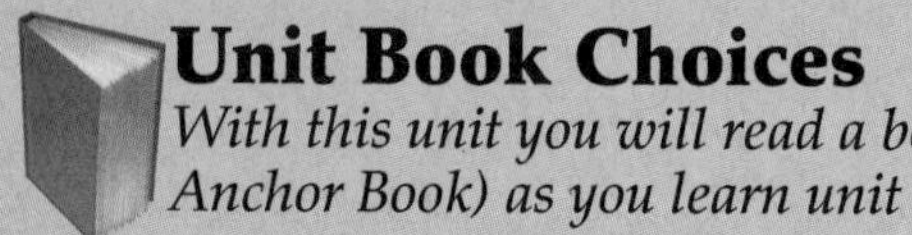

Unit Book Choices

With this unit you will read a book (your Anchor Book) as you learn unit skills. Here are six books that complement the unit well.

- Hiroshima
- Spies
- Myths and Monsters
- The Story of Muhammad Ali
- The Emperor's Silent Army
- Paths to Peace

Free-Choice Book

Enrich and extend your learning with a free-choice book.

Before Reading Your Anchor Book

While Reading Your Anchor Book

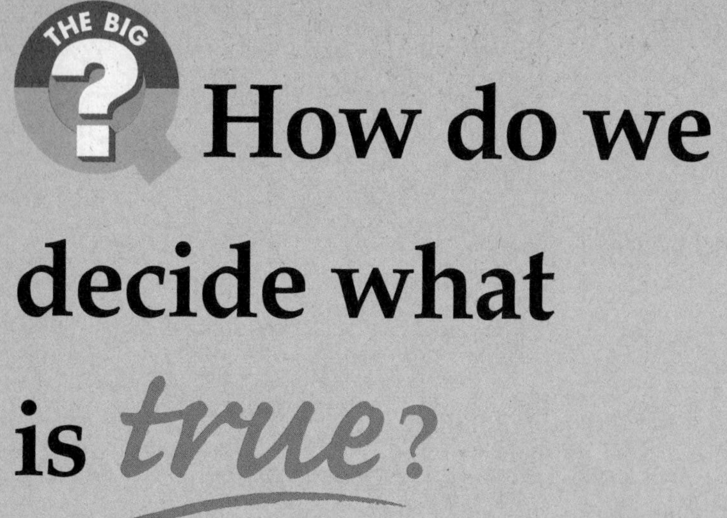

How do we decide what is *true*?

Unit 1 Genre focus:
Fiction and Nonfiction

Unit Book Choices
With this unit you will read one book as an Anchor Book. There are many good books that would work well with this unit. The following pages offer six suggestions.

Free-Choice Reading
Later in this unit you will be given an opportunity to choose another book to read. This is called your Free-Choice Book.

You might read...

A Racing the Past
B Going Home
C Jim Thorpe: Original All-American
D Leon's Story
E BEHIND THE BLUE AND GRAY
F Edgar Allan

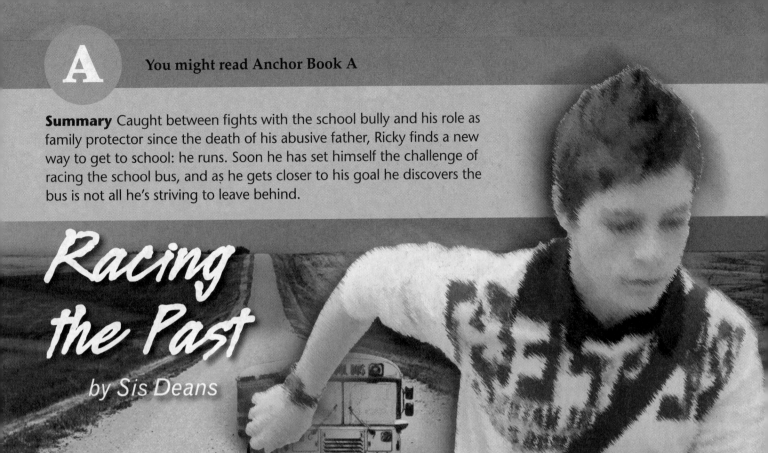

A You might read Anchor Book A

Summary Caught between fights with the school bully and his role as family protector since the death of his abusive father, Ricky finds a new way to get to school: he runs. Soon he has set himself the challenge of racing the school bus, and as he gets closer to his goal he discovers the bus is not all he's striving to leave behind.

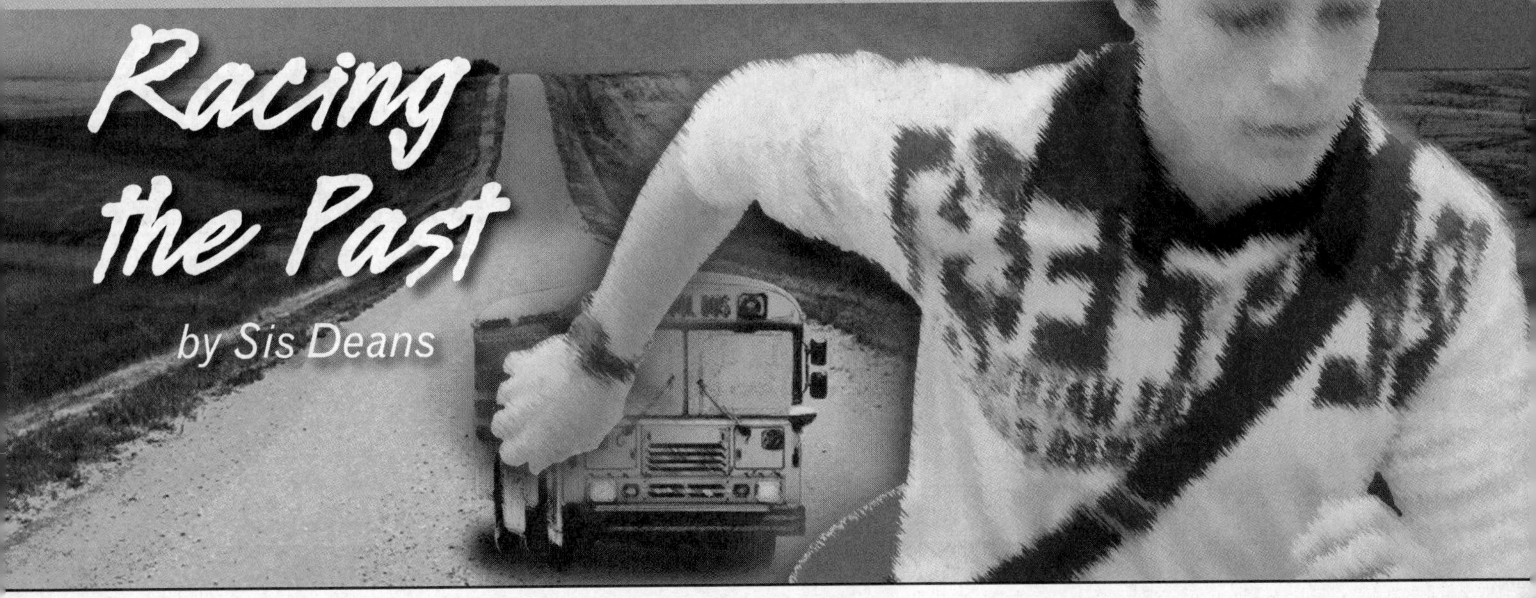

Racing the Past

by Sis Deans

B You might read Anchor Book B

Summary When eleven-year-old Felita visits her relatives in Puerto Rico one summer, she feels like an outsider. Her uncle's village is boring, and the other kids resent her as a "Nuyorican." But as the summer wears on, her New York background and Puerto Rican heritage begin to integrate into an emerging new identity.

Going Home

by Nicholasa Mohr

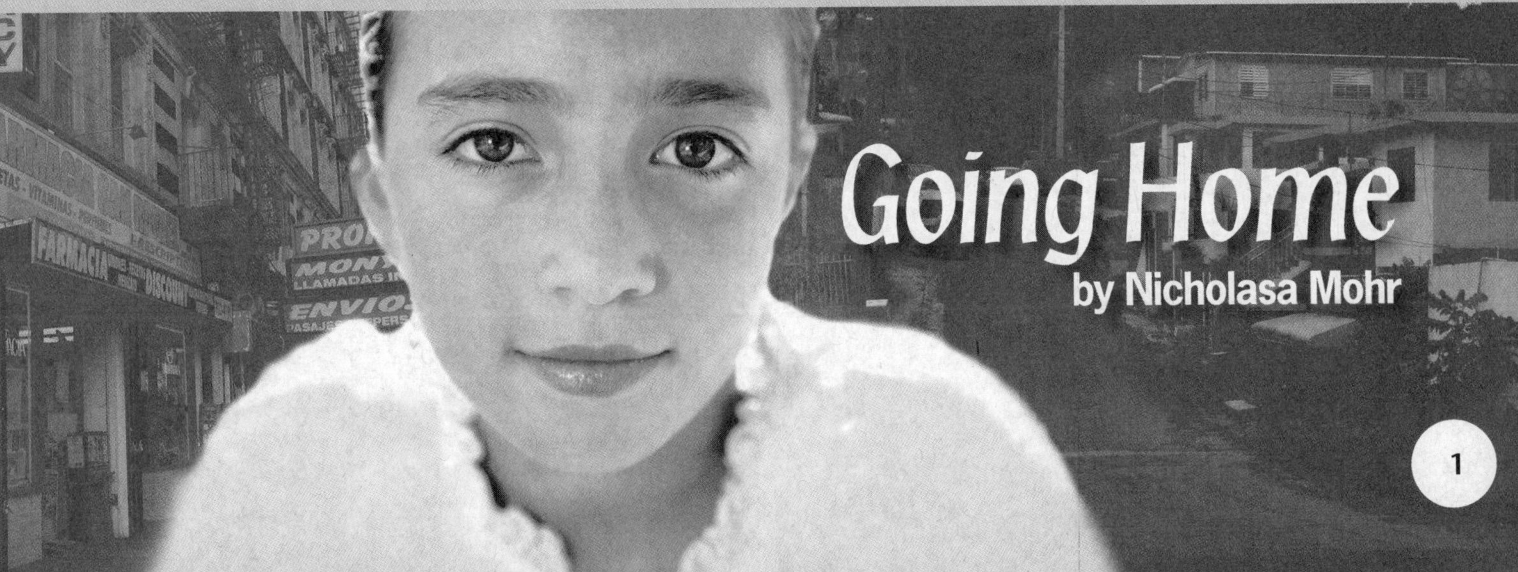

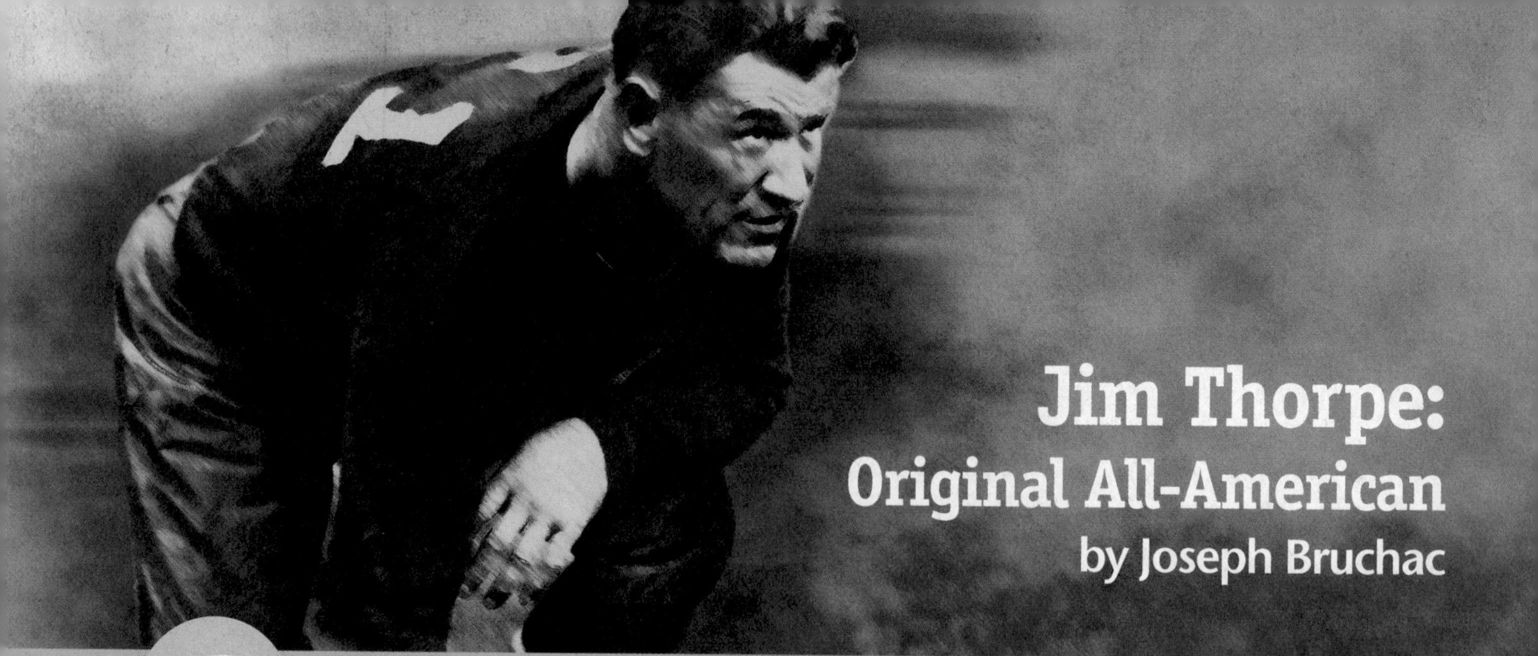

Jim Thorpe: Original All-American

by Joseph Bruchac

C You might read Anchor Book C

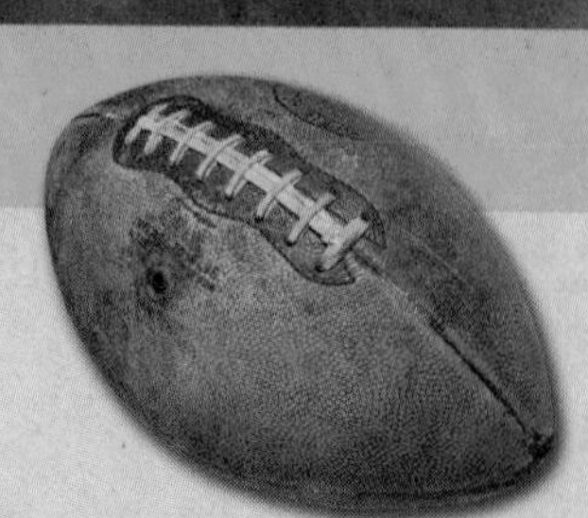

Summary One of the best days in Jim Thorpe's life was when he drove a ball straight through the middle of the goal during a football game between a little, unknown Native American team and Harvard. He won the game for his team and went on to become one of the greatest athletes that ever lived.

D You might read Anchor Book D

Summary For Leon, growing up in North Carolina in the 1940s is tough. His father is a sharecropper, and getting an education is hard: he has to walk miles to get to school while the white kids ride in a bus. Then he witnesses the murder of his father by a group of drunken teenagers, and the kids aren't brought to justice.

Leon's Story

by Leon Walter Tillage

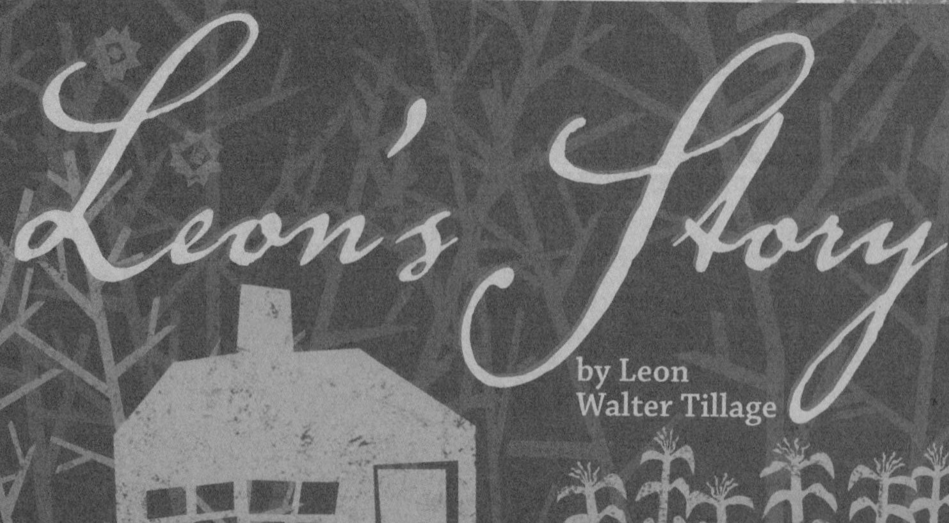

E

You might read Anchor Book E

Summary Civil War soldiers came from all walks of life—there were Native American volunteers, an all-black regiment from the North, and German, Irish, and other foreign-born fighters. But all—whether Union blue or Confederate gray—endured battle, disease, prison, and even boredom during the long war between the North and the South.

BEHIND THE BLUE AND GRAY: THE SOLDIER'S LIFE IN THE CIVIL WAR

BY DELIA RAY

F

You might read Anchor Book F

Summary When twelve-year-old Michael Ficketts gets a new foster brother, he's not too fazed. He's already got two sisters and another brother, and anyway, he thinks little Edgar Allan—or "E. A."—is kind of cute. But when the Ficketts decide to adopt E. A., they aren't prepared for the racism they encounter from their neighbors.

Edgar Allan

by John Neufeld

1-1 Understanding the Big Question

How do we decide what is true?

You've heard the word *truth* many times, but what does it really mean? What exactly makes something true? In this unit, you will learn terms and techniques to help you decide what is true and what is not.

Do you think it is easy to tell what is true and what isn't? In the following activity, you will test your classmates to see if they know what is true about you.

On the following lines below, write three statements about your achievements, past experiences, or family. Write two statements that are true and one that is made up. Be sure your made-up statement sounds convincing and as true as possible. Your group members will have to decide which statement is false!

As you write your statements, think of the following.

- **Avoid** writing overly specific or obvious statements, such as "My favorite color is purple," "I have two eyes," or "I don't like winter."
- **Try** writing statements that require your group members to think about how realistic the statement seems, such as "I once swallowed a bee," "I have never seen the ocean," or "My ancestors came over on the *Mayflower*."

Statement 1:

Statement 2:

Statement 3:

Directions Read your statements to your group members. Then ask your group members which statements they think are true and which one is false. Discuss the answers with your group.

1 Choose three true statements that either you or your group members wrote. On the lines below, describe how each statement could be proven. Consider the following sources that could provide the necessary information.

- **Historical document**
- **Photograph**
- **Personal letter**
- **Report card**
- **Newspaper article**
- **Birth certificate**
- **Magazine**
- **Certificate of award**

Statement 1: ______________________________

____

Statement 2: ______________________________

____

Statement 3: ______________________________

____

2 Discuss your made-up statements. Which statement was the most believable? Explain why it was believable. Which statement was the least believable? Explain why it was not very believable.

____

____

____

3 Based on what you learned in this activity, work with your group to write a definition of the word *true* without using a dictionary. Then share your group's definition with the class.

____

____

____

As you read your Anchor Book and other literary texts, think about how you can decide if something is true or not.

You will start reading your Anchor Book soon. The next few pages in this book give you some background information plus a reading skill.

Introduction to Fiction and Nonfiction

It isn't always easy to tell whether a story is real or imaginary. If a story is about purple people with six arms living in outer space, you *know* it's not real. But what if the story is about a person walking on the moon? Then, it can be hard to tell.

People have been telling stories long before they were able to put them on paper. These stories were passed from one generation to the next, both to entertain and to share cultural beliefs and traditions. In some cases, the stories were fictional, or made up. In other cases, the stories were nonfiction—descriptions of events that actually happened.

The diagram compares some characteristics of fiction and nonfiction.

	FICTION	NONFICTION
What it is	stories or writings that are made up	accounts of real people, places, and events
Characteristics	realistic or fantasy; can include real people, places, and events	factual; may contain the actual words of a person or historical document
Types of Fiction / Types of Nonfiction	folk tales, myths, realistic fiction, historical fiction, science fiction	manuals, biographies, historical accounts, speeches, letters, journals, reference books
Examples of Texts	short story, novella, novel, drama	newspapers, magazines, encyclopedias, original documents, textbooks

Often, it can be hard to distinguish a **fictional** story from an account of a real event. Many types of fiction contain characters that seem real. The setting might be a place that is real. The story might be based on a real event. Although the characters and their dialogue are made up, the story may include, or be based on, real people.

Nonfiction, however, tells about real people, places, and events. Nonfiction includes facts, ideas, and opinions, but it doesn't include anything that has been made up. The facts in a piece of nonfiction can be verified, or proven to be true.

As you read, you can ask questions to help you identify whether you're reading fiction or nonfiction.

- *Is the text about a real person? Is it a biography?*
- *Is there something on the cover of the book or in the title that makes me think the story is real or made up?*
- *What has happened so far in the story?*
- *Does the text give real dates and places that an event took place?*

Directions Read the passage below. Underline the parts that could be made up and circle the parts that could be true.

> Finally, after weeks of begging his dad to take him, on July 4, 1965, Jason was sitting in the NASA viewing room watching the spacecraft Mariner 4 perform the first successful flyby of the planet Mars. The spacecraft had cameras on board programmed to send photos back to Earth—the first photos anyone had *ever* seen of the Red Planet.
>
> Jason watched the scientists nervously staring at the screen. They all hoped to see some form of life on Mars. But were they surprised when the images started to appear—a frozen world covered in a purple and pink haze with hundreds of people—double-headed purple people—walking around!

Now decide: Is the passage fiction or nonfiction? Why do you think so?

before reading your anchor book

1-2 Reading Skills
Making Predictions

In learning new reading skills, you will use special academic vocabulary. Knowing the right words will help you demonstrate your understanding.

Academic Vocabulary

Word	Meaning	Example Sentence
verify *v.* *Related words:* verified, verification, verifiable	to confirm	She can *verify* her prediction by reading the rest of the book.
revise *v.* *Related words:* revised, revision	to change something based on new ideas and information	I will *revise* my story after you comment on it.
assist *v.* *Related words:* assisted, assistant, assistance	to give help or support	Everything you've ever learned will *assist* you in the future.

When you **make predictions**, you make logical guesses about what will happen next in a text. First, look for clues in the text, title, headings, and images. Then think about what you already know about the topic. Finally, use this information to **assist** you in guessing, or predicting, what will happen next.

As you read, **verify** your predictions by checking them against what happens in the text. **Revise** your predictions if they are not accurate.

You can use a diagram like this one to help you make predictions.

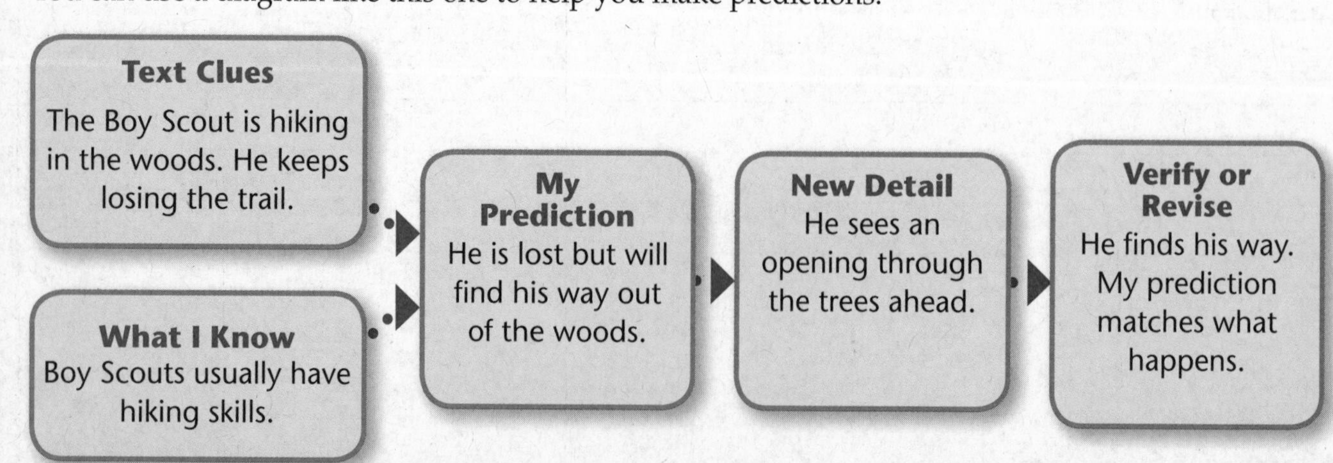
Text Clues
The Boy Scout is hiking in the woods. He keeps losing the trail.
What I Know
Boy Scouts usually have hiking skills.
My Prediction
He is lost but will find his way out of the woods.
New Detail
He sees an opening through the trees ahead.
Verify or Revise
He finds his way. My prediction matches what happens.

before reading your anchor book

Directions Read the first paragraph of the selection. Then fill in the *What I Know* and *My Prediction* boxes in the diagram below. Read on to see whether or not your prediction was correct. Finally, complete the *Verify or Revise Prediction* box.

Won't Know Till I Get There

by Walter Dean Myers

TO WHOM IT MAY CONCERN: Last year we studied what our English teacher called "personal" writing. Mainly they were diaries and journals, stuff like that. One of the reasons people write that way, she said, is that the writing helps them bring things together, to see where they fit in life. Right now that seems like a good idea. The English teacher said that I write well, and I know I need to get some things together in my own head, so I figured a journal would be cool.

When I thought I was going into coin collecting in a big way (which I didn't), I bought a little fireproof safe. I can keep the journal in there and keep it locked up. Also, I can write it in my father's den. It's his den, but the three of us share it, really. Whoever is in there first has first rights, and the others don't intrude. Usually we don't use it that much. I guess the four of us will be sharing it now. That's more or less what the journal is about—how come there's four of us now.

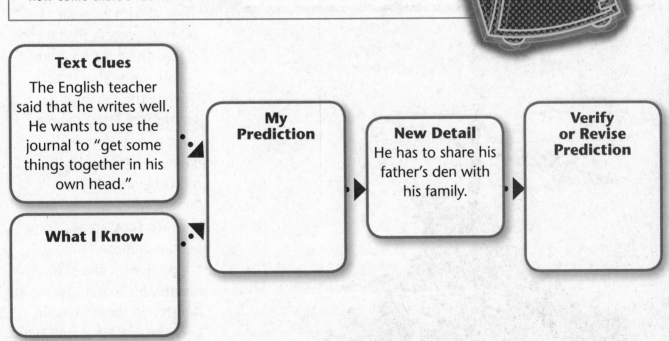

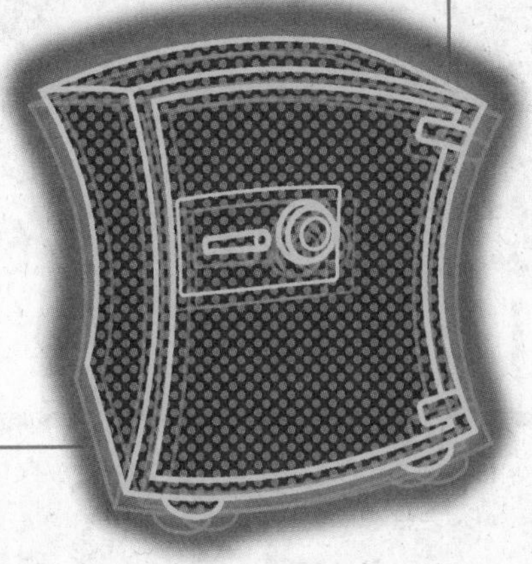

Text Clues
The English teacher said that he writes well. He wants to use the journal to "get some things together in his own head."

What I Know

My Prediction

New Detail
He has to share his father's den with his family.

Verify or Revise Prediction

before reading your anchor book

Before you read the article, look at the title, images, and headings. Make a prediction and write it on a separate sheet of paper. Then, read the article. ***Guiding Question:*** **What do you know to be true about protecting the environment?**

Environmental Issues

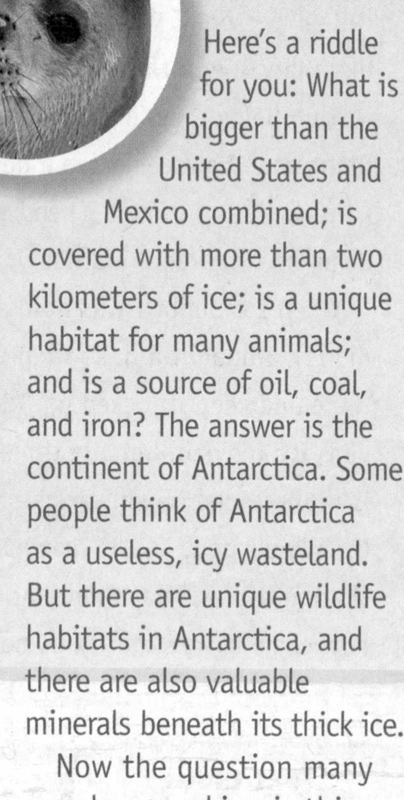

Here's a riddle for you: What is bigger than the United States and Mexico combined; is covered with more than two kilometers of ice; is a unique habitat for many animals; and is a source of oil, coal, and iron? The answer is the continent of Antarctica. Some people think of Antarctica as a useless, icy wasteland. But there are unique wildlife habitats in Antarctica, and there are also valuable minerals beneath its thick ice.

Now the question many people are asking is this: What is the best use of Antarctica? Many people want access to its rich deposits of minerals and oil. Others worry that mining will harm its delicate ecosystems. Some people propose building hotels, parks, and ski resorts. But others feel that Antarctica should remain undeveloped. It is not even clear who should decide Antarctica's fate.

The debate about Antarctica's future is just one environmental issue that people face today. Environmental issues fall into three general categories: resource use, population growth, and pollution. Because these three types of issues are interconnected, they are very difficult to study and solve.

Resource Use

Anything in the environment that is used by people is called a natural resource. Some natural resources are renewable. Renewable resources are always available or they are naturally replaced in a relatively short period of time. Renewable resources include sunlight, wind, fresh water, and trees. Some people think that renewable resources can never be used up, but this is not true for some renewable resources. For example, if people cut down trees faster than they can grow back, the supply of this resource will decrease and could possibly run out completely.

Natural resources that are not replaced for a long time are called nonrenewable resources. As nonrenewable resources such as coal or oil are used, the supply continues to decrease.

Population Growth

The human population in the world has changed dramatically over the last 3,000 years. You can see from the maps on the right that the population grew very slowly until about A.D. 1700. Around that time, improvements in medicine, agriculture, and waste disposal enabled people to live longer. The human population has been growing faster and faster since then.

When a population grows, the demand for resources also grows. Water shortages sometimes happen in areas with fast-growing populations. The water supplies in such areas were designed to serve fewer people than they now do, so shortages sometimes occur during unusually warm or dry weather.

Pollution

The contamination of Earth's land, water, or air is called pollution. Pollution can be caused by a variety of factors, including chemicals, wastes, noise, heat, and light.

Pollution can be related to resource use. The burning of gasoline releases pollutants into the air. With more cars on the road today, more gasoline is used and more pollutants are released into the air. Pollution can also be related to population growth. For example, as populations grow and more people need to be fed, more fertilizers and other chemicals may be used to produce that food. As these chemicals run off the land, they can pollute bodies of water.

Making Environmental Decisions

Dealing with environmental issues means making decisions. These decisions can be made at personal, local, national, or global levels. Your decision to walk to your friend's house rather than ride in a car is made at a personal level. A town's decision about how to dispose of its trash is made at

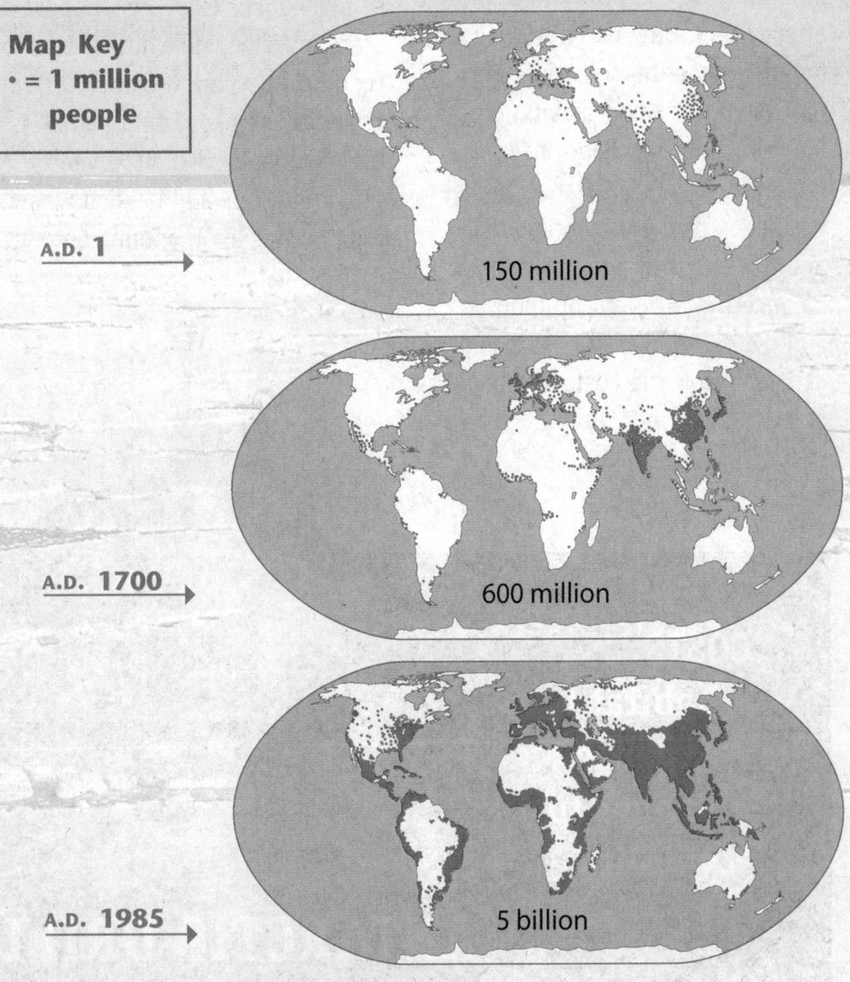

a local level. A decision about whether the United States should allow oil drilling in a wildlife refuge is a decision made on a national level. Decisions about how to protect Earth's atmosphere are made on a global level.

Every decision has some impact on the environment. Your personal decisions of what to eat or how to travel have a small impact. But when the personal decisions of millions of people are combined, they have a huge impact on the environment.

Balancing Needs

Lawmakers work with many groups, such as environmental scientists, to make environmental decisions. Environmental science is the study of natural processes in the environment and how humans can affect them. But the data provided by environmental scientists are only part of the decision-making process. Environmental decision-making requires a delicate balance between the needs of the environment and the needs of people. To help balance the different opinions on an environmental issue, decision-makers weigh the costs and benefits of a proposal very carefully.

Drilling for oil in Antarctica could disrupt wildlife, such as these penguins.

Costs and Benefits

Costs and benefits decisions are often made for economic reasons. For example, will a proposal provide jobs or will it cost too much money? But costs and benefits are not only measured in terms of money. For example, suppose a state must decide whether to allow logging in a park. Removing trees changes the ecosystem, which is an ecological cost. However, by providing jobs and needed wood, logging has an economic benefit.

It is also important to consider the short-term and long-term costs and benefits of an environmental decision. A plan's short-term costs might be outweighed by its long-term benefits.

Weighing the Consequences

Once the potential costs and benefits of a decision have been identified, they are closely analyzed. Consider the costs and benefits of drilling for oil in Antarctica. It would be very expensive to set up a drilling operation in such a cold, distant place. Transporting the oil would also be difficult and costly. An oil spill in the seas around Antarctica could harm the animals that live there.

However, there would be benefits to drilling for oil in Antarctica. Oil drilling would provide a new supply of oil for heat, electricity, and transportation. If the worldwide supply of oil were larger, the price might drop, making oil available to more people. The plan would also create many new jobs. Would the benefits of drilling for oil in Antarctica outweigh the costs? This is the kind of complicated question lawmakers must ask before they make any environmental decision.

ANTARCTIC DRILLING

COSTS
- **habitat loss**
- **expense**
- **danger to wildlife**

BENEFITS
- **jobs**
- **oil for heat, electricity, and transportation**

Thinking About the Selection

Environmental Issues

1 **Verify** Look at the prediction you wrote before you read the article. Was your prediction correct? Use the graphic organizer to help you to verify or revise your prediction.

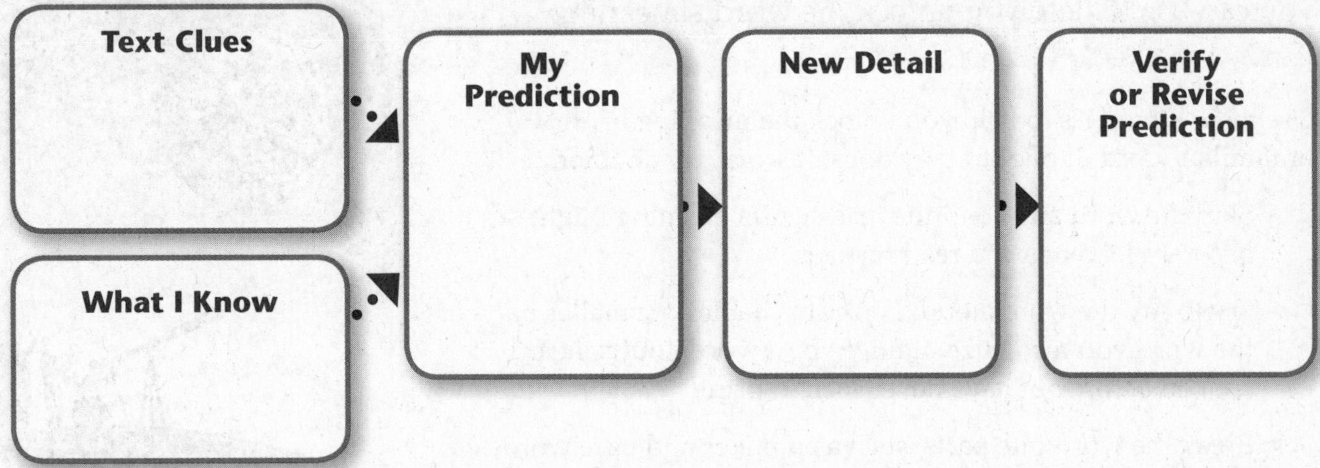

2 **Explain** Was your prediction accurate, or did you have to revise it while reading? Use details from the article to explain your answer.

3 **Predict** Based on what you read, do you think people will find a balance between our need for energy and the planet's needs so that the environment is not threatened? Explain.

Write Answer the following questions in your Reader's Journal.

4 **Respond** What do you know to be true about protecting the environment?

5 **Predict** Look at the title, chapter headings, images, and other text features in your Anchor Book. Make a prediction about what you think will happen. Revise your prediction as you read.

before reading your anchor book

1-3 Vocabulary Building Strategies
Unlocking Word Meanings

If you run into words whose meaning you don't know, don't get discouraged. There are many options, or strategies, you can use to help you unlock the word's meaning.

Use these strategies to help you unlock the meaning of an unfamiliar word. If one strategy doesn't work, try another.

- Skip the word and continue reading. Its meaning might become clearer as you read further.
- Try to say the word aloud. Look at syllables or smaller parts of the word you recognize. It might be a word you've heard spoken before but have never seen in print.
- Break the word into parts, such as prefixes and base words.
- Look for clues—such as other words in the sentence, pictures, or illustrations—that suggest the word's meaning.
- Think about the subject of the text or the situation a character is dealing with. What word or words would make sense when describing that subject or situation?

  His *steed* took off and galloped through the prairie.

  Question: What animal gallops?

  Answer: A horse. A steed must be a horse.

- When all else fails, use a dictionary, thesaurus, or electronic resource to find the meaning of the word.

1 Which of the strategies above do you already use? Give an example of when you used one.

____

____

____

2 Why is it useful to know more than one strategy?

____

____

____

____

before reading your anchor book

Using Prefixes

Prefixes are word parts added to the beginning of a base word. The letters *pre-* in *prefix*, for example, mean "before." Knowing the meaning of some common prefixes can help you unlock the meaning of new words. Using prefixes can also make your writing more precise.

Prefix	Prefix Meaning	Base Word	New Word	Meaning of New Word
dis- *un-*	opposite of	trust tangle	distrust untangle	not able to trust to free from tangles
ex-	from, out	claim	exclaim	to shout out
mis-	wrong	spell	misspell	to spell incorrectly
pre-	before	school	preschool	school before required school
re-	again, back	heat	reheat	to heat again

Directions Revise the underlined part of each sentence using a prefix from the chart.

1 The man gasped in lack of belief.

____

2 Rather than bake a cake, I bought one that was made beforehand.

____

Directions Use what you have learned about prefixes to figure out the meaning of the following words. Locate the prefix and its meaning in the chart. Then, write what you think the word means on the first line. Check your guess by looking up each word in a dictionary or an online resource. Write the definition on the second line.

3 **prevent**

My guess: ______________________________

Definition: ______________________________

4 **misplace**

My guess: ______________________________

Definition: ______________________________

Ready? Start Reading Your Anchor Book *It's time to get started. As you learn from this worktext, your teacher will also give you reading assignments from your Anchor Book.*

1-4 Writing about Your Anchor Book

Reader's Journal

Introduction Throughout the year, you will keep a Reader's Journal for your Anchor Book. You will use your journal for several purposes, such as the following.

- Writing questions you have about what you're reading
- Listing new words you encounter, along with their meanings
- Drawing diagrams or webs to help you understand what you're reading
- Answering questions your teacher assigns

Your teacher may ask you to use a notebook or a computer to create your Reader's Journal. In either case, be sure to set up your page as shown below. If you are keeping your Reader's Journal in a notebook, save four pages at the beginning for a table of contents.

How to Set Up Your Reader's Journal

Name of Anchor Book: **Date:**

Question:

Answer:

Tips for Writing a Strong Response

- Use examples from the book. Include quotations when they support an answer.
- Tell what you think the author means to say, or give your opinion about the information you read.
- Evaluate the information and tell what you believe is true.

Directions Look at the model of the Reader's Journal and use the rubric to evaluate the response.

Student Model

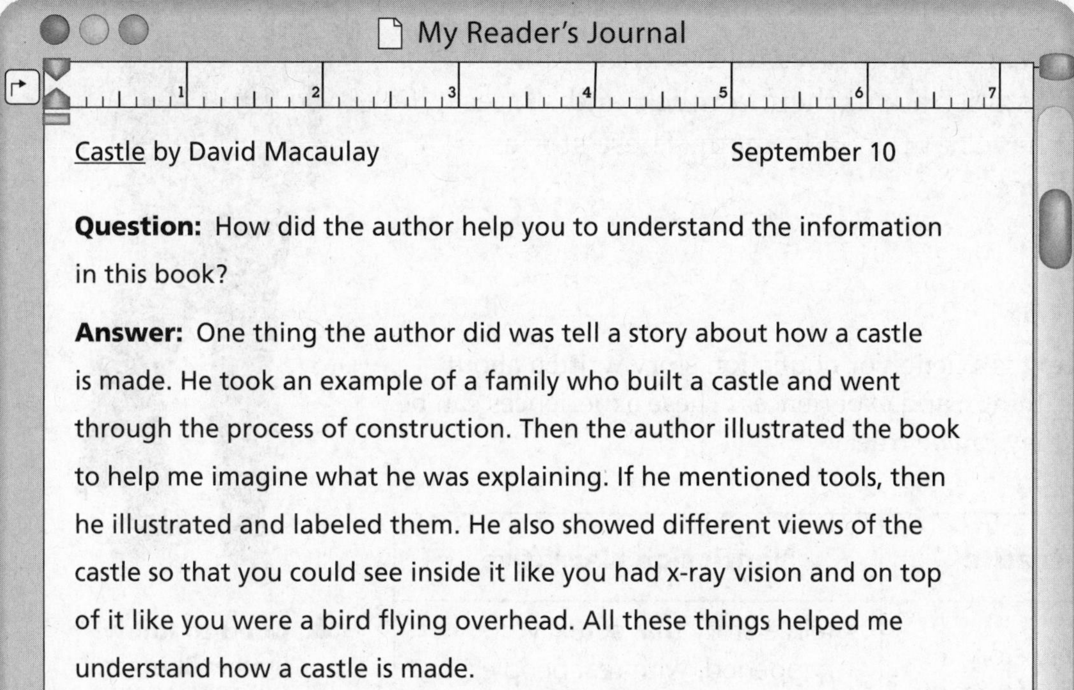

Rubric for Reader's Journal Responses

Your Response . . .	Excellent Job	Nice Work	Okay	Can Do Much Better
shows proof of understanding the information	4	3	2	1
shows evidence of understanding text features in a nonfiction book	4	3	2	1
fully explains ideas and reasoning	4	3	2	1
is written neatly with correct spelling and grammar	4	3	2	1

Evaluate What score would you give the student's Reader's Journal response? Support your answer with details from the response.

____

____

while reading your anchor book

1-5 Literary Analysis
Narrative Texts

For thousands of years, people have told stories—stories about themselves, stories about their families, and stories about things that have happened to them. These stories are called **narratives.**

Literary Terms

- A **narrative text** is a fiction or nonfiction story written about people, places, things, and experiences. These experiences can be imaginary, or they can be true.

Fiction Narrative	Nonfiction Narrative
• tells an imaginary story, often with made-up people, places, things, and events	• tells a story that actually happened, with real people, places, things, and events • contains true facts and ideas
• an author's purpose for writing is to entertain	• an author's purpose for writing can be to entertain, to inform, to persuade, to share thoughts and experiences, or to explain
Fiction and Nonfiction Narrative	
• tell about interesting or notable events • are generally told in chronological order—from beginning to end • can feature cause and effect, where one event leads to the next • include **characters**—people or animals the story is about; **plot**—the series of events in a story; **setting**—the time and place an event takes place; and **conflict**—the story's central problem	

▲ **Good to Know!** Brother Blue, the official storyteller of Boston and Cambridge, Massachusetts, uses the streets as his stage and the public as his audience.

Directions Ask your teacher for a few examples of brief narrative texts. With a partner, choose one and read it together. List specific details from the text. Use the chart above as a checklist to help you determine whether the details are elements of fiction or nonfiction writing. Share your list with the class and explain why the narrative is fiction or nonfiction.

There are different kinds of narrative texts. Here are some examples.

Folk tales are fiction stories that were told from one generation to the next. They entertain, reflect cultural values and beliefs, and pass on universal themes or messages about life.

Historical fiction is a type of made-up story that includes real settings, characters, or events.

Biographies are true stories of another person's life, focusing on the most interesting parts. **Autobiographies** are real stories an author tells about his or her own life.

Fables are brief stories or poems, usually with animal characters, that teach a lesson stated directly at the end.

Marking the text as you read can help you determine whether the elements in the story are fiction or nonfiction. Read the guidelines for marking a text below. Then look at the student model on page 20.

Guidelines for Marking the Text

- Underline words and phrases that tell you something about the story's setting or main character(s).
- Note what you think might be real information and look for ways to confirm that it is true.
- Circle actual dates and real places in the text.
- Ask yourself questions as you read and write them in the margin.

Sample questions:

- What makes the events in the story interesting or notable?
- How do I know if the events are true?
- How does one event lead to the next?
- What do I expect to happen at the end of the story?

- Draw a box around unfamiliar words. Look for clues in the selection or look for parts of each word that will help you unlock its meaning.
- Write down questions you have about the selection.

Directions Read the narrative text. Notice how a student used the guidelines on page 19 to mark the text and make notes in the margin to help him or her determine whether the elements are fiction or nonfiction. Then answer the questions.

About the Author
Visit: PHSchool.com
Web Code: exe-6101

from ***The Drive-In Movies*** *by Gary Soto*

For our family, moviegoing was rare. But if our mom, tired from a week of candling eggs, woke up happy on a Saturday morning, there was a chance we might later scramble to our blue Chevy and beat nightfall to the Starlight Drive-In. My brother and sister knew this. I knew this. So on Saturday we tried to be good. We sat in the cool shadows of the TV with the volume low and watched cartoons, a prelude of what was to come.

candling eggs — a method of checking eggs by holding them in front of a light (Does the author's mother work on an egg farm?)

prelude — something that happens before a larger event

Is he writing about a real family, maybe his own—nonfiction?

1 **Evaluate** Do you think the narrative text is fiction or nonfiction? Use details from the text to explain your answer.

2 **Analyze** How does the author help you predict the ending of the story?

3 **Describe** Describe why might it be difficult to distinguish this text as fiction or nonfiction writing.

while reading your anchor book

Directions Read the narrative text. As you read, mark the text according to the guidelines on page 19.

from The Roswell Incident *by Philip Brooks*

Date: July 3, 1947 **Place:** Roswell, New Mexico

William "Mac" Brazel rode his horse across the dry desert land of his ranch. He thought about the explosion he had heard last night during a storm. Now he wanted to find out what had caused it.

Something silver glinted in the sunlight, catching Mac's eye. The ground around him was littered with shiny metal pieces. He stopped to pick one up.

The fragment was extremely lightweight but unbendable. And it was covered with hieroglyphs[1].

Mac felt uneasy. The metal looked like nothing on earth. He telephoned the air force base at nearby Roswell.

Staff from the Roswell base arrived at Mac's ranch. They posted guards around the area where the metal was found.

On July 8, the air force base issued an amazing news statement—they said that the wreckage was from a flying saucer!

Later that day, the base released a second statement. It said that the first story was a mistake. The crashed object was in fact a weather balloon[2]. But was it? Were the authorities covering something up?

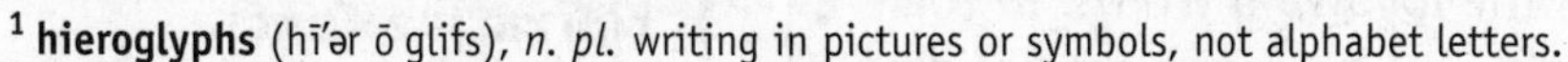

[1] **hieroglyphs** (hī′ər ō glifs), *n. pl.* writing in pictures or symbols, not alphabet letters.

[2] **weather balloon** (we*th*′ər bə lo͞on′), *n.* a balloon that carries instruments for gathering information about weather and sends the information back over radio waves.

while reading your anchor book

1 **Analyze** Does this selection contain main elements of a fiction or nonfiction narrative? Use details from the text in your answer.

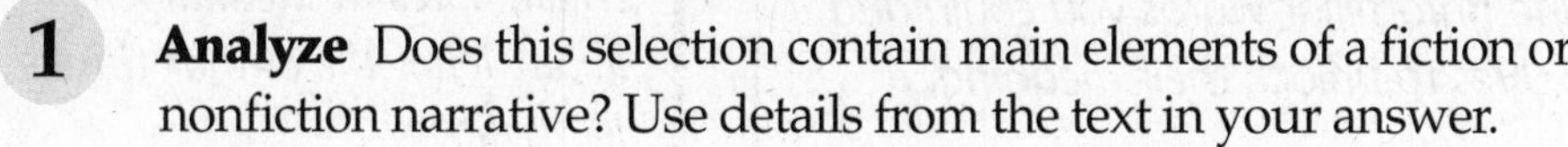

2 **Interpret** Do you think people today would be more or less likely to believe that a UFO had crashed in Roswell? Explain why or why not.

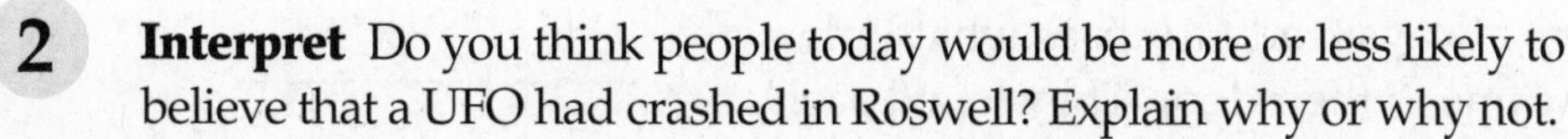

The following narrative text is a folk tale. As you read, look for the characteristics that make the folk tale a fiction narrative. *Guiding Question:* **How can a fiction narrative tell something that is true even though it does not contain facts?**

The Three Wishes

Puerto Rican Folk Tale retold by Ricardo E. Alegría

Background *Folk tales are popular around the world. Each culture has its own stories that are told to generation after generation. Folk tales were spread by word of mouth and have certain common characteristics, such as taking place "long ago" or "once upon a time," involving both good and bad characters, and using magic or supernatural forces to change events.*

Vocabulary Builder

Before you read, *you will discuss the following words. In the Vocabulary Builder box in the margin, use a vocabulary building strategy to make the words your own.*

grace   scarcely   covetousness   repentance   bestow

As you read, *draw a box around unfamiliar words you could add to your vocabulary. Use context clues to unlock their meaning.*

Marking the Text

Narrative Texts

As you read, *underline sentences and details that let you know this is a folk tale. Make notes in the margin about what the author thinks is "true."*

Many years ago, there lived a woodsman and his wife. They were very poor but very happy in their little house in the forest. Poor as they were, they were always ready to share what little they had with anyone who came to their door. They loved each other very much and were quite content with their life together. Each evening, before eating, they gave thanks to God for their happiness.

One day, while the husband was working far off in the woods, an old man came to the little house and said that he had lost his way in the forest and had eaten nothing for many days. The woodsman's wife had little to eat herself, but, as was her custom, she gave a large portion of it to the old man. After he had eaten everything she gave him, he told the woman that he had been sent to test her and that, as a reward for the kindness she and her husband showed to all who came to their house, they would be granted a special **grace.** This pleased the woman, and she asked what the special grace was.

The old man answered, "Beginning immediately, any three wishes you or your husband may wish will come true."

When she heard these words, the woman was overjoyed and exclaimed, "Oh, if my husband were only here to hear what you say!"

The last word had **scarcely** left her lips when the woodsman appeared in the little house with the ax still in his hands. The first wish had come true.

The woodsman couldn't understand it at all. How did it happen that he, who had been cutting wood in the forest, found himself here in his house? His wife explained it all as she embraced him. The woodsman just stood there, thinking over what his wife had said. He looked at the old man who stood quietly, too, saying nothing.

Suddenly he realized that his wife, without stopping to think, had used one of the three wishes, and he became very annoyed when he remembered all of the useful things she might have asked for with the first wish. For the first time, he became angry with his wife. The desire for riches had turned his head[1], and he scolded his wife, shouting at her, among other things, "It doesn't seem possible that you could be so stupid! You've wasted one of our wishes, and now we have only two left! May you grow ears of a donkey[2]!"

He had no sooner said the words than his wife's ears began to grow, and they continued to grow until they changed into the pointed, furry ears of a donkey.

When the woman put her hand up and felt them, she knew what had happened and began to cry. Her husband was very ashamed and

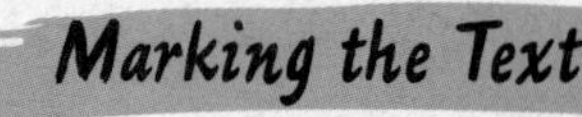

Vocabulary Builder

grace
(grās) *n.*

Meaning

scarcely
(skers'lē) *adv.*

Meaning

while reading your anchor book

[1] **turned his head** affected his judgment in a negative way.

[2] **ears of a donkey** In many folk tales, donkeys are a symbol of foolishness.

sorry, indeed, for what he had done in his temper, and he went to his wife to comfort her.

The old man, who had stood by silently, now came to them and said, "Until now, you have known happiness together and have never quarreled with each other. Nevertheless, the mere knowledge that you could have riches and power has changed you both. Remember, you have only one wish left. What do you want? Riches? Beautiful clothes? Servants? Power?"

The woodsman tightened his arm about his wife, looked at the old man, and said, "We want only the happiness and joy we knew before my wife grew donkey's ears."

No sooner had he said these words than the donkey ears disappeared. The woodsman and his wife fell upon their knees to ask forgiveness for having acted, if only for a moment, out of **covetousness** and greed. Then they gave thanks for all their happiness.

The old man left, but before going, he told them that they had undergone this test in order to learn that there can be happiness in poverty just as there can be unhappiness in riches. As a reward for their **repentance**, the old man said that he would **bestow** upon them the greatest happiness a married couple could know. Months later, a son was born to them. The family lived happily all the rest of their lives.

Vocabulary Builder

covetousness
(kuv'ət əs nes) *n.*

Meaning

repentance
(ri pen'təns) *n.*

Meaning

bestow
(bē stō') *v.*

Meaning

Vocabulary Builder

After you read, *review the words you decided to add to your vocabulary. Write the meaning of words you have learned in context. Look up the other words in a dictionary, glossary, thesaurus, or electronic resource.*

Ricardo Alegría grew up in San Juan, Puerto Rico. He is a social scientist and archaeologist who has studied the Taino culture—the native culture of Puerto Rico. He is also an author who has written down the common folk tales of the island, as well as nonfiction books about his archaeological digs. In 1993, President Bill Clinton awarded him the prestigious Charles Frankel Award for his lifelong contributions to Puerto Rican learning and culture.

Thinking About the Selection

The Three Wishes

1 **Respond** Why do you think the story ends with the couple remaining in poverty instead of being granted an easier life?

2 **Analyze** What main elements of a fiction narrative are present in this selection? Give details from the text as examples for each element.

3 **Predict** How do you think the couple would have handled material wealth if the old man had bestowed it on them?

4 **Interpret** In what ways did the couple's argument help them to understand what was important to them?

5 **Predict** If the old man returns and again grants the family a special grace, what do you think they will wish for this time?

Write Answer the following questions in your Reader's Journal.

6 **Discuss** How can a fiction narrative tell something that is true even though it does not contain facts?

7 **Interpret** Describe the elements of a fiction or nonfiction narrative that appear in your Anchor Book. Give examples of how what is true is communicated through the text.

while reading your anchor book

1-6 Comparing Literary Works
Sensory Language

You can describe a raindrop simply, as in *fell from the sky,* or vividly, as in *hit the baking pavement with a crisp sizzle.* Which statement appeals more to your senses? If your answer was the second statement, then you are reacting to the **sensory language** the author used in describing the rain.

Sensory language is the words and phrases an author uses to create images in the reader's mind. Sensory language appeals to all five senses—smell, sight, sound, taste, and touch. Good sensory language can bring to life the setting, characters, and actions in a story.

Directions Read the student model. Notice how the student marked the text for sensory language. Then answer the question that follows.

Student Model: Marking the Text

Marcos didn't know what to expect as he stepped out of the bus—he had never been to the beach before. The first thing he noticed was the salty smell that poured in from beyond the parking lot. As he stepped barefoot onto the blacktop, the hot tar singed his feet. He quickly stepped toward the boardwalk, keeping pace with the shouting kids alongside him.

As he finally reached the beach, he peered down onto the scene below, soaking in the sea of sunbathers, the circling seagulls, and the endless expanse of the sea. The sound of the crashing waves thrilled him. Marcos tore off his shirt, and taking in the sun's warm embrace, he went searching for a spot from which to explore.

smell
touch
sound
sight
sound
touch

Explain How does the author's use of sensory language affect your understanding of Marcos' experience at the beach?

Read the poem "Blackberry Eating" to compare the sensory language it uses to the sensory language in "The Sand Castle."
Guiding Question: **How does sensory language make poems and fictional stories seem true?**

Vocabulary Builder

Before you read, *you will discuss the following words. In the Vocabulary Builder box in the margin, use a vocabulary building strategy to make the words your own.*

unbidden **cumbersome** **hostile**

As you read, *draw a box around unfamiliar words you could add to your vocabulary. Use context clues to unlock their meaning.*

Marking the Text

Sensory Language

As you read, *underline words that excite your senses. In the margin, note the words that appeal to taste, touch, sight, sound, or smell.*

while reading your anchor book

Blackberry Eating

by Galway Kinnell

I love to go out in late September
among the fat, overripe, icy, black blackberries
to eat blackberries for breakfast,
the stalks very prickly, a penalty
they earn for knowing the black art
of blackberry-making; and as I stand among them
lifting the stalks to my mouth, the ripest berries
fall almost **unbidden** to my tongue,
as words sometimes do, certain peculiar words
like *strengths* or *squinched*[1],
many-lettered, one-syllabled lumps,
which I squeeze, squinch open, and splurge well
in the silent, startled, icy, black language
of blackberry-eating in late September.

unbidden
(un'bid''n) *adj.*

Meaning

[1] **squinched** (skwincht) *v.* squinted.

Now read the short story. Write examples of sensory language in the margin at the right.

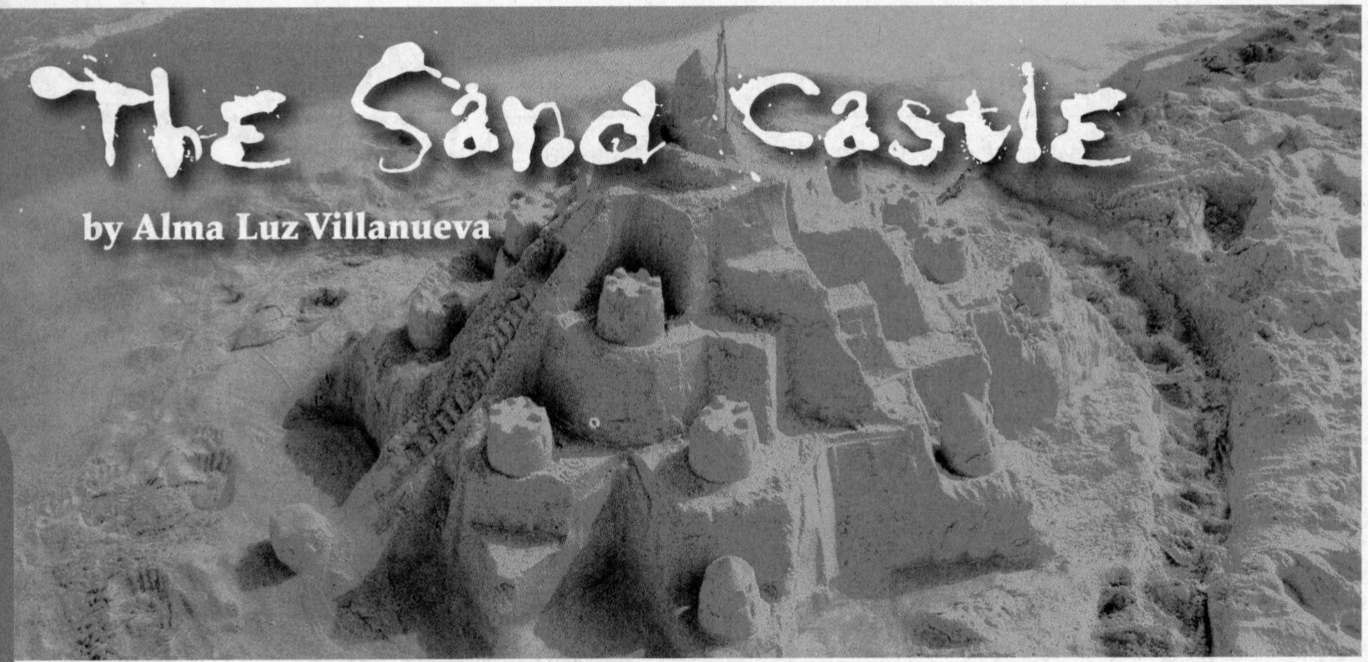

The Sand Castle

by Alma Luz Villanueva

Background *This science fiction story takes place about 100 years in the future. The main character remembers what life was like before the Earth's climate changed.*

"Have you dressed yet?" their grandmother called. "Once a month in the sun and they must almost be forced," she muttered. "Well, poor things, they've forgotten the warmth of the sun on their little bodies, what it is to play in the sea, yes … ." Mrs. Pavloff reached for her protective sun goggles that covered most of her face.

It screened all ultraviolet light[1] from the once life-giving sun; now, it, the sun, scorched the Earth, killing whatever it touched. The sea, the continents, had changed. The weather, as they'd called it in the last century, was entirely predictable now: warming.

Mrs. Pavloff slipped on the thick, metallic gloves, listening to her grandchildren squabble and she heard her mother's voice calling her, "Masha, put your bathing suit under your clothes. It's so much easier that way without having to go to the bathhouse first. Hurry! Father's waiting!" She remembered the ride to the sea, the silence when the first shimmers of water became visible. Her father had always been first into the chilly water. "Good for the health!" he'd yell as he dove into it, swimming as far as he

Marking the Text

Sensory Language

As you read, *underline words that help you to see, hear, taste, smell, and feel parts of the story. How do these sensory details support the author's message about the Earth's climate? What feelings or thoughts do the details stir in you?*

---

[1] **ultraviolet light** (ul' trə vī' ə lit līt) (*n.*) a type of invisible light from the Sun that is harmful to people.

could, then back. Then he'd lie exhausted on the sand, stretched to the sun. Such happiness to be warmed by the sun.

Then the picnic. She could hear her mother's voice, "Stay to your knees, Masha! Only to your knees!" To herself: "She'd be a mermaid if I didn't watch," and she'd laugh. Masha would lie belly down, facing the sea and let the last of the waves roll over her. She hadn't even been aware of the sun, only that she'd been warm or, if a cloud covered it, cold. It was always there, the sun: its light, its warmth. But the sea—they traveled to it. So, she'd given all of her attention to the beautiful sea.

She saw her father kneeling next to her, building the sand castle they always built when they went to the sea. Her job was to find seashells, bird feathers, and strips of seaweed to decorate it. How proud she'd felt as she placed her seashells where she chose, where they seemed most beautiful. Only then was the sand castle complete. She heard her father's voice, "The Princess's castle is ready, now, for her Prince! Come and look, Anna! What do you think?" She saw herself beaming with pride, and she heard her mother's laugh. "Fit for a queen, I'd say! Can I live in your castle, too, Masha? Please, Princess Masha?"

"Of course, Mother! You can live with me always. . . ." She remembered her mother's laughing face, her auburn hair lit up by the sun, making her look bright and beautiful.

All vehicles were solar powered. The populations took buses when they needed transportation and people emerged mainly at night. So, most human activity was conducted after the sun was gone from the sky. Those who emerged during the day wore protective clothing. Everything was built to screen the sun's light. Sometimes she missed the natural light of her childhood streaming through the windows so intensely the urge to just run outside would overtake her. She missed the birds, the wild birds.

But today they were going out, outside in the daytime, when the sun was still in the sky. Masha knew they were squabbling because they hated to dress up to go outside. The clothing, the gloves, the goggles were uncomfortable and **cumbersome.** She sighed, tears coming to her eyes. Well, they're coming, Masha decided. They can remove their goggles, and gloves on the bus.

The sea was closer now and the bus ride was comfortable within the temperature controlled interior. Those with memories of the sea signed up, bringing grandchildren, children, friends, or just went alone. Masha had taken her grandchildren before, but they'd sat on the sand, listlessly[2], sifting it through their gloved hands with bored little faces. She'd tried to interest them in the sea with stories of her father swimming in it as far as he could. But they couldn't touch it, so it, the sea, didn't seem real to them. What was it: a mass of undrinkable, **hostile** water. Hostile like

[2] **listlessly** (list'lis'lē) *adv.* with little energy, interest, or concern.

Marking the Text

Vocabulary Builder

cumbersome
(kum'bər səm) *adj.*

Meaning

hostile
(häs'təl) *adj.*

Meaning

while reading your anchor book

Literature in Context
Global Warming

Climate change is a "hot" topic these days. People are realizing the effects global warming is having on Earth's atmosphere and its natural patterns in the ecosystem. Recently, the plight of polar bears captured worldwide attention. Climate change has affected their Arctic habitat. Northern ice now breaks up earlier than it had broken in the past. As a result, seals—the bears' main food source—are not around for as long, so the bears face starvation. The threats to these great animals serve as a reminder to everyone that global warming is very real.

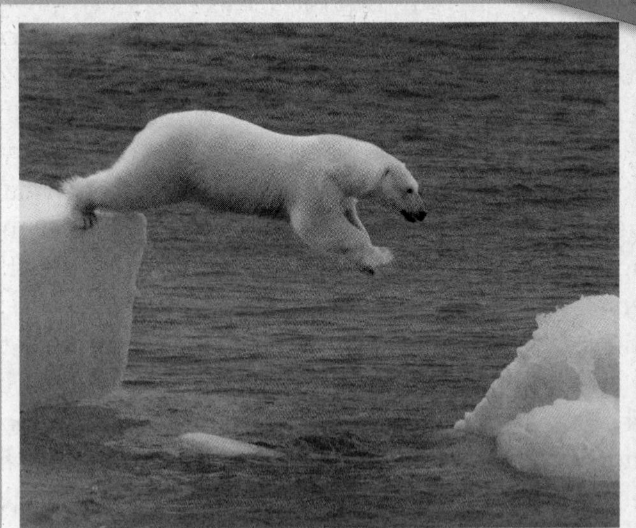

the sun. They'd taken no delight, no pleasure, in their journey to the sea.

But today, yes, today we will build a sand castle. Masha smiled at her secret. She'd packed everything late last night to surprise them at the sea.

Why haven't I thought of it before? Masha asked herself, and then she remembered the dream, months ago, of building a sand castle with her father at the sea. It made her want to weep because she'd forgotten. She'd actually forgotten one of the most joyful times of her girlhood. When the sea was still alive with life.

Today we will build a sand castle.

They trudged[3] on the thick, dense sand toward the hiss of pale blue. Only the older people picked up their step, excited by the smell of salt in the air. Masha's grandchildren knew they'd be here for two hours and then trudge all the way back to the bus. The darkened goggles made the sunlight bearable. They hated this forlorn place where the sun had obviously drained the life out of everything. They were too young to express it, but they felt it as they walked, with bored effort, beside their grandmother.

"We're going to build a sand castle today—what do you think of that?" Masha beamed, squinted to see their faces.

"What's a sand castle?" the boy mumbled.

"You'll see, I'll show you. . . ."

"Is it fun, Grandmama?" the girl smiled, taking her grandmother's hand.

"Yes, it is so much fun. I've brought different sized containers to mold the sand, and, oh, you'll see!"

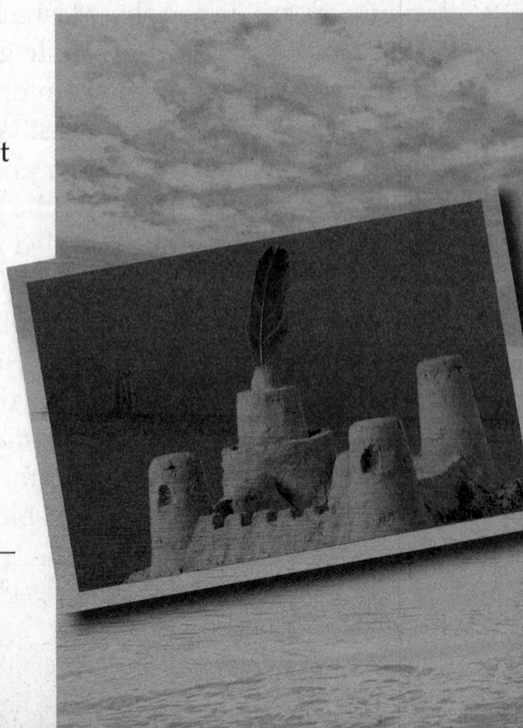

[3] **trudged** (trujd) *v.* walked steadily but with great effort.

The boy gave an awkward skip and nearly shouted, "Show us, Grandmama, show us what you mean!"

Masha laughed, sounding almost like a girl. "We're almost there, yes, we're almost there!"

The first circle of sandy shapes was complete, and the children were so excited by what they were building they forgot about their protective gloves.

"Now, we'll put a pile of wet sand in the middle and build it up with our hands and then we'll do another circle, yes, children?"

The children rushed back and forth from the tide line carrying the dark, wet sand. They only had an hour left. Their eyes, beneath the goggles, darted with excitement.

"Just don't get your gloves in the water, a little wet sand won't hurt, don't worry, children. When I was a girl there were so many birds at the sea we'd scare them off because they'd try to steal our food. Seagulls, they were, big white birds that liked to scream at the sea, they sounded like eagles to me. . . ."

"You used to eat at the sea, Grandmama?" the girl asked incredulously[4].

"We used to call them picnics. . . ."

"What are eagles, Grandmama?" the boy wanted to know, shaping the dark sand with his gloved hands.

"They used to be one of the largest, most beautiful wild birds in the world. My grandfather pointed them out to me once. . . ."

Until that moment, she'd forgotten that memory of nearly sixty years ago. They'd gone on a train, then a bus, to the village where she'd been born. She remembered her grandfather looking up toward a shrill, piercing cry that seemed to come from the sky. She'd seen the tears in her grandfather's eyes and on his cheeks.

[4] **incredulously** (in krej' oo ləs' lē) *adv.* having a hard time believing.

Marking the Text

while reading your anchor book

He'd pointed up to a large, dark flying-thing in the summer blue sky: "That's an eagle, my girl, the spirit of the people."

Sadness overtook Masha, but she refused to acknowledge its presence. The sand castle, Masha told herself sternly—the sand castle is what is important now. "I've brought a wonderful surprise, something to decorate the sand castle with when we're through building it."

"Show us, Grandmama, please?"

"Yes, please, please show us now!"

Masha sighed with a terrible, sudden happiness as she brought out the plastic bag. Quickly, she removed each precious shell from its protective cotton: eight perfect shells from all over the world.

"But Grandmama, these are your special shells! You said the sea doesn't make them anymore. . . ."

"It will, Anna, it will." Masha hugged her granddaughter and made her voice brighten with laughter. "Today we will decorate our sand castle with the most beautiful shells in the world, yes!"

Vocabulary Builder

After you read, *review the words you decided to add to your vocabulary. Write the meaning of words you have learned in context. Look up the other words in a dictionary, glossary, thesaurus, or electronic resource.*

while reading your anchor book

Alma Luz Villanueva

(b. 1944)

Alma Luz Villanueva was born in California. She faced poverty and hardship in her early life. Just surviving was a struggle. In her twenties, Villanueva went to college and became a serious writer. Her poetry and fiction have won many awards. Her writing reflects her concern with the place of women in society, with poverty, and with nature.

Thinking About the Selections

Blackberry Eating *and* The Sand Castle

About the Author
Visit: PHSchool.com
Web Code: exe-6104
exe-6105

1 **Connect** Think about a fun experience you've had on summer vacation and about what it's like to eat your favorite fruit. How do these experiences help you to connect to the story and poem?

2 **Analyze** Alma Luz Villanueva suggests that people's treatment of the Earth could have disastrous effects in the future. How does her sensory language help to support this message?

3 **Take a Position** Do you agree or disagree with this statement? *Galway Kinnell and Alma Luz Villanueva seem to share similar feelings about nature.* Explain your opinion.

4 **Infer** Look at the image of blackberries on page 27. Galway Kinnell describes them as "many-lettered, one-syllable lumps." What do you think he means?

5 **Make a Judgment** Do you think that Villanueva's view of a possible future on the Earth is valid? Why or why not?

Write Answer the following questions in your Reader's Journal.

6 **Analyze** How does sensory language make poems and fictional stories seem true?

7 **Apply** Select a passage from your Anchor Book that has lots of sensory language. How does the sensory language affect your understanding of the passage you chose?

while reading your anchor book

1-7 Analyzing an Informational Text
Employment Application

Forms such as an employment application might not be the most fascinating reading—but knowing how to read them will help you get ahead in life!

The purpose of an employment application is to let a potential employer know why you qualify for a particular job. It is important to read and answer all the questions on the form carefully.

Directions Read the application. Answer the questions that follow.

Link to Real Life

EMPLOYMENT APPLICATION FORM

Date: *6/9/08*

Name *Whittleby* (Last) *Doug* (First) *Alexander* (Middle)

Address *260 Curve Street* (Street) *Rockford* (City) *Maine* (State) *97039* (Zip)

Telephone *(219) 301-5523* **Email** *DougAW@mailme.com*

Position Applying for *dog walker* **Rate of Pay** *$6/hour*

Date Available *6/21/08* **Days and Hours Available** *Monday–Friday, 3 p.m. to 8 p.m.*

The employer will use your days and hours to make your schedule.

Are you 18 years of age or older? Yes ☐ No ☑

Employment History			
Name of Employer *The Feldman Family*	**Employment Dates**	**Job Title/Duties**	**Pay**
	From: *6/07* **To:** *8/07*	*Dog walker: Walk two dogs three afternoons every week*	*$6/hour*
	Reason for Leaving *Month long preparation for finals*		
Name of Employer *The Edison Family*	**Employment Dates**	**Job Title/Duties**	**Pay**
	From: *7/07* **To:** *9/07*	*Dog walker: Walk one dog two afternoons every week*	*$5/hour*
	Reason for Leaving *Family moved away*		

It is important to write clearly and neatly.

Are you or have you been involved in volunteer work? *Last summer, I volunteered at my town's pool. I helped watch little kids who came in for swimming lessons, and I cleaned up around the snack bar.*

while reading your anchor book

Thinking About the Selection

Employment Application

1 **Explain** Why does the application ask for your address, telephone number, and e-mail address?

2 **Explain** Why is it important to give accurate information on an employment application?

3 **Analyze** Why do you think an employer wants to know who your previous employers were?

4 **Analyze** What is the purpose of describing your duties at past jobs?

5 **Explain** What do you think is the most important section in this employment application? Why?

6 **Respond** If you were an employer reading this application, would you hire the applicant? Why or why not?

1-8 Language Coach
Grammar and Spelling

Common and Proper Nouns

A **noun** is a word used to name a person, place, or thing. All nouns are considered either *common* or *proper*.

A **common noun** is used to name any one of a group of people, places, or things. For example the noun *river* can be used to name any river. Common nouns are not capitalized unless they are at the beginning of a sentence or in a title.

Example This *river* is wider than that *river.*

A **proper noun** is used to name a specific person, place, or thing. Proper nouns are always capitalized.

Example The *Nile River* is wider than the *Charles River.*

Directions Read the sentences below. Underline each common noun and circle each proper noun.

1. Paul Revere rode on a horse through Lexington, Massachusetts.
2. Ben Franklin was an inventor and a writer.
3. His friend went to see the Statue of Liberty.
4. The family went to a museum on Fifth Ave.

Directions Write three or four sentences about a day trip you have taken. Use common and proper nouns to tell about where you went, what you did, and what you saw. When you are finished, underline the proper nouns and circle the common nouns.

Go Online
Learn More
Visit: PHSchool.com
Web Code: exp-6101

Author's Craft

Folk tales usually seem as though they could have happened to anyone, at any time, anywhere. One way authors create this effect is to use common nouns so that people and places are vague. Reread "The Three Wishes" on pages 22–24. Choose a paragraph from the folk tale and change some common nouns to proper nouns to make it seem that the story is about specific people, in a specific place and time.

Singular and Plural Nouns

Singular nouns refer to one person, place, or thing. **Plural nouns** refer to more than one person, place, or thing. There are different ways to form plural nouns.

- To make most nouns plural, add *-s* or *-es* to the end of the word.
- Nouns that end in *ch, s, x,* or *z* can be made plural by adding *-es.*
- To make many nouns that end in *o* plural, such as *hero,* add *-es.*

Singular athlete, branch, tomato

Plural athletes, branches, tomatoes

- If a noun ends in a consonant and is followed by *y,* to make it plural, change the *y* to *i* and add *-es.*

Singular canary

Plural canaries

- In some nouns that end in *f,* change the *f* to *v* and add *-es.*

Singular knife, thief, calf

Plural knives, thieves calves

- Other nouns have their own special plural forms.

Singular woman, goose, child, mouse

Plural women, geese, children, mice

Author's Craft

Good authors are also good proofreaders. They know that publishers aren't going to take a text seriously if it is submitted with spelling errors, even if the writing is excellent in every other way. Reread "Environmental Issues" on page 10. Then write four sentences about the passage, using incorrectly spelled plurals. Trade papers with a partner and see if you can spot your partner's mistakes.

Directions Rewrite the sentences below by changing each noun in parentheses to its plural form.

1. All (generation) have their (hero) and (ideal).

____

____

2. (Police officer) protect the (life) of (person).

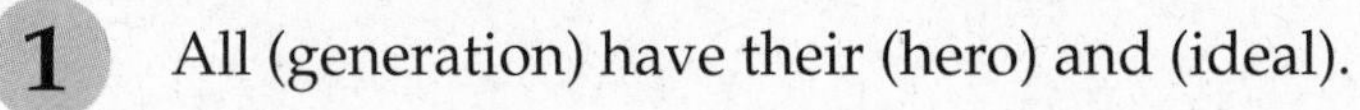

____

3. Some people admire the (lifestyle) of (actor) and (actress).

____

____

4. Television (personality) and (musician) have their (follower).

____

____

Possessive Nouns

Possessive nouns are used to show ownership. To make most singular nouns possessive, add an apostrophe and an *s*. Be careful not to leave out an apostrophe or place it incorrectly.

Examples the *moon's* orbit; *Ross's* new car

Many plural nouns end in *s*. To make most plural nouns possessive, add an apostrophe after the *s*.

Examples my *grandparents'* home; the *players'* uniforms

Some plural nouns do not end in *s*. To make these nouns possessive, add an apostrophe and an *s*.

Examples the *women's* clothing; the *people's* choice

Directions Rewrite each sentence using the possessive form of the underlined noun.

1. He admired the medal of the athlete.

2. It was a decision made by James.

3. Do not go near the den of the foxes.

4. The judge heard the complaint of the lawyer.

5. It was the hat of that gentleman.

6. The storm swept over the crew of the ship.

Directions In the paragraph below, underline each incorrect possessive noun. Write the correct form of each noun on the line below.

7. In 1899, Alaskas' gold attracted many prospectors. For years, rubber was the region's most important product. Most sharecropper's wages never rose during those years. Eventually, the territorys' population increased. About sixty years later, oil became the state's new gold.

Spelling: Easily Confused Words

Some words are easily confused with other words. *Then* and *than* are often confused because they have similar spellings. They also sound alike—so it makes it even more confusing to keep them straight. Here are two more examples.

Words	Example
accept **except**	I *accept* the invitation to the party. I took all the clothes *except* the socks.
our **are**	We had to take all of *our* books with us. Jason's friends *are* waiting for him.

If you have a question about the correct spelling or use of a word, use a dictionary to help you.

Directions Complete each sentence using the correct word from the pair given. Rewrite the entire sentence on the line.

1. (Our, Are) team must work very hard if we (are, our) to win the championship.

2. I usually get better grades in math (then, than) my sister, but (then, than), she gets better grades in science.

3. I have to be careful not to (loose, lose) my purse. The handle is very (loose, lose).

4. Nick must (except, accept) that he is at the top of his class for all subjects (except, accept) math.

Directions Circle the correct words in the paragraph below.

(Our, are) class will go on a field trip to the Museum of Art this year. None of us (accept, except) Tanya has been there before. I (know, now) I will enjoy it. I will never (lose, loose) my love of art. I (accept, except) that not everyone loves art as much as I do. (Know, Now) I will get to see paintings by some of my favorite artists. I will see famous works of art, and (than, then) I will be happy.

1-9 Writer's Workshop
Narration: Autobiographical Narrative

Sometimes a writer will tell the story of an event in his or her life. This type of writing is called an **autobiographical narrative.** Letters, journals, persuasive essays, and anecdotes can be autobiographical narratives. Follow the steps in this workshop to write your own autobiographical narrative about an important event in your life.

What to include Your autobiographical narrative should include the following elements.

- a clear, well-ordered sequence of events
- a central problem or conflict that you or someone else resolves
- a consistent use of first-person point of view
- vivid details that describe the people, places, and events
- error-free writing, including correct use of nouns

Purpose To write an autobiographical narrative about an event that taught you a lesson or helped you to grow

Audience You, your teacher, and your classmates

Prewriting—Plan It Out

The following steps will help you plan and organize your thoughts before you begin writing.

Choose a broad topic. Try one of these prewriting strategies.

- **Freewrite.** Jot down thoughts that occur to you about a general topic in your life, such as *relationships*, *adventures*, or *solving problems*. Read over your thoughts, and choose a topic.
- **Make a memory quicklist.** Think about special times or people in your life. List these memories in the first column of the chart. Then describe the event, person, or experience. In the last column, tell why this memory is important to you. For example, did it teach you a lesson? Did it help you to grow? Choose one memory as your broad topic.

Memories	Description	Why Is It Important?
I got my first job.	I delivered the paper to all the subscribers in my town.	I have experience in working with customers, so in future jobs, I'll be prepared.

Narrow your topic. Once you have a broad topic, focus on one aspect of the experience that stands out in your mind. Use this specific topic as the basis for your autobiographical narrative.

Gather details. Use an **idea web** to gather details for your narrative. On a separate sheet of paper, draw an idea web like the one shown. Write your topic in the center and details in the ovals around it.

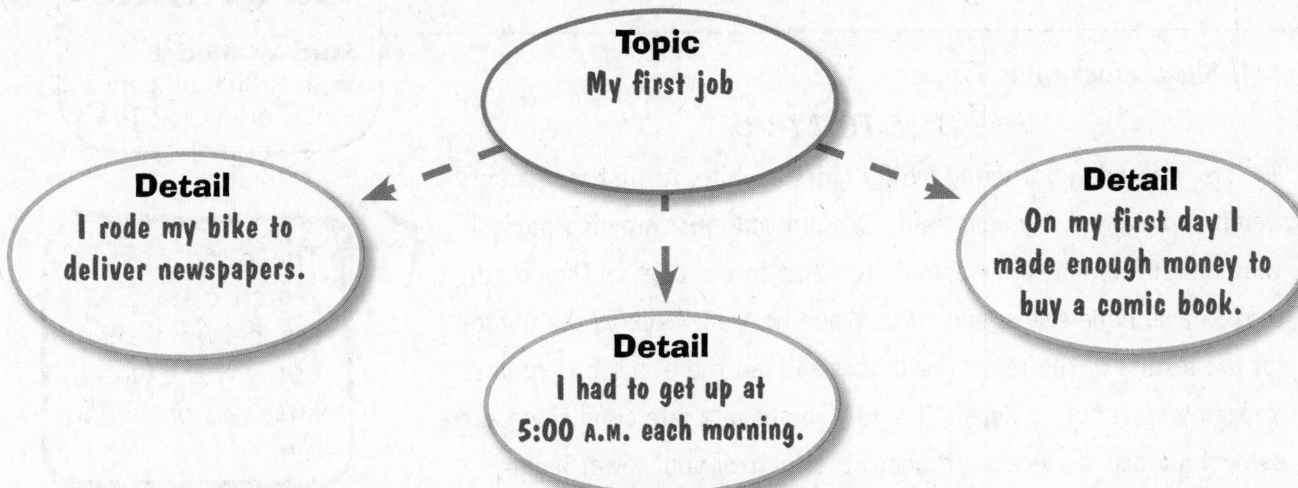

Drafting—Get It on Paper

Use your idea web as an outline to write your first draft. The following steps will help you to make it interesting and organized.

Shape your writing. Here are some ways you can organize your narrative.

- One way that you can organize your narrative is by using **chronological order.** Begin with the first event. Then add other events in the order that they happened.
- Use **flashback.** Begin at the end of your story and flash back to the beginning. Then tell the rest of the story in chronological order through flashback.

Clarify your point of view. Your narrative is an account of an event in your life, so like all autobiographical writing, it should be written from first-person, or your own point of view.

Provide elaboration. Decide the tone of your narrative. Do you want it to be humorous, serious, formal, or informal? Use descriptive words and phrases to create your own style. Varying your sentence length helps to develop style and tone. Also, use dialogue to help bring life to your characters.

Directions Read this student autobiographical narrative as a model for your own.

Student Model: Writing

Kyle Shea, Clackamas, OR

A Time to Heal

My knee had been bothering me for quite a while. At first my parents weren't concerned. My mom said, "It's probably just growing pains." The pain continued so my parents took me to the doctor. The doctor took x-rays, bone scans, and MRIs. When we went back to the doctor for the results of the tests, the doctor entered the examining room looking very serious. "Kyle," he said, "you have a rare condition called osteochondritis dissecans. It means that part of your lower femur has died because there is no longer a blood supply to that area." He explained that this could be a very serious condition. My parents and I were in shock! I was very afraid.

The doctor gave me two options. He said, "You can have six months of complete rest—except walking or swimming—or you can have surgery to regenerate the blood supply to that area of the bone." The surgery involves drilling microscopic holes in the bone. I wasn't thrilled with either choice. . . .

. . . After six months of rest, I had more bad news—my leg had not gotten better so the doctor said, "Kyle, we have no other choice but to move forward with the surgery." The surgery will take about three months to heal. My recovery will require me to be on crutches for a month then gradually over the next two months start putting weight back on my leg. At the end of three months I will be back on my feet in time for spring baseball.

"Hey, Kyle," my friend Alex asked, "isn't it hard not to play sports?"

"Alex," I said, "The thing I miss the most is just being around you guys. It's been really lonely. I can't wait to get back into it again."

I realize how fortunate I am . . . Mine is an injury that can be corrected with surgery. I feel very lucky because I have an excellent chance of a complete recovery. A year off from sports taught me to appreciate what I took for granted like friends and being part of a team.

Go Online
Student Model
Visit: PHSchool.com
Web Code: exr-6101

The introductory sentence makes readers want to find out why the writer's knee was bothering him.

Here, the writer introduces the central problem that is the focus of his autobiographical narrative.

Transitions such as *before* and *after* help readers follow the chronological order of events.

Revising—Make It Better

Revise your draft. Be certain your opening paragraph is an attention-grabber. Link your paragraphs using transition words, such as *then, next, before,* and *after*.

Revise your conclusion. Bring a sense of closure to your narrative.

Peer Review Read your autobiographical narrative aloud to a partner. Identify at least three goals for the revision of your narrative.

Editing—Be Your Own Language Coach

Before you hand in your autobiographical narrative, review it for grammatical errors. Pay special attention to noun usage.

Publishing—Share It!

A work is published for a specific audience. Consider sharing your work using one of the following ideas.

Deliver a speech. Use your autobiographical narrative as the basis for a dramatic presentation.

Get it published. Mail your narrative to a magazine that publishes student writing.

Reflecting on Your Writing

Rubric for Self-Assessment Assess your essay. For each question, circle a rating.

CRITERIA	RATING SCALE
	NOT VERY — VERY
IDEAS Is your narrative clear and focused with rich details?	1 2 3 4 5
ORGANIZATION How logical and consistent is your organization?	1 2 3 4 5
VOICE How well do you draw the reader in with your tone and style?	1 2 3 4 5
WORD CHOICE How appropriate is the language for your audience?	1 2 3 4 5
SENTENCE FLUENCY How varied is your sentence structure?	1 2 3 4 5
CONVENTIONS How accurate is your grammar, especially your use of nouns?	1 2 3 4 5

1-10 Discussing Your Anchor Book
Literature Circles

Introduction A Literature Circle is a small group of students who meet to discuss what they are reading. Together, your group will talk about topics and complete activities that help you get the most of your Anchor Book.

You have one topic in this Literature Circle. Carefully read the Discussion Guidelines on the following page before beginning your discussion.

Symbolism

A **symbol** is anything that stands for or represents something else. In literature, symbols often stand for abstract ideas, such as love or hope. Some commonly recognized symbols are $, which stands for money, and a dove, which stands for peace.

Symbolism is the use of symbols that an author uses to emphasize certain ideas in a story. Authors emphasize ideas with symbolism to add levels of meaning to their story. Readers can interpret the same symbols differently. Sometimes, the symbols that authors use may have more than one meaning.

Below are some common symbols and their meanings.

voyage	is a symbol for	journey of life
rose	is a symbol for	beauty
heart	is a symbol for	love
vulture	is a symbol for	death

With your group, discuss symbols in your Anchor Book and the author's purpose for using them. Consider the following in your discussion.

- What message do you think the author is trying to convey through the symbols he or she used?
- Explain the effect the author's use of symbolism has on the meaning of the text in your Anchor Book.

DISCUSSION GUIDELINES

1 LISTEN

Wait until a person has finished speaking before you respond. Be courteous when a person is sharing his or her ideas within your Literature Circle. Also, respect the age, gender, social position, and cultural traditions of others.

2 BUILD

Think of ways to build on each other's comments. You could make a connection to a big question or give examples that support what the Literature Circle member said. Always maintain a positive tone in all your responses, even if you disagree with someone.

Sentence Starters for Building Discussion

- When Ramon suggested that . . . it reminded me of. . . .
- When Elena thought that . . . I remembered that. . . .
- When Jake emphasized that . . . I made a connection to. . . .

Example When Anita pointed out that the author uses a lot of rocks to tell the story, I realized that rocks probably symbolize steadiness, strength, or things that last forever.

3 QUESTION

Sometimes you might want to know more about a Literature Circle member's comments, and sometimes you may disagree with his or her ideas. Asking questions is a good way to have a member clarify unknown vocabulary or expand upon ideas, which leads to more productive discussions.

Sentence Starters for Asking Questions

To ask for more information or explanation of an idea

- I don't understand what you meant when you said. . . . Could you explain that idea in more detail?
- Could you give me an example of what you mean?
- Please tell me more about . . .

To show polite disagreement

My opinion/experience/perspective is different from yours. Does it seem possible that . . . ?

Example I'm not sure why you feel that the character is not telling the truth. Can you give me an example of when you think she is lying?

Standardized Test Practice

Reading Skills: Making Predictions

Directions Read the following passage. Then answer the questions.

Mark breezed through the swim meet's first round of elimination. He was confident that the next events would be no problem because he had made the finals in the last two events. He thought he had a good chance at winning the entire competition—until he saw the swimmer two lanes over. Vin Franklin was the four-time state champion in the 100-yard freestyle swim. If there was one competitor who could get in the way of Mark's victory, it was Vin. A hint of doubt began to creep into his confidence.

The judge called the swimmers to their ready positions. "On your mark. Get set—." The starter's gun went off. The swimmers hit the water with a graceful force. As soon as he entered the water, Mark began to question his speed.

1 After reading the passage, what **prediction** can you make?

A. Mark will win the race.

B. Vin will be disqualified for a false start.

C. Mark won't finish the race.

D. Mark will lose the race to Vin.

2 Which of the following does *not* support your **prediction** from question 1?

F. "A hint of doubt began to creep into his confidence."

G. "The judge called the swimmers to their ready positions."

H. ". . . Mark began to question his speed."

J. "Vin Franklin was the four-time state champion . . ."

3 Which of the following is a text clue that *supports* your **prediction** from question 1?

A. ". . . breezed through the swim meet's first round . . ."

B. "He was confident . . ."

C. "Mark began to question his speed."

D. "On your mark. Now set—."

4 What is the first clue in the text that helped you make a **prediction?**

F. "Mark breezed through the swim meet's first round of elimination."

G. ". . . he had made the finals in the last two events."

H. ". . . —until he saw the swimmer two lanes over."

J. "A hint of doubt began to creep into his confidence."

Literary Analysis: Elements of Fiction and Nonfiction

Read the following passage. Then answer the questions.

> The cool breeze didn't give Amy any relief from the heat. The sun beat down on her ears, shoulders, and neck. Beads of sweat slid down her face and stung her eyes. Amy didn't care about the sweat blurring her vision or the heat rising in waves from the pavement. She only heard the rhythmic grinding of the gears, the bike chain smoothly turning round and round with the motion of the pedals.
>
> There were five more miles left in the bike race before Amy had to hop off and begin the seven-mile run. She couldn't think about that right now. She had to focus on finishing the bike race. Fans cheering and clapping along the trail broke her concentration at times, but her aching body quickly brought her back to the reality of the situation: The race wasn't over. Ignoring the piercing cramps and growing fatigue, Amy pumped her legs harder and faster and surged ahead.

5 What type of writing is this passage?

A. folk tale

B. autobiography

C. short story

D. journal or diary

6 The hot sun described in the selection is a part of the __________.

F. plot

G. climax

H. setting

J. characters

7 Which senses does the passage mainly appeal to?

A. touch and sight

B. sound and taste

C. touch and taste

D. sound and touch

8 What mood or atmosphere does the **sensory language** in this passage create?

F. laziness

G. boredom

H. fear

J. exhaustion

Timed Writing: Description

Directions Use what you have learned about sensory language to write a paragraph that appeals to at least three of the five senses. Your paragraph should create a strong mental picture for the reader about a special place you have visited. **(20 minutes)**

1-11 Reading Skills
Fact and Opinion

In learning new reading skills, you will use special academic vocabulary. Knowing the right words will help you demonstrate your understanding.

Academic Vocabulary

Word	Meaning	Example Sentence
claim *v.* *Related words:* claimed, claiming	to state that something is true, often without evidence	Sunny Juice's ad *claims* that kids like their juice more than any other kind.
distinguish *v.* *Related words:* distinguished, distinguishing	to recognize a difference in something or someone	The twins' personalities are so different that even a stranger can easily *distinguish* Dena from Dana.
influence *v.* *Related words:* influenced, influencing	to persuade, or to pressure into doing something	I tried to *influence* my little sister's taste in music by playing my favorite artists at home.

Sometimes it's not easy to tell whether a statement you read is a fact or an opinion.

- A **fact** is a statement that can be proved. You can determine if something is a fact by checking reference sources such as encyclopedias, almanacs, atlases, or reliable Web sites.
- An **opinion** expresses a person's judgment or belief, but it cannot be proved. To recognize statements of opinion, look for clue words or phrases, such as *best*, *worst*, *most*, *least*, and *I think*.

Many advertisers make **claims** about their products to **influence** people to buy them. For example, words on a cereal box might claim that the cereal has all the vitamins you need. To **distinguish** between fact and opinion, read the information that tells about the ingredients. You might find that the cereal does have all the vitamins you need, but that there is very little of each vitamin in the cereal.

Fact That Can Be Proven Contains oats, cranberries, and almonds.

Opinion That Cannot Be Proven The best cereal you'll ever try!

Directions Study the label below. Underline statements that are facts and circle words that indicate opinions. Then complete the chart below.

STATEMENT OR PHRASE	FACT OR OPINION	EXPLANATION
Most delicious applesauce anywhere . . . you'll love it!	opinion	The phrase *most delicious* signals an opinion. People's tastes differ, so some may not like it.
Servings per Container 4		
We know our apples. You should, too.		
Net Wt. 15 oz.		
INGREDIENTS: APPLES, SUGAR, CORN SYRUP, WATER.		

while reading your anchor book

Newspaper reports can influence public opinion.
Guiding Question: **How true is the information in a newspaper article?**

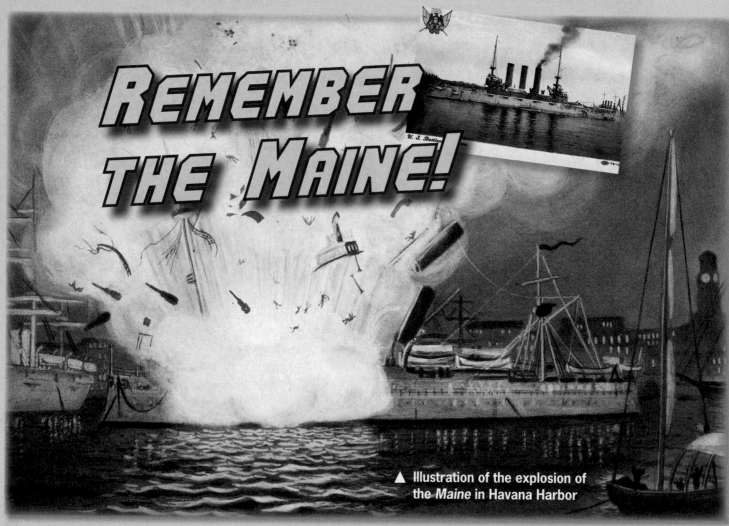

Remember the Maine!

▲ Illustration of the explosion of the *Maine* in Havana Harbor

Dangers to Peace

In the beginning of 1898, the United States was at peace. The United States had not fought in a major war since the Civil War, more than 30 years earlier. A generation had grown up without knowing the horrors of war. The nation took peace for granted.

Several events, however, were occurring that were about to upset that peace. Some Americans wanted the United States to become a world power by controlling more land. They were called imperialists, or empire builders. They dreamed of an American empire. At the same time, American jingoists (people who support a policy favoring war) demanded that the United States show its strength by being more aggressive. Another danger to the peace in America came from several of the leading U.S. newspapers. These newspapers tried to sway their readers' emotions to support a war. They paid little attention to facts in their news stories. These newspapers had a great influence on public opinion. They played an important role in the story of the *Maine*.

Cuba

The island of Cuba is 90 miles (145 kilometers) off the southeastern coast of the United States. In the 1890s, it became a focus of American interest. Businesses had invested money in Cuba's sugar fields. Politicians recognized Cuba's geographic and military importance to the United States. In general, Americans were concerned about the political situation in Cuba.

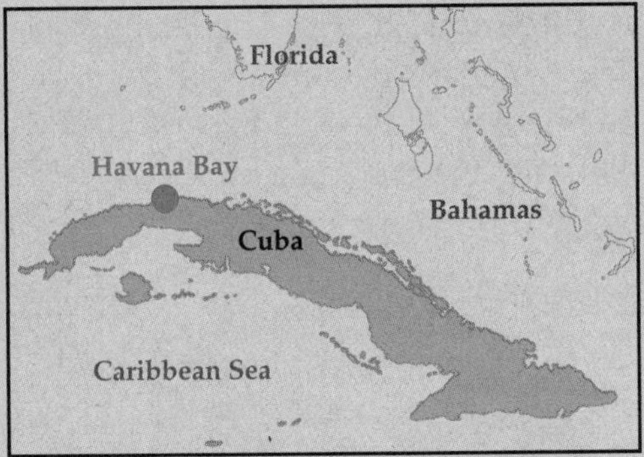

For years, Cuba had been under Spanish rule. Many Cubans wanted independence. In 1895, some Cubans attempted a revolt against Spain. The revolt failed. Spain sent a new governor, General Weyler, to the island. He treated the rebels cruelly and set up detention camps where many Cuban prisoners became sick and died.

Americans were shocked by the news from Cuba and they wanted to know more. Two New York newspapers saw a chance to sell more copies—they made Cuba a hot news topic.

Yellow Journalism

The two New York newspapers were Joseph Pulitzer's *The World* and William Randolph Hearst's *Journal*. These newspapers competed for stories about Cuba. They printed shocking stories with screaming headlines where Spain was always the villain. A group of Cubans in New York was giving information to the papers. The information was slanted, or biased, in favor of the rebels. It told only one side of the story.

The stories in *The World* and the *Journal* had little to do with the facts. Instead they tried to catch the readers' attention and sway their emotions. This kind of journalism became known as yellow journalism.

With great emotion, the newspapers reported about conditions in Cuba. One article read: "You would sicken at the sight of thousands of women and children starving to death in Cuba today . . . filthy skeletons dying on bare, foul boards." Another paper stated in an editorial piece: "If Spain will not put an end to murder in Cuba, the United States must."

The two newspapers urged the United States to go to war with Spain. Hearst told one photographer who was headed for Cuba, "You supply the pictures. I'll supply the war." The stories that the New York newspapers printed were picked up by newspapers all over the country and they had a great effect on the American people. Public opinion became set against Spain.

The Sinking of the Maine

In 1898, riots erupted in the city of Havana, the capital of Cuba. President McKinley wanted to protect American citizens in Cuba, so he ordered the battleship *Maine* into Havana Harbor. Shortly after the *Maine* arrived in Havana, it exploded.

Captain Sigsbee was the officer in charge of the *Maine*. He made the following report about the explosion.

> Maine *blown up in Havana Harbor at nine-forty tonight and destroyed. Many wounded and doubtless more killed or drowned. Wounded and others on board Spanish man-of-war and Ward Line steamer. Send lighthouse tenders from Key West for crew and the few pieces of equipment above water. No one has clothing other than that upon him.*

863,956 WORLDS CIRCULATED YESTERDAY

The World

Department of State

"Circulation Books Open to All."

NEW YORK, THURSDAY, FEBRUARY 17, 1898.

MAINE EXPLOSION CAUSED BY BOMB OR TORPEDO?

Capt. Sigsbee and Consul-General Lee Are in Doubt---The World Has Sent a Special Tug, With Submarine Divers, to Havana to Find Out---Lee Asks for an Immediate Court of Inquiry---Capt. Sigsbee's Suspicions.

CAPT. SIGSBEE, IN A SUPPRESSED DESPATCH TO THE STATE DEPARTMENT, SAYS THE ACCIDENT WAS MADE POSSIBLE BY AN ENEMY.

Dr. E. C. Pendleton, Just Arrived from Havana, Says He Overheard Talk There of a Plot to Blow Up the Ship---Capt Zalinski, the Dynamite Expert, and Other Experts Report to The World that the Wreck Was Not Accidental---Washington Officials Ready for Vigorous Action if Spanish Responsibility Can Be Shown---Divers to Be Sent Down to Make Careful Examinations.

The New York World a day after

who had been Populists and those who became Progressives — clamored for the United States to rescue the Cuban people from the Spanish malefactors.

President William McKinley and the conservative Republican leaders in Congress reluctantly gave way before this pressure. Senator Henry Cabot Lodge warned ... "If the war in Cuba drags on through the summer with ... party] shall go down in the greatest ...

Already, in ...

Front page headline in *The World* newspaper on February 17, 1898

. . . Public opinion should be suspended until further report . . . Many Spanish officers, including representatives of General Blanco, now with me to express sympathy.

The newspapers reported the explosion to the American people in a very different way. Only two days after the explosion, the front page headline of *The World* on February 17, 1898, read, "*Maine* Explosion Caused by Bomb or Torpedo?"

War Fever

No one was ever able to prove that Spain had caused the sinking of the *Maine*. The explosion may have been an accident, or it may have been planned. Whatever the cause, American public opinion was turned against Spain.

President McKinley tried to keep war from breaking out. He made an offer to Spain demanding that they end their presence in Cuba. Spain turned down McKinley's plan.

War fever ran high in the United States. The newspapers continued printing stories against Spain. Finally President McKinley recognized Cuba as an independent country and as a result, Spain declared war on the United States. The next day, Congress declared war on Spain, and the Spanish-American War had officially begun.

People lined the sidewalks in Washington, D.C. to view the funeral procession for the USS *Maine* victims.

Link to Social Studies

Literature in Context

On February 15, 1898, the United States battleship *Maine* sat in the harbor of Havana, Cuba. Suddenly a huge explosion caused the *Maine* to blow apart. More than 260 American sailors were killed. The ship's captain gave no cause for the explosion in his report, and a navy investigation failed to uncover any clear evidence. To this day, no one is sure what caused the explosion. So why did most Americans believe that Spain caused the explosion that blew up the ship?

Thinking About the Selection

Remember the *Maine!*

1 **Distinguish** Complete the chart. Decide if each statement is fact or opinion. Explain your decision.

Statement	Fact or Opinion	Explanation
"If Spain will not put an end to murder in Cuba, the United States must." —newspaper editorial		
"*Maine* blown up in Havana Harbor at nine-forty tonight and destroyed."— Captain Sigsbee		

2 **Interpret** A newspaper report stated, "You would sicken at the sight of . . . children starving to death in Cuba . . ." How do you think that report influenced its readers' opinions about the situation in Cuba?

3 **Speculate** Why do you think newspapers and magazines are able to convince people to agree with a certain opinion?

Write Answer the following questions in your Reader's Journal.

4 **Evaluate** How true is the information in a newspaper article?

5 **Support** Write three facts and three opinions you have about a character from your Anchor Book. Use details from the text to support your facts and opinions.

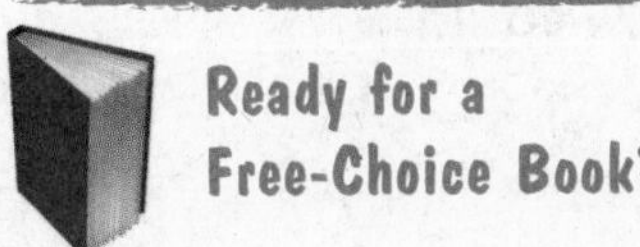

Ready for a Free-Choice Book? *Your teacher may ask you if you would like to choose another book to read on your own. Select a book that fits your interest and that you'll enjoy. As you read, think about how your new book compares with your Anchor Book.*

while reading your anchor book

1-12 Literary Analysis
Narrator and Point of View

Imagine watching a friend race at a swimming competition. After the race, you might say to her, "That was awesome! You looked so confident! "But your friend might respond, "I was terrified! My stomach was churning, and I almost missed the turn on the last lap." Why are the retellings of the same event so different? You each have a different point of view.

Literary Terms

- The **narrator** is the speaker or character who tells the story.
- The **point of view** is the position or angle from which a narrator tells a story.
  - In a **first-person point of view** account, the narrator participates in the action of the story and refers to himself or herself as "I." You only know what the narrator sees, thinks, or feels.
  - In a **third-person point of view** account, the narrator does not participate in the action of the story. A third-person narrator is an outside observer and can tell you how all the characters think or feel and what they see.
- In nonfiction writing, an **author's perspective** is the viewpoint from which he or she writes. This perspective reveals the author's attitudes, opinions, background, feelings, or personal interest in a subject. The author's perspective is reflected in the content of the writing and in the language he or she uses.

Usually, the point of view remains consistent throughout a passage. Look at the examples below.

Consistent *I'm* nervous when *I* skate. *I* feel like *I* could lose my balance.

Inconsistent *I'm* nervous when *I* skate. *You* feel like *you* could lose *your* balance.

Directions Read the following passage. Underline information that helps you identify the point of view. Then, answer the questions on the next page.

Go Online
About the Author
Visit: PHSchool.com
Web Code: exe-6106

from Tangerine *by Edward Bloor*

Once we dump this garbage bag, that will be it. That will be the last evidence that the Fisher family ever lived in Houston. Dad and my brother, Erik, are already gone. They've been living in Florida for a week now, with the sleeping bags, suitcases, and chairs that they stuffed into Dad's Range Rover. The rest of our furniture left yesterday, professionally packed by two guys who came to really hate Mom. By now it should be over halfway to our new address—a place called Lake Windsor Downs in Tangerine County, Florida.

I set the garbage bag down and leaned against the station wagon, staring east, directly into the rising sun. I'm not supposed to do that because my glasses are so thick. My brother, Erik, once told me that if I ever look directly into the sun with these glasses, my eyeballs will burst into flame, like dry leaves under a magnifying glass.

I don't believe that. But I turned back around anyway, and I looked west down our street at the receding line of black mailboxes. Something about them fascinated me. I leaned my chin against the top of the station wagon and continued to stare. An old familiar feeling came over me, like I had forgotten something. What was it? What did I need to remember?

Somewhere behind me a car engine started up, and a scene came back to me:

I remembered a black metal mailbox, on a black metal pole.

I was riding my bike home at dinnertime, heading east down this street, with the sun setting behind me. I heard a loud roar like an animal's, like a predator snarling. I swiveled my head around, still pedaling, and looked back. All I could see was the red sun, huge now, setting right over the middle of the street. I couldn't see anything else. But I could hear the roar, even louder now, and I recognized it: the roar of an engine revved up to full throttle.

while reading your anchor book

1 **Identify** What point of view is used in this passage? Use details from the text to explain how you know. How might the text be different if another point of view was used?

2 **Analyze** Why do you think the author chose not to use Erik as the narrator to convey the information in the passage?

3 **Apply** Suppose you are telling the story. Rewrite the second paragraph. Use a consistent third-person point of view.

4 **Infer** What can you infer about Erik from the way he told his brother not to look at the sun?

5 **Predict** What do you think is the next thing the narrator will say in the story? Provide details from the selection to support your prediction.

while reading your anchor book

The narrator of the next selection is an eleven-year-old girl in a war-torn city. *Guiding Question:* **Why is it important to know true accounts of children who have lived through a war?**

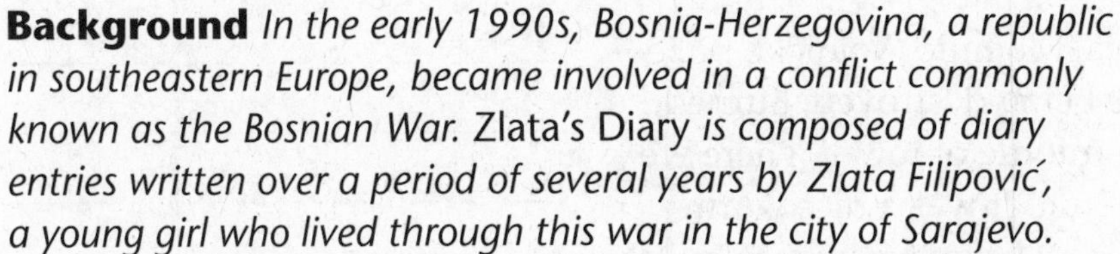

From Zlata's Diary

by Zlata Filipović

Background *In the early 1990s, Bosnia-Herzegovina, a republic in southeastern Europe, became involved in a conflict commonly known as the Bosnian War. Zlata's Diary is composed of diary entries written over a period of several years by Zlata Filipović, a young girl who lived through this war in the city of Sarajevo.*

Vocabulary Builder

Before you read, *you will discuss the following words. In the Vocabulary Builder box in the margin, use a vocabulary building strategy to make the words your own.*

humanity edgy shrapnel vanity case

As you read, *draw a box around unfamiliar words you could add to your vocabulary. Use context clues to unlock their meaning.*

Marking the Text

Narrator and Point of View

As you read, *underline details that tell how the writer feels about war. Circle words that indicate the point of view from which the story is told. In the margin, write notes about how the writer's feelings change as the war continues.*

Monday, March 30, 1992

Hey, Diary! You know what I think? Since Anne Frank[1] called her diary Kitty, maybe I could give you a name too. What about:

ASFALTINA PIDZAMETA
SEFIKA HIKMETA
SEVALA MIMMY or something else???
I'm thinking, thinking . . .
I've decided! I'm going to call you
MIMMY
All right, then, let's start.

[1] **Anne Frank** In 1942, thirteen-year old Anne Frank began a diary while hiding from the Nazis in an attic in Amsterdam. Anne died in a concentration camp in 1945. Her father published parts of the diary in 1947.

while reading your anchor book

Dear Mimmy,

It's almost half-term. We're all studying for our tests. Tomorrow we're supposed to go to a classical music concert at the Skenderija Hall. Our teacher says we shouldn't go because there will be 10,000 people, pardon me, children, there, and somebody might take us as hostages or plant a bomb in the concert hall. Mommy says I shouldn't go. So I won't.

Hey! You know who won the Yugovision Song Contest?! EXTRA NENA!!!???

I'm afraid to say this next thing. Melica says she heard at the hairdresser's that on Saturday, April 4, 1992, there's going to be BOOM-BOOM, BANG-BANG, CRASH Sarajevo. Translation: they're going to bomb Sarajevo.

Love, Zlata

Sunday, April 12, 1992

Dear Mimmy,

The new sections of town—Dobrinja, Mojmilo, Vojnicko polje—are being badly shelled. Everything is being destroyed, burned, the people are in shelters. Here in the middle of town, where we live, it's different. It's quiet. People go out. It was a nice warm spring day today. We went out too. Vaso Miskin Street was full of people, children. It looked like a peace march. People came out to be together, they don't want war. They want to live and enjoy themselves the way they used to. That's only natural, isn't it? Who likes or wants war, when it's the worst thing in the world?

I keep thinking about the march I joined today. It's bigger and stronger than war. That's why it will win. The people must be the ones to win, not the war, because war has nothing to do with **humanity.** War is something inhuman.

Zlata

Tuesday, April 14, 1992

Dear Mimmy,

People are leaving Sarajevo. The airport, train and bus stations are packed. I saw sad pictures on TV of people parting.

Families, friends separating. Some are leaving, others staying. It's so sad. Why? These people and children aren't guilty of anything. Keka and Braco[2] came early this morning. They're in the kitchen with Mommy and Daddy, whispering. Keka and Mommy are crying. I don't think they know what to do—whether to stay or to go. Neither way is good.

Zlata

[2] **Keka and Braco** nicknames of a husband and wife who are friends of Zlata's parents.

Marking the Text

Vocabulary Builder

humanity
(hyo͞o man´ətē) *n.*

Meaning

Critical Viewing What emotions do you see on the faces of these peace demonstrators?

Saturday, May 2, 1992

Dear Mimmy,

Today was truly, absolutely the worst day ever in Sarajevo. The shooting started around noon. Mommy and I moved into the hall. Daddy was in his office, under our apartment, at the time. We told him on the intercom to run quickly to the downstairs lobby where we'd meet him. We brought Cicko[3] with us. The gunfire was getting worse, and we couldn't get over the wall to the Bobars'[4] so we ran down to our own cellar.

The cellar is ugly, dark, smelly. Mommy, who's terrified of mice, had two fears to cope with. The three of us were in the same corner as the other day. We listened to the pounding shells, the shooting, the thundering noise overhead. We even heard planes. At one moment I realized that this awful cellar was the only place that could save our lives. Suddenly, it started to look almost warm and nice. It was the only way we could defend ourselves against all this terrible shooting. We heard glass shattering in our street. Horrible. I put my fingers in my ears to block out the terrible sounds. I was worried about Cicko. We had left him behind in the lobby. Would he catch cold there? Would something hit him? I was terribly hungry and thirsty. We had left our half-cooked lunch in the kitchen.

When the shooting died down a bit, Daddy ran over to our apartment and brought us back some sandwiches. He said he could smell something burning and that the phones weren't working. He brought our TV set down to the cellar. That's when

[3] **Cicko** (chek´ o) Zlata's canary.

[4] **Bobars'** (Bo´ bërs) Zlata's next-door neighbors.

▲ **Critical Viewing** What do you think the person who took this photo was trying to tell the viewer?

we learned that the main post office (near us) was on fire and that they had kidnapped our President. At around 8:00 we went back up to our apartment. Almost every window in our street was broken. Ours were all right, thank God. I saw the post office in flames. A terrible sight. The fire-fighters battled with the raging fire. Daddy took a few photos of the post office being devoured by the flames. He said they wouldn't come out because I had been fiddling with something on the camera. I was sorry. The whole apartment smelled of the burning fire. God, and I used to pass by there every day. It had just been done up. It was huge and beautiful, and now it was being swallowed up by the flames. It was disappearing. That's what this neighborhood of mine looks like, my Mimmy. I wonder what it's like in other parts of town? I heard on the radio that it was awful around the Eternal Flame.[5] The place is knee-deep in glass. We're worried about Grandma and Granddad. They live there. Tomorrow, if we can go out, we'll see how they are. A terrible day. This has been the worst, most awful day in my eleven-year-old life. I hope it will be the only one. Mommy and Daddy are very **edgy.** I have to go to bed.

Ciao![6] *Zlata*

Marking the Text

Vocabulary Builder

edgy
(ej´ē) *adj.*

Meaning

[5] **Eternal Flame** Sarajevo landmark that honors those who died resisting the Nazi occupation during World War II.

[6] **Ciao!** (chou) *interj.* hello or goodbye.

while reading your anchor book

Tuesday, May 5, 1992

Dear Mimmy,

The shooting seems to be dying down. I guess they've caused enough misery, although I don't know why. It has something to do with politics. I just hope the "kids" come to some agreement. Oh, if only they would, so we could live and breathe as human beings again. The things that have happened here these past few days are terrible. I want it to stop forever. PEACE! PEACE!

I didn't tell you, Mimmy, that we've rearranged things in the apartment. My room and Mommy and Daddy's are too dangerous to be in. They face the hills, which is where they're shooting from. If only you knew how scared I am to go near the windows and into those rooms. So, we turned a safe corner of the sitting room into a "bedroom." We sleep on mattresses on the floor. It's strange and awful. But, it's safer that way. We've turned everything around for safety. We put Cicko in the kitchen. He's safe there, although once the shooting starts there's nowhere safe except the cellar. I suppose all this will stop and we'll all go back to our usual places.

Ciao! Zlata

Thursday, May, 7 1992

Dear Mimmy,

I was almost positive the war would stop, but today . . . Today a shell fell on the park in front of my house, the park where I used to play and sit with my girlfriends. A lot of people were hurt. From what I hear Jaca, Jaca's mother, Selma, Nina, our neighbor Dado and who knows how many other people who happened to be there were wounded. Dado, Jaca and her mother have come home from the hospital, Selma lost a kidney but I don't know how she is, because she's still in the hospital. AND NINA IS DEAD. A piece of **shrapnel** lodged in her brain and she died. She was such a sweet, nice little girl. We went to kindergarten together, and we used to play together in the park. Is it possible I'll never see Nina again? Nina, an innocent eleven-year-old little girl—the victim of a stupid war. I feel sad. I cry and wonder why? She didn't do anything. A disgusting war has destroyed a young child's life. Nina, I'll always remember you as a wonderful little girl.

Love, Zlata

Marking the Text

Vocabulary Builder

shrapnel
(shrap´nəl) *n.*

Meaning

while reading your anchor book

▲ **Critical Viewing**
How does this photo compare to how you picture someone who lives in a war-torn country?

Monday, June 29, 1992

Dear Mimmy,

BOREDOM!!! SHOOTING!!! SHELLING!!! PEOPLE BEING KILLED!!! DESPAIR!!! HUNGER!!! MISERY!!! FEAR!!!

That's my life! The life of an innocent eleven-year-old schoolgirl!! A schoolgirl without a school, without the fun and excitement of school. A child without games, without friends, without the sun, without birds, without nature, without fruit, without chocolate or sweets, with just a little powdered milk. In short, a child without a childhood. A wartime child. I now realize that I am really living through a war, I am witnessing an ugly, disgusting war. I and thousands of other children in this town that is being destroyed, that is crying, weeping, seeking help, but getting none. God, will this ever stop, will I ever be a schoolgirl again, will I ever enjoy my childhood again? I once heard that childhood is the most wonderful time of your life. And it is. I loved it, and now an ugly war is taking it all away from me. Why? I feel sad. I feel like crying. I am crying.

Your Zlata

Marking the Text

Thursday, October 29, 1992

Dear Mimmy,

Mommy and Auntie Ivanka (from her office) have received grants to specialize in Holland. They have letters of guarantee,[7] and there's even one for me. But Mommy can't decide. If she accepts, she leaves behind Daddy, her parents, her brother. I think it's a hard decision to make. One minute I think—no, I'm against it. But then I remember the war, winter, hunger, my stolen childhood and I feel like going. Then I think of Daddy, Grandma and Granddad, and I don't want to go. It's hard to know what to do. I'm really on edge, Mimmy, I can't write anymore.

Your Zlata

Monday, November 2, 1992

Dear Mimmy,

Mommy thought it over, talked to Daddy, Grandma and Granddad, and to me, and she's decided to go. The reason for her decision is—ME. What's happening in Sarajevo is already too much for me, and the coming winter will make it even harder. All right. But . . . well, I suppose it's better for me to go. I really can't stand it here anymore. I talked to Auntie Ivanka today and she told me that this war is hardest on the children, and that the children should be got out of the city. Daddy will manage, maybe he'll even get to come with us.

Ciao! Zlata

Thursday, December 3, 1992

Dear Mimmy,

Today is my birthday. My first wartime birthday. Twelve years old. Congratulations. Happy birthday to me!

The day started off with kisses and congratulations. First Mommy and Daddy, then everyone else. Mommy and Daddy gave me three Chinese **vanity cases**—with flowers on them!

As usual there was no electricity. Auntie Melica came with her family (Kenan, Naida, Nihad) and gave me a book. And Braco Lajtner came, of course. The whole neighborhood got together in the evening. I got chocolate, vitamins, a heart-shaped soap (small, orange), a key chain with a picture of Maja and Bojana, a pendant made of a stone from Cyprus, a ring (silver) and earrings (bingo!).

Vocabulary Builder

vanity case
(van´tē kās) *n.*

Meaning

[7] **letters of guarantee** *n.* letters from people or companies promising to help individuals leave the country during the war.

Literature in Context
Remembering

"Aftershocks: Art and Memoirs of Growing Up in the Aftermath" is an exhibit created by teen survivors of the Bosnian War. The exhibit contains artwork and writing about the teens' experiences during the war. This collage was created by five Sarajevo teenagers to represent their dark memories from the past and hopeful thoughts for the future. The teens created this "self portrait" to show the experiences they have in common with other children of war.

The exhibit also includes pieces by students who witnessed the World Trade Center tragedy in 2001.

Good To Know!
The collage at right was created by five Sarajevo teenagers as a "group self-portrait" to reflect the experiences they have in common as children of war.

The table was nicely laid, with little rolls, fish and rice salad, cream cheese (with Feta), canned corned beef, a pie, and, of course—a birthday cake. Not how it used to be, but there's a war on. Luckily there was no shooting, so we could celebrate.

It was nice, but something was missing. It's called peace!

Your Zlata

Tuesday, July 27, 1993

Dear Mimmy,

Journalists, reporters, TV and radio crews from all over the world (even Japan). They're interested in you, Mimmy, and ask me about you, but also about me. It's exciting. Nice. Unusual for a wartime child.

My days have changed a little. They're more interesting now. It takes my mind off things. When I go to bed at night I think about the day behind me. Nice, as though it weren't wartime, and with such thoughts I happily fall asleep.

But in the morning, when the wheels of the water carts wake me up, I realize that there's a war on, that mine is a wartime life. SHOOTING, NO ELECTRICITY, NO WATER, NO GAS, NO FOOD. Almost no life.

Zlata

Marking the Text

Thursday, October 7, 1993

Dear Mimmy,

Things are the way they used to be, lately. There's no shooting (thank God), I go to school, read, play the piano . . .

Winter is approaching, but we have nothing to heat with.

I look at the calendar and it seems as though this year of 1993 will again be marked by war. God, we've lost two years listening to gunfire, battling with electricity, water, food, and waiting for peace.

I look at Mommy and Daddy. In two years they've aged ten. And me? I haven't aged, but I've grown, although I honestly don't know how. I don't eat fruit or vegetables, I don't drink juices, I don't eat meat . . . I am a child of rice, peas and spaghetti. There I am talking about food again. I often catch myself dreaming about chicken, a good cutlet, pizza, lasagna . . . Oh, enough of that.

Zlata

Tuesday, October 12, 1993

Dear Mimmy,

I don't remember whether I told you that last summer I sent a letter through school to a pen-pal in America. It was a letter for an American girl or boy.

Today I got an answer. A boy wrote to me. His name is Brandon, he's twelve like me, and lives in Harrisburg, Pennsylvania. It really made me happy.

I don't know who invented the mail and letters, but thank you whoever you are. I now have a friend in America, and Brandon has a friend in Sarajevo. This is my first letter from across the Atlantic. And in it is a reply envelope, and a lovely pencil.

A Canadian TV crew and journalist from *The Sunday Times* (Janine) came to our gym class today. They brought me two chocolate bars. What a treat. It's been a long time since I've had sweets.

Love,
Zlata

Marking the Text

▼ **Critical Viewing**
What do you think the people in line are waiting for? What can you infer about the situation from their body language and the emotion in their facial expressions?

December 1993

Dear Mimmy,

PARIS. There's electricity, there's water, there's gas. There's, there's . . . life, Mimmy. Yes, life; bright lights, traffic, people, food . . . Don't think I've gone nuts, Mimmy. Hey, listen to me, Paris!? No, I'm not crazy, I'm not kidding, it really is Paris and (can you believe it?) me in it. Me, my Mommy and my Daddy. At last. You're 100% sure I'm crazy, but I'm serious, I'm telling you, dear Mimmy, that I have arrived in Paris. I've come to be with you. You're mine again now and together we're moving into the light. The darkness has played out its part. The darkness is behind us; now we're bathed in light lit by good people. Remember that—good people. Bulb by bulb, not candles, but bulb by bulb, and me bathing in the lights of Paris. Yes, Paris. Incredible. You don't understand. You know, I don't think I understand either. I feel as though I must be crazy, dreaming, as though it's a fairy tale, but it's all TRUE.

Love,
Zlata

Marking the Text

Vocabulary Builder

After you read, *review the words you decided to add to your vocabulary. Write the meaning of words you have learned in context. Look up the other words in a dictionary, glossary, thesaurus, or electronic resource.*

Zlata Filipović

When asked why she began her diary, Zlata Filipović responded, "I wanted to have one place where I could keep my memories." These "memories" were a young girl's day-to-day impressions of life in the war-torn city of Sarajevo, the capital of Bosnia-Herzegovina. *Zlata's Diary* has been translated into more than twenty languages and published in countries throughout the world. Zlata and her parents promote peace by speaking all over the world. Zlata has used earnings from the sale of her book to begin a charity to help victims of the Bosnian war.

Thinking About the Selection

Zlata's Diary

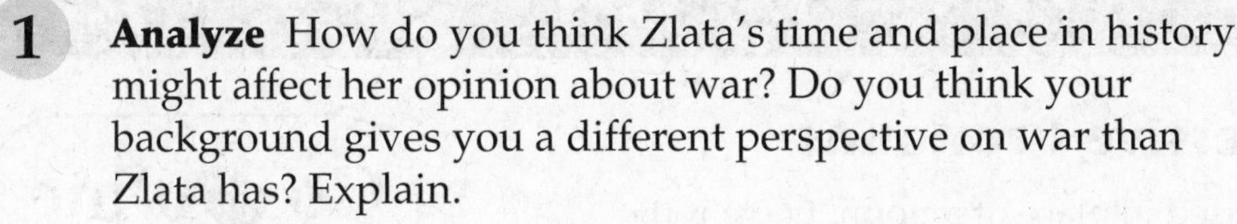

1. **Analyze** How do you think Zlata's time and place in history might affect her opinion about war? Do you think your background gives you a different perspective on war than Zlata has? Explain.

2. **Infer** Use sensory details—smells, sights, sounds—from Zlata's description to tell what you think it would be like to retreat to a cellar for protection.

3. **Interpret** What do you think Zlata meant in the last entry of the excerpt when she talks about "moving into the light" and "the darkness has played out its part"?

4. **Explain** On May 5, 1992, Zlata writes that she hopes "the 'kids' come to some agreement." What do you think Zlata means by "the kids"?

Write Answer the following questions in your Reader's Journal.

5. **Assess** Why is it important to know true accounts of children who have lived through a war?

6. **Apply** If your Anchor Book is fiction, identify the narrator's point of view. Use details from the text to explain your answer. If your Anchor Book is nonfiction, describe the author's perspective.

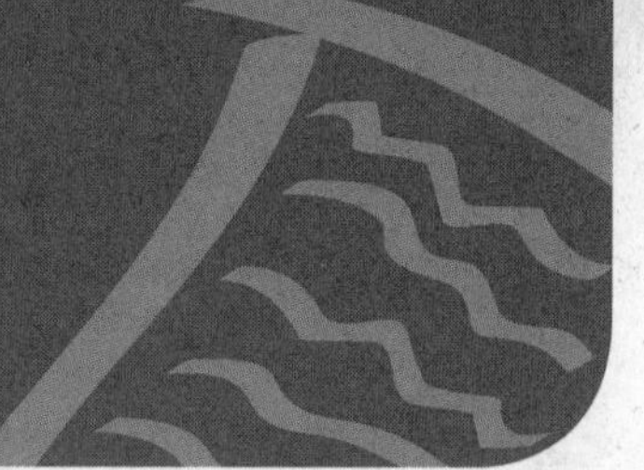

1-13 Language Coach
Grammar and Spelling

Personal and Possessive Pronouns

A **pronoun** is a word that is used in place of a noun. Look at the sentences below.

- *Sandra* went shopping at the farmer's market, where *she* bought four different types of apples. She used them to make an apple crunch.

In this example, the pronoun *she* takes the place of the noun *Sandra*.

The **antecedent** is the noun that the pronoun refers to or replaces. *Sandra* is the antecedent of *she*.

A **personal pronoun** takes the place of a noun that appears somewhere else in the sentence or paragraph. *Them* is a personal pronoun because it refers to the noun *apples*.

Personal Pronouns	I, me, he, she, him, her, you, it, they, them, we

Like personal pronouns, **possessive pronouns** refer to a noun. Possessive pronouns function as adjectives. They answer the question *Whose?*

Possessive Pronouns	my, mine, his, her, your, yours, its, our, ours, their, theirs

Directions Revise the following paragraph by replacing some of the nouns with personal and possessive pronouns. Circle the personal pronouns in your new paragraph. Underline the possessive pronouns.

One morning, Pedro looked out Pedro's window. In the tree in Pedro's yard, Pedro saw three baby birds. The birds seemed to be crying for the birds' mother. The birds quieted down a moment later when the mother arrived with worms for the birds to eat. Once the mother was finished feeding the baby birds, the mother flew out of the tree. Pedro was excited—Pedro had never seen anything like what Pedro saw.

Go Online

Learn More
Visit: PHSchool.com
Web Code: exp-6105

Author's Craft

How important are personal pronouns? To find out, scan "Remember the *Maine*" on page 50. Choose a paragraph that contains several personal pronouns. Cross out each one and replace it with its antecedent. Then, read your revised paragraph to a partner, and listen to your partner's paragraph. How do they sound? What does the difference in sound tell you about the importance of pronouns?

Pronoun and Antecedent Agreement

Remember that a **pronoun** is a word that is used in place of a noun and an **antecedent** is the noun that the pronoun refers to or replaces. Pronouns keep writers from repeating the same noun over and over.

- *Sal* went to the beach. *He* was looking for shells to collect. (The pronoun *he* takes the place of the noun *Sal*.)

A pronoun and its antecedent must agree in number, person, and gender. Use a singular pronoun with a singular antecedent and a plural pronoun with a plural antecedent.

Singular Pronoun and Antecedent	Plural Pronoun and Antecedent
The *film* won several awards for *its* special effects.	Those *beans* will not cook properly unless you soak *them* first.

Directions Identify each pronoun and its antecedent.

1 Many of the girls on the softball team bring their own gloves.

The pronoun __________ takes the place of the noun ________.

2 Take care of my plants, but do not give them too much water.

The pronoun __________ takes the place of the noun ________.

3 One of the boys in the class has left his backpack on the floor.

The pronoun __________ takes the place of the noun ________.

4 As the sun set, it cast a shadow across the valley.

The pronoun ________ takes the place of the noun ______.

Directions Rewrite the following paragraph so that the pronouns and antecedents agree in number, person, and gender.

5 The dog walked up to Bill, wagging their tail. Bill reached out its hand to pet the dog. As Bill looked down at her shoes, he noticed that it were untied. As he leaned over to tie it, she was face to face with the dog. For a moment, we stared into each other's eyes. "What are you looking at?" Bill joked.

____

____

____

____

____

Interrogative and Indefinite Pronouns

An **interrogative pronoun** is another type of pronoun. It is used to introduce a question. In the sentence below, the interrogative pronoun *who* represents the person or people with whom Daniel went fishing.

▸ *Who* went fishing with Daniel?

Interrogative Pronouns	who, whom, whose, what, which

Indefinite pronouns do not take the place of a particular noun. Instead, they refer to people, places, or things in a general way. Some indefinite pronouns are singular and others are plural. Depending on how they are used, a few may be singular or plural.

Type	Pronouns	Example
Singular Indefinite Pronouns	anyone, anything, each, either, everyone, everything, much, nobody, nothing, one, other, somebody, someone	*Everyone* is ready to go.
Plural Indefinite Pronouns	both, few, many, others, several	*Both* of my sisters are in the car.
Singular or Plural Indefinite Pronouns	all, more, most, none, some	*All* of them are fast. *All* of it is exciting.

Directions Write a sentence using the type of pronoun shown in the parentheses. Then underline the pronoun.

1 (plural indefinite) ______________________________

2 (interrogative) ______________________________

3 (singular indefinite) ______________________________

4 (singular or plural indefinite) ______________________________

Go Online
Learn More
Visit: PHSchool.com
Web Code: exp-6107

Author's Craft

Good authors recognize when it is better to use indefinite pronouns and when it is better to use specific details. Turn to "Zlata's Diary" on page 57. Working with a partner, find one indefinite pronoun that you think is appropriate, and one that you think should be replaced with specific detail. Explain your choices.

Indefinite Pronoun-Antecedent Agreement

Sometimes an antecedent is not a noun but an indefinite pronoun, such as *anyone.* Below is a list of some indefinite pronouns.

Singular Indefinite Pronouns	Plural Indefinite Pronouns
another, everything, each, everyone, one, someone, something, nothing, anyone	both, few, many, others, several, all

Singular Indefinite Pronoun as Antecedent	Plural Indefinite Pronoun as Antecedent
Can *anyone* lend me *his* or *her* jacket?	*Many* of the cats recovered after *they* were treated by a vet.

It is important to be sure pronouns and their antecedents agree in number—that they are both singular or both plural. When they do not agree, writing becomes confusing or awkward.

Incorrect Someone (antecedent) took their (pronoun) hat but forgot her gloves.

Correct Someone (antecedent) took her (pronoun) hat but forgot her gloves.

Pronouns and their antecedents must also agree in gender. Sometimes, though, the gender of the antecedent is unclear. When you do not know the gender of a singular indefinite pronoun, use *his or her* or *him or her*.

Everyone (antecedent) is allowed to have his or her (pronoun) own opinion.

Directions Rewrite the following sentences to correct pronoun-antecedent agreement. Then underline the pronoun and circle the antecedent. If the sentence is correct, write *correct*.

1 Everyone in the library was quietly working on their research.

____

2 That one is a favorite with teens because of their theme.

____

3 Few of the students returned their permission slips the next day.

____

4 Several of the students in class were really disappointed in his or her grades.

____

1-14 Writer's Workshop
Research: News Report

A **news report** is a factual telling of an event or situation usually found in a newspaper or magazine. People read news reports differently than they read a short story or a novel. Readers skim magazines and newspapers for news reports that contain information they want to know more about. The eye-catching headlines and to-the-point text help readers spot what they want to read. In this Writer's Workshop, you will write your own news report about an event at school.

Purpose To write a news report about a school event

Audience You, your teacher, and your classmates

To create an effective news report, include the following elements.

- an attention-grabbing headline
- answers to the questions *Who? What? When? Where? Why? How?*
- accurate retelling of the facts surrounding an event
- clear organizational format
- concise, informative, and direct statements
- eyewitness accounts from people at the event
- error-free punctuation, grammar, and correct use of pronouns

Prewriting—Plan It Out

Here are some strategies to help you plan your news report.

Choose your topic. In the chart, list events that have recently occurred at your school. Give details that tell what makes the events interesting. Choose one event as the topic of your report.

What's Going On?	Why Is This Interesting?
Basketball team goes to state finals.	It's been five years since the team made it to the state finals.

Identify and interview sources. Think of someone involved with the event, and interview him or her to gather information. For a story about a basketball game, you might interview a member of the team, the coach, or an audience member. Think of questions that will help your interview subject provide more detail.

Organize information. Start organizing your information. Write details in information blocks like the ones following below.

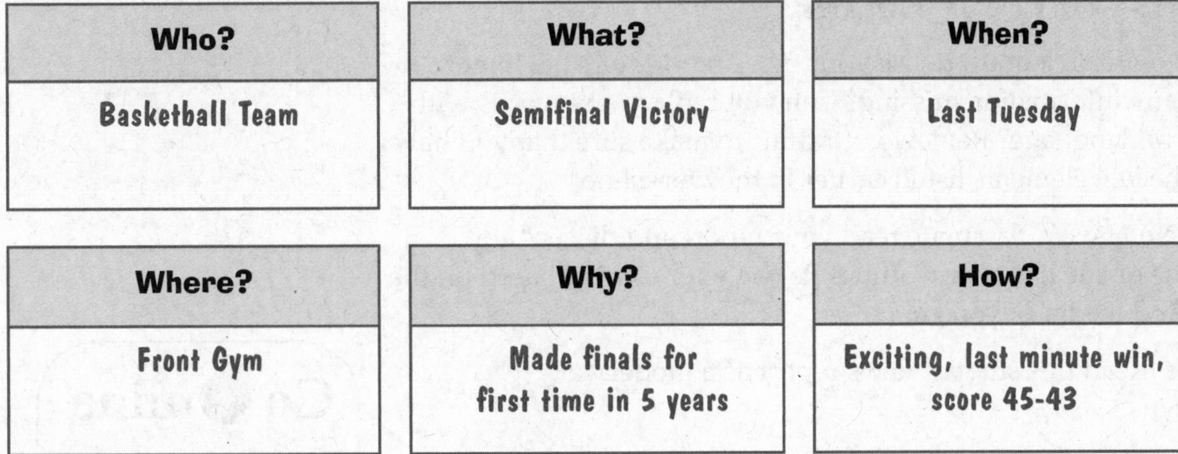

Who?	What?	When?
Basketball Team	Semifinal Victory	Last Tuesday

Where?	Why?	How?
Front Gym	Made finals for first time in 5 years	Exciting, last minute win, score 45-43

Drafting—Get It on Paper

News reports are written using an inverted pyramid format. The most important information is at the top—the beginning of your report—and the least important information is at the bottom—the end.

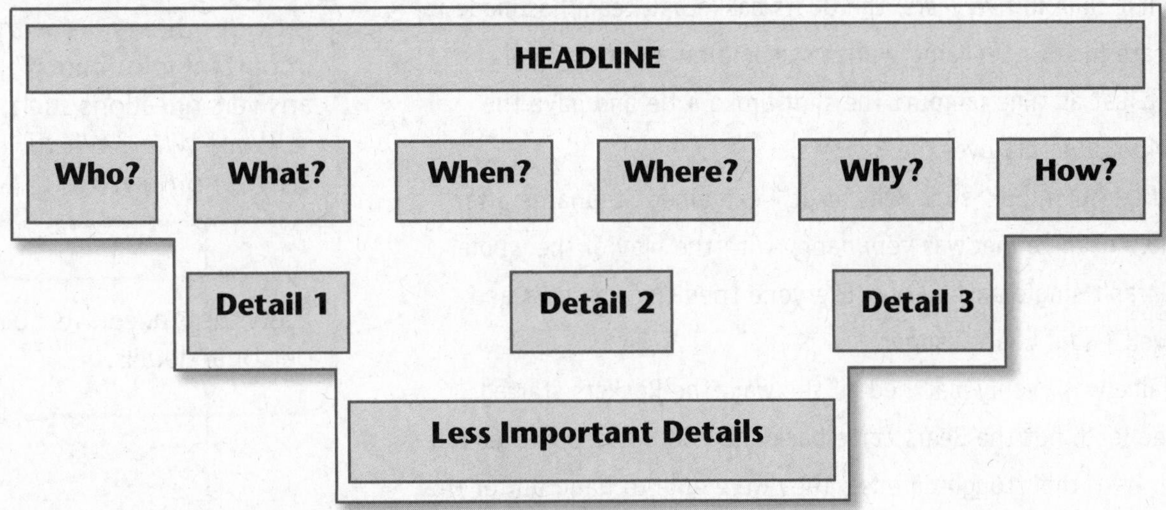

The **headline** should grab your reader's attention. It should be compact, very specific, and clearly focused. Which headline would grab your attention and keep you reading?

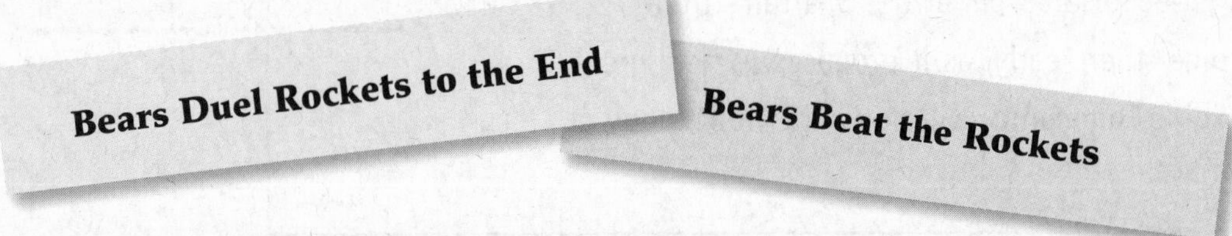

The first, or lead, sentence or paragraph should answer questions such as *Who? What? When? Where? Why?* and *How?* The sentences or paragraphs that follow should provide more details, with the most important details presented first.

Revising—Make It Better

Now that you have a draft, revise your news report to make it more precise. Is any information missing? Can you replace any words with more colorful language? Review your draft to make sure that you have followed the key elements listed earlier in the workshop.

Peer Review Have a classmate read your report and discuss any questions he or she has after reading. Revise your writing based on the questions and feedback you get.

Directions Read this student news report as a model for your own.

Go Online
Student Model
Visit: PHSchool.com
Web Code: exr-6102

Student Model: Writing

Bears Duel Rockets to the End

by Andy Rubin

For the first time in five years, the Bears basketball team has made it to the state finals! Stephanie Williams scored on an open jump shot yesterday just as time ran out. The shot broke a tie and gave the Bears a 45-43 victory over the Rockets.

"I had an open look, so I went for it," explained Stephanie after the game. Coach Launer was very happy with the play of the whole team. "I can't single anyone out. Everyone tried their hardest and played well," said Coach Launer.

The game was evenly matched all the way. The Rockets started out in the lead, but the Bears came back and had a five-point lead at halftime. With their tough defense, they were able to hang on for the win.

The Bears will face the Spartans in the state finals this Saturday. These two have met twice before this season, each team winning one game. The tip-off is set for 2:05 pm at the Spartan's front gymnasium. Be sure to get there early, as it promises to be a great game. As always, the Spirit Community will be in the front lobby of the gym with concessions.

The first sentence provides the reader with important information. It answers questions such as *Who? What? When? Why?* and *How?*

Eyewitness accounts add personal details.

The writer adds important details about the upcoming event.

Editing—Be Your Own Language Coach

Before you hand in your news report, review it for language convention errors. Pay special attention to your use of pronouns.

Publishing—Share It!

When you publish a work, you produce it for a specific audience. Consider one of the following ideas to share your writing.

Submit your article. Give your article to the school or local newspaper.

Put it on poster board. Mount your article so your friends can read it.

Present your article. Read your article aloud to the class or to the people involved in the event you wrote about.

Reflecting on Your Writing

1. Respond to the following question on the back of your final draft. What new insights did you gain about the form of the news report by writing one?

2. **Rubric for Self-Assessment** Assess your news report. For each question, circle a rating.

CRITERIA	RATING SCALE
	NOT VERY — VERY
IDEAS Is your news report clear and focused with rich details?	1 2 3 4 5
ORGANIZATION How logical and consistent is your organization?	1 2 3 4 5
VOICE Is your writing lively and engaging, drawing the reader in?	1 2 3 4 5
WORD CHOICE Do your words convey a message in a powerful way?	1 2 3 4 5
SENTENCE FLUENCY Does your writing have an easy flow and rhythm with varied sentence structure?	1 2 3 4 5
CONVENTIONS How correct is your grammar, especially your use of pronouns?	1 2 3 4 5

1-15 Discussing Your Anchor Book
Literature Circles

Writing a narrative is like building a house. There are certain things that every house has, but in the end each house is unique. The same goes for writing a narrative. How it is built is up to the author. These choices the author makes for building a narrative determine the **narrative structure.**

The structure of a narrative—the way the author plans out the story being told or the events taking place—depends on the type of narrative. For example, a short story might start in the middle of the action, while a biography might begin with lots of background about the subject's family.

Here are a few questions that you can ask about the structure of a narrative. Knowing the structure can help you identify the type of narrative you are reading.

- Does the text include lots of background information?
- Does it build slowly, or start in the middle of the action?
- Is it organized in chronological order, or in a different order?
- Does it cover a long or short period of time?
- Does it tell about one event, or a group of related events?

1 Identify

- Read the descriptions of the narratives in the chart. With your group, discuss the clues about the narrative structure. Identify what type of narrative it is. Then think of a book title that fits this type of narrative or make up a title and write it in the right-hand column.

1	**Type of narrative:** ______	**Sample titles:**
	______ ► nonfiction ► first-person point of view ► tells story of narrator's life	______ ______ ______ ______

while reading your anchor book

2 Type of narrative: ______	Sample titles:
▸ fiction ▸ brief; meant to be read in one sitting ▸ includes character, setting, plot ▸ contains single conflict	

3 Type of narrative: ______	Sample titles:
▸ nonfiction ▸ third-person point of view ▸ narrative is mostly chronological, with some flashbacks ▸ tells the story of someone's life	

2 Discuss

▸ Now think about the narrative structure of your Anchor Book. Discuss with your group the questions on the previous page. Then answer the following questions about your Anchor Book.

1 How is your Anchor Book organized?

2 How much time is covered?

3 Does the book focus on one main story or event or more than one?

4 Why do you think the author chose this narrative structure? Do you think this structure was effective?

while reading your anchor book

1-16 Connecting to Your Anchor Book

Anchor Book Projects

Now that you have completed reading your Anchor Book, it is time to get creative! Complete one of the following projects.

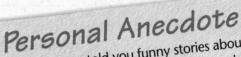

A Personal Anecdote

Have your family members ever told you funny stories about their lives? These stories, called anecdotes, are short narratives about biographical events. Besides being entertaining, anecdotes can help to explain information that might not be familiar to others. For example, your grandmother might tell you how she was involved in the civil rights movement. For this project, use your own experiences to write a personal anecdote that helps explain a topic or issue from your Anchor Book.

1. List events, characters, or places from your Anchor Book. Choose one that relates to your life as the subject of your anecdote.
2. Write your personal anecdote. Make it no longer than one page. Use sensory language and a clear voice.

Your personal anecdote should include the following.

- A topic from your Anchor Book that relates to your own life
- A well-developed story that provides information about your life
- Sensory language that captures the reader's interest

Give a Speech

Speeches are an effective way to communicate information. *How* it is said is just as important as *what* is said. Gestures, body language, and eye contact help to emphasize the message of the speech. These elements also help to capture and maintain an audience's attention. Write a speech about a conflict or issue faced by a character in your Anchor Book. Then deliver a speech to the class, using proper gestures, body language, and eye contact.

1. Think about a conflict faced by a character in your Anchor Book. How might you handle the conflict differently? List your ideas.
2. Determine the purpose of your speech. Will it be to entertain, to persuade, or to inform your audience?
3. Write your speech. Make sure the tone matches its purpose.
4. Recite your speech to the class.

Your speech should include the following.

- A well-reasoned response to an issue or conflict a character faces
- Strong delivery, including appropriate language choice, body language, and eye contact

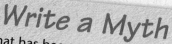

Write a Myth

C

A myth is a narrative that has been passed down verbally from generation to generation. Myths often explain events in nature or how something came to be. For example, one myth explains the Sun's movements throughout the day with a story about Apollo who drives a golden chariot across the sky from east to west. Other myths might explain why bears have short tails or why the Sun and Moon live in the sky. Consider the setting in your Anchor Book. Write a myth that explains the existence of one detail of the setting, such as a river, a mountain, a special type of bird, or season.

1. Choose a detail of the setting, such as moonlight, as the focus of your myth. On a separate sheet of paper, describe how this detail came to be. Feel free to create your own mythical beings or heroes.
2. Create a myth that explains or tells a story about that detail and its significance, its origins, or its destruction.

Your myth should include the following.

- A detail from your Anchor Book
- A thoughtful and creative story that explains how that detail came to be
- Features in a myth, such as gods and heroes

Free-Choice Book Reflection

You have completed your free-choice book. Before you take your test, read the following instructions to write a brief reflection of your book.

My free-choice book is ______________________________.

The author is ______________________________.

1 Would you recommend this book to a friend? Yes _____ No _____

Why or why not?

____

____

Write Answer the following question in your Reader's Journal.

2 **Compare and Contrast** *How do we decide what is true?* Compare and contrast how your Anchor Book and free-choice book help to answer this question. Use specific details from both books to support your answer.

Standardized Test Practice

Answer the questions below to check your understanding of this unit's skills.

Reading Skills: Making Predictions

Read this selection. Then answer the questions that follow.

> As Heather walked to school, she spotted a squirrel gathering acorns. She remembered that she had been scurrying around the night before just like the squirrel. She had been trying to finish writing note cards for the speech that she would give in front of the whole school today. She was certain that she remembered placing the note cards in her bag. As she entered the school, she remembered that she took some things out of her bag right before she left home. She began to feel butterflies in her stomach.

1 Which of the following do you **predict** will happen to Heather?

A. She will finish writing her note cards.

B. She will empty out her bag and not find her note cards.

C. She will trip over the squirrel that she saw earlier.

D. She will find the squirrel eating her note cards.

2 Which detail BEST supports your **prediction?**

F. She was trying to finish up her note cards for the speech.

G. She spotted a squirrel gathering acorns.

H. She had been scurrying around the night before.

J. She remembered she took some things out of her bag.

Reading Skills: Fact and Opinion

Read this selection. Then answer the questions that follow.

> Every year, thousands of kids in the United States are injured. This is one of the most important issues for parents. The injury could be as simple as a bruised shin that can be treated with ice at home. Other injuries can be more serious and need the attention of a hospital nurse or doctor. In some cases, an injury could even require surgery. This is a concern because there are always risks when an operation is involved. In general, kids just aren't as careful as they should be. Parents also need to teach safety tips to their children.

3 Which of these statements is a **fact?**

A. Parents also need to teach safety tips to their children.

B. Every year, thousands of kids in the United States are injured.

C. In general, kids just aren't as careful as they should be.

D. This is one of the most important issues for parents.

4 Which is a good source for proving facts?

F. encyclopedia

G. novel

H. conversation with a friend

J. advertisements

5 Which phrase helps you recognize an **opinion?**

A. "require surgery"

B. "can be treated"

C. "most important issues"

D. "teach safety"

6 Which will help you recognize a fact?

F. words that determine feelings, such as *I believe*

G. words that determine judgment, such as *wonderful*

H. words that determine viewpoint, such as *always*

J. words that provide dates and statistics, such as *on this day in 1900*

Literary Analysis: Elements of Fiction and Nonfiction

Read this selection and answer the questions that follow.

> When I first arrived here, it was right in the middle of the hottest, driest summer on record. I could feel the grimy, dry dust covering my clothes like a blanket whenever a car drove by, and when I breathed in really, really deep it felt like sand paper scratching the inside of my throat. At night, the strange symphony of noises that came from the creaky, crackling woods across the street were enough to cause me to cry myself to sleep almost every night for a week! I muffled wet sniffles in my soggy pillow so my mom wouldn't hear me. I didn't want her to know how much I missed my best friend Janine, my school, my own bed—my whole life!

Choose the best answer for the following questions.

7 Which example of **sensory language** from the passage helps you understand what the narrator was hearing?

A. sand paper scratching

B. hottest, driest summer

C. creaky, crackling woods

D. grimy, dry dust

8 What is the **point of view** of the passage?

F. third person

G. first person

H. first person and third person

J. second person

9 Which of the following is always found in **fiction narrative** writing?

A. comparisons

B. conflict

C. danger

D. author's perspective

10 Which of these elements is found in nonfiction writing?

F. accounts of people and places

G. fantasy

H. strong opinions

J. science fiction

11 Which genre is an example of **nonfiction narrative** writing?

A. novel

B. novella

C. autobiography

D. short story

12 What point of view is used if the narrator is not a part of the story's action?

F. second person

G. third person

H. first person

J. first and third person

Language Skills: Vocabulary

Choose the best answer.

13 Which of the following is NOT a strategy for unlocking word meanings?

A. Ignore the word and continue reading.

B. Say the word aloud.

C. Break the word into parts, such as prefixes and base words.

D. Look for pictures or illustrations that might suggest the word's meaning.

14 Choose the word that has the same meaning as the words underlined in the sentence.

Buffalo were <u>introduced again</u> to their native habitat once enough had been bred in captivity.

F. returned

G. revealed

H. reintroduced

J. reinstated

15 What does the word *misunderstand* mean?

A. to understand before

B. to understand incorrectly

C. to understand again

D. to understand well

16 What does the **prefix** *dis-* mean?

F. from

G. out

H. opposite of

J. wrong

Language Skills: Grammar

Choose the best answer.

17 Which word is a **proper noun?**

A. encyclopedia

B. bottled water

C. Tuesday

D. apple pie

18 Which word is a **common noun?**

F. river

G. Statue of Liberty

H. President Washington

J. Elm Street

19 Nouns that end in *ch, s, x,* or *z* are made **plural** by adding ________.

A. *-es*

B. *-s*

C. *-ies*

D. *-oes*

20 What is the possessive form of the noun "boxes"?

F. boxes

G. boxes's

H. box'es

J. boxes'

21 What is the **antecedent** of the pronoun *they* in this sentence?

I remembered to shut the windows before the storm so they wouldn't let in the rain.

A. I

B. windows

C. storm

D. rain

22 Complete the following sentence using the correct **indefinite pronoun.**

Can anyone lend me ________ book?

F. his or her

G. his and her

H. his

J. their

Language Skills: Spelling

Choose the best answer.

23 Choose the correct words to complete the following sentence:

My cousin got higher scores ________ my brother, but ________ they played again.

A. than, then

B. then, then

C. then, than

D. than, than

24 Choose the correct words to complete the following sentence:

________ family dogs are sad because they ________ not coming to the beach.

F. Are, are

G. Are, our

H. Our, our

J. Our, are

THE BIG ? Is *conflict* always bad?

Unit 2 Genre focus: The Novel

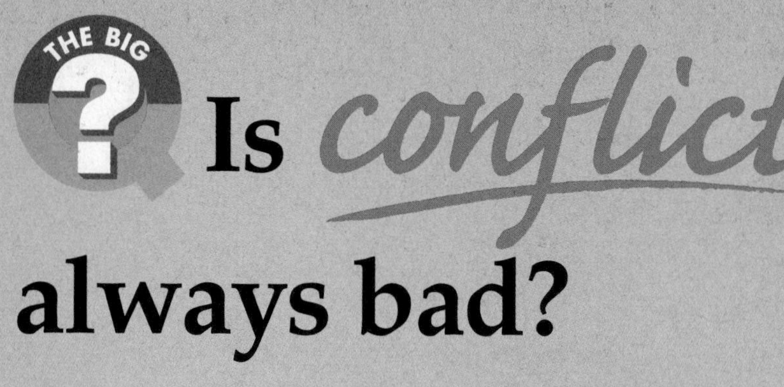

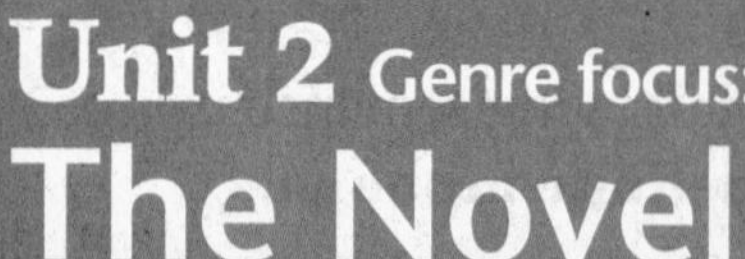

Unit Book Choices
With this unit you will read one book as an Anchor Book. There are many good books that would work well with this unit. The following pages offer six suggestions.

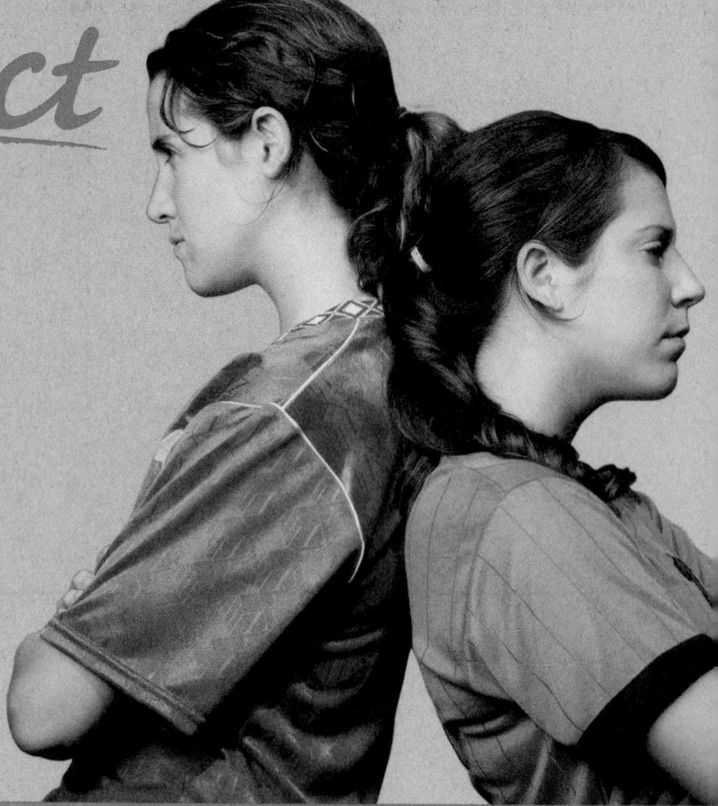

Free-Choice Reading
Later in this unit you will be given an opportunity to choose another book to read. This is called your Free-Choice Book.

You might read...

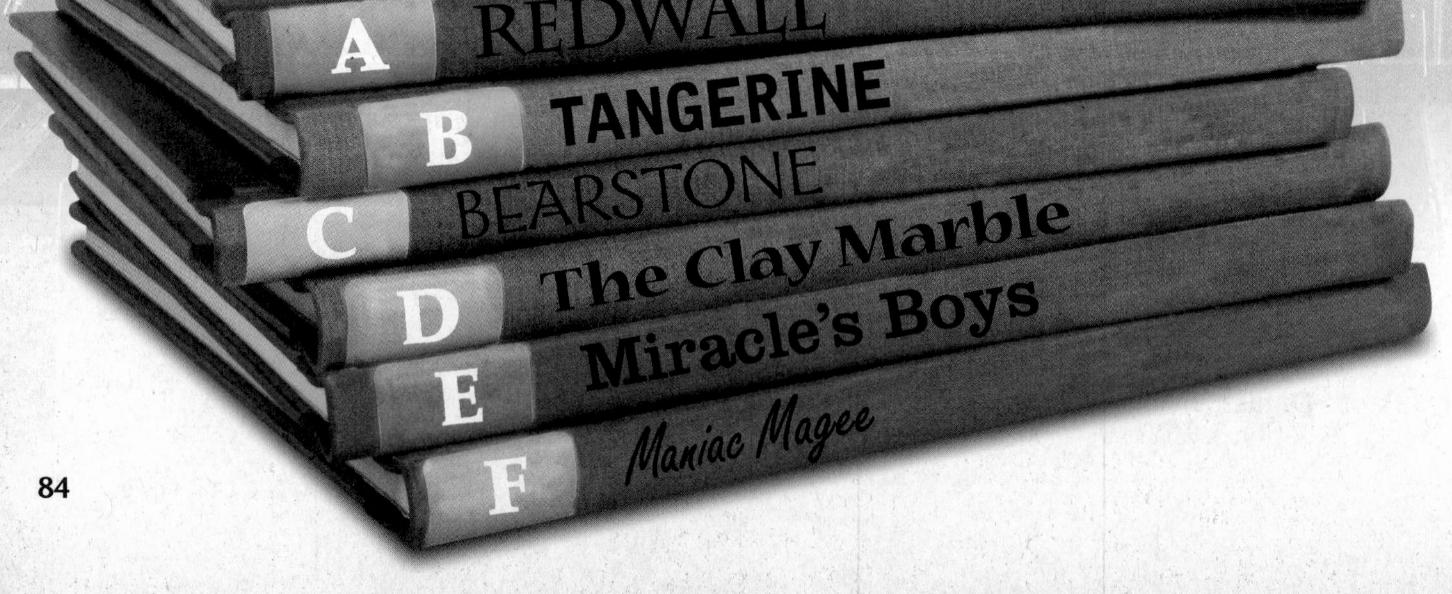

A REDWALL
B TANGERINE
C BEARSTONE
D The Clay Marble
E Miracle's Boys
F Maniac Magee

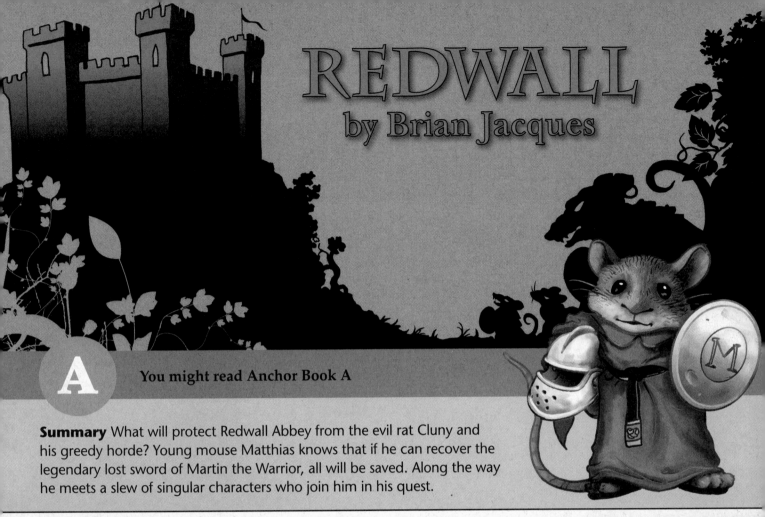

REDWALL
by Brian Jacques

A

You might read Anchor Book A

Summary What will protect Redwall Abbey from the evil rat Cluny and his greedy horde? Young mouse Matthias knows that if he can recover the legendary lost sword of Martin the Warrior, all will be saved. Along the way he meets a slew of singular characters who join him in his quest.

TANGERINE
BY EDWARD BLOOR

B

You might read Anchor Book B

Summary A mysterious injury has left Paul Fisher wearing ultrathick glasses—so thick his brother Erik has warned him not to look up at the sun in case his eyes catch on fire. But Paul can see a lot more than people think. He sees that Erik is no hero, even if he is a high school football star, and he can see that Tangerine, Florida is a very strange place.

C You might read Anchor Book C

Summary When fourteen-year-old Cloyd ran away from his group home in Colorado to find his father, he wasn't expecting to see him hooked up to a bunch of tubes in a hospital. Now he's been sent to work on a ranch for an old man he's never even met. Then he finds an ancestral burial ground, and it begins to look as if his summer might not turn out so bad after all.

BEARSTONE

by Will Hobbs

The Clay Marble

by Minfong Ho

D You might read Anchor Book D

Summary It is 1980, and twelve-year-old Dara and her family have fled their war-torn Cambodian village for a refugee camp. Then Dara is separated from her family during battle, and she sets off on her own, determined to find her lost mother and brother.

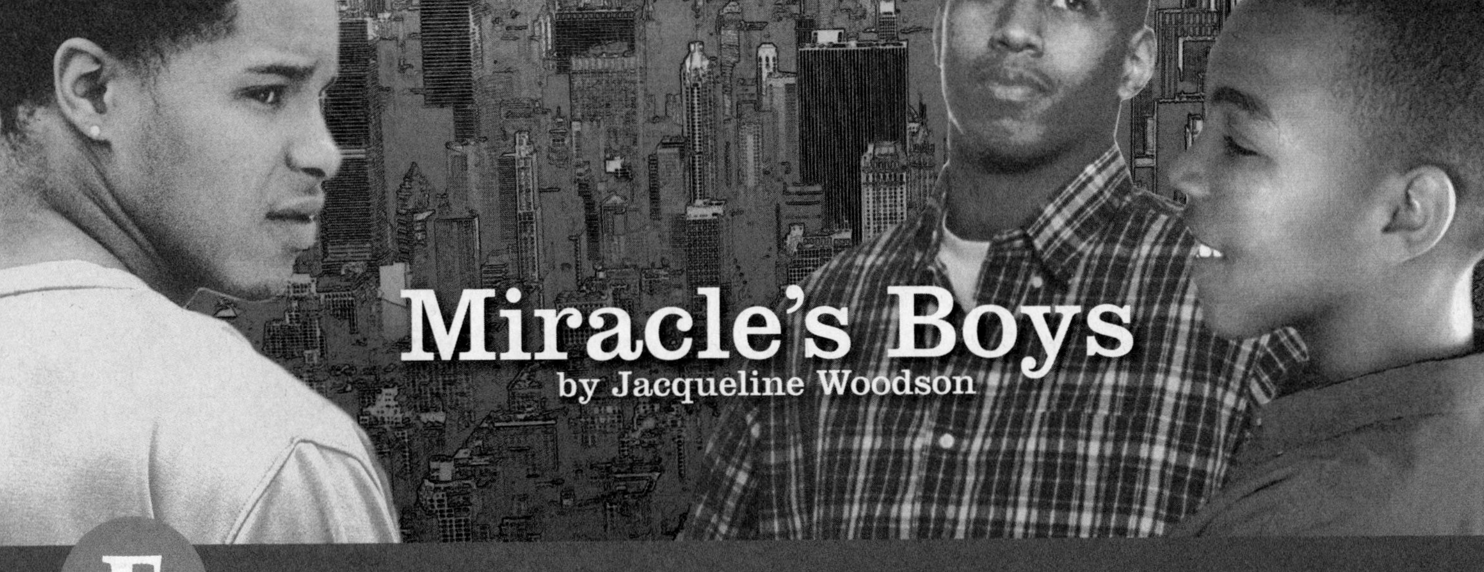

Miracle's Boys

by Jacqueline Woodson

E You might read Anchor Book E

Summary Things just haven't been the same since Lafayette's mother died. Big brother Charlie has turned into a hateful stranger, and Ty'ree, who should be going to college, has to work full time to keep the family together. But difficult as things are, the Bailey boys' survival depends on pulling together "brother to brother."

Maniac Magee

by Jerry Spinelli

F You might read Anchor Book F

Summary When Jeffrey Lionel Magee runs away from home and begins living in Two Mills, he quickly becomes a legend. First he catches a pass meant for a high school football star; then he rescues Arnold Jones from disaster. But when "Maniac" Magee moves in with the Beales, there are those who think a white kid has no business in a black neighborhood.

2-1 Understanding the Big Question

Is Conflict Always Bad?

When you think of conflicts in history, such as the civil rights movement, do you think of the dangerous confrontations, or do you think of the opportunities and positive changes that resulted from the conflict? It often takes a **conflict**—a struggle between people or opposing forces—to make a change for the better.

In this activity, you and your classmates will examine and analyze a situation involving a conflict. By examining the situation, you may better understand how conflicts have positive outcomes as well as negative ones. You will also learn how knowing these outcomes can help you to resolve, or settle, a conflict the best way.

The following are situations of conflict that might occur in your life. Your teacher will assign your group one of the conflicts. Put a ✓ next to the conflict your group is assigned.

☐ **Conflict 1** Your best friend is hanging out with a new group at school and doesn't want to include you. What should you do?

☐ **Conflict 2** Your little brother's birthday party is on the same day that your friends are going to the amusement park. Your parents expect you to attend the family party. What should you do?

☐ **Conflict 3** You know that a classmate cheated on a test. What do you do?

☐ **Conflict 4** Two best friends are competing for first place in a swim meet. The competition is threatening their friendship. What should they do?

Directions Discuss your conflict with your group. Identify the opposing forces by asking these questions. *What is the struggle? Who is involved in the struggle?* Use the graphic organizer on the next page to answer these questions.

Now think about the possible outcomes of the conflict. List the positive outcomes on the left and the negative outcomes on the right.

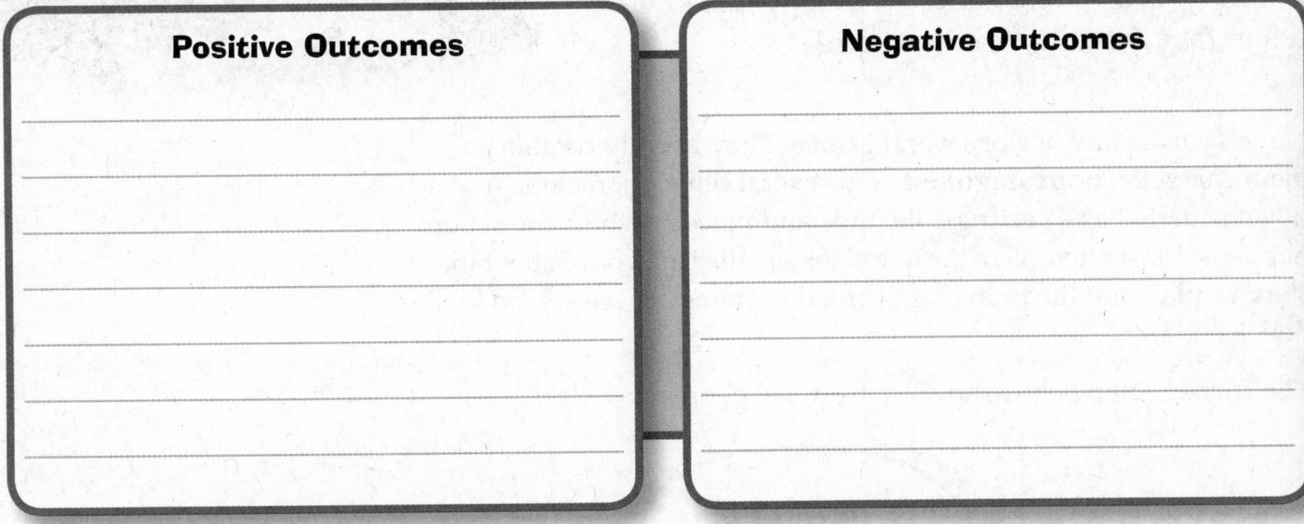

1 **Make a Judgment** Decide with your group how you would resolve, or settle, the conflict. Write your decision on the lines.

2 **Discuss** How does knowing all the possible outcomes help you resolve a conflict?

As you read your Anchor Book and the related readings, pay attention to the conflicts characters face and the ways they try to resolve them. Think about ways a different outcome might have been produced.

before reading your anchor book

Getting Ready for Your Anchor Book

You will start reading your Anchor Book soon. The next few pages in this book give you some background information plus a reading skill.

Introduction to the Novel

Have you read a good book just for fun lately? If so, there's a good chance it was a novel. A **novel** is a full-length work of fiction. Because a novel tells a story, it is often the kind of book people choose when they want to be entertained.

Novels can be any one of several genres. They usually contain a main character, or **protagonist,** and several other characters. A novel usually has a **setting**—the time and place in which the action happens. Most often, all of the questions a reader may have about the story, or **plot,** and the problems facing the characters are solved by the novel's end.

The concept map below shows some novel genres.

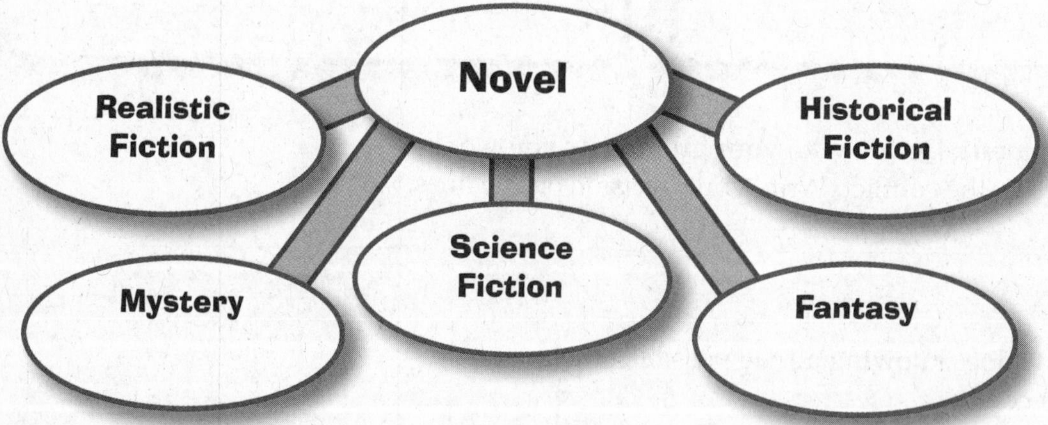

The Novel and the Short Story

A short story is another kind of fictional work. Short stories are always much shorter than novels, and they usually have fewer characters and a simpler plot. Short stories can also be any one of the genres listed on the concept map above. Since they are shorter works of fiction, myths, fables, and folk tales are usually considered short stories.

The chart below will help you understand the similarities and differences between novels and short stories.

What Novels and Short Stories Have in Common

- **are fictional works**
- **contain characters**
- **follow a plot**
- **are narrative text**
- **describe a setting**
- **communicate a mood**
- **contain a theme**

What Makes Them Different

Novel

- **is usually more than 100 pages long**
- **has many subplots**
- **has many characters**
- **major characters develop throughout the story**
- **protagonist has a main problem and other related problems**

Short Story

- **intended to be read in one sitting**
- **has no subplots**
- **has a limited number of characters**
- **protagonist has a single problem**

Directions Read each of the descriptions below. Use the graphic organizer above to help you decide if a novel or a short story is being described. On the lines below each description, write *N* for novel or *SS* for short story and the reason for your answer.

1 A 287-page piece of science fiction that tells the story of a group of aliens and their leaders, who live on the planet Zuricon.

2 A ten-page myth about how the character, Anansi, tricked the Sun.

3 A work of historical fiction that takes place around the time of the Civil War. The protagonist is a girl named Honor who is one of five sisters. The story follows the girls from the time they were children through young adulthood.

before reading your anchor book

2-2 Reading Skills
Making Inferences

In learning new reading skills, you will use special academic vocabulary. Knowing the right words will help you demonstrate your understanding.

Academic Vocabulary

Word	Meaning	Example Sentence
refer *v.* *Related words:* referred, reference	to direct attention to something	You can *refer* to a dictionary to find out what the word means.
speculate *v.* *Related words:* speculated, speculation	to make a prediction	We *speculate* that the hero of the story will win the race.
interpret *v.* *Related words:* interpreted, interpretation	to explain the meaning of something	Can you help me *interpret* the last two lines of this poem?

An author doesn't always tell you everything you need to know. Sometimes you have to **interpret** information by making a logical guess, or **inference,** about information that is not directly stated. To make an inference, you **refer** to information in the text and combine it with prior knowledge, or what you already know about the topic. Look at the example below. Use the clues and prior knowledge to make an inference.

Clues in the Text (It says...)	+	Prior Knowledge (I know...)	=	Inference (So I think...)
The boy on the phone is laughing out loud.	+	I know that people laugh when they have heard or seen something funny.	=	

before reading your anchor book

Directions Read the following article. The notes written in the margin show the student's prior knowledge on the topic. Fill in the graphic organizer to help you make an inference. Then, answer the questions on the next page.

Showdown at Victoria Falls

Just before the Zambezi River makes its famous plunge, there lies a small, undeveloped stretch of Zambia's Mosi-Oa-Tunya National Park. It's a crucial elephant crossing and it's the only riverfront spot in the park that people can enjoy without paying a fee.

National parks are home to wildlife.

South African developer Legacy Holdings Zambia, with the support of the Zambia Wildlife Authority, has different plans for the site: two hotels, 400 villas, and a golf course. In a nod to wildlife, the plans do include an elephant right-of-way that flanks the Maramba River. Critics find this laughable. "Elephant corridors have never worked anywhere," says conservationist Mike Musgrave.

Hotels will mean more people.

Developments can ruin natural areas.

Since the proposal became public last summer, Zambians, ranging from local government officials to a bike-tour guide, have rallied in opposition. Area residents welcome development, just not so close to the Falls that it jeopardizes the park's status as a UNESCO World Heritage site. They hope grassroots pressure and a legal challenge will save the park's last riverfront open space. "Even 30 years ago Victoria Falls was overdeveloped," says Ian Manning, a former park warden. "This would be a disaster."

—Karen E. Lange

1 **Infer** Complete this graphic organizer that a student created.

Clues in the Text (It says...)	+	Prior Knowledge (I know...)	=	Inference (So I think...)
A developer wants to build hotels, villas and a golf course where a free park is located. Residents support development if it doesn't harm the park's status.	+	Development can bring lots of traffic and trash to a beautiful place.	=	

2 **Infer** Do you think the developer will be able to gain support for the development? Why or why not?

3 **Deduce** What does the phrase "grassroots pressure" mean in the article? List clues from the article, along with prior knowledge, that helped you find the meaning.

4 **Speculate** What do you think will happen to the elephants if they are forced to use the elephant right-of-way crossing?

5 **Interpret** What do you think the idiom "a nod to wildlife" means?

6 **Analyze** A "showdown" is a term for a confrontation between two people or groups. Why do you think the selection is titled "Showdown at Victoria Falls"?

As you read the following article, pay attention to clues in the text that help you make inferences. *Guiding Question:* **How can the conflict surrounding the possible extinction of antelopes have a positive result?**

Link to Science

Antelopes

Background *Antelopes are hoofed animals with hollow horns. They are diverse in their range, size, and appearance. Antelopes live on grasslands, mountains, wetlands, and in deserts. Today, some groups are threatened with extinction.*

Antelopes are deer-like animals that live in the grassy plains of east and southern Africa and in parts of Asia and the Middle East. Like deer, antelopes are herbivorous animals because they eat grass, leaves, and fruit. Antelopes have two-toed hoofs and hollow horns. Some antelopes have spiral horns, whereas others have slightly curved horns. Unlike deer, which shed their antlers every year to grow a new set, antelopes have permanent horns that they keep their entire lives.

Size and Speed

dik-dik

There are about 100 different kinds of antelopes, and most of them live in Africa. Antelopes range in size from the large eland to the tiny dik-dik. The eland may stand up to 6 feet (1.8 meters) tall at the shoulder and can weigh more than 1,500 pounds (680 kilograms)—more than the weight of an average car! The dik-dik is only about 14 inches (35 centimeters) tall and weighs up to 12 pounds (5 kilograms). All antelopes are built for running, and they use speed to get away from their enemies. They can usually outrun wild dogs, cheetahs, leopards, and lions. Antelopes can often run at high speeds for a longer time than the big cats can.

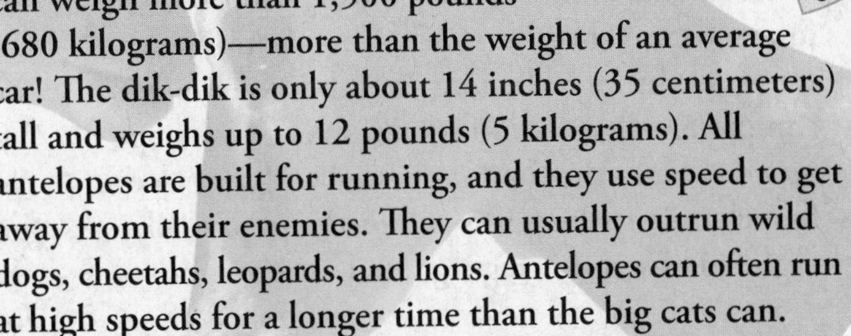

Antelope species can be found in parts of Africa, Asia, and the Middle East. Antelopes' habitat varies widely and can include savannas, woodlands, marshes, swamps, and deserts, depending on the species.

Gazelles and impalas are two of the fastest and most graceful antelopes. Gazelles stand 2 to 3 feet (60 to 90 centimeters) tall at the shoulder, but they can run as fast as 60 miles (96 kilometers) per hour for short distances. Impalas are about 3 feet (90 centimeters) tall at the shoulder, and they can cover 30 feet (9 meters) in one single leap.

The Ruminants

Antelopes are in the animal group called ruminants. Ruminants include cattle, goats, deer, and giraffes. Ruminants are different from other hoofed animals. They have a stomach with four separate chambers. Anything a ruminant eats goes through the four chambers before it is completely digested. Rumination is a two-step process. First, the food is chewed and sent to the first chamber where it is softened and partially digested. Then it is regurgitated, or brought back up to the mouth. This semi-digested food, called cud, is chewed again and sent directly to the other chambers where microorganisms help complete the digestion.

Headed for Extinction

Unlike many of their ruminant relatives, some types of antelopes are in danger of becoming extinct. Overgrazing by animals, such as cattle, uses up land that was once populated by the antelopes. Expanding urban centers are causing a loss of the antelope's natural habitat, while other antelopes fall victim to hunters. For example, the Tibetan antelope is hunted and killed for its fur, which is sold and woven into fashion scarves. However, there are environmental groups and individuals working toward making some of these practices illegal, to help prevent the extinction of the antelopes and keep them on Earth for a long, long time.

Thinking About the Selection

Antelopes

1 **Contrast** How are antelopes and other ruminants different from other hoofed animals? Give examples from the text in your answer.

2 **Infer** Do you think antelopes have strong leg muscles? Use the graphic organizer to answer this question.

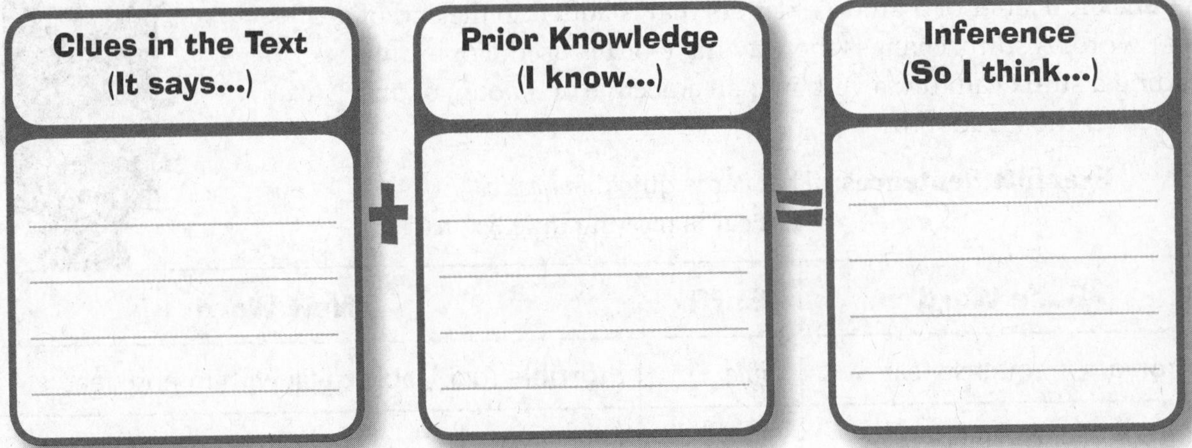

3 **Speculate** Do you think all antelopes can live in the same environment? Use the text and the text features to explain.

4 **Speculate** Do you think people planning urban centers should be responsible for helping the wildlife that live in the areas they are developing? Explain your answer.

Write Answer the following question in your Reader's Journal.

5 **Draw Conclusions** How can the conflict surrounding the possible extinction of antelopes have a positive result?

before reading your anchor book

2-3 Vocabulary Building Strategies
Suffixes

When you read, you might come to a stop when you reach an unfamiliar word. Before you grab a dictionary, look a little more closely. The word might be made up of two or more parts. Knowing the meaning of each of these parts can help you unlock the meaning of many words.

A **suffix** is a letter or a group of letters that is added to the end of a base word. A suffix changes the way the word is used. For example, adding a suffix can turn a verb into an adjective or a noun, or an adjective into an adverb.

Example Sentences: That car is quick! *(adjective)*
That car is moving quickly. *(adverb)*

Base Word	Suffix	New Word
horror *(n.)* intense fear	*-ible*	**horrible** *(adj.),* able to fill with intense fear
move *(v.)* to change position	*-able*	**movable** *(adj.),* able to change position
loud *(adj.)* noisy	*-ly*	**loudly** *(adv.),* in a way that is noisy
govern *(v.)* to rule over	*-ment*	**government** *(n.),* state or way of ruling over
participate *(v.)* to take part	*-ion*	**participation** *(n.),* state or way of taking part

Directions Write the new word and use it to write a sentence.

Adjective		**Suffix**		**Adverb**
solemn	+	-ly	=	________

Sentence: ______________________________

Verb		**Suffix**		**Noun**
reflect	+	-ion	=	________

Sentence: ______________________________

before reading your anchor book

Directions Follow the directions below to change the way each word is used by adding a suffix. Write the word and its definition on the line.

1 Change "slow" into an adverb.

2 Change "notice" into an adjective.

3 Change "merry" into an adverb.

4 Change "arrange" into a noun.

Directions Underline one phrase in each sentence that can be replaced with a word with a suffix. Then rewrite the sentence using the word with the suffix.

5 I bought a mattress that is able to be inflated.

6 The storm clouds were approaching in a rapid way.

7 In my state of being confused, I forgot my keys.

Directions Underline the phrases in the following sentences that could be replaced with words with suffixes. Then rewrite the paragraph using words with suffixes.

I had no idea that the lamp was able to be broken until it came crashing down in a noisy way. I waited for Mom to come over and tell me my state of being punished. Instead, she gave me a look that was like a friend. "It was headed for the garbage anyway," she said with a sigh. It wasn't the way of reacting that I was expecting.

Ready? Start Reading Your Anchor Book

It's time to get started. As you learn from this worktext, your teacher will also give you reading assignments from your Anchor Book.

2-4 Writing about Your Anchor Book

Reader's Journal

Keeping Track of Important Information Sometimes it is difficult to keep track of details in the text—or your own ideas—as you read. It helps to write those details and ideas in the book by marking the text. However, you can't always write directly on the page. Self-stick notes allow you to place your notes on the page without damaging the book.

How to Use Self-Stick Notes Using self-stick notes helps you keep track of important details as you read. It also makes it easier for you to go back and find those details after you have finished reading. This will come in handy as you plan to write your Reader's Journal response about your Anchor Book.

- **As you read,** track important details from your Anchor Book, such as details about conflict, by sticking the notes directly on the pages where you found the information. On each note, draw an arrow pointing to the text and explain why you think the details are important.
- **After you read,** go back and review all your self-stick notes. Identify the notes that have information you want to include in your Reader's Journal response. You can put a star or checkmark on the most important details so they will be the easiest to find when you get ready to write your response.

In the passage on the next page, the student wrote the words *Character Traits* to indicate what type of details she would list on the self-stick note.

Directions Read this passage and examine the self-stick note.

Student Model: Using Self-Stick Notes

It seemed as if every time Dawn began to feel at home in a new place, it was time to pick up and move again.

"Do we really have to move?" she asked, fearful that the question might upset her father.

"We can't stay here without a job," her father replied with a shrug of his broad shoulders. He was a husky man, but he looked weak now as he slouched sadly in his favorite chair.

Dawn clasped her hands tightly together and held them under her chin, thinking. She was not looking forward to the prospect of starting over again as the new kid in some unfamiliar city. She decided to explore her options thoroughly. She felt she needed to try everything. Then she remembered what her friend said about the job available at their family's mill.

Character Traits

- Dawn doesn't want to move.
- She respects her father.
- She is determined to stay.

1 **Defend** What details from the passage support the student's ideas about Dawn's character?

2 **Predict** What do you think Dawn will do next? Use details listed on the self-stick note to help you make a prediction.

3 **Analyze** Look at earlier Reader's Journal responses you made without using self-stick notes. How will the note method of tracking details make it easier for you to analyze your Anchor Book?

2-5 Literary Analysis
Characterization

How do you get to know the characters in a story? That's up to the author! The author must bring the characters to life through characterization. If the author does a good job, the characters seem believable and familiar to the reader.

Literary Terms

- **Characters** are the people or animals that take part in a story.
- **Characterization** is the way an author creates and develops characters and reveals their traits or qualities. An author can use characterization in two ways.

Direct characterization	An author makes straightforward statements about a character. **Example:** Freddy was very competitive.
Indirect characterization	An author presents a character's thoughts, words, and actions and reveals what others think and say about the character. **Example:** Two days before the game, Freddy gathered his teammates and laid out his plan. Then he looked at them and said, "We are going to win this one. No excuses."

Directions Read the following passage about a dog's memory of Bunnicula, a rabbit vampire. Underline words that provide clues about the dog Harold. In the margin, note whether the words are those of Harold or those of someone else in the story.

Go Online
About the Author
Visit: PHSchool.com
Web Code: exe-6200

from *Bunnicula* by *Deborah and James Howe*

I shall never forget the first time I laid these now tired old eyes on our visitor. I had been left home by the family with the admonition to take care of the house until they returned. That's something they always say to me when they go out: "Take care of the house, Harold. You're the watchdog." I think it's their way of making up for not taking me with them. As if I wanted to go anyway. You can't lie down at the movies and still see the screen. And people think you're being impolite if you fall asleep and start to snore, or scratch yourself in public. No thank you, I'd rather be stretched out on my favorite rug in front of a nice, whistling radiator.

1 Fill in the web with things you learned about the character of Harold. An example is shown.

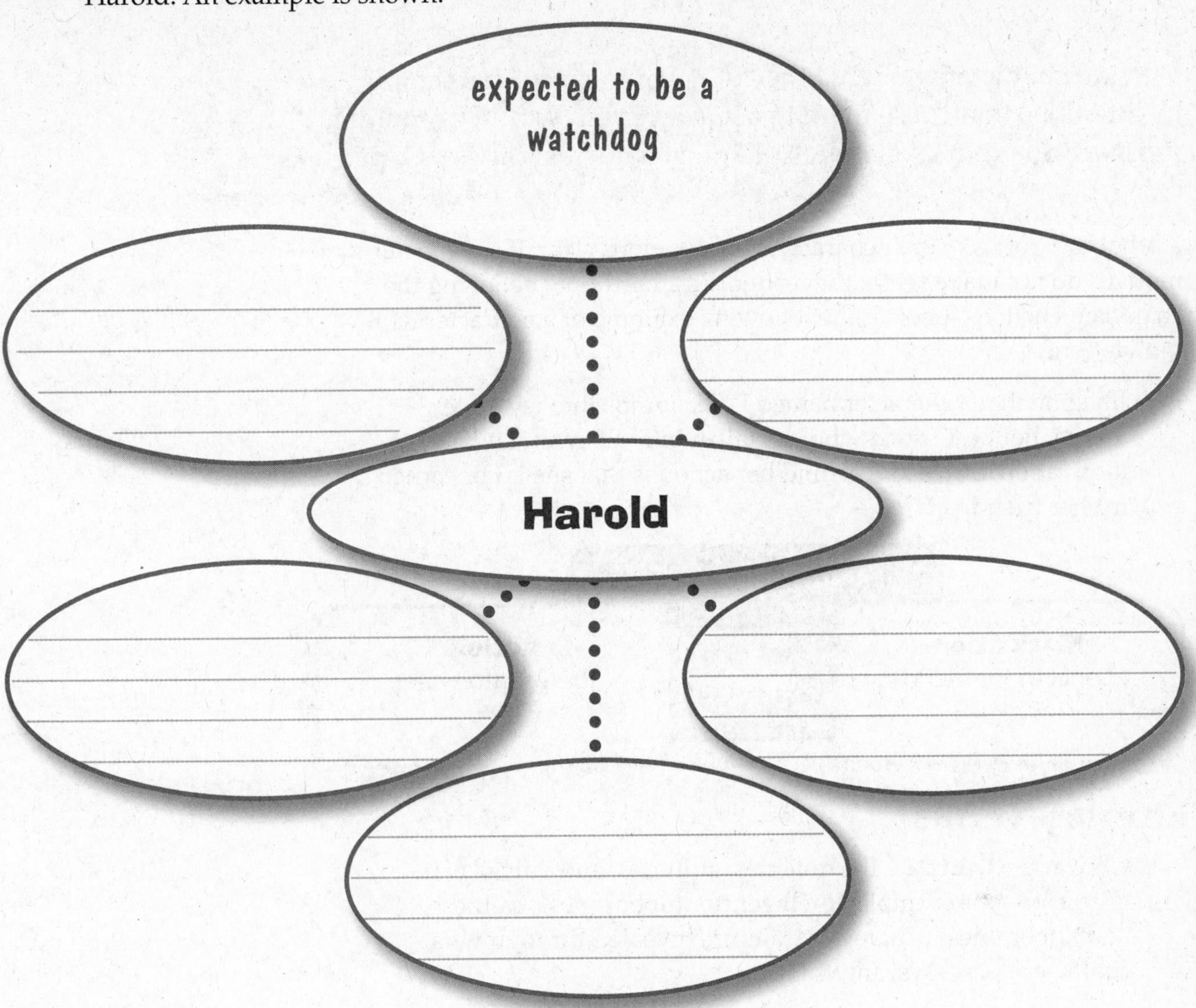

2 **Analyze** How does the author reveal what others think about Harold? Is this an example of direct or indirect characterization?

3 **Create** Write two sentences that use direct characterization to describe Harold's personality.

while reading your anchor book

Character Motivation

Why do characters do what they do? Authors put characters in situations that cause them to act in a certain way. **Character motivation** is a reason that explains a character's actions.

Authors try to make their characters' motivations clear. If a character's motives do not make sense, the reader has a hard time believing the character's actions. Look at the following example of a character's motivation.

- Imagine that a character named Lydia jumps into icy water to save her best friend who has fallen into the river. Lydia's motivation, or reason, behind her action is that she is concerned for her friend.

Literary Terms

- **Character traits** are the qualities, attitudes, and values of a character—for example, intelligence, stubbornness, sadness, and hopefulness. Character traits are revealed through what a character does, says, and thinks.
- **Character motivation,** or reason for doing something, can be driven by a need (for shelter or food), by a feeling (jealousy or fear), or by a desire (for power or money).

To help you identify a character's motivation you can ask yourself these questions.

- *What do the characters want?*
- *What do the characters need?*
- *What do the characters do to get what they want or need?*

Directions Read the following passage. Underline details that explain what motivates Sparky to keep pursuing his dream. Then, answer the questions.

Go Online
About the Author
Visit: PHSchool.com
Web Code: exe-6202

from ***Sparky*** *by Earl Nightingale*

. . . one thing was important to Sparky—drawing. He was proud of his artwork. Of course, no one else appreciated it. In his senior year of high school, he submitted some cartoons to the editor of the yearbook. The cartoons were turned down. Despite this particular rejection, Sparky was so convinced of his ability that he decided to become a professional artist.

After completing high school, he wrote a letter to Walt Disney Studios. He was told to send some samples of his artwork, and the subject for a cartoon was suggested. Sparky drew the proposed cartoon. He spent a great deal of time on it and on all the other drawings he submitted.

Finally, the reply came from Disney Studios. He had been rejected once again. Another loss for the loser.

So Sparky decided to write his own autobiography in cartoons. He described his childhood self—a little boy loser and chronic underachiever. The cartoon character would soon become famous worldwide. For Sparky, the boy who had such lack of success in school and whose work was rejected again and again, was Charles Schultz. He created the "Peanuts" comic strip and the little cartoon character whose kite would never fly and who never succeeded in kicking a football, Charlie Brown.

1 **Analyze** Use information from the passage to complete the graphic organizer.

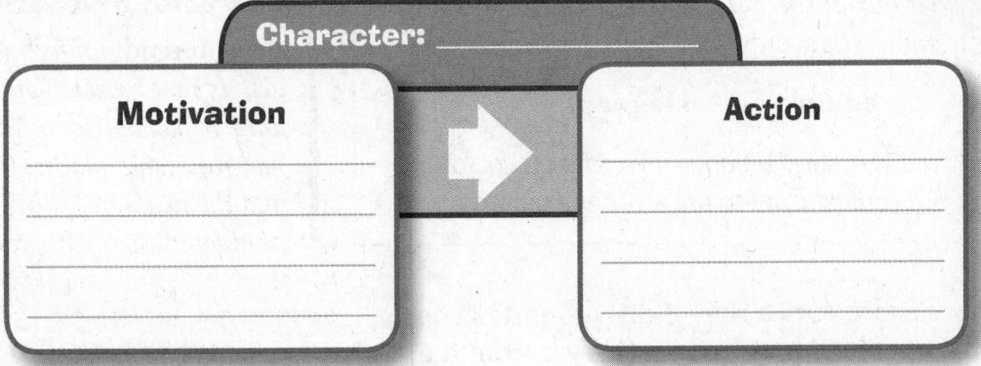

2 **Apply** What have you learned from Sparky's story that might motivate a friend who is about to give up on reaching a goal?

______

______

Now that you have learned about characterization and character motivation, read this story. *Guiding Question:* **How do the boys' different character traits and motivations create conflict in the story?**

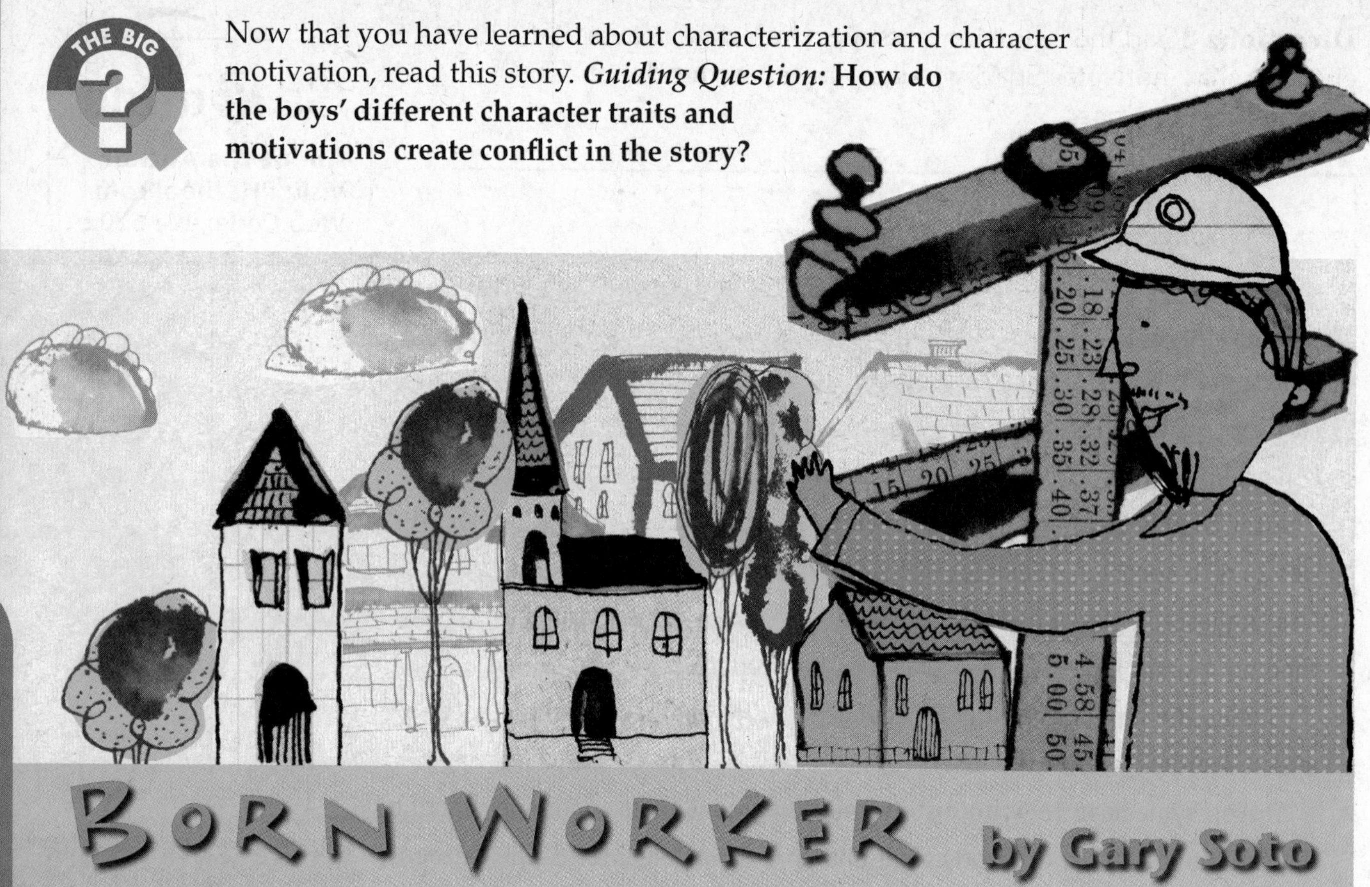

BORN WORKER by Gary Soto

Background *José and his cousin Arnie share a Mexican American background. But José believes in hard work, while his cousin is a fast-talker. Soon after the boys agree to be partners in a small business, a crisis reveals how different the cousins are, and José learns a few things about himself.*

Vocabulary Builder

Before you read, *you will discuss the following words. In the Vocabulary Builder box in the margin, use a vocabulary building strategy to make the words your own.*

retort **pumice** **stagnant**

As you read, *draw a box around unfamiliar words you could add to your vocabulary. Use context clues to unlock their meaning.*

Marking the Text

Characterization and Character Motivation

As you read, *underline details that reveal what José and Arnie are like. In the margin, name character traits and the needs or feelings that motivate these characters.*

They said that José was born with a ring of dirt around his neck, with grime under his fingernails, and skin calloused from the grainy twist of a shovel. They said his palms were already rough by the time he was three, and soon after he learned his primary colors, his squint was the squint of an aged laborer. They said he was a born worker. By seven he was drinking coffee slowly, his mouth pursed the way his mother sipped. He wore jeans, a shirt with sleeves rolled to his elbows. His eye could measure a length of board, and his knees genuflected[1] over flower beds and leafy gutters.

They said lots of things about José, but almost nothing of his parents. His mother stitched at a machine all day, and his father, with a steady job at the telephone company, climbed splintered, sun-sucked poles, fixed wires and looked around the city at tree level.

"What do you see up there?" José once asked his father. "Work," he answered. "I see years of work, mi'jo[2]." José took this as a truth, and though he did well in school, he felt destined to labor. His arms would pump, his legs would bend, his arms would carry a world of earth. He believed in hard work, believed that his strength was as ancient as a rock's.

"Life is hard," his father repeated from the time José could first make out the meaning of words until he was stroking his fingers against the grain of his sandpaper beard.

His mother was an example to José. She would raise her hands, showing her fingers pierced from the sewing machines. She bled on her machine, bled because there was money to make, a child to raise, and a roof to stay under.

One day when José returned home from junior high, his cousin Arnie was sitting on the lawn sucking on a stalk of grass. José knew that grass didn't come from his lawn. His was cut and pampered, clean.

" José!" Arnie shouted as he took off the earphones of his CD Walkman.

"Hi, Arnie," José said without much enthusiasm. He didn't like his cousin. He thought he was lazy and, worse, spoiled by the trappings of being middle class. His parents had good jobs in offices and showered him with clothes, shoes, CDs, vacations, almost anything he wanted. Arnie's family had never climbed a telephone pole to size up the future.

Arnie rose to his feet, and José saw that his cousin was wearing a new pair of high-tops. He didn't say anything.

"Got an idea," Arnie said cheerfully. "Something that'll make us money."

José looked at his cousin, not a muscle of curiousity twitching in his face.

Still, Arnie explained that since he himself was so clever with words, and his best cousin in the whole world was good at working with his hands, that maybe they might start a company.

"What would you do?" José asked.

"Me?" he said brightly. "Shoot, I'll round up all kinds of jobs for you. You won't have to do anything." He stopped, then started again. "Except—you know—do the work."

[1] **genuflected** (jen'yə flékt' id) *v.* to kneel respectfully, as in church.

[2] **mi'jo** (mī yo) *n.* stands for the Spanish phrase *mi hijo*, which means "my son."

Marking the Text

while reading your anchor book

"Get out of here," José said.

"Don't be that way," Arnie begged. "Let me tell you how it works."

The boys went inside the house, and while José stripped off his school clothes and put on his jeans and a T-shirt, Arnie told him that they could be rich.

"You ever hear of this guy named Bechtel?" Arnie asked.

José shook his head.

"Man, he started just like us," Arnie said. "He started digging ditches and stuff, and the next thing you knew, he was sitting by his own swimming pool. You want to sit by your own pool, don't you?" Arnie smiled, waiting for José to speak up.

"Never heard of this guy Bechtel," José said after he rolled on two huge socks, worn at the heels. He opened up his chest of drawers and brought out a packet of Kleenex.

Arnie looked at the Kleenex.

"How come you don't use your sleeve?" Arnie joked.

José thought for a moment and said, "I'm not like you." He smiled at his **retort**.

"Listen, I'll find the work, and then we can split it fifty-fifty."

José knew fifty-fifty was a bad deal.

"How about sixty-forty?" Arnie suggested when he could see that José wasn't going for it. "I know a lot of people from my dad's job. They're waiting for us."

José sat on the edge of his bed and started to lace up his boots. He knew that there were agencies that would find you work, agencies that took a portion of your pay. They're cheats, he thought, people who sit in air-conditioned offices while others work.

"You really know a lot of people?" José asked.

"Boatloads," Arnie said. "My dad works with this millionaire—honest—who cooks a steak for his dog every day."

He's a liar, José thought. No matter how he tried, he couldn't picture a dog grubbing on steak. The world was too poor for that kind of silliness.

"Listen, I'll go eighty-twenty," José said.

"Aw, man," Arnie whined. "That ain't fair."

José laughed.

"I mean, half the work is finding the jobs," Arnie explained, his palms up as he begged José to be reasonable.

José knew this was true. He had had to go door-to-door, and he disliked asking for work. He assumed that it should automatically be his since he was a good worker, honest, and always on time.

"Where did you get this idea, anyhow?" José asked.

"I got a business mind," Arnie said proudly.

"Just like that Bechtel guy," José retorted.

"That's right."

Vocabulary Builder

retort
(ri tôrt′) *n.*

Meaning

Marking the Text

while reading your anchor book

José agreed to a seventy-thirty split, with the condition that Arnie had to help out. Arnie hollered, arguing that some people were meant to work and others to come up with brilliant ideas. He was one of the latter. Still, he agreed after José said it was that or nothing.

In the next two weeks, Arnie found an array of jobs. José peeled off shingles from a rickety garage roof, carried rocks down a path to where a pond would go, and spray-painted lawn furniture. And while Arnie accompanied him, most of the time he did nothing. He did help occasionally. He did shake the cans of spray paint and kick aside debris so that José didn't trip while going down the path carrying the rocks. He did stack the piles of shingles, but almost cried when a nail bit his thumb. But mostly he told José what he had missed or where the work could be improved. José was bothered because he and his work had never been criticized before.

But soon José learned to ignore his cousin, ignore his comments about his spray painting, or about the way he lugged rocks, two in each arm. He didn't say anything, either, when they got paid and Arnie rubbed his hands like a fly, muttering, "It's payday."

Then Arnie found a job scrubbing a drained swimming pool. The two boys met early at José's house. Arnie brought his bike. José's own bike had a flat that grinned like a clown's face.

"I'll pedal," José suggested when Arnie said that he didn't have much leg strength.

With Arnie on the handlebars, José tore off, his pedaling so strong that tears of fear formed in Arnie's eyes.

"Slow down!" Arnie cried.

José ignored him and within minutes they were riding the bike up a gravel driveway. Arnie hopped off at first chance.

"You're scary," Arnie said, picking a gnat from his eye.

José chuckled.

When Arnie knocked on the door, an old man still in pajamas appeared in the window. He motioned for the boys to come around to the back.

"Let me do the talking," Arnie suggested to his cousin. "He knows my dad real good. They're like this." He pressed two fingers together.

José didn't bother to say OK. He walked the bike into the backyard, which was lush with plants—roses in their last bloom, geraniums, hydrangeas, pansies with their skirts of bright colors. José could make out

Marking the Text

while reading your anchor book

the splash of a fountain. Then he heard the hysterical yapping of a poodle. From all his noise, a person might have thought the dog was on fire.

"Hi, Mr. Clemens," Arnie said, extending his hand. "I'm Arnie Sanchez. It's nice to see you again."

José had never seen a kid actually greet someone like this. Mr. Clemens said, hiking up his pajama bottoms, "I only wanted one kid to work."

"Oh," Arnie stuttered. "Actually, my cousin José really does the work and I kind of, you know, supervise."

Mr. Clemens pinched up his wrinkled face. He seemed not to understand. He took out a pea-sized hearing aid, fiddled with its tiny dial, and fit it into his ear, which was surrounded with wiry gray hair.

"I'm only paying for one boy," Mr. Clemens shouted. His poodle click-clicked and stood behind his legs. The dog bared its small crooked teeth.

"That's right," Arnie said, smiling a strained smile. "We know that you're going to compensate only one of us."

Mr. Clemens muttered under his breath. He combed his hair with his fingers. He showed José the pool, which was shaped as round as an elephant. It was filthy with grime. Near the bottom some grayish water shimmered and leaves floated as limp as cornflakes.

"It's got to be real clean," Mr. Clemens said, "or it's not worth it."

"Oh, José's a great worker," Arnie said. He patted his cousin's shoulders and said that he could lift a mule.

Mr. Clemens sized up José and squeezed his shoulders, too.

Marking the Text

"How do I know you, anyhow?" Mr. Clemens asked Arnie, who was aiming a smile at the poodle.

"You know my dad," Arnie answered, raising his smile to the old man. "He works at Interstate Insurance. You and he had some business deals."

Mr. Clemens thought for a moment, a hand on his mouth, head shaking. He could have been thinking about the meaning of life, his face was so dark.

"Mexican fella?" he inquired.

"That's him," Arnie said happily.

José felt like hitting his cousin for his cheerful attitude. Instead, he walked over and picked up the white plastic bottle of bleach. Next to it were a wire brush, a **pumice** stone, and some rags. He set down the bottle and, like a surgeon, put on a pair of rubber gloves.

"You know what you're doing, boy?" Mr. Clemens asked.

José nodded as he walked into the pool. If it had been filled with water, his chest would have been wet. The new hair on his chest would have been floating like the legs of a jellyfish.

"Oh, yeah," Arnie chimed, speaking for his cousin. "José was born to work."

José would have drowned his cousin if there had been water. Instead, he poured a bleach solution into a rag and swirled it over an area. He took the wire brush and scrubbed. The black algae came up like a foamy monster.

"We're a team," Arnie said to Mr. Clemens.

Arnie descended into the pool and took the bleach bottle from José. He held it for José and smiled up at Mr. Clemens, who,

Vocabulary Builder

pumice
(pum′is) *n.*

Meaning

Marking the Text

hands on hips, watched for a while, the poodle at his side. He cupped his ear, as if to pick up the sounds of José's scrubbing.

"Nice day, huh?" Arnie sang.

"What?" Mr. Clemens said.

"Nice day," Arnie repeated, this time louder. "So which ear can't you hear in?" Grinning, Arnie wiggled his ear to make sure that Mr. Clemens knew what he was asking.

Mr. Clemens ignored Arnie. He watched José, whose arms worked back and forth like he was sawing logs.

"We're not only a team," Arnie shouted, "but we're also cousins."

Mr. Clemens shook his head at Arnie. When he left, the poodle leading the way, Arnie immediately climbed out of the pool and sat on the edge, legs dangling.

"It's going to be blazing," Arnie complained. He shaded his eyes with his hand and looked east, where the sun was rising over a sycamore, its leaves hanging like bats.

José scrubbed. He worked the wire brush over the black and green stains, the grime dripping like tears. He finished a large area. He hopped out of the pool and returned hauling a garden hose with an attached nozzle. He gave the cleaned area a blast. When the spray got too close, his cousin screamed, got up, and, searching for something to do, picked a loquat[3] from a tree.

"What's your favorite fruit?" Arnie asked.

José ignored him.

Arnie stuffed a bunch of loquats into his mouth, then cursed himself for splattering juice on his new high-tops. He returned to the pool, his cheeks fat with the seeds, and once again sat at the edge. He started to tell José how he had first learned to swim. "We were on vacation in Mazatlán[4]. "You been there, ain't you?"

José shook his head. He dabbed the bleach solution onto the sides of the pool with a rag and scrubbed a new area.

"Anyhow, my dad was on the beach and saw this drowned dead guy," Arnie continued. "And right there, my dad got scared and realized I couldn't swim."

Arnie rattled on about how his father had taught him in the hotel pool and later showed him where the drowned man's body had been.

"Be quiet," José said.

"What?"

"I can't concentrate," José said, stepping back to look at the cleaned area.

Arnie shut his mouth but opened it to lick loquat juice from his fingers. He kicked his legs against the swimming pool, bored. He looked around the backyard and spotted a lounge chair. He got

---

[3] **loquat** (lō'kwät') *n.* a small, tangy fruit native to China.

[4] **Mazatlán** (mä'sät län') *n.* a seaport in western Mexico.

Marking the Text

while reading your anchor book

Literature in Context
Mazatlán

Today the city of Mazatlán, Mexico, is a popular tourist destination, but hundreds of years ago it was home to native people called the Totorames. Many changes have occurred since the Totorames created clay objects, hunted, and fished along the coastline.

When the Spanish conquered Mexico, the area fell under their control. Spanish galleons shipped out gold, attracting the attention of pirates. At various times in its history, Mazatlán was occupied by United States troops, the French, and the British. German immigrants left their mark as well.

Over the years, the Mazatlán port has grown, the fishing industry has prospered, railroad and highway transportation has developed, and the area has flourished. Each year, Mazatlán hosts thousands of visitors.

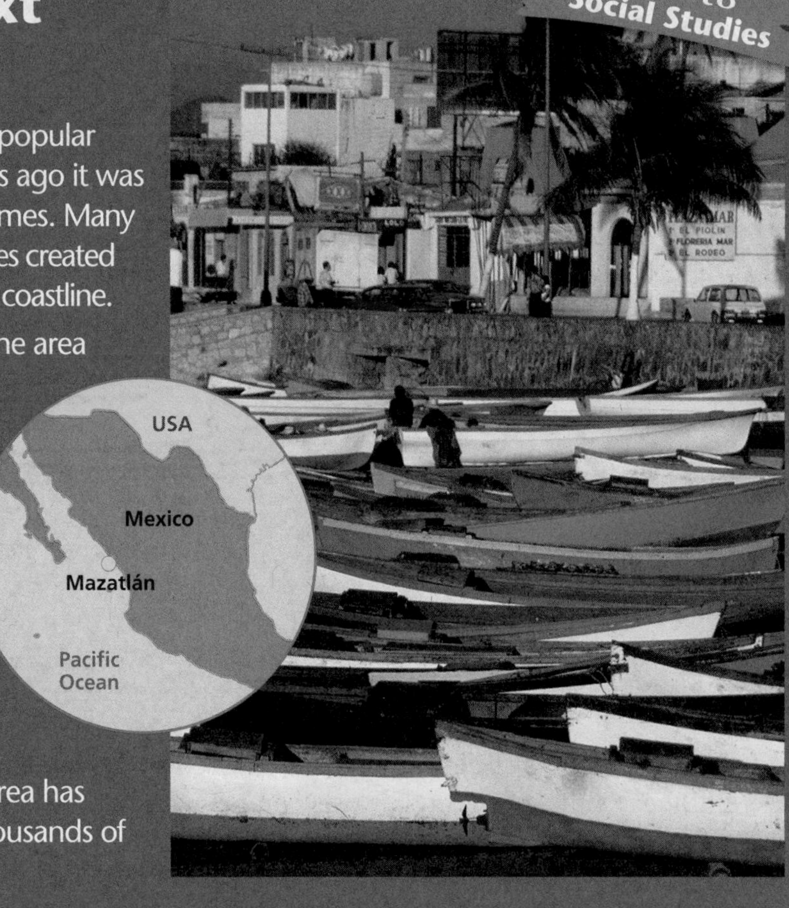

up, dusting off the back of his pants, and threw himself into the cushions. He raised and lowered the back of the lounge. Sighing, he snuggled in. He stayed quiet for three minutes, during which time José scrubbed. His arms hurt but he kept working with long strokes. José knew that in an hour the sun would drench the pool with light. He hurried to get the job done.

Arnie then asked, "You ever peel before?"

José looked at his cousin. His nose burned from the bleach. He scrunched up his face.

"You know, like when you get sunburned."

"I'm too dark to peel," José said, his words echoing because he had advanced to the deep end. "Why don't you be quiet and let me work?"

Arnie babbled on that he had peeled when on vacation in Hawaii. He explained that he was really more French than Mexican, and that's why his skin was sensitive. He said that when he lived in France, people thought that he could be Portuguese or maybe Armenian, never Mexican.

José felt like soaking his rag with bleach and pressing it over Arnie's mouth to make him be quiet.

Marking the Text

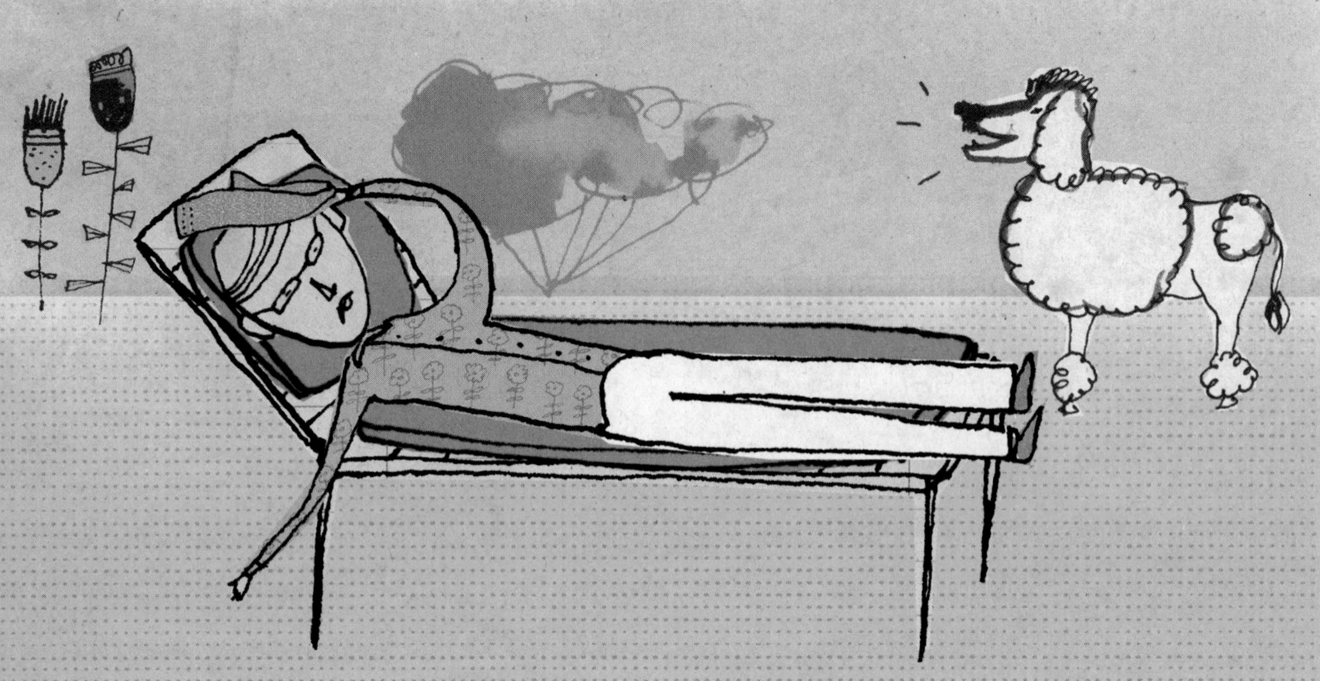

Then Mr. Clemens appeared. He was dressed in white pants and a flowery shirt. His thin hair was combed so that his scalp, as pink as a crab, showed.

"I'm just taking a little rest," Arnie said.

Arnie leaped back into the pool. He took the bleach bottle and held it. He smiled at Mr. Clemens, who came to inspect their progress.

" José's doing a good job," Arnie said, then whistled a song.

Mr. Clemens peered into the pool, hands on knees, admiring the progress.

"Pretty good, huh?" Arnie asked.

Mr. Clemens nodded. Then his hearing aid fell out, and José turned in time to see it roll like a bottle cap toward the bottom of the pool. It leaped into the **stagnant** water with a plop. A single bubble went up, and it was gone

"Dang," Mr. Clemens swore. He took shuffling steps toward the deep end. He steadied his gaze on where the hearing aid had sunk. He leaned over and suddenly, arms waving, one leg kicking out, he tumbled into the pool. He landed standing up, then his legs buckled, and he crumbled, his head striking against the bottom. He rolled once, and half of his body settled in the water.

"Did you see that!" Arnie shouted, big-eyed.

José had already dropped his brushes on the side of the pool and hurried to the old man, who moaned, eyes closed, his false teeth jutting from his mouth. A ribbon of blood immediately began to flow from his scalp.

Marking the Text

Vocabulary Builder

stagnant
(stag′ nənt) *adj.*

Meaning

"We better get out of here!" Arnie suggested. "They're going to blame us!"

José knelt on both knees at the old man's side. He took the man's teeth from his mouth and placed them in his shirt pocket. The old man groaned and opened his eyes, which were shiny wet. He appeared startled, like a newborn.

"Sir, you'll be all right," José cooed, then snapped at his cousin. "Arnie, get over here and help me!"

"I'm going home," Arnie whined.

"You punk!" José yelled. "Go inside and call 911."

Arnie said that they should leave him there.

"Why should we get involved?" he cried as he started for his bike. "It's his own fault."

José laid the man's head down and with giant steps leaped out of the pool, shoving his cousin as he passed. He went into the kitchen and punched in 911 on a telephone. He explained to the operator what had happened. When asked the address, José dropped the phone and went onto the front porch to look for it.

"It's 940 East Brown," José breathed. He hung up and looked wildly about the kitchen. He opened up the refrigerator and brought out a plastic tray of ice, which he twisted so that a few of the cubes popped out and slid across the floor. He wrapped some cubes in a dish towel. When he raced outside, Arnie was gone, the yapping poodle was doing laps around the edge of the pool, and Mr. Clemens was trying to stand up.

"No, sir," José said as he jumped into the pool, his own knees almost buckling. "Please, sit down."

Mr. Clemens staggered and collapsed. José caught him before he hit his head again. The towel of ice cubes dropped from his hands. With his legs spread to absorb the weight, José raised the man up in his arms, this fragile man. He picked him up and carefully stepped toward the shallow end, one slow elephant step at a time.

"You'll be all right," José said, more to himself than to Mr. Clemens, who moaned and struggled to be let free.

The sirens wailed in the distance. The poodle yapped, which started a dog barking in the neighbor's yard.

"You'll be OK," José repeated, and in the shallow end of the pool, he edged up the steps. He lay the old man in the lounge chair and raced back inside for more ice and another towel. He returned outside and placed the bundle of cubes on the man's head, where the blood flowed. Mr. Clemens was awake, looking about. When the old man felt his mouth, José reached into his shirt pocket and pulled out his false teeth. He fit the teeth into Mr. Clemens's mouth and a smile appeared, something bright at a difficult time.

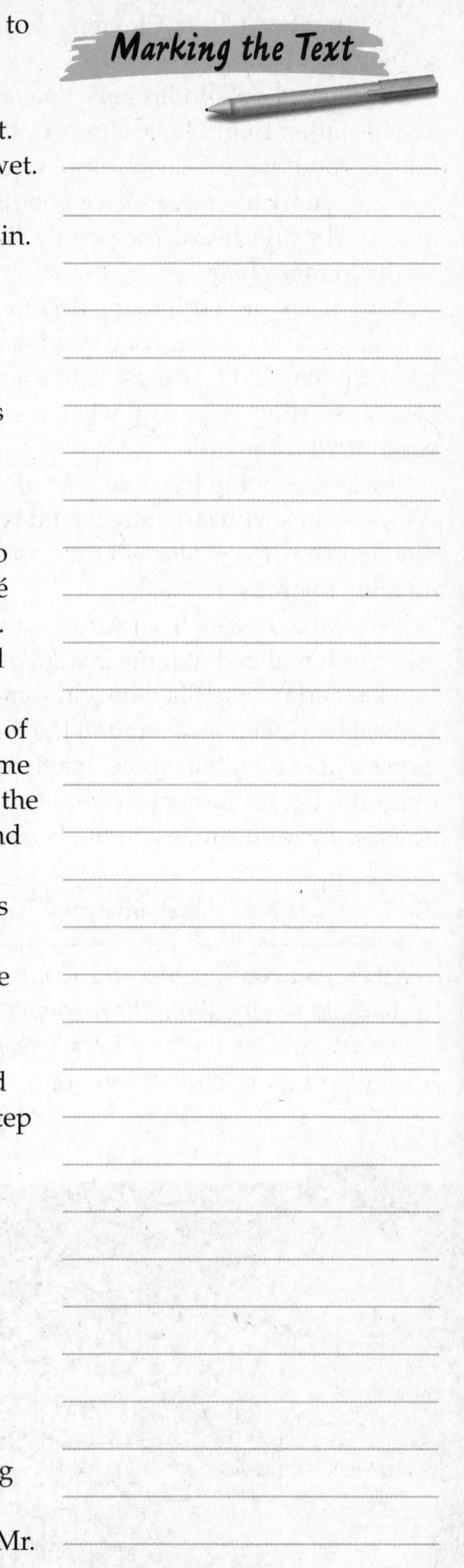

"I hit my head," Mr. Clemens said after smacking his teeth so that the fit was right.

José looked up and his gaze floated to a telephone pole, one his father might have climbed. If he had been there, his father would have seen that José was more than just a good worker. He would have seen a good man. He held the towel to the old man's head. The poodle, now quiet, joined them on the lounge chair.

A fire truck pulled into the driveway and soon they were surrounded by firemen, one of whom brought out a first-aid kit. A fireman led José away and asked what had happened. He was starting to explain when his cousin reappeared, yapping like a poodle.

"I was scrubbing the pool," Arnie shouted, "and I said, 'Mr. Clemens, you shouldn't stand so close to the edge.' But did he listen? No, he leaned over and . . . Well, you can just imagine my horror."

José walked away from Arnie's jabbering. He walked away, and realized that there were people like his cousin, the liar, and people like himself, someone he was getting to know. He walked away and in the midmorning heat boosted himself up a telephone pole. He climbed up and saw for himself what his father saw—miles and miles of trees and houses, and a future lost in the layers of yellowish haze.

Marking the Text

while reading your anchor book

Vocabulary Builder

After you read, *review the words you decided to add to your vocabulary. Write the meaning of words you have learned in context. Look up the other words in a dictionary, glossary, thesaurus, or electronic resource.*

GARY SOTO (b. 1952)

Gary Soto gathers ideas for his writing from his experience growing up in a Mexican-American neighborhood in Fresno, California. Often his work uses realistic details to tell about the everyday lives of Mexican-American boys and girls. Soto is the author of fiction, short stories, poetry, and children's picture books. His hobbies include karate and Aztec dancing.

Thinking About the Selection

Born Worker

1 **Contrast** José and Arnie both have a Mexican-American heritage. In what ways are their backgrounds different?

2 **Explain** Why does José help Mr. Clemens? Why does Arnie run away?

3 **Identify** What is the conflict between José and Arnie? How is it resolved?

4 **Speculate** Suppose José and Arnie are looking to find a job in the help-wanted ads. What kind of ad would interest José? What kind of ad would interest Arnie? On a separate sheet of paper, show what the ads might look like and what they might say.

Write Answer the following questions in your Reader's Journal.

5 **Analyze** How do the boys' different character traits and motivations create conflict in the story? Which side of the conflict do you agree with? Why?

6 **Apply** Write a paragraph describing the motives of a character in your Anchor Book.

2-6 Comparing Literary Works
Conflict

Life would be great if there were no conflict. A story without conflict, however, can be pretty boring. Conflict is what makes a story interesting—it creates tension between characters and moves the plot along.

Literary Terms

In a story, **conflict**—a problem or a struggle between opposing forces—helps to create action, keep the reader interested, and move the plot forward. A story can have more than one conflict. These are the two types of conflict.

- An **internal conflict** occurs within a person when he or she struggles to make a choice, take action, or overcome a feeling. The guilt a person feels over telling a lie is an internal conflict.
- An **external conflict** occurs between two characters or between one character and an outside force such as nature or society. A person caught in a blizzard while on a hike is experiencing an external conflict.

When looking for conflict in a story, ask these questions.

- ▸ What does the main character want?
- ▸ Why can't the main character get what he or she wants?

To identify the type of conflict, ask yourself the following questions.

Internal conflict	External conflict
• Does the character have a difficult decision to make? • Is the character having opposing thoughts or feelings that are preventing him or her from taking action?	• Is there an argument or disagreement between two or more characters? • Are there elements in nature or society that are preventing the character from taking action?

while reading your anchor book

Directions Read the following excerpt. Notice how the student has used self-stick notes to identify language that shows conflict. Then answer the questions that follow.

About the Author
Visit: PHSchool.com
Web Code: exe-6204

Student Model: Marking the Text

from The Diary of Anne Frank

by Frances Goodrich and Albert Hackett

Background *For hundreds of years, the Star of David has been recognized as a symbol of Judaism. In Nazi-occupied Europe during World War II, it became a source of humiliation and a labeling device for the Jews. Nazis required all Jews to wear the Star on their clothing, and many were attacked and persecuted because of it.*

ANNE. *[. . . as she pulls off her star, the cloth underneath shows clearly the color and form of the star]* Look! It's still there! *[PETER goes over to the stove with his star.]* What're you going to do with yours?

PETER: Burn it.

ANNE. *[She starts to throw hers in, and cannot.]* It's funny, I can't throw mine away. I don't know why.

PETER. You can't throw. . . ? Something they branded you with…? That they made you wear so they could spit on you?

ANNE. I know. I know. But after all, it is the Star of David, isn't it?

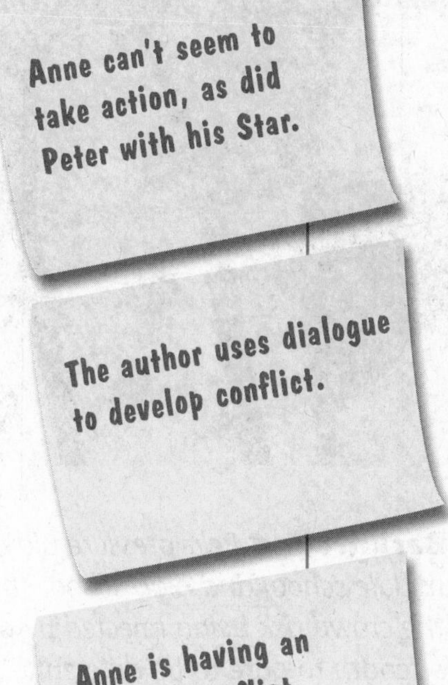

Anne can't seem to take action, as did Peter with his Star.
The author uses dialogue to develop conflict.
Anne is having an internal conflict.

1 **Identify** Why does the student describe Anne's conflict as internal?

2 **Interpret** Why do you think Anne experiences this conflict during this time in history?

3 **Apply** On a separate sheet of paper, rewrite the dialogue so that the type of conflict Anne experiences is external instead of internal.

while reading your anchor book

Identify and analyze the conflict in this excerpt from *Stargirl.*
***Guiding Question:* How does an author use conflict to help a character better understand himself or herself?**

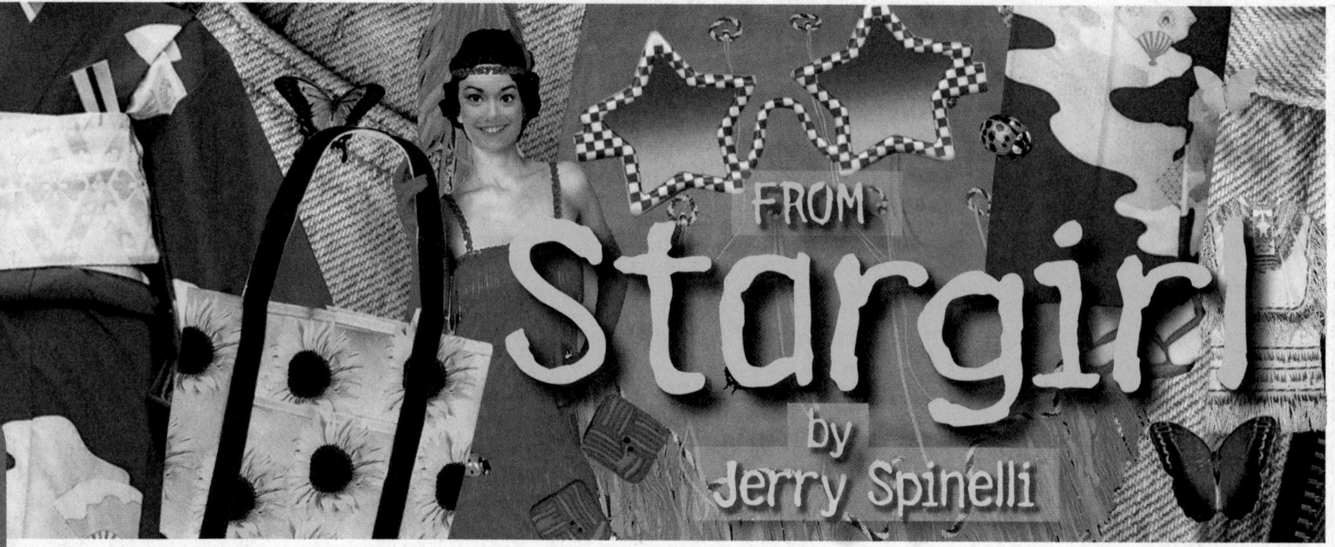

Background *Peer pressure plays a major role in the lives of middle school and high school students. Those who stand out from the crowd risk being rejected by others. It takes a certain inner strength to dare to be different.*

Vocabulary Builder

Before you read, *you will discuss the following words. In the Vocabulary Builder box in the margin, use a vocabulary building strategy to make the words your own.*

nonconformity **serenaded** **acquired**

As you read, *draw a box around unfamiliar words you could add to your vocabulary. Use context clues to unlock their meaning.*

Marking the Text

Conflict

As you read, *think about what kind of conflict the narrator experiences. Underline phrases that reveal the conflict.*

Mica Area High School—MAHS—was not exactly a hotbed of **nonconformity.** There were individual variants[1] here and there, of course, but within pretty narrow limits we all wore the same clothes, talked the same way, ate the same food, listened to the same music. Even our dorks and nerds had a MAHS stamp on them. If we happened to somehow distinguish ourselves, we quickly snapped back into place, like rubber bands.

Kevin was right. It was unthinkable that Stargirl could survive—or at least survive unchanged—among us. But it was

Vocabulary Builder

nonconformity
(nän-kən fôrm ə tē) *n.*

Meaning

[1] **variants** (ver′ē ənts) *n.* Things that differ slightly in form from other things.

also clear that Hillari Kimble was at least half right: this person calling herself Stargirl may or may not have been a faculty plant for school spirit, but whatever she was, she was not real.

She couldn't be.

Several times in those early weeks of September, she showed up in something outrageous. A 1920s flapper dress. An Indian buckskin. A kimono. One day she wore a denim miniskirt with green stockings, and crawling up one leg was a parade of enamel ladybug and butterfly pins. "Normal" for her were long, floorbrushing pioneer dresses and skirts.

Every few days in the lunchroom she **serenaded** someone new with "Happy Birthday." I was glad my birthday was in the summer.

In the hallways, she said hello to perfect strangers. The seniors couldn't believe it. They had never seen a tenth-grader so bold.

In class she was always flapping her hand in the air, asking questions, though the question often had nothing to do with the subject. One day she asked a question about trolls—in U.S. History class.

She made up a song about isosceles triangles. She sang it to her Plane Geometry class. It was called "Three Sides Have I, But Only Two Are Equal."

She joined the cross-country team. Our home meets were held on the Mica Country Club golf course. Red flags showed the runners the way to go. In her first meet, out in the middle of the

Vocabulary Builder

serenaded
(ser'ə nād' ed) *v.*

Meaning

Marking the Text

course, she turned left when everyone else turned right. They waited for her at the finish line. She never showed up. She was dismissed from the team.

One day a girl screamed in the hallway. She had seen a tiny brown face pop up from Stargirl's sunflower canvas bag. It was her pet rat. It rode to school in the bag every day.

One morning we had a rare rainfall. It came during her gym class. The teacher told everyone to come in. On the way to the next class they looked out the windows. Stargirl was still outside. In the rain. Dancing.

We wanted to define her, to wrap her up as we did each other, but we could not seem to get past "weird" and "strange" and "goofy." Her ways knocked us off balance. A single word seemed to hover in the cloudless sky over the school:

HUH?

Everything she did seemed to echo Hillari Kimble: She's not real . . . She's not real . . .

And each night in bed I thought of her as the moon came through my window. I could have lowered my shade to make it darker and easier to sleep, but I never did. In that moonlit hour, I **acquired** a sense of the otherness of things. I liked the feeling the moonlight gave me, as if it wasn't the opposite of day, but its underside, its private side, when the fabulous purred on my snow-white sheet like some dark cat come in from the desert.

It was during one of these nightmoon times that it came to me that Hillari Kimble was wrong. Stargirl was real.

Marking the Text

Vocabulary Builder

acquired
(ə kwīr′ ed) *v.*

Meaning

Vocabulary Builder

After you read, *review the words you decided to add to your vocabulary. Write the meaning of words you have learned in context. Look up the other words in a dictionary, glossary, thesaurus, or electronic resource.*

Jerry Spinelli (b. 1941)

Newbury-award winning author Jerry Spinelli dreamed of becoming a cowboy and a major league baseball player while growing up in Norristown, Pennsylvania. At age 16, his poem about the local football team's big win was published in his local newspaper—that's when Jerry knew he wanted to become a writer. When he was 41 years old, Jerry published his first book. Since then he has written more than 15 books for young readers. Spinelli gets his ideas from his everyday life—with the help of his six children, his many grandchildren, his childhood memories, and his imagination.

Thinking About the Selections

from Stargirl *and* Born Worker

About the Author
Visit: PHSchool.com
Web Code: exe-6205

1 **Explain** Both the narrator in *Stargirl* and José in "Born Worker" learn something important about themselves or about the character traits of another person in the story. How do they both come to this realization?

2 **Connect** Make a personal connection with a character in one of the stories. Tell about an event or incident in which you or a friend experienced something similar to the character's experiences.

3 **Infer** At the end of "Born Worker," José climbs up a telephone pole and sees "what his father saw—miles and miles of trees and houses, and a future lost in the layers of yellowish haze." Describe what you think this statement means. Then make an inference about the kind of external conflicts you think José deals with in his life.

4 **Explain** José experiences more than one conflict in "Born Worker." What internal and external conflicts does he have?

Write Answer the following questions in your Reader's Journal.

5 **Analyze** How does an author use conflict to help a character better understand himself or herself?

6 **Compare and Contrast** Think about a conflict in either *Stargirl* or "Born Worker." How is this conflict similar to, or different from, a conflict in your Anchor Book?

2-7 Language Coach
Grammar and Spelling

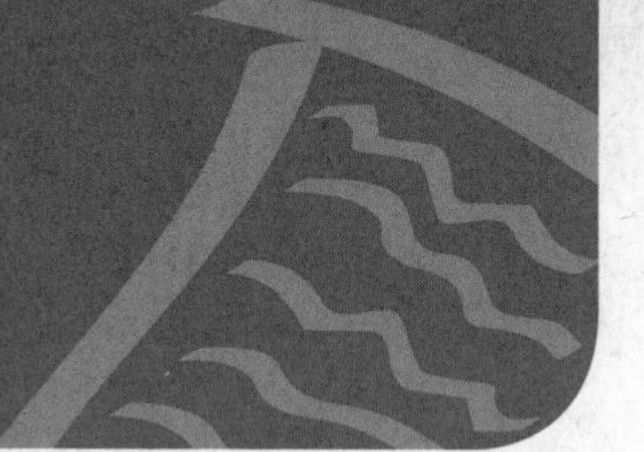

Simple Verb Tenses

A **tense** is a form of verb that is used to show time of action or a state of being. The **present tense** can be used to describe different things.

- something that occurs regularly: *I get up every day at six-thirty.*
- something that is common knowledge: *The sun rises in the east.*
- to express feelings: *I feel like going for a jog.*
- something that is happening now: *We are walking through the mall.*

Sometimes a present tense is formed using a **helping verb,** (for example, *am, are, is*), and *-ing*. Helping verbs work with the main verb and tell the reader when the action occurs.

The **past tense** shows an action that happened at some point in the past and has finished. To form the past tense of **regular verbs,** add *-ed* or *-d* to the base form of the word. The past tense of **irregular verbs** does not follow a pattern, so you will need to memorize these words.

The **future tense** shows an action that will happen. To form the future tense, use the helping verb *will* before the base form of the word.

Go Online
Learn More
Visit: PHSchool.com
Web Code: exp-6201

Author's Craft

Turn to "Showdown at Victoria Falls," on page 93, and reread the second sentence. *It's* is a contraction that stands for *it is*. What tense is *it's*? Can you rewrite it in the other tenses? Is it regular or irregular?

Verb Tense	Regular	Irregular	Irregular
Present	I (am) dream (*–ing*)	I (am) fall (*–ing*)	I (am) eat (*–ing*)
Past	I dreamed	I fell	I ate
Future	I will dream	I will fall	I will eat

Directions Rewrite the sentence using a verb tense from the chart.

1. I am dreaming of a summer on the lake. (past)

____

2. Ann fell into the pool. (future)

____

3. He stood at the gate. (present)

____

Perfect Verb Tenses

The **perfect tense** of a verb is created by using a form of the word *have* before the past participle of the verb. You can use different verb tenses within sentences to explain the order in which events occur. Usually, authors use one verb tense to set the time in which a story takes place, and then they show changes in time by shifting tenses.

Present Perfect (*have* or *has* + past participle)	▸ action that happened recently and continues into the present	They have voted.
Past Perfect (*had* + past participle)	▸ past action or condition that ended before another action began ▸ used with **past tense**	They had voted by the time we arrived.
Future Perfect (*will have* + past participle)	▸ future action or condition that will end before another begins ▸ used with **present tense**	They will have voted by the time the booth closes.

Directions Write sentences using each verb in the verb tenses shown in parentheses. Review the chart for clues.

1. *spend* (present perfect); *take* (present)

2. *begin* (past perfect); *eat* (past tense)

3. *finish* (future perfect); *see* (present)

Directions Read the following passage. Underline shifts in verb tenses. On a separate sheet of paper, rewrite the passage using the correct verb tenses.

> Faneuil Hall in Boston was built in 1742 by Peter Faneuil, who later will have given it to the city. Nineteen years later, it burns down. However, it was rebuilding soon after. Before the Revolutionary War, it will be a theater. Later it was called "the cradle of liberty." The name was given to it because it has been the scene of many important meetings during the Revolutionary War. It now had contained many historical paintings and is an exciting place.

2-8 Writer's Workshop
Exposition: Compare-and-Contrast Essay

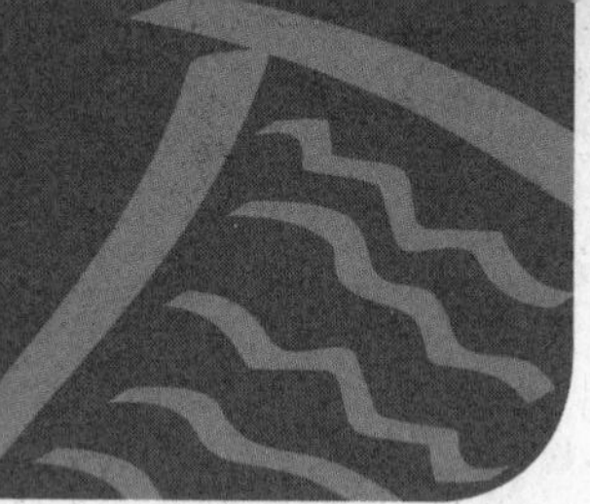

A **compare-and-contrast essay** uses factual details to examine similarities and differences between two or more related topics. This form of writing may be used to compare and contrast products, movies, vacation spots, and many other items. Follow the steps in this workshop to write a compare-and-contrast essay in which you examine the similarities and differences between two subjects.

Purpose To write an essay in which you compare and contrast two subjects

Audience You, your teacher, and your classmates

Your essay should include the following elements.

- two or more subjects that are alike and different in notable ways
- an organization that highlights similarities and differences
- a strong opening paragraph that grabs the reader's attention
- facts, descriptions, and examples that show how the two subjects are alike and different
- error-free writing, including correct use of verb tenses

Prewriting—Plan It Out

To help you choose a topic for your essay and write your draft, use one of these strategies.

Quicklist Fold a sheet of paper into two columns. In the first column, list broad topics—for example, pets, foods, things, or hobbies—that are interesting to you. In the second column, list specific subjects within each topic that you could compare and contrast.

Topic	Possible Subjects
Symbols	letters, pictures and numbers

Look at how one student used the chart to come up with a subject for a compare-and-contrast essay.

Narrow your topic. Review your list, looking for which topic and subjects would be most interesting for your compare-and-contrast essay. Finally, choose two subjects to compare and contrast.

Topic: Symbols

Subject: I would like to compare and contrast letters and numbers.

Gather details. Use the Venn diagram to list details that show similarities and differences between your two subjects. In the two outside sections, list how the topics are different. In the center overlapping area, list how they are similar.

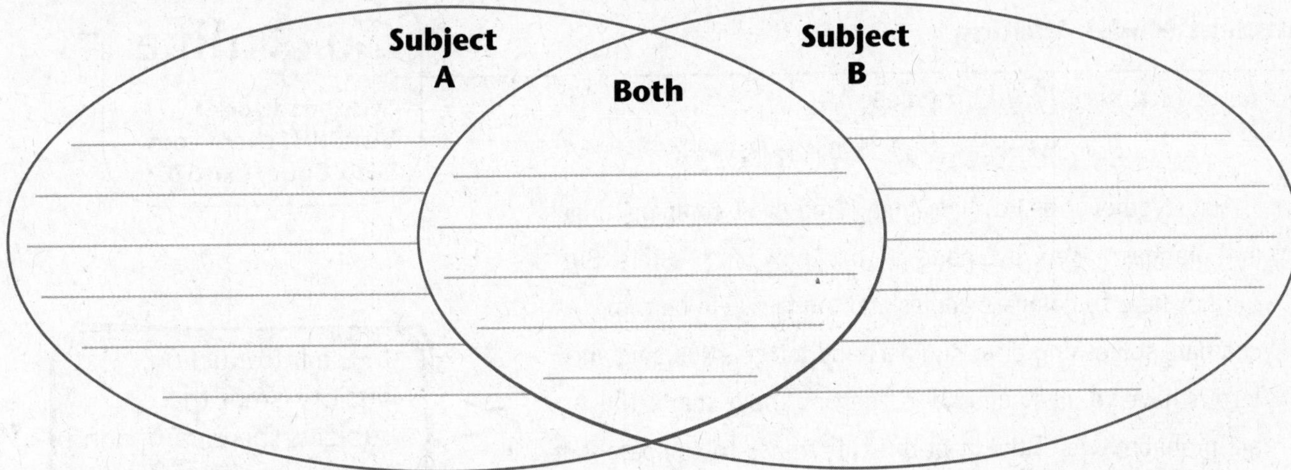

Shape your writing. Before writing your first draft, choose one of the following methods to organize your essay.

- **Block Method** Present all the details about one subject first, and then present all the details about the second subject. The block method works well if you are writing about different types of details.
- **Point-by-Point Method** Present individual details of each subject in turn. For example, if you are comparing an eagle to a hawk, you might first discuss the diet of each one, then their size and mobility, and so on.

Block Method

1. Introduction
2. Letters: purpose and use
3. Numbers: purpose and use
4. Conclusion

Point-by-Point Method

1. Introduction
2. Purpose of letters vs. purpose of numbers
3. Use of letters vs. use of numbers
4. Conclusion

Provide elaboration. Use specific details to help you focus on similarities and differences. Compare the following examples.

General letters are used in many languages

Specific letters are used in English, Hebrew, Spanish, Greek and more

Using specific details will make your writing more interesting and capture your audience's attention.

Revising—Make It Better

Reread your draft several times to check that you gave equal attention to each subject in your essay. Add or rearrange details for a more effective balance. It may help to put your draft away and return to it later to make sure you haven't missed anything.

Peer Review Read your essay aloud to a partner. Identify at least three goals for the revision of your essay.

Directions Read this student compare-and-contrast essay as a model for your own.

Student Model: Writing

Jessica Kursan, Franklin Lakes, NJ

Letters...Or Numbers?

Have you ever heard the saying, "You can't compare apples and oranges?" Well, I've done it, so I know it's possible. But I'm not here to compare apples and oranges. I'm here to compare something else: numbers and letters. Numbers and letters have so many unusual properties about them. They are probably two of the most difficult things to compare, but I'll tackle them anyway.

We'll start off with their differences. Numbers and letters have a lot of differences, obviously, but I'm only going to name a few. For one thing, letters are used to spell words, and numbers are used to, well, write numbers! Also, how many letters you have in your alphabet, whether it's Hebrew, Spanish, Greek, or anything else, it will always end somewhere. But numbers just keep right on going.

Also, letters can represent numbers, but not the other way around, unless you're a computer programmer. For example, you could have a list of instructions, and the step could be labeled A, B, C instead of 1, 2, 3. But you can't say that 586 spells *car*.

Numbers and letters have about as many similarities as they do differences, and they are just as simple. For one thing, words and numbers are both used in everyday speech. For example, you could say, "Mr. Johnson, may I walk your dog?" "But I have two dogs." Just the words themselves that you speak are made up of letters and numbers... .

As you see, numbers and letters have many differences, but also many similarities. If you take the time, I'm sure you can find even more on your own.

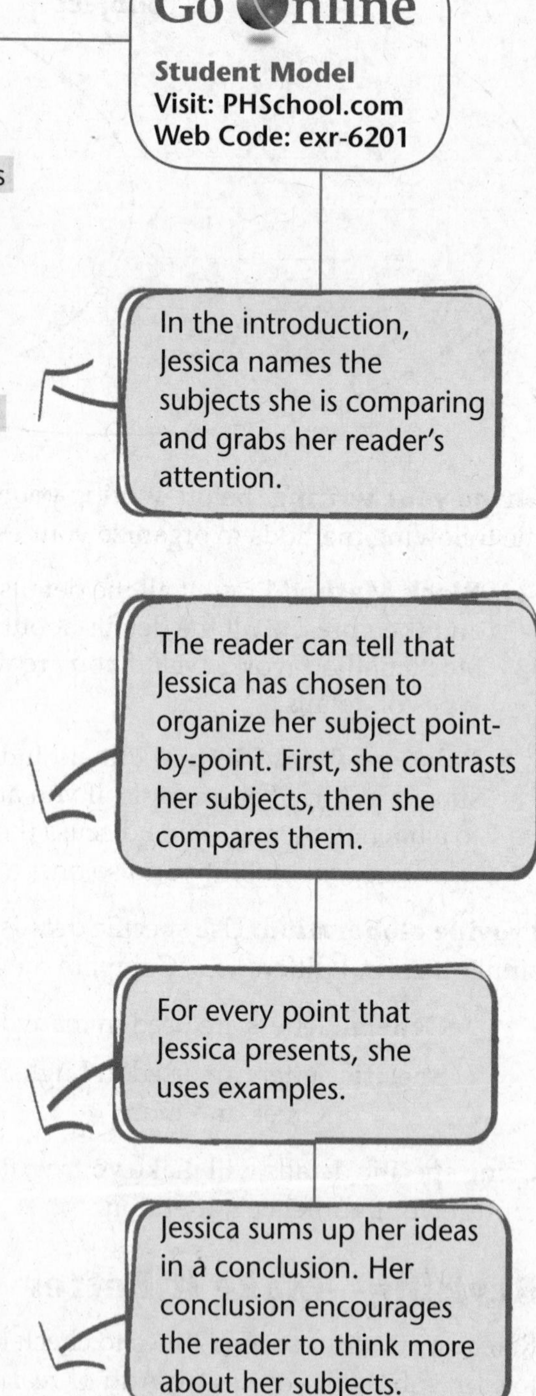

Go Online
Student Model
Visit: PHSchool.com
Web Code: exr-6201
In the introduction, Jessica names the subjects she is comparing and grabs her reader's attention.
The reader can tell that Jessica has chosen to organize her subject point-by-point. First, she contrasts her subjects, then she compares them.
For every point that Jessica presents, she uses examples.
Jessica sums up her ideas in a conclusion. Her conclusion encourages the reader to think more about her subjects.

Editing—Be Your Own Language Coach

Before you hand in your essay, proofread it. Review it on your own or with an adult for language convention errors. Pay special attention to correct verb tenses.

Publishing—Share It!

When you publish a work, you produce it for a specific audience. Consider one of the following ways to share your writing.

Create a picture essay. Find or draw images to illustrate the similarities and differences you have discussed.

Create an audio recording. Read your essay aloud, slowly and clearly, emphasizing the strongest points. At the end, include a brief description of your writing process. Record it and share it with your class.

Reflecting on Your Writing

Respond to the following question on a separate sheet of paper. What new insights did you gain about the form of a compare-and-contrast essay by writing one?

Rubric for Self-Assessment Assess your essay. For each question, circle a rating.

CRITERIA	RATING SCALE				
	NOT VERY				VERY
IDEAS How well do your subjects interest the reader?	1	2	3	4	5
ORGANIZATION How clearly and effectively are your ideas organized?	1	2	3	4	5
CONTENT How well do you use facts and descriptions to show how the two subjects are alike and different?	1	2	3	4	5
WORD CHOICE How appropriate is the language for your audience?	1	2	3	4	5
SENTENCE FLUENCY How varied is your sentence structure?	1	2	3	4	5
CONVENTIONS How correct is your grammar, especially your use of verb tenses?	1	2	3	4	5

2-9 Discussing Your Anchor Book

Literature Circles

Setting and Mood Imagine a scary story that is set in a small, happy town during spring, with the birds chirping and the flowers in bloom. How can the story be scary when it takes place in such a bright and cheerful setting? Now erase that happy scene from your mind and change it to a place where you think a good scary story might occur.

Literary Terms

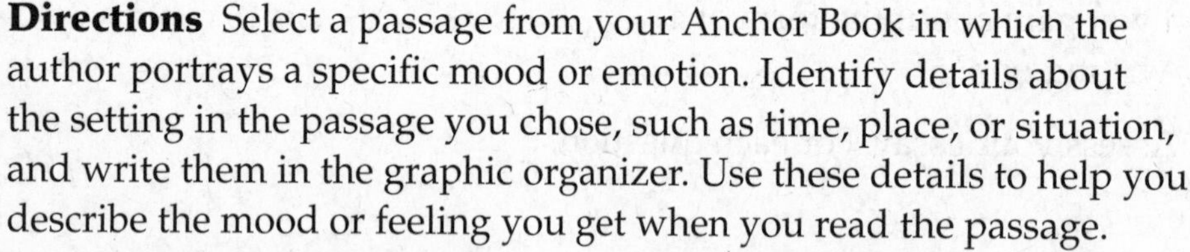

- The **setting,** or time and location of a story, helps make the story seem more real. It can also help set the mood for a story. The **mood** is the overall feeling created by the story or essay. A strong setting can help set a mood that is cheerful, lonely, or frightening.

Directions Select a passage from your Anchor Book in which the author portrays a specific mood or emotion. Identify details about the setting in the passage you chose, such as time, place, or situation, and write them in the graphic organizer. Use these details to help you describe the mood or feeling you get when you read the passage.

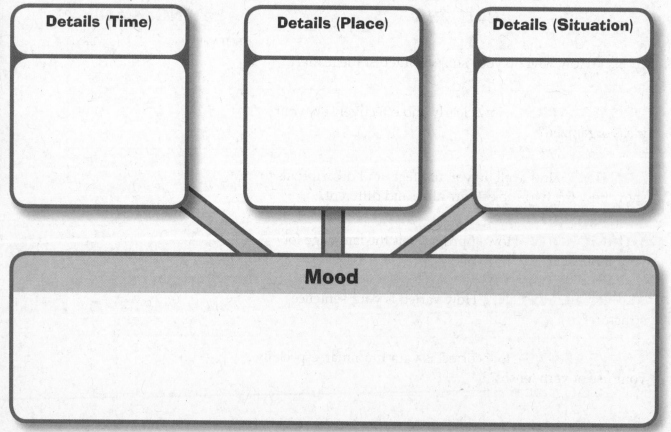

Details (Time)	Details (Place)	Details (Situation)

Mood

while reading your anchor book

Use the details and ideas from your graphic organizer to answer the following questions.

1 **Describe** What is the setting of the passage you chose? Use examples from your Anchor Book in your answer.

2 **Analyze** Choose a detail that relates to setting, such as the time or place. How is this detail important to the story's plot?

3 **Interpret** How does this setting affect the mood of the passage?

With Your Group

Now meet with your group members. Take turns sharing the passages you chose. Participate in a discussion to define how the setting of each passage contributes to the mood. Ask probing questions to get the opinion of each member. Then, as a group, complete the graphic organizer. Include details about the setting from each passage and describe the overall mood of your Anchor Book.

Page ____ **Setting**	**Mood of passage**
Page ____ **Setting**	**Mood of passage**
Page ____ **Setting**	**Mood of passage**

Overall mood of your Anchor Book:

while reading your anchor book

Monitoring Your Progress
Standardized Test Practice

Reading Skill: Making Inferences

Directions Read the following passage. Then answer the questions.

As we do every Saturday evening, our family was getting ready to go out to a concert together. All of us were ready but my sister Bret. She was always making us late, and tonight was no exception. While the rest of the family waited, I went upstairs to check on her. Judging from the pile of clothes on her bed, I figured it would be another half-hour before we could leave for the concert.

It didn't help that the sky was quickly turning a dark gray. Ever since last year, my dad takes the back roads in bad weather. It would take us an extra fifteen minutes to reach the concert hall.

My mom gazed out the window as the rain started pouring down. "That does it," she said. She took off her coat and tossed her keys on the table. I didn't mind. I don't like getting caught in the rain anyway.

1 Which of the following **inferences** can you make based on the clues in the passage?

A. Bret is going to get dressed on time.

B. The concert will be entertaining.

C. Bret has not finished dressing.

D. The family called a taxi.

2 What most likely happened to the narrator's father last year?

F. He became a composer.

G. He got in a car accident.

H. He got lost by taking the back roads in his car.

J. He bought Bret lots of new clothes.

3 What can you **infer** about what happened at the end of this passage?

A. It rains on Saturday nights.

B. The family decided to stay home that night.

C. Bret has never been late.

D. The family was late to the concert.

4 What causes the narrator's mom to say, "That does it"?

F. She sees that it has started to rain.

G. She wants to go to the concert.

H. She is tired of waiting for Bret.

J. She sees someone she knows out the window.

Literary Analysis: Elements of the Novel

Directions Read the following passage. Then answer the questions.

> Oksana wanted perfection—she wouldn't let anyone else make a single decision about her day. But the bridesmaids were not happy about their dresses. The color didn't look good on the bridesmaids. According to everyone, the style was quite outdated. They were also painfully expensive. It was decided that Kristin should talk to Oksana about the dresses.
>
> Kristin was the perfect woman for the job. She had always been the peacemaker, the diplomat of the group. It's a good thing, too, because Oksana was not known for being the easiest person to deal with. Once she made a decision, it was usually set in stone. And so, with a humble knock at her door, Kristin timidly let herself into Oksana's bedroom and calmly said, "Oksana, I think we need to talk."

5 Which of the following is an example of **direct characterization**?

- **A.** "Oksana, I think we need to talk."
- **B.** She had always been the peacemaker, the diplomat of the group.
- **C.** Kristin timidly let herself into Oksana's bedroom and calmly said
- **D.** They were also painfully expensive.

6 Based on the story, what is Kristin's **motivation** when she enters Oksana's room?

- **F.** She wants to congratulate her.
- **G.** She wants to let her know that the dresses are beautiful.
- **H.** She thinks that the reception hall is beautiful.
- **J.** She wants to tell her how the bridesmaids feel about their dresses.

7 What creates the **conflict** that develops in this story?

- **A.** The wedding date is the same as another event.
- **B.** It is an outdoor wedding and the weather forecast calls for rain.
- **C.** There is no conflict in this story.
- **D.** The bridesmaids don't like the dresses, but the bride is very stubborn.

8 Which of the following is an example of **indirect characterization**?

- **F.** Kristin timidly let herself into Oksana's bedroom and calmly said . . .
- **G.** It was decided that Kristin should talk to Oksana about the dresses.
- **H.** They were also painfully expensive.
- **J.** But the bridesmaids were not happy about their dresses.

Timed Writing: Interpretation of Literature

Directions Write a brief conversation about what Kristin and Oksana might have said about the bridesmaids' dresses in Oksana's bedroom. Think about the author's characterizations of both characters as you write. **(20 minutes)**

2-10 Reading Skills
Drawing Conclusions

In learning new reading skills, you will use special academic vocabulary. Knowing the right words will help you demonstrate your understanding.

Academic Vocabulary

Word	Meaning	Example Sentence
conclude *v.* *Related words:* conclusion, conclusive	to make a final decision	When Miguel told me the milk was sour, I *concluded* that it had been sitting on the counter too long.
examine *v.* *Related words:* examination, exam	to give special attention; stress	You should *examine* the new floor carefully and make sure there are no scratches.
contribute *v.* *Related words:* contribution, contributed	to give or supply to others	Each week I *contribute* two hours of my time to the dog shelter.

When reading, sometimes you have to **draw conclusions,** or form ideas or opinions about what you read. To draw a conclusion, you must **examine** evidence from the text and from information you already know about the topic. In life, people draw conclusions all the time. Look at the graphic organizer to see how someone might draw a conclusion based on supporting evidence.

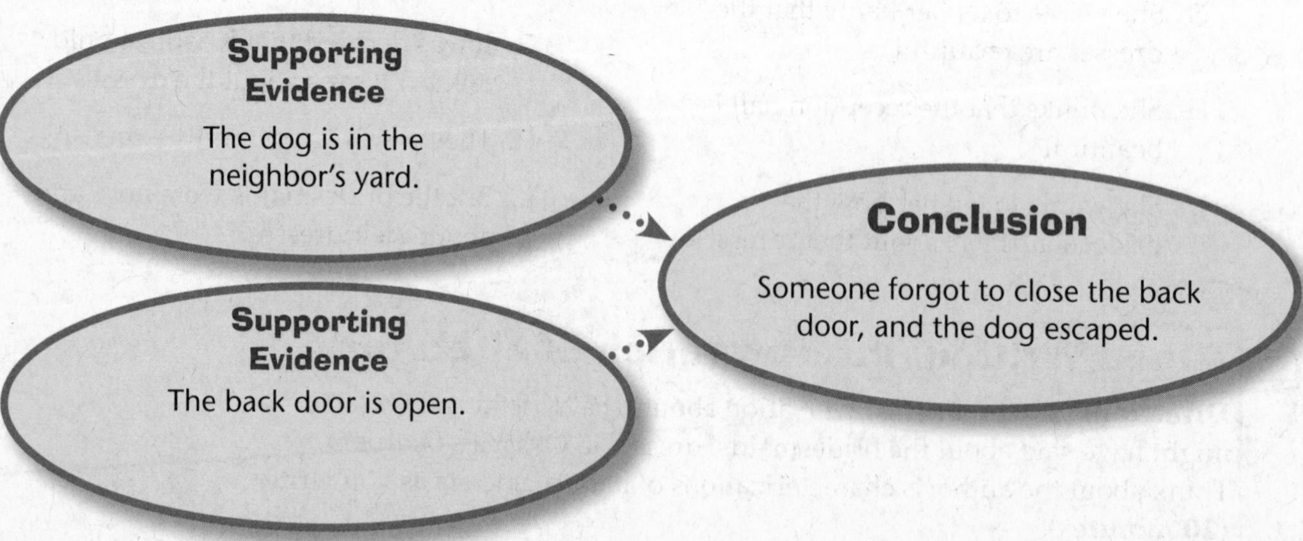
Supporting Evidence
The dog is in the neighbor's yard.
Supporting Evidence
The back door is open.
Conclusion
Someone forgot to close the back door, and the dog escaped.

while reading your anchor book

Directions Read the article and underline facts and details. Then answer the questions that follow.

Space Trash and Treasure by Michael Klesius

Even a tiny paint flake left floating in orbit can pit the window of a space shuttle traveling 17,500 miles an hour. To avoid catastrophic collisions, the Department of Defense tracks pieces of orbiting space junk larger than two inches. Debris[1] orbiting relatively close to Earth, such as a glove that drifted away in 1965 from Edward White or an eyebolt[2] shaken loose from a solar panel on a Russian spacecraft in 2004, quickly burn up in the atmosphere. Items in higher orbit remain aloft[3] for generations: The Vanguard 1 satellite will fly for centuries. Space agencies are pondering ways to sweep such junk out of the path of collision. Meanwhile, Australian archaeologist Alice Gorman is lobbying for the creation of an international treaty that would designate certain satellites, such as the Vanguard 1, as treasures of cultural heritage. One day, she says, they may even beckon[4] space tourists.

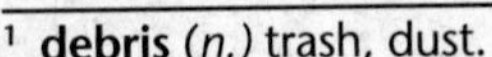

[1] **debris** (*n.*) trash, dust.
[2] **eyebolt** (*n.*) a bolt with a loop in the head.
[3] **aloft** (*adj.*) high up above the earth.
[4] **beckon** (*v.*) to signal to or appear inviting.

1 **Conclude** Complete this graphic organizer. Find evidence in the text and draw a conclusion about the Vanguard 1.

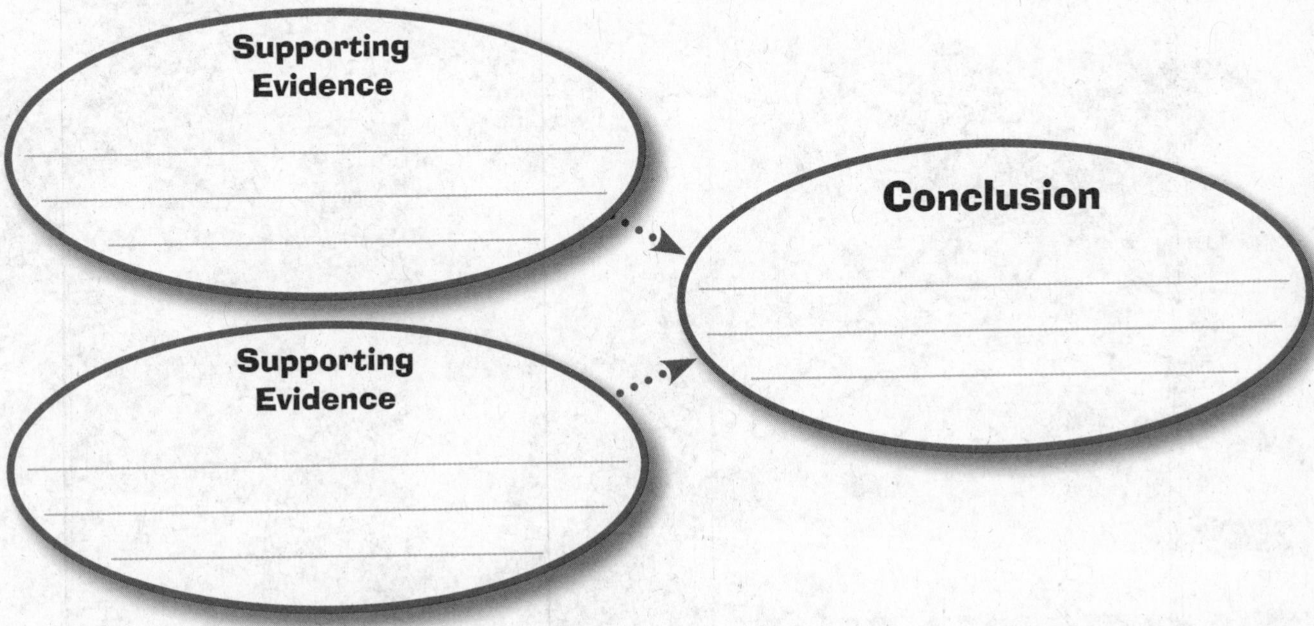

while reading your anchor book

As you read this social studies textbook excerpt, draw conclusions based on important details. ***Guiding Question:* What positive outcomes came out of the conflicts of the war?**

Link to Social Studies

Conflict Between the North and South

The Civil War began because of many differences between the North and the South. These differences existed since the early 1800s. Tensions grew for several decades. When the war started in 1861, most Americans believed that it would not last long. Instead, it stretched into four years of bloody fighting. In the end, more Americans died in the Civil War than in any other previous war.

The problems between the North and the South centered on five major issues. These issues were slavery, tariffs, taxes, power in the House of Representatives, and power in the Senate. People in the North had strong feelings about these issues, as did the people in the South.

Three million soldiers fought in the Civil War. Of those, 180,000 were African Americans fighting for the North.

▲ **Crops, such as cotton, were picked by slave labor on the Southern plantations in the 1800s.**

Slavery

The North and the South had different beliefs about slavery. These beliefs were based on differences in their economies. The economy of a region is the way most people in that area earn their money.

Manufacturing was the most important part of the North's economy. Many people there earned their livings by making things in factories. The North had many workers for its factories because it had a larger population than the South. All of the states in the South produced less than one quarter of the goods (in dollar value) that were produced in the North.

The South's economy was based on agriculture, or growing plants. The most important farms in the South were plantations. These were large farms that grew cotton and tobacco. Plantation owners depended on slaves to take care of their huge crops.

Many people in the North did not believe in slavery. They thought the people of the South should not own slaves. Although some Southerners opposed slavery, most believed they needed slaves for their plantations. They said that ending slavery would be a threat to their economy.

Tariffs

Congress has always placed tariffs on manufactured goods imported into the United States. Tariffs raise the price of foreign products. Foreign products then cost more than U.S. products. Northerners liked tariffs, because more Americans bought cheaper U.S. products made in the North.

Southerners hated tariffs. They needed to sell their cotton in Europe to make money. In exchange, they agreed to buy goods from Europe. Tariffs raised the prices of these European products. That is why Southerners saw tariffs as a kind of tax on them. Their representatives in Congress had argued against tariffs since the early 1800s. However, Congress continued to increase the tariffs.

▼ **In the 1800s, many women in the North worked in textile factories where they made items such as clothing and shoes, as shown here.**

Taxes

Taxes for road building were also an issue between the North and the South. People in the North needed good roads to ship their products to other parts of the country. Money to build these roads came from taxes paid by both Northerners and Southerners. The South, however, had many rivers that were good for shipping. Southerners used steamboats to ship their crops to the coast. Southerners did not need as many roads. Therefore they objected to paying the taxes needed to build roads. They thought the states should have more say in how to use the money from taxes.

Power in the House of Representatives

Another difference of opinion arose over control of the House of Representatives. In the North, the growing number of factories meant an increasing demand for workers. Many immigrants from Europe settled in the North because of the jobs there. As a result, the population of the North grew quickly. The greater a state's population, the more House representatives it has. Soon the North had more representatives in the House than the South did. This advantage gave Northerners more power to pass laws in the House of Representatives.

The South wanted to have more power in the House. However, its population was smaller than that of the North. Southerners argued for the right to count slaves as part of the population. This way, the South would get more representatives. The North believed that slaves should not be counted just to give Southerners more representatives. In order to count the slaves, the North argued, Southerners must first free them.

▲ **Congress debates the California Compromise of 1850.**

Power in the Senate

By 1819, there were 11 Northern free states and 11 Southern slave states. Each state had two senators. While the Southerners knew that they could not control the House, they struggled with the North for control of the Senate.

In 1850, the territory of California asked to join the Union as a free state. After much heated debate, Congress passed the Compromise of 1850. This compromise allowed California to be admitted as a free state. However, the rest of the southwestern territory would be open to slavery if the people who settled there voted for it.

Gradually the tensions between the North and the South grew worse. The Southern states decided that they had no future in the Union and withdrew from it. The country soon divided. In the Civil War that followed, Northerners fought against Southerners. After four years of fighting, the North won the war. The Union was saved. The task of reunion, however, proved to be long and difficult.

▼ **The Union army employed military textile workers to make awnings, harnesses, and other items during the Civil War.**

Directions Read the following selection. As you read, underline and label the most important parts of the plot.

The Tortoise and the Hare

The hare was once boasting of his speed before the other animals. "I have never yet been beaten," said he, "when I put forth my full speed. I challenge anyone here to race with me."

The tortoise said quietly, "I accept your challenge."

"That is a good joke," said the hare. "I could dance around you all the way."

"Keep your boasting until you've beaten me," answered the tortoise. "Shall we race?"

So a course was fixed and a start was made. The hare darted almost out of sight at once, but soon stopped, and to show his contempt for the tortoise, lay down to have a nap. The tortoise plodded on and plodded on, and when the hare awoke from his nap, he saw the tortoise nearing the finish line, and he could not catch up in time to save the race.

The moral of the story? Slow and steady wins the race.

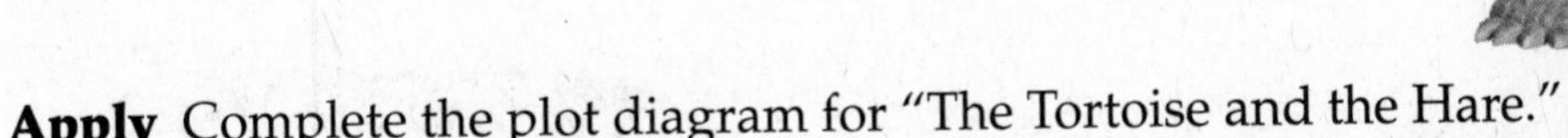

Apply Complete the plot diagram for "The Tortoise and the Hare."

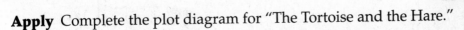

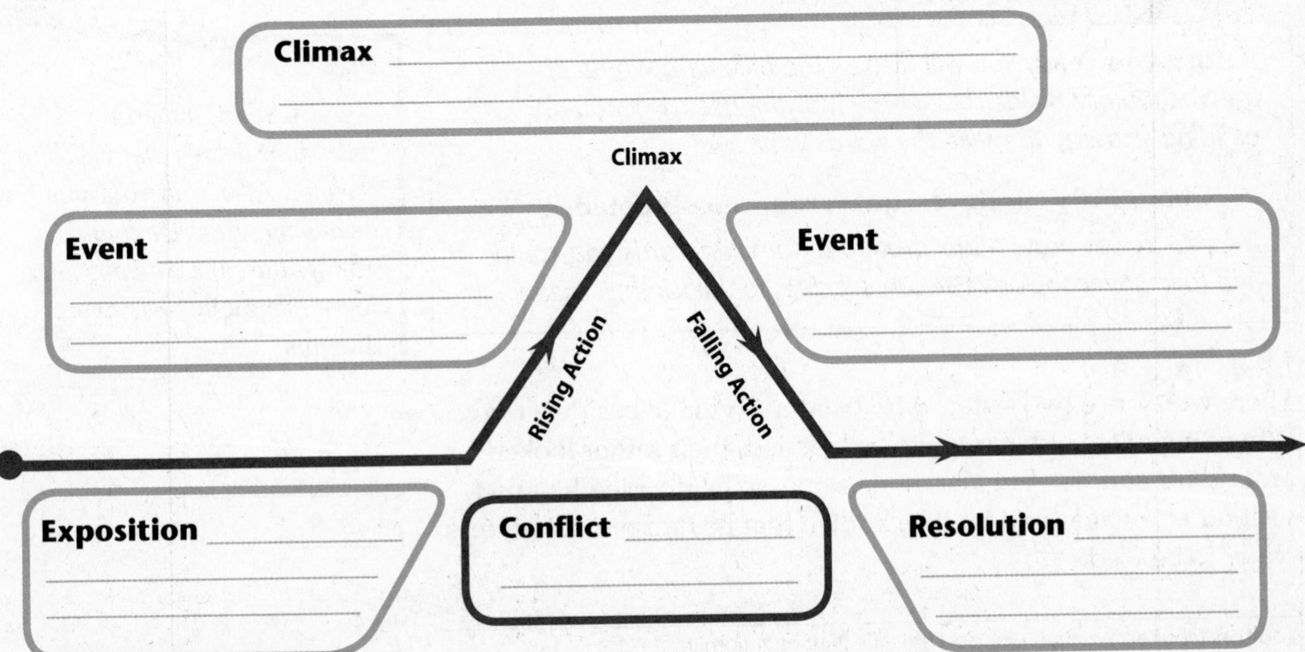

As you read this folk tale, pay special attention to how the plot unfolds. *Guiding Question:* **How does the conflict in the plot have a positive and negative effect on the situation?**

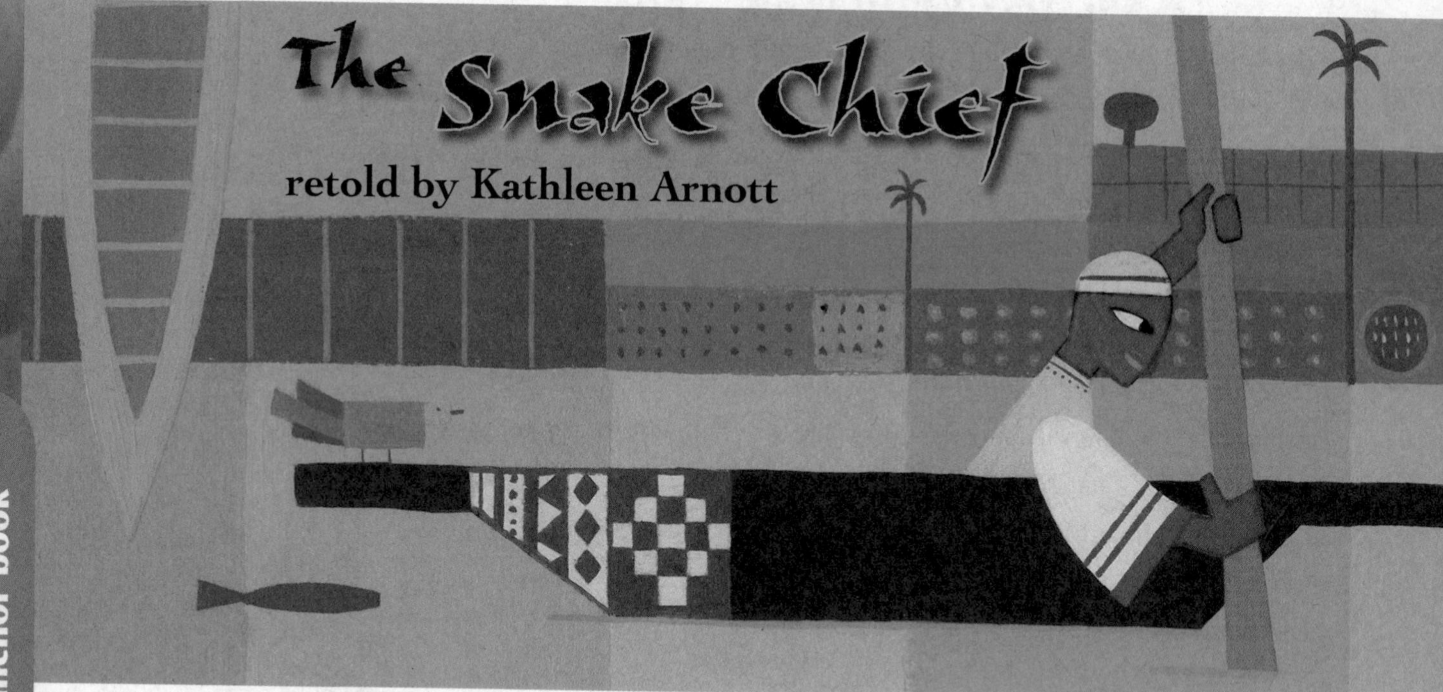

The Snake Chief

retold by Kathleen Arnott

Background *A folk tale is a story or legend shared orally with an audience. In this African folk tale, two sisters with very different personalities prepare for marriage. The ways the sisters approach their marriages sets the story in motion.*

Vocabulary Builder

Before you read, *you will discuss the following words. In the Vocabulary Builder box in the margin, use a vocabulary building strategy to make the words your own.*

haughtily induce quavered incompetence

As you read, *draw a box around unfamiliar words you could add to your vocabulary. Use context clues to unlock their meaning.*

Marking the Text

Plot

As you read, *underline important details that make up the plot. Also, underline any details that describe conflict. You will use these details later to complete a five-part plot diagram.*

There were once two sisters who lived in a village beside a river. When they were old enough to be married, their father looked around for suitors[1], but alas, none came, so he decided he must visit other villages and let it be known that he had two daughters ready to be wed.

[1] **suitors** (so͞ot'erz) *n.* men who seek the affection of a woman.

while reading your anchor book

One day, he took his small canoe and crossed the big river. Then he walked along a path until he came to a village. It appeared to be a happy place and the people greeted him kindly.

"Welcome!" they cried. "What news have you brought?"

"I have no news of importance," he replied. "Have you?"

"Our chief is looking for a wife," the people replied, "otherwise nothing we can think of is worth repeating."

Now the man had found out what he wanted to know, and he told the people that he would send a wife for the chief the next day.

He re-crossed the river and went to his house, smiling contentedly. When his daughters came back from their work in the fields he called them and said:

"At last I have found a man who is worthy to be the husband of one of my daughters. The chief in the village across the water is looking for a wife. Which of you shall I send?"

The elder[2] daughter said quickly: "I shall go, of course, since I am the elder."

"Very well," replied the man. "I shall call all my friends and bid the drummers lead you to your husband's home."

"Indeed you will not," said the girl **haughtily.** "When I go to the home of my husband, I shall go alone."

Now in that part of Africa it was unheard of for a bride to go to her wedding without a host of friends and relations all singing and dancing for joy. So the father was astonished when his daughter said she would go alone, even though he knew that she had been proud and headstrong from childhood.

"But, my daughter," he pleaded, "no woman ever goes alone to her marriage. It is not the custom."

"Then I shall start a new custom," said the girl. "Unless I go alone, I shall not go at all."

At last the father, realizing that no amount of persuasion would **induce** the girl to change her mind, agreed to her going alone, and early the next morning she set out. He took her across the river and pointed out the way, then returned home unhappily.

The girl began her journey without looking back and after a little while she met a mouse on the path. It stood up on its hind-legs, and rubbing its two front paws together, asked politely:

"Would you like me to show you the way to the chief's village?"

The girl scarcely stopped walking and almost trod on the mouse as she replied:

"Get out of my sight! I want no help from you."

Then she continued on her way while the mouse screeched after her:

"Bad luck to you!"

---

[2] **elder** (el'dər) *adj.* an older person.

Marking the Text

Vocabulary Builder

haughtily
(hôt' ē lī) *adv.*

Meaning

induce
(in do͞os') *v.*

Meaning

while reading your anchor book

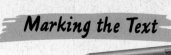

A little further on the girl met a frog, sitting on a stone at the side of the path.

"Would you like me to show you the way?" he croaked.

"Don't you speak to me!" answered the girl, tipping the frog off the stone with her foot. "I am going to be a chief's wife and am far too important to have anything to do with a mere frog."

"Bad luck to you then," croaked the frog, as he picked himself up from where he had fallen and jumped off into the bush.

Soon after this the girl began to feel tired and she sat down under a tree to rest. In the distance she could hear goats bleating[3] and presently a herd of them passed by, driven by a little boy.

"Greetings, sister," he said politely. "Are you going on a long journey?"

"What business is that of yours?" demanded the girl.

"I thought you might be carrying food with you," replied the boy, "and I hoped you might give me something to eat for I am so hungry."

"I have no food," said the girl, "and even if I had I should not dream of giving any to you."

The boy looked disappointed and hurried after his goats, turning back to say over his shoulder:

"Bad luck to you then."

Presently the girl got to her feet and continued her journey. Suddenly she found herself face to face with a very old woman.

---

[3] **bleating** (blēt [ng]) *n.* the sound a goat makes, similar to whining or crying.

"Greetings, my daughter," she said to the girl. "Let me give you some advice.

"You will come to some trees which will laugh at you, but do not laugh back at them.

"You will find a bag of thick, curdled[4] milk, but do not on any account drink it.

"You will meet a man who carries his head under his arm, but you must not drink water if he offers you any."

"Be quiet, you ugly old thing!" exclaimed the girl, pushing the old woman aside. "If I want any advice from you, I'll ask for it."

"You will have bad luck if you don't listen to me," **quavered** the old woman, but the girl took no notice and went on her way.

Sure enough she soon came to a clump of trees which began to laugh loudly as she approached them.

"Stop laughing at me," she commanded, and when they did not, she laughed noisily at them in return as she passed them by.

A little further on, she saw a bag made from a whole goatskin, lying at her feet. On picking it up, she discovered it was full of curdled milk and since this was something she was particularly fond of, she drank it with relish, exclaiming:

"How lucky I found this! I was getting so thirsty with such a long journey."

Then she threw the bag into the bush and continued on her way. As she walked through a shady grove, she was a little taken aback at the strange sight of a man coming towards her, carrying

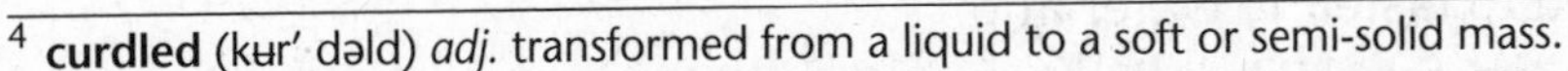

4 **curdled** (kur' dəld) *adj.* transformed from a liquid to a soft or semi-solid mass.

Marking the Text

Vocabulary Builder

quavered
(kwā'vərd) *v.*

Meaning

while reading your anchor book

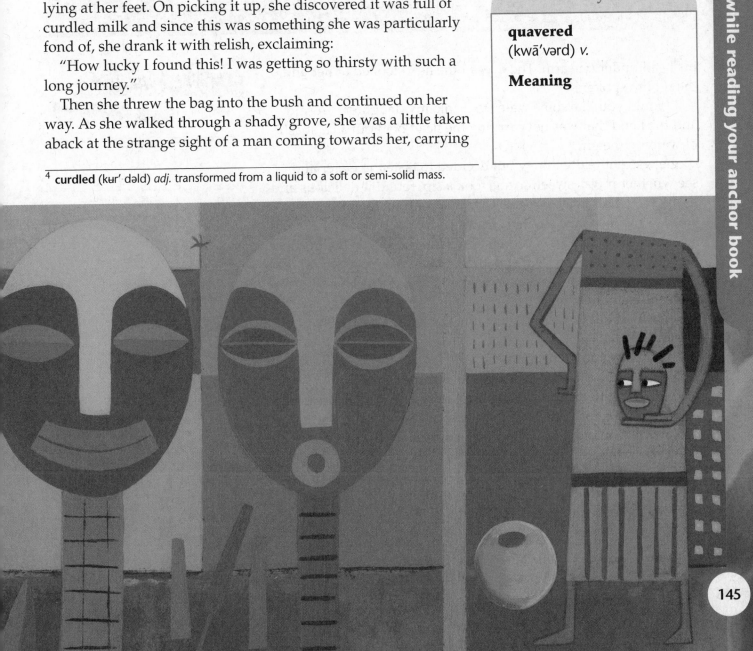

Literature in Context

Link to Social Studies

Voices About the Past

Today, people still understand the importance of passing on and preserving traditions, events, and beliefs that document our culture. On October 27, 2000, the Library of Congress initiated the Veterans History Project. This ongoing project is aimed at capturing and preserving the memories of life in combat. Soldiers and citizens throughout the United States are dedicated to interviewing, collecting, and recording memories and anecdotes of the men and women who were in combat at different periods of time throughout U.S. history. Preserving these memories is important in preserving our history. It allows future generations to get a sense of what wartime was like in the past.

Allen, Robert Wayne

Allen, James W.

James Allen saluting the colors at his retirement ceremony (September 1980)

War: Korean War, 1950-1955; Vietnam War, 1961-1975
Branch: Army
Unit: 7th Infantry Division
Service Location: Union Station; Korea; Germany; Vietnam
Highest Rank: First Sergeant
Place of Birth: Ocala,FL

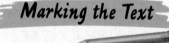

VIEW FULL DESCRIPTION

his head under one arm. The eyes in the head looked at her and the mouth spoke:

"Would you like some water to drink, my daughter?" it said, and the hand that was not carrying the head held out a calabash[5] of water to the girl.

She was not really thirsty but decided to taste the water and see whether it was sweet, so she took a sip, found it delicious and drank the whole calabash full. Then she continued, without a word of thanks to the strange creature.

As she turned the next bend in the path, she saw in the distance the village she was seeking and knew that her journey was almost over. She had to cross a small stream and found a girl bending there, filling her water-pot.

She was about to pass on when the village girl greeted her and asked:

"Where are you going, pray?"

With scarcely a glance at her questioner she replied:

"I am going to that village to marry a chief. You have no right to speak to me, for I am older than you and far more important."

Now the younger girl was the chief's sister, but she did not boast about this. She merely said:

"Let me give you some advice. Do not enter the village from this side. It is unlucky to do so. Go right round past those tall trees and enter it on the far side."

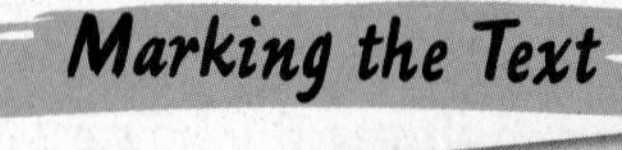

[5] **calabash** (kal′ ə bash′) *n.* a dried, hollowed-out gourd, used as a ladle or bottle.

The girl took no notice at all but just walked on to the nearest entrance with her head in the air. When she arrived, the women crowded round her to find out who she was and what she wanted.

"I have come to marry your chief," she explained. "Get away, and let me rest."

"How can you be a bride if you come alone?" they asked. "Where is the bridal procession, and are there no drummers with you?"

The girl did not answer, but she sat down in the shade of a hut to rest her aching legs.

Presently some of the older women came over to her.

"If you are to be the wife of our chief," they said, "then you must prepare his supper, as all good wives do."

The girl realized that this was true, so she asked:

"And from where shall I get the millet to cook my husband's supper?"

They gave her some millet and told her to grind it, showing her where the grinding stones were, but unlike most women, she only ground the corn for a very short time, so that the flour was coarse and gritty. Then she made some bread, and when the other women saw it, they went away together and laughed at her **incompetence**.

As the sun set, a mighty wind blew up. The roof of the hut shook and shivered and the girl crouched against the mud walls in fear. But worse was to come. A huge snake with five heads suddenly appeared, and coiling itself up at the door of the hut, told her to bring it the supper she had cooked.

Marking the Text

Vocabulary Builder

incompetence
(in käm'pə təntz) *n.*

Meaning
inadequate ability

"Did you not know that I am the chief?" asked the snake, as it began to eat the bread. Then it uttered a fearful scream, spat the food from its mouth and hissed:

"This supper is so badly cooked, I refuse to have you for a wife! So I shall slay you!" and with a mighty blow from his tail, he killed her.

When the news of her death at last reached her father, he still had not found a husband for his younger daughter, whose name was Mpunzanyana.

"Let me go to this chief," she begged him. "I am sure I could please him if I tried."

Rather reluctantly the father called together all his relations and friends and asked them to make up a bridal procession for his second daughter. They were all delighted and went away to put on their best clothes, while the father summoned the musicians and drummers who were to lead the way.

They set off early in the morning, and crossing the big river, they sang joyfully as they went. They began the long journey along the same little path that the eldest daughter had taken not so long ago, and presently they met a mouse.

"Shall I tell you how to get there?" it asked of Mpunzanyana, as she stopped to avoid treading on it.

Marking the Text

"Thank you very much," she replied, and listened courteously as the tiny animal told them which path to take.

On they went until they came to a deep valley and found a very old woman sitting beside a tree. The ugly old creature rose shakily to her feet to stand before the girl. Then she said:

"When you come to a place where two paths meet, you must take the little one, not the big one as that is unlucky."

"Thank you for telling me, grannie." Mpunzanyana answered. "I will do as you say and take the little path."

They journeyed on and on, meeting no one for some time, until suddenly a coney stood on the path in front of them all. Stretching up its head, it looked at the girl and said:

"You are nearly there! But let me give you some advice. Soon you will meet a young girl carrying water from the stream. Mind you speak politely to her.

"When you get to the village they will give you millet to grind for the chief's supper. Make sure you do it properly.

"And finally, when you see your husband, do not be afraid. I beg you, have no fear, or at least, do not show it."

"Thank you for your advice, little coney," said the girl. "I will try to remember it all and do as you say."

Sure enough, as they turned the last bend in the path, they caught sight of the village, and coming up from the stream they overtook a young girl carrying a pot of water on her head. It was the chief's sister, and she asked:

"Where are you bound for?"

"We are going to this village where I hope to be the chief's bride," answered Mpunzanyana.

"Let me lead you to the chief's hut," said the younger girl, "and do not be afraid when you see him."

Mpunzanyana followed the girl, and the bridal party followed Mpunzanyana, so that all the people came out of their huts to see what the joyful noise was about. They welcomed the visitors politely and gave them food to eat. Then the chief's mother brought millet to Mpunzanyana and said:

"If you are to be the wife of our chief, then you must prepare his supper, as all good wives do."

So the girl set to work and ground the millet as finely as she could, then made it into light, delicious bread.

As the sun set, a strong wind arose which shook the house and when Mpunzanyana heard the people saying: "Here comes our chief," she began to tremble. Then she remembered what she had been told and even when one of the poles which supported the roof fell to the ground, she did not run inside in a panic but stood quietly waiting for her husband to come home.

She almost cried out when she saw the huge snake, but when it asked her for food, she gave it the bread she had baked and it ate it with obvious enjoyment.

"This bread is delicious," said the snake. "Will you be my wife?"

Marking the Text

while reading your anchor book

For one moment, Mpunzanyana was struck dumb, but she yelled bravely when she thought of all the advice she had heard, and replied:

"Yes, O chief, I will marry you."

At her words, the shining snake-skin fell from the chief and he rose up, a tall, handsome man.

"By your brave words, you have broken the spell," he explained.

That night a feast was begun in the chief's village which lasted for twenty days. All the time the sound of music and drumming made the people's hearts glad.

So Mpunzanyana became the wife of a rich and splendid chief, and in course of time they had many sons, while the village prospered under her husband's wise rule.

Marking the Text

Vocabulary Builder

After you read, *review the words you decided to add to your vocabulary. Write the meaning of words you have learned in context. Look up the other words in a dictionary, glossary, thesaurus, or electronic resource.*

Thinking About the Selection

The Snake Chief

Go Online
About the Author
Visit: PHSchool.com
Web Code: exe-6206

1 **Apply** Look at the parts of the story that you underlined. Use these details to create a plot diagram for "The Snake Chief."

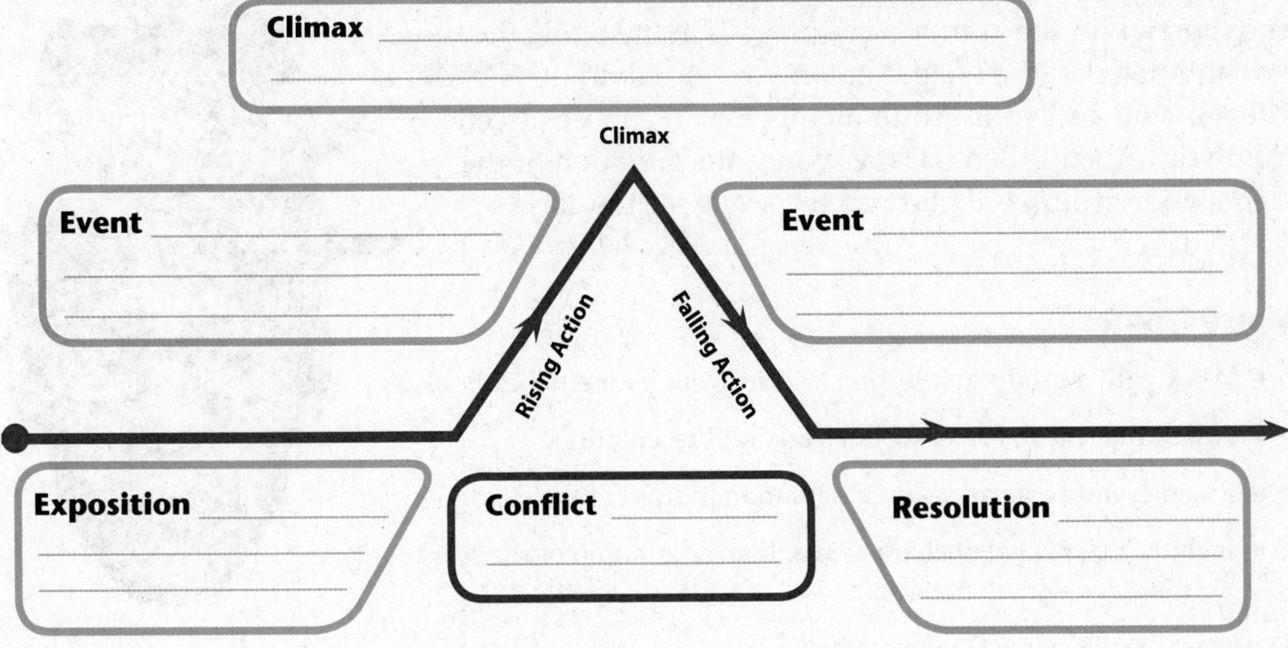

2 **Identify** How do the elder daughter's actions create conflict in the story? Give examples from the text in your answer.

3 **Speculate** The conflict the elder daughter created caused the second daughter to volunteer to become the wife of the chief. Why do you think she volunteered to do this?

Write Answer the following question in your Reader's Journal.

4 **Analyze** How does the conflict in the plot have a positive and a negative effect on the situation?

5 **Apply** Use a plot diagram to identify the parts of the plot in your Anchor Book.

while reading your anchor book

2-12 Listening and Speaking Workshop
Reader's Theater

Reading a good book is like watching a movie in your head. The more vivid the author's language is in the book, the more real and detailed the images are in your mind. In this Reader's Theater, you and your group members will choose a scene from your Anchor Book. Using your interpretation of the scene, your group will perform the scene for the class.

Your Task

- Work with a group to interpret a scene from your Anchor Book.
- Adapt the text so it will work as an oral presentation.
- Practice and perform your presentation in front of the class.
- Include a portrayal of characters and an adaptation of the scene for the stage—your classroom.

Organize Your Presentation

1 **Select a scene from your Anchor Book.** As a group, choose a scene that has some action or conflict. Be sure the scene includes several characters and engaging dialogue.

2 **Think about your character.** Think about the traits that make your character unique. Use a character web to help you understand your character's actions, words, and thoughts. Fill in the circles with words that describe your character.

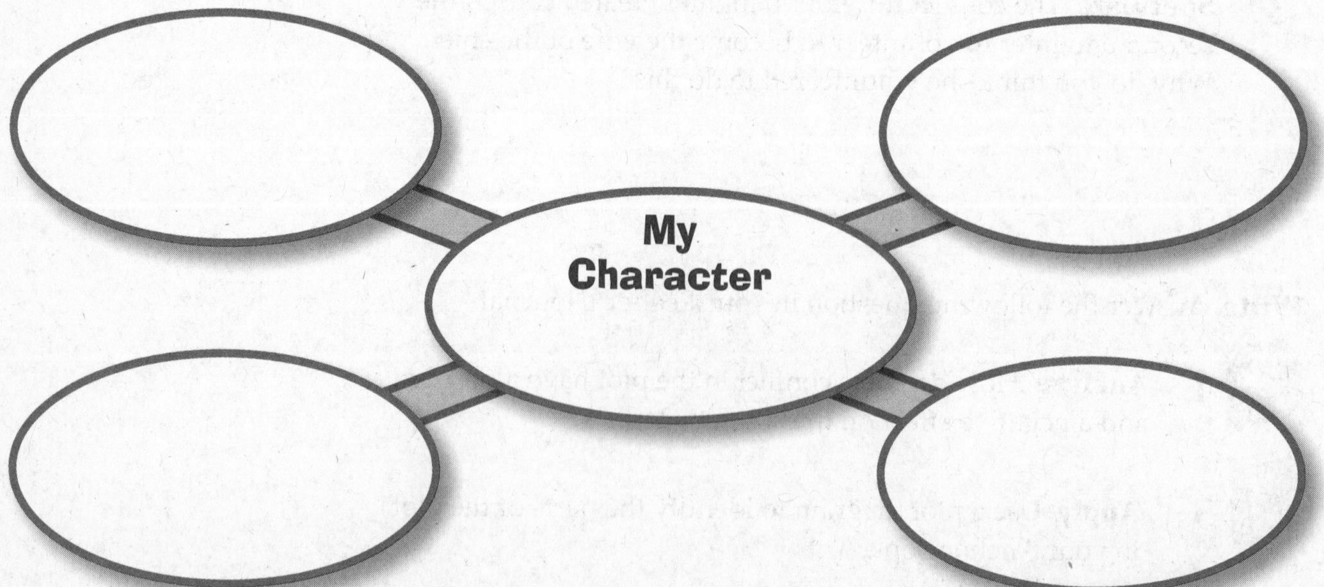

while reading your anchor book

3 **Reread the scene.** As a group, list actions, events, and important details from your Anchor Book. Then list your thoughts about, and reactions to, the scene. Use these notes to make revisions.

4 **Practice your scene.** As you practice your presentation, think about your character's personality and how he or she interacts with the other characters. Practice your speech, expression, and movements to capture the personality of your character.

5 **Present your scene to the class.** Use simple props that will help convey the characters, setting, mood, and action to your audience. Don't rush through your scene. Remember to speak clearly and to project your voice.

Directions Assess your performance. For each question, circle a rating.

SPEAK: Rubric for Oral Interpretation

CRITERIA	RATING SCALE
CONTENT How well did the group portray the characters and the scene?	NOT VERY … VERY 1 2 3 4 5
ORGANIZATION How well did the group prepare for the presentation?	1 2 3 4 5
DELIVERY How well did the group connect with the audience while performing?	1 2 3 4 5
DELIVERY How well did the group demonstrate clear speech and expression?	1 2 3 4 5
COOPERATION How well did the group work together?	1 2 3 4 5

LISTEN: Rubric for Audience Self-Assessment

CRITERIA	RATING SCALE
ACTIVE LISTENING How well did you focus your attention on the speakers? Did you ask questions at the end?	NOT VERY … VERY 1 2 3 4 5
ACTIVE LISTENING How well did you respond to what you heard?	1 2 3 4 5

2-13 Language Coach
Grammar and Spelling

Action and Linking Verbs

Go Online
Learn More
Visit: PHSchool.com
Web Code: exp-6203

A **verb** is a word that shows an action or links the subject of the sentence to a description. An **action verb**, such as *play* or *jump*, names an action of a person or thing.

Example **Toni played the bass guitar.** (The action is *playing*.)

A **linking verb**, such as *is* or *feels*, links a noun or pronoun to a word that identifies, renames, or describes the noun or pronoun. Other common linking verbs are *seem, look,* and *become*.

Example **Mr. Byrne is the mayor of Norwood.** (*Mayor* renames *Mr. Byrne*.)

To determine whether a verb is a **linking verb** or an **action verb**, replace it in the sentence with the correct form of *be*. If the sentence still makes sense, it is a linking verb. If it doesn't make sense, it is an action verb.

Linking verb **The soup tastes delicious.**
Replaced with form of *be* **The soup is delicious.** (makes sense)

Action verb **The pitcher threw the ball.**
Replaced with form of *be* **The pitcher was the ball.** (does not make sense)

Action verbs make sentences more direct and to the point. This makes action verbs useful in listing a subject's accomplishments or actions. Authors use linking verbs when the subject that is receiving the action is more important than the character doing that action.

Directions Fill in the blanks in the following passage with linking or action verbs to complete the story.

1. Everyone in the living room __________________ something sweet in the air. Mother __________________ with bread from the oven. The brown, crisp loaf __________________ delicious. Suddenly, Kim __________________ very hungry. She eagerly __________________ the bread.

2. On a separate sheet of paper, use action and linking verbs to write a three- or four-sentence story about participating in a sports event.

Author's Craft

Authors use both action and linking verbs to describe characters. Action verbs tell what the characters *do*, and linking verbs link to descriptions of what the characters *are like*. Scan "The Snake Chief" on page 142. Find two examples of action verbs and two examples of linking verbs that help describe a character. Which verb type do you think tells more about the character?

Principal Parts of Verbs

Every verb has four main forms, or **principal parts.** These parts are used to form verb tenses, which indicate when an action takes place. The example below shows the four principal parts of the **regular verb** *walk*.

Principal Part	Example
Present	walk, walks
Present Participle	(am, is, are) walking
Past	walked
Past Participle	(have, had) walked

Directions Use the provided principal part to create original sentences.

Example Past participle: *think* **I have thought about writing a story.**

1. Past: *live*

____

2. Past participle: *spend*

____

3. Present participle: *try*

____

4. Present: *sing*

____

Directions Rewrite the passage. Replace the underlined word with its past participle.

Oliver climbs the ladder up to the loft. He wants to see if the bat is hanging in the corner. He looks up but sees nothing. Then, all of a sudden, he hears a flapping of wings. Oliver glances up at the roof, and there it is all along—a little brown bat!

____

____

____

____

Learn More
Visit: PHSchool.com
Web Code: exp-6205

Irregular and Troublesome Verbs

Irregular verbs are verbs in which the past tense and the past participle are not formed by adding *–ed* or *–d* to the present form. The verbs *be* and *gone* are examples of irregular verbs.

Principal Part	Forms of *be*	Forms of *go*
Present	am, are, is	go, goes
Present Participle	(am, is, are) being	(am, is, are) going
Past	was	went
Past Participle	(have, had) been	(have, had) gone

Troublesome verbs are verb pairs that are easily confused with each other. *Lay* and *lie* are examples of these verbs.

Lay means to "put or place something." It directs an action to another person or thing.

Examples **I must lay the violin gently on the counter.**
Monroe laid his book on the table.

Lie means "to rest in a reclining position" or "to be situated." It does not direct an action to another person or thing.

Examples **Manuel likes lying in the snow.**
I have lain in the shade today.

Directions On a separate sheet of paper, rewrite the following paragraph. Change each underlined verb from present (or present participle) to past (or past participle).

My family is going on a weekend camping trip. I am so excited about sitting around the campfire and telling stories all night. We go to the same campgrounds every year. My sister is upset because there are no showers there and she is very concerned about her appearance. My dad says that everyone there has the same facilities and she shouldn't worry about it.

Author's Craft

Present verbs and present participle verbs may seem almost identical. To find out how different they are, reread "Space Trash and Treasure" on page 135. Find two present participles with helping verbs, and change them to present tense verbs. Then, choose two present tense verbs and change them to present participles. How does the meaning of the sentences change?

Spelling with Suffixes

Adding a suffix to the end of a word can change its spelling along with the way the word is used. For instance, the noun *color* becomes the adjective *colorless* when the suffix *–less* is added. Suffixes can also help you infer the meaning of an unfamiliar word. Here are six rules for spelling words when adding suffixes.

- Change *y* to *i* when adding a suffix to a word ending in *y* and preceded by a consonant. (*lazy* + *ness* = *laziness*)
- Do not change a final *y* to *i* before the suffix *–ing*. (*hurry* + *ing* = *hurrying*)
- Double the last letter when the word is one syllable and ends in a consonant. (*fog* + *y* = *foggy*)
- Never double the last letter if the last syllable is unstressed. (*order* + *ed* = *ordered*)
- Never double the last letter when a word ends in more than one consonant. (*remark* + *able* = *remarkable*)

Directions Use the rules above to add the suffixes *–y*, *–ing*, *-ed*, or *–able* to each word. Make as many words as you can.

1 cancel

____

2 try

____

3 stop

____

Directions Rewrite each word using the suffix in parentheses. Write a sentence using the new word.

4 helpful (*-less*)

____

5 happily (*–ness*)

____

6 realism (*–ity*)

____

7 caring (*–ful*)

____

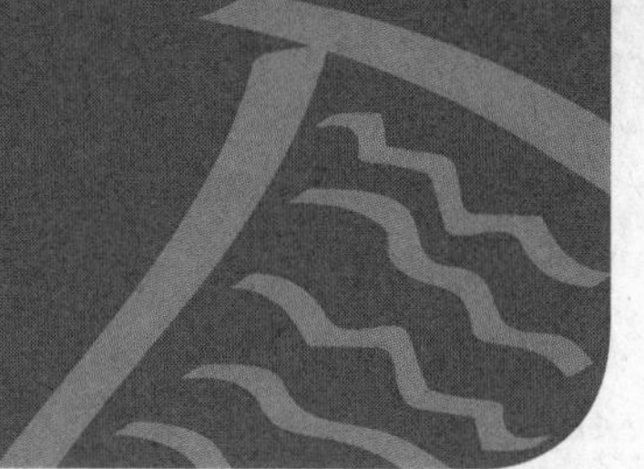

2-14 Writer's Workshop
Narration: Short Story

Short stories are shorter works of fiction than novels. They often contain a clear theme, or message, and they often feature a conflict faced by one or more characters. In this workshop, you will write a short story about a person who faces a difficult challenge.

Purpose To write a short story about a person who faces a difficult challenge

Audience You, your teacher, and your classmates

To be effective, your short story should include the following elements.

- one or more well-rounded characters
- an interesting conflict or problem
- a plot that moves toward a resolution of the conflict
- concrete and sensory details that establish the setting
- dialogue between characters
- error-free grammar, including proper use of verb tenses

Prewriting—Plan It Out

To decide what your story should be about, use these steps.

Choose your topic. Think about some challenges that you or someone you know has faced. For example, have you ever gone for a bike ride and gotten a flat tire? What happened? What did you do? Take five minutes to create a list of these challenges. Then choose one of these ideas for your story.

Create a main character. Develop your main character by noting characteristics in the chart below. Use the sample chart at right for guidance.

Name	Physical Traits	Personality	Likes	Dislikes
Cristina	short, blonde, braces	funny, friendly, caring	telling jokes, ice cream	noise, reality television

Name	Physical Traits	Personality	Likes	Dislikes

Identify a conflict. Ask yourself questions about your story to identify its conflict—the struggle between two opposing forces.

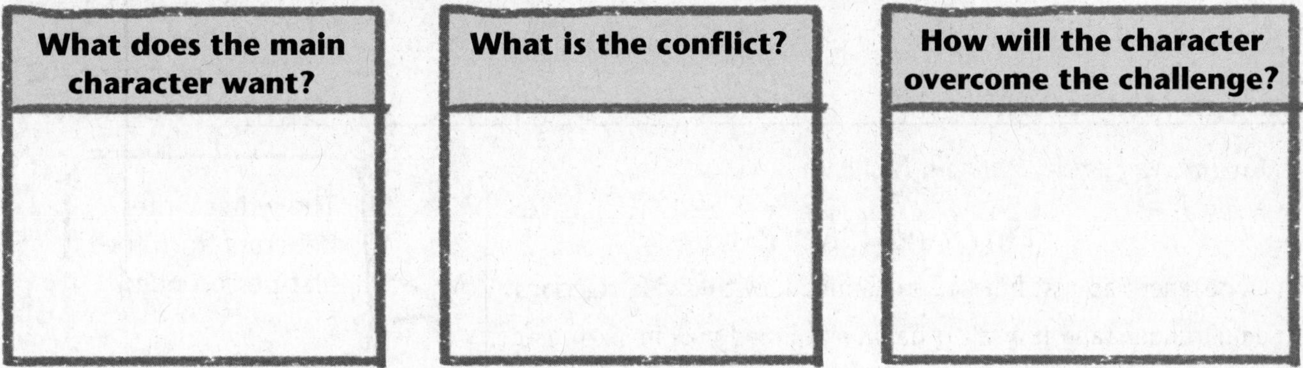

What does the main character want?
What is the conflict?
How will the character overcome the challenge?

Drafting—Get It on Paper

Develop a plot. Think of your audience and purpose for writing when drafting your story. In the beginning, or *exposition,* introduce your characters, setting, and the challenge your main character will face. Develop the conflict during the *rising action* to create suspense until you reach the *climax,* the point of highest tension. During the *falling action,* describe what happens after the climax. Conclude your story with a *resolution.* On a separate piece of paper, create a plot diagram like the one on p. 140 to help you construct your plot.

Use sensory details. Use specific language to describe how things look, sound, feel, taste, and smell. Write a sentence, then revise it to make it more vivid in the space below.

Dull	The sky looked stormy.
Vivid	The sky boiled with black clouds and loud thunder.
Dull	
Vivid	

Use a consistent point of view. Tell your story from a specific point of view. A participant in the story would tell it from a first-person point of view. An observer of the story would tell it from a third-person point of view.

Revising—Make It Better

Show, don't tell. Use dialogue to develop your characters and to show what they are feeling.

Peer Review Ask for a partner's response to your short story. Revise to achieve the reaction you had intended.

Go Online
Student Model
Visit: PHSchool.com
Web Code: exr-6202

Directions Read this student's short story as a model for your own.

Student Model: Writing

Karina McKorkle, Raleigh, NC

Math Mackerel

My teacher had just finished explaining how to divide fractions. I didn't understand it at all. I hated math, and now in sixth grade, math was much harder.

> The writer writes her story from the first-person point of view.

"I wish someone could help me understand math," I whispered. Suddenly, a fish appeared out of thin air. I stared at him.

> The conflict and characters are introduced early in the story.

"W-who are you?" I stammered.

"I am Math Mackerel. I thought I heard someone asking for help with math," the fish stated proudly.

"Oh, that was me," I said.

"I'll see you at recess," Math Mackerel said as he disappeared with a swish of his tail and a flick of his fins...

> The writer creates suspense during the rising action.

Outside, I sat in a secluded spot behind a bush and waited. Suddenly, Math Mackerel appeared.

"Greetings," said Math Mackerel happily. "I am here to help you with math."

"Are you going to give me all the knowledge I need?" I asked curiously.

> The writer adds dialogue between the characters.

"I could do that, but that would be cheating," scoffed Math Mackerel. He whipped out a deck of cards. I raised my eyebrows at him. I couldn't see how a deck of cards could help me with math.

"Do you know how to play Go Fish?" asked Math Mackerel.

"Yes, but how is..." I tried to ask.

"Good, I'll go first." He began to deal the cards with his fins.

Twenty minutes later, we were still playing a hearty game of Go Fish.

"Got any nines?" I asked, peering over my cards.

"Yes, what is one and seven ninths divided by two thirds?" he asked.

"Two and two thirds," I answered.

"Good job!" Math Mackerel said as he slammed his nines on the ground. I heard my teacher's whistle. It was time to go inside. . . .

All week, I dreaded Friday. I gulped as the teacher passed out papers. I worked through the problems and found them easy as I thought about Go Fish. My teacher returned the tests on Monday. I picked mine up and saw an A!

The writer includes an exciting climax and ends with a resolution.

Editing—Be Your Own Language Coach

Before you hand in your short story, review it for language convention errors. Pay attention to your use of verb tenses and keep a consistent point of view.

Publishing—Share It!

When you publish a work, you produce it for a specific audience. Consider one of the following ideas to share your writing.

Give a reading. Get together with a group of classmates, family members, or adults, and present a literary reading.

Act it out. Perform your story in front of your class.

Reflecting On Your Writing

Respond to the following questions on the back of your final draft. What did you learn about the form of the short story by writing one? What do you do well? What do you need to work on? Set a goal you can meet in your next workshop.

Rubric for Self-Assessment Assess your story. For each question, circle a rating.

CRITERIA	RATING SCALE
IDEAS How interesting are your plot, characters, and setting?	NOT VERY — VERY 1 2 3 4 5
ORGANIZATION How clearly is your story organized, especially by developing conflict and building to a climax?	1 2 3 4 5
VOICE How well do you set a tone in telling the story?	1 2 3 4 5
WORD CHOICE How vivid is the language you use?	1 2 3 4 5
SENTENCE FLUENCY How varied is your sentence structure?	1 2 3 4 5
CONVENTIONS How correct is your grammar, especially your use of verb tenses?	1 2 3 4 5

2-15 Discussing Your Anchor Book
Literature Circles

The **theme** of a story is its central message. Some themes are about personal growth, courage, or overcoming a challenge. In this Literature Circle, you and your group members will compare and discuss the theme of your Anchor Book.

1 **Analyze** To find the theme of your Anchor Book, ask yourself the following questions and write your answers in the chart. Use the well-known example of *Pinocchio* to help you.

Questions	Pinocchio	My Anchor Book
What ideas seem to come up again and again in the text?	Many characters tempt Pinocchio to make bad choices.	
How do the main characters respond to the conflict?	Pinocchio learns from his mistakes and returns to save Geppetto.	
How do the characters change over the course of the story?	Pinocchio changes from a puppet who acts carelessly to a boy who makes smart choices.	
What is one lesson you can learn from the story?	Growing up means learning to make smart choices and being considerate of others.	

The answers to the first three questions help you to answer the last question about the message, or theme. However, there can be more than one theme. Brainstorm a few possible ideas. Choose the theme you think is most important.

2 **Support** A theme should be supported by events in the text. For example, Pinocchio's adventures away from home and his return to search for Geppetto all relate to the theme that growing up means learning to be responsible and considerate. Think of a few events from your Anchor Book that relate to its theme. Write them in the following graphic organizer.

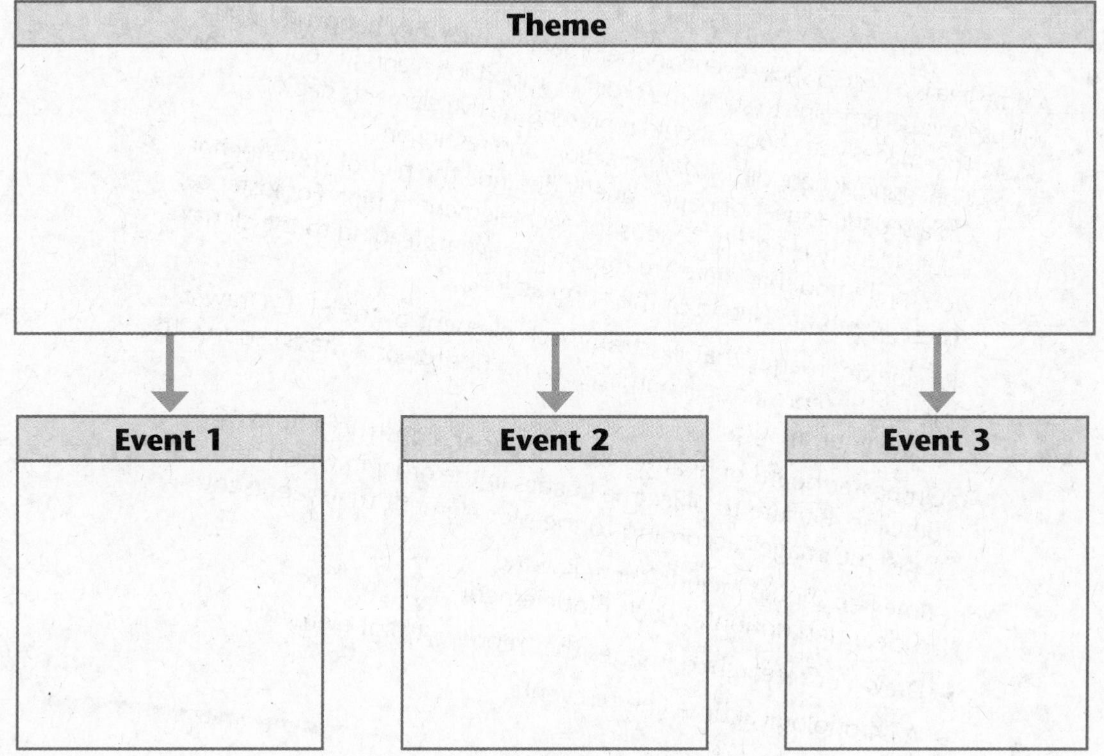

3 **Compare** List each group member's theme on a sheet of paper. Explain how the events and ideas presented in the story relate to your theme. Listen respectfully as your group members share their ideas.

4 **Explore** Choose one theme from your anchor book and explore it further with your group members. What other events and ideas relate to this theme? Think of the important events in the beginning, middle, and end. Decide how each event supports the theme.

5 **Discuss** Talk about the characters in the book. How does each respond to the conflict? How do they change over the course of the story? Think about how your answers relate to the themes your group has discussed.

6 **Connect** Relate the themes to real life. How can you apply the themes to your life? What real-life situations have you experienced that are like the events in the book? If you do not think the themes apply, explain why.

2-16 Connecting to Your Anchor Book

Anchor Book Projects

Now that you have finished reading your Anchor Book, get creative! Complete one of the following projects.

A

Picture This!

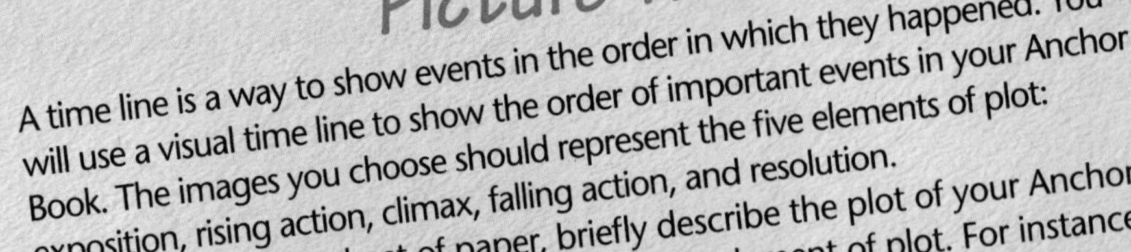

A time line is a way to show events in the order in which they happened. You will use a visual time line to show the order of important events in your Anchor Book. The images you choose should represent the five elements of plot: exposition, rising action, climax, falling action, and resolution.

1. On a separate sheet of paper, briefly describe the plot of your Anchor Book. Identify events or actions for each element of plot. For instance, you might find that there are three main events leading to the climax. These events are all part of the rising action.
2. Decide on images that illustrate each element of the plot. Draw a picture to represent each image, using photos or a media source to create your images.
3. On poster board or a large sheet of paper, construct your visual timeline. Be sure to place the images in the order in which they occur. Label the images according to the plot element they represent.

Your time line should include the following.

- A clear description of each plot element
- Drawn or researched images that represent plot elements
- A chronological time line of events

B

Master the Media

Many books, such as *The Wizard of Oz* and *The Lord of the Rings,* are retold in the movies using digital technology. Think about a character in your Anchor Book and how the author used characterization to bring the character to life. Then create a multimedia representation of that character.

1. Choose a character from your Anchor Book. Think of your character's traits, personality, and appearance. Select a medium you can use that will capture the feeling of your character. For example, for a funny character, you might record some silly music and present it with a collage of images that show people laughing.
2. Work with a partner to create a presentation of your character. You can record a CD, create a collage, use computer animation, make a slide show, or any other medium for your presentation.
3. Deliver your presentation to the class.

Your multimedia presentation should include the following.

- A detailed analysis of your character
- Creative representation of your character through multimedia

See Through a Character's Eyes C

One of the great things about reading a good story is that you get to see through the eyes of different characters. Choose an event in your Anchor Book. Think about how one character sees or reacts to the event. Compare the character's reaction to the way you would react to the same event.

1. Select a character and an event in which the character has a major part. Consider how that character feels, thinks, and acts. Then think about how you would feel, think, or act.
2. Become the character and rewrite the event from a first-person point of view. Be creative—you can add details, actions, and descriptions.

Your visual should include the following.

- A description of a specific event or situation in your Anchor Book
- Specific details of how the character handles the situation
- A thoughtful, clear description of how you would handle the situation if you were the character

Free-Choice Book Reflection

You have completed your free-choice Book. Before you take your test, read the following instructions to write a brief reflection of your book.

My free-choice Book is ____________________

The author is ____________________

1 Would you recommend this book to a friend? Yes _____ No _____

Briefly explain why.

____

____

Write Answer the following question in your Reader's Journal.

2 **Compare and Contrast** *Is conflict always bad?* Compare and contrast how your Anchor Book and free-choice book help to answer this question. Use specific details from both books to support your answer.

Standardized Test Practice

Answer the questions below to check your understanding of this unit's skills.

Reading Skill: Making Inferences

Read the following passage. Then answer the questions.

> Tom quickly twisted the knobs on the beat-up, old radio. All he heard was static. There were only a few minutes left in the program, and he just had to hear what happened at the end. He shifted the antenna, but it did nothing. Why had he let his brother Mike leave him with this heap of junk? Now Mike was away at college, probably listening to Tom's digital radio. Tom tried to think fast.

1 What can you **infer** about Tom from this passage?

A. He is a fan of a radio program.

B. He likes old radios.

C. He knows how radios work.

D. He has never visited Mike at college.

2 What details in the paragraph support your answer to Question 1?

F. "He shifted the antenna, but it did nothing."

G. "Why had he let his brother Mike leave him with this heap of junk?"

H. ". . . and he just had to hear what happened at the end."

J. ". . . twisted the knobs on the beat up radio. . . . All he heard was static."

3 What can you **infer** about what Tom is thinking at the end of the passage?

A. how to contact Mike

B. where to buy a radio

C. what else he could be doing

D. how to hear the end of the program

4 Why does Tom shift the radio's antenna?

F. to make the radio loud

G. to help him find a station

H. to get them out of the way

J. to try to clear the static

Reading Skills: Drawing Conclusions

Read this selection. Then answer the questions that follow.

> The crowd held its breath in anticipation. It was the end of a long double-header and the Rockets' pitcher had not allowed the Giants to score all game. Only one out remained in the final game of the series. It seemed that every time a ball had been

smacked, the winds would come to knock it down into an outfielder's glove. The Giants' last hope was a rookie who was just happy to be playing in the game.

5 What **conclusion** can you draw from the information provided in the selection?

A. The game will be called off because of rain.

B. The Rockets expect to win the game.

C. The crowd was not interested in the game.

D. The batter will hit a home run.

6 Which detail acts as supporting evidence to this conclusion?

F. The Rockets' pitcher had not allowed the Giants to score all game.

G. The crowd held its breath.

H. The rookie was left-handed.

J. It was the final game of the series.

Literary Analysis: Elements of the Novel

Read this selection. Then answer the questions that follow.

All day long, the grasshopper hopped around the field and played games. He laughed as he watched the ant working away, gathering food and building a home for the winter. "Don't work so hard! Come play with me!" the grasshopper said. The ant grunted but said nothing, and went back to work.

Soon winter came, and the grasshopper grew cold and hungry. He came knocking at the door of the ant. "Can I come in with you?" he asked. "I'm sorry," the ant replied. "I have just enough food for myself. You shouldn't have spent all summer playing games." The grasshopper wandered off, bracing himself against the winter wind.

7 Which event is part of the **exposition** of the story?

A. The ant grunted.

B. The grasshopper played in the field.

C. The winter came.

D. The grasshopper asked for food.

8 What is the grasshopper's **motivation** for going to the ant's house?

F. to come in from the cold

G. to hop around the field

H. to brace against the heat

J. to watch the ant work

9 Which **character traits** does the ant show?

A. hard-working and organized

B. silly and playful

C. sad and moody

D. helpful and sincere

10 Which of the following best describes the **climax** of a story?

F. the ending

G. the point when the conflict is introduced

H. the point of the highest tension

J. the point when the characters are described

11 Which element of a **plot** is a struggle between two forces?

A. introduction

B. resolution

C. rising action

D. conflict

12 The disagreement between the grasshopper and the ant is an example of which element of the **plot?**

F. exposition

G. internal conflict

H. resolution

J. external conflict

Language Skills: Vocabulary

13 Which **suffix** means "able to be"?

A. *-ment*

B. *-ly*

C. *-ible*

D. *-ous*

14 Which revision changes an adjective into an adverb?

F. changing *sing* to *singing*

G. changing *quick* to *quickly*

H. changing *react* to *reaction*

J. changing *noise* to *noisy*

15 Which meaning defines the word *visible?*

A. able to be divided

B. able to be seen

C. to do in a happy way

D. to be able to deduce

16 One way to change the word *comfort* into an adjective is to ________________.

F. add *-ing*

G. add *-ly*

H. add *-ily*

J. add *-able*

Language Skills: Spelling

17 Which is the correct spelling of *happy* + the **suffix** *-ly*?

A. happilly

B. hapily

C. happily

D. happyly

18 How do you add a **suffix** to a word that has one syllable and ends in a consonant?

F. change the consonant to an *i*

G. double the final consonant

H. never double the final consonant

J. leave the consonant as it is

Language Skills: Grammar

19 Which is the **past tense** of the verb *to dream*?

A. dreamed

B. dreaming

C. will dream

D. will have dreamed

20 Which is the **past perfect tense** of the verb *to eat*?

F. eating

G. had eaten

H. ate

J. will be eating

21 Which of the following is an example of **future perfect**?

A. We will have eaten by the time you get to the party.

B. No one will know if you don't bring any chips.

C. We had eaten before we got there.

D. No one knew that you hadn't brought any chips.

22 Which is the **action verb** in this sentence?

Chris rode his bike to school.

F. Chris

G. bike

H. rode

J. school

23 Complete the sentence with the **past tense** of the verb *to stand*.

Rachael _______________ at the front of the line.

A. will stand

B. is standing

C. stood

D. has been standing

24 The **present perfect tense** of the verb *smile* is

F. will be smiling

G. was smiling

H. has smiled

J. smiles

25 How is the **present perfect** constructed?

A. *have* or *has* + present participle

B. *have* or *has* + past participle

C. *will have* + past participle

D. past participle

26 Complete the following sentence with a **linking verb**.

Marcie __________ taller than me.

F. looks

G. grows

H. has

J. jumps

What is important to *know*?

Unit 3 Genre focus: Types of Nonfiction

Unit Book Choices
With this unit you will read one book as an Anchor Book. There are many good books that would work well with this unit. The following pages offer six suggestions.

Free-Choice Reading
Later in this unit you will be given an opportunity to choose another book to read. This is called your Free-Choice Book.

You might read...

A *Amistad: The Story of a Slave Ship*

B *You Want Women to Vote, Lizzie Stanton?*

C Thura's Diary

D The Tarantula in My Purse

E *Under the Royal Palms*

F A STRONG RIGHT ARM

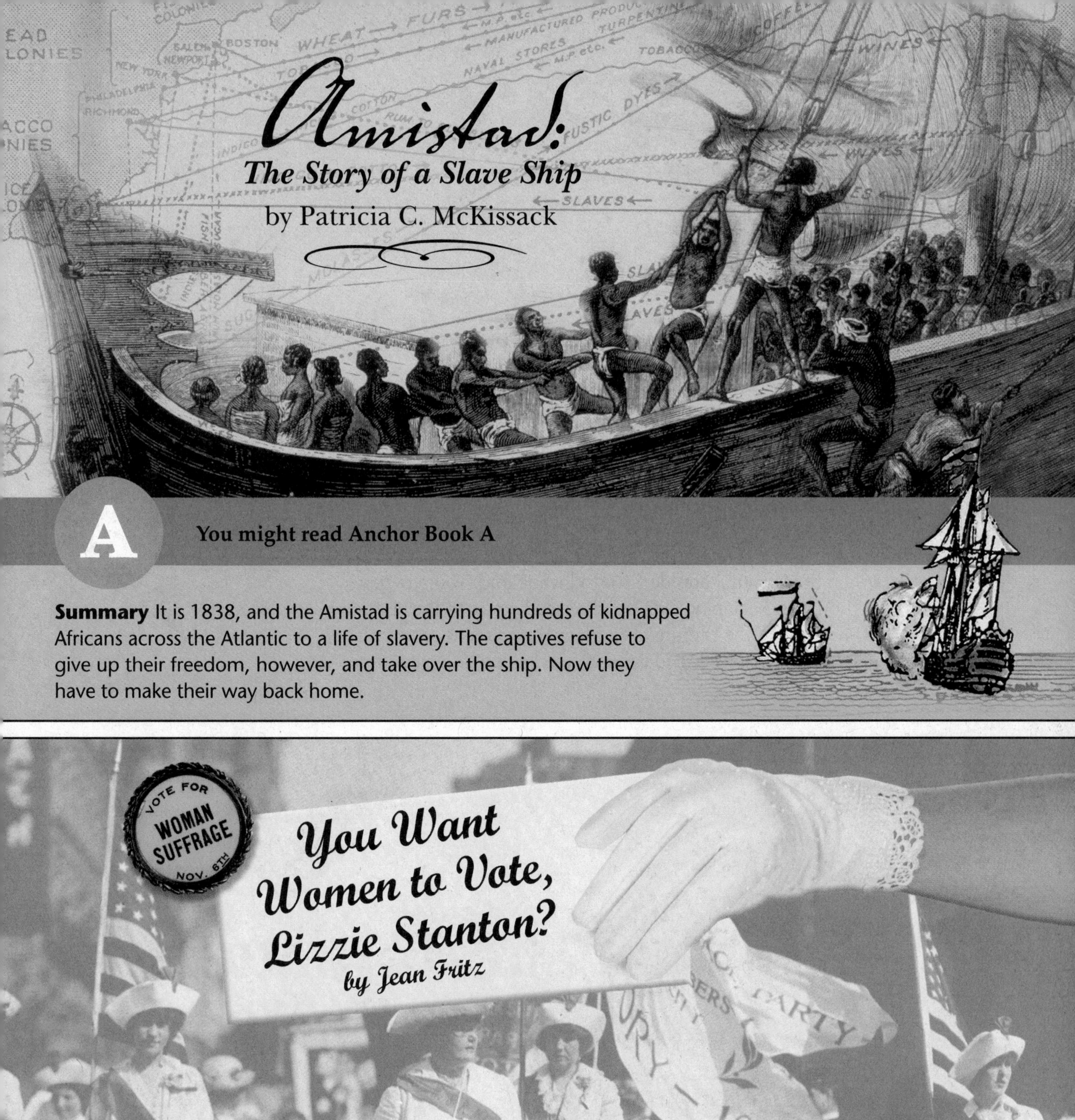

Amistad: The Story of a Slave Ship

by Patricia C. McKissack

A You might read Anchor Book A

Summary It is 1838, and the Amistad is carrying hundreds of kidnapped Africans across the Atlantic to a life of slavery. The captives refuse to give up their freedom, however, and take over the ship. Now they have to make their way back home.

You Want Women to Vote, Lizzie Stanton?

by Jean Fritz

B You might read Anchor Book B

Summary It is nineteenth-century New York, and Lizzie Stanton believes girls are just as good as boys—contrary to public opinion. She sets out to prove the fact: first to her father, and then to the world.

Thura's Diary: My Life in Wartime Iraq

by Thura Al-Windawi

C

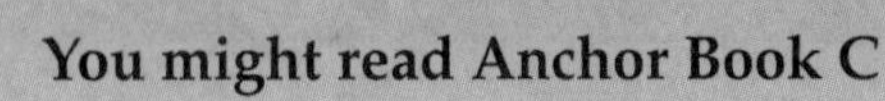

You might read Anchor Book C

Summary When the United States decided to invade Iraq, Thura began recording her thoughts. Beginning with the days leading up to the attack on Baghdad and ending with the capture of Saddam Hussein nine months later, Thura's diary describes what it's like to live with war in one's own country.

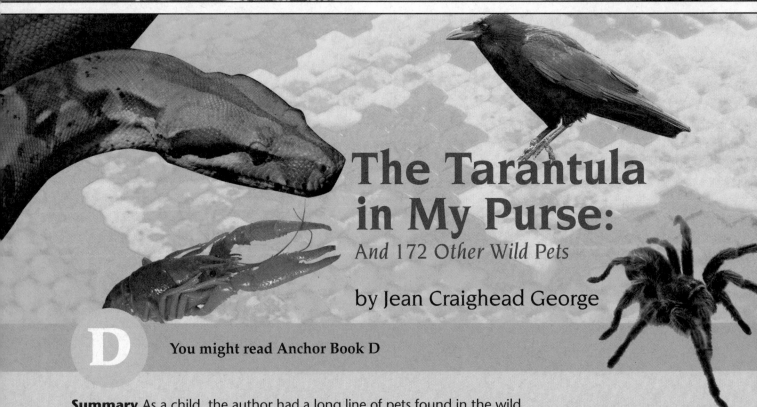

The Tarantula in My Purse:

And 172 Other Wild Pets

by Jean Craighead George

D

You might read Anchor Book D

Summary As a child, the author had a long line of pets found in the wild, beginning with a baby vulture. Now her kids have inherited the family tradition. One owl, six ducklings, a weasel, a skunk, and, yes, a tarantula are just a few of the pets that make up the family's wild menagerie.

E
You might read Anchor Book E
Under the Royal Palms: A Childhood in Cuba
by Alma Flor Ada
A STRONG RIGHT ARM: THE STORY OF MAMIE "PEANUT" JOHNSON
by Michelle Y. Green
F
You might read Anchor Book F

Summary In these ten stories from the author's girlhood in Cuba, Camagüey is a city of both funny and painful memories: of feeding baby bats, mourning the death of a beloved uncle, and getting lost—and found—in a *marabú* field.

Summary Ever since she can remember, Mamie "Peanut" Johnson had a baseball in her hand—she even slept with one under her pillow. One of only three women to play professional baseball, her response to the discrimination from all sides was clear: it doesn't matter if you're black or white, a boy or a girl—a ball's still a ball.

3-1 Understanding the Big Question
What is important to know?

From the moment you get up in the morning until you go to sleep at night, you are bombarded with information. "The temperature is 70 degrees." "Buy Toasty Crunchies!" "There are 212 bones in the human body." "The Jets play tonight." Some of this information might seem overwhelming—or even useless. In this unit, you will learn to recognize the information you need to know and understand why you need to know it.

Most people agree that certain information is important for everyone to know, such as how to stay healthy and safe. There are other kinds of information, though, that are more important for some people to know than for others, depending on their jobs, interests, or hobbies. For example, to do his or her job well, a heart doctor must know how all the veins and arteries inside the body function. However, the same information is not important to a carpenter.

Directions Work with your group to complete the following activity.

With your group, choose three of the following careers to compare. Write your choices in the chart on the following page.

ASTRONAUT

FARMER

TEACHER

BASEBALL PLAYER

NURSE

CHEF

BALLET DANCER

ARCHITECT

Discuss with your group what type of information the people in each career you chose need to know. List the information in the chart on the next page. Then list information that's important for people in all three careers to know.

Career 1	Career 2	Career 3
What this worker needs to know	**What this worker needs to know**	**What this worker needs to know**

What all three workers need to know

1 What did you learn about the three different careers you chose by completing the chart?

2 What is some information that people in *all* careers need to know?

THE BIG ?

As you read your Anchor Book and the related readings, think about how you can decide what information is important for you to know.

before reading your anchor book

Getting Ready for Your Anchor Book

You will start reading your Anchor Book soon. The next few pages in this book give you some background information plus a reading skill.

Types of Nonfiction

Nonfiction writing provides information about real people, places, events, and ideas. By reading nonfiction, you learn about the world around you because the information is based on facts, actual experiences, and real-life situations.

Nonfiction Writing With a Purpose

Nonfiction writing reflects an **author's purpose,** or reason for writing. That purpose can be to entertain, inform, persuade, or reflect. An author chooses a formal or an informal style of writing depending on his or her purpose. Look at the different types of nonfiction writing and purposes of each.

Type	Examples	Definition	Purpose
Narrative	Biography Autobiography	Tells the story of a person's life	To entertain or inform
Expository	Essay Newspaper article How-to writing	Gives facts and ideas, or explains a process	To inform
Persuasive	Editorial Advertisement Sales brochure	Tries to persuade the reader to take a point of view or change his or her opinions about a topic	To persuade
Reflective	Diary Letter	Offers insights into why an event or idea is important to an author	To reflect

1 **Apply** What would you write about if you were writing a nonfiction piece to persuade your audience?

2 **Infer** Neela is writing about what influenced her to become an artist. What is her purpose for writing?

Organization

A nonfiction author organizes information in a way that will reflect his or her purpose for writing and will make it easy to understand. The chart shows different ways an author can organize information.

Organization Pattern	Reason for Organization	Example
Chronological	Gives details in time order, from first to last	A biography of a president's life
Cause-and-effect	Shows the relationship among causes and effects	An article about pesticides and their effects on the environment
Compare-and-contrast	Presents two or more subjects and tells how they are alike and different	A magazine article describing how two games are similar and different
Problem-and-solution	Focuses on a problem and discusses a possible solution	A newspaper editorial that discusses the hazards at an old playground and proposes building a new one

3 Within the topic of "Pets," write a narrow topic for each organization pattern. The first one has been done for you.

Chronological	The development of a dog from a puppy to an adult dog.
Cause-and-effect	
Compare-and-contrast	
Problem-and-solution	

4 If an author did not use a chronological pattern while writing a biography, how might it affect his or her purpose of informing a reader about the subject's life?

3-2 Reading Skills
Main Idea

In learning new reading skills you will use special academic vocabulary. Knowing the right words will help you demonstrate your understanding.

Academic Vocabulary

Word	Meaning	Example Sentence
restate *v.* *Related words:* restated, restating	to state again or in another way	To help her readers understand the experiment, the scientist *restated* it in a simpler way.
identify *v.* *Related words:* identification, identified	to recognize as being; to point out the person or thing described	The astronomer *identified* an entirely new solar system.
determine *v.* *Related words:* determined, determining	to decide or conclude	The purpose of the student council meeting is to *determine* how much money is available for the dance.

The **main idea** is the most important idea in a text. It is supported by **details** found throughout the selection. Often, the main idea is stated in one of the first paragraphs. Sometimes the author will **restate** the main idea in the final paragraph.

If it is stated directly in the text, then the main idea is not hard to **identify.** Otherwise, the reader has to rely on key details in the text to **determine** the main idea. Look at the following pattern many authors use when writing nonfiction texts.

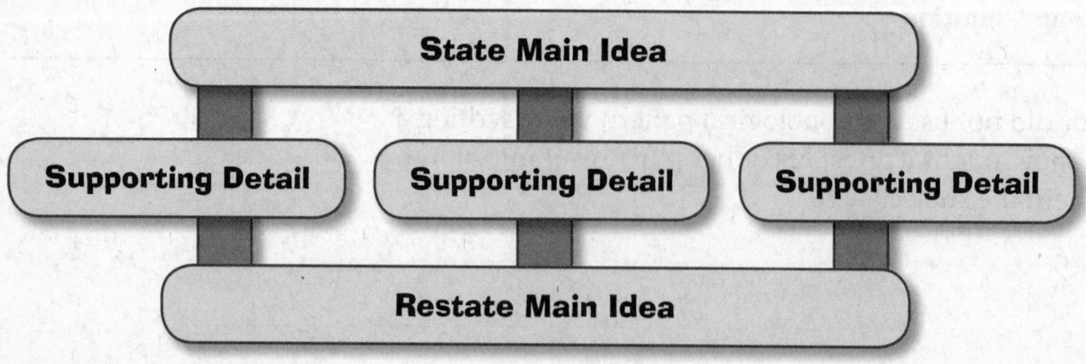

Directions Read this poem and circle the main idea. As you read, underline supporting details.

One *by James Berry*

Only one of me
and nobody can get a second one
from a photocopy machine.
Nobody has the fingerprints I have.
Nobody can cry my tears, or laugh my laugh
or have my expectancy when I wait.
But anybody can mimic my dance with my dog.
Anybody can howl how I sing out of tune.
And mirrors can show me multiplied
many times, say, dressed up in red
or dressed up in grey.
Nobody can get into my clothes for me
or feel my fall for me, or do my running.
Nobody hears my music for me, either.
I am just this one.
Nobody else makes the words
I shape with sound, when I talk.
But anybody can act how I stutter in a rage.
Anybody can copy echoes I make.
And mirrors can show me multiplied
many times, say, dressed up in green
or dressed up in blue.

1 **Restate** Restate the main idea of the poem in your own words. How were you able to determine the main idea?

___

___

2 **Defend** Explain three details in the poem that support the main idea.

___

___

___

In this article, Rosa Parks explains why she acted the way she did on a segregated bus more than fifty years ago. ***Guiding Question:*** **Why is it important to know Rosa Parks's thoughts about her role in the bus boycott?**

'I Was Not Alone'

The bus on which Rosa Parks rode and refused to give up her seat is now in the Henry Ford Museum in Dearborn, Michigan.

Before the civil rights movement in the South, schools, shops, diners, public bathrooms, and even water fountains were segregated, or separated, according to race. White people had access to better services and cleaner facilities, whereas African Americans were often ignored or had to wait for those same services. One African American, Rosa Parks, had had enough and decided to act.

An interview with Rosa Parks by Brian Lanker from *I Dream a World*

As far back as I can remember, being black in Montgomery we were well aware of the inequality of our way of life. I hated it all the time. I didn't feel that, in order to have some freedom, I should have to leave one part of the United States and go to another part of the same country just because one was South and one was North.

My mother believed in freedom and equality even though we didn't know it for reality during our life in Alabama.

In some stores, if a woman wanted to go in to try a hat, they wouldn't be permitted to try it on unless they knew they were going to buy it, or they put a bag on the inside of it. In the shoe stores they had this long row of seats, and all of those in the front could be vacant, but if one of us would go in to buy, they'd always take you to the last one, to the back of the store. There were no black salespersons.

At the Montgomery Fair [a department store] I did men's alterations. Beginning in December coming up to the Christmas holiday, the work was a bit heavy. When I left the store that evening, I was tired, but I was tired every day. I had planned to get an electric heating pad so I could put some heat to my shoulder and my back and neck. After I stepped up on the bus, I noticed this driver as the same one who had evicted me from another bus way back in 1943.

Just back of the whites there was a black man next to one vacant seat. So I sat down with him. A few white people boarded the bus and they found seats except this one man. That is when the bus driver looked at us and asked us to let him have those seats. After he saw we weren't moving immediately, he said, "Y'all make it light on yourselves and let me have those seats."

When he saw that I was still remaining in the seat, the driver said, "If you don't stand up, I'm going to call the police and have you arrested." I said, "You may do that."

Two policemen came and wanted to know what was the trouble. One said, "Why don't you stand up?" I said, "I don't think I should have to." At that point I asked the policemen, "Why do you push us around?" He said, "I don't know, but the law is the law and you're under arrest."

The decision was made by the three of us, my husband, my mother, and me, that I would go on and use my case as a test case, challenging segregation on the buses.

When I woke up the next morning I realized I had to go to work and it was pouring down rain, the first thing I thought about was the fact that I never would ride a segregated bus again. That was my decision for me and not necessarily for anybody else.

People just stayed off the buses because I was arrested, not because I asked them. If everybody else had been happy and doing well, my arrest wouldn't have made any difference at all.

The one thing I appreciated was the fact that when so many others, by the hundreds and by the thousands, joined in, there was a kind of lifting of a burden from me individually. I could feel that whatever my individual desires were to be free, I was not alone. There were many others who felt the same way.

The first thing that happened after the people stayed off was the black cab companies were willing to just charge bus fare instead of charging cab fare. Others who had any kind of car at all would give people rides. They had quite a transportation system set up. Mass meetings were keeping the morale up. They were singing and praying and raising money in the collection to buy gasoline or tires.

▼ Rosa Parks was arrested by the Montgomery police in 1955 for "refusing to obey orders of bus driver."

There was a lot of humor in it, too. Somebody told a story about a [white] husband who had fired the family cook because she refused to ride the bus to work. When his wife came home, she said, "If you don't go get her, you better be on your way." Some white people who were not wanting to be deprived of their domestic help would just go themselves and pick up the people who were working for them.

The officials really became furious when they saw that the rain and bad weather or distance or any other problem didn't matter.

Many whites, even white Southerners, told me that even though it may have seemed like the blacks were being freed, they felt more free and at ease themselves. They thought that my action didn't just free blacks but them also.

Some have suffered much more than I did. Some have even lost their lives. I just escaped some of the physical—maybe not all—but some of the physical pain. And the pain still remains. From back as far as I can remember.

When people made up their minds that they wanted to be free and took action, then there was a change. But they couldn't rest on just that change. It was to continue.

It just doesn't seem that an older person like I am should still have to be in the struggle, but if I have to be in it then I have no choice but to keep on.

I've been dreaming, looking, for as far back as I had any thought, of what it should be like to be a human being. My desires were to be free as soon as I had learned that there had been slavery of human beings and that I was a descendant from them. If there was a proclamation setting those who were slaves free, I thought they should be indeed free and not have any type of slavery put upon us.

▼ **Rosa Parks's arrest sparked a protest against segregation. For 381 days, people boycotted the Montgomery bus station.**

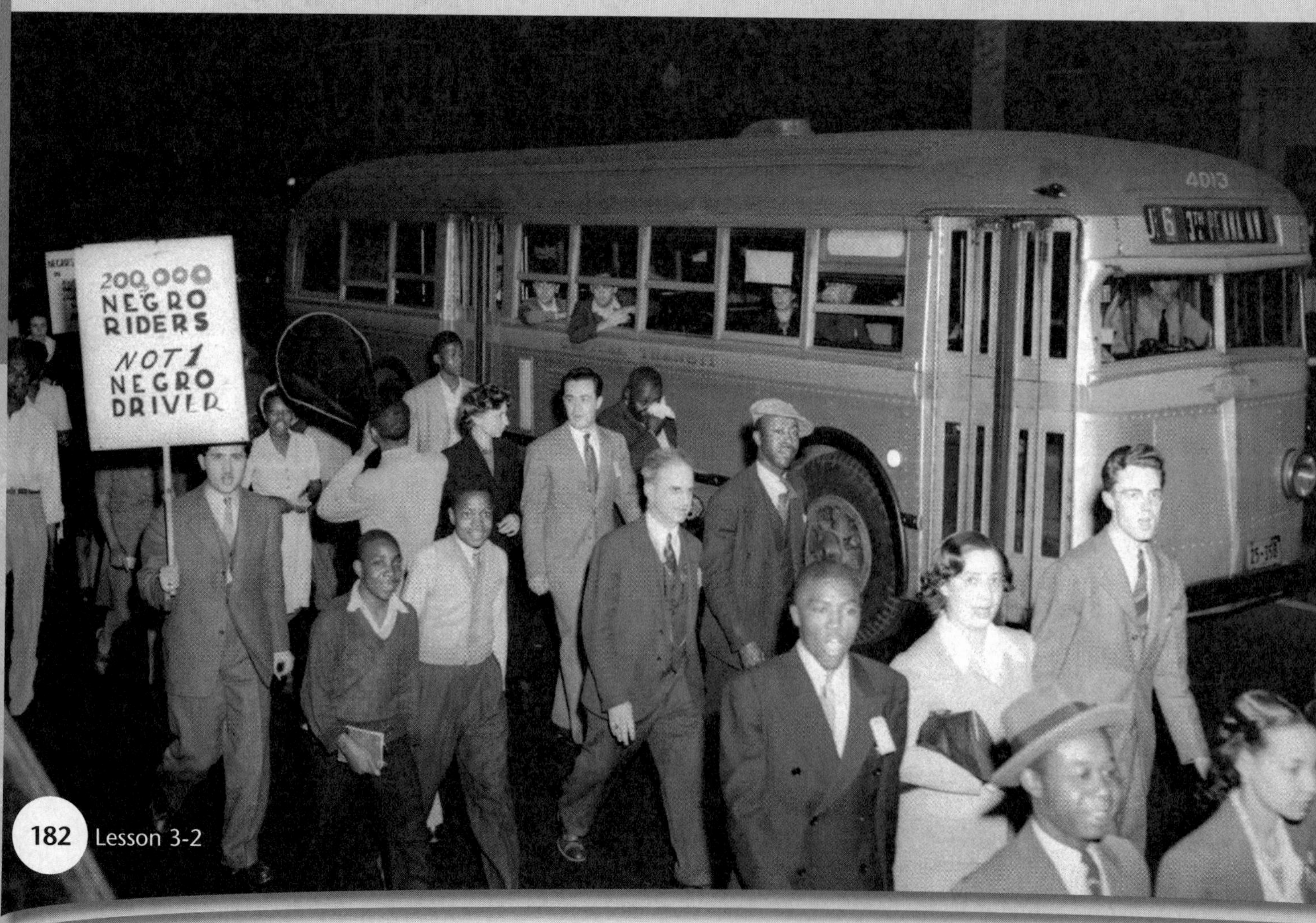

Thinking About the Selection

I Was Not Alone

1 **Apply** Complete the graphic organizer. Identify the main idea and three supporting details.

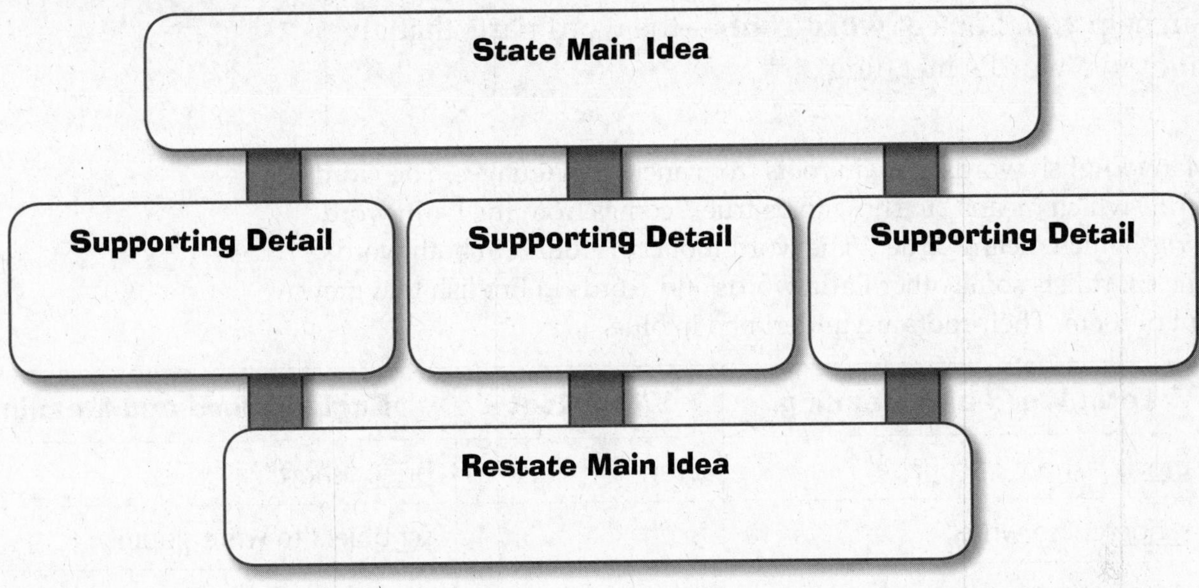

2 **Respond** How did you determine the main idea?

3 **Infer** Why do you think some white people felt freed by Parks's actions and the results that followed?

4 **Analyze** Suppose the interview took place immediately after Parks's arrest. Do you think she would have felt the same way? Explain your answer.

Write Answer the following question in your Reader's Journal.

5 **Infer** Why is it important to know Rosa Parks's thoughts about her role in the bus boycott?

before reading your anchor book

3-3 Vocabulary Building Strategies
Word Roots

Puzzling over the meaning of a word? Here is a strategy that can help you. Look at **word roots**—the word parts that give clues to a word's meaning.

Many English words contain roots from ancient languages. The word *verify,* which means "to show to be true," comes from the Latin word *verus,* which means "true." The word root *ver* is found in both words. The chart lists some other Latin words and words in English that grew out of them. Their roots are underlined in blue.

Latin Word and Meaning	Word Root	English Word and Meaning
brevis: "short"; "concise"	*brev*	brief: "short"
scribere: "to write"	*scrib*	scribble: "to write sloppily"
dictare: "to speak assertively"	*dict*	dictation: "words to be transcribed"
portare: "to carry"	*port*	import: "bring in goods"
spectare: "to watch"	*spect*	spectator: "a witness"

Directions Think of words you know that have a root found in the table above. Use a dictionary if you need help. Write the word, its root, and its meaning.

My Word	Its Root	Its Meaning

Directions Read each sentence and write a definition for the underlined word. Use word roots and context clues to help you find the meaning of each word.

1 Give me an abbreviated version rather than a long list.

2 The doctor prescribed medicine for my headaches.

3 Good diction is important for getting your message across.

4 A porter stood ready to carry the senator's luggage when she entered the airport.

5 Suddenly feeling introspective, I decided to write how I felt in my journal.

6 The Fourth of July is always a huge spectacle, with colorful fireworks and patriotic music.

7 Public transportation allows many people to travel without using so many cars.

Directions Read the paragraph. Then rewrite it using your own words. Be sure to replace the underlined words with different words.

8 The scribe sat at his desk and took off his spectacles. A load of mangoes had just been imported from overseas, and it was almost closing time. "I'll never get this done in time!" he cried. "I wish I had a portable counting tool so I could go home and finish these calculations."

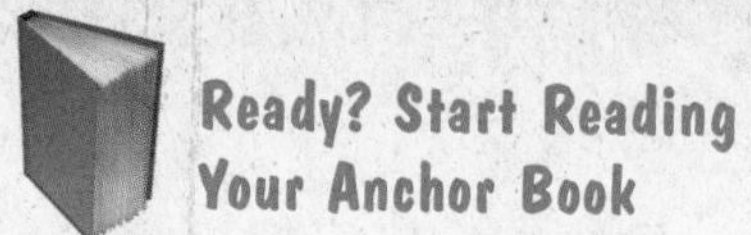

It's time to get started. As you learn from this worktext, your teacher will also give you reading assignments from your Anchor Book.

3-4 Literary Analysis
Narrative Nonfiction Writing

Have you ever written a story about an event that really happened to you or to a relative? If so, you have written a piece of narrative nonfiction. Narrative nonfiction writing can take many forms, such as a biography or an autobiography. It can include researched facts or facts the author knows from personal experience.

Literary Terms

As you learn these terms, remember that a narrative is something that tells about a series of events in the order that they occur.

- A **biography** is an account of someone's life story written by another person.
- An **autobiography** is the author's story of his or her own life.
- A **narrative essay** is a true story told by the author. The story tells about real events that happened to real people. The author may or may not have been involved in the events.

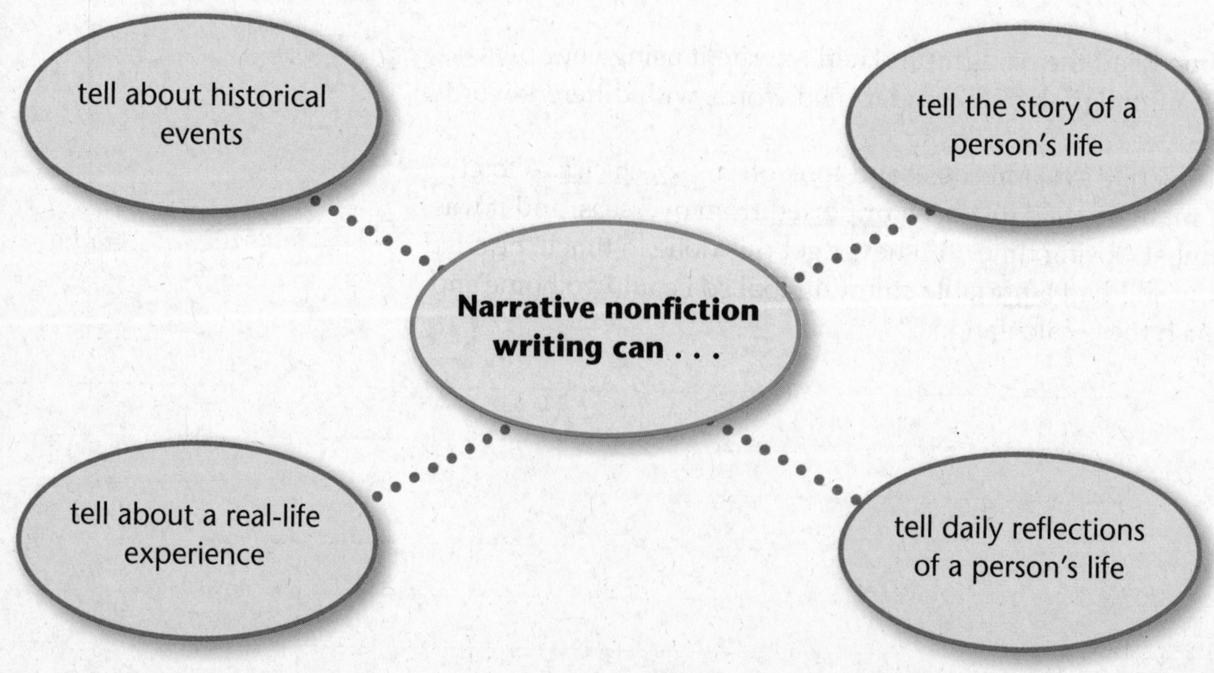

Directions Read the narrative nonfiction excerpt. Notice the main idea the student circled. Then, underline the events that happened over two weeks that support the main idea.

About the Author
Visit: PHSchool.com
Web Code: exe-6301

from *"The Case of the Monkeys That Fell From the Trees"* *by Susan E. Quinlan*

When the incidents began in August 1972, biologist Ken Glander and his wife, Molly, had been studying the eating habits of a troop of howling monkeys in northwestern Costa Rica for nearly three months. Then, over a two-week period, seven monkeys from various troops in the area fell out of trees and died. Another fell but climbed back up.

One morning the Glanders watched a female howling monkey with a ten-day-old baby turn in tight circles on a tree branch. Abruptly, she fell off the branch. For a moment she hung upside down, suspended by her long tail. Then her grip failed and she plunged thirty-five feet to the forest floor. Dazed but still alive, she climbed back up, carrying her clinging infant. She stopped on a thick branch and sat there without eating for the next twenty-four hours.

Normally, howling monkeys are skilled, nimble climbers. They often leap ten feet or more between tree limbs, and they almost never fall. Why were monkeys suddenly falling from trees?

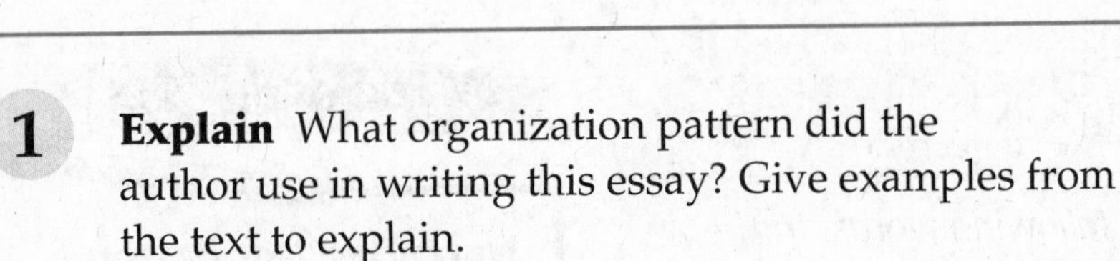

1 **Explain** What organization pattern did the author use in writing this essay? Give examples from the text to explain.

2 **Apply** What form of nonfiction narrative is "The Case of the Monkeys That Fell From the Trees?" Use details from the text in your answer.

while reading your anchor book

In this narrative essay, the author, as the founder of a bird sanctuary, shares her experiences helping a wounded vulture. *Guiding Question:* **Why do you think it is important to know about the Sanctuary's experience with the vulture?**

The Vulture's Flight

from *Through Animals' Eyes*

by Lynn Marie Cuny

Background *Wildlife sanctuaries provide help for orphaned, injured, and displaced wildlife such as wolves, bears, vultures, and eagles. Thousands of animals are brought to sanctuaries every year. The animals are cared for until they are well enough to reenter their world. If an animal's health doesn't return and allow it to reenter the wild, the sanctuary becomes its permanent home.*

Vocabulary Builder

Before you read, *you will discuss the following words. In the Vocabulary Builder box in the margin, use a vocabulary building strategy to make the words your own.*

sanctuary captivity lofty impact consolation

As you read, *draw a box around unfamiliar words you could add to your vocabulary. Use context clues to unlock their meaning.*

Marking the Text

Narrative Nonfiction

As you read, *underline words that help show what organization pattern the author uses. In the margin, state what pattern is used and why the underlined words support the pattern.*

Several years ago, when WRR[1] was located at the four-acre site near Leon Springs, we received a call from a man who had found a large injured black bird in his field. I asked him if the bird was a grackle. He wasn't sure what a grackle was, but he said it seemed likely that this was one. I asked him to cover the bird gently with

[1] **WRR** *n.* Wildlife Rescue & Rehabilitation, Inc.

a towel or pillowcase, place her in a box and bring her to the **Sanctuary.** The man replied that all he had was a minnow net and he would do what he could with that.

Within the hour, an old blue pickup truck arrived in our driveway. The man stepped out of the truck and said, "Lady, I've got your grackle." I immediately went to the back of the truck and opened the camper door. There, sitting with a minnow net draped like a mantilla[2] over her head and down to her very large feet, was one very disgruntled black vulture. She cocked her head and looked up at me as if to say: "Please tell this gentleman that I am *not* a grackle!"

Once I removed the tangled headdress from the vulture's body, it was easy to see that someone had used her for target practice. Whoever had shot off most of her right wing had also left her for dead. The wound was infected, and the bird was quite emaciated[3] and dehydrated[4].

Once we cleaned her wounds and medicated her for the infection, it was time to find our new patient something to eat. Contrary[5] to what most people think, vultures can be picky about their diet, especially in **captivity.** But this vulture was not interested in being picky. She was interested only in eating. After consuming a huge platter of fresh meat, she was ready to sit back and rest.

For the next several weeks, we kept her in a large flight cage. Even though she could no longer fly, she did enjoy climbing about

[2] **mantilla** (man til' ə) *n.* lace or silk scarf worn over the hair and shoulders.

[3] **emaciated** (ē mā shē āt' ed) *adj.* extremely thin.

[4] **dehydrated** (dē hī' drāt' ed) *adj.* when the body has excessive loss of water.

[5] **contrary** (kän' tre rē) *adj.* conflicting with.

Marking the Text

Vocabulary Builder

sanctuary
(sa[ng]k' cho͞o er' ē) *n.*

Meaning

captivity
(kap tiv' i tē) *n.*

Meaning

while reading your anchor book

◀ **Critical Viewing**
Why do you think vultures need such large eyes and keen eyesight?

the tree in her new home. It wasn't long before she adapted to life without flight. She had developed a remarkable way of getting into the very top of the tree. She would use her beak and feet the way a parrot does and climb to the heights of the tall oak.

One day, I decided to let her out of her enclosure to walk around the Sanctuary grounds. Since the property was completely fenced, she would be safe. After about an hour, the vulture was nowhere to be found. We looked everywhere . . . except up. This amazing bird had climbed to the top of the tallest oak tree, which grew just outside the back door of the Sanctuary house. At the foot of the tree was a large pool for the ducks. There was no doubt about it. The black vulture had chosen her new home.

Every morning, she'd climb down from her tree, wade in the pool, often right alongside the ducks, then have her breakfast of fresh meat before returning to her **lofty** perch. She would often come down in the middle of the day to play her game of pick-up sticks: running around and gathering up small twigs, carrying them over to the side of the pool, dropping them in one by one, then dancing around them with her wings spread. She would entertain herself for about an hour before jumping into the pool and splashing about.

It was a joy to watch this beautiful black bird come alive again and make the best of her less-than-perfect situation. Little did we

Vocabulary Builder

lofty
(lôft ē) *adj.*

Meaning

Good to Know!
A vulture has a bare, featherless head. This adaptation is great for an animal that constantly sticks its head inside the bodies of animals it eats. Its wide, open nostrils allow it to breathe while its head is inside its latest meal!

◀ **Good to Know!**
Vultures live between 5 and 15 years in the wild, but if they are kept in captivity—like the one in this story—they can live up to 30 years.

know that she had not seen the end of her days in the air. On April 1st of the following year, our black vulture was to have one more grand flight.

The day started out as most do. There were babies to feed, dishes to wash, phones to answer, animals to rescue and treat. Everything was normal . . . except that at approximately 2:00 in the afternoon, a severe storm warning was issued for our area. High winds and heavy rains were predicted. Preparing for the worst, we had all the animals in sheltered areas by noon. All the ones living in enclosures were secured. The free-roaming ducks and one large black vulture were finding their own shelter and weren't interested in any man-made protection. As it turned out, the weather forecasters were half right. There wasn't any rain, but there were very high winds of seventy miles per hour. I do not remember actually watching the wind sweeping anyone into the sky, but the trees bent down to the ground and a blinding dust filled the air.

When everything finally quieted down and it was time to survey the damage, there was only one real noticeable difference. We were missing one black vulture. She was not in her tree. She was not on the ground. She wasn't anywhere to be found on our four acres.

I called volunteers to form a search party. We put up signs as far as five miles away and notified store owners, residents, newspapers and anyone else we could think of.

Day one passed with no word. Days two, three and four passed and still no sign of our precious vulture. By day five, I had decided that, after being blown away in the storm, she must have landed so hard she had been killed on **impact.** The only **consolation** was that perhaps in the moment of becoming airborne, she felt once again united with the sky, the very place that used to be her home.

Vocabulary Builder

impact
(im′ pakt) *n.*

Meaning

consolation
(kän′sə lā′shən) *n.*

Meaning

Marking the Text

while reading your anchor book

One week after she disappeared, I was at the Sanctuary, standing at the back door, talking on the phone. Out of the corner of my eye, I saw something dark by the gate, which seemed to be moving toward me. I thought it was a garbage bag blowing in the wind. When I finally looked up, I was thrilled to see that the garbage bag was actually one extremely exhausted black vulture!

This remarkable bird barely noticed me. She trotted by, intent on her pool. As she hopped in and cooled her feet, she had the most relieved look on her face that I have ever seen on a bird. After being blown away, she managed to find her way home once again, tired and hungry.

For years after her final flight, the black vulture, now living at the Sanctuary, has spent her days with other flightless vultures, sitting in the tops of trees. One thing still makes her unique. Every time the wind picks up, she comes down from the tree, sits quietly on the ground, and waits for the danger to pass. I feel certain that neither of us will ever forget her exciting adventure.

Marking the Text

Vocabulary Builder

After you read, *review the words you decided to add to your vocabulary. Write the meaning of words you have learned in context. Look up words in a dictionary, glossary, thesaurus, or electronic resource.*

Lynn Marie Cuny (b. 1951)

Lynn Marie Cuny was born in Texas and writes about her experiences with animals. In 1978 she established the WRR Sancturary to help injured and abandoned animals. She has run it ever since while writing about her experiences with a variety of its animal guests. By writing her stories, Cuny tries to help people see that animals have emotions and compassion. The stories in her book *Through Animals' Eyes: True Stories From a Wildlife Sanctuary* tell about animals that won't give up, such as a raccoon with burned feet; and animals that take care of others, such as a mockingbird that adopted an orphaned sparrow.

Thinking About the Selection

The Vulture's Flight

1 **Explain** Check what form of narrative nonfiction "The Vulture's Flight" is.

☐ Autobiography ☐ Essay ☐ Biography

What was the author's purpose for writing the narrative? Why do you think she chose this form?

2 **Analyze** What is the main idea of the selection? Write the main idea and three supporting details in the graphic organizer.

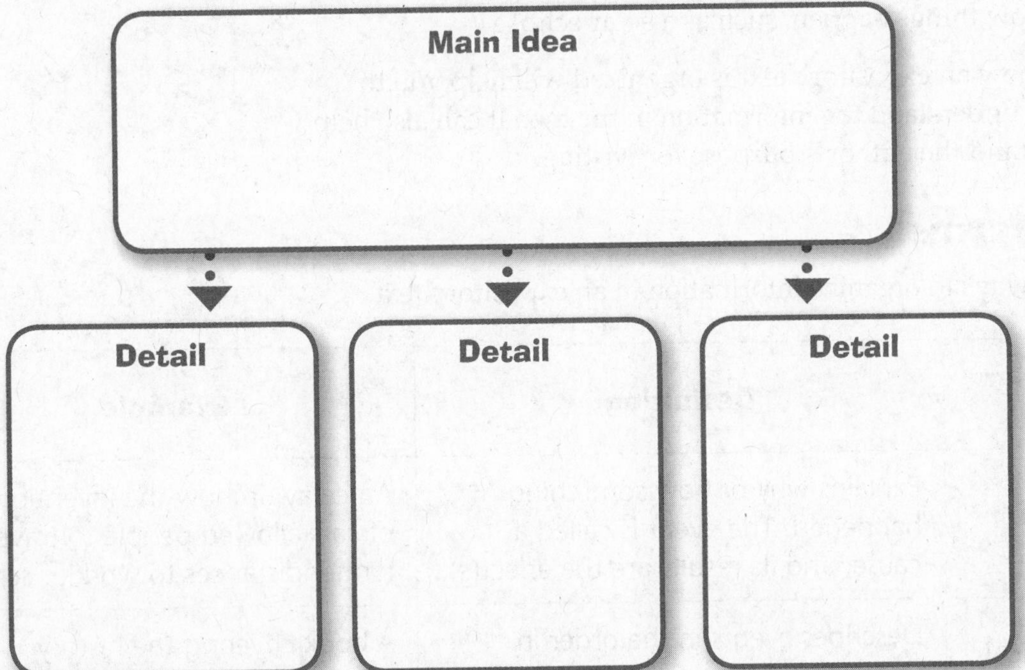

Write Answer the following questions in your Reader's Journal.

3 **Evaluate** Why do you think it is important to know about the Sanctuary's experience with the vulture?

4 **Compare and Contrast** How does the purpose of this selection compare to the purpose of your Anchor Book? Include examples from the selection and your Anchor Book in your answer.

while reading your anchor book

3-5 Literary Analysis
Expository Writing

If you want to find information about the eating habits of polar bears, what kind of text would be the most helpful to you? To find accurate information about a topic like this, your best bet is to read texts that are based on facts and are free of opinions. This type of nonfiction is called **expository writing.**

Expository texts describe, inform, and explain facts. An author's purpose for choosing this type of writing might be to

- describe what things are like, such as a rain forest
- tell what things can do, such as a rocket
- describe where things are found, such as kiwis
- explain how things happen, such as a solar eclipse

Determining how an expository text is organized will help you to recognize and understand the information in the text. It can also help you to understand the author's purpose for writing.

Literary Terms

Here are four ways to organize information in an expository text.

Organization Pattern	Definition	Example
Cause-and-effect	Explains why or how something happened. The event is called a cause, and its results are the effect(s).	An essay on how the invention of cars allowed people to travel longer distances to work or school
Chronological	Describes events in the order in which they happen	A book covering the history of the car
Compare-and-contrast	Shows how two or more subjects are similar and different	A magazine article that compares and contrasts a gasoline-powered car with a gas-electric hybrid car
Problem-and-solution	Gives a problem and then identifies a solution	An essay that discusses the threat car emissions have on our atmosphere and proposes alternatives such as hybrid cars

Directions Read the following passage from an expository essay. Then answer the questions that follow.

Keeping It Quiet

A construction worker uses a jackhammer; a woman waits in a noisy airport; a spectator watches a rock concert. All three experience noise pollution. In fact, millions of people in the United States face danger to their health because of noise pollution.

Noise levels are measured in decibels: the louder the noise, the higher the decibel level. People start to feel pain at about 120 decibels—a car horn creates this level of noise. But noise that doesn't hurt your ears can still damage your hearing. Sounds louder than 85 decibels—such as a screaming child—can slowly damage the hair cells in your inner ear. In America, as many as 10 million people have some hearing loss caused by noise. What can be done about noise pollution?

1 **Speculate** What is the author's purpose in writing this article?

2 **Analyze** What argument does the author use to convince readers that something should be done about noise pollution? What evidence in the passage supports the author's argument?

3 **Distinguish** What organization pattern does the author use to organize the information in the passage? Explain your response with examples from the text.

As you read this expository text, think about why the author chose to organize the information the way she did. *Guiding Question:* **How does the essay's organization help you to know what is important about the changing color of leaves?**

"Why Leaves Turn Color in the Fall"

by Diane Ackerman

Background *Every year, people travel many miles to witness the fall foliage. However, there's more to the color-changing ritual than beauty. It's a process that is necessary for the trees' survival. In this selection, Diane Ackerman uses both poetic and scientific language to explain why leaves change color in the fall.*

Vocabulary Builder

Before you read, *you will discuss the following words. In the Vocabulary Builder box in the margin, use a vocabulary building strategy to make the words your own.*

stealth **macabre** **edicts** **sublime**

As you read, *draw a box around unfamiliar words you could add to your vocabulary. Use context clues to unlock their meaning.*

Marking the Text

Expository Writing

As you read, *underline important details about the essay's subject. In the margin, note the organization patterns the author uses within the essay.*

Vocabulary Builder

stealth
(stelth) *n.*

Meaning

The **stealth** of autumn catches one unaware. Was that a goldfinch perching in the early September woods, or just the first turning leaf? A red-winged blackbird or a sugar maple closing up shop for the winter? Keen-eyed as leopards, we stand still and squint hard, looking for signs of movement. Early-morning frost sits heavily on the grass, and turns barbed wire into a string of stars. On a distant hill, a small square of yellow appears to be

while reading your anchor book

a lighted stage. At last the truth dawns on us: Fall is staggering in, right on schedule, with its baggage of chilly nights, **macabre** holidays, and spectacular, heart-stoppingly beautiful leaves. Soon the leaves will start cringing on the trees, and roll up in clenched fists before they actually fall off. Dry seedpods will rattle like tiny gourds. But first there will be weeks of gushing color so bright, so pastel, so confettilike, that people will travel up and down the East Coast just to stare at it—a whole season of leaves.

Where do the colors come from? Sunlight rules most living things with its golden **edicts.** When the days begin to shorten, soon after the summer solstice on June 21, a tree reconsiders its leaves. All summer it feeds them so they can process sunlight, but in the dog days of summer the tree begins pulling nutrients back into its trunk and roots, pares down, and gradually chokes off its leaves. A corky layer of cells forms at the leaves' slender petioles, then scars over. Undernourished, the leaves stop producing the pigment chlorophyll[1], and photosynthesis[2] ceases. Animals can migrate, hibernate, or store food to prepare for winter. But where can a tree go? It survives by dropping its leaves, and by the end of autumn only a few fragile threads of fluid-carrying xylem hold leaves to their stems.

A turning leaf stays partly green at first, then reveals splotches of yellow and red as the chlorophyll gradually breaks down. Dark green seems to stay longest in the veins, outlining and defining them. During the summer, chlorophyll dissolves in the heat and light, but it is also being steadily replaced. In the fall, on the other hand, no new pigment is produced, and so we notice the other colors that were always there, right in the leaf, although chlorophyll's shocking green hid them from view. With their camouflage gone, we see these colors for the first time all year, and marvel, but they were always there, hidden like a vivid secret beneath the hot glowing greens of summer.

The most spectacular range of fall foliage occurs in the northeastern United States and in eastern China, where the leaves are robustly colored thanks in part to a rich climate. European maples don't achieve the same flaming reds as their American relatives, which thrive on cold nights and sunny days. In Europe, the warm, humid weather turns the leaves brown or mildly yellow. Anthocyanin, the pigment that gives apples their red and turns leaves red or red-violet, is produced by sugars that remain in the leaf after the supply of nutrients dwindles. Unlike the carotenoids, which color carrots, squash, and corn, and turn leaves orange and yellow, anthocyanin varies from year to year, depending on the temperature and amount of sunlight. The

Marking the Text

Vocabulary Builder

macabre
(mə käb′ rə) *adj.*

Meaning

edicts
(ē′dikts′) *n.*

Meaning

1 **chlorophyll** (klôr′ə fil) *n.* a green pigment, or coloring, present in all green plants.

2 **photosynthesis** (fōt′ō sin′ thə sis) *n.* the process by which a plant uses the energy from sunlight to produce sugar.

fiercest colors occur in years when the fall sunlight is strongest and the nights are cool and dry (a state of grace scientists find vexing to forecast). This is also why leaves appear dizzyingly bright and clear on a sunny fall day: The anthocyanin flashes like a marquee.

Not all leaves turn the same color. Elms, weeping willows, and the ancient ginkgo all grow radiant yellow, along with hickories, aspens, bottlebrush buckeyes, cottonweeds, and tall, keening poplars. Basswood turns bronze, birches bright gold. Water-loving maples put on a symphonic display of scarlets. Sumacs turn red, too, as do flowering dogwoods, black gums, and sweet gums. Though some oaks yellow, most turn a pinkish brown. The farmlands also change color, as tepees of cornstalks and bales of shredded-wheat-textured hay stand drying in the fields. In some spots, one slope of a hill may be green and the other already in bright color, because the hillside facing south gets more sun and heat than the northern one.

An odd feature of the colors is that they don't seem to have any special purpose. We are predisposed to respond to their beauty, of course. They shimmer with the colors of sunset, spring flowers, the tawny buff of a colt's pretty rump, the shuddering pink of a blush. Animals and flowers color for a reason—adaptation to their environment—but there is no adaptive reason for leaves to color so beautifully in the fall any more than there is for the sky or ocean to be blue. It's just one of the haphazard marvels the planet bestows every year. We find the sizzling colors thrilling, and in a sense they dupe us. Colored like living things, they signal death and disintegration. In time, they will become fragile and, like the body, return to dust. They are as we hope our own fate will be when we die; not to vanish, just to **sublime** from one beautiful state into another. Though leaves lose their green life, they bloom

Marking the Text

Vocabulary Builder

sublime
(səb līm′) *v.*

Meaning

with urgent colors, as the woods grow mummified day by day, and Nature becomes more carnal, mute, and radiant. We call the season "fall," from the Old English *feallan*, to fall, which leads back through time to the Indo-European *phol*, which also means to fall. So the word and the idea are both extremely ancient, and haven't really changed since the first of our kind needed a name for fall's leafy abundance. As we say the word, we're reminded of that other Fall, in the Garden of Eden, when fig leaves never withered and scales fell from our eyes. Fall is the time when leaves fall from the trees, just as spring is when flowers spring up, summer is when we summer, and winter is when we whine from the cold.

Children love to play in piles of leaves, hurling them into the air like confetti, leaping into soft unruly mattresses of them. For children, leaf fall is just one of the odder figments of Nature, like hailstones or snowflakes. Walk down a lane overhung with trees in the never-never land of autumn, and you will forget about time and death, lost in the sheer delicious spill of color . . . But how do the colored leaves fall? As a leaf ages, the growth hormone, auxin, fades, and cells at the base of the petiole divide. Two or three rows of small cells, lying at right angles to the axis of the petiole, react with water, then come apart, leaving the petioles hanging on by only a few threads of xylem. A light breeze, and the leaves are airborne. They glide and swoop, rocking in invisible cradles. They are all wing and may flutter from yard to yard on small whirlwinds or updrafts, swiveling as they go. Firmly tethered to earth, we love to see things rise up and fly—soap bubbles, balloons, birds, fall leaves. They remind us that the end of a season is capricious, as is the end of life. We especially like the way leaves rock, careen, and swoop as they fall. Everyone knows the motion. Pilots sometimes do a maneuver called a "falling

▲ Critical Viewing
Would you describe these photographs as scientific, poetic, or both?

Marking the Text

leaf," in which the plane loses altitude quickly and on purpose, by slipping first to the right, then to the left.

The machine weighs a ton or more, but in one pilot's mind it is a weightless thing, a falling leaf. She has seen the motion before, in the Vermont woods where she played as a child. Below her the trees radiate gold, copper, and red. Leaves are falling, although she can't see them fall, as she falls, swooping down for a closer view.

At last the leaves leave. But first they turn color and thrill us for weeks on end. Then they crunch and crackle underfoot. They shush, as children drag their small feet through leaves heaped along the curb. Dark, slimy mats of leaves cling to one's heels after a rain. A damp, stuccolike mortar of semidecayed leaves protects the tender shoots with a roof until spring, and makes a rich humus. An occasional bulge or ripple in the leafy mounds signals a shrew or a field mouse tunneling out of sight. Sometimes one finds in fossil stones the imprint of a leaf, long since disintegrated, whose outlines remind us how detailed, vibrant, and alive are the things of this earth that perish.

Marking the Text

Vocabulary Builder

After you read, *review the words you decided to add to your vocabulary. Write the meaning of words you have learned in context. Look up words in a dictionary, glossary, thesaurus, or electronic resource.*

Diane Ackerman (b. 1948)

Diane Ackerman is a poet, essayist, and naturalist. Her writings on science and natural history reflect her wonder at the natural world. She has said that she writes "about nature and human nature. And . . . about that twilight zone where the two meet and have something they can teach each other." Ackerman has received many awards for her writing, including a Guggenheim Fellowship, the John Burroughs Nature Award, and the Lavan Poetry Prize. She also has the unusual distinction of having a molecule named after her—dianeackerone.

Thinking About the Selection

Why Leaves Turn Color in the Fall

1 **Identify** The author uses sensory language—language that appeals to your senses of sight, sound, smell, touch, or taste—throughout the essay. Write two examples of sensory language from the essay and tell which sense each one appeals to.

2 **Explain** Why do you think the author uses such strong sensory language?

3 **Analyze** What is the author's purpose for writing the essay?

4 **Deduce** What is one organization pattern the author uses to structure the information in the essay? Use details from the text to support your answer.

Write Answer the following questions in your Reader's Journal.

5 **Evaluate** How does the essay's organization help you to know what is important about the changing color of leaves?

6 **Describe** Pick a selection from your Anchor Book. How does the author organize information? Why do you think the author uses that particular organization pattern? Explain with details from your book.

while reading your anchor book

3-6 Language Coach
Grammar and Spelling

Adjectives

If authors relied only on nouns to identify people, places, or things, their writing might be dry and boring. Which sentence would make you want to continue reading?

- There were houses on the lot.
- The two broken-down houses on the empty, littered lot looked scary.

You probably chose the one with the adjectives. **Adjectives** describe people, places, or things and answer the questions *What kind? Which one? How many? How much?* They can be called modifiers because they modify, or make clearer, the meaning of a noun or pronoun. Authors use adjectives to help bring their characters and settings to life.

Sentence	Question	Adjective
Judith will read three novels.	How many?	three
The red notebook is mine.	Which one?	red
Andrew ate a blueberry muffin.	What kind?	blueberry
José ate the entire bowl of soup.	How much?	entire

Learn More
Visit: PHSchool.com
Web Code: exp-6301

Author's Craft

Using adjectives makes writing more vivid, but sometimes authors choose not to use them. Review the passage "The Vulture's Flight" beginning on on page 188. Which people, places, or things did the author chose *not* to use adjectives to describe? Why do you think she made this choice?

Articles

An **article** is a special kind of adjective. There are three articles—*a, an,* and *the. A* and *an* refer to any person place or thing, while *the* refers to a specific person, place, or thing.

That is **a** pretty dress. That was **an** easy test. **The** dog ate my shoe!

Directions Revise the following passage using articles and adjectives.

They arrived at field and set up tent. First night was clear, but rains flooded tent on second night. On third day, sun came out and Gerald tried to build fire, but wood was wet.

Comparisons With Adjectives

Authors often use adjectives to compare people or things. Most adjectives have three forms to show different degrees of comparison. These are **positive, comparative,** and **superlative.** The form used depends on how many things are being compared.

Adjective Form	Definition	Example
Positive	no comparison is being made	Joe is tall.
Comparative	compares two things	Sharon is taller than Joe.
Superlative	compares three or more things	Franz is the tallest one in our class.

- For most one- and two- syllable adjectives, use *-er* or *more* to form the comparative degree and *-est* or *most* to form the superlative degree.
- The most common way to form the comparative degree is by adding *-er*. The most common way to form the superlative degree is by adding *-est*. But you can also use *more* and *most* with many one- and two- syllable adjectives. Don't use *more* or *most* if the use sounds awkward, such as "The bike goes *more fast* on the road."
- For adjectives that have three or more syllables, use the words *more* and *most* to form the comparative and superlative.

Author's Craft

Return to "Why Leaves Turn Color in the Fall," beginning on page 196. Where does the author use the superlative form of an adjective to compare things? How do these comparisons make her descriptions stronger?

Positive	Comparative	Superlative
fast	faster	fastest
happy	happier	happiest
handsome	more handsome	most handsome
wonderful	more wonderful	most wonderful

Directions Choose three words and their degree of comparison from the list below. Write a three- to four-sentence paragraph using the words.

warm (positive)	dangerous (comparative)	large (superlative)
lucky (positive)	small (comparative)	creepy (superlative)

Troublesome Modifiers

Modifiers are adjectives and adverbs that add detail and description to your writing. It can be easy to confuse the two types of modifiers. The information in the charts below should help you decide whether an adjective or an adverb is the correct choice for what you're writing.

When to Use Adjectives or Adverbs	Example
Use adjectives to modify nouns and pronouns.	The car in the driveway is *new*. He has *many* friends.
Use adverbs to modify action verbs.	The game ended *suddenly.*

To identify and fix errors related to the modifiers *good* and *well*, review these rules.

When to Use *Good* and *Well*	Example
Good is an adjective that modifies only nouns and pronouns.	The plans sound *good* to me.
Well is an adverb that modifies action verbs.	The orchestra played *well.*

To identify and fix errors related to the modifiers *better* and *best*, determine the number of things or actions.

When to Use *Better* and *Best*	Example
Use *better* when two things or actions are being compared.	I think spaghetti is *better* than rice.
Use *best* when three or more things or actions are being compared.	I think spaghetti is the *best* food of all.

Directions Write a sentence using each modifier.

1 good ______________________
well ______________________

2 better ______________________
best ______________________

3 slow ______________________
slowly ______________________

Spelling Base Words and Endings

A **base word** can be changed by adding a prefix before the word or a suffix at the end of the word. Follow these spelling rules for adding the suffix *-ed* or *-ing* to base words.

Spelling Rule	Example
For most verbs, do not double the final consonant.	read + *-ing* = reading
For most one-syllable verbs ending in one vowel and one consonant, double the final consonant.	run + *-ing* = running
For verbs that end in a vowel plus *y*, generally keep the *y*.	play + *-ed* = played
For verbs that end in a consonant plus *y*, keep the *y* when adding *-ing*, but change the *y* to *i* when adding *-ed*.	carry + *-ing* = carrying; carry + *-ed* = carried

When you want to make a noun refer to more than one thing, you have to turn the base word into the **plural** form. There are some rules you have to learn that go along with this, too. To spell the plural of most nouns, you can simply add *-s* or *-es* to the base word. However, there are some exceptions to this rule.

Spelling Rule	Example
For many words ending in *f*, change *f* to *v* and add *-es*.	calf, calves (*exception:* chief, chiefs)
For some words, the plural and singular forms are the same.	deer, deer
Some plurals are irregular and add a special ending or have special forms.	child, children; man, men; ox, oxen; mouse, mice

Directions Add the suffix in parentheses to each underlined base word, or make the underlined word plural. Rewrite each sentence correctly.

1. I paint my bedroom blue. *(-ing)*

____

2. We stop the game so we could eat lunch. *(-ed)*

____

3. There are seven half of melon left. *(plural)*

____

3-7 Writer's Workshop
Exposition: How-To Essay

You've probably read step-by-step instructions before. Maybe you were preparing food, assembling a toy, or playing a new board game. Step-by-step instructions help you understand how to do unfamiliar things. Instructions in a **how-to essay** teach someone the steps of doing or making something. Follow the steps outlined in this workshop to write your own how-to essay.

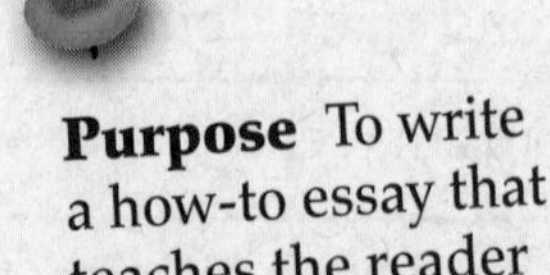

Purpose To write a how-to essay that teaches the reader the steps for doing something

Audience You, your teacher, and your classmates

Your essay should include the following elements.

- a list of all the materials needed
- a clear sequence of steps, presented in the correct order
- transitional words and phrases to make the order clear
- a result that is specific and achievable
- illustrations, charts, or maps to help explain difficult steps
- error-free writing, especially the correct use of modifiers

Prewriting—Plan It Out

You can use one of these ideas to help you choose a topic for your essay and plan your draft.

Brainstorm. Make a list of some things you're good at, games you like to play, or crafts you like to make. Review your list. Select an activity that you would enjoy teaching to someone else.

Gather details. On an index card, list all the materials needed for the activity. Number and list the steps in the order in which they should be done.

How to

Materials:

Steps:
1.
2.
3.
4.
5.
6.
7.

Drafting—Get It on Paper

Use your list of steps as an outline for your first draft. The following ideas will help you keep your essay organized.

Start with a catchy introduction. Write a brief, interesting, one-paragraph introduction. First, identify the task and build your reader's interest in a fun, creative way. Then, move into the procedure.

Give step-by-step directions. Describe the materials needed in the order in which they will be used. Then, write the steps in order, adding details and illustrations as needed. Use numbered steps or transition words such as *first, next,* and *finally*.

End it with a send-off. Describe for readers the benefits of following these steps and encourage them to enjoy the final product.

Revising—Make It Better

Reread your draft several times to check that your instructions are clear and in order. Consider the following to make your essay better.

Use visual aids. Use highlighting or boldface type to emphasize important steps. Illustrations or graphics such as charts can clarify your instructions.

Establish reader interest. Make sure your essay interests your reader. Check that the steps are clear, and use vivid details to describe the process.

Peer Review Have a classmate read your essay and tell you if your steps are easy to follow. Revise to achieve the reaction you intended.

Directions Read this how-to essay as a model for your own.

Student Model: Writing

Sara Noë, LaPorte, IN

How to Write a Poem

The technique of writing poetry varies among different poets. My format depends on the mood I'm in, the environment around me, and what my inspiration is. I can't think of a poem whenever I want to; I have to let it come to me on its own. However, there are many other ways to write poems that rhyme. The most common process I've seen follows these steps:

1. picking a topic you're good at or having knowledge about the subject
2. brainstorming for words that relate to your topic

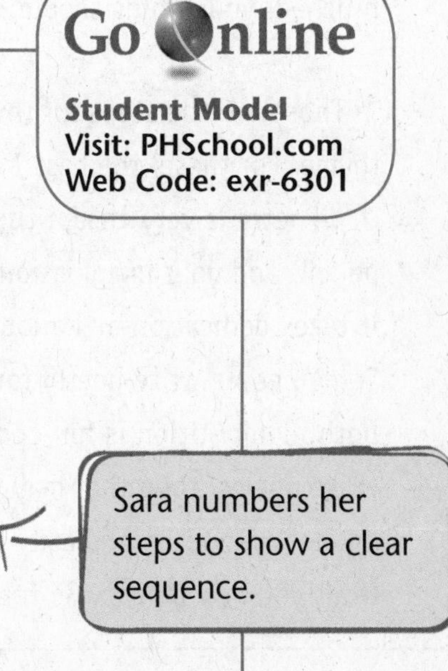

Go Online
Student Model
Visit: PHSchool.com
Web Code: exr-6301
Sara numbers her steps to show a clear sequence.

3. thinking up more words that rhyme with your first list and that also describe your topic
4. creating phrases that include your rhyming words at the end
5. finally, combining your phrases into one and trying to get the words to flow together

If you choose a topic you don't like or don't know a lot about, your poem may end up being dull or boring . . . Word webs and lists are the best way to brainstorm for words. If another way helps you more, go for it!

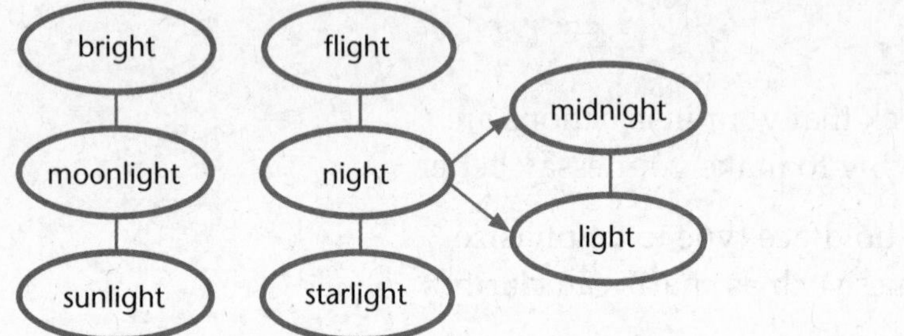

Sara uses a word web to explain her idea.

Remember to make sure your words relate to your topic. For rhyming words, just go through the alphabet until you have plenty. Once you have your list done, sit down in a quiet place and begin organizing the words into phrases. The rhyming words from your list should be at the end of each phrase. Here is where the words and ideas need to flow together. Finally, put all of your phrases together. When you are finished, your words should blend together in one smooth poem.

Those are the steps for rhyming poems, but free-form poems don't rhyme. For these, the best I can tell you is to use your imagination . . . Poetry is very cheap; the only materials you need are paper, a pencil, and your imagination. Pretty much anybody can write poetry, but it takes dedication and a lot of determination to make it a good poem. Some people write poetry for competition. Some people, like me, do both. Competition is fun occasionally, but if that's the only reason you write poems, then that may take all the excitement out of it. Poetry is my hobby, and it can easily be yours. Just do your best, and be proud of what you accomplish. Go for it!

Sara lists the materials needed for writing poetry.

She describes the rewards of writing poetry and encourages the reader.

Editing—Be Your Own Language Coach

Before you hand in your essay, proofread it. Review it on your own or with an adult for language convention errors or errors in spelling and grammar. Pay special attention to your use of modifiers.

Publishing—Share It!

When you publish a work, you produce it for a specific audience. Consider the following ideas to share your writing.

Give a demonstration. Use the information in your essay to perform a demonstration. Make visual aids such as posters, diagrams, and photographs to use with your presentation.

Create a "How-To" Web page. Work with a teacher to design a Web page presenting the how-to essays written by your class.

Reflecting on Your Writing

1. Respond to the following questions on a separate sheet of paper and hand it in with your final draft. What new insights did you gain about the form of a how-to essay by writing one? What did you do well? What do you need more work on?

2. **Rubric for Self-Assessment** Assess your essay's strengths and weaknesses using the criteria. For each question, circle a rating.

CRITERIA	RATING SCALE
IDEAS How well have you focused your topic?	NOT VERY — VERY 1 2 3 4 5
ORGANIZATION How organized are the sequence of steps and the list of materials?	1 2 3 4 5
VOICE How interesting and engaging is your introductory paragraph?	1 2 3 4 5
WORD CHOICE How well do you use transitions to make the steps clear?	1 2 3 4 5
CONVENTIONS How correct is your grammar, especially your use of modifiers?	1 2 3 4 5

3-8 Discussing Your Anchor Book
Literature Circles

Descriptive Writing An author always has a reason for writing. Most often it's to inform, entertain, reflect, or persuade. The author's purpose, or main reason for writing, often determines the way in which he or she writes.

Authors use **descriptive writing** to grab the reader's attention by directly appealing to the five senses—sight, sound, smell, taste, and touch. Which sentence below would make you want to keep reading?

He stepped out of the swamp. **or** *With a sharp sucking sound, he yanked his cold and muddy foot out of the murky swamp.*

The sentence on the right grabs you immediately because of its descriptive language. You can almost hear the sucking sound and see the murkiness as the person pulls his foot out of the swamp.

Descriptive writing also affects the **mood** of a text—the feeling the reader has as he or she reads it. Depending on the descriptive language used, the mood can be serious, sad, happy or hopeful.

while reading your anchor book

1 ON YOUR OWN

Find five sentences in your Anchor Book that contain descriptive writing. Identify which senses the words appeal to. Write each sentence in the corresponding column in the chart that follows. Note the page where you found the sentence.

Sight	page ______
Smell	page ______
Touch	page ______
Sound	page ______
Taste	page ______

2 WITH YOUR GROUP

Meet with your group members to discuss your examples of descriptive language. Then answer the questions.

1 **Analyze** As a group, choose your three favorite examples of descriptive writing from section 1 on page 210. Record each example in the chart. Identify the mood that each example of descriptive writing helps to create.

Descriptive Writing	Mood Created
Example 1	
Example 2	
Example 3	

2 **Assess** How did the author use the descriptive language in Example 1 to set the mood for the scene?

3 **Synthesize** With your group, find a passage of three or four sentences in your Anchor Book that has little or no descriptive writing. Rewrite the passage to include descriptive writing.

Passage:

Rewritten passage:

Standardized Test Practice

Reading Skills: Main Idea

Directions Read the following passage. Then answer the questions.

For centuries, people have been interested in studying outer space. Space exploration began with Galileo's invention of the telescope in the early seventeenth century. The first telescopes were not strong, but they improved over the next three hundred years. Today the Hubble space telescope is one of the most powerful. It orbits above Earth's atmosphere, allowing us to see far into space. Yet the planets and asteroids of our solar system still hold many mysteries.

One way to learn about space is to send ships into space. The first planetary missions of the National Aeronautics and Space Administration (NASA) were "fly-bys." The spacecraft zoomed by a planet, taking pictures and gathering atmospheric data. Then they continued on into deep space. They paved the way for later space probes that orbited the planets.

1 What is the **main idea** of the passage?

A. the job of the Hubble telescope

B. NASA's role in space exploration

C. the role of telescopes and spacecrafts in space exploration

D. the first planetary mission

2 What **detail** could be added to support the passage's main idea?

F. People began venturing into space in the 1960s.

G. Our galaxy is known as the Milky Way.

H. The Hubble telescope did not work properly at first.

J. Microscopes can help us study very small objects.

3 Where is the main idea of a selection *usually* found?

A. in a footnote

B. in the middle

C. on the cover page

D. in the topic sentence

4 The main idea of a selection is often **restated** in the __________.

F. first paragraph

G final paragraph

H. in the title

J. supporting details

Literary Analysis: Elements of Nonfiction

Read the following passage. Then answer the questions.

> As he grew old, William Randolph Hearst, a very powerful publisher of newspapers and magazines, became weary of the profession. He went into politics. When he was not elected as the mayor of New York City in 1909, Hearst chose to retire. In 1919, he built a magnificent castle in California called San Simeon and filled it with art treasures from around the world. This impressive home was the site of huge, lavish banquets. Hearst loved to invite the biggest movie stars in Hollywood to San Simeon and serve them fancy dinners. When Hearst died in 1951, he was one of the richest and most powerful men in America. The Hearst Corporation still owns many of the country's newspapers and magazines.

5 What **organization pattern** was used to write this selection?

A. cause-and-effect

B. compare-and-contrast

C. chronological

D. problem-and-solution

6 Which organization pattern would an author most likely use to write an autobiography?

F. chronological

G. problem-and-solution

H. compare-and-contrast

J. cause-and-effect

7 Which of the following is this selection an example of?

A. autobiography

B. biography

C. how-to essay

D. narrative essay

8 Why would a writer use a **cause-and-effect** organization pattern?

F. to show a problem and a solution

G. to show how two things are different

H. to tell the order of events

J. to tell why something happened

Timed Writing: Exposition

Directions What is the main idea of this selection? Does the organization pattern help you understand the main idea? Would another organization pattern work better? Use specific examples from the text to support your answer. **(20 minutes)**

3-9 Reading Skills
Author's Purpose

In learning new reading skills, you will use special academic vocabulary. Knowing the right words will help you demonstrate your understanding.

Academic Vocabulary

Word	Meaning	Example Sentence
analyze *v.* *Related words:* analyzed, analysis	to examine something very carefully	We *analyze* fiction and nonfiction to discover the author's purpose.
emphasize *v.* *Related words:* emphasizing, emphasis	to stress or bring out	A poet uses repetition and rhyme to *emphasize* certain words or phrases.
intent *n.* *Related words:* intently, intention	purpose	The author's *intent* is the same as the author's purpose: to inform, persuade, entertain, or reflect.

An author always has a reason for writing. Most often, the author's **intention** is to inform, entertain, reflect, or persuade. The **author's purpose,** or reason for writing, often determines his or her writing style. For example, if the author's purpose is to inform, he or she may use a serious style and **emphasize** certain facts to prove a point.

Directions Read each sentence to determine the author's purpose. Put a check mark in the correct box.

	Inform	Entertain	Persuade	Reflect
I know you agree that we should protect sea turtles.				
Place a screen over a turtle's nest to protect it.				
Dora the turtle yawned and went to bed.				
I remember it was rainy when I lost my turtle.				

while reading your anchor book

Directions The following poem was written with a specific purpose. Read it to determine whether the author's purpose is to inform, to entertain, to reflect, or to persuade.

Face It *by Janet S. Wong*

My nose belongs
to Guangdong, China—
short and round, a Jang family nose.

My eyes belong
to Alsace, France—
wide like Grandmother Hemmerling's.

But my mouth, my big-talking mouth, belongs
to me, alone.

1 **Analyze** What do you think is the author's purpose for writing "Face It"? Give examples from the poem in your answer.

2 **Speculate** Look at your answer to question 1. Why did the author use poetry as a way of emphasizing this purpose?

3 **Compare** Compare the wording of the three stanzas, or groups of lines in the poem. How does the wording help the author get across her purpose for writing?

while reading your anchor book

The following interview gives an account of an adventure very few people will ever experience in their own lives and reveals the author's purpose. ***Guiding Question:* Why is it important to know a person's own account of a real event in his or her life?**

ICE DOGS EXPLORER ON SIBERIA–TO–U.S. DOGSLED ATTEMPT

by Brian Handwerk
for *National Geographic Ultimate Explorer*

Background *Many explorers travel to remote places to discover something new. Benedict Allen takes this idea one step further: He lives with the people of a region, learning their way of life in order to gain their trust and acceptance. He also travels completely alone, and he records his adventures as a video diary.*

November 7, 2003—English explorer Benedict Allen has crossed the Amazon Basin, lived with isolated[1] peoples in Papua New Guinea, and walked the harsh Gobi Desert with a group of reluctant[2] camels. But his latest journey was his perhaps most extreme yet: an attempted solo crossing of the frozen Bering Strait from Siberia to Alaska. Solo, that is, except for a team of trusty sled dogs that were essential to his survival.

National Geographic News recently spoke with Allen about his Arctic odyssey[3] as he warmed up in Washington, D.C. Excerpts:

You have a long background in exploration, but this was something new. What drew you to the Arctic?

My technique is to live with local people and learn their skills, because the places others see as exotic or scary they see as home. In the Gobi, I learned to travel with camels and had an extraordinary amount of freedom in a place which should have perhaps killed me. I thought, "Can I carry it further? Can I go to perhaps the most extreme place, the Arctic, and survive there with the help of dogs?"

You spent months living and traveling with local Chukchi people in Siberia who taught you about handling a dog team and surviving the Arctic. What was life like among people who herd reindeer and hunt walrus and seals?

I was trying to hone in[4] immediately on their ability with dogs, but I was also struck with how they seemed to read the landscape so easily. It can be terribly disorienting[5] in a blizzard that's come from nowhere. Yet the local people had grown up in this place where the line between life and death is so fine. They knew when bad winds were coming and so on. That's what struck me first.

---

1 **isolated** (ī'sō lāt'ed) *adj.* far away from other people.

2 **reluctant** (rē luc tənt) *adj.* unwilling.

3 **odyssey** (äd'i sē) *n.* an extended wandering or journey.

4 **hone in** (hōn in) *phrasal v.* to focus attention on a goal.

5 **disorienting** (dis ôr'ē ent'[ng]) *adj.* causing confusion and the feeling of being lost.

But perhaps above all I was struck by their ability to deal mentally with harsh conditions. They were always making jokes. There is a danger when you're stuck in a blizzard, when you don't know where you are and it's minus 40° Fahrenheit [minus 40° Celsius], that you can sort of turn in on yourself. You can begin feeling sorry for yourself, and you just want to go to sleep and forget the numbing cold. The Chukchi were always getting me to jump about and have a good laugh. They made me keep moving, keep thinking and be positive. For example, they once started lighting distress flares during a blizzard, and I was thinking, "My God, I'm trusting them as guides and they are firing flares where we have no hope of being rescued." But it was all about having fun, just a bit of fireworks to keep things light.

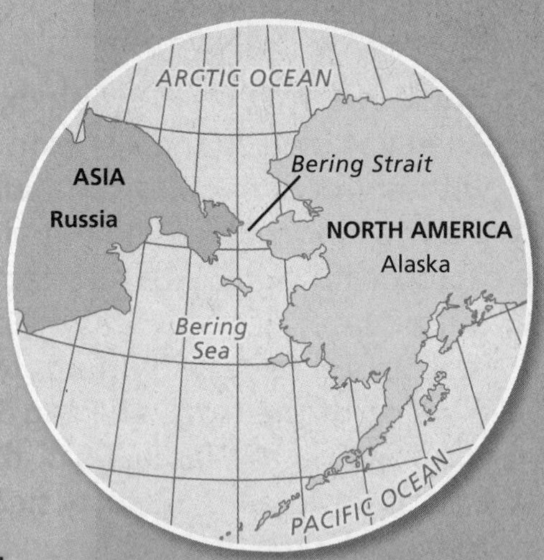

▲ **Map** The Bering Strait is a sea passage between Asia and North America. It freezes over to form an ice bridge between the continents.

Did they think you were a bit crazy?

They did, especially because I was such a total beginner. They couldn't understand why I was aiming to be out there in the Bering Strait alone. They don't go on expeditions alone, and they couldn't see the point of it. They were also doubtful that I'd gain enough skills over two or three months to cope alone for even a day. Maybe they're right [that the trip was crazy]. Lots of people in our culture can't see the "why" either. In the end, only certain sorts of people feel that they want to push themselves to the limit.

▼ **Close Call** Allen did not complete his journey across the Bering Strait. One night, he lost the dogs when he went ahead to check the route. He thought he might die alone in the Arctic. However, the dogs were waiting for him the next morning. That's when he decided to turn back and return to the mainland.

What did you first think of the dogs?

I knew I'd have to prove myself to the Chukchis, but I found that the dogs were not going to obey me until I'd earned their respect. I hadn't expected that, and it was quite startling. You don't have to prove yourself to a pet dog, but these dogs are tough creatures—they knew the rules of the Arctic. It was humbling to see how adept they were out there. Top Dog, the lead dog, really ignored me for six weeks. He ran, but didn't heed[6] my commands to turn right or left.

[6] **heed** (hēd) *v.* to pay attention.

Thinking About the Selection

Ice Dogs Explorer on Siberia-to-U.S. Dogsled Attempt

1 **Analyze** What do you think the author's purpose is for writing this article? Give examples from the text to support your answer.

2 **Infer** What can you infer about Allen's personality by this statement: "In the end, only certain sorts of people feel that they want to push themselves to the limit"?

3 **Compare** List details that support the purpose of writing "Face It" and "Ice Dogs." Did the forms of poetry and interview help you understand each purpose for writing? Why?

Title	Purposes	Detail that Informs	Detail that Entertains
Face It	to entertain to inform		
Ice Dogs	to inform		

Write Answer the following questions in your Reader's Journal.

4 **Explain** Why is it important to know a person's own account of a real event in his or her life?

5 **Deduce** What was the author's purpose for writing your Anchor Book? Give details from the text in your answer.

Ready for a Free-Choice Book? *Your teacher may ask you if you would like to choose another book to read on your own. Select a book that fits your interest and that you'll enjoy. As you read, think about how your new book compares with your Anchor Book.*

3-10 Literary Analysis
Author's Style

When you think of style, what comes to mind? Do you think of different clothing, personal styles, or musical styles? Authors have different styles, too. They use style to get a point across or to share their feelings about a story or character.

An **author's style** is the way he or she uses words to make ideas come alive on the page. There are several styles of writing. For example, an author can use comical words to sound humorous, or use sensory and descriptive language to create a dark, scary mood. The style used depends on the author's purpose for writing.

Literary Terms

An author uses many techniques to develop a style. The following are some techniques that influence an author's style.

Technique	Examples
Words can be formal or informal.	▸ *Informal:* Jason's friends dissed him. ▸ *Formal:* Jason's friends voted against him.
Sentence lengths and structures can vary.	▸ Janice went to the store. She bought a scarf. ▸ Janice went to the department store and bought a woolen scarf.
Dialogue shows the reader how the characters speak and can indicate the character's background.	▸ "I flipped right outta the wagon after he jammed his foot on the brakes." ▸ "I am confident the hours he spent sailing the yacht enabled him to pass the exam."
Tone tells what the author's attitude toward the subject is. Formal language creates a serious tone. Informal language creates a light hearted tone.	▸ Tarantulas lurk in hidden places in the desert. ▸ Beware of creepy crawlers in the desert!
Mood is the atmosphere or feeling that the author establishes in the story.	▸ Maria wore a black veil to cover her tears. ▸ The child giggled as she danced around.
Sensory language appeals to the five senses and creates a certain style.	▸ The breeze tossed her golden curls around her head, while the fragrant blossoms entwined in her hair quivered and bounced.

while reading your anchor book

Directions Read the following folk tale. As you read, notice the sentences a student underlined to identify the author's style. Circle words and phrases in the text that give the story a formal tone. Then answer the question.

About the Author
Visit: PHSchool.com
Web Code: exe-6303

The Mustard Seed

retold by Marilyn McFarlane

The Buddha was walking on a dusty country road one day when he stopped at the edge of a river to splash cooling water on his face. When he finished washing, he looked up and saw an old woman kneeling beside him. Her clothes were ragged and her face was worn. Her arms were covered with sores.

"Oh, Master," she wailed. "I suffer so. Please help me."

"What troubles you?" the Buddha asked, looking at her with compassion in his eyes.

"Look at me! See my sad lot!" She touched her rags, and she pointed with skinny fingers to her blistered arms. "I am poor, my clothes are torn, I am ill. Once I was prosperous, with a farm, and now I am old and have only a bowl of rice to eat. Won't you heal me and bring back my riches?"

"You have described life as it is," the Buddha answered. "We are all born to suffering."

The old woman shook her head, weeping. "No, no, I won't listen. I was not born to suffer."

The Buddha saw that she could not understand. "Very well, I will help you," he said. "You must do as I say."

"Anything, anything!" she gasped.

Analyze What techniques did the author use to develop the formal style of the folk tale?

while reading your anchor book

The following myth tells how a goddess's imprisonment in the underworld affects the people and the world around her. *Guiding Question:* **Why is it important to know about myths and the cultures that created them?**

The Origin of the Seasons

by Olivia Coolidge

Background The Origin of the Seasons *is a retelling of an ancient Greek myth. Olivia Coolidge, the author, studied Latin and Greek at Oxford University in England. Her studies influenced her style of writing and her ability to bring ancient mythical characters to life today.*

while reading your anchor book

Vocabulary Builder

Before you read, *you will discuss the following words. In the Vocabulary Builder box in the margin, use a vocabulary building strategy to make the words your own.*

fate **immortal** **stature** **decreed**

As you read, *draw a box around unfamiliar words you could add to your vocabulary. Use context clues to unlock their meaning.*

Marking the Text

Author's Style

As you read, *circle specific words and underline sentences that indicate the author's style. In the margin, identify the author's style.*

Demeter, the great earth mother, was goddess of the harvest. Tall and majestic was her appearance, and her hair was the color of ripe wheat. It was she who filled the ears with grain. In her honor white-robed women brought golden garlands of wheat as first fruits to the altar. Reaping, threshing, winnowing, and the long tables set in the shade for the harvesters' refreshment—all these were hers. Songs and feasting did her honor as the hard-working farmer gathered his abundant fruit. All the laws which the farmer knew came from her: the time for plowing, what land would best bear crops, which was fit for grapes, and which to leave for pasture. She was a goddess whom men called the great mother because of her generosity in giving. Her own special daughter in the family of the gods was named Persephone.

Persephone was the spring maiden, young and full of joy. Sicily[1] was her home, for it is a land where the spring is long and lovely, and where spring flowers are abundant. Here Persephone played with her maidens from day to day till the rocks and valleys rang with the sound of laughter, and gloomy Hades[2] heard it as he sat on his throne in the dark land of the dead. Even his heart of stone was touched by her young beauty, so that he arose in his awful majesty and came up to Olympus[3] to ask Zeus[4] if he might have Persephone to wife. Zeus bowed his head in agreement, and mighty Olympus thundered as he promised.

Thus it came about that as Persephone was gathering flowers with her maidens in the vale of Enna, a marvelous thing happened. Enna was a beautiful valley in whose meadows all the most lovely flowers of the year grew at the same season. There were wild roses, purple crocuses, sweet-scented violets, tall irises, rich narcissus, and white lilies. All these the girl was gathering, yet fair as they were, Persephone herself was fairer by far.

As the maidens went picking and calling to one another across the blossoming meadow, it happened that Persephone strayed apart from the rest. Then, as she looked a little ahead in the meadow, she suddenly beheld the marvelous thing. It was a flower so beautiful that none like it had ever been known. It seemed a kind of narcissus, purple and white, but from a single root there sprang a hundred blossoms, and at the sweet scent of it the very heavens and earth appeared to smile for joy. Without calling to the others, Persephone sprang forward to be the first to pick the precious bloom. As she stretched out her hand, the earth opened in front of her, and she found herself caught in a stranger's arms. Persephone shrieked aloud and struggled, while the armful of flowers cascaded down to earth. However, the dark-eyed Hades was far stronger than she. He swept her into his golden chariot, took the reins of his coal-black horses, and was gone amid the rumbling sound of the closing earth before the other girls in the valley could even come in sight of the spot. When they did get there, nobody was visible. Only the roses and lilies of Persephone lay scattered in wild confusion over the grassy turf.

Marking the Text

1 **Sicily** (sis'ə lē) *n.* an island off the coast of Italy.

2 **Hades** (hā'dēz') *n.* the god of the underworld.

3 **Olympus** (ō lim'pəs) *n.* a mountain where Greek gods lived.

4 **Zeus** (zo͞os) *n.* the supreme god.

Bitter was the grief of Demeter when she heard the news of her daughter's mysterious **fate.** Veiling herself with a dark cloud, she sped, swift as a wild bird, over land and ocean for nine days, searching everywhere and asking all she met if they had seen her daughter. Neither gods nor men had seen her. Even the birds could give no tidings, and Demeter in despair turned to Phoebus Apollo, who sees all things from his chariot in the heavens.

"Yes, I have seen your daughter," said the god at last. "Hades has taken her with the consent of Zeus, that she may dwell in the land of mist and gloom as his queen. The girl struggled and was unwilling, but Hades is far stronger than she."

When she heard this, Demeter fell into deep despair, for she knew she could never rescue Persephone if Zeus and Hades had agreed. She did not care any more to enter the palace of Olympus, where the gods live in joy and feasting and where Apollo plays the lyre[5] while the Muses[6] sing. She took on her the form of an old woman, worn but stately, and wandered about the earth, where there is much sorrow to be seen. At first she kept away from the homes of people, since the sight of little children and happy mothers gave her pain. One day, however, as she sat by the side of a well to rest her weary feet, four girls came down to draw water. They were kind-hearted and charming as they talked with her and concerned themselves about the fate of the homeless stranger-woman who was sitting at their gates. To account for herself, Demeter told them that she was a woman of good family from Crete[7] across the sea, who had been captured by pirates and was to have been sold for a slave. She had escaped as they landed once to cook a meal on shore, and now she was wandering to find work.

▲ Critical Viewing
Does this illustration match the author's style? Explain how.

Vocabulary Builder

fate
(fāt) *n.*

Meaning

Marking the Text

---

[5] **lyre** (līr) *n.* a Greek stringed instrument made like a harp with strings attached to a crossbar.

[6] **Muses** (myo͞oz əs) *n.* goddesses who take care of the arts and music.

[7] **Crete** (krēt) *n.* an island off Greece.

The four girls listened to this story, much impressed by the stately manner of the strange woman. At last they said that their mother, Metaneira, was looking for a nurse for their new-born brother, Demophoon. Perhaps the stranger would come and talk with her. Demeter agreed, feeling a great longing to hold a baby once more, even if it were not her own. She went therefore to Metaneira, who was much struck with the quiet dignity of the goddess and glad to give her charge of her little son. For a while thereafter Demeter was nurse to Demophoon, and his smiles and babble consoled[8] her in some part for her own darling daughter. She began to make plans for Demophoon: He should be a great hero; he should become an **immortal**, so that when he grew up she could keep him with her.

Presently the whole household was amazed at how beautiful Demophoon was growing, the more so as they never saw the nurse feed him anything. Secretly Demeter would anoint him with ambrosia[9], like the gods, and from her breath, as he lay in her lap, he would draw his nourishment. When the night came, she would linger by the great fireside in the hall, rocking the child in her arms while the embers burned low and the people went off to sleep. Then, when all was still, she would stoop quickly down and put the baby into the fire itself. All night long the child would sleep in the red-hot ashes, while his earthly flesh and blood changed slowly into the substance of the immortals. In the morning when people came, the ashes were cold and dead, and by the hearth sat the stranger-woman, gently rocking and singing to the child.

Presently Metaneira became suspicious of the strangeness of it all. What did she know of this nurse but the story she had heard from her daughters? Perhaps the woman was a witch of some sort who wished to steal or transform the boy. In any case it was

8 **consoled** (kan'sōld') *v.* gave comfort to.

9 **ambrosia** (am brō' zhə) *n.* food of the gods.

Marking the Text

Vocabulary Builder

immortal
(i môrt'l) *adj.*

Meaning

while reading your anchor book

Literature in Context
Greek Mythology

Link to Mythology

Ancient Greeks did not always understand nature, so they told stories about gods and goddesses whom they believed controlled events on Earth. Travelers spread these stories while wandering around the country. Greek mythology features all-powerful gods and goddesses who have human feelings and thoughts, but who can control human behavior, weather, and events. The plots feature war, betrayal, love, wanderings, and humans that earn the right to become gods by exemplary behavior. Today, we call these stories myths.

◀ This Greek vase from the sixth century was used at banquets.

wise to be careful. One night, therefore, when she went up to her chamber, she set the door ajar and stood there in the crack silently watching the nurse at the fireside crooning over the child. The hall was very dark, so that it was hard to see clearly, but in a little while the mother beheld the dim figure bend forward. A log broke in the fireplace, a little flame shot up, and there clear in the light lay the baby on top of the fire.

Metaneira screamed loudly and lost no time in rushing forward, but it was Demeter who snatched up the baby. "Fool that you are," she said indignantly to Metaneira, "I would have made your son immortal, but that is now impossible. He shall be a great hero, but in the end he will have to die. I, the goddess Demeter, promise it." With that old age fell from her and she grew in **stature**. Golden hair spread down over her shoulders so that the great hall was filled with light. She turned and went out of the doorway, leaving the baby on the ground and Metaneira too amazed and frightened even to take him up.

All the while that Demeter had been wandering, she had given no thought to her duties as the harvest goddess. Instead she was almost glad that others should suffer because she was suffering. In vain the oxen spent their strength in dragging the heavy plowshare through the soil. In vain did the sower with his bag of grain throw out the even handfuls of white barley in a wide arc as he strode. The greedy birds had a feast off the seed corn that season; or if it started to sprout, sun baked it and rains washed it away. Nothing would grow. As the gods looked down, they saw threatening the earth a famine[10] such as never had been known.

Marking the Text

Vocabulary Builder

stature
(stach′ər) *n.*

Meaning

[10] **famine** (fam′in) *n.* extreme scarcity of food.

Even the offerings to the gods were neglected by despairing men who could no longer spare anything from their dwindling stores.

At last Zeus sent Iris, the rainbow, to seek out Demeter and appeal to her to save mankind. Dazzling Iris swept down from Olympus swift as a ray of light and found Demeter sitting in her temple, the dark cloak still around her and her head bowed on her hand. Though Iris urged her with the messages of Zeus and offered beautiful gifts or whatever powers among the gods she chose, Demeter would not lift her head or listen. All she said was that she would neither set foot on Olympus nor let fruit grow on the earth until Persephone was restored to her from the kingdom of the dead.

At last Zeus saw that he must send Hermes of the golden sandals to bring back Persephone to the light. The messenger found dark-haired Hades sitting upon his throne with Persephone, pale and sad, beside him. She had neither eaten nor drunk since she had been in the land of the dead. She sprang up with joy at the message of Hermes, while the dark king looked gloomier than ever, for he really loved his queen. Though he could not disobey the command of Zeus, he was crafty, and he pressed Persephone to eat or drink with him as they parted. Now, with joy in her heart, she should not refuse all food. Persephone was eager to be gone, but since the king entreated[11] her, she took a pomegranate[12] from him to avoid argument and delay. Giving in to his pleading, she ate seven of the seeds. Then Hermes took her with him, and she came out into the upper air.

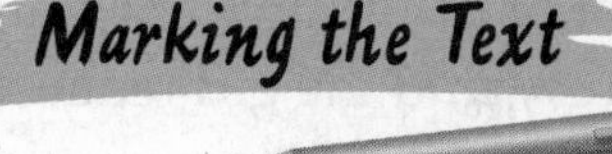

[11] **entreated** (en trēt′ed) *v.* asked in an earnest manner.

[12] **pomegranate** (päm′ ə gran′it) *n.* a fruit filled with many seeds, each surrounded by a reddish sweet pulp.

When Demeter saw Hermes with her daughter, she started up, and Persephone too rushed forward with a glad cry and flung her arms about her mother's neck. For a long time the two caressed each other, but at last Demeter began to question the girl. "Did you eat or drink anything with Hades?" she asked her daughter anxiously, and the girl replied:

"Nothing until Hermes released me. Then in my joy I took a pomegranate and ate seven of its seeds."

"Alas," said the goddess in dismay, "my daughter, what have you done? The Fates[13] have said that if you ate anything in the land of shadow, you must return to Hades and rule with him as his queen. However, you ate not the whole pomegranate, but only seven of the seeds. For seven months of the year, therefore, you must dwell in the underworld, and the remaining five you may live with me."

Thus the Fates had **decreed**, and even Zeus could not alter their law. For seven months of every year, Persephone is lost to Demeter and rules pale and sad over the dead. At this time Demeter mourns, trees shed their leaves, cold comes, and the earth lies still and dead. But when, in the eighth month, Persephone returns, her mother is glad and the earth rejoices. The wheat springs up, bright, fresh, and green in the plowland. Flowers unfold, birds sing, and young animals are born. Everywhere the heavens smile for joy or weep sudden showers of gladness upon the springing earth.

[13] **Fates** (fāts) *n.* three goddesses who rule over the life and death of humans.

Marking the Text

Vocabulary Builder

decreed
(dē krēd') *v.*

Meaning

Vocabulary Builder

After you read, *review the words you decided to add to your vocabulary. Write the meaning of words you have learned in context. Look up the other words in a dictionary, glossary, thesaurus, or electronic resource.*

Thinking About the Selection

The Origin of the Seasons

1 **Apply** In the chart below, list words and phrases that show different techniques the author used to create her writing style.

Example	Technique and Style
"Hades has taken her with the consent of Zeus, that she may dwell in the land of mist and gloom as his queen."	The dialogue reflects the style of the myth and makes the story feel like it takes place in another time and place.

2 **Analyze** How does Demeter feel when Hades takes her daughter? How do her feelings contribute to the mood of the story?

____

____

____

3 **Distinguish** Many English words come from Greek and Roman myths. For example *Vulcan* is the god of fire, from which the English word *volcano* is derived. Use a dictionary or online resource to find which mythological god these words come from.

January: ________ is the god of ____________________.

Cereal: ________ is the goddess of ____________________.

Write Answer the following questions in your Reader's Journal.

4 **Discuss** Why is it important to know about myths and the cultures that created them?

5 **Apply** Describe the author's mood in your Anchor Book. What describing words, dialogue, or sensory language reflect the mood?

while reading your anchor book

3-11 Literary Analysis

Persuasive Writing

When people feel strongly about a subject, they often want to persuade others to feel the same way. Strong feelings or beliefs alone, however, may not be enough to change someone's mind. Writers and speakers need to offer good reasons and facts to support their views—and to convince their audience.

Literary Terms

In **persuasive writing,** an author tries to convince readers to agree with his or her view, or to take action for or against something.

An author can use different tools or methods to persuade an audience. Below is a list of some of these tools.

Tools of Persuasion

Opinions are statements based on feelings or beliefs. They cannot be proven.
Example: Book clubs are lots of fun.

Facts are true statements containing details or other information that can be proven.
Example: Studies show that people in book clubs read more.

Humor is a light or witty approach to a subject. Authors and speakers may use humor and **personification**—giving human traits to nonhuman things—to get their **audience** to pay attention to a serious message.
Example: These books are crying out to be discussed!

Some authors use **propaganda,** or misleading information, to promote their message and get people to change their opinion. It's important to recognize—and not be influenced by—propaganda.
Example: You're not cool if you're not in a book club.

Ethical appeals stir the reader's feelings of justice or fairness.
Example: It's only fair for the school to offer a book club for its eager readers.

Emotional appeals try to make the reader feel sympathy for a cause or an idea.
Example: What will our poor students do without a book club?

Directions Read the following example of persuasive writing. Then answer the questions.

Wash, Don't Spread Germs

I'm about to reveal three words that could transform your life. Are you ready? Okay, then: *Wash your hands.*

Don't get me wrong. I'm not suggesting that you scrub until the skin peels. Nor am I advocating that you lather up every hour on the hour. My recommendation is this: Gently cleanse, at specific times of the day.

Figuring out when to wash your hands doesn't require much thought. Do it before meals. Do it after you sneeze into your hands or blow your nose. Wash after spending time in public places, such as a bus or grocery store. Last, but certainly not least, wash your hands after any visit to the bathroom.

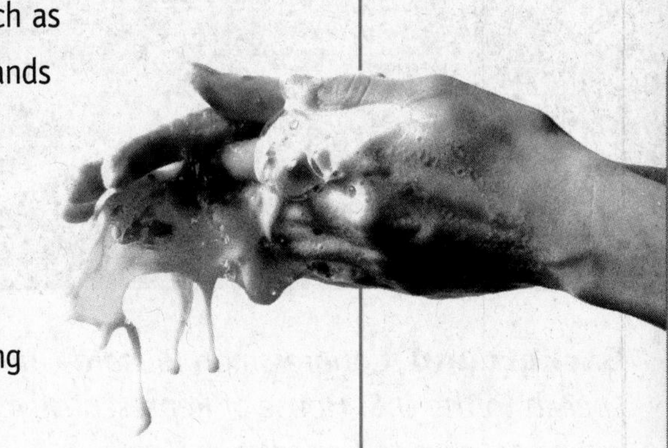

Washing hands isn't like writing a long essay, or running the marathon, or eating a pound of raw spinach. It's quick and easy. It's also very good for you—and for the people you care about. As professionals at the Centers for Disease Control put it, "Keeping hands clean is one of the most important steps we can take to avoid getting sick and spreading germs to others."

1 **Analyze** What is the author's opinion about handwashing?

2 **Identify** What facts does the author use to support this opinion?

3 **Conclude** Why does the author quote the Centers for Disease Control in his or her argument?

4 **Evaluate** Is humor an effective tool for persuading readers to wash their hands? Give your reasons.

In this selection, a member of the U.S. Congress argues that one small part of an all-American sport should remain unchanged. *Guiding Question:* **Why is it important to know as much as you can about a topic before trying to persuade others to agree with you?**

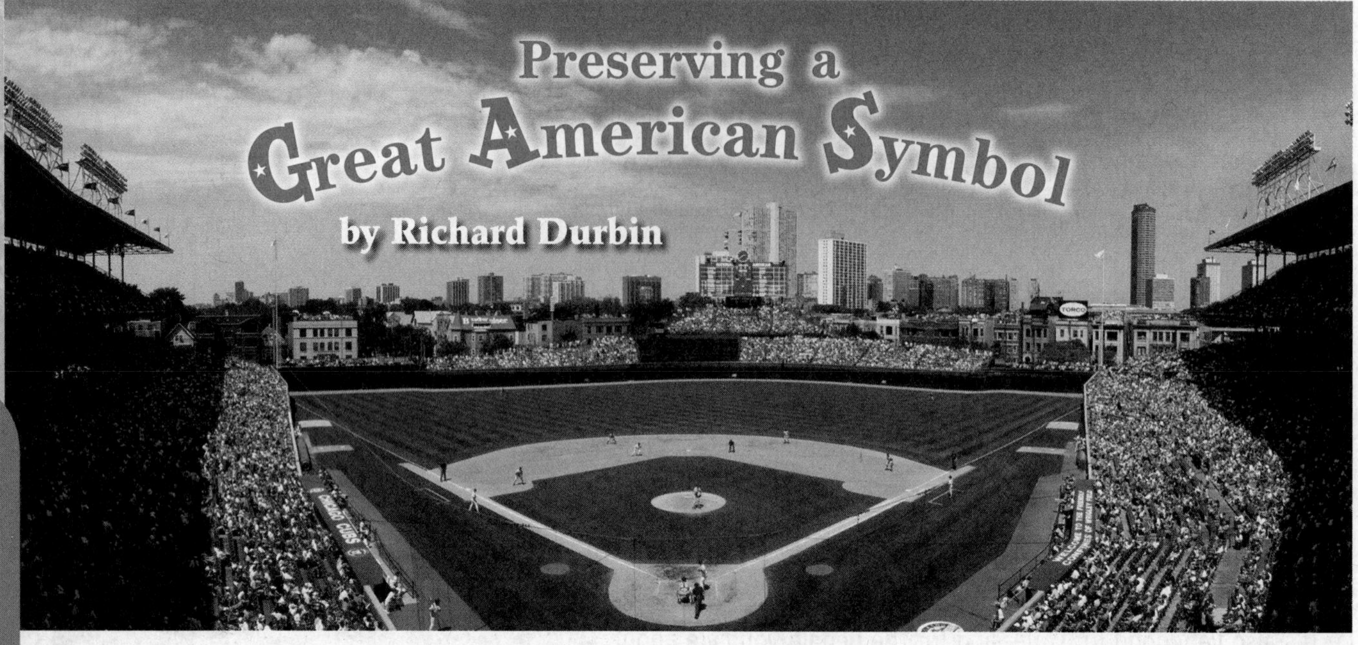

▲ A baseball game at Chicago's Wrigley Field

Preserving a Great American Symbol

by Richard Durbin

Background *Congressman Richard Durbin gave the following speech to the U.S. House of Representatives on July 26, 1989. While most speeches to Congress are serious, Durbin's is humorous, yet persuasive. His humor helps to drive home the point that metal baseball bats should not replace old-fashioned wooden ones.*

Vocabulary Builder

Before you read, *you will discuss the following words. In the Vocabulary Builder box in the margin, use a vocabulary building strategy to make the words your own.*

condemn **extinction** **notion**

As you read, *draw a box around unfamiliar words you could add to your vocabulary. Use context clues to unlock their meaning.*

Marking the Text

Persuasive Language

As you read, *underline facts that Congressman Durbin uses to make his argument. Take notes in the margin about the effects of his persuasion.*

Mr. Speaker, I rise to **condemn** the desecration[1] of a great American symbol. No, I am not referring to flagburning; I am referring to the baseball bat.

[1] **desecration** (des′i krā′shən) *n.* ruin.

Vocabulary Builder

condemn
(kən dem′) *v.*

Meaning

Several experts tell us that the wooden baseball bat is doomed to **extinction**, that major league baseball players will soon be standing at home plate with aluminum bats in their hands. Baseball fans have been forced to endure countless indignities[2] by those who just cannot leave well enough alone: designated hitters, plastic grass, uniforms that look like pajamas, chicken clowns dancing on the base lines, and, of course, the most heinous[3] sacrilege[4], lights in Wrigley Field[5].

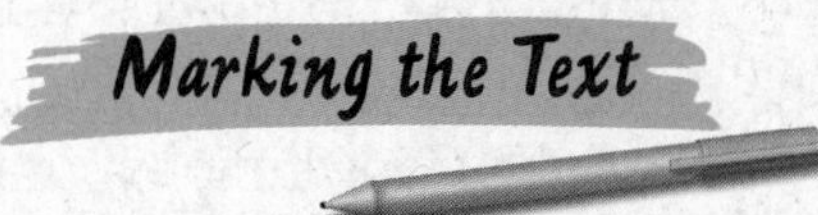

[2] **indignities** (in dig'nə tēz) *n.* examples of shame and dishonor.

[3] **heinous** (hā'nəs) *adj.* wicked.

[4] **sacrilege** (sak'rə lij') *n.* disrespect.

[5] **Wrigley Field** (rig'lē' fēld) *n.* historic baseball field in Chicago, built in 1914.

Vocabulary Builder

extinction
(ek stink'shən) *n.*

Meaning

Marking the Text

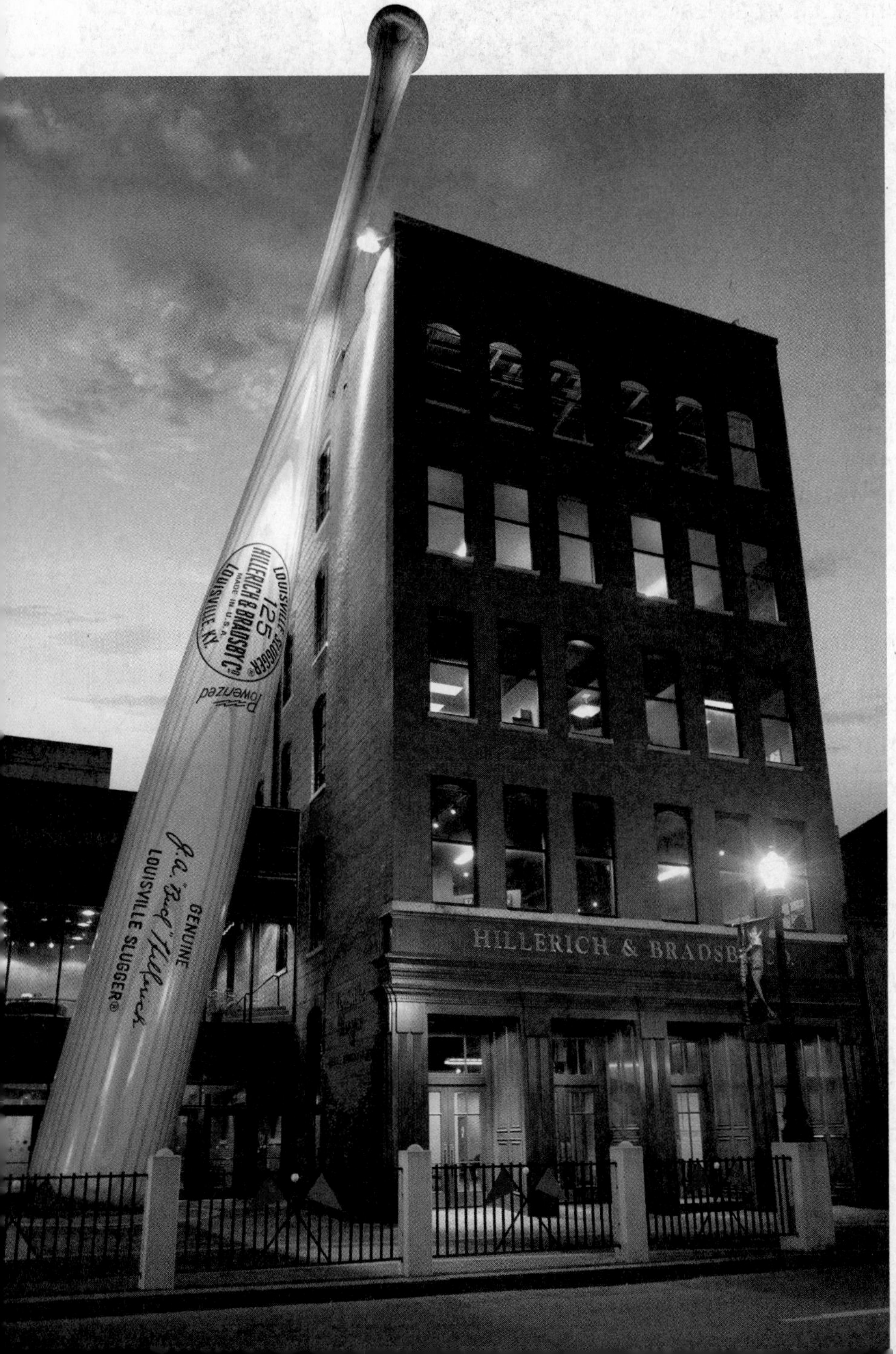

◀ Batter Up!
The Louisville Slugger Museum and Factory in Louisville, Kentucky, is home to the largest bat in the world. It stands 120 feet tall. About one million bats a year are produced at the Louisville factory.

while reading your anchor book

Literature in Context
Sports and the Law

Durbin is exaggerating when he wonders whether it will take a constitutional amendment to keep baseball traditions alive. The Constitution is the basis for the United States government. Any change, or amendment, is serious business. Because the process is so hard, there have only been 27 amendments since 1787, when the Constitution was written.

The speech may not have persuaded representatives to amend the Constitution, but it may have helped Durbin get elected to the U.S. Senate seven years later. Just days before the election, Durbin had a small lead in the race. His staff broadcast the speech during rush hour—and at the peak of baseball season—to reach voters through sports. Days later, Durbin was voted in to the Senate with 56 percent of the vote.

Are we willing to hear the crack of a bat replaced by the dinky ping? Are we ready to see the Louisville Slugger replaced by the aluminum ping dinger? Is nothing sacred?

Please do not tell me that wooden bats are too expensive, when players who cannot hit their weight are being paid more money than the President of the United States.

Please do not try to sell me on the **notion** that these metal clubs will make better hitters.

What will be next? Teflon baseballs? Radar-enhanced gloves? I ask you.

I do not want to hear about saving trees. Any tree in America would gladly give its life for the glory of a day at home plate. I do not know if it will take a constitutional amendment to keep our baseball traditions alive, but if we forsake the great Americana of broken-bat singles and pine tar, we will have certainly lost our way as a nation.

Marking the Text

Vocabulary Builder

notion
(nō'shen) *n.*

Meaning

Vocabulary Builder

After you read, *review the words you decided to add to your vocabulary. Write the meaning of words you have learned in context. Look up the other words in a dictionary, glossary, thesaurus, or electronic resource.*

Thinking About the Selection

Preserving a Great American Symbol

1 **Analyze** List the changes in baseball Durbin mentions in his speech. What can you infer about these changes?

2 **Describe** What details does Durbin use to convince his audience that aluminum bats are not as good as wooden bats?

3 **Evaluate** Do you think that Durbin makes a strong argument in favor of keeping wooden bats? Explain your reasons.

4 **Speculate** Why did Durbin use personification, or human characteristics, to describe trees when referring to them as a source of baseball bats? How did this help him persuade his audience?

5 **Analyze** What are two tools of persuasion that Durbin used in this speech? Support your answer with examples from the text.

Write Answer the following questions in your Reader's Journal.

6 **Explain** Why is it important to know as much as you can about a topic before trying to persuade others to agree with you?

7 **Connect** Find a section in your Anchor Book where a character is voicing an opinion. Do you agree or disagree with that character's opinion? Explain your answer.

while reading your anchor book

3-12 Comparing Literary Works
Mood

People sometimes choose vague words to describe their mood. They say, "I'm in a good mood today," or "I'm in a bad mood." What do they really mean? A good mood might be peaceful, happy, or even joyous. A bad mood might be sad, angry, or depressed. A skillful author carefully chooses words to communicate the **mood,** or the overall feeling, of his or her literary work.

while reading your anchor book

Literary Terms

- **Mood** is the general feeling that a literary work gives the reader. Strong words and vivid details help to set the mood.
- **Setting** is the time and place in which a story occurs. The setting helps to set the mood in a story.

One thing that affects the mood of a literary work or piece of text is the author's choice of details. An author uses details to describe the setting and characters, and also to support his or her message.

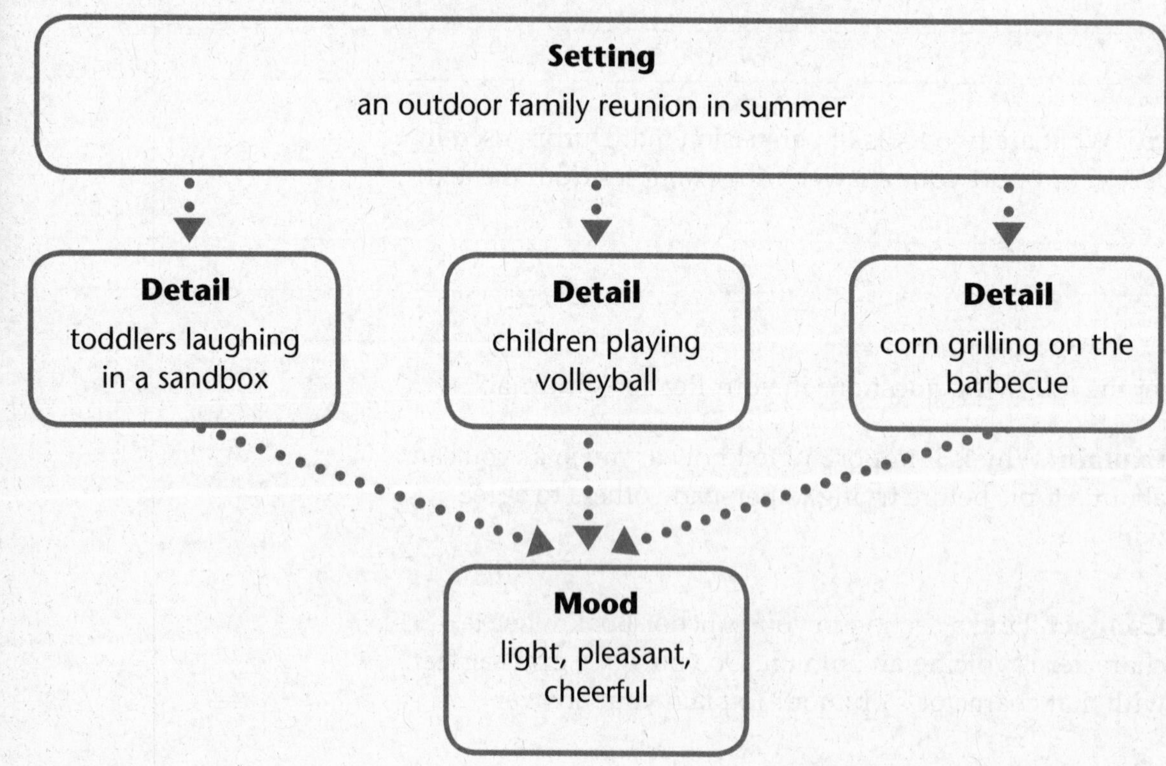

Directions As you read the story, underline details that establish the setting and mood. Then answer the questions.

In the semi-darkness of dawn, Lila slipped out of the camper, carrying a small pail. She planned to surprise her family with fresh blueberries. Everybody said that blueberries grew all over the campgrounds.

Lila headed into the thicket behind the camper, thinking it might lead to a blueberry patch. Snaking vines snatched the sun's early morning rays. The path was nearly as dark as her bedroom at night. Lila walked uncertainly. She had never explored this part of the campsite before.

A clump of ferns rustled. *A squirrel?* she wondered. No, whatever had moved was bigger than a squirrel. Crows, upset by the noise, cawed angrily in a giant gnarled oak. Lila's heart pounded. Sweat beaded over her upper lip. She shouldn't have left the camper alone, so early.

Lila began to run back toward her family. It wasn't far. As she emerged into the sunlight, her foot caught in a root. Lila fell onto a big bush.

Her legs were scratched and she felt like crying. But then she noticed that the bush was full of berries—thick, ripe blueberries.

1 **Recall** What is the story's setting?

2 **Infer** What is the general mood of the story?

3 **Analyze** Which details help to create this mood?

4 **Explain** How do the character's feelings contribute to this mood?

while reading your anchor book

You have read the speech "Preserving a Great American Symbol." Now read "The Talking Skull," and compare the moods of the two selections.
***Guiding Question:* What message does the author want you to know and understand from reading this fable?**

while reading your anchor book

Background *A fable is a simple story with a message or lesson that is stated directly. Like other kinds of folk tales, fables were originally told by word of mouth. "The Talking Skull" is a fable from Cameroon, a country in central-west Africa on the Atlantic Ocean.*

Vocabulary Builder

Before you read, *you will discuss the following words. In the Vocabulary Builder box in the margin, use a vocabulary building strategy to make the words your own.*

scholar **brandishing** **pompous**

As you read, *draw a box around unfamiliar words you could add to your vocabulary. Use context clues to unlock their meaning.*

Marking the Text

Mood

As you read, *underline words that help to set the mood of the fable. Take notes in the margin about the effect the vivid details produce.*

Once a man was walking down the road toward his village. He was not paying attention to anything around him. This man considered himself a **scholar** of life. He was always deep in thought. He liked to think about important things. He did not put his mind to ordinary problems. If it wasn't impossible, or at least very complicated, he didn't care about it at all.

Vocabulary Builder

scholar
(skäl′ er) *n.*

Meaning

This man spent all day looking out over the ocean, and he only noticed things he thought were useful. He didn't notice the beauty of the ocean. The only things he considered were sharks and shipwrecks. He didn't notice the clear blue sky. He was thinking about all the storms that must have been churning far away. He did not notice the wonderful songs of the birds. He only thought about how many of their nests had been robbed. He didn't notice the playful animals swinging through branches or rustling in the grass. He only wondered whether or not the great cats were on the prowl. That was the kind of man he was.

As he walked back toward the village that day, he happened to pass a pile of bones. They were bleached white and they gleamed in the bright sun. He stopped and stared down at them. He was the sort of man who would stop to stare down at a pile of bones. The skull on the pile was resting above all the other bones, and it seemed to be watching the man just as intently as he was watching it.

The man reached out and picked up the skull. He held it one way and then another. He looked gravely into the empty eye sockets and said, "What brought you here, brother?"

"Talking," the skull replied without much interest.

The man was so shocked, he dropped the skull and jumped back. He watched the skull for a few minutes before he managed to stammer[1] out, "You can talk!"

"Yes," said the skull. "Talking is very easy. All you have to do is open up your mouth and out it comes. Talking is easy. Finding something worthwhile to say is not."

The man was amazed. He had never seen a talking skull before, let alone one that could spout[2] such wisdom. "I must take you to the village!" the man exclaimed.

He scooped up the skull and ran as fast as he could. The villagers saw him coming, and a great many of them ran for their homes. You see, he was the kind of man who was always getting busy people into useless conversations when there was work to be done. He never seemed to be quiet, and he never spoke about anything anyone ever wanted to hear.

As he entered the village, he called out to his neighbors, "Come quickly! I have something wonderful to show you!" No one came.

The man was so excited that he did not even realize that the few people in sight were moving away from him. "Put down whatever you are doing, everyone! I have a marvelous mystery to show all of you, the likes of which you have never before seen!"

---

1 **stammer** (stam′ ər) *v.* to repeat the same sound several times while trying to say a word.

2 **spout** (spout) *v.* to speak rapidly.

Marking the Text

while reading your anchor book

When the man said the word "mystery," you can be sure he got the attention of some of the villagers. They started poking their heads out of their houses. Women left their yams cooking, men put down their digging sticks, and children stopped their playing. They all began to gather around the man.

When he saw that he had everyone's attention, he drew out the skull. He could not have prepared himself for what happened next.

Everyone stared at the skull for a moment. Then they all started yelling.

"Mama! What is he doing?" cried a little boy.

"How dare you bring that thing here!" his mother howled, waving a spoon.

"Somebody do something!" said another, clutching her child.

"Send him away!" demanded a third mother.

The men who still had gardening tools in their hands started waving them.

▲ **Critical Viewing**
How does this illustration help you predict what the villagers' reactions will be to the man with the talking skull?

Marking the Text

"Move out of the way!" yelled a man with a digging stick.

"Somebody get the chief!" said an old man holding his grandson's hand.

There was so much commotion[3], the chief came to see what was happening.

"What is going on?" the chief roared. He was a very orderly chief, and he did not like all this yelling and **brandishing** of gardening tools in the middle of the village.

All the people were silent except for one villager. He stood up and pointed to the man with the skull.

"This man told us he had something to show us. Then he pulled out that awful skull. We thought he was trying to call the Dark Spirits to the village, and we were trying to stop him."

"Oh," said the chief, eyeing the man with the skull. "And were you going to call Dark Spirits to my village?"

"Certainly not!" the scholar declared, glad that the chief was there. He was sure the chief would understand this intellectual[4] matter.

"Then what were you doing?" the chief asked with curiosity.

"Well," the man said in a **pompous** voice, "I was on my way home from the ocean when I came across a pile of bones. On top of the heap was this skull. It spoke to me! I brought it here to share this wonder with the village."

The chief did not look convinced.

"I'll show you," the man said, raising the skull so that it looked at the chief. "Say something to the chief," he commanded.

The skull said nothing. The chief frowned.

"Speak!" the man said. "I command you!"

The skull remained silent. One of the children laughed.

"Speak!" he said. "You must speak!" The man started getting nervous.

The skull said nothing. The man begged and pleaded with the skull. The skull remained silent. The people began to get angry again, and the chief got angry right along with them.

"You are always a troublemaker in my village, and now you come here with this nonsense!" The chief and the people had had enough. They took the skull from the man, found the mound of bones he had taken it from, and put it back there.

That very day the villagers held a meeting with the chief and decided to throw the man out of their village. They watched him collect his few belongings and said to him, "Since you found that skull so much company, why don't you go live with it!"

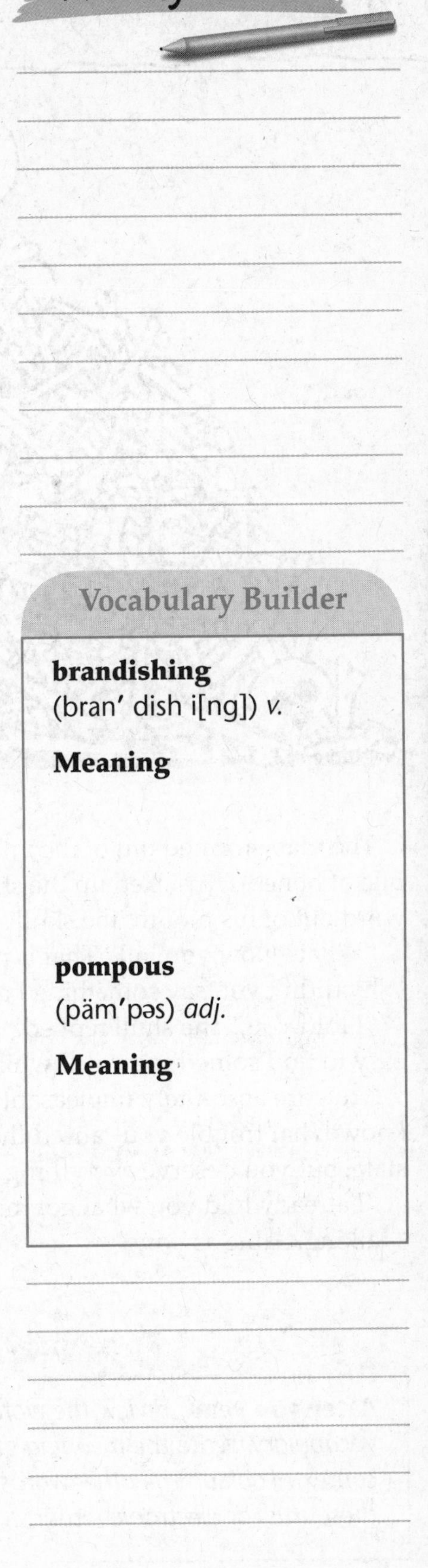

---

[3] **commotion** (kə mō' shən) *n.* noisy rushing around; confusion.

[4] **intellectual** (in'tə lek' cho͞o əl) *adj.* requiring thought and understanding.

The man stormed out of the village and down the road to the pile of bones. He picked up the skull. Before he could get one word out of his mouth, the skull said, "Sorry about that."

"What? Now you talk! That is not going to do me much good! Why didn't you say something back in the village?"

"I told you," the skull replied. "It is easy to talk. It is not always easy to find something worthwhile to say."

"You are absolutely unpleasant!" the man screamed. "I don't know what trouble you caused that brought you to this sorry state, but you deserve everything you got!"

"I already told you what got me into trouble," the skull replied. "Talking. Same as you."

▲ **Critical Viewing**
How does this illustration help you understand the message the fable is trying to portray?

Marking the Text

Vocabulary Builder

After you read, *review the words you will add to your vocabulary. Write the meaning of words you have learned in context. Look up the other words in a dictionary, glossary, thesaurus, or electronic resource.*

while reading your anchor book

Thinking About the Selections

Preserving a Great American Symbol *and* The Talking Skull

1 **Analyze** "The Talking Skull" is set in an African village. Which details help the reader to understand what this village is like?

____

____

2 **Describe** What words describe the mood of "Preserving a Great American Symbol" and "The Talking Skull"? Fill in the details to help you identify a similar mood in the two selections.

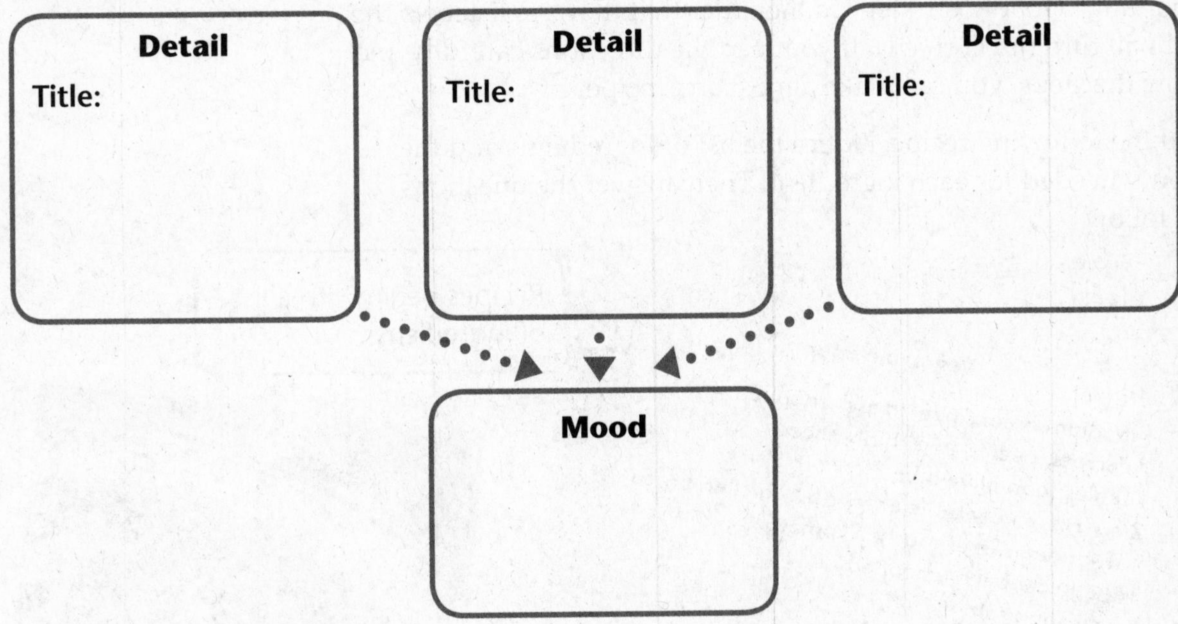

3 **Contrast** Both selections personify objects, or give them human characteristics. Contrast the use of personification in the two selections.

____

____

____

Write Answer the following questions in your Reader's Journal.

4 **Draw Conclusions** What message does the author want you to know and understand from reading this fable?

5 **Compare and Contrast** Compare and contrast the mood of "The Talking Skull" or "Preserving a Great American Symbol" with the mood of your Anchor Book. Use details from both texts to support your answers.

while reading your anchor book

3-13 Analyzing an Informational Text
Reading a Recipe

Maps, Web sites, schedules, how-to booklets, and recipes all have something in common. They are all informational texts—that is, they all present facts or explain a process.

You've probably seen someone baking a cake by following a recipe. A **recipe** explains how to make something to eat or drink. The ingredients tell you what you need and how much to use. These are listed after the recipe's title. Next come the steps in the process. It is important to follow the steps in the order that they are listed so the food will turn out correctly. If you read the directions carefully and follow the steps, you can make almost any recipe.

Read the following recipe. Notice the list of ingredients and the amount needed for each ingredient. Then answer the questions that follow.

Vegetable Soup

1 medium onion, peeled and chopped
3 carrots, peeled and thinly sliced
1 tablespoon olive oil
2 quarts of vegetable or low-fat chicken broth
1 15-ounce can of crushed tomatoes
1/2 cup cabbage, chopped
1 teaspoon salt
1/2 teaspoon pepper
1 teaspoon dried thyme
1 tablespoon fresh or dried parsley
3/4 cup fresh or frozen peas
1 cup frozen corn
3/4 cup green beans, cut into 1-inch pieces

1. In large pot, over low heat, cook onion and carrots in olive oil until soft, but not browned.
2. Add broth, crushed tomatoes, cabbage, salt, pepper, thyme, and parsley. Simmer for 25 minutes, stirring occasionally.
3 Add peas, corn, and green beans. Simmer another 5–10 minutes until frozen vegetables thaw.

Makes 6-8 servings

Recipes begin with a list of ingredients.

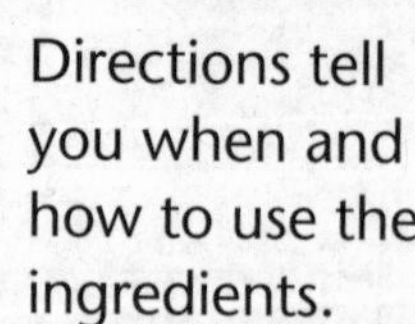

Directions tell you when and how to use the ingredients.

A recipe tells you how many people it serves.

Thinking About the Selection

Reading a Recipe

1 **Explain** Why is it important to read recipe directions before you begin to cook?

2 **Describe** Why does cooking require you to pay close attention to details, such as measurements and time?

3 **Predict** What would happen if you didn't follow the directions in the correct order?

4 **Speculate** What do you think will happen if you leave an ingredient out of a recipe?

5 **Apply** Place a number from 1 to 6 on each line to order the steps you take in making vegetable soup.

_______ Buy ingredients.

_______ Add frozen peas and corn.

_______ Cook onion and carrots.

_______ Add crushed tomatoes.

_______ Read recipe.

_______ Simmer until frozen vegetables are heated.

6 **Create** Complete the following task on a separate sheet of paper. What's your favorite sandwich? Write a recipe so others will know how to make a sandwich just like it. Be creative in your instructions. Add drawings or diagrams if you wish.

while reading your anchor book

3-14 Language Coach
Grammar and Spelling

Adverbs

Authors liven up their writing by using words that describe other words. **Adverbs** are words that do this. An adverb can modify, or describe, a verb, an adjective, or another adverb. Look at the sentences below. Which gives the reader a better picture of what is happening?

Adverb Modifying a Verb
The crowd cheered for the team. The crowd cheered **enthusiastically** for the team. [The adverb *enthusiastically* modifies the verb *cheered*.]
Adverb Modifying an Adjective
I thought the movie was sad. I thought movie was **extremely** sad. [The adverb *extremely* modifies the adjective *sad*.]
Adverb Modifying an Adverb
He reads slowly. He reads **very** slowly. [The adverb *very* modifies the adverb *slowly*.]

Go Online
Learn More
Visit: PHSchool.com
Web Code: exp-6305

Author's Craft

Adverbs can have a significant influence on the mood of a piece of writing, but how much difference can one word make? Turn to "Ice Dogs" beginning on page 216. Choose a sentence, and add an adverb to convey a strong mood. Then try replacing your adverb with another adverb that conveys the opposite mood.

Directions An adverb and the part of speech it modifies are given. Write a sentence using both the adverb and its modifier.

1 adverb *so* modifies *tasty* (adjective)

____

2 adverb *usually* modifies *play* (verb)

____

3 adverb *very* modifies *quickly* (adverb)

____

Adverbs are used to tell different things about a verb, an adjective, or another adverb. They answer several questions when they modify a word. The chart below shows some examples.

Where?	I live close to town.
When?	Yesterday I went on a long bike ride.
How?	Luisa sang beautifully.
To what extent?	The victory made the coach very happy.

Go Online
Learn More
Visit: PHSchool.com
Web Code: exp-6306

Directions The verb in each sentence below is underlined. Fill in the blank with an adverb that modifies the verb. The hints in parentheses tell you what question the adverb should answer.

4 Coach blew the whistle____________________. (How?)

5 The team will play its first match ____________________. (When?)

6 The plane flew __________________ low in the sky. (To what extent?)

7 The field is__________________ from my house. (Where?)

Directions Rewrite each sentence using an adverb that will make the sentence more interesting.

8 She walked across the street.

____

9 The pizza was hot.

____

10 I sent the letter.

____

11 The puppies fought with each other.

____

12 I swam in the ocean.

____

Coordinating Conjunctions and Interjections

Learn More
Visit: PHSchool.com
Web Code: exp-6307

Coordinating conjunctions are connectors. Sometimes they connect single words. Other times they connect groups of words or even full sentences. Some of the most common conjunctions are *and, or, but, nor, for, yet,* and *so.*

What the Conjunction Connects	Example Sentence
words	Rupert **and** I watch every baseball game.
groups of words	I like swimming in the lake **or** playing on the beach.
sentences	My sister likes skating, **but** I prefer biking.

Author's Craft

Interjections are especially useful in creating realistic dialogue. Reread "The Origin of the Seasons" beginning on page 222. Choose a scene from the story and write a conversation that could have occurred between two of the characters. Use appropriate interjections.

Writers use different kinds of words to express feelings and emotions. **Interjections** are words that express strong feelings or excitement.

Example *Oh gosh,* I made the same mistake again!

There are many interjections. Some common ones are *ah, aha, golly, hey, oh, oops, whew, wow,* and *yikes.*

Directions Underline the conjunction in each sentence. Write what the conjunction connects—words, groups of words, or sentences.

1. My brother and I are twins.

____

2. The novel was long but very interesting

____

Directions Write a sentence using the conjunction and the interjection.

3. conjunction: *and* + interjection: *wow*

____

4. conjunction: *yet* + interjection: *gosh*

____

5. conjunction: *and* + interjection: *shh*

____

Combining Sentences Using Coordinating Conjunctions

Learn More
Visit: PHSchool.com
Web Code: exp-6308

Writing that uses too many short, simple sentences can feel choppy and boring to a reader.

Short and Choppy We went to the store. We went to the park.

Combined We went to the store and the park.

You can make sentences longer and more interesting by joining them with coordinating conjunctions. Not all sentences can be joined with coordinating conjunctions. Here are a few rules to follow when joining sentences.

- To combine sentences with a coordinating conjunction, make sure the two sentences are closely related. If the sentences share the same subject, do not use a comma before the conjunction.
- Use a comma, plus *and, or,* or *but,* if the conjunction connects two independent clauses, or sentences that have different subjects.

Related Sentences	Combined
I bought the rabbit cage. My sister bought the rabbit food.	I bought the rabbit cage, **and** my sister bought the rabbit food.
Ricardo likes football. Shawna prefers soccer.	Ricardo likes football, **but** Shawna prefers soccer.
We could go swimming. We could watch TV.	We could go swimming **or** watch TV.
Jenna got her chores done. She was able to go to the party.	Jenna got her chores done, **so** she was able to go to the party.

Author's Craft

Good writers use a variety of methods to combine sentences. Scan "Preserving a Great American Symbol" beginning on page 232. Find an example of sentences that have been combined without using a coordinating conjunction. Separate the sentences and recombine them using a coordinating conjunction.

Directions Rewrite the following paragraph using coordinating conjunctions to combine sentences where appropriate.

Dana Goodman is talented. She is friendly. She enjoys painting. She likes to create charcoal drawings. The student vice-president moved to a different school. Dana joined the student government to fill his place. In her two months as vice-president, Dana formed an art club. She also formed a community-service club that volunteers at the animal shelter.

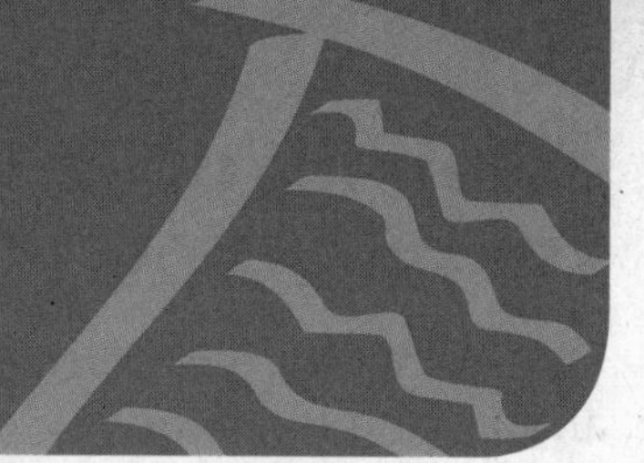

3-15 Writer's Workshop
Persuasion: Persuasive Essay

Do you ever wish everyone agreed with you? One way to make that happen is to write an essay that convinces people of your point of view. In this workshop, you will write a **persuasive essay** designed to persuade others to share your position on an issue.

Your essay should include the following elements.

- a clear focus statement that presents a position on an issue
- facts, examples, and reasons that support your position
- powerful language that appeals to your audience
- evidence and arguments to address readers' concerns
- a clear organization, including an introduction, body, and conclusion
- error-free writing, including correct use of adverbs, coordinating conjunctions, and interjections

Purpose To write a persuasive essay about a topic that matters to you

Audience Your teacher and your classmates

Prewriting—Plan It Out

You will do your best writing if you choose a topic that you care about. Follow these steps to plan your essay.

Choose your topic. Make a list of issues you feel strongly about, such as "Why trees are important." The issues you choose can involve different things in your life, such as your school, your town, or your friends. Choose one issue as the topic of your essay.

Prepare arguments. Make a two-column chart with arguments for and against your position. By considering different points of view, you may create a stronger case. Use the chart on the right as an example.

For	Against
Trees filter out impurities, cleansing the air.	The amount of pollution trees filter is small and makes little difference.

Gather details. You must be knowledgeable about your topic in order to successfully persuade others to agree with your opinion. Collect facts, statistics, quotations, personal observations, and other information that supports your position. Be sure to take notes on the sources of your information, because you will need to give credit for any ideas or words that are not your own.

Drafting—Get It on Paper

The following steps will help make your essay focused.

Organize your thoughts. Include your focus statement—a sentence that states your issue and expresses your opinion—in your introduction, then support it in the main body. Organize supporting information into paragraphs. Make sure each paragraph contains one reason for your position. Conclude with a restatement of your position.

Use persuasive techniques. You can use a variety of techniques to keep your audience interested and to help you convince them. Here are a few different techniques you can use.

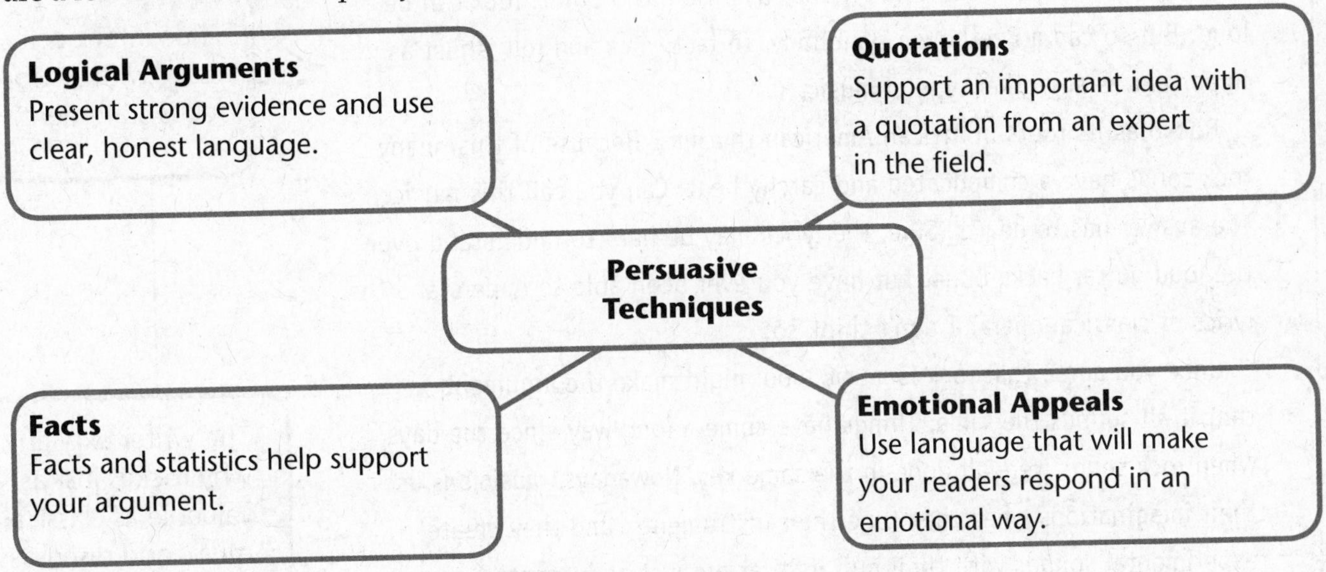

Persuasive Techniques

Logical Arguments
Present strong evidence and use clear, honest language.

Quotations
Support an important idea with a quotation from an expert in the field.

Facts
Facts and statistics help support your argument.

Emotional Appeals
Use language that will make your readers respond in an emotional way.

Target your audience. It helps to know something about your readers' ages and their knowledge of your topic. If you do, you can develop your draft with this information in mind.

Revising—Make It Better

Use the following strategy to make your draft even stronger.

Add more support. Review your draft. Strengthen a weak argument by using a fact, a statistic, or a quotation.

Student Model: Adding Support

```
We need better sidewalks on Johnson Street. ~~Lots of students~~ [At least 50 students]
walk down that street every day on the way to school.
```

The student adds a statistic to show how many students use the street.

Peer Review Read your essay aloud to a partner or small group. Do your listeners understand your arguments? Discuss your essay, and make changes based on the feedback you receive.

Directions Read this student's persuasive essay as a model for your own.

Student Model: Writing

Go Online
Student Model
Visit: PHSchool.com
Web Code: exr-6302

Tyler Miller, Cape Girardeau, MO

Not All Music Has to Be Classical

My dad always complains whenever I play something from my rock and roll collection. "Turn down that noise," he says. He has a point: rock can be loud. But so can a Beethoven symphony. In fact, rock and roll is just as important as any other type of music.

The writer begins his essay with a strong focus statement.

Rock has its roots in African American rhythms. Because of this, many rock songs have a complicated and catchy beat. Can you call this music? The answer has to be *yes*. Sure, the lyrics may be hard to understand over the loud guitar background, but have you ever been able to understand the lyrics of classical opera? I don't think so.

Once you agree that rock is music, you might make the argument that it all sounds the same. Things have come a long way since the days when rock songs were all done in the same key. Nowadays, musicians use their imaginations when they tune their instruments, and they create experimental sounds with their guitars that are just as intricate as any classical composer's compositions.

The writer explains why rock is just as valuable as classical music and discusses what the two have in common.

Even though it has ancient roots, rock and roll hasn't been treated as a musical art form for as long as classical music. But its themes are for everyone: making the world a better place, conflicts within yourself or with others, or just plain growing up. It can make you feel sad, mellow, or joyful about living. But oftentimes, people who don't understand rock disapprove or ban it. Many people may not realize this, but some older forms of classical music were misunderstood, too.

The author considers the audience's point of view.

I think anyone who is open-minded about music can appreciate both classical and rock music. For a richer life, you need them both. To ignore either type of music would be unfair. I listen to both types of music because each one makes a contribution to my life. Classical music is like an elegant meal, and rock is like a hot fudge sundae with toppings galore. Both are uniquely delicious. So, the next time you sit down to listen to a CD, I invite you to open your ears and consider rock music.

Strong images help readers understand the writer's position.

Editing—Be Your Own Language Coach

Before you hand in your persuasive essay, review it for grammatical errors, especially your use of adverbs, conjunctions, and interjections. Refer to a language or style handbook if you have usage questions.

Publishing—Share It!

When you publish your work, you produce it for a specific audience. Consider one of the following ideas to share your writing.

Send it out. E-mail your persuasive essay to friends and family. Write the title in the subject line. Ask them for their honest opinions.

Stage a debate. Read your essay aloud, inviting your class to debate it with you. Bring additional facts and ideas to help support your position.

Reflecting on Your Writing

1. Respond to the following questions on a separate sheet of paper and hand it in with your final draft. What new insights did you gain about the form of a persuasive essay by writing one? What did you do well? What do you need more work on?

2. **Rubric for Self-Assessment** Assess your essay's strengths and weaknesses using the criteria. For each question, circle a rating.

CRITERIA	RATING SCALE				
	NOT VERY				VERY
IDEAS How well did you state your position and support it with reasons and evidence?	1	2	3	4	5
ORGANIZATION How organized is your essay?	1	2	3	4	5
VOICE How well do you use lively language?	1	2	3	4	5
WORD CHOICE How well do you use emotional appeal?	1	2	3	4	5
SENTENCE FLUENCY How well do you vary your sentence structure?	1	2	3	4	5
CONVENTIONS How correct is your grammar, especially your use of adverbs, conjunctions, and interjections?	1	2	3	4	5

3-16 Discussing Your Anchor Book
Literature Circles

Author's Purpose You have learned that authors write for many reasons. They might write to inform, entertain, reflect, or persuade. In this Literature Circle, you and your group members will discuss the author's purpose in your Anchor Book.

The author's purpose is the main reason the author writes a work. Certain details in the text can help you identify the author's purpose.

If the text contains...		...then the purpose is most likely to...
facts, statistics, technical terms, and no opinions	→	inform
facts, statistics, and opinions	→	persuade
stories about experiences	→	entertain
opinions and thoughts	→	reflect on an experience

1 ON YOUR OWN

Choose a passage from your Anchor Book. Identify three details and what they contain, and write them in the graphic organizer. Then determine the purpose of each detail.

Detail From Your Anchor Book	Detail Contains	Purpose of Detail

Draw Conclusions Based on the details you found, what do you think the author's purpose is for writing this passage?

____

____

2 WORK WITH YOUR GROUP

With your group members, discuss these questions.

1 **Discuss** Discuss your analysis of the passage from your Anchor Book. Consider these questions.

- How did the details each member chose help to identify the author's purpose for the passage?
- Did your group members agree on the author's purpose?

2 **Draw Conclusions** Discuss the following questions with your group.

- What is the author's purpose for writing the book?
- Did the author achieve this purpose? Why or why not?

3 **Evaluate** Sometimes an author does not succeed in carrying out his or her purpose. Have a volunteer read the passage below. Then, with your group, fill out the graphic organizer to determine the purpose of the passage.

> My neighbor and I used to venture into the woods to catch bullfrogs. We wanted these croaking amphibians as pets so badly. A frog starts its life underwater. Many species of frogs lay their eggs in jellied clusters right in the water. I bet it's interesting to watch them lay eggs. When the baby frogs hatch, they don't look like frogs at all. They have tails and swim like fish. I like to watch fish swim.

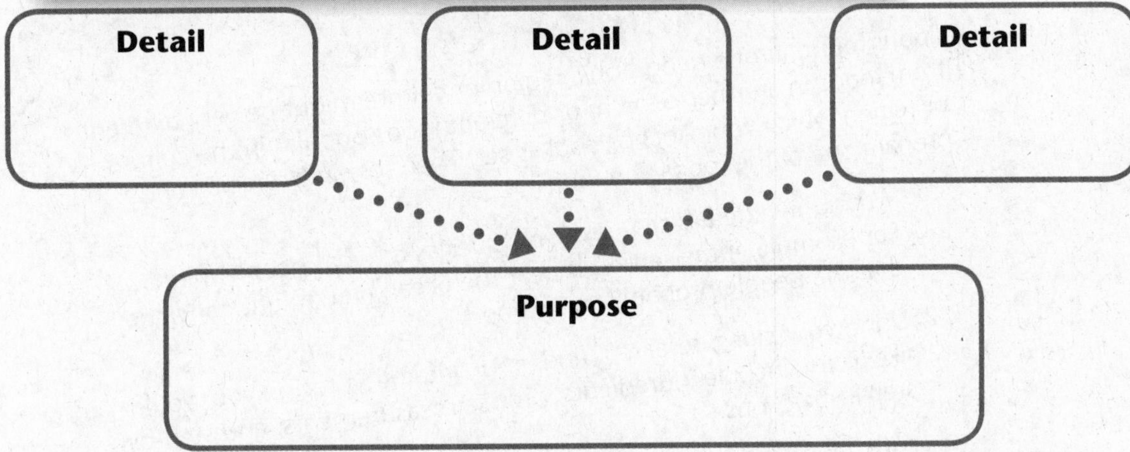

Underline details in the passage that stray from the main purpose. With your group members, determine how this author could have stayed focused.

while reading your anchor book

3-17 Connecting to Your Anchor Book

Anchor Book Projects

Now that you have completed reading your Anchor Book, get creative! Choose one of the following projects.

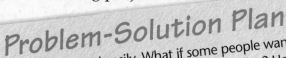

A Problem-Solution Plan

Not all problems can be solved easily. What if some people want to build a new ball field, and others living nearby are against the idea? How do you solve the problem? You can start by discussing the problem, writing out a plan, discussing the plan, and suggesting a solution. By using these steps, you can draw up a plan to solve a problem in your Anchor Book.

1. Think about a problem raised in your Anchor Book. Write down the problem. Write any reactions the characters have—or the author has—toward the problem.
2. Using these reactions and ideas, write a plan that would offer a solution to the problem. The first part of your proposal should describe the problem. The second part should offer a solution.

Your problem-solution proposal should include the following elements.

- a problem from your Anchor Book
- a clear description of the problem using examples from the text
- a realistic and workable solution that fully addresses the problem

B Find a Recipe

Foods found in one geographic region or culture might be very different from foods in another. Search for different foods popular in the culture or region which your Anchor Book is set. Then research a recipe and prepare one of the foods you find.

1. Write down details that give you clues as to what people might eat. For example, if the setting is near the ocean, you might conclude that the people probably eat seafood.
2. Using your clues, research, find, and write out a recipe you would like to try. Include ingredients, precise measurements, and step-by-step instructions.
3. With an adult, prepare your recipe in the school kitchen or at home. Then share your creation with your classmates.

Your research and recipe should include the following elements.

- details related to a culture or region discussed in your Anchor Book
- a clearly written recipe that includes ingredients, measurements, and instructions

Persuade Your Audience

C

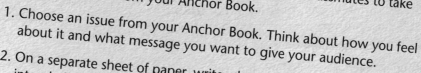

Every day you probably spend some time trying to persuade someone to let you do something. You may try to convince your friends to join you somewhere. You can use those same skills to create a persuasive speech. In this project, you will try to persuade your classmates to take your side of an issue from your Anchor Book.

1. Choose an issue from your Anchor Book. Think about how you feel about it and what message you want to give your audience.
2. On a separate sheet of paper, write what your issue and your intended message are. Then write your feelings on the issue. Gather facts that support your side and write them below your message.
3. Write a persuasive speech using the methods and techniques you learned when you wrote a persuasive essay. Have a partner read your speech to determine how effective it is.

Your persuasive speech should include the following elements.

- a clear and well-defined point of view on your issue
- a clearly communicated message on your issue
- error-free writing that contains elements of persuasive writing

Free-Choice Book Reflection

You have completed your free-choice book. Before you take your test, read the following instructions to write a brief reflection of your book.

My free-choice book is ______________________________.

The author is ______________________________.

1 Would you recommend this book to a friend? Yes _____ No _____
Briefly explain why.

____

____

Write Answer the following question in your Reader's Journal.

2 **Compare and Contrast** *What is important to know?* Compare and contrast how your Anchor Book and free-choice book help to answer this question. Use specific details from both books to support your answer.

Unit Review
Standardized Test Practice

Answer the questions below to check your understanding of this unit's skills.

Reading Skills: Main Idea

Read this selection. Then answer the questions that follow.

> Becoming a teacher is a job that many people grow up wanting to do. The steps to becoming a teacher are challenging, however. If you plan to be a teacher, you must graduate from college, complete education courses, and spend time practice teaching. A middle school or high school teacher often has to take courses in a special area, such as language arts, science, or math. A person who wants to teach at a four-year college or university has to take courses after they graduate from college. That may make a total of six or more years of study.

1 Which of the following is the **main idea** of the passage?

A. Schooling for college or university teaching may take six or more years of study.

B. People have to spend a lot of time studying to become a teacher.

C. Some teachers study math, science, or language arts.

D. University professors are inexperienced teachers.

2 What could you expect to read about in the next paragraph of this passage?

F. dress codes for teachers and students

G. how to become an engineering teacher

H. how most teachers do not usually like their work

J. details about daily life as a teacher

Reading Skills: Author's Purpose

Read this selection. Then answer the questions that follow.

> Marbles have been around for thousands of years. How do we know this? Archaeologists have discovered them in ancient burial sites in Egypt, North America, and Aztec pyramids. The oldest marbles date back to 3,000 B.C. and were made of semiprecious stones. Romans gave marbles as gifts at Saturnalia—the winter solstice holiday. Children have been playing the game of marbles for thousands of years.

3 What is the **author's purpose** in the passage?

A. to inform

B. to entertain

C. to persuade

D. to reflect

4 Which of these clues tells you the author's purpose?

F. marbles are fun to play

G. the passage contains facts

H. semiprecious stones are valuable

J. the author uses a rhetorical question

Literary Analysis: Elements of Nonfiction

Read this selection. Then answer the questions that follow.

"The Stars and Stripes Forever!" had always reminded me of summer. Every Fourth of July, the smashing cymbal, blasting brass, and trilling piccolo caused us to rise up out of our seats cheering! Since very few people in the crowd knew the more traditional words to the song, we would serenade the community band with "Be Kind to Your Web-Footed Friends." We could only guess what Sousa's reaction would be.

5 Which word describes the **mood** of the passage?

A. excited

B. dreamlike

C. formal

D. suspenseful

6 How does the **setting** convey the mood?

F. It is dark and brooding.

G. It is formal.

H. It is festive and colorful.

J. It is told in the first person.

Read this selection and answer the questions that follow.

Childhood obesity is becoming an epidemic. According to the *Journal of Pediatrics*, between 5 and 25 percent of children and teenagers are overweight. Decreased physical activity, eating high-calorie snacks, heredity, and making poor eating choices have each contributed to the disease.

Luckily, childhood eating habits are easier to modify than adult habits. Families can learn to create good habits, such as monitoring television watching and choosing low-fat snacks. In the fight for maintaining a healthy weight, prevention gets better results than weight loss.

7 This is an example of which type of nonfiction writing?

A. expository

B. a flashback

C. cause-and-effect method

D. narrative

8 Which tool of **persuasion** does the author use?

F. ethical appeals

G. opinion

H. facts

J. emotional appeals

9 Write a short essay persuading the reader to start a recycling program in his or her neighborhood.

____

____

____

____

____

____

____

____

Choose the best answer for the following questions.

10 **Descriptive writing** can appeal to ______.

A. the reader's sense of ethics

B. the reader's problem-solving skills

C. the cost of a publication

D. the reader's five senses

11 Which organization pattern would you use to write a recipe?

F. compare-and-contrast

G. chronological

H. problem-and-solution

J. cause-and-effect

Language Skills: Vocabulary

Choose the best answer.

12 Why is it important to learn word **roots?**

A. to find out how to use a word in a sentence

B. to unlock the meaning of a word

C. to identify prefixes and suffixes

D. to find out how a word is spelled

13 The root of a word often comes from ______.

F. an ancient language

G. a modern language

H. another part of speech

J. a thesaurus

14 The root of the word "scribble" is probably

A. scribbling

B. scribere

C. dribble

D. inscription

15 The Latin root *spectare* means

F. to give

G. to want

H. to watch

J. to speak

Language Skills: Grammar

Choose the best answer.

16 Identify the part of speech of the italicized word in the following sentence:

Raphael is *an* excellent student.

A. adverb

B. article

C. adjective

D. present tense

17 Which word correctly completes the following sentence?

I am not feeling ____ today.

F. good

G. well

H. welly

J. goodly

18 An **adverb** can be used to __________.

A. modify action verbs

B. describe a place

C. connect two clauses

D. describe a noun or pronoun

19 Identify the part of speech of the italicized word in the following sentence:

Raphael is an *excellent* student.

F. adverb

G. article

H. adjective

J. past participle

Language Skills: Spelling

Choose the best answer.

20 To add *-ed* to *carry,* you must __________.

A. keep the *y* and add *-ed*

B. change the *y* to *i* and add *-ed*

C. double the *y* and add *-ed*

D. drop the *y* and add *-ed*

21 The plural of *half* is __________.

F. halves

G. whole

H. halfs

J. halfes

THE BIG ?

Do we need words to communicate?

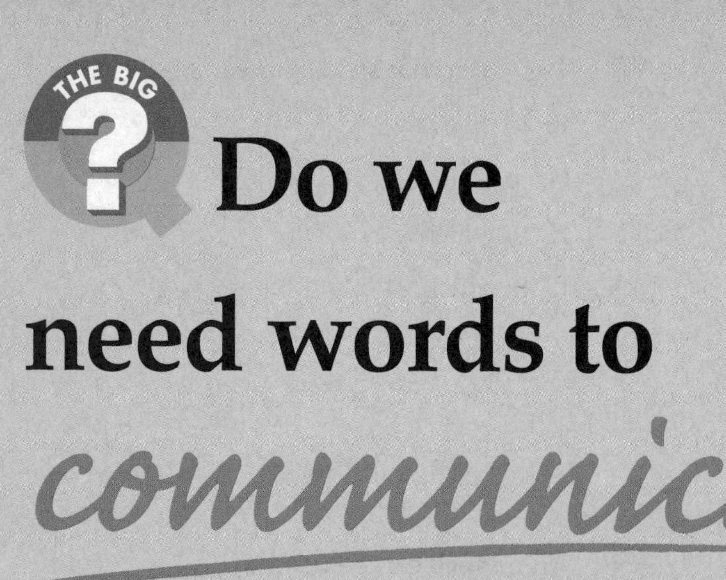

Unit 4 Genre focus: Prose and Poetry

Unit Book Choices
With this unit you will read one book as an Anchor Book. There are many good books that would work well with this unit. The following pages offer six suggestions.

Free-Choice Reading
Later in this unit you will be given an opportunity to choose another book to read. This is called your Free-Choice Book.

You might read...

A The Westing Game

B The Hero's Trail

C Cheaper by the Dozen

D Fearless Fernie

E Number the Stars

F The Liberation of Gabriel King

The Westing Game
by Ellen Raskin

A You might read Anchor Book A

Summary After the unexpected death of an eccentric millionaire, sixteen very different characters come together for the reading of his will. They discover that in order to claim their inheritance, they must solve the murder mystery.

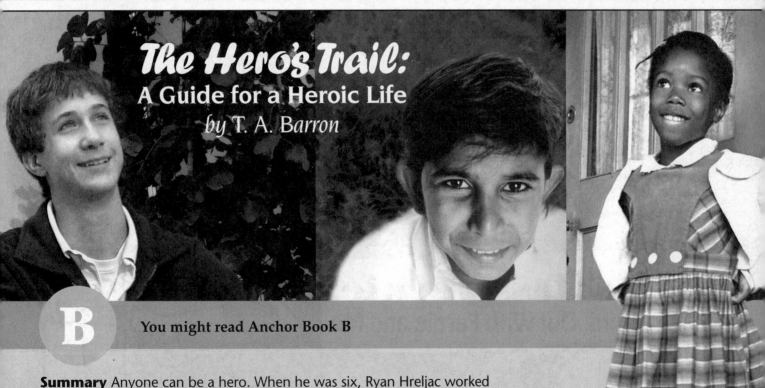

The Hero's Trail:
A Guide for a Heroic Life
by T. A. Barron

B You might read Anchor Book B

Summary Anyone can be a hero. When he was six, Ryan Hreljac worked to improve conditions in a Ugandan village. Iqbal Masih, who escaped bondage when he was ten, fought against child slavery worldwide. And courageous Ruby Bridges, also just six at the time, became the first African American child to enter an all-white school.

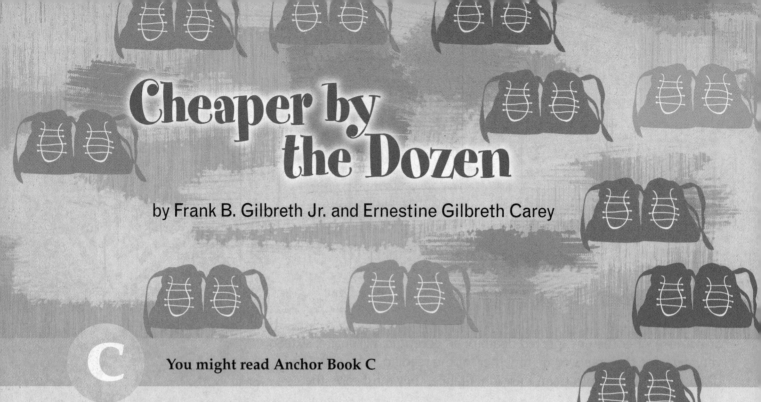

Cheaper by the Dozen

by Frank B. Gilbreth Jr. and Ernestine Gilbreth Carey

C

You might read Anchor Book C

Summary In the Gilbreth household, there are charts to initial in the morning after bathing, brushing teeth, combing hair, and making beds. At night, charts are initialled after homework and washing up. This practice may seem a little overzealous, but with a dozen kids and a wife who doesn't believe in discipline, what's a dad to do?

D

You might read Anchor Book D

Summary Fernie and "Me" have been best friends since they were born. Now in middle school, they experience the fun—and the humiliations—together. From sports tryouts to school dances and from bad moods to crazy antics, they find that life is pretty comical when you're stumbling through it together.

Fearless Fernie: Hanging Out With Fernie and Me

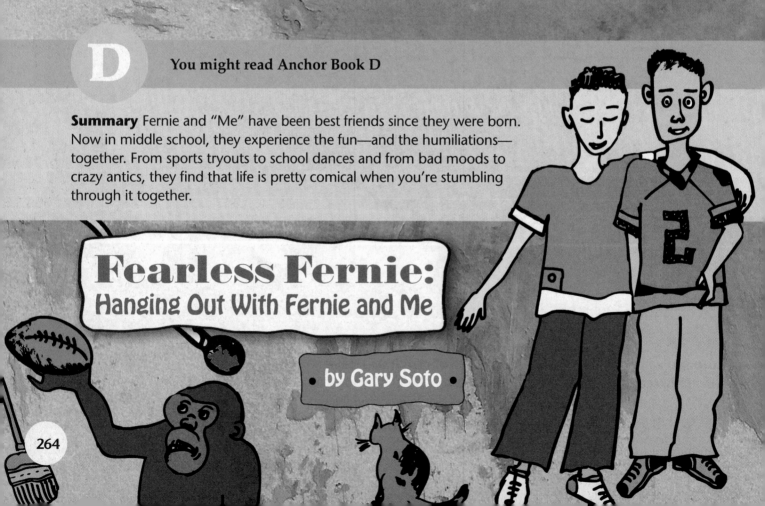

• by Gary Soto •

E

You might read Anchor Book E

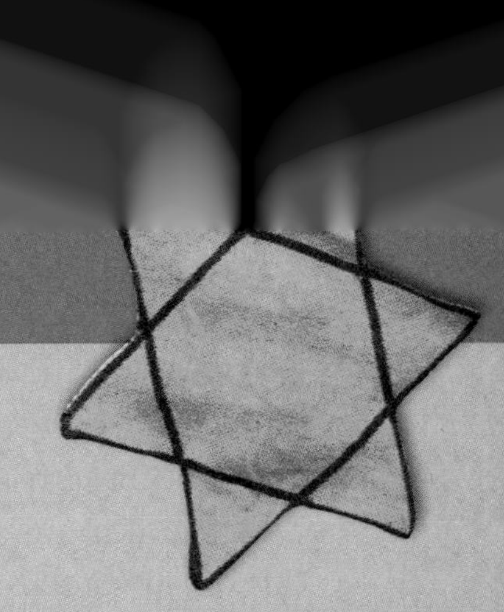

Summary It is 1943 in Copenhagen, Denmark, and ten-year-old Annemarie witnesses the Nazi soldiers marching into town. When the Jewish population is rounded up for "relocation," Annemarie's best friend Ellen moves in with her and pretends to be her sister. Then, Annemarie is called upon to perform a very brave feat.

Number the Stars
by Lois Lowry

The Liberation of Gabriel King
by K. L. Going

F

You might read Anchor Book F

Summary The school year is about to end, and Gabe King knows it's going to be the best summer ever. He's going to ride his bike, camp out, and go swimming in the pond. His best friend Frita has other ideas. She's going to help Gabe face his fears: corpses, cows on the loose, and sixth-grade bullies, to name a few. It turns out, though, that Frita has a fear of her own.

4-1 Understanding the Big Question
Do we need words to communicate?

People talk to one another all day long. You might discuss movies with your parents, describe a homework assignment to a friend, or tell your sister how to bake cookies. Talking is the main way we communicate our thoughts and feelings—but it's not the only way. Let's take a look at another way of communicating.

When a dog wags its tail, it's using body language to communicate how happy and excited it is. People use body language, too. For example, you might smile to say "I'm happy," or clap to say "Good job!" There are many ways to communicate ideas or feelings without using words. For example, you can . . .

- raise your eyes to show surprise
- cross your arms to show stubbornness
- turn your back on someone to show anger
- hug someone to show you love them

In this activity, you and your group will communicate emotions without using any words. Discuss with your group members how you can communicate using body language. Think about these emotions.

Directions Think of how you can communicate each emotion without using words. Then act out one of the emotions for your group. Invite group members to guess which emotion you used. Use the chart on the next page to identify how you and the other group members used body language to communicate each emotion. Then answer the questions that follow.

Emotion	Body Language Used
Happiness	**Example:** I used my face and arms to show happiness. I had a big smile on my face, and I flung my arms open as if to say, "That was great!"

1 **Assess** How well were you and your group members able to communicate these emotions using body language? Explain your answer.

2 **Compare** Think of a second way to use body language to communicate one of the emotions above. Does one way express your emotion more strongly than the other? Why or why not?

THE BIG ?

As you read your Anchor Book and the related readings, think about the ways characters communicate, both with and without speaking.

Getting Ready for Your Anchor Book *You will start reading your Anchor Book soon. The next few pages in this book give you some background information plus a reading skill.*

Introduction to Prose and Poetry

All authors use language to create images, tell stories, and describe events. Authors who write prose—such as essays, novels, short stories, and articles—organize their writing in sentences and paragraphs. Poets, however, decide how each line of a poem will end and how to make every word count.

It is important to know that when you read poetry, you may have to read more carefully than you would when reading prose. Prose usually follows a specific structure, but often poetry does not. You might find that you need to read a poem several times in order to better understand it.

The Venn diagram below shows a few similarities and differences between prose and poetry.

Prose

- usually follows conventional rules of grammar
- is organized by sentences and paragraphs
- structure helps explain the content
- is written in paragraph form

Both

- can use figurative language such as personification, simile, and metaphor
- can use sensory language

Poetry

- doesn't necessarily follow conventional rules of grammar
- fixed line endings determined by author
- structure helps express the author's thoughts and feelings
- often uses sound devices such as repetition, alliteration, rhyme, and rhythm

Distinguish Prose from Poetry

Compare "One" on page 179 with "I Was Not Alone" on page 180. One selection is a poem and the other is prose—but how do you know which is which? Fill in the charts below.

Title	
Poet	
I know it is a poem because . . .	

Title	
Author	
I know it is prose because . . .	

Change Prose to Poetry

Prose and poetry can be used to describe the same topic or event, but they do this in different ways. Complete this exercise to see what happens when you turn prose into poetry.

1 Find a short prose passage—about fifty words long. Look for one that has a lot of description about the setting or about a character's feelings and emotions.

2 Choose words and phrases from the prose passage that are the most powerful and meaningful. Turn them into a poem by arranging them in a way that you think best expresses the message of the passage. Since poetry does not necessarily follow conventional grammatical rules, you are free to use single words, phrases, or sentences to write your poem. Be creative! Write your poem on a separate sheet of paper.

3 Read your poem aloud to see if your arrangement and word choices reflect the message you intended. Make changes if necessary.

before reading your anchor book

4-2 Reading Skills
Paraphrasing

In learning new reading skills, you will use special academic vocabulary. Knowing the right words will help you demonstrate your understanding.

Academic Vocabulary

Word	Meaning	Example Sentence
convey *v.* *Related words:* conveyed; conveying	to communicate or make known	Please *convey* my concerns about homework to the principal.
paraphrase *v.* *Related words:* paraphrased; paraphrasing	to restate or reword a text or passage using different words	After I *paraphrased* the scientific article on mosquitoes, it was much easier to understand.
represent *v.* *Related words:* represented; representing	to stand for or describe	This lyric poem *represents* my thoughts on nature.

Many poems contain language that may not sound familiar. If you **paraphrase** poetry, or take the words a poet wrote and restate them in your own words, you can better understand the ideas that the poet is trying to **convey**.

Look at the example from T.S. Eliot's poem, "The Naming of Cats."

Poet's Words	The Naming of Cats is a difficult matter. It isn't just one of your holiday games.
Student's Paraphrase	Finding just the right name for a cat is not an easy thing to do.

- "difficult matter" means something that's hard to do
- "holiday games" are silly, fun, and easy

Use the steps on the following page to help you paraphrase to make the meaning of a poem clear.

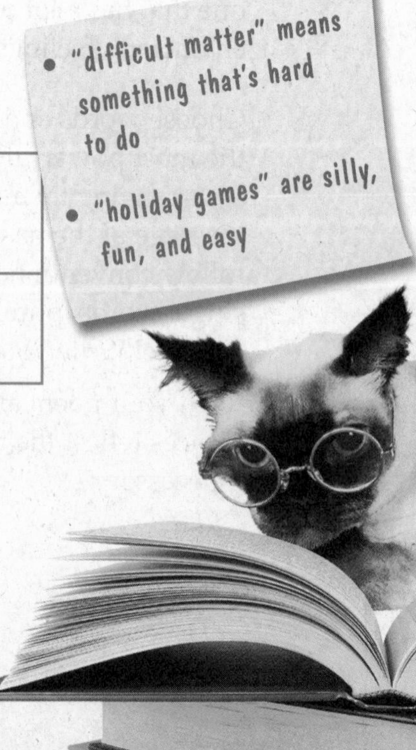

before reading your anchor book

How to Paraphrase

Step 1 Reread difficult or confusing lines or parts of the selection. This will help you to check your understanding.

Step 2 Learn the meaning of unfamiliar words by reading words and phrases around them. Refer to a dictionary if needed.

Step 3 Restate difficult text with easier, everyday language. Your paraphrase should be easier to read than the original text.

Step 4 Read what you paraphrased to be sure it makes sense and **represents** the author's original text.

Directions The poem below is in two parts, or stanzas. Read the first stanza and the way in which it was paraphrased. Then paraphrase the second stanza and answer the questions.

Original Text "Count That Day Lost" by George Eliot	Unfamiliar Words or Phrases	Paraphrase
If you sit down at set of sun And count the acts that you have done, And, counting, find One self-denying deed, one word That eased the heart of him who heard, One glance most kind That fell like sunshine where it went— Then you may count that day well spent.	"Self-denying deed" means *to do something for someone else.* "One glance most kind" means *a kind look.*	At the end of a day, think about all you have done. If you have done something kind for someone else, then you can say you spent your day well.
But if, through all the livelong day, You've cheered no heart, by yea or nay— If, through it all You've nothing done that you can trace That brought the sunshine to one face— No act most small That helped some soul and nothing cost— Then count that day as worse than lost.		

Analyze What is the theme of the poem? How does paraphrasing the poem help you to understand its theme?

before reading your anchor book

Now that you have learned how to paraphrase, read the following article. *Guiding Question:* **How does paraphrasing the selection help you to communicate its message?**

Link to Science

ALIEN INVADERS

Many plants and animals have been brought into the United States from different parts of the world. Some end up taking food and territory from the plants and animals that have always lived here!

◀ Kudzu is known as the "mile-a-minute weed" and "the vine that ate the South."

One hundred years ago, there were no muskrats in the Netherlands. Then in 1906, Dutch fur traders released six muskrats that they had brought from the United States. The fur traders hoped the muskrats would multiply so they could trap the mammals for their fur.

The fur traders were not disappointed. There were no natural predators, or enemies, to bother the muskrats. The earth dikes of the Netherlands, which kept out the sea, made a fine habitat for the animals. As a result, millions of muskrats were soon tunneling through the dikes.

Over time, the muskrats weakened the dikes. The Dutch had to repair and rebuild the dikes at great cost. They also hired hundreds of trappers to catch muskrats. Even so, no permanent solution to the Dutch muskrat problem has been found yet.

The story of the muskrats is not unique. All over the world, nonnative, or alien, plants and animals are introduced into new habitats.

SPECIES ON THE MOVE

Animals and plants have always migrated, or moved from place to place. Seeds float on the wind and are carried by birds and animals. Animals have crossed ice bridges and, clinging to driftwood, have been carried across the ocean. Few species, however, moved very far in these ways.

During the last few centuries, advances in transportation and worldwide trade have helped plants and animals move around the world. It is not uncommon, for example, for snakes to crawl into the wheel wells of airplanes and hop from country to country.

Some animals, like the Dutch muskrats, are deliberately introduced into new habitats. Other introductions are accidental. Either way, the effects can be dramatic.

IMPORT FROM AUSTRALIA

Over thousands of years, certain plants and animals have learned to share the same space. They make connections that allow them all to survive. This type of ecosystem ticks along like a smoothly running clock.

For thousands of years, the Florida Everglades was such an ecosystem. Countless insects lived in the many plants and trees. The insects provided food for birds and reptiles. Larger animals then ate the birds and reptiles.

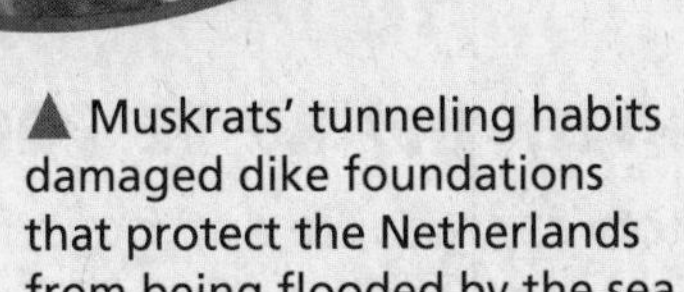

▲ Muskrats' tunneling habits damaged dike foundations that protect the Netherlands from being flooded by the sea.

In 1936, melaleuca trees were imported from Australia. Florida lumberjacks hoped the new trees would produce inexpensive lumber in the Everglades wetlands. Today melaleuca trees have taken more than 500,000 acres of the Everglades. They crowd out native plants and drain water from the swamps.

To make matters worse, the Australian trees drive away Florida's insects. So melaleuca forests provide no food or habitats for insect-eating birds and reptiles. The invasion of the melaleucas has disrupted the ecosystem in the Everglades environment.

▼ Nonnative melaleuka trees can grow 3 to 6 feet per year, displacing the Everglades cypress trees and sawgrass.

GOOD EFFECTS AND BAD EFFECTS

Not all imported species are dangerous. In fact, 98 percent of the American food supply comes from plants and animals that are not native to North America. Wheat, rice, and oats, for example, were brought here by early settlers. Beef and chicken are imports, too. So are many of our favorite fruits and vegetables.

Other alien species are cause for serious concern. These species threaten our environment and damage our economy.

ALIEN PESTS

Alien weeds cost the U.S. about $35.5 billion a year. One of the worst weeds is kudzu. At the 1876 Philadelphia Exhibition, Japan featured this exotic plant. Kudzu attracted many admirers, who took cuttings of the plant to grow at home.

Kudzu grew best in the South. The vine was attractive, with purple flowers and the scent of grapes. Cattle and other livestock ate the fast-growing plant. Kudzu also restored nitrogen to worn-out soil. The government was so impressed that it paid people to plant kudzu.

Today kudzu is a serious problem in the South. Kudzu covers road signs, causes accidents, and has killed off entire forests. People spray, burn, and cut kudzu. So far, it has been a losing battle.

Starlings are shiny black birds with starlike white spots. The first starlings were brought to New York City from Europe in 1890. These black birds adapted quickly in the United States. Spreading from coast to coast, they numbered more than 200 million by 1960. During those same years, the population of native songbirds declined.

Why were the starlings thriving? For one thing, starlings have better vision than most birds and can find food faster. Starlings are also strong enough to push other birds from their own nests. By taking over much of the available food in many habitats, starlings have made it difficult for other birds to survive.

▲ Kudzu will take over almost anything that is not moving, but many people are finding the plant has many good uses, such as in medicine, cooking, paper-making, and mosquito repellent.

What Should Be Done?

How can people and governments stop the spread of destructive alien species? Today governments check imported food for alien species. Pets and other animals from overseas are quarantined, or kept separate, for a period of time to make sure they are safe. People can no longer introduce new species just because they think it is a good idea.

Some nonnative species have been wiped out in this country. During the 1920s, Eurasian water chestnuts were grown in the pools on the mall in Washington, D.C. Somehow, the species spread to the Potomac River and other waterways. More than 10,000 acres of water were soon choking under the plants. Luckily, swift action removed them before the situation got out of control.

Using other species to control unwanted aliens is another solution. In California, for example, an insect called the cotton scale threatened to destroy the state's crop of oranges. Growers brought in a type of beetle from Australia, a natural predator of the cotton scale. The crop was saved.

Controlling one new species with another new species has its dangers, though. In Hawaii, rats arrived in the 1870s and became a big problem. Farmers imported mongooses from India to fight the rats. The rats, however, were nocturnal, or active during the night. The mongooses hunted by day. Since the mongooses rarely saw the rats, they feasted on native birds instead. As a result, several types of birds almost became extinct.

All living things are connected in a delicate web of life. It is up to all of us to protect the balance of nature around us. Alien species remind us how easily this balance can be upset.

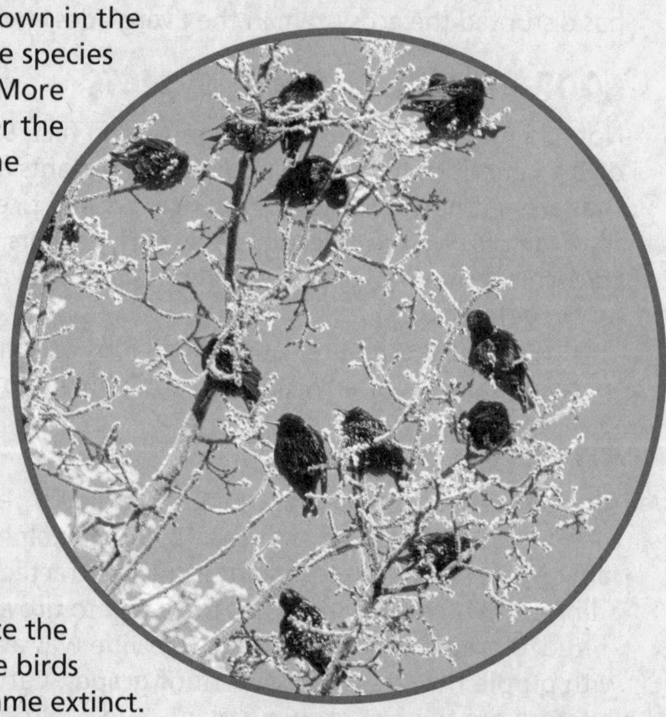

▲ Starling flocks can destroy an entire fruit crop in a few hours.

Thinking About the Selection

Alien Invaders

1 **Apply** Reread the information about muskrats in the article. List unfamiliar words and their meanings in the chart below. In two or three sentences, paraphrase how muskrats have become such a problem in the Netherlands.

Unfamiliar Words or Phrases	Definition
Paraphrase	

2 **Explain** How do the visual features of the article, such as boldface headings, photos, and captions, help you better understand the text?

3 **Infer** Paraphrasing can help you identify the main idea of the text. What is the main idea of the selection?

Write Answer the following question in your Reader's Journal.

4 **Apply** How does paraphrasing the selection help you to communicate its message?

before reading your anchor book

4-3 Vocabulary Building Strategies
Idioms and Multiple-Meaning Words

Sometimes you will come across a phrase in which you recognize each individual word, but together, the words don't make much sense. You might also read words that are familiar, but seem out of place in the text. In this lesson, you will learn how to make sense of these words and phrases.

Idioms

An **idiom** is an expression or phrase used in a particular way. An idiom is not meant to be taken literally—it doesn't mean exactly what the words say. For example, instead of describing a person as "very sad," you could say the person is "down in the dumps." Idioms often suggest visual images that make writing more colorful and easier to understand.

Sometimes you can figure out what an idiom means by reading the words around it and rewriting the phrase in your own words.

Idiom When I found out I had gotten an A on the test, I was *walking on air.*

Rewritten Phrase I know when I get a good grade on a test, I am very happy. *Walking on air* probably means "very happy and satisfied."

Directions In each sentence below, the idiom is underlined. Circle words in each sentence that help you understand the meaning of the idiom. Then write the meaning of each idiom.

1. My Aunt Sarah <u>has her hands full</u> running two different businesses, and never has time to visit.

   ____

2. When we wanted tickets to the baseball game, my dad <u>pulled some strings</u> to get front-row seats from the team's manager.

   ____

3. After missing the first two questions, I <u>bounced back</u> with three correct answers in the trivia game.

   ____

before reading your anchor book

Multiple-Meaning Words

Sometimes in your reading you will find a familiar word that is used in an unfamiliar way. Look at these examples.

I always *share* my favorite oatmeal bars with my sister.

▶ The word *share* is a verb meaning "to give a portion of something to others."

My sister received a *share* of the books left over from the yard sale.

▶ Here the word *share* is a noun meaning "a portion belonging to something or someone."

Share is a **word with multiple meanings.** Sometimes a word's multiple meanings are related, as in the word *sign*. The multiple meanings of other words, such as *key*, are not related.

Words With Multiple Meanings

Word	Meaning	Another Meaning
sign	a notice or signal (noun)	to write your name (verb)
key	a device that opens a lock (noun)	important (adjective)
stage	part of a theater (noun)	one of a series (noun)

Directions Read each sentence. Decide which meaning of the underlined word is used. Then write a new sentence using a different meaning of the same word.

1 Be sure to sign your name on the back of the card.

____

2 The first stage of the experiment was completed with success.

____

Directions Write each meaning of the underlined word.

The day was cold for spring (1). When we became thirsty on our hike, we walked to the spring (2) in the valley to get a fresh drink. Most of us were tired, except for one energetic group member who wanted to spring (3) ahead to the pond.

Meaning 1: ______________________________

Meaning 2: ______________________________

Meaning 3: ______________________________

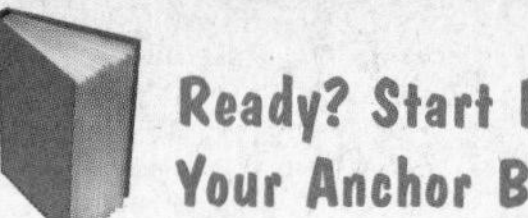

Ready? Start Reading Your Anchor Book *It's time to get started. As you learn from this worktext, your teacher will also give you reading assignments from your Anchor Book.*

4-4 Comparing Literary Works
Figurative Language

Have you ever heard someone say they were "frozen with fear" or "hungry as a horse"? These phrases are not meant to be taken literally because they don't mean exactly what the words say. Both are examples of **figurative language**—language that helps create a clear picture of something in a reader's mind.

Literary Terms

Figurative language is not meant to be taken literally, but it does communicate meaning in a vivid, imaginative way. Examples of figurative language include the following.

- A **simile** uses *like* or *as* to compare two different things.
- A **metaphor** describes one thing as if it were something else.
- **Personification** gives human qualities or abilities to something that is nonhuman.

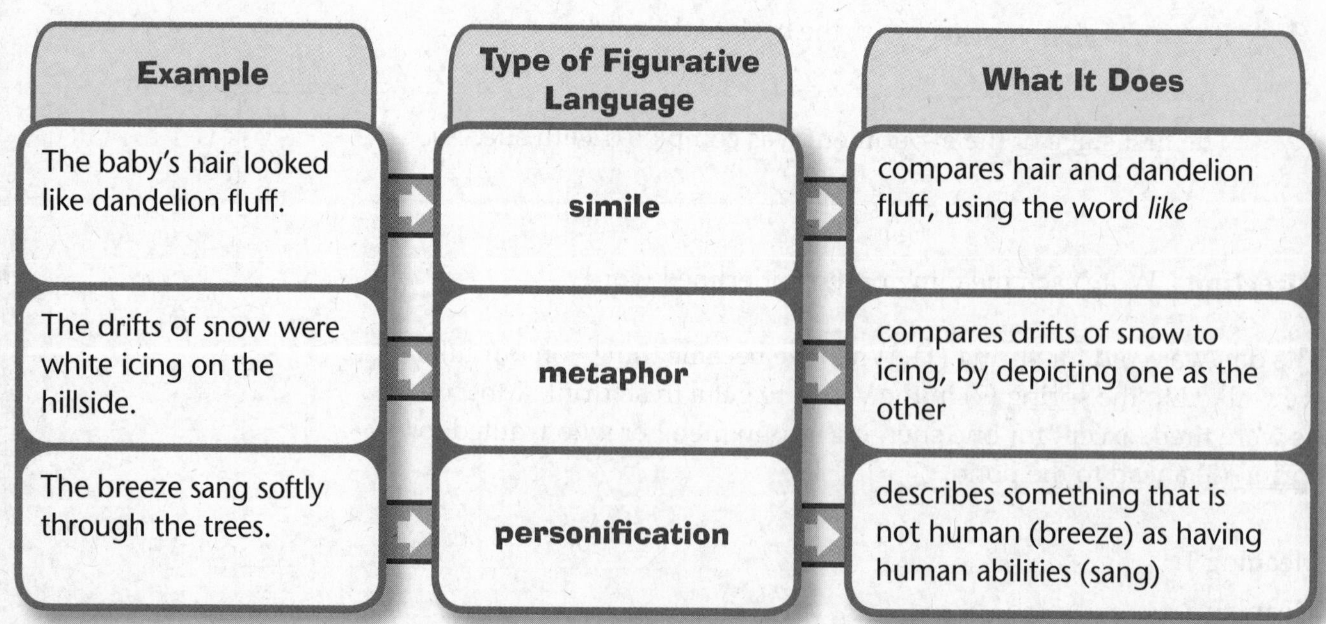

Example	Type of Figurative Language	What It Does
The baby's hair looked like dandelion fluff.	**simile**	compares hair and dandelion fluff, using the word *like*
The drifts of snow were white icing on the hillside.	**metaphor**	compares drifts of snow to icing, by depicting one as the other
The breeze sang softly through the trees.	**personification**	describes something that is not human (breeze) as having human abilities (sang)

Directions Read the following poem. Notice how the student marked the metaphors. Then answer the questions that follow.

Go Online
About the Author
Visit: PHSchool.com
Web Code: exe-6401

from "The Love Song of J. Alfred Prufrock"

by T.S. Eliot

The yellow fog that rubs its back upon the window-panes,
The yellow smoke that rubs its muzzle[1] on the window-panes
Licked its tongue into the corners of the evening,
Lingered upon the pools that stand in drains,
Let fall upon its back the soot that falls from chimneys,
Slipped by the terrace, made a sudden leap,
And seeing that it was a soft October night,
Curled once about the house, and fell asleep.

[1] **muzzle** (muz'əl) *n.* the mouth, nose, and jaws of an animal.

1 **Interpret** Eliot describes the fog using a metaphor. What do you think he is comparing the fog to? Which words does he use to describe it?

2 **Evaluate** Think about a time when you have seen fog. Do you think Eliot does a good job describing fog using this metaphor? Explain your answer.

3 **Analyze** What lines of text are similar to each other? Why do you think Eliot wrote the lines this way? Explain.

Now that you have learned about figurative language, read the following selections to see how authors use figurative language to state ideas in creative and vivid ways.
Guiding Question: **How do authors use figurative language to communicate messages in poetry and prose?**

Vocabulary Builder

Before you read, *you will discuss the following words. In the Vocabulary Builder box in the margin, use a vocabulary building strategy to make the words your own.*

etching **crude** **abode** **draped** **tendril**

As you read, *draw a box around unfamiliar words you could add to your vocabulary. Use context clues to unlock their meaning.*

Marking the Text

Figurative Language

As you read, *underline examples of figurative language. In the margin, name the type of figurative language. Write what each example compares or means.*

while reading your anchor book

April Rain Song

by Langston Hughes

Let the rain kiss you.
Let the rain beat upon your head with silver liquid drops.
Let the rain sing you a lullaby.

The rain makes still pools on the sidewalk.
The rain makes running pools in the gutter.
The rain plays a little sleep-song on our roof at night—
And I love the rain.

Simile: Willow and Ginkgo

by Eve Merriam

Marking the Text

The willow is like an **etching,**
Fine-lined against the sky.
The ginkgo[1] is like a **crude** sketch,
Hardly worthy to be signed.

The willow's music is like a soprano,
Delicate and thin.
The ginkgo's tune is like a chorus,
With everyone joining in.

The willow is sleek as a velvet-nosed calf;
The ginkgo is leathery as an old bull.
The willow's branches are like silken thread;
The ginkgo's like stubby rough wool.

The willow is like a nymph[2] with streaming hair;
Wherever it grows, there is green and gold and fair.
The willow dips to the water,
Protected and precious, like the king's favorite daughter.

The ginkgo forces its way through gray concrete;
Like a city child, it grows up in the street.
Thrust against the metal sky,
Somehow it survives and even thrives.

My eyes feast upon the willow,
But my heart goes to the ginkgo.

---

1 **ginkgo** (gi[ng]k' gō) *n.* large tree with fan-shaped leaves and edible nuts.

2 **nymph** (nimf) *n.* a beautiful young woman or goddess.

Vocabulary Builder

etching
(ech'i[ng]) *n.*

Meaning

crude
(kro͞od) *adj.*

Meaning

Good to Know! Different species of ginkgo trees have existed on Earth for more than 200 million years.

while reading your anchor book

The Little Rain

by Tu Fu

Marking the Text

Vocabulary Builder

abode
(ə'bōd) *n.*

Meaning
a house or home

Oh! she is good, the little rain! and well she knows our need
Who cometh in the time of spring to aid the sun-drawn seed;
She wanders with a friendly wind through silent nights unseen,
The furrows[1] feel her happy tears, and lo! the land is green.

Last night cloud-shadows gloomed the path that winds to my **abode**,
And the torches of the river-boats like angry meteors glowed.
To-day fresh colours break the soil, and butterflies take wing
Down broidered[2] lawns all bright with pearls in the garden of the King.

1 **furrows** (fûr'ōz) *n.* deep wrinkles in the skin

2 **broidered** (broi'dərd) *v.* ornamented with needlework

from

Esperanza Rising

by Pam Muñoz Ryan

Aguascalientes, Mexico, 1924

"Our land is alive, Esperanza," said Papa, taking her small hand as they walked through the gentle slopes of the vineyard. Leafy green vines **draped** the arbors and the grapes were ready to drop. Esperanza was six years old and loved to walk with her papa through the winding rows, gazing up at him and watching his eyes dance with love for the land.

"This whole valley breathes and lives," he said, sweeping his arm toward the distant mountains that guarded them. "It gives us the grapes and then they welcome us." He gently touched a wild **tendril** that reached into the row, as if it had been waiting to shake his hand. He picked up a handful of earth and studied it. "Did you know that when you lie down on the land, you can feel it breathe? That you can feel its heart beating?"

"Papa, I want to feel it," she said.

"Come." They walked to the end of the row, where the incline of the land formed a grassy swell.

Papa lay down on his stomach and looked up at her, patting the ground next to him.

Esperanza smoothed her dress and knelt down. Then, like a caterpillar, she slowly inched flat next to him, their faces looking at each other. The warm sun pressed on one of Esperanza's cheeks and the warm earth on the other.

She giggled.

"Shhh," he said. "You can only feel the earth's heartbeat when you are still and quiet."

She swallowed her laughter and after a moment said, "I can't hear it, Papi."

Marking the Text

Vocabulary Builder

draped
(drāpt) *v.*

Meaning

tendril
(ten′drəl) *n.*

Meaning

while reading your anchor book

"Aguántate tantito y la fruta caerá en tu mano," he said. "Wait a little while and the fruit will fall into your hand. You must be patient, Esperanza."

She waited and lay silent, watching Papa's eyes.

And then she felt it. Softly at first. A gentle thumping. Then stronger. A resounding thud, thud, thud against her body.

She could hear it, too. The beat rushing in her ears. *Shoomp, shoomp, shoomp.*

She stared at Papa, not wanting to say a word. Not wanting to lose the sound. Not wanting to forget the feel of the heart of the valley.

She pressed closer to the ground, until her body was beating with the earth's. And with Papa's. The three hearts beating together.

She smiled at Papa, not needing to talk, her eyes saying everything.

And his smile answered hers. Telling her that he knew she had felt it.

Vocabulary Builder

After you read, *review the words you decided to add to your vocabulary. Write the meaning of words you have learned in context. Look up the other words in a dictionary, glossary, thesaurus, or electronic resource.*

Pam Muñoz Ryan (b. 1951)

Pam Muñoz Ryan was born and raised among a large extended family in the San Joaquin Valley of California. The hot summers in the valley helped Ryan get hooked on reading. Because her family did not have air-conditioning or a swimming pool, Ryan biked to the library—where it was nice and cool!

It wasn't until after college that Ryan started writing books. A friend at work asked her to help write one, and since then, Ryan has written more than 25 books. Her books include fiction, nonfiction, and picture books for young children. Ryan has won many awards for her work, particularly her bestseller, Esperanza Rising, which she based on the life of her grandmother, who grew up in Mexico.

while reading your anchor book

Thinking About the Selections

April Rain Song, Simile: Willow and Ginkgo, The Little Rain, *and* Esperanza Rising

Go Online
About the Author
Visit: PHSchool.com
Web Code: exe-6402
6403
6404
6405

1 **Contrast** Use the graphic organizer to list figurative language used in "Simile: Willow and Gingko" and "The Little Rain." For each example, list a line from the poem, the type of figurative language used, and what the figurative language does.

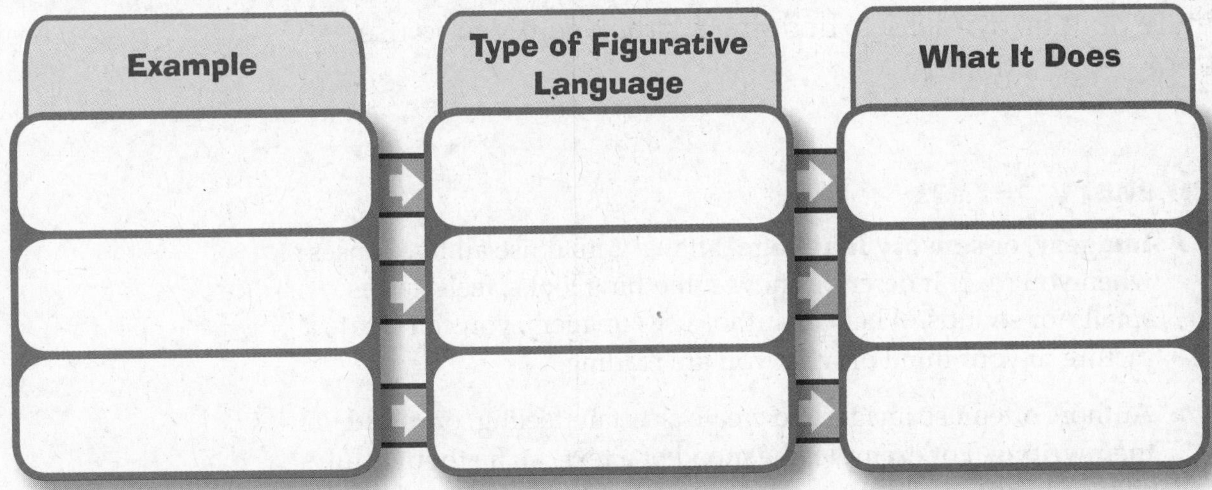

Example
Type of Figurative Language
What It Does

2 **Interpret** Why do you think the author of "April Rain Song" gives the rain a human voice in the line "Let the rain sing you a lullaby"?

3 **Speculate** Why do you think Ryan says that Esperanza and her father can actually hear the earth's heartbeat?

Write Answer the following questions in your Reader's Journal.

4 **Apply** How do authors use figurative language to communicate messages in poetry and prose?

5 **Analyze** Identify three examples of figurative language in your Anchor Book. What is the author's purpose for using this figurative language?

while reading your anchor book

4-5 Literary Analysis
Imagery

Listening to a friend describe her day at the beach might bring to your mind the coconut fragrance of suntan lotion, the screeches of gulls, and the grittiness of sand grains on your skin. Authors also use words that appeal to one or more of your five senses. In doing so, they help you to use your imagination.

Literary Terms

- **Imagery**, or **sensory language**, allows you to use all five senses when you read. It describes how something looks, feels, tastes, smells, or sounds. When an author uses imagery, you can create a picture in your mind of what you are reading.
- Authors often use imagery to create a certain feeling, or **mood**, in their writing. For example, the mood of a text can be thoughtful, silly, or happy.

Sense	Imagery	Mood
sight	We sat silently as we watched the **crimson red** sun sink into the horizon.	mellow
sound	I had to listen to the **shriek** of the car horns while stuck in a traffic jam.	annoyed
smell	The tomato sauce bubbling on the stove released a **sharp, earthy** scent of basil—just the way Mom's special sauce did when she made it years ago.	longing
taste	Morsels of **bittersweet** chocolate melted in my mouth.	satisfied
touch	The wind on my face was so cold it **stung** my cheeks, nose, and lips.	uncomfortable

Writing that uses imagery helps you feel as if you are taking part in the action. When an author uses strong sensory language, you might actually feel like you can taste the sweet, juicy slice of watermelon that he or she is describing. Imagery helps an author bring characters, settings, and events to life on the page.

Directions Read the poem. Notice how the student has marked the imagery. Then answer the questions that follow.

Dust of Snow by Robert Frost

The way a <u>crow</u>
<u>Shook</u> down on me
The <u>dust of snow</u>
From a <u>hemlock tree</u>

Has given my heart
A change of mood
And saved some part
Of a day I had rued[1].

[1] **rued** (rōōd) *v.* bitterly regretted.

About the Author
Visit: PHSchool.com
Web Code: exe-6406

while reading your anchor book

1 **Apply** Identify words the poet used to create an image in your mind. Write the words in the table below. Include all the senses the words appealed to.

These words . . .	. . . appealed to my sense of . . .

2 **Describe** What image does the poem form in your mind? Use examples from the poem in your description.

3 **Analyze** How does the incident with the crow in the beginning of the poem affect the author's mood at the end of the poem?

Authors in all genres of writing use imagery to appeal to the five senses. The essay and the poem that follow both rely on imagery to create pictures in the reader's mind. *Guiding Question:* **How do authors use imagery to communicate ideas?**

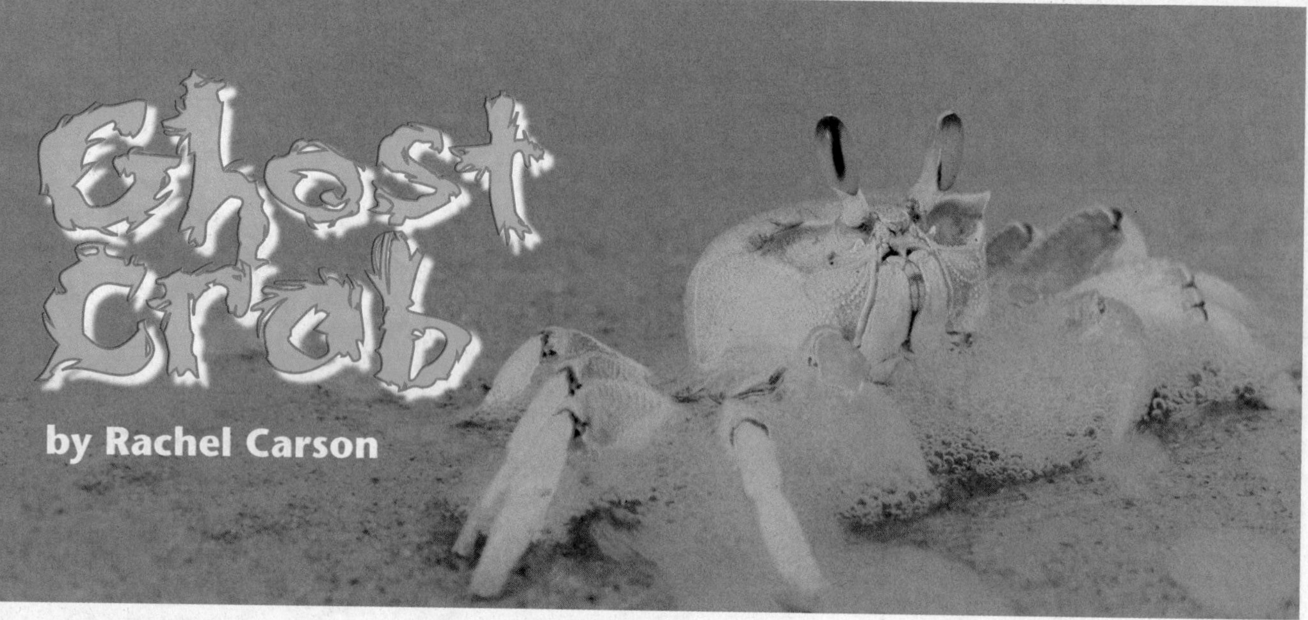

Ghost Crab

by Rachel Carson

Vocabulary Builder

Before you read, *you will discuss the following words. In the Vocabulary Builder box in the margin, use a vocabulary building strategy to make the words your own.*

distractions **all-enveloping** **shriveled** **scarred**

As you read, *draw a box around unfamiliar words you could add to your vocabulary. Use context clues to unlock their meaning.*

Marking the Text

Imagery

As you read, *underline words and phrases that show imagery. In the margin, write which of the five senses they appeal to.*

The shore at night is a different world, in which the very darkness that hides the **distractions** of daylight brings into sharper focus the elemental[1] realities. Once, exploring the night beach, I surprised a small ghost crab in the searching beam of my torch. He was lying in a pit he had dug just above the surf, as though watching the sea and waiting. The blackness of the night possessed water, air, and beach. It was the darkness of an older world, before Man. There was no sound but the **all-enveloping,** primeval[2] sounds of wind blowing over water and sand, and of waves crashing on the beach. There was no other visible life—just one small crab near the sea. I have seen hundreds of ghost crabs

[1] **elemental** (el'ə ment'əl) *adj.* essential, basic.

[2] **primeval** (prī mē'vəl) *adj.* ancient, prehistoric.

Vocabulary Builder

distractions
(di strak' shənz) *n.*

Meaning

all-enveloping
(ôl en vel' əp' i[ng]) *adj.*

Meaning

Literature in Context

Link to Science

Haunting the Beach

The ghost crab is a crustacean that usually appears only at night. As quickly as the crab appears, it disappears again into the sand—like a ghost! Equally haunting is the fact that the ghost crab is known to face the full moon as it scurries along the beach at night.

The ghost crab is small, about two inches wide. Its size and its pale color blend in with the sand, making it difficult for predators and people to spot. When it is not wandering across the beach or scavenging for food, it is hiding out in its burrow. To escape the heat, the ghost crab closes the opening of the burrow. But when it is too cold, the crab encloses itself within the warm walls of its sandy home.

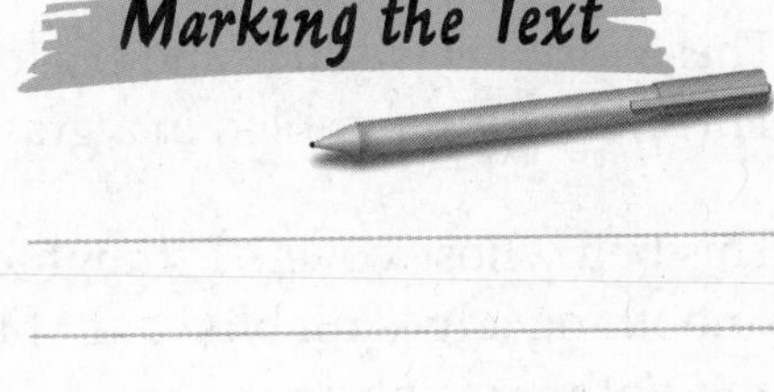

in other settings, but suddenly I was filled with the odd sensation that for the first time I knew the creature in its own world—that I understood, as never before, the essence of its being. In that moment time was suspended; the world to which I belonged did not exist and I might have been an onlooker from outer space. The little crab alone with the sea became a symbol that stood for life itself—for the delicate, destructible, yet incredibly vital force that somehow holds its place amid the harsh realities of the inorganic[3] world.

Marking the Text

[3] **inorganic** (in'ôr gan'ik) *adj.* not composed of living matter.

Rachel Carson (1907–1964)

Growing up on a Pennsylvania farm, Rachel Carson loved the outdoors. Her other love was writing. She entered college with plans to become a writer, but a course in biology caused her to change her mind. As an adult, she was employed by the U.S. Bureau of Fisheries (later the U.S. Fish and Wildlife Service).

Rachel Carson wrote in poetic language about science and nature. Her best-known book, Silent Spring, tells about the dangers pesticides pose for animals. Many people give this book credit for opening America's eyes to environmental issues and starting the environmental movement.

DAILY

by Naomi Shihab Nye

These **shriveled** seeds we plant,
corn kernel, dried bean,
poke into loosened soil,
cover over with measured fingertips

These T-shirts we fold into
perfect white squares

These tortillas we slice and fry to crisp strips
This rich egg scrambled in a gray clay bowl

This bed whose covers I straighten
smoothing edges till blue quilt fits brown blanket
and nothing hangs out

This envelope I address
so the name balances like a cloud
in the center of the sky
This page I type and retype
This table I dust till the **scarred** wood shines
This bundle of clothes I wash and hang and wash again
like flags we share, a country so close
no one needs to name it

The days are nouns; touch them
The hands are churches that worship the world

Marking the Text

Vocabulary Builder

shriveled
(shriv'əld) *adj.*

Meaning

scarred
(skärd) *adj.*

Meaning

Vocabulary Builder

After you read, *review the words you decided to add to your vocabulary. Write the meaning of words you have learned in context. Look up the other words in a dictionary, glossary, thesaurus, or electronic resource.*

Thinking About the Selections

Ghost Crab *and* Daily

1 **Speculate** What do you think the author of "Ghost Crab" was referring to when she used the words "the harsh realities of the inorganic world"?

2 **Evaluate** What do you think the author's purpose was for writing the poem "Daily"? Use examples from the poem to explain your answer.

3 **Compare** In the chart, list examples of imagery from "Ghost Crab" and "Daily." Tell what senses they appeal to.

"Ghost Crab"		"Daily"	
Example	Sense	Example	Sense

4 **Connect** On a separate sheet of paper, write a letter to Naomi Shihab Nye. Use imagery to describe an event or daily occurrence that comes from your heritage.

Write Answer the following questions in your Reader's Journal.

5 **Analyze** How do authors use imagery to communicate ideas?

6 **Compare and Contrast** Tell how the author's use of sensory language in your Anchor Book creates a mood that is like or unlike the mood created by Carson or Nye.

while reading your anchor book

4-6 Literary Analysis
Point of View

Imagine your sister tells you all about a school play she saw. The next day, a friend who is in the play tells you about it—but the way she describes it is very different. How can two stories about the same thing be so different? Each story is told from a different perspective, or **point of view.** Your sister was *watching* the play and your friend was *in* the play—so they each have a different point of view on it.

Literary Terms

The **narrator** is the person telling a story. The **point of view** is the position, or perspective, from which the narrator tells the story. Below are the two most common points of view.

- In the **first-person point of view** the narrator is a character in the story and refers to himself or herself as *I*. The narrator only tells the reader what he or she sees, thinks, or feels.
- In the **third-person point of view** the narrator is outside the story—he or she does not participate in the action. The narrator refers to characters as *he, she, they, him, her,* and *them* throughout the story and can share the actions, thoughts, and feelings of any of the characters.

First-Person Point of View	Third-Person Point of View
I watched the struggle between my two friends unfold as though it was happening in slow motion.	Amy watched the struggle between her two friends unfold as though it was happening in slow motion.

A narrator presenting a third-person point of view can take one of two positions.

- In an **omniscient third-person point of view,** the narrator knows every character's thoughts and feelings, as well as everything that goes on.
- In a **limited third-person point of view,** the narrator knows the thoughts and feelings of only one character—usually the main character.

Directions Read the following passage. Notice the details a student underlined to help her determine the point of view of the story. Then answer the questions.

Go Online
About the Author
Visit: PHSchool.com
Web Code: exe-6409

from ***"Madam C.J. Walker"*** *by Jim Haskins*

Madam C. J. Walker was the first American woman to earn a million dollars. There were American women millionaires before her time, but they had inherited their wealth, either from their husbands or from their families. Madam Walker was the first woman to earn her fortune by setting up her own business and proving that women could be financially independent of men. . . .

Madam C. J. Walker was born Sarah Breedlove on December 23, 1867. She grew up in the South under very racist conditions. Her parents, Owen and Minerva Breedlove, had been slaves until President Abraham Lincoln's Emancipation Proclamation and the Union victory in the Civil War had freed the slaves.

1 **Apply** Is this story told in the first-person or third-person point of view? Use details from the passage to explain your answer.

2 **Recall** What made Madam C.J. Walker different from other women millionaires?

3 **Interpret** Rewrite the first paragraph of the passage in a different point of view. Refer to your answer to question 1, if necessary.

while reading your anchor book

Now that you have learned about point of view, read two selections that have different points of view. *Guiding Question:* **How does point of view help communicate thoughts, feelings, and ideas in a poem or story?**

Vocabulary Builder

Before you read, *you will discuss the following words. In the Vocabulary Builder box in the margin, use a vocabulary building strategy to make the words your own.*

submitted grappling hovered monitors

As you read, *draw a box around unfamiliar words you could add to your vocabulary. Use context clues to unlock their meaning.*

Marking the Text

Point of View

As you read, *underline words that indicate point of view. In the margin, explain from what point of view the narrator is telling the story.*

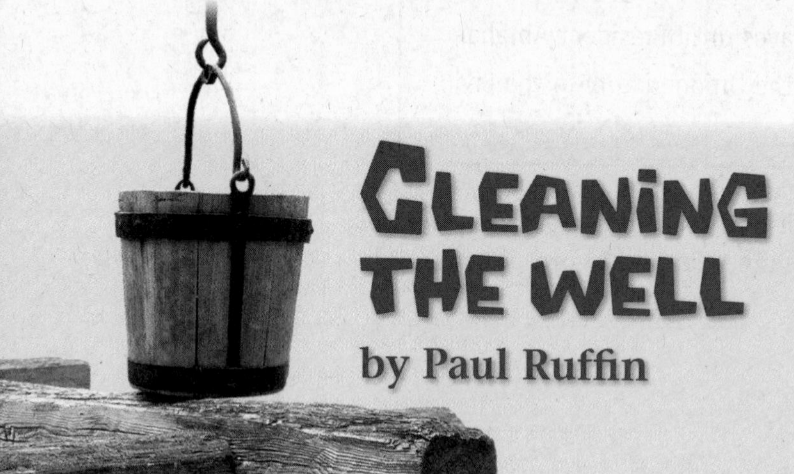

Cleaning the Well

by Paul Ruffin

Each spring there was the well to be cleaned.
Once a day my grandfather would say,
"It's got to be done. Let's go." This time
I dropped bat and glove, **submitted** to the rope,
and he lowered me into the dark and cold
water of the well. The sun
slid off at a crazy cant[1] and I
was there, thirty feet down, waist deep
in icy water, **grappling** for whatever
was not pure and wet and cold.
The sky **hovered** like some pale moon
above, eclipsed by his heavy red face
bellowing down to me not to dally[2],
to feel deep and load the bucket.

[1] **cant** (kant) *n.* angle.

[2] **dally** (dal' ē) *v.* waste time.

Vocabulary Builder

submitted
(səb mit'ed) *v.*

Meaning

grappling
(grap' lē[ng]) *v.*

Meaning

hovered
(huv' ərd) *v.*

Meaning

My feet rasped[3] against cold stone,
toes selecting unnatural shapes, curling
and gripping, raising them to my fingers,
then into the bucket and up to him:
a rubber ball, pine cones, leather glove,
beer can, fruit jars, an indefinable bone.
It was a time of fears: suppose he
should die or forget me, the rope break,
the water rise, a snake strike, the
bottom give way, the slick sides crumble?
The last bucket filled, my grandfather
assured, the rope loop dropped to me
and I was delivered by him who
sent me down, drawn slowly to sun
and sky and his fiercely grinning face.
"There was something else down there:
a cat or possum skeleton, but it
broke up, I couldn't pick it up."

He dropped his yellow hand on my head.
"There's always something down there
you can't quite get in your hands.
You'd know that if it wasn't your first
trip down. You'll know from now on."

"But what about the water?
Can we keep on drinking it?"

"You've drunk all that cat
you're likely to drink. Forget it
and don't tell the others. It's just
one more secret you got to live with."

Marking the Text

[3] **rasped** (rasp'd) *v.* rubbed against something rough.

Geraldine Moore the Poet

by Toni Cade Bambara

Background *In this story, Geraldine Moore, a young girl living in poverty, discovers that poetry isn't just about flowers, rainbows, or other pretty things. Poetry is about life—whether it is beautiful, ugly, sad, or, in Geraldine's case, not easy at all.*

Geraldine paused at the corner to pull up her knee socks. The rubber bands she was using to hold them up made her legs itch. She dropped her books on the sidewalk while she gave a good scratch. But when she pulled the socks up again, two fingers poked right through the top of her left one.

"That stupid dog," she muttered to herself, grabbing at her books and crossing against traffic. "First he chews up my gym suit and gets me into trouble, and now my socks."

Geraldine shifted her books to the other hand and kept muttering angrily to herself about Mrs. Watson's dog, which she minded two days a week for a dollar. She passed the hotdog man on the corner and waved. He shrugged as if to say business was very bad.

> *Must be, she thought to herself. Three guys before you had to pack up and forget it. Nobody's got hot-dog money around here.*

Geraldine turned down her street, wondering what her sister Anita would have for her lunch. She was glad she didn't have to eat the free lunches in high school any more. She was sick of the funny-looking tomato soup and the dried-out cheese sandwiches and those oranges that were more green than orange.

When Geraldine's mother first took sick and went away, Geraldine had been on her own except when Miss Gladys next door came in on Thursdays and cleaned the apartment and made a meat loaf so Geraldine could have dinner. But in those days Geraldine never quite managed to get breakfast for herself. So she'd sit through social studies class, scraping her feet to cover up the noise of her stomach growling.

Marking the Text

Now Anita, Geraldine's older sister, was living at home waiting for her husband to get out of the Army. She usually had something good for lunch—chicken and dumplings if she managed to get up in time, or baked ham from the night before and sweet-potato bread. But even if there was only a hot dog and some baked beans—sometimes just a TV dinner if those soap operas kept Anita glued to the TV set—anything was better than the noisy school lunchroom where **monitors** kept pushing you into a straight line or rushing you to the tables. Anything was better than that. Geraldine was almost home when she stopped dead. Right outside her building was a pile of furniture and some boxes. That wasn't anything new. She had seen people get put out in the street before, but this time the ironing board looked familiar. And she recognized the big, ugly sofa standing on its arm, its under-belly showing the hole where Mrs. Watson's dog had gotten to it.

Miss Gladys was sitting on the stoop[1], and she looked up and took off her glasses. "Well, Gerry," she said slowly, wiping her glasses on the hem of her dress, "looks like you'll be staying with me for a while." She looked at the men carrying out a big box with an old doll sticking up over the edge. "Anita's upstairs. Go on up and get your lunch."

Geraldine stepped past the old woman and almost bumped into the superintendent[2]. He took off his cap to wipe away the sweat.

"Darn shame," he said to no one in particular. "Poor people sure got a hard row to hoe."

"That's the truth," said Miss Gladys, standing up with her hands on her hips to watch the men set things on the sidewalk.

Upstairs, Geraldine went into the apartment and found Anita in the kitchen.

"I dunno, Gerry," Anita said. "I just don't know what we're going to do. But everything's going to be all right soon as Ma gets well." Anita's voice cracked as she set a bowl of soup before Geraldine.

"What's this?" Geraldine said.

"It's tomato soup, Gerry."

Geraldine was about to say something. But when she looked up at her big sister, she saw how Anita's face was getting all twisted as she began to cry.

That afternoon, Mr. Stern, the geometry teacher, started drawing cubes and cylinders on the board. Geraldine sat at her desk adding up a column of figures in her notebook—the rent, the light and gas bills, a new gym suit, some socks. Maybe they would move somewhere else, and she could have her own room. Geraldine turned the squares and triangles into little houses in the country.

---

1 **stoop** (sto͞op) *n.* small porch with steps at the front of a building.

2 **superintendent** (so͞o'pər in ten'dənt) *n.* person who takes care of a building.

Vocabulary Builder

monitors
(män'i tərz) *n.*

Meaning

Marking the Text

"For your homework," Mr. Stern was saying with his back to the class, "set up your problems this way." He wrote GIVEN: in large letters, and then gave the formula for the first problem. Then he wrote TO FIND: and listed three items they were to include in their answers.

Geraldine started to raise her hand to ask what all these squares and angles had to do with solving real problems, like the ones she had. Better not, she warned herself, and sat on her hands. *Your big mouth got you in trouble last term.*

In hygiene[3] class, Mrs. Potter kept saying that the body was a wonderful machine. Every time Geraldine looked up from her notebook, she would hear the same thing. "Right now your body is manufacturing all the proteins and tissues and energy you will need to get through tomorrow."

And Geraldine kept wondering, *How? How does my body know what it will need, when I don't even know what I'll need to get through tomorrow?*

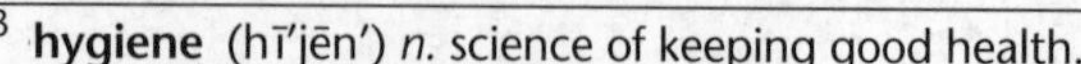

[3] **hygiene** (hī'jēn') *n.* science of keeping good health.

while reading your anchor book

As she headed down the hall to her next class, Geraldine remembered that she hadn't done the homework for English. Mrs. Scott had said to write a poem, and Geraldine had meant to do it at lunchtime. After all, there was nothing to it—a flower here, a raindrop there, moon, June, rose, nose. But the men carrying off the furniture had made her forget.

"And now put away your books," Mrs. Scott was saying as Geraldine tried to scribble a poem quickly. "Today we can give King Arthur's knights a rest. Let's talk about poetry."

Mrs. Scott moved up and down the aisles, talking about her favorite poems and reciting a line now and then. She got very excited whenever she passed a desk and could pick up the homework from a student who had remembered to do the assignment.

"A poem is your own special way of saying what you feel and what you see," Mrs. Scott went on, her lips moist. It was her favorite subject.

"Some poets write about the light that . . . that . . . makes the world sunny," she said, passing Geraldine's desk.

"Sometimes an idea takes the form of a picture—an image."

For almost half an hour, Mrs. Scott stood at the front of the room, reading poems and talking about the lives of the great poets. Geraldine drew more houses, and designs for curtains.

"So for those who haven't done their homework, try it now," Mrs. Scott said. "Try expressing what it is like to be . . . to be alive in this . . . this glorious world."

"Oh, brother," Geraldine muttered to herself as Mrs. Scott moved up and down the aisles again, waving her hands and leaning over the students' shoulders and saying, "That's nice," or "Keep trying." Finally she came to Geraldine's desk and stopped, looking down at her.

"I can't write a poem," Geraldine said flatly, before she even realized she was going to speak at all. She said it very loudly, and the whole class looked up.

"And why not?" Mrs. Scott asked, looking hurt.

"I can't write a poem, Mrs. Scott, because nothing lovely's been happening in my life. I haven't seen a flower since Mother's Day, and the sun don't even shine on my side of the street. No robins come sing on my window sill."

Geraldine swallowed hard. She thought about saying that her father doesn't even come to visit any more, but changed her mind. "Just the rain comes," she went on, "and the bills come, and the men to move out our furniture. I'm sorry, but I can't write no pretty poem."

Teddy Johnson leaned over and was about to giggle and crack the whole class up, but Mrs. Scott looked so serious that he changed his mind.

Marking the Text

"You have just said the most . . . the most poetic thing, Geraldine Moore," said Mrs. Scott. Her hands flew up to touch the silk scarf around her neck. "'Nothing lovely's been happening in my life.'" She repeated it so quietly that everyone had to lean forward to hear.

"Class," Mrs. Scott said very sadly, clearing her throat, "you have just heard the best poem you will ever hear." She went to the board and stood there for a long time staring at the chalk in her hand.

"I'd like you to copy it down," she said. She wrote it just as Geraldine had said it, bad grammar and all.

Nothing lovely's been happening in my life.
I haven't seen a flower since Mother's Day,
And the sun don't even shine on my side of the street.
No robins come sing on my window sill.
Just the rain comes, and the bills come,
And the men to move out our furniture.
I'm sorry, but I can't write no pretty poem.

Mrs. Scott stopped writing, but she kept her back to the class for a long time—long after Geraldine had closed her notebook.

And even when the bell rang, and everyone came over to smile at Geraldine or to tap her on the shoulder or to kid her about being the school poet, Geraldine waited for Mrs. Scott to put the chalk down and turn around. Finally Geraldine stacked up her books and started to leave. Then she thought she heard a whimper—the way Mrs. Watson's dog whimpered sometimes—and she saw Mrs. Scott's shoulders shake a little.

Vocabulary Builder

After you read, *review the words you decided to add to your vocabulary. Write the meaning of words you have learned in context. Look up the other words in a dictionary, glossary, thesaurus, or electronic resource.*

Thinking About the Selections

Cleaning the Well *and* Geraldine Moore the Poet

1 **Speculate** Suppose the speaker's grandfather told the story in "Cleaning the Well." How might the poem be different?

2 **Speculate** How do you think the speaker feels as he is being pulled up out of the well? Support your answers with examples from the poem.

3 **Analyze** Identify the point of view of "Geraldine Moore the Poet." How does this point of view affect how you feel about Geraldine's conflict?

4 **Interpret** "Geraldine Moore the Poet" contains several idioms. Using clues from the story, determine the meaning of the idiom *stopped dead* on page 297. Find another idiom and determine its meaning.

Write Answer the following questions in your Reader's Journal.

5 **Infer** How does point of view help communicate thoughts, feelings, and ideas in a poem or story?

6 **Evaluate** What point of view did the author of your Anchor Book write in? Choose a paragraph from the book and rewrite it using a different point of view. What effect might this change have on the story?

while reading your anchor book

4-7 Language Coach
Grammar and Spelling

Simple and Compound Subjects

Every sentence has a subject and predicate. The **subject** is the word or words that tell you who or what a sentence is about. The **predicate** is the last part of the sentence, beginning at the verb, which tells what the subject does.

Paul rides a bike to school.
subject predicate

When a sentence has only one subject, that subject is known as a **simple subject.**

Sentence	Simple Subject
The baby cried all night long.	baby

A **compound subject** is two or more subjects that have the same verb and are joined by a conjunction such as *and* or *or.*

Sentence	Compound Subject
Kyle and Maura will participate in the science fair.	Kyle, Maura
Jenny or Mary will wash the car tonight.	Jenny, Mary

Directions Use the subject or subjects given to write simple or compound sentences.

1 dog, cat

2 cell phone

3 beach, pool

4 Ezra, Alec

Sentence Types

There are four types of sentences—**declarative, interrogative, imperative,** and **exclamatory.** Each type has a different purpose. You can look for certain clues to help you figure out what type of sentence you are reading.

Sentence Type	Function	End Punctuation	Example
declarative	makes a statement	period	The lizard is healthy.
interrogative	asks a question	question mark	Where are you going?
imperative	gives an order	period or exclamation mark	Do your homework. Come here now!
exclamatory	expresses strong emotion	exclamation mark	What a great idea!

Directions Write the sentence type for each of the examples below. Then add the correct end punctuation.

1 ______________ Cory has a dog, two cats, and a parakeet.__

2 ______________ Will your aunt run in the marathon this year__

3 ______________ Get out on that soccer field right now__

4 ______________ I'm so excited to go on vacation__

Directions Change each sentence type into the type listed in parentheses. Write the new sentence. Make sure that you use correct end punctuation in your new sentences.

5 Will you wait for me by the stage door? (imperative sentence)

____

6 That game was exciting. (interrogative sentence)

____

7 Is John going to compete in next week's hockey tournament? (exclamatory sentence)

____

8 Does your mother work every weekend? (declarative sentence)

____

Go Online
Learn More
Visit: PHSchool.com
Web Code: exp-6403

Revising for Stronger Sentences

As you've just learned, end punctuation is very important in all sentences. When you write, it's important to use correct end punctuation, so that your readers understand the purpose of each sentence.

When you revise your writing, reread each sentence carefully to make sure that it does what you want it to do. If your writing is not clear, revise it by changing the end punctuation, reorganizing your sentences, making sure you use the correct words, and adding details.

Directions Rewrite the paragraph with the correct end punctuation. If the punctuation is already correct, do not change it.

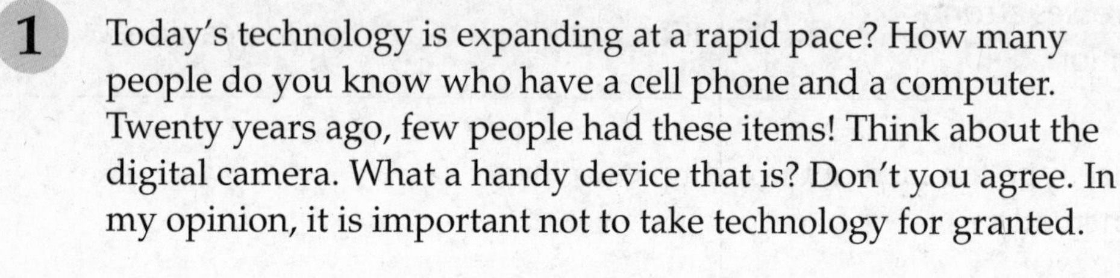

1 Today's technology is expanding at a rapid pace? How many people do you know who have a cell phone and a computer. Twenty years ago, few people had these items! Think about the digital camera. What a handy device that is? Don't you agree. In my opinion, it is important not to take technology for granted.

Author's Craft

Have you ever seen a passage without any declarative sentences? Reread "Ghost Crab" beginning on page 288. Change all of the declarative sentences to a different sentence type. How does the passage sound? How important do you think declarative sentences are?

Directions Write a four- or five-sentence paragraph about your favorite book or movie. Use a declarative, an interrogative, an imperative, and an exclamatory sentence at least once. Make sure to use the correct end punctuation.

2

Spelling Words With Prefixes and Suffixes

Go Online
Learn More
Visit: PHSchool.com
Web Code: exp-6404

Prefixes are word parts added to the beginning of a base word. When you add a prefix to a base word, the meaning of the word changes, but the spelling of the base word remains the same.

Prefix	Prefix Meaning	Base Word	New Word
dis- *un-*	opposite of	trust tangle	distrust untangle
mis-	wrong	spell	misspell
pre-	before	school	preschool
re-	again, back	heat	reheat

Directions Divide each word into its prefix and base word.

1 ______ + ______ = preview

2 ______ + ______ = misinterpret

Suffixes are word parts added to the end of a base word. Adding a suffix changes the way a word is used in a sentence. Here are ways that adding a suffix can affect the spelling of a word.

- When you add a suffix that starts with a consonant (*-ful, -ness, -ly*), sometimes you change a *y* to *i* in the base word.
- When you add a suffix that starts with a vowel (*-ion, -al, -able*), you usually drop the final *e* in the base word. You change a *y* to *i* in the base word unless a consonant precedes the *y*.
- In many cases, you do not change the spelling of the base word.

Suffix	Suffix Meaning	Base Word	New Word
-ful	full of	fancy	fanciful
-ness	quality	silly	silliness
-ly	in a way, like	noise	noisily
-ion	the state of	hesitate	hesitation

Author's Craft

How many words can you create by adding prefixes or suffixes to a single base word? Reread "Cleaning the Well" beginning on page 294. Working with a small group, choose words from the poem and add prefixes and/or suffixes to see how many words you can make. Compare lists with other groups. Which base words worked best?

Directions Combine each base word and suffix to form a new word.

3 season, -al ______

4 commit, -ment ______

5 hungry, -ly ______

6 meaning, -ful ______

4-8 Writer's Workshop
Description: Descriptive Essay

A **descriptive essay** is an essay that tells the reader how an experience or event looks, feels, smells, tastes, or sounds. This type of essay uses words that give the reader a mental picture of what is being described, and that allow readers to feel they are having the same experience. Follow the steps in this workshop to write a descriptive essay about a setting you know well.

Purpose To write a descriptive essay about a setting you know well

Audience Your teacher and your classmates

Your descriptive essay should include the following elements.

- a clear image of the setting that is supported by details
- rich sensory details that appeal to one or more of the five senses
- an organization that helps readers picture the setting
- language that creates vivid images and comparisons appropriate to the tone, style, and mood of your essay
- error-free writing, with correct use of simple and compound subjects

Prewriting—Plan It Out

Use these strategies to start planning your essay.

Choose your topic. Make a list of general topics, such as *vacation*, *celebration*, or *family members*. Make notes about specific places and events from your life that you associate with each of the topics. Review your list and choose the place or event that is most interesting to you.

Gather details. How many ways can you think of to describe your setting or event? One way is to describe it in terms of the five senses. Use a sensory chart to help you gather details. Look at this student's examples. Then add your own.

Sights	Scents	Textures	Sounds	Tastes
pine trees	clear air, smoke	crunchy pine needles	hoot of owls	smoky flavor of food

Drafting—Get It on Paper

Use these steps to help you write your first draft.

Organize the details. Before you write, organize the details that help the reader picture the setting. Combine related details about the experience as this student did.

smoky smell of hot dogs cooking over a crackling campfire

a tent that is slightly lopsided or sagging in the middle

Provide elaboration. Use figurative language, such as similes and metaphors, to create vivid images and comparisons.

Simile: The dried *wood* crackled *like fireworks* on the Fourth of July.

Metaphor: The *rain* was a steady *waterfall.*

Write your own simile or metaphor in the box.

My figurative language:

Revising—Make It Better

Review and revise your work when your first draft is finished.

Check sentence length. Be sure your sentences vary in length and complexity. Short sentences can be choppy and seem awkward. Combine two sentences, or break long sentences into shorter ones to emphasize unique details. Also check your paragraph development, consistency of verb tenses, word choice, and organization.

There is so much darkness. There is a small light. It is a streetlight. It is tall and gives off a silvery glow.

Though there is so much darkness, a tall streetlight gives off a silvery glow.

The writer combined several short, choppy sentences to create one longer sentence.

Peer Review Ask for a classmate's response to your descriptive essay. Revise to achieve the reaction you had intended.

Directions Read this student descriptive essay as a model for your own.

Go Online
Student Model
Visit: PHSchool.com
Web Code: exr-6401

Student Model: Descriptive Writing

Hailley White, Somerset, NY

The Night Life

As I sit here on my cold, damp patio in early fall, I look up at the clear, dark sky. I see the beautiful bright stars as they twinkle. I am always in awe as I look up there, and my heart sometimes skips a beat. In such a vast sky, the expanse of it all makes me feel as though I am as small as a tiny ant. . . .

I love the sounds of nature at nighttime. The sound of crickets rubbing their thin legs together makes the most lovely noise. Then there is the big owl perched in a distant tree, hooting a lonesome tune. Off in the distance is the bullfrog. All of these wonderful sounds are like a luring lullaby that could rock me to sleep . . . .

The air smells like freshly cut grass. In the dim light, the grass looks like asphalt, it is so black. When I take a step, it is cold and damp from the fallen dew, and the wetness gives everything a shimmery look. There is also the smell of decaying leaves. They make a crunching noise underneath my feet. I feel so free just running around my backyard barefoot in the dark. The leaves and the dew feel absolutely refreshing. You should really try it sometime.

House after house surrounds me. One has its lights on, showing that someone is still awake. The other houses' lights are completely out, and everyone is probably snug in their beds. I can see red blinking lights over the hills and valleys. They must be towers for cell phones, so people can communicate—even in the dark . . . .

There is a slight breeze blowing, but that is okay. I wish I could stand here forever, staring up at the total darkness, except for the light of a few stars.

In the first sentence, Hailley presents the setting she will describe.

Hailley creates a vivid image with a simile that compares night sounds to a lullaby.

Hailley brings her setting to life by using sensory images that appeal to the senses of smell, sight, touch, and hearing.

By organizing her essay to focus on sensory images, Hailley makes readers feel as though they were in the setting she describes.

Editing—Be Your Own Language Coach

Before you hand in your descriptive essay, review it for language convention errors. Pay special attention to your use of simple and compound subjects. Also check for the spelling of previously studied words, word patterns, and usage.

Publishing—Share It!

When you publish a work, you produce it for a specific audience. Consider one of the following ideas to share your writing.

Record it. Make an audio recording of your description. Ask classmates to imagine the setting as they listen to the recording.

Illustrate it. Create a book for a young child. Write one or two sentences on each page along with a drawing of what you describe.

Reflecting on Your Writing

1 Respond to the following questions on a separate sheet of paper and hand it in with your final draft. What new insights did you gain about the form of a descriptive essay by writing one? What did you do well? What do you need to work on?

2 **Rubric for Self-Assessment** Assess your essay's strengths and weaknesses using the criteria. For each question, circle a rating.

CRITERIA	RATING SCALE
	NOT VERY — VERY
IDEAS How clear are your images of the setting and supporting details?	1 2 3 4 5
ORGANIZATION How clear and logical is your organization?	1 2 3 4 5
VOICE How lively and engaging is your writing?	1 2 3 4 5
WORD CHOICE How effective is your use of descriptive language?	1 2 3 4 5
SENTENCE FLUENCY How varied is your sentence structure?	1 2 3 4 5
CONVENTIONS How correct is your spelling, grammar, and use of simple and compound subjects?	1 2 3 4 5

Monitoring Your Progress
Standardized Test Practice

Reading Skill: Paraphrasing

Read the passage. Then answer the questions.

Tea is one of the main beverages consumed around the world. Aside from water, the most popular beverage is tea. Like water, tea has many benefits.

The Chinese began the practice of drinking tea more than 1,000 years ago. Today, people in China still meet over cups of tea in teahouses. Tea drinking has developed into an art form in China, focusing on taste rather than on how to drink tea.

The Chinese have benefited from tea for a long time. Tea aids in relaxation and has many chemicals that help the body. It has less caffeine than coffee and reduces the risk of heart attack, stroke, and cancer. Tea helps build strong bones and a strong immune system. It is naturally calorie-free, and it can increase your metabolism. Maybe scientists will discover more benefits to drinking tea.

1 When you **paraphrase** a sentence from this passage, you ______.

A. summarize it

B. give your opinion

C. use your own words

D. cite sources

2 Which statement best **paraphrases** the first sentence?

F. Tea is better for you than coffee.

G. Tea is one of the most popular drinks in the world.

H. More people in China drink tea than anywhere else.

J. Tea has no calories, so it can help you lose weight.

3 Which best **paraphrases** the author's views about the role of tea in China?

A. Tea is an important part of Chinese life.

B. The Chinese drink tea because it reduces the chance of heart attacks.

C. People in China realize that tea has less caffeine than coffee.

D. The Chinese live longer because they drink more tea.

4 What is most likely the meaning of "immune system"?

F. the practice of visiting teahouses

G. series of exercises for relaxation

H. system for making tea

J. what protects the body from sickness

5 Paraphrase the last sentence in the passage.

____

____

Literary Analysis: Elements of Prose and Poetry

Read the passage. Then answer the questions.

Kiri dipped one end of the gnarled oar into the water, braced her sun-baked arms, and slowly propelled the canoe forward across the pane of glass her parents called the sea. She looked behind her, at the ripples and bubbles calling her name—*Kiri, Kiri, Kiri*—but they soon settled down once the canoe was far enough away. Kiri liked to think of the ocean as a great child, whispering to her and splashing water up at her flushed face. Her parents didn't think like Kiri did, though. They frowned when she slapped the crests of frolicking waves with the palm of her hand. To them, the ocean was a mirror that separated two worlds. Her parents warned her not to break the surface of the sea, or she might be lost forever to the world under the water. Kiri wasn't sure if her parents were right. But she knew, as she shifted the oar to the other side and heard the bubbly chatter again—*Kiri, Kiri, Kiri*—a child was calling her name.

6 Why does the author use **figurative language** in this passage?

A. to illustrate Kiri's relationship with the sea and with her parents

B. to help the reader understand unfamiliar words

C. to help the reader form a picture of what Kiri's parents are like

D. to help the reader understand how to use a canoe

7 Which is an example of a **metaphor?**

F. bubbles calling her name

G. slapped the crests of frolicking waves

H. the ocean was a mirror

J. she might be lost forever

8 The author used **personification** to describe what?

A. canoe

B. oar

C. ocean

D. Kiri

9 From which **point of view** is the passage told?

F. first person

G. second person

H. omniscient third person

J. limited third person

Timed Writing: Interpretation of Literature

Directions Write about an experience using first-person point of view. Be sure to use the pronouns *I, me, mine,* and *my.* Then describe that same experience using a different point of view. **(20 minutes)**

4-9 Reading Skills
Context Clues

In learning new reading skills, you will use special academic vocabulary. Knowing the right words will help you demonstrate your understanding.

Academic Vocabulary

Word	Meaning	Example Sentence
confirm *v.* *Related words:* confirming, confirmation	to prove to be true; to verify	I called my friend to *confirm* that we were meeting at 7:00.
preview *v.* *Related words:* previewed, previewing	to look at or view in advance	Tonight we saw a *preview* of the movie that is coming out this weekend.
clarify *v.* *Related words:* clarified, clarification	to make clear or understandable	Jenny was confused by the directions, until her teacher *clarified* them for her.

When you come across an unfamiliar word while reading, try to determine the meaning of the word without using a dictionary. Look for **context clues**—the words, phrases, or sentences around the unfamiliar word that can help you determine the word's meaning. Then you can use a dictionary to **confirm** whether or not your meaning is correct. To use context clues, **preview** the text and ask yourself these questions about the word.

- What type of word is it?
- What other words in the sentence might help me **clarify** its meaning?
- What simpler word can I use in its place?

Example	Students are allowed to go to the museum as long as a student brings in a parent's written *consent*.
Clues from text	"Are allowed" tells me that students need permission to go on the trip. I can infer that a parent's permission, or *consent*, allows a student to go on the trip.

Directions Read the following passage. Then answer the questions.

from **"La Leña Buena"** *by John Phillip Santos*

Good wood is like a jewel, Tío Abrán, my great-grandfather Jacobo's twin brother, used to say. Huisache burns fast, in twisting yellow flames, engulfing the log in a cocoon of fire. It burns brightly, so it is sought after for Easter bonfires. But it does not burn hot, so it's poor wood for home fires. On a cold morning in the sierra, you can burn a whole tree by noon. Mesquite, and even better, cedar—these are noble, hard woods. They burn hot and long. Their smoke is fragrant. And if you know how to do it, they make exquisite charcoal.

"La leña buena es como una joya."

Good wood is like a jewel. And old Tío Abrán knew wood the way a jeweler knows stones, and in northern Coahuila, from Múzquiz to Rosita, his charcoal was highly regarded for its sweet, long-burning fire.

1 **Apply** Use the graphic organizer to help you determine the meaning of an unfamiliar word in the passage.

Unfamiliar word	
Type of word	
Clues from text	
Meaning	

2 **Infer** What is the meaning of *huisache?* Underline context clues from the passage that help you determine its meaning. Why do you think the author uses this word in the passage?

3 **Clarify** The author uses the simile "Good wood is like a jewel." What context clues explain what the author is saying? Rewrite the statement using your own words.

while reading your anchor book

In the following selection, use context clues to determine the meaning of unfamiliar words. *Guiding Question:* **How does the author communicate the meaning of unfamiliar words?**

Link to Science

WIPING OUT YELLOW FEVER

Background *Yellow fever is a deadly disease found in the tropics. Long ago, scientists did not know what caused it, so they could not stop it from spreading. Research by several scientists from 1796 to 1950 finally led to a vaccine that could prevent the disease.*

Yellow fever is a tropical disease that is caused by a virus. Many people from Central America, South America, Africa, and tropical islands have died from the disease. The disease is spread to humans by infected mosquitoes. It can damage the liver and cause a person's skin to take on a yellow color. Scientists from all over the world have found ways to prevent the disease.

EDWARD JENNER

Edward Jenner (1749–1823) was the first scientist to vaccinate people in order to protect them from disease. In vaccinating people, he injected a weakened form of the disease into their bodies. The injected germs caused the body to go into alert and to produce special cells that would fight off the disease. Once a person was infected, the body would become immune, or more likely to resist the disease.

Jenner was an English doctor who had watched many people die from smallpox. He noticed that another group of people, those who contracted cowpox disease, never got the smallpox virus. Cowpox was similar to smallpox, but the symptoms were much milder. From this observation, Jenner concluded that the cowpox germ must have protected people from getting smallpox.

In 1796, Jenner injected a young boy with cowpox germs by forcing the germs into the boy's body through a hollow needle. A few months later, he injected the boy with smallpox germs, but the boy never developed smallpox. Edward Jenner had found a way to stop the spread of smallpox. At first, people were afraid to try vaccination, but soon this new form of prevention was saving lives around the world.

LOUIS PASTEUR

Other scientists inspired by Jenner's work began searching for new vaccines to protect people from disease. Jenner had vaccinated people by using weaker germs from a less serious disease. In 1881, French scientist Louis Pasteur (1822–1895) took Jenner's work a step farther. He found a way to take powerful germs and make them weaker. Then he began experimenting with these germs using sheep and chickens.

Pasteur divided the animals into two groups and injected one group with the weakened germs. The other group of animals was not injected at all. In scientific experiments, this group is called the control group. The animals in the control group usually caught the serious disease and died, but the animals that were injected with the germ did not catch the disease.

Four years later, Pasteur was ready to battle a deadly human disease called rabies. He began by making a weakened form of the rabies germ. He injected this vaccine into a 9-year-old boy who had been bitten by a dog with rabies. Louis Pasteur and his vaccine saved the boy's life.

CARLOS FINLAY

Scientists were eager to find the germ that caused the spread of yellow fever. If they found it, perhaps they could create a vaccine to stop the spread of this deadly disease. But no one could figure out where the disease originated or how it was spread.

In 1881, Carlos Finlay (1833–1915), a Cuban doctor, had a new idea. After investigating yellow fever for almost 10 years, he had a breakthrough. He read that some diseases needed a host plant or animal to transport the disease. Through further study, he came up with the idea that mosquitoes carried the disease—but his idea proved to be too advanced for its time. Finlay tested his idea and presented his theory at an international scientific conference in 1886. Unfortunately, he could not convince the scientific world of his idea, and they ignored his work for years. It wasn't until almost 20 years later that an American doctor named Walter Reed finally proved that Finlay was right.

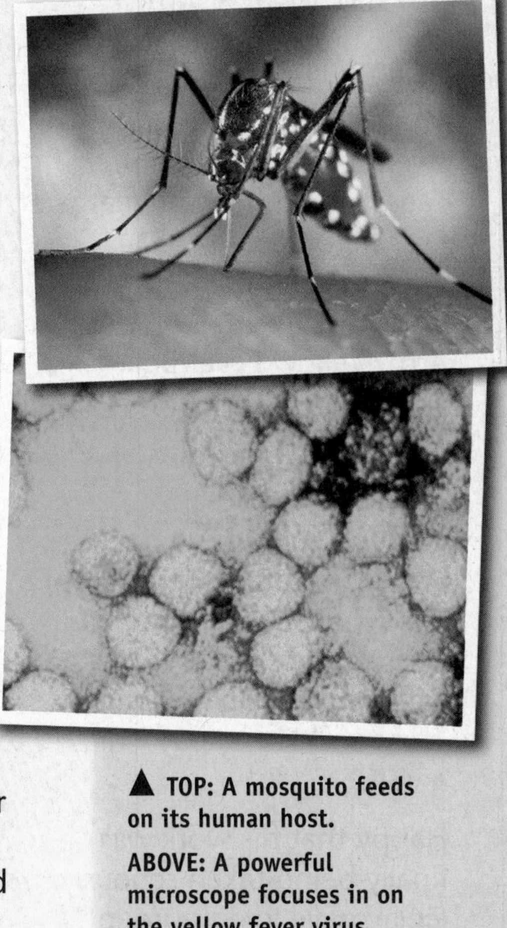

▲ **TOP: A mosquito feeds on its human host.**

ABOVE: A powerful microscope focuses in on the yellow fever virus.

WALTER REED

In 1900, the U.S. Army chose a group of men to study yellow fever in Cuba. The disease had recently swept across the island, causing hundreds of deaths. Dr. Walter Reed (1851–1902) was appointed to head the group—the U.S. Army Yellow Fever Board.

At that time, the U.S. Army still believed that objects such as bedding and clothing spread the disease. With few options remaining, Reed and several other doctors considered Carlos Finlay's work on mosquitoes. They decided to pay Finlay a visit.

Happy that his work was finally being taken seriously, Finlay gave Reed's group mosquito eggs on which they could experiment. At the lab in Havana, Cuba, Reed's group of doctors began the experiment—on themselves. First, the doctors allowed the mosquitoes to feed on the blood of patients infected with the virus. Then the mosquitoes would bite the healthy doctors. None of the doctors got sick until Dr. James Carroll fell ill. He was diagnosed with yellow fever but later recovered. This daring experiment established proof that certain mosquitoes were the agents that carried the yellow fever virus.

WILLIAM GORGAS

The next step was to find out how to get rid of the mosquitoes that carried yellow fever. William Gorgas (1854–1920), a U.S. Army doctor, knew that mosquitoes' breeding grounds were in areas that included trash heaps, garbage dumps, unused wells, old tin cans, puddles, ponds, and swamps. With this information, he began a program in Cuba to clean up garbage and other wastes that promoted the disease. This sanitation program helped stop the yellow fever epidemic. Gorgas then went on to Panama to duplicate his efforts and wipe out yellow fever there. His work in Panama saved hundreds of workers who were building the Panama Canal.

MAX THEILER

The final step in solving the yellow fever mystery took scientists back to the discoveries of Jenner and Pasteur. Could scientists now find the yellow fever germ in infected mosquitoes and make a weaker form of the germ to be used for vaccinations?

Max Theiler (1899–1972), a South African doctor working in the United States, achieved this final step. In the 1930s, he created a weak form of the yellow fever germ. For more than 20 years, he continued to improve his vaccine. Because of his work, doctors could now protect people from yellow fever even if mosquitoes that carried the disease still remained.

Today yellow fever is under control in most of the world. Doctors cannot cure the disease, but they can prevent it from spreading by using vaccinations and better sanitary conditions.

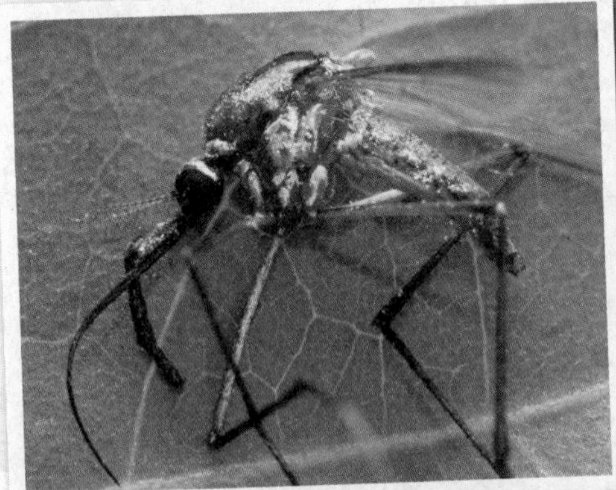

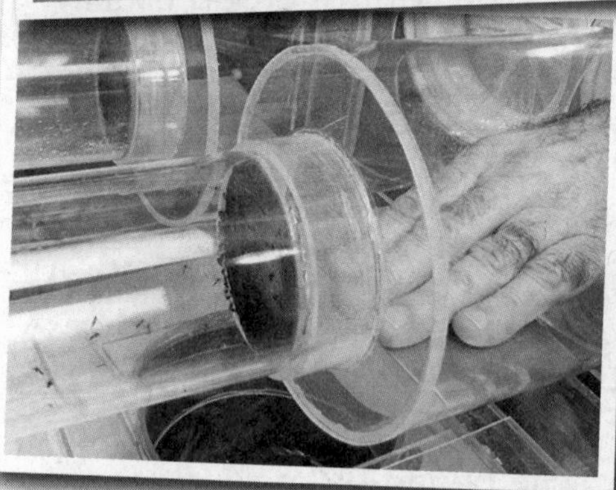

▲ **TOP: Spraying mosquitoes such as this swamp mosquito can help prevent diseases like yellow fever from spreading.**

BOTTOM: A scientist demonstrates how strongly a yellow fever mosquito is attracted to the scent of his hand. The mosquitoes are separated from his hand by a screen.

Thinking About the Selection

Wiping Out Yellow Fever

1 **Apply** Use context clues to define the meaning of each boldfaced word. In your own words, tell what the word means.

Unfamiliar Word	Context Clue(s)	Meaning
. . . he **injected** a weakened form of the disease into their bodies.	A virus was put into their bodies by a needle.	to put something into a person's body using a needle
. . . some diseases needed a **host** plant or animal to transport the disease.		
This **sanitation** program helped stop the epidemic.		

2 **Analyze** How did the author organize the information in the article?

Write Answer the following questions in your Reader's Journal.

3 **Explain** How does the author communicate the meaning of unfamiliar words?

4 **Apply** Use context clues to define an unfamiliar word in your Anchor Book. Write its meaning in your journal.

Ready for a Free-Choice Book? *Your teacher may ask you if you would like to choose another book to read on your own. Select a book that fits your interest and that you'll enjoy. As you read, think about how your new book compares with your Anchor Book.*

while reading your anchor book

4-10 Literary Analysis
Sound Devices

When you listen to music, can you figure out the mood the composer is trying to get across? Is it sadness? Excitement? Anger? Delight? As in music, if you listen to the different sounds in a poem, you can figure out what mood the poet is trying to communicate.

Literary Terms

One way a poet tries to bring a poem to life is by appealing to your sense of hearing. **Sound devices** give poetry a musical quality and help to create a poem's mood, tone, and meaning. Listed below are a few kinds of sound devices.

- **Repetition** is when an author uses words, sounds, phrases, or rhythms more than once to highlight an idea. Look at the example from Edgar Allan Poe's poem "The Raven."

  As of someone gently rapping, rapping at my chamber door.—
  "Tis some visitor," I muttered, "tapping at my chamber door."

- **Rhyme** is the repeating of sounds at the ends of words. Rhyming words usually appear at the end of lines in a poem. *Jewel, pool, rule,* and *fool* are rhyming words.

  Some poems have a regular, predictable pattern of rhyming words known as a **rhyme scheme.** You can use letters to label the pattern. In a poem with a rhyme scheme of *abab,* for example, the words at the end of every other line rhyme.

  The following poem has the rhyme scheme *abcb.* The second and fourth lines rhyme, but the first and third lines do not.

  A lonely man walked into **town** *a*
  Dragging his feet all the **way.** *b*
  He never stopped, or said a **word** *c*
  Because after all, what would he **say?** *b*

- **Rhythm** is the pattern of strong and weak stresses, or beats, you hear as you read a poem. Some poetry has a regular rhythm that's easy to identify—for example, *da da DUM da da DUM da da DUM.* In other poems, you have to look a little harder for a rhythm that captures the natural rise and fall of the words as you speak.

Directions Read the following poem. Underline the rhyming words.

Go Online
About the Author
Visit: PHSchool.com
Web Code: exe-6412

The Question *by Karla Kuskin*

People always say to me
"What do you think you'd like to be
When you grow up?"
And I say "Why,
I think I'd like to be the sky
Or a plane or train or mouse
Or maybe a haunted house
Or something furry, rough and wild . . .
Or maybe I will stay a child."

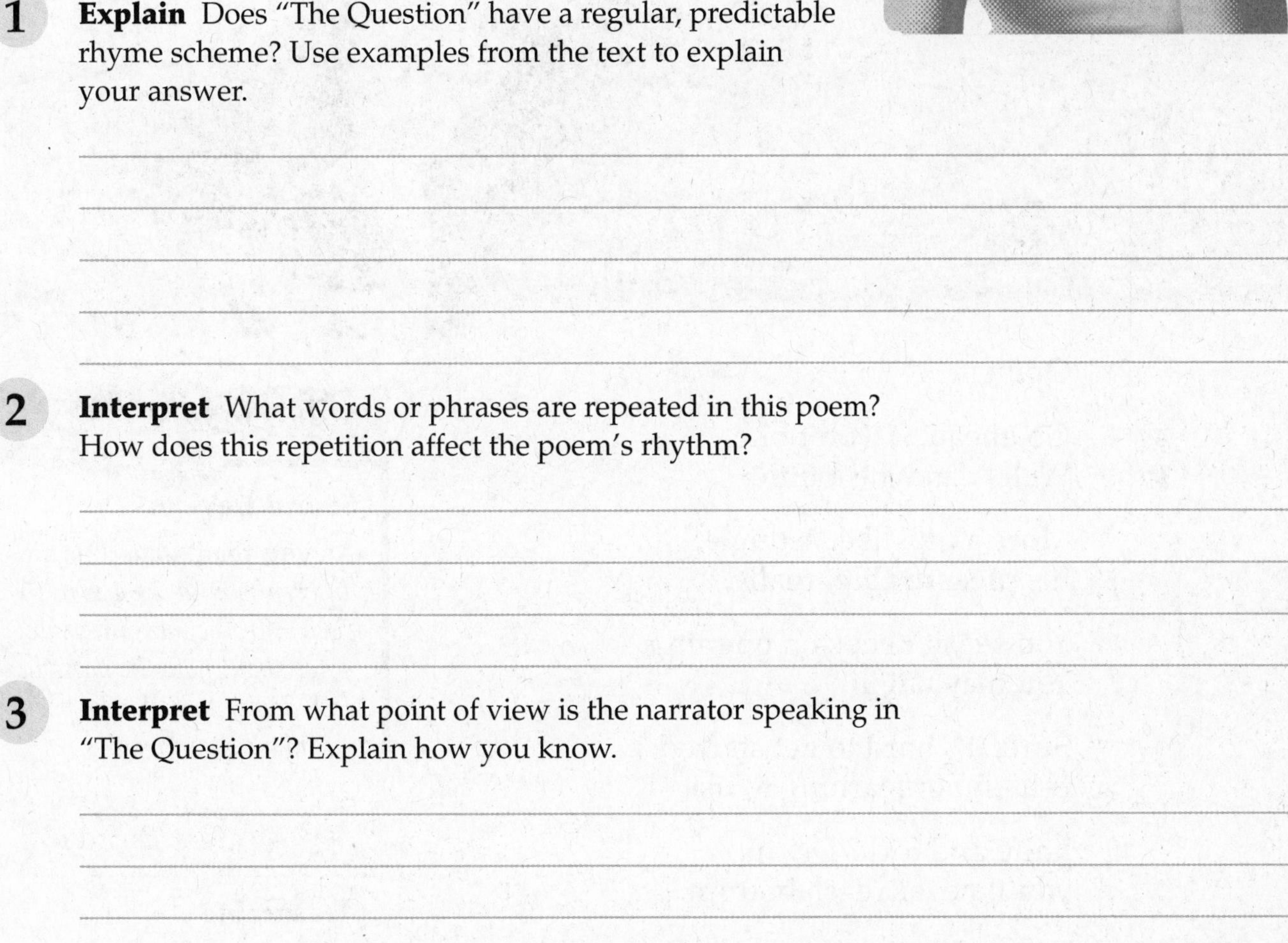

1 **Explain** Does "The Question" have a regular, predictable rhyme scheme? Use examples from the text to explain your answer.

2 **Interpret** What words or phrases are repeated in this poem? How does this repetition affect the poem's rhythm?

3 **Interpret** From what point of view is the narrator speaking in "The Question"? Explain how you know.

while reading your anchor book

Read the following poems aloud. Listen for the musical quality brought out in each poem by the sound devices the poet uses. *Guiding Question:* **How do poets, like musicians, use sound devices to communicate their ideas?**

Vocabulary Builder

Before you read, *you will discuss the following words. In the Vocabulary Builder box in the margin, use a vocabulary building strategy to make the words your own.*

pleasurable **beset** **profound**

As you read, *draw a box around unfamiliar words you could add to your vocabulary. Use context clues to unlock their meaning.*

Open it.

Go ahead, it won't bite.
Well . . .maybe a little.

More a nip, like. A tingle.
It's **pleasurable,** really.

You see, it keeps on opening.
You may fall in.

Sure, it's hard to get started;
remember learning to use

knife and fork? Dig in:
you'll never reach bottom.

It's not like it's the end of the world—
just the world as you think

you know it.

Marking the Text

Sound Devices

As you read, *underline the different sound devices in the poems. In the margin, write notes about how the poets use each device to make the poem sound a certain way.*

Vocabulary Builder

pleasurable
(plezh'ər ə bəl) *adj.*

Meaning

Literature in Context
Martin Luther King, Jr.

Link to History

Martin Luther King, Jr. was born in Atlanta, Georgia, in 1929. He grew up when segregation was a leading issue in the United States. African Americans had to attend different schools, drink from different water fountains, and use different restrooms than white people. This separation by race influenced King to join the civil rights movement. He led the movement by using peaceful action to bring about change. Not everyone agreed with his ideas, and in 1968 in Memphis, Tennessee, he was shot and killed. Today we remember him each year on Martin Luther King, Jr. Day.

while reading your anchor book

MARTIN LUTHER KING

by Raymond Patterson

Marking the Text

He came upon an age
Beset by grief, by rage—

His love so deep, so wide,
He could not turn aside.

His passion, so profound,
He would not turn around.

He taught a suffering earth
The measure of man's worth.

For this he was slain,
But he will come again.

Vocabulary Builder

beset
(bē set′) *v.*

Meaning

profound
(prō found′) *adj.*

Meaning

Marking the Text

Who Am I?

by Felice Holman

The trees ask me,
And the sky,
And the sea asks me
    Who am I?

The grass asks me,
And the sand,
And the rocks ask me
    Who I am.

The wind tells me
At nightfall,
And the rain tells me
Someone small.

Someone small
Someone small
But a piece
    of
    it
    all.

Vocabulary Builder

After you read, *review the words you decided to add to your vocabulary. Write the meaning of words you have learned in context. Look up the other words in a dictionary, glossary, thesaurus, or electronic resource.*

The First Book, Martin Luther King, *and* Who Am I?

Go Online
About the Author
Visit: PHSchool.com
Web Code: exe-6413
6414
6415

1 **Analyze** How does the poet capture the natural speaking rhythm and tone of the narrator in "The First Book"? Give examples from the poem.

2 **Interpret** What is the tone of the poem "Martin Luther King"? How does the author's choice of rhyme words help to convey this tone?

3 **Apply** What is the rhyme scheme of "Martin Luther King"?

4 **Analyze** How does repetition in "Who Am I?" help you to understand how the narrator feels about her place in the world around her?

Write Answer the following questions in your Reader's Journal.

5 **Explain** How do poets, like musicians, use sound devices to communicate their ideas?

6 **Compare and Contrast** What are some examples of sound devices used in your Anchor Book? How are they similar to, or different from, those used in the poems you just read?

while reading your anchor book

4-11 Literary Analysis
Forms of Poetry

You have learned that fiction and nonfiction writing can take on many forms. Poetry can, too. The form of a poem reflects the author's purpose for writing it.

Literary Terms

- A **narrative poem** tells a story in verse. Narrative poems often have the same elements that are found in short stories and novels, such as plots and characters.
- A **lyric poem** expresses the thoughts and feelings of a single speaker. These poems are usually short and musical-sounding.
- A **concrete poem** is shaped to look like the subject of the poem. For example, the words in a concrete poem about the moon would be arranged in the shape of the moon.
- A **limerick** is a funny poem with five lines. Lines 1, 2, and 5 rhyme, and have three beats, or stressed syllables. Lines 3 and 4 rhyme and have two beats.

  There WAS an old MAN with a BEARD,
  Who SAID, "It is JUST as I FEARED!
  Two OWLS and a HEN,
  Four LARKS and a WREN,
  Have ALL built their NESTS in my BEARD!"

  A limerick's *aabba* rhyme scheme, along with its playful language, gives it a fun and humorous sound.
- **Haiku** is a Japanese form of poetry with three lines. The poet uses figurative and sensory language to create images that often relate to nature. Lines 1 and 3 have five syllables, while line 2 has seven syllables.

while reading your anchor book

Directions Read the limerick. Notice the details a student underlined to identify the stressed syllables, as well as the notes the student wrote on the self-stick note that tell about the structure and rhyme pattern.

Anonymous

Limerick

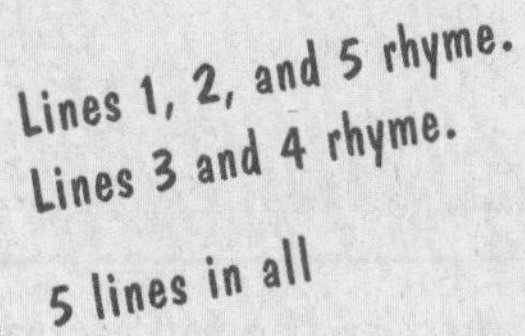

Lines 1, 2, and 5 rhyme.
Lines 3 and 4 rhyme.
5 lines in all

A flea and a fly in a flue[1]
Were caught, so what could they do?
Said the fly, "Let us flee."
"Let us fly," said the flea.
So they flew through a flaw[2] in the flue.

1 **flue** (flo͞o) *n.* pipe for smoke, hot air, or exhaust fumes, especially in a chimney.

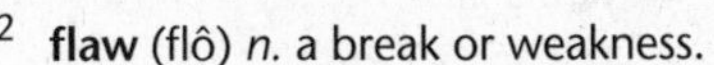

2 **flaw** (flô) *n.* a break or weakness.

1 **Describe** What tricks does the poet use to add humor to the poem?

2 **Explain** What is personified in this poem? How do you know?

3 **Analyze** What elements of the poem make it a limerick? Support your answer with details from the poem.

The following selections represent different forms of poetry—concrete, haiku, and narrative poetry. *Guiding Question:* **How do you think poets decide which form of poetry to use to communicate their purpose?**

Vocabulary Builder

Before you read, *you will discuss the following words. In the Vocabulary Builder box in the margin, use a vocabulary building strategy to make the words your own.*

rage **locomotion**

As you read, *draw a box around unfamiliar words you could add to your vocabulary. Use context clues to unlock their meaning.*

Marking the Text

Forms of Poetry

In the margin, *name the form of poetry. Underline things in each poem—or write notes in the margin about things—that helped you to decide the form of poetry.*

CONCRETE CAT

by Dorthi Charles

A A
e r e r

eYe eYe stripestripestripestripe
whisker whisker stripestripestripe tail
whisker m h whisker stripestripestripestripe tail
o t stripestripestripe
U stripestripestripestripe

paw paw paw paw mouse

dishdish litterbox
litterbox

Literature in Context
History of Haiku

Link to Social Studies

Short poems have been around for centuries in Japan. At one time, people would get together and compose poems the way we might get together to play board games. To create *linked poems,* one person would start a poem and someone else would finish it. At first, there were many complicated rules, but eventually, the popular poetry form known as *haiku* evolved. Haiku is characterized by language that describes an image from nature, uses simple words, and has a set pattern of syllables. Today, haiku is popular not only in Japan, but also in countries around the world.

Haikus

Over the wintry
Forest, winds howl in a **rage**
With no leaves to blow.

—Musō Soseki

Bearing no flowers,
I am free to toss madly
Like the willow tree.

—Chiyojo

Marking the Text

while reading your anchor book

Vocabulary Builder

rage
(rāj) *n.*

Meaning

How I Got My Name

from *Locomotion* by Jacqueline Woodson

Marking the Text

Whenever that song came on that goes
Come on, baby, do the Locomotion, Mama
would make us dance with her.
We'd do this dance called the **Locomotion**

when we'd bend our elbows and move
our arms in circles at our sides.
Like arms were train wheels.
I can see us doing it now—in slow motion.

Mama grinning and singing along
Saying all proud "my kids got rhythm!"
Sometimes Lili got behind me and we'd
do the Locomotion around our little living room.

Till the song ended.
And we fell out on the couch
Laughing. Mama would say
You see why I love that song so much, Lonnie?

See why I had to make it your name?
Lonnie Collins Motion, Mama would say.
Lo Co Motion
Yeah.

while reading your anchor book

Vocabulary Builder

locomotion
(lō′ kō mō′ shən) *n.*

Meaning

Vocabulary Builder

After you read, *review the words you decided to add to your vocabulary. Write the meaning of words you have learned in context. Look up the other words in a dictionary, glossary, thesaurus, or electronic resource.*

Thinking About the Selections

Concrete Cat, Haikus, *and* How I Got My Name

About the Author
Visit: PHSchool.com
Web Codes: exe-6416
6417
6418
6419

1 **Evaluate** Which form of poetry did you find most enjoyable? Explain why.

2 **Make a Judgment** In your opinion, which words in "Concrete Cat" are placed most cleverly? Explain.

3 **Interpret** What is the mood of Soseki's haiku? Explain how the language communicates that mood.

4 **Analyze** What significance does the song "Locomotion" have for the speaker of the poem? How does the speaker feel about the song? Use details to explain your answer.

Write Answer the following questions in your Reader's Journal.

5 **Assess** How do you think poets decide which form of poetry to use to communicate their purpose?

6 **Analyze** Choose a poem or a section of your Anchor Book and think about the form of writing the author used. How does the form match the author's purpose?

4-12 Listening and Speaking Workshop
Reading Poetry Aloud

In this activity, you and your group members will read a poem aloud to the class. With your group, you will decide the best way to communicate the poem's meaning. Pay special attention to poetic elements, such as sound devices, figurative language, and sensory language.

Your Task

- Work with your group to choose a poem.
- Study the poem and identify elements that contribute to the poem's meaning.
- Read the poem to the class and give a brief explanation of its meaning. Be prepared to answer questions to help your classmates understand the poem's meaning.

Organize and Practice Your Presentation

1. **Choose a poem.** With your group, select a poem from this unit, or one that your teacher provides.
2. **Read and discuss the poem.** Read the poem to yourself and figure out what it means.
    - As you read, identify elements of poetry. Mark the poem where these elements are used. Check each one off in the chart to the right. Then describe it in the "Examples" column.
    - Think of how your poem represents diverse cultures, ethnicities, or time periods. How does this add to the poem's meaning?
    - Discuss your ideas with your group members. Agree upon an action for explaining the meaning of the poem.

My Poem Has	Examples
☐ sound devices	
☐ figurative language	
☐ sensory language	
☐ imagery	

3. **Create a visual.** Create a visual to help audience members understand the types of elements found in the text. For example, if the poem contains examples of literary devices, you might make a poster to illustrate the examples.
4. **Plan your delivery.** How you read the poem affects your audience's understanding of it. Consider the following questions.

- Which parts of the poem will be read individually? Which will be spoken with another reader?
- Will you speak quickly or slowly? When will you pause?
- When will you lower or raise your voice?
- Which words will you emphasize?
- What gestures will you use?

Experiment with different ideas. Remember that each group member should read at least one line of the poem.

5. **Practice and present.** Practice until all members are comfortable reading their parts. Remember to speak clearly. Speak together when you are reading as a group. Review the following rubric to make sure you are meeting all criteria.

Directions Assess your performance. For each question, circle a rating.

Speak: Rubric for Oral Interpretation

CRITERIA	RATING SCALE
CONTENT How well did the group convey the poem's meaning through its explanation of the poetic elements used?	NOT VERY — VERY 1 2 3 4 5
CONTENT How well did the group convey the poem's meaning through its analysis of culture, ethnicity, or time period?	1 2 3 4 5
ORGANIZATION How well did group members know when and how to read their lines?	1 2 3 4 5
DELIVERY How well did the group adjust their voices and expressions to communicate the poem's meaning?	1 2 3 4 5
COOPERATION How well did the group work together?	1 2 3 4 5

Listen: Rubric for Audience Self-Assessment

CRITERIA	RATING SCALE
ACTIVE LISTENING How well did you focus your attention on the speakers?	NOT VERY — VERY 1 2 3 4 5
ACTIVE LISTENING How well did you demonstrate active listening with appropriate silence, responses, and body language?	1 2 3 4 5

while reading your anchor book

4-13 Language Coach
Grammar and Spelling

Direct and Indirect Objects

A **direct object** is a noun, pronoun, or group of words that directly receives the action of the verb. The direct object answers the questions *Whom?* or *What?*

Example: Isabelle ate spaghetti for dinner.
(The direct object is *spaghetti*, which tells what Isabelle ate for dinner.)

An **indirect object** is a noun, pronoun, or group of words that tells to whom or for whom the action is being done. An indirect object is often located between an action verb and a direct object.

Example: I bought my mother flowers for her birthday.
(The indirect object is *my mother*, which tells for whom I bought the flowers.)

Directions Identify the underlined word by writing *direct object* or *indirect object* on the line.

1 Pedro wrote me a long letter. ______________

2 Mr. Chang rented a video for his family. ______________

3 Dad walked the dog for almost an hour last night. ______________

4 The instructor handed the swimmer the scuba gear. ______________

Now, go back to the above sentences. If the underlined word is the direct object, is there an indirect object? If so, circle it. If the underlined word is an indirect object, underline the direct object twice.

Directions Write a complete sentence using the direct objects and indirect objects listed. Then circle the direct objects and underline the indirect objects.

5 direct object: *bath*; indirect objects: *cat, guinea pig*

____

6 direct object: *popcorn*; indirect objects: *brother, sister*

____

7 direct objects: *flowers, balloons*; indirect object: *me*

____

Go Online
Learn More
Visit: PHSchool.com
Web Code: exp-6405

Author's Craft

Are direct objects important? Turn to "How I Got My Name" on page 328 and read the second stanza. Cross out all the direct objects and reread the new version. How do direct objects affect the meaning of a text?

Predicate Nouns and Adjectives

A **complement** is a word or a group of words that complete the meaning of a subject and a verb.

Toni brought *cookies.*

One type of complement, a **subject complement,** follows a linking verb and tells something about the subject.

Juan was the *speaker.*

Speaker follows the linking verb *was* and tells about the subject *Juan*.

There are two types of subject complements—*predicate nouns* and *predicate adjectives*.

A **predicate noun** renames or identifies the subject of the sentence.

Lucinda has become a teacher.

[Lucinda] has become <a teacher.>

subject **linking verb** **predicate noun**

A **predicate adjective** describes the subject of the sentence. Like a predicate noun, it comes after a subject and a linking verb.

[Sarah] was <thrilled> with her grades.

subject **linking verb** **predicate adjective**

Directions For each sentence below, underline the subject complement. Put a check in the box to show whether it is a **predicate noun** or a **predicate adjective.**

	Sentence	Predicate	
		Noun	Adjective
1	The winner of the poetry award is Jen Weinstein.		
2	My grandmother seems especially proud today.		
3	That garbage smells disgusting!		
4	Maria is the soloist at tonight's concert.		

Directions On a separate sheet of paper, write a five-sentence paragraph describing someone important to you. Share your paragraph with a partner and have him or her identify the direct and indirect objects and predicate nouns and adjectives.

Learn More
Visit: PHSchool.com
Web Code: exp-6407

Revising Choppy Sentences

If you write a paragraph containing several short sentences, your writing might sound choppy.

One way to eliminate choppy writing is to create **compound complements**—two complements joined by *or, and,* or *but*. Remember that a complement is a word or group of words that completes the meaning of a subject and a verb.

- **Direct objects** and **indirect objects** are complements used with action verbs.
- **Predicate nouns** and **predicate adjectives** are complements used with linking verbs.

Author's Craft

Turn to "Wiping Out Yellow Fever" beginning on page 314. Work with a partner to rewrite the first paragraph using many small, choppy sentences. Which version would you rather read? Why?

Choppy	Type of Complement	Compound Complement
I washed the floor. I washed the windows.	direct object	I washed the floor and the windows.
Danny may sell Marco his guitar. Danny may sell Isabel his guitar.	indirect object	Danny may sell Marco or Isabel his guitar.
Pam is a pianist. Pam is a singer.	predicate noun	Pam is a pianist and a singer.
Playing music is fun. It is challenging.	predicate adjective	Playing music is fun but challenging.

Directions Combine the pairs of sentences by creating a compound complement. Use the connecting words *or, and,* or *but*.

1. Sue may become a lawyer. She may become a judge.

2. The fireworks were beautiful. They were too loud.

3. Mom will give me a ride. She will give Ben a ride.

4. They sell fruit at the farm stand. They sell vegetables at the farm stand.

Directions Combine each pair of sentences according to the directions in parentheses. Write the new sentence on the line.

Go Online
Learn More
Visit: PHSchool.com
Web Code: exp-6408

5 Jorge wrote the lyrics. He also wrote the melody.
(Use *and* to make a compound direct object.)

6 The ice cream tasted sweet. The ice cream tasted delicious.
(Use *and* to make a compound predicate adjective.)

7 Mr. Garcia will tell Sid a story. He will tell me a story.
(Use *or* to make a compound indirect object.)

8 Jennifer looked tired today. She looked happy.
(Use *but* to make a compound predicate adjective.)

9 Ms. DeMaria is a science teacher. She is also a gymnastics coach.
(Use *and* to make a compound predicate noun.)

10 My aunt sells furniture. She sells fabrics.
(Use *and* to make a compound direct object.)

Directions Rewrite the paragraph by joining some of the choppy sentences.

11 The awards ceremony was held on Thursday night. Mr. Grimes was the organizer. He was also the emcee. Mr. Wisnewski, our school principal, presented Mindy Chang with an award for English. He gave Russ Hill an award for math. Most of the acceptance speeches were brief. They were also entertaining.

4-14 Writer's Workshop
Narration: Narrative Poem

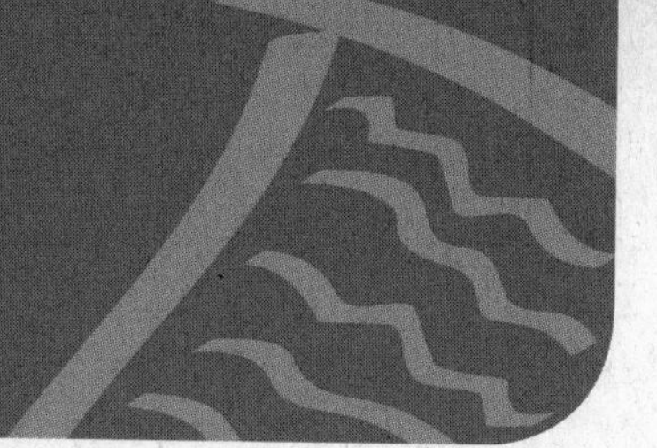

A **narrative poem** is a poem that tells a story. It has elements that are similar to those of a short story, such as plot, characters, and conflict. A narrative poem may be short, but, as in all poems, every word counts. In this workshop, you will write a poem that tells a story about a memorable event from your life.

Purpose To write a narrative poem about a memorable event

Audience You, your teacher, and your classmates

To be effective, your narrative poem should include the following.

- characters and a clear plot
- a series of real events in chronological order—the order in which the events occurred
- sound devices such as repetition, rhyme, rhyme scheme, and rhythm.
- an appropriate use of figurative language and imagery
- error-free grammar, including correct use of compound complements

Prewriting—Plan It Out

To choose the topic of your poem, use the following strategies.

Choose a topic. On a separate sheet of paper, make a chart like the one below. Fill in the first column with special events from your life that you have vivid memories and strong feelings about. For example, you may want to write about a holiday celebration or a sporting event.

Gather ideas. Complete your chart by adding memorable moments, images, and feelings that you associate with each event you listed. When you have finished, review your chart and choose the event that would make the most interesting poem.

Events	Memorable Moments	Images	Feelings
Andrea's birthday party	listening to the band, eating cake, talking to friends	birthday cake, streamers, magician, presents, barbeque	happy, excited, entertained

Drafting—Get It on Paper

Follow these steps as you write your draft.

1. **Elaborate on the details and mood.** Look over the details of your selected event. On a separate sheet of paper, create a chart like the one below. Write down which sentence types (interrogative, imperative, declarative, or exclamatory) would be most appropriate to create the mood of your chosen event.

Mood	Sentence
excited	exclamatory (!)

2. **Think about the words.** Create a list of words that relate to your chosen event. Think of two or three additional words that rhyme with each word on your list.
3. **Narrate the text.** Begin writing your poem. Think of lines that have a set rhythm and end with the rhyming words from your list. Make sure that the lines tell a story. Check that the lines not only rhyme but also make sense. Give your poem a title.

Revising—Make It Better

Check the rhythm. Read your poem aloud to check the rhythm. If a line seems too long or short, revise it to give the poem a steady rhythm.

Instead of We had fun and ran around.
A happier, more fun-loving group could never be found!

Try We talked and laughed and ran around.
No happier group could ever be found!

Describe Take your revisions one step further by introducing some figurative language, such as similes and metaphors, to better describe your event.

Instead of The flames from the candles on the cake
lit up the night sky.

Try The candles flickered like stars in the sky.

Peer Review Read your poem to a partner and ask for a response. Revise to achieve the reaction you intended.

Directions Read this student narrative poem as a model for your own.

Go Online
Student Model
Visit: PHSchool.com
Web Code: exr-6402

Student Model: Writing

Kimberly Rolle, Seal Beach, CA

Party Cake

We talked and laughed and ran around.
No happier group could ever be found!
Hearing the band, the cheering crowd
Roared like thunder from the clouds!
When they were done, and said goodbye,
the candles flickered like stars in the sky.
The ice cream cooled us off from the sun—
never before have I had so much fun!

The student chose words that help to create an exciting, playful mood.

The student uses a simile to figuratively describe the actions of the partygoers.

The use of an exclamation mark shows that this sentence is exclamatory and helps create excitement.

Editing—Be Your Own Language Coach

Before you hand in your narrative poem, review it for language convention errors. Pay special attention to the correct use of compound complements.

Publishing—Share It!

When you publish a work, you produce it for a specific audience. Consider one of the following ideas to share your writing.

Create an anthology. Collect submissions from your classmates and create an anthology of narrative poems for your class.

Submit your work. Ask your teacher about, or investigate on your own, local magazines or newspapers that could publish your poem. Submit your poem and share your narrative style with the community.

Perform it! Read your poem to the class, or record yourself reading it with expression.

Reflecting on Your Writing

1 Respond to the following questions on a separate sheet of paper and hand it in with your final draft. What new insights did you gain about the form of a narrative poem by writing one? What did you do well? What do you need more work on?

2 **Rubric for Self-Assessment** Assess your poem's strengths and weaknesses using the criteria. For each question, circle a rating.

CRITERIA	RATING SCALE
	NOT VERY / VERY
IDEAS How well does your poem focus on a real-life event?	1 2 3 4 5
ORGANIZATION How well does the sequence of lines tell a story?	1 2 3 4 5
VOICE How well do you draw the reader in with your tone and style?	1 2 3 4 5
WORD CHOICE How appropriate is your use of figurative language and imagery?	1 2 3 4 5
SENTENCE FLUENCY How varied is your sentence structure?	1 2 3 4 5
CONVENTIONS How accurate is your grammar, especially your use of compound complements and figurative language?	1 2 3 4 5

4-15 Discussing Your Anchor Book

Literature Circles

Sound Devices When you read the sentence *Sandra slowly slurped the slippery spaghetti*, do you form a familiar picture in your mind? Now read the sentence aloud. Was it hard to say because so many of the words started with the same letter? In this literature circle, you will discuss sound devices and how an author's choice of sound devices influences the way we interpret their writing.

Alliteration is the repeated use of the same consonant sounds at the beginning of words. For example, *Charlie chomped on the chewy chocolate chip cookie.* In addition to making a poem sound musical, alliteration often adds humor and lightens the mood of a text.

Onomatopoeia is the use of a word that sounds like the object it names or the sound an object makes. Poets use this sound device to create musical effects and help readers form images in their minds. For example, the sound of bacon frying in a pan is hard to describe. It's much easier to imitate the sound with the word *sizzle* to help the reader better imagine the image of bacon cooking.

while reading your anchor book

1 ON YOUR OWN

On your own find examples of sound devices in your Anchor Book. On the chart, record the sentence from the book and the page where the sound device appears. Tell whether it is an example of alliteration or onomatopoeia.

Words From Text	Sound Device
Page ________	
Page ________	
Page ________	

2 ASKING GOOD QUESTIONS

Now that you have identified some sound devices, think of some good questions to ask about each one. Your questions should do the following.

- help your Literature Circle better understand both the sound devices and your Anchor Book.
- encourage your Literature Circle to see something about your Anchor Book in a different way.
- have more than one possible answer, other than "yes" or "no"

3 YOUR QUESTIONS

____

____

____

4 WITH YOUR GROUP

Use your examples of sound devices and questions as the basis for a Literature Circle discussion. After your discussion, answer the following questions.

1 What new understanding of sound devices did you gain? What new understanding of your Anchor Book did you gain?

____

____

____

2 Which questions created the best discussion?

____

____

____

3 Strong questions encourage you to think deeply about a topic or issue. Questions, however, can also be weak. What makes questions strong or weak? Discuss your ideas with your Literature Circle. On a sheet of paper, list some characteristics of strong and weak questions.

4-16 Connecting to Your Anchor Book

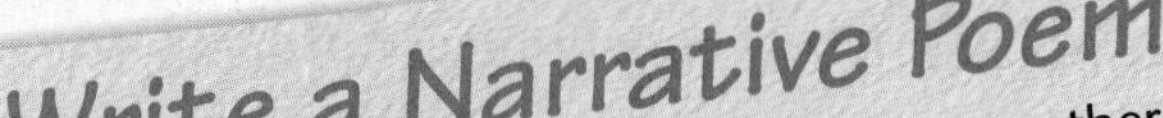

Anchor Book Projects

Now that you have completed reading your Anchor Book, it's time to get creative! Choose one of the following projects.

A Write a Narrative Poem

Families and friends love to tell stories when they get together. Pretend you are a character from your Anchor Book. Write a narrative poem that the character would share with his or her family about a conflict that occurred.

1. Choose a character and a conflict from your Anchor Book as the topic of your poem.
2. Refer to Lesson 11 in this unit to refresh your memory of what a narrative form includes.
3. Write your poem using the first-person point of view from the perspective of a character in your Anchor Book. Use sensory and figurative language to add details and creativity.

Your poem should include the following elements.

- a clear reference to a character and event from your Anchor Book
- characteristics that reflect a narrative poem
- consistent use of first-person point of view
- error-free writing that contains figurative language and/or sensory language and captures the reader's interest

B Create a Picture

Choose a passage or poem from your Anchor Book that contains a lot of imagery and figurative language. Create a visual representation of it. Ask yourself, "When I read this, what do I see, hear, feel, smell, or taste? What is the mood of the passage or poem?"

1. Create a list of words and phrases that describe what you imagine when you read the passage or poem you chose from your Anchor Book.
2. Decide how you can visually represent the passage or poem. Draw, paint, create a collage, photograph images, or make a video.
3. Create your visual. Use your notes as reference. Write a brief statement explaining your representation.

Your visual should include the following elements.

- an image that represents a passage or poem from your Anchor Book
- a brief explanation of your representation of the passage or poem

Write a Haiku

C

As you've learned, a haiku is a Japanese poem consisting of three lines. Haikus contain rich details and simple, strong imagery. Make a setting or character from your Anchor Book come alive in the form of a haiku.

1. Choose a character or setting from your Anchor Book that you found memorable. Create a list of images, feelings, and sensory details that come to mind to describe that character or setting.
2. Look at your list and circle the strongest and most descriptive details.
3. Use these circled details to write a descriptive haiku.

Your haiku should include the following elements.

- a subject that is related to your Anchor Book
- thoughtful, strong, descriptive images and details
- three lines: five syllables in the first and third lines, and seven syllables in the second

Free-Choice Book Reflection

You have completed your free-choice book. Before you take your test, read the following instructions to write a brief reflection of your book.

My free-choice book is ______________________________.

The author is ______________________________.

1 Would you recommend this book to a friend? Yes _____ No _____

Briefly explain why.

____

____

____

Write Answer the following question in your Reader's Journal.

2 **Compare and Contrast** *Do we need words to communicate?* Compare and contrast how your Anchor Book and free-choice book help to answer this question. Use specific details from both books to support your answer.

Unit Review
Standardized Test Practice

Answer the questions below to check your understanding of this unit's skills.

Reading Skills: Paraphrasing

Read the selection. Then, answer the questions that follow.

John Vincent Atanasoff invented the electronic digital computing device in 1939. Since original computational machines of the time were slow and inaccurate, Atanasoff decided to design an electronic digital computer to speed up mathematical computations. Out of that development came a new age—the age of computers.

Imagine life without computers: there would be no Internet, no word processing, no E-mail. That's the obvious conclusion. But do you realize that without computers, it wouldn't be possible to turn on the television, drive a car, land an airplane, listen to the radio, or make a telephone call? All of these items use computer technology. In the world in which we live, it is almost impossible to do anything without a computer.

1 Which sentence best **paraphrases** the first paragraph?

A. Atanasoff knew computers would affect all of our lives.

B. In 1939, computational devices were slow and inaccurate.

C. Atanasoff invented the electronic computing device to speed up mathematical computations.

D. Without computers, there would be no Internet.

2 Which statement best **paraphrases** the second paragraph?

F. Computers play an important role in our everyday lives.

G. We need computers so we can send E-mails.

H. Without a computer, we couldn't drive a car.

J. We need computers to communicate to people in the world.

3 Use your own words to paraphrase the second sentence of the passage.

Reading Skills: Context Clues

Read the selection. Then answer the questions that follow.

> It can take millions of years for water erosion to occur. The force of water slowly removes tiny fragments from stone. Because stone is motionless, it cannot escape the friction of the water. The water flows as the stone stands still, and this puts pressure upon the stone. This water pressure removes tiny pieces of stone. If a rough piece of stone is exposed to water for a long enough time, it will be sculpted smooth. The water will shape the stone.

3 What is the meaning of *water erosion?*

A. the flowing of water

B. the sharpening of a stone's edges

C. the wearing away of stone by water

D. the effect that stones have on water

4 What is the meaning of *friction?*

F. the rubbing of one surface on another

G. the removal of stone from water

H. the attraction between two surfaces

J. the smoothing out of a surface

Literary Analysis: Elements of Prose and Poetry

Read the poem and answer the questions that follow.

> It began to flurry as
> I walked to school.
> The snowflakes danced daintily on my tongue
> as I tried to catch them.
> They fell harder and harder
> until they blinded me like a blanket over my eyes.
> I finally reached the building
> and gladly walked into its warm, welcoming arms.

5 Which of these phrases is a **simile?**

A. fell harder and harder

B. blinded me like a blanket

C. the snowflakes danced

D. gladly walked into

6 From which **point of view** is the poem written?

F. first-person

G. limited third-person

H. omniscient third-person

J. third-person

7 Which of these phrases is an example of **repetition?**

A. danced daintily

B. into its warm, welcoming arms

C. harder and harder

D. like a blanket over my eyes

8 Which **sound device** is used in the sentence "The snowflakes danced daintily on my tongue"?

F. alliteration

G. onomatopoeia

H. rhyme scheme

J. repetition

9 **Imagery** is language that ________.

A. creates excitement

B. appeals only to the sense of sight

C. appeals to the five senses

D. uses the imagination

10 Which of the following defines a **concrete poem?**

F. A poem that describes something concrete

G. A poem that takes the shape of its subject

H. A poem that has no particular rhyme scheme

J. A poem that tells a story in verse

Language Skills: Vocabulary

Choose the best answer.

11 Which word has **multiple meanings?**

A. bat

B. sing

C. pencil

D. desk

12 My family took a **trip.** What is another meaning for the word *trip*?

F. stumble

G. take

H. trick

J. day

13 Which of the following describes an **idiom?**

A. It is a true statement.

B. It should not be taken literally.

C. It should be taken literally.

D. It tells you how and why something happened.

14 Which of the following is an **idiom?**

F. quite upset

G. on cloud nine

H. rather anxious

J. very happy

Language Skills: Spelling

Circle the letter that contains the correctly spelled word to complete the sentence.

15 Adding the suffix *-ness* to the word *crazy* creates the word

A. crazness
C. crazeness
B. crazyness
D. craziness

16 Adding the prefix *mis-* to the word *spoke* creates the word

F. mispoke
H. misspoke
G. mis-spoke
J. misaspoke

Language Skills: Grammar

Choose the best answer.

17 When there is only one subject in a sentence, it is called a __________.

A. simple subject
B. compound subject
C. single subject
D. primary subject

18 "Put your coat on before you go outside." is an example of a(n) __________ sentence.

F. declarative
G. interrogative
H. exclamatory
J. imperative

19 Which sentence has a **predicate noun** in it?

A. The doctor was studious.
B. Raul Morales is a doctor.
C. The doctor walked briskly and with determination.
D. I went to see the doctor.

20 Which of the following sentences contains a **predicate adjective?**

F. Minnesota is freezing in the winter.
G. Sometimes you need several hours to shovel your driveway.
H. Exhausted, I had to stop working.
J. I wish spring were here!

21 Identify the **direct object** in this sentence.

Joshua wrote his mother a letter.

A. Joshua
B. wrote
C. mother
D. letter

22 An **indirect object** usually is located __________.

F. after the linking verb
G. between an action verb and the direct object
H. between the subject and a linking verb
J. at the beginning of the sentence

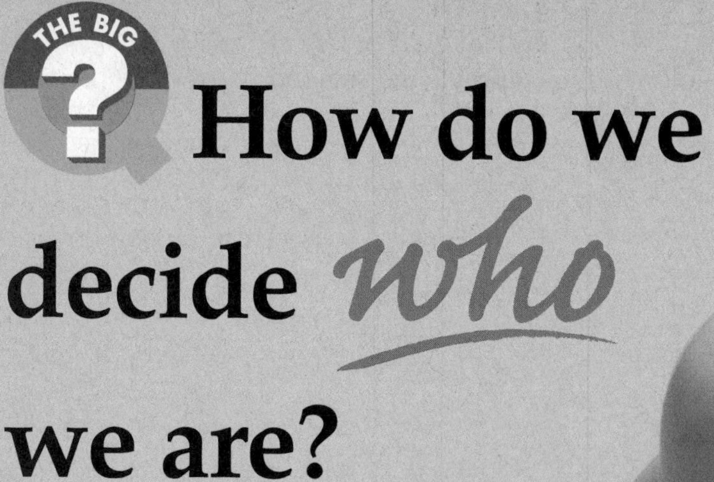

How do we decide *who* we are?

Unit 5 Genre focus: Drama

Unit Book Choices

With this unit you will read one book as an Anchor Book. There are many good books that would work well with this unit. The following pages offer six suggestions.

Free-Choice Reading

Later in this unit you will be given an opportunity to choose another book to read. This is called your Free-Choice Book.

You might read...

A Escape to Freedom

B Pushing Up the Sky

C I Never Saw Another Butterfly

D Play to Win

E Mother Hicks

F The Mousetrap and Other Plays

A You might read Anchor Book A

Summary The young Frederick Douglass understood early on that the road from slavery to freedom lay in learning how to read. Forbidden even to pick up a book, he found a way to accomplish his goal, secretly trading food for learning.

Escape to Freedom: A Play About Young Frederick Douglass

by Ossie Davis

Seven Native American Plays for Children

by Joseph Bruchac

B You might read Anchor Book B

Summary From "A" (the Abenaki story "Gluskabe and Old Man Winter") to "Z" (the Zuni story "The Strongest One"), these stories from the oral tradition of seven Native nations abound with heroes, villains, and tricksters.

C

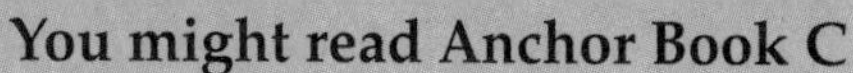

You might read Anchor Book C

Summary When young Raja Englanderova is sent to Terezin, a stopping-off place for hundreds of thousands of Jews on their way to Auschwitz concentration camp, she is one of more than 15,000 children who have passed through its gates. She becomes one of its only survivors.

I Never Saw Another Butterfly

by Celeste Raspanti

BLOCK A

D

You might read Anchor Book D

Summary This is the story of Hall of Famer Jackie Robinson, the man who crossed the color line in professional sports when he was inducted into Major League Baseball in 1947. Robinson faced bigotry and death threats on and off the field, but he took on the historical civil rights challenge with grace and determination.

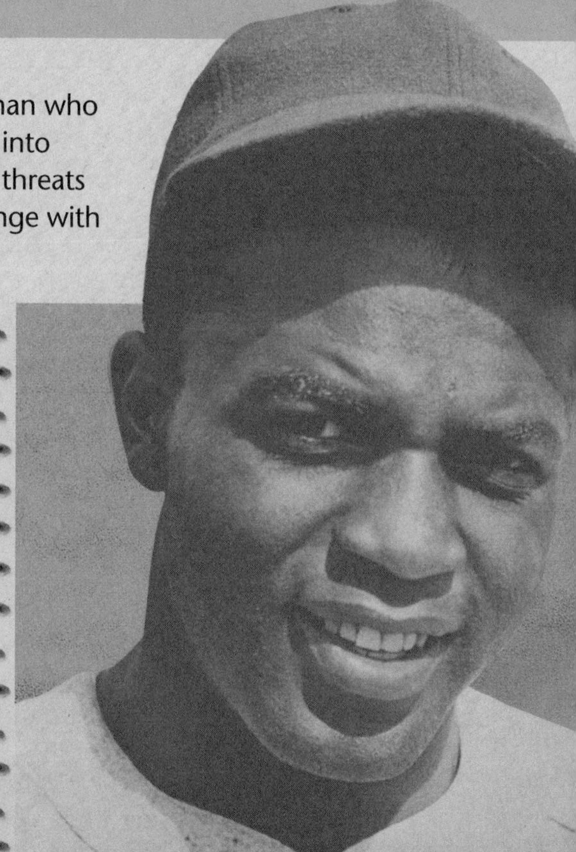

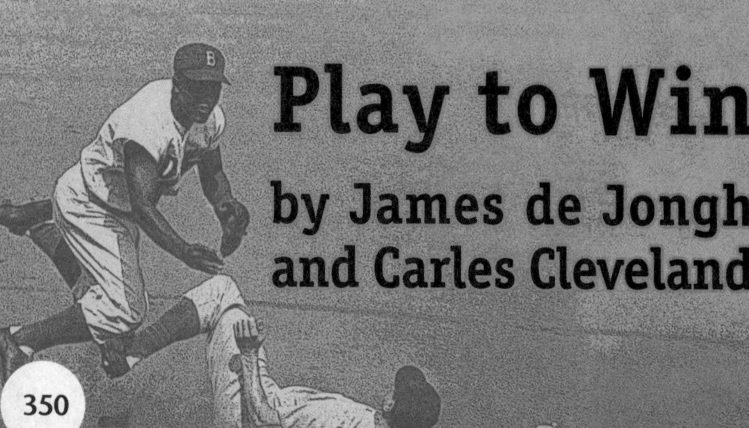

Play to Win

by James de Jongh and Carles Cleveland

E

You might read Anchor Book E

Summary Strange events have been occurring in Ware, Illinois, and the townspeople think witchery is the cause. Then Girl, a rebellious orphan raised by the town, and Tuc, a young deaf and mute man, wind up in the care of the town's number one suspect, the eccentric recluse Mother Hicks.

F

You might read Anchor Book F

Summary Seven characters are stranded in a small hotel during a snowstorm. Detective Sergeant Trotter arrives on skis with the warning that a killer is on his way to the hotel, but when one of the guests is murdered, it becomes clear that the killer is already there.

5-1 Understanding the Big Question

How do we decide who we are?

Describe yourself using three words. Now think: Would your parents describe you in the same way? How about your friends? We often see ourselves very differently from the way others see us. By looking at how we are viewed by others, we can learn more about ourselves.

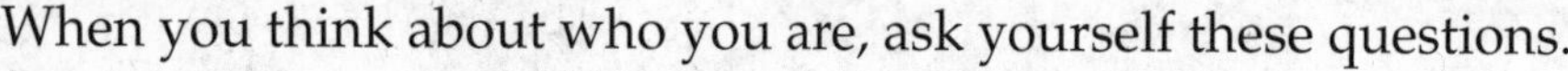

Let's compare how a classmate views you to how you view yourself. Start by thinking of three words to describe yourself. Some words might describe personality traits, such as *serious, laid-back,* or *funny*. Others might describe abilities, such as *athletic, artistic,* or *graceful*. Be sure you choose each word for a good reason.

When you think about who you are, ask yourself these questions.

- *What do I like to do?*
- *What am I good at?*
- *How do I express myself?*

Directions Write your name in the chart. Write your three words in the "How I Describe Myself" column. Then cover the left-hand column with a sheet of paper. Have a classmate write his or her name in the title "How __________ Describes Me" and then write three words that he or she thinks best describe you.

Name: ______________________________

How I Describe Myself	How __________ Describes Me

before reading your anchor book

Once your classmate has described you, remove the sheet of paper. Compare the words you wrote about yourself to the words your classmate wrote about you. Circle any words that match. Did your classmate choose a word that you don't agree with?

Directions In the graphic organizer, write one of the words that was on your classmate's list. In the bottom left-hand box, explain how this word does or does not describe you. Have your classmate write his or her name on the line in the bottom right-hand box and explain his or her reason for choosing this word. Then answer the questions that follow.

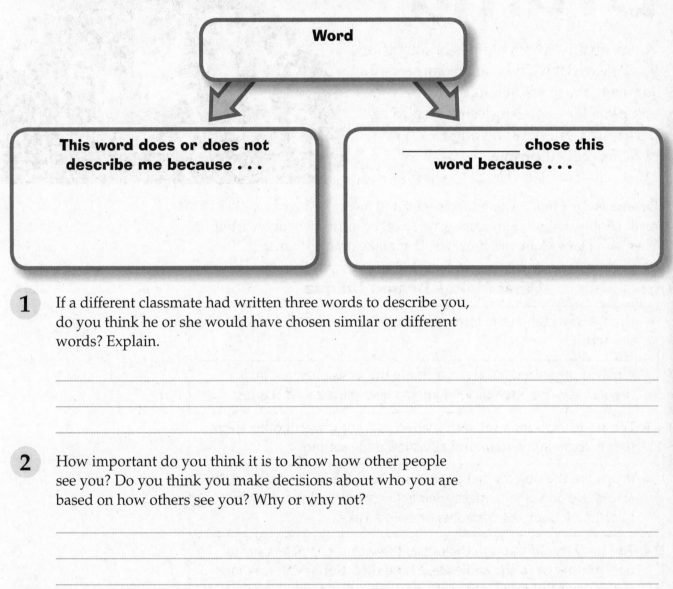

Word

This word does or does not describe me because . . .	**____________ chose this word because . . .**

1 If a different classmate had written three words to describe you, do you think he or she would have chosen similar or different words? Explain.

____

____

____

2 How important do you think it is to know how other people see you? Do you think you make decisions about who you are based on how others see you? Why or why not?

____

____

____

3 **Apply** As you read your Anchor Book and the related readings, think about how people decide who they are. Do they see themselves differently from the way others see them?

You will start reading your Anchor Book soon. The next few pages in this book give you some background information plus a reading skill.

Introduction to Drama

You probably watch movies or television shows each day. These are examples of stories that are written in the form of a play. Plays are stories written to be performed. All plays belong to a type of fiction called **drama.**

Drama is a form of writing that is meant to be performed as well as read. Drama is similar in many ways to other forms of fiction writing. There are many elements, however, that make drama unique.

What Makes Drama Unique
▸ Drama is written in the form of a **play.** The written text of a play is the **script.**
▸ A play is organized in **acts,** which are the units of action in a drama. Acts are often divided into smaller parts called **scenes.**
▸ The stage includes a **set** with scenery, backdrops, and other items that help an audience member visualize the setting.
▸ **Props** are the objects that appear on the stage or the objects that actors use on stage to make their actions look realistic. A prop might be a book, a telephone, or even a cake.
▸ The story is told through **dialogue,** the words characters say to one another or to the audience. **Stage directions**—information about what the stage looks like and how the characters move and speak—are also part of the script.
▸ Not all scripts are performed live on stage. A **screenplay** is a movie script. A **teleplay** is a screenplay written for television. A **radio play** is a script written for radio broadcasts.

Types of Drama

Most drama can be divided into two categories.

- A **comedy** is a play that has a happy ending. Comedies are usually meant to be funny and to entertain, but they can also address serious issues in society or human weaknesses.
- A **tragedy** is a play that ends with the main character's downfall or death. In ancient Greek and Shakespearean plays, this character is always a very important person—often a king or hero. In modern times, this character is often an ordinary person.

What Makes Drama Unique

Because drama and novels are both forms of fiction, they share some similarities. However, they also have many differences. The graphic organizer shows some differences and similarities.

How are they different?

Drama	Novel
• script • props • usually performed • divided into acts and/or scenes • contains stage directions	• more than 100 pages • points of view • usually read silently • usually divided into chapters • contains descriptive language

How are they the same?

Drama and Novel

characters • plot • conflict
setting • dialogue

Book or Movie?

Sometimes books, such as the *Harry Potter* series, are turned into movies. Think of a book you have read that has been made into a movie. In what ways was the movie similar to or different from the book? Which did you like better? Explain your answer.

5-2 Reading Skills
Summarize

In learning new reading skills, you will use special academic vocabulary. Knowing the right words will help you demonstrate your understanding.

Academic Vocabulary

Word	Meaning	Example Sentence
recall *v.* *Related words:* recalled, recalling	to remember	The new student was introduced to the class just yesterday, but I still couldn't *recall* her name.
review *v.* *Related words:* reviewed, reviewing	to look at or examine again	To help us study for the test, Ms. DeSalle *reviewed* the literary terms.
describe *v.* *Related words:* description, describes	to explain or depict	The author uses vivid language to *describe* how leaves change color.

A **summary** is a short statement that presents the main idea and most important details of a piece of writing. When you summarize in your own words, you recognize what information is most important to know and leave out what is not. Summarizing a story or an article can help you better understand what you're reading.

Follow these important steps to create a good summary of fiction and nonfiction texts.

1. As you read, identify and record the most important information, or main idea, and details that support the main idea.

2. Use your own words to briefly **describe** the main idea and events in the text. Organize your description so that the details and events appear in chronological order.

3. Reread your summary to make sure you've included the most important information and left out unnecessary information. Then **review** and revise your summary.

Directions Read the passage below. Use the important details underlined in the text to answer the questions.

from "La Bamba" *by Gary Soto*

Manuel was the fourth of seven children and looked like a lot of kids in his neighborhood: black hair, brown face, and skinny legs scuffed from summer play. But summer was giving way to fall: The trees were turning red, the lawns brown, and the pomegranate trees were heavy with fruit. Manuel walked to school in the frosty morning, kicking leaves and thinking of tomorrow's talent show. He was still amazed that he had volunteered. He was going to pretend to sing Ritchie Valens's[1] "La Bamba" before the entire school.

Why did I raise my hand? he asked himself, but in his heart he knew the answer. He yearned for the limelight. He wanted applause as loud as a thunderstorm and to hear his friends say, "Man, that was bad!" And he wanted to impress the girls, especially Petra Lopez, the second-prettiest girl in his class. The prettiest was already taken by his friend Ernie. Manuel knew he should be reasonable since he himself was not great-looking, just average.

[1] **Ritchie Valens** (1941–1959) was the first Mexican American rock star. Valens died in a plane crash in 1959 when he was only 17 years old.

1 **Apply** Use the graphic organizer to identify the main idea and supporting details in "La Bamba." Then summarize the passage.

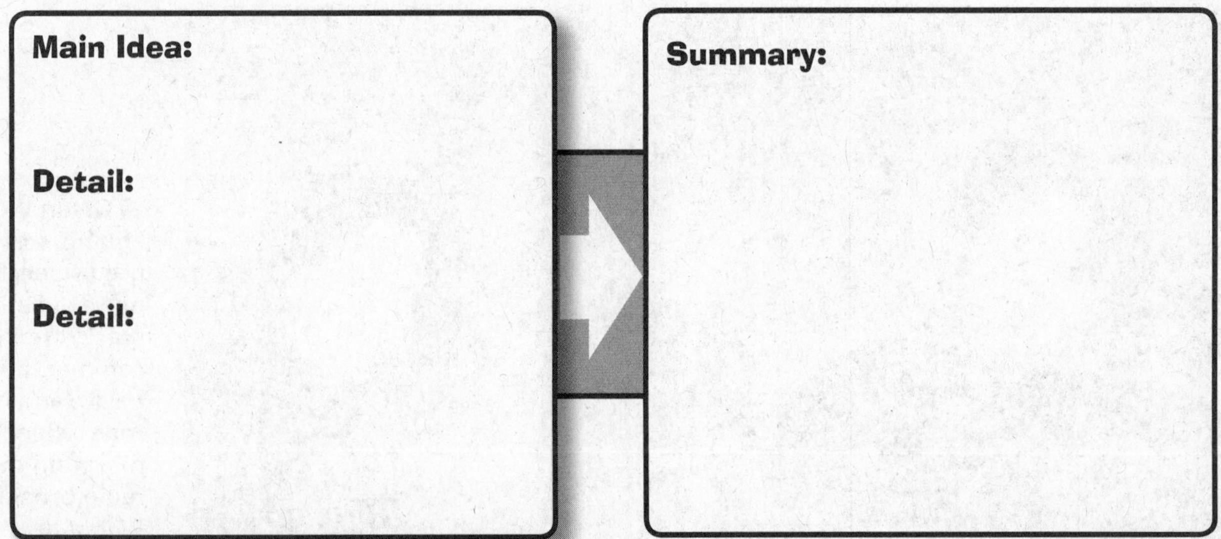

before reading your anchor book

Use the skills you have learned to summarize the following article. *Guiding Question:* **How do media broadcasts, such as *War of the Worlds,* shape who we are and how we behave?**

Link to Real Life

THE PANIC BROADCAST

On October 30, 1938, Earth was invaded by creatures from Mars! At least that's what thousands of radio listeners in the United States believed. Actually, on that evening a man named Orson Welles directed and starred in a radio broadcast entitled *War of the Worlds.* The radio play was based on a book with the same title by H. G. Wells, an English author. The performance described a fictional attack on New Jersey by invaders from Mars. The broadcast was not about a real event. However, it seemed so real that it caused a national panic.

In the 1930s, radio had a great influence on life in the United States. Television sets were not yet available for home use, so there were no live TV broadcasts to show people events as they happened. It was, therefore, not totally surprising that so many radio listeners believed what they heard in *War of the Worlds*.

◀ **Orson Welles and his company used screeching news bulletins and quick, breathless commentary to create an urgent tone when narrating the 1938 radio broadcast of *War of the Worlds.***

▲ **Grovers Mill, NJ, is shown intact on October 30, 1938, the day after the town was supposed to have been "destroyed" by invaders from Mars.**

The story of the Martians' invasion, only a small part of the original story of *War of the Worlds*, was used for the radio program. Playwright Howard Koch, who rewrote the story for radio, had picked up a map at a New Jersey gas station to find a location in the United States for the Martians' landing. He opened the map, closed his eyes, and pointed his pencil. The pencil landed on the town of Grovers Mill, New Jersey.

The radio play was presented like a regular radio broadcast—with music, a weather report, and then a series of special news bulletins. An introduction before the show began identified it as fiction: "The Columbia Broadcasting System and its affiliated stations present Orson Welles and the Mercury Theatre of the Air in *War of the Worlds* by H. G. Wells." However, many listeners missed or did not listen to the introduction of the program. The newspaper listing for the show also identified the title of the program. In addition, three announcements during the program stated that the broadcast was fiction.

The first "news bulletins" and "eyewitness accounts" during the broadcast described a meteor that was supposed to have landed near Princeton, New Jersey. Later "reports" changed the meteor to a metal cylinder containing creatures from Mars armed with death rays. The creatures finally burst into flames, and the whole field where they had landed caught fire, spreading destruction.

Because radio listeners were used to interruptions in broadcasts during the recent threats of war in Europe, the program seemed real and caused fright and panic. Some families grabbed their personal belongings and fled into the streets. Traffic came to a standstill.

Once radio listeners realized that Earth was not under Martian attack, they were angry that they had been fooled. Outraged citizens flooded radio stations, newspapers, and police headquarters with

◀ In a CBS studio, Orson Welles rehearses his depiction of the science fiction story *War of the Worlds.*

▼ Many historians claim that newspaper accounts of the hysteria caused by the broadcast were exaggerated. But almost 70 years later, people like Mabel Dey hold on to the proof they have of the effect of the broadcast.

telephone calls. For days afterward, the broadcast was the topic of newspaper headlines.

Following the broadcast, a Grovers Mill farmer collected a 50-cent parking charge from each of the hundreds of carloads of people who wanted to see where the invaders had attacked. Even 30 years later, land in Grovers Mill was being sold at high prices because it was advertised as the site of the Martians' landing. The choice of Grovers Mill, New Jersey, as the town where the Martians landed helped to create new business opportunities there.

One New Jersey woman summed up many people's feelings when she said, "I thought it was all up with us. I grabbed my boy and just sat and cried." Believing that the entire human race faced death, many a person reached for someone nearby, not wishing to die alone. Others merely accepted their fate. A woman who had some leftover chicken in her icebox[1] said to her nephew, "We may as well eat this chicken—we won't be here in the morning." Her remark was an attempt to make life go on as usual.

One woman said, "My only thought was delight that if the Martians came, I wouldn't have to pay the butcher's bill." A man who enjoyed spreading news said, "It was the most exciting thing that ever happened to me. I ran all through my apartment building telling everybody the Martians were here."

Thousands of the estimated 6 million listeners believed that the broadcast was fact. Surprisingly, many listeners failed to change to another station to check whether the broadcast was true. Why were so many people ready to believe this outrageous fantasy, and why did they react in panic? As one person remarked, "Being in a trouble-some world, anything is liable to happen . . . So many things we hear are unbelievable." If we can learn anything from the public reaction to the broadcast of *War of the Worlds*, it is that we should not be quick to believe everything that we hear over the airwaves and read in print.

[1] **icebox** (īs' bäks') **n.** an early refrigerator that kept food cold with a block of ice.

Thinking About the Selection

The Panic Broadcast

1 **Recall** In the chart, list other important events and details described in "The Panic Broadcast" that occurred before, during, and after the broadcast of *War of the Worlds*.

Before the Broadcast	During the Broadcast	After the Broadcast
• In the 1930s, radio had a great influence on life in the United States.	• Orson Welles presented the radio play as a regular radio broadcast, even though announcements called it fiction.	• Angry citizens called radio stations, newspapers, and police headquarters.

2 **Summarize** Write a summary of the article "The Panic Broadcast." Use details from the chart to help you.

3 **Synthesize** Why is it helpful to organize details and events in the order they are presented before you write a summary?

Write Answer the following question in your Reader's Journal.

4 **Speculate** How do media broadcasts, such as *War of the Worlds*, shape who we are and how we behave? Use examples from "The Panic Broadcast" to support your answer.

before reading your anchor book

5-3 Vocabulary Building Strategies
Borrowed Foreign Words

Where do English words come from? Our language contains many words that have been borrowed from different languages and many words that originated from other languages.

Many common English words were borrowed letter-for-letter from other languages. These words have found a place in our everyday speech. Look at these familiar words: *taco* (Spanish), *lasagna* (Italian), and *lacrosse* (French)—each of them was borrowed!

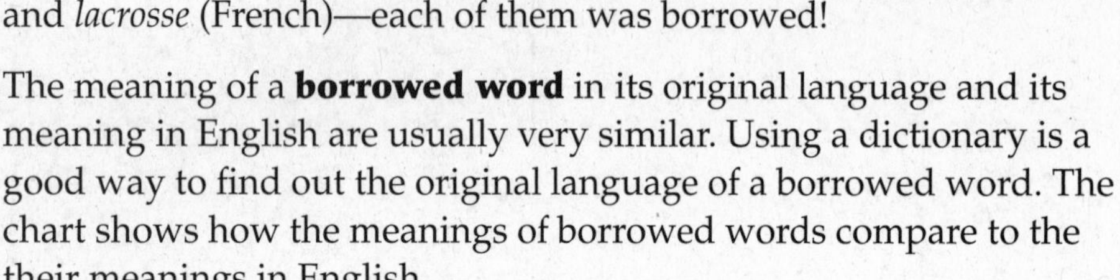

The meaning of a **borrowed word** in its original language and its meaning in English are usually very similar. Using a dictionary is a good way to find out the original language of a borrowed word. The chart shows how the meanings of borrowed words compare to the their meanings in English.

Borrowed Word	Language of Origin	Meaning in Original Language	Meaning in English
café	French	coffee	a place that sells refreshments, such as coffee
chorus	Greek	in drama, a group of singers and dancers who comment on the action of the play	a group of singers who perform together
tornado	Spanish	thunderstorm	a violent windstorm

Directions Look up each borrowed word in a dictionary. Identify its origin as French, Greek, or Spanish. Write the origin on the line. Then write a sentence that shows the meaning of each word.

1 petite

____

2 theater

____

3 tortilla

____

Word Origins

Many English words come from other languages, such as Greek and Latin. Knowing the origin of these unfamiliar words can help you to unlock their meaning. Some words, such as *stone,* started out in another language but changed throughout time to become the word we use today. Look at the diagram to see how two Greek words became the English words we know today.

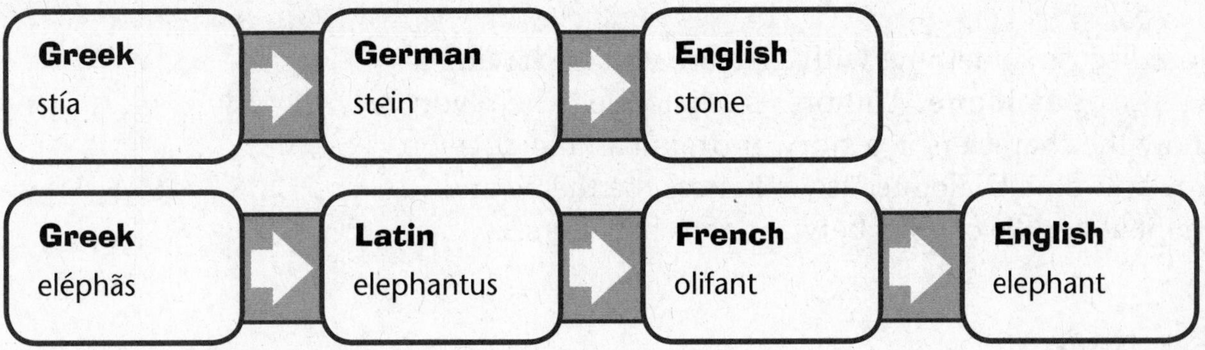

Directions Use the word origins from the following charts, along with context clues, to help you determine the meaning of the underlined word in each sentence. Write the meaning on the line. Use a dictionary to check each meaning.

Word Origin	Meaning in Original Language
áthlon (Greek)	athlete
ūnus (Latin)	one

Word Origin	Meaning in Original Language
nõmen (Latin)	name
manus (Latin)	hand

1 Most cars shift gears automatically; some cars, though, require the driver to shift the gears <u>manually</u>.

______

2 After the Civil War, the North and the South were <u>unified</u> once more, but tensions between the two regions were still high.

______

3 In order to become class president, you have to be <u>nominated</u> by your classmates first.

______

before reading your anchor book

Ready? Start Reading Your Anchor Book *It's time to get started. As you learn from this worktext, your teacher will also give you reading assignments from your Anchor Book.*

5-4 Literary Analysis
Dialogue

When you discuss something with a friend, you are having a conversation, or **dialogue.** Authors use dialogue to help you get to know the characters in a story or drama and to develop the setting and plot. Dialogue also enhances the theme and reveals a lot about the conflict between the characters.

Literary Terms

- **Dialogue** is the words that characters speak. In a novel, the characters' dialogue is set off with quotation marks. In drama, dialogue usually follows the character's name, which is often written in capital letters.

Novel	Samantha questioned, "What do you mean you can't go tomorrow?"
Drama	SAMANTHA: What do you mean you can't go tomorrow?

- A **script** is the written text of a play, movie, or broadcast.
- A **playwright** is a person who writes plays.

Directions Read the scene from the play on the following page. Think about how the playwright develops the characters and setting through dialogue. Then answer the questions that follow.

from The Governess *by Neil Simon*

Go Online
About the Author
Visit: PHSchool.com
Web Code: exe-6501

MISTRESS. Julia! [*Calls again*] Julia!

[*A young governess, JULIA, comes rushing in. She stops before the desk and curtsies.*]

JULIA. [*Head down*] Yes, madame?

MISTRESS. Look at me, child. Pick your head up. I like to see your eyes when I speak to you.

JULIA. [*Lifts her head up*] Yes, madame. [*But her head has a habit of slowly drifting down again*]

MISTRESS. And how are the children coming along with their French lessons?

JULIA. They're very bright children, madame.

MISTRESS. Eyes up... They're bright, you say. Well, why not? And mathematics? They're doing well in mathematics, I assume?

JULIA. Yes, madame. Especially Vanya.

MISTRESS. Certainly. I knew it. I excelled in mathematics. He gets that from his mother, wouldn't you say?

JULIA. Yes, madame.

MISTRESS. Head up... [*She lifts her head up*] That's it. Don't be afraid to look people in the eyes, my dear. If you think of yourself as inferior, that's exactly how people will treat you.

JULIA. Yes, madame.

1 **Explain** How does the playwright use dialogue to develop the setting in the play? Give examples from the play.

2 **Classify** What part of the dialogue makes you think Mistress feels superior to Julia?

3 **Apply** If you were writing this scene and wanted to show a change in Julia's character, what would you have her say to Mistress?

while reading your anchor book

Dialect

When you want a soft drink, do you ask for a soda or a pop? Or do you use another word? Your answer depends on where you are from and how the people around you speak. The specific words and pronunciations people in a particular region use are known as **dialect.**

Literary Term

- **Dialect** is the unique words, phrases, and pronunciations used in a specific geographical region. Often, you can tell where a person is from based on his or her accent and the words he or she uses. Can you tell from which region of the country this speaker might be?

> **MARGARET:** [*laughing*] So y'all think the way I speak is funny? Maybe it's y'all who talk funny!

The contraction *y'all* indicates that Margaret is most likely from the South.

Drama and Dialect

Playwrights use dialogue to make their characters seem real, but use dialect to give the characters personality on the page or on stage. A playwright can use the following to make characters come alive.

Words used in a specific area	A character from New York City might refer to a sandwich as a *hero*, while a character from Rhode Island might call it a *grinder*.
Phrases used in a specific area	A play that takes place in London, England, might include the phrase *rang her*, which means "called her on the telephone."
Ways of pronouncing common words	A character from Boston might use an accent in which *r*'s are not pronounced, so a word such as *car* would be written as *ca'* or *cah*.

Directions With a partner, think of examples of dialect you have encountered in your life, from the region in which you live or from somewhere else. On a separate sheet of paper, write a line of dialogue for each example of dialect.

In the following selection, the author uses dialogue to develop the characters and the conflict between the characters. *Guiding Question:* **How do authors use dialogue and dialect to show who their characters are?**

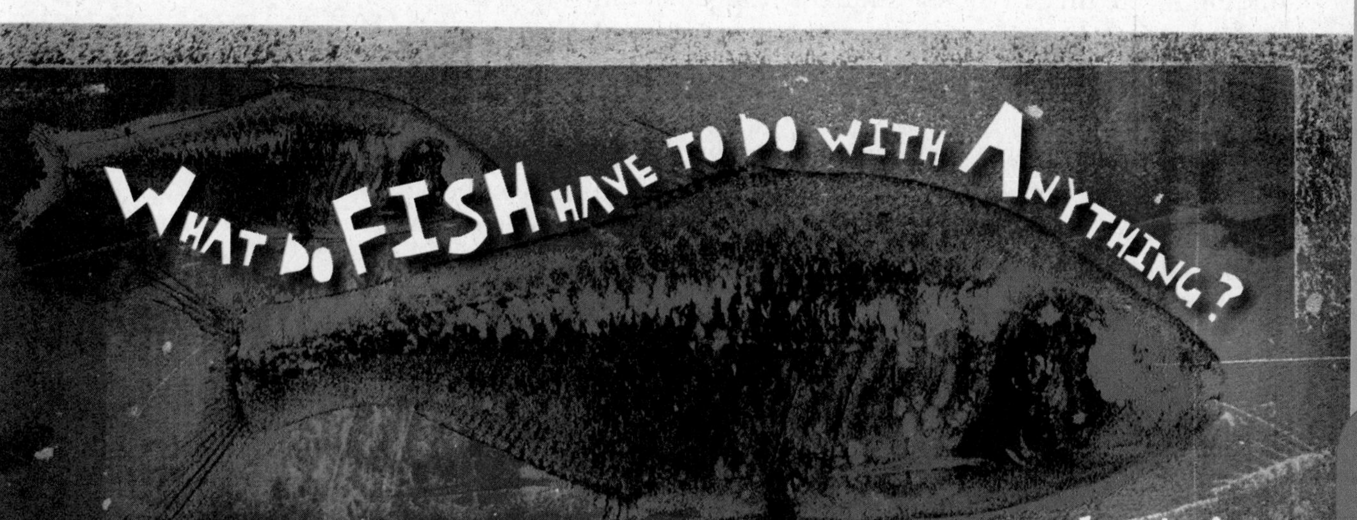

Background *The fish in this story are not the typical fish that might come to your mind, such as trout, bass, or sunfish. They live in dark caves where no light can reach, so over thousands of years, these fish gradually lost their need for eyes. So, you might wonder, what do these fish have to do with anything?*

Vocabulary Builder

Before you read, *you will discuss the following words. In the Vocabulary Builder box in the margin, use a vocabulary building strategy to make the words your own.*

threshold **interval** **strained** **contemplated**

As you read, *draw a box around unfamiliar words you could add to your vocabulary. Use context clues to unlock their meaning.*

Marking the Text

Dialogue and Dialect

As you read, *underline the dialogue that helps to develop the characters of Mrs. Markham, Willie, and the old man on the street. Also, make notes of character traits that you can infer from people's actions.*

Every day at three o'clock Mrs. Markham waited for her son, Willie, to come out of school. They walked home together. If asked why she did it, Mrs. Markham would say, "Parents need to watch their children."

As they left the schoolyard, Mrs. Markham inevitably asked, "How was school?"

Willie would begin to talk, then stop. He was never sure his mother was listening. She seemed preoccupied with her own

while reading your anchor book

thoughts. She had been like that ever since his dad had abandoned them six months ago. No one knew where he'd gone. Willie had the feeling that his mother was lost too. It made him feel lonely.

One Monday afternoon, as they approached the apartment building where they lived, she suddenly tugged at him. "Don't look that way," she said.

"Where?"

"At that man over there."

Willie stole a look back over his shoulder. A man, whom Willie had never seen before, was sitting on a red plastic milk crate near the curb. His matted,[1] streaky gray hair hung like a ragged curtain over his dirty face. His shoes were torn. Rough hands lay upon his knees. One hand was palm up. No one seemed to pay him any mind. Willie was certain he had never seen a man so utterly alone. It was as if he were some spat-out piece of chewing gum on the pavement.

"What's the matter with him?" Willie asked his mother in a hushed voice.

Keeping her eyes straight ahead, Mrs. Markham said, "He's sick." She pulled Willie around. "Don't stare. It's rude."

"What kind of sick?"

As Mrs. Markham searched for an answer, she began to walk faster. "He's unhappy," she said.

"What's he doing?"

[1] **matted** (mat'id) *adj.* hair that's tangled in a thick mass.

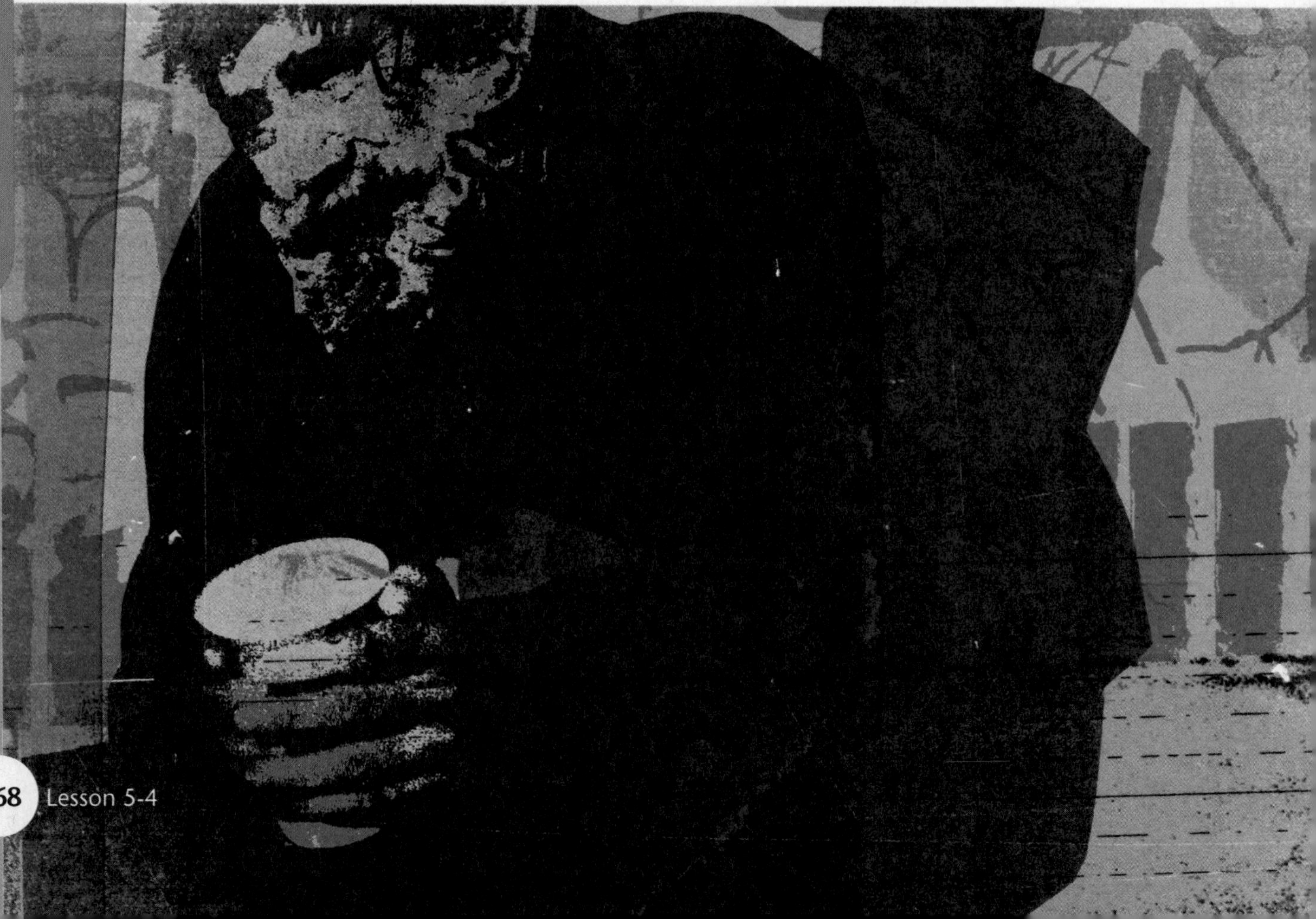

"Come on, Willie, you know perfectly well. He's begging."

"Do you think anyone gave him anything?"

"I don't know. Now come on, don't look."

"Why don't you give him anything?"

"We have nothing to spare."

When they got home, Mrs. Markham removed a white cardboard box from the refrigerator. It contained pound cake.[2] Using her thumb as a measure, she carefully cut a half-inch piece of cake and gave it to Willie on a clean plate. The plate lay on a plastic mat decorated with images of roses with diamondlike dewdrops. She also gave him a glass of milk and a folded napkin. She moved slowly.

Willie said, "Can I have a bigger piece of cake?"

Mrs. Markham picked up the cake box and ran a manicured pink fingernail along the nutrition information panel. "A half-inch piece is a portion, and a portion contains the following health requirements. Do you want to hear them?"

"No."

"It's on the box, so you can believe what it says. Scientists study people, then write these things. If you're smart enough you could become a scientist. Like this." Mrs. Markham tapped the box. "It pays well." Willie ate his cake and drank the milk. When he was done he took care to wipe the crumbs off his face as well as to blot his milk moustache with the napkin. His mother liked him to be neat.

His mother said, "Now go and do your homework. Carefully. You're in sixth grade. It's important."

Willie gathered up his books that lay on the empty third chair. At the kitchen entrance he paused and looked back at his mother. She was staring sadly at the cake box, but he didn't think she was seeing it. Her unhappiness made him think of the man on the street.

"What *kind* of unhappiness do you think he has?" he suddenly asked.

"Who's that?"

"That man."

Mrs. Markham looked puzzled.

"The begging man. The one on the street."

"Oh, could be anything," his mother said, vaguely. "A person can be unhappy for many reasons." She turned to stare out the window, as if an answer might be there.

"Is unhappiness a sickness you can cure?"

"I wish you wouldn't ask such questions."

"Why?"

After a moment she said, "Questions that have no answers shouldn't be asked."

"Can I go out?"

"Homework first."

---

[2] **pound cake** (pound' kāk') *n.* a rich cake originally made with ingredients that included a pound of butter, flour, and sugar.

Marking the Text

while reading your anchor book

Willie turned to go again.

"Money," Mrs. Markham suddenly said. "Money will cure a lot of unhappiness. That's why that man was begging. A salesperson once said to me, 'Maybe you can't buy happiness, but you can rent a lot of it.' You should remember that."

"How much money do we have?"

"Not enough."

"Is that why you're unhappy?"

"Willie, do your homework."

Willie started to ask another question, but decided he would not get an answer. He left the kitchen.

The apartment had three rooms. The walls were painted mint green. Willie walked down the hallway to his room, which was at the front of the building. By climbing up on the windowsill and pressing against the glass, he could see the sidewalk five stories below. The man was still there.

It was almost five when he went to tell his mother he had finished his school assignments. He found her in her dim bedroom, sleeping. Since she had begun working the night shift at a convenience store—two weeks now—she took naps in the late afternoon.

For a while Willie stood on the **threshold,** hoping his mother would wake up. When she didn't, he went to the front room and looked down the street again. The begging man had not moved.

Willie returned to his mother's room.

"I'm going out," he announced—softly.

Willie waited a decent **interval** for his mother to waken. When she did not, Willie made sure his keys were in his pocket. Then he left the apartment.

By standing just outside the building door, he could keep his eyes on the man. It appeared as if he had still not moved. Willie wondered how anyone could go without moving for so long in the chill October air. Was staying still part of the man's sickness?

During the twenty minutes that Willie watched, no one who passed looked in the beggar's direction. Willie wondered if they even saw the man. Certainly no one put any money into his open hand.

A lady leading a dog by a leash went by. The dog **strained** in the direction of the man sitting on the crate. His tail wagged. The lady pulled the dog away. "Heel!"[3] she commanded.

The dog—tail between his legs—scampered to the lady's side. Even so, the dog twisted around to look back at the beggar.

Willie grinned. The dog had done exactly what Willie had done when his mother told him not to stare.

Pressing deep into his pocket, Willie found a nickel. It was warm and slippery. He wondered how much happiness you could rent for a nickel.

[3] **heel** (hēl) *v.* a command that means "stay closely behind me."

Marking the Text

Vocabulary Builder

threshold
(thresh′ ōld) *n.*

Meaning

interval
(in′tər vəl) *n.*

Meaning

strained
(strānd) *v.*

Meaning

Squeezing the nickel between his fingers, Willie walked slowly toward the man. When he came before him, he stopped, suddenly nervous. The man, who appeared to be looking at the ground, did not move his eyes. He smelled bad.

"Here." Willie stretched forward and dropped the coin into the man's open right hand.

"God bless you," the man said hoarsely, as he folded his fingers over the coin. His eyes, like high beams on a car, flashed up at Willie, then dropped.

Willie waited for a moment, then went back up to his room. From his front room he looked down on the street. He thought he saw the coin in the man's hand but was not sure.

After supper Mrs. Markham readied herself to go to work, then kissed Willie good night. As she did every night, she said, "If you have regular problems, call Mrs. Murphy downstairs. What's her number?"

"274-8676," Willie said.

"Extra bad problems, call Grandma."

"369-6754."

"Super special problems, you can call me."

"962-6743."

"Emergency, the police."

"911."

"Lay out your morning clothing."

"I will."

"Don't let anyone in the door."

"I won't."

"No television past nine."

"I know."

"But you can read late."

Marking the Text

while reading your anchor book

"You're the one who's going to be late," Willie reminded her.

"I'm leaving," Mrs. Markham said.

After she went, Willie stood for a long while in the hallway. The empty apartment felt like a cave that lay deep below the earth. That day in school Willie's teacher had told them about a kind of fish that lived in caves. These fish could not see. They had no eyes. The teacher had said it was living in the dark cave that made them like that.

Willie had raised his hand and asked, "If they want to get out of the cave, can they?"

"I suppose."

"Would their eyes come back?"

"Good question," she said, but did not give an answer.

Before he went to bed, Willie took another look out the window. In the pool of light cast by the street lamp, Willie saw the man.

On Tuesday morning when Willie went to school, the man was gone. But when he came home from school with his mother, he was there again.

"*Please* don't look at him," his mother whispered with some urgency.

During his snack, Willie said, "Why shouldn't I look?"

"What are you talking about?"

"That man. On the street. Begging."

"I told you. He's sick. It's better to act as if you never saw him. When people are that way, they don't wish to be looked at."

"Why not?"

Mrs. Markham pondered for a while. "People are ashamed of being unhappy."

Willie looked thoughtfully at his mother. "Are you sure he's unhappy?"

Marking the Text

"You don't have to ask if people are unhappy. They tell you all the time."

"How?"

"The way they look."

"Is that part of the sickness?"

"Oh, Willie, I don't know. It's just the way they are."

Willie **contemplated** the half-inch slice of cake his mother had just given him. A year ago his parents seemed to be perfectly happy. For Willie, the world seemed easy, full of light. Then his father lost his job. He tried to get another but could not. For long hours he sat in dark rooms. Sometimes he drank. His parents began to argue a lot. One day, his father was gone.

For two weeks his mother kept to the dark. And wept.

Willie looked at his mother. "You're unhappy. Are *you* ashamed?"

Mrs. Markham sighed and closed her eyes. "I wish you wouldn't ask that."

"Why?"

"It hurts me."

"But are you ashamed?" Willie persisted. He felt it was urgent that he know. So that he could do something.

She only shook her head.

Willie said, "Do you think Dad might come back?"

She hesitated before saying, "Yes, I think so."

Willie wondered if that was what she really thought.

"Do you think Dad is unhappy?"

"Where do you get such questions?"

"They're in my mind."

"There's much in the mind that need not be paid attention to."

"Fish who live in caves have no eyes."

"What are you talking about?"

"My teacher said it's all that darkness. The fish forget how to see. So they lose their eyes."

"I doubt she said that."

"She did."

"Willie, you have too much imagination."

After his mother went to work, Willie gazed down onto the street. The man was there. Willie thought of going down, but he knew he was not supposed to leave the building when his mother worked at night. He decided to speak to the man the next day.

That afternoon—Wednesday—Willie stood before the man. "I don't have any money," Willie said. "Can I still talk to you?"

The man lifted his face. It was a dirty face with very tired eyes. He needed a shave.

"My mother," Willie began, "said you were unhappy. Is that true?"

"Could be," the man said.

Marking the Text

"What are you unhappy about?"

The man's eyes narrowed as he studied Willie intently. He said, "How come you want to know?"

Willie shrugged.

"I think you should go home, kid."

"I am home." Willie gestured toward the apartment. "I live right here. Fifth floor. Where do you live?"

"Around."

"*Are* you unhappy?" Willie persisted.

The man ran a tongue over his lips. His Adam's apple bobbed. "A man has the right to remain silent," the man said, and closed his eyes.

Willie remained standing on the pavement for a while before retreating back to his apartment. Once inside he looked down from the window. The man was still there. For a moment Willie was certain he was looking at the apartment building and the floor where Willie lived.

The next day, Thursday—after dropping a nickel in the man's palm, Willie said, "I've never seen anyone look so unhappy as you do. So I figure you must know a lot about it."

The man took a deep breath. "Well, yeah, maybe."

Willie said, "And I need to find a cure for it."

"A *what?*"

"A cure for unhappiness."

The man pursed his cracked lips and blew a silent whistle. Then he said, "Why?"

"My mother is unhappy."

"Why's that?"

"My dad went away."

"How come?"

"I think because he was unhappy. Now my mother's unhappy too—all the time. So if I found a cure for unhappiness, it would be a good thing, wouldn't it?"

"I suppose. Hey, you don't have anything to eat on you, do you?"

Willie shook his head, then said, "Would you like some cake?"

"What kind?"

"I don't know. Cake."

"Depends on the cake."

On Friday Willie said to the man, "I found out what kind of cake it is."

"Yeah?"

"Pound cake. But I don't know why it's called that."

"Long as it's cake it probably don't matter."

Neither spoke. Then Willie said, "In school my teacher said there are fish who live in caves and the caves are so dark the fish don't have eyes. What do you think? Do you believe that?"

"Sure."

"You do? How come?"

"Because you said so."

"You mean, just because someone *said* it you believe it?"

"Not someone. You."

Willie was puzzled. "But, well, maybe it *isn't* true."

The man grunted. "Hey, do you believe it?"

Willie nodded.

"Well, you're not just anyone. You got eyes. You see. You ain't no fish."

"Oh." Willie was pleased.

"What's your name?"

"Willie."

"That's a boy's name. What's your grown-up name?"

"William."

"And that means another thing."

"What?"

"I'll take some of that cake."

Willie started. "You will?" he asked, surprised.

"Just said it, didn't I?"

Willie suddenly felt excited. It was as if the man had given him a gift. Willie wasn't sure what it was except that it was important and he was glad to have it. For a moment he just gazed at the man. He saw the lines on the man's face, the way his lips curved, the small scar on the side of his chin, the shape of his eyes, which he now saw were blue.

"I'll get the cake," Willie cried and ran back to the apartment. He snatched the box from the refrigerator as well as a knife, then hurried back down to the street. "I'll cut you a piece," he said, and he opened the box.

"Hey, that don't look like a pound of cake," the man said.

Marking the Text

while reading your anchor book

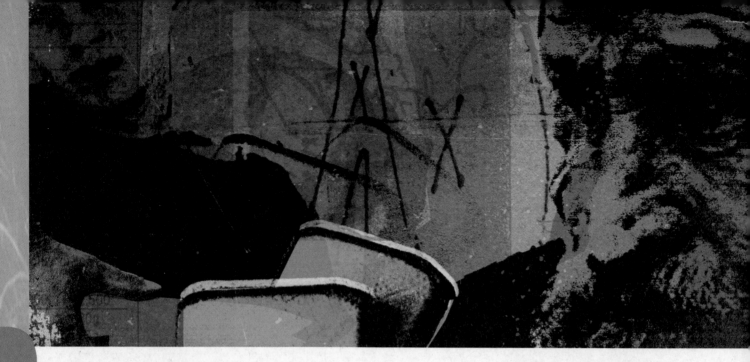

Willie, alarmed, looked up.

"But like I told you, it don't matter."

Willie held his thumb against the cake to make sure the portion was the right size. With a poke of the knife he made a small mark for the proper width.

Just as he was about to cut it, the man said, "Hold it!"

Willie looked up. "What?"

"What were you doing there with your thumb?

"I was measuring the size. The right portion. A person is supposed to get only one portion."

"Where'd you learn that?"

"It says so on the box. You can see for yourself." He held out the box.

The man studied the box then handed it back to Willie. "That's just lies," he said.

"How do you know?"

"William, how can a box say how much a person needs?"

"But it does. The scientists say so. They measured, so they know. Then they put it there."

"Lies," the man repeated.

Willie began to feel that this man knew many things. "Well, then, how much should I cut?" he asked.

The man said, "You have to look at me, then at the cake, and then you're going to have to decide for yourself."

"Oh." Willie looked at the cake. The piece was about three inches wide. Willie looked up at the man. After a moment he cut the cake into two pieces, each an inch and a half wide. He gave one piece to the man and kept the other in the box.

"God bless you," the man said, as he took the piece and laid it in his left hand. He began to break off pieces with his right hand

Marking the Text

and put them into his mouth one by one. Each piece was chewed thoughtfully. Willie watched him eat.

When the man was done, he licked the crumbs on his fingers.

"Now I'll give you something," the man said.

"What?" Willie said, surprised.

"The cure for unhappiness."

"You know it?" Willie asked, eyes wide.

The man nodded.

"What is it?"

"It's this: What a person needs is always more than they say."

"Who's *they?*" Willie asked.

The man pointed to the cake box. "The people on the box," he said.

In his mind Willie repeated what he had been told, then he gave the man the second piece of cake.

The man took it, saying, "Good man," and he ate it.

Willie grinned.

The next day was Saturday. Willie did not go to school. All morning he kept looking down from his window for the man, but it was raining and he did not appear. Willie wondered where he was, but could not imagine it.

Willie's mother woke about noon. Willie sat with her while she ate her breakfast. "I found the cure for unhappiness," he announced.

"Did you?" his mother said. She was reading a memo from the convenience store's owner.

"It's 'What a person needs is always more than they say.'"

His mother put her papers down. "That's nonsense. Where did you hear that?"

"That man."

"What man?"

"On the street. The one who was begging. You said he was unhappy. So I asked him."

"Willie, I told you I didn't want you to even look at that man."

"He's a nice man . . . ."

"How do you know?"

"I've talked to him."

"When? How much?"

Willie shrank down. "I did, that's all."

"Willie, I forbid you to talk to him. Do you understand me? Do you? Answer me!" She was shrill.

"Yes," Willie said, but he'd already decided he would talk to the man one more time. He needed to explain why he could not talk to him anymore.

On Sunday, however, the man was not there. Nor was he there on Monday.

"That man is gone," Willie said to his mother as they walked home from school.

Marking the Text

"I saw. I'm not blind."

"Where do you think he went?"

"I couldn't care less. But you might as well know, I arranged for him to be gone."

Willie stopped short. "What do you mean?"

"I called the police. We don't need a nuisance like that around here. Pestering kids."

"He wasn't pestering me."

"Of course he was."

"How do you know?"

"Willie, I have eyes. I can see."

Willie glared at his mother. "No, you can't. You're a fish. You live in a cave."

"Fish?" retorted Mrs. Markham. "What do fish have to do with anything? Willie, don't talk nonsense."

"My name isn't Willie. It's William. And I know how to keep from being unhappy. I do!" He was yelling now. "What a person needs is always more than they say! *Always!*"

He turned on his heel and walked back toward the school. At the corner he glanced back. His mother was following. He kept going. She kept following.

Marking the Text

Vocabulary Builder

After you read, *review the words you decided to add to your vocabulary. Write the meaning of words you have learned in context. Look up the other words in a dictionary, glossary, thesaurus, or electronic resource.*

while reading your anchor book

AVI (b. 1937)

Avi was born in New York City. He has a twin sister who gave him the name Avi when she was about one year old. The name stuck and now it is the only name he uses. Reading and playing imaginative games were two activities he loved to do as a child. In giving advice to young writers, Avi believes that the key to writing is in reading, and the more you read, the better your writing will be.

Thinking About the Selection

What Do Fish Have to Do With Anything?

About the Author
Visit: PHSchool.com
Web Code: exe-6502

1 **Contrast** How do Mrs. Markham and the beggar treat Willie differently?

2 **Synthesize** Mrs. Markham says to Willie, "I couldn't care less. But you might as well know, I arranged for him to be gone." Suppose she said it this way: "Who cares? FYI, I gave him the boot." How might the change in dialect change the meaning and tone of her dialogue? Explain.

3 **Apply** How would the dialogue below be written if it appeared in a script?

Fiction	"You're the one who's going to be late," Willie said. "I'm leaving," Mrs. Markham said.
Script	

4 **Interpret** What is the author's purpose for telling the story of the blind fish?

Write Answer the following questions in your Reader's Journal.

5 **Discuss** How do authors use dialogue and dialect to show who their characters are?

6 **Evaluate** Find an example of dialogue in your Anchor Book. Tell how the dialogue helps you understand who the characters are and what kind of conflict they share.

while reading your anchor book

5-5 Language Coach
Grammar and Spelling

Prepositions and Prepositional Phrases

A **preposition** is a word that tells the relationship between a noun or pronoun and another word in a sentence. In the following example, the preposition *to* relates the noun *school* to the verb *walks*.

Example: Adi walks to school.

Common Prepositions				
above	below	from	off	until
among	between	into	on	with
behind	during	like	than	without

A **prepositional phrase** is a group of words that includes a preposition and a noun or pronoun, which is called the **object of the preposition**. In the sentence *The cat sat out in the rain,* the words *in the rain* are a prepositional phrase and the noun *rain* is the object of the preposition.

Prepositions allow you to add detail to your writing and bring more meaning to what you're trying to say. Look at the example from "What Do Fish Have to Do With Anything?" Notice how the author gave the sentence more detail by using prepositional phrases.

Without Prepositional Phrases	When he was done, he took care to wipe the crumbs as well as to blot his milk moustache.
With Prepositional Phrases	When he was done, he took care to wipe the crumbs *off his face* as well as to blot his milk moustache *with the napkin.*

Directions Write a preposition or an object of the preposition on each line to complete the passage.

We pulled the board ________ (prep.) the door so no one could get in. We dragged the wood from the ________ (obj. of prep.), heaved it up the ________ (obj. of prep.), and nailed it ________ (prep.) the thin wall. We waited ________ (prep.) Gertrude saw us in the tree high above her ________ (obj. of prep.). Then we laughed ________ (prep.) we could hardly breathe.

Go Online

Learn More
Visit: PHSchool.com
Web Code: exp-6501

Author's Craft

Can you use prepositions and prepositional phrases to transform the meaning of a text? To experiment, scan "What Do Fish Have to Do With Anything?" beginning on page 367. Choose a paragraph and cross out all of the prepositions and prepositional phrases. Then rewrite the paragraph, replacing the prepositions and prepositional phrases with new ones. Make sure the text still makes sense.

Spelling: Syllables With No Sound Clues

Syllables are word parts that contain a single vowel sound. The word *ago* has two syllables. The first syllable has the vowel sound "uh." This vowel sound is called the *schwa* sound. The schwa sound is used in unstressed syllables in multi-syllable words.

com pute´ (the unstressed syllable with the schwa sound is *com*, pronounced "kumm")
lik´ a ble (the unstressed syllable with the schwa sound is *a*, pronounced "uh")

The schwa sound is spelled many different ways. For this reason, it can be difficult to spell words containing the schwa sound. Here are some examples of words that use the schwa sound.

alien	calendar	elegant	done
opposite	contain	purpose	apologize

To help you remember how to spell a word containing the schwa sound, break the word into syllables. Then identify the schwa sound.

envelope	en ve lope	"ve" has the schwa sound
system	sys tem	"tem" has the schwa sound

Directions Break each word into syllables. Then circle the unstressed syllable that is pronounced with the schwa sound. You may use a dictionary to help you.

Example: harmony   har mo ny

1 polite ______________________________

2 career ______________________________

3 horrible ______________________________

Directions Make a list of five words containing the schwa sound on a separate sheet of paper. Check the spelling of the words in the dictionary. Then write a paragraph containing all five words you chose. When you are done, reread the paragraph and circle the words containing the schwa sound.

____
____
____
____

Author's Craft

How many ways can the schwa sound be spelled? Which are most common? Working with a group, search one page of "The Panic Broadcast" beginning on page 358. Find words with the schwa sound and list each spelling of the syllable. When you find a repeat of the same spelling, draw a checkmark next to it on your list. How many spellings did you find? Which were the most common?

5-6 Writer's Workshop
Exposition: Writing for Assessment

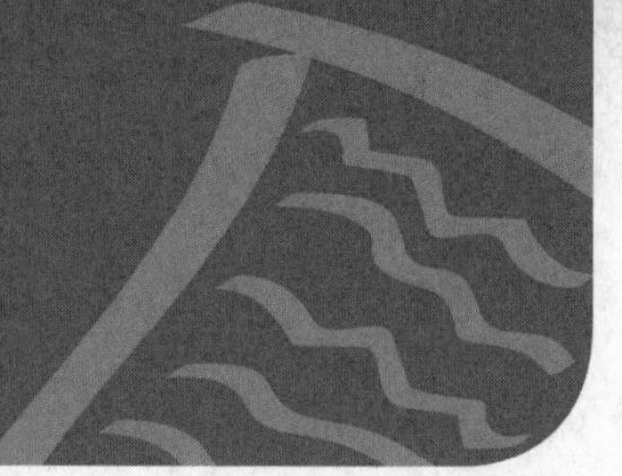

Throughout the year, your teachers measure how much you have learned and how well your writing skills are progressing. One way to measure your progress is to have you **write for assessment,** or respond to a question in writing. In essay tests or standardized tests, you might be given a **writing prompt,** or a statement for which you are asked to write a response. This lesson provides you with steps you can follow to practice writing these responses.

Purpose To write for assessment, taking a clear position that addresses the writing prompt

Audience You, your teacher, and your classmates

To be effective, your writing should include the following elements.

- a response that addresses the writing prompt and is directed to a specific audience
- a main idea and supporting details that are clear and concise throughout
- a consistent, appropriate organization pattern
- a complete response written within a limited time
- error-free writing, including the correct use of prepositional phrases

Prewriting—Plan It Out

For your essay, use the writing prompt in the box to the right. To completely address the writing prompt, spend about one quarter of your assigned time prewriting. Use these strategies to help plan your response.

Your writing prompt:

Think of an experience you have had that taught you something. Describe the experience and what you learned.

Analyze the writing prompt. It is important to figure out exactly what the writing prompt is asking you to do. To do this, look for and circle keywords in the prompt. The following chart lists some common keywords found in writing prompts.

Keyword	What You Should Do
Convince	Be clear on a position you take on an issue and give strong reasons to support where you stand.
Describe	Paint a clear image of a person, place, or thing using vivid sensory details.
Explain	Give a clear, accurate account of something.

Gather details. Once you understand what the writing prompt is asking you to do, you need to decide how you want to answer it. Use these steps and the student model as a guide for your own process.

1. Create a list of ideas that you could use to answer the writing prompt.
2. Choose from your list the idea that you think best addresses the writing prompt.
3. Brainstorm details that will support your idea.

My ideas:
- -took babysitting class
- -worked at Girl Scout car wash
- -helped out at the Special Olympics

Details about babysitting class:
- -how to do CPR and the Heimlich maneuver
- -got numbers to call in case of an emergency
- -identified household poisons

Drafting—Get It on Paper

Spend about half your assigned time drafting your essay. Write clearly and make sure you understand your notes. Keep your eye on the clock so you have enough time to revise and edit.

Find a focus. Review the prompt and use your notes to write one sentence that describes your main idea.

Choose an organization pattern. Match the type of prompt to an organization pattern that will answer the prompt most effectively.

- Use **compare-and-contrast** organization if the prompt asks you to look at the similarities and differences of two or more issues.
- Use **problem-solution** organization if the prompt presents an issue that you must resolve.
- Use **chronological** organization if the prompt asks you to describe an event in the order in which it happened.

Add details. If you have time, add additional facts or examples from previous readings or class discussions to support your ideas.

Revising—Make It Better

Spend the rest of your time revising and editing your response.

Compare and check. Your response should address the keywords you circled in the writing prompt. Revise to directly respond to all parts of the prompt. Be sure your response is clearly written.

Peer Review Ask for a partner's response to your essay. Revise to achieve the reaction you had intended.

Directions Read this student's writing for assessment as a model for your own.

Writing Prompt: Write an essay describing your community for a competition in the local paper. Give details about what you like and don't like about your community.

Go Online
Student Model
Visit: PHSchool.com
Web Code: exr-6501

Student Model: Writing

Liz Dzialo, Tiverton, RI

Cheers and Jeers

At my school and in my community, there are some things that make me happy and some things that make me unhappy. Here are some of my opinions on local issues—a list of cheers for the things I like and jeers for things I do not like.

In the first paragraph, Liz clearly outlines the topic of her essay.

Cheers to my school for holding a successful charity supper. They made more than $1,000, and a local family in need is getting the majority of it. I am really glad that so many people came and I am sure that the family was also very grateful.

Jeers to my school for making students wait outside before school. It is not fair that the students have to stand outside and freeze. It has been really cold lately, and we should be allowed to go inside to get warm . . . I think they should consider letting us in before the weather gets even colder.

By discussing both positive and negative news events, Liz addresses all aspects of the writing prompt.

Cheers to the town of Tiverton for building the Muddy Moose! It's a great place to get ice cream, coffee, pastries, and other food. Even though they only serve one type of ice cream—soft-serve—the food is very good . . . It is bad that they put Dairy Dip out of business, but you have to admit Muddy Moose is better!

Jeers to Tiverton for building a new bank. Even though it will be good to have a bank nearby, it will bring much more traffic. In the morning, on the way to school it will be horrible. We do not need any more new buildings in Tiverton. Soon Tiverton will start looking like a big city!

Liz follows a logical organization by alternating "cheers" with "jeers." She also supports ideas with evidence.

On reviewing these local news events, it seems Tiverton has a balance of good and bad news—at least there is enough good news for it to remain a good place to live.

Editing—Be Your Own Language Coach

Review your essay for language convention errors before handing it in. Revise your sentences for correct use of prepositional phrases.

Publishing—Share It!

When you publish a work, you produce it for a specific audience. Consider one of the following ideas to share your writing.

Organize a class discussion. Compare your essay with those of your classmates. Conduct a small group discussion about how using rubrics for self-assessment can improve your work.

Make a test-prep booklet. Include your essay in a booklet that contains your classmates' essays. Read through the booklet and note the different techniques your classmates used in their essays. Review the essays as practice for your next writing assessment.

Reflecting on Your Writing

1 **Reflecting on Your Writing** Respond to the following questions on a separate sheet of paper and hand it in with your final draft. What new insights did you gain about writing for assessment? What did you do well? What do you need to work on?

2 **Rubric for Self-Assessment** Assess your essay. For each question, circle a rating.

CRITERIA	RATING SCALE
	NOT VERY VERY
IDEAS How clearly do you address the keywords of the writing prompt?	1 2 3 4 5
ORGANIZATION How well did you organize your time in prewriting, drafting, and revising your essay?	1 2 3 4 5
VOICE How lively and engaging is your writing? How consistent is your tone?	1 2 3 4 5
WORD CHOICE How appropriate is the language for your audience?	1 2 3 4 5
SENTENCE FLUENCY How varied is your sentence structure?	1 2 3 4 5
CONVENTIONS How correct is your grammar, especially your use of prepositional phrases?	1 2 3 4 5

Monitoring Your Progress

Standardized Test Practice

Reading Skill: Summarizing

Read the passage. Then answer the questions.

As the twentieth century came to a close, many people were concerned about the coming of the next century. Since the 1950s, computers had recorded the date using only the last two digits of the year to save time and money. When the year 2000 arrived, it was thought that computers would get confused, interpreting the "00" in 2000 as 1900. Because the government, economy, and transportation relied on computers, this error could be disastrous. For instance, your supermarket might run out of food because the computers that check its inventory would "think" the next delivery wasn't due for 100 years.

Corporate and government programs spent an estimated $600 billion upgrading their software to recognize all four digits in a year. While the problem was serious, some predicted widespread panic—and even the end of the world. On New Year's Eve 1999, many people gathered stockpiles of food and prepared for the worst. But January 1, 2000, rolled around and not much happened. People breathed a sigh of relief knowing that their worst fears had not come to pass.

1 What is the **main idea** of this passage?

A. Many companies spent a lot of money to avoid the problem.

B. Some people thought the world would end in the year 2000.

C. People worried their bank accounts could be at risk in 2000.

D. Many people feared a major computer failure when the calendar hit 2000.

2 Which of these is a **supporting detail** of the main idea?

F. The government, economy, and transportation relied on computers, so an error could be disastrous.

G. Computers used the last two digits of the year to record the date.

H. People avoided using computers.

J. January 1, 2000, rolled around and not much happened.

3 On the lines below, summarize the passage in a few sentences.

____

____

____

____

____

Literary Analysis: Elements of Drama

Read the passage. Then answer the questions.

[CAPTAIN ARAMUS *enters the holding dock.* TARALA *is already there.*]

TARALA: Captain, it has chewed through the wires in the holding bay. We can not contain the Cateravite much longer.

CAPTAIN ARAMUS: [*Nods*] These aliens have been following us since we left the Duchu System. [*Peers through the viewing screen and watches the creature lick its striped coat.*]

TARALA: I don't get it. The Cateravite are not suited for space travel.

CAPTAIN ARAMUS: This alien's behavior is unlike the description of the Cateravite in the *Galacticon*—[CAPTAIN ARAMUS *is distracted by the creature's yawn. It walks up to the viewing screen and twitches its tail.*]—It is not fierce at all. Tarala, I am letting it in.

TARALA: [*Widens her eyes*] Captain?

[CAPTAIN ARAMUS *pushes a button to open the large, alloyed door. First there is silence. Then there is the sound of nails clicking on the ship's floor as the creature trots to the captain.* CAPTAIN ARAMUS *hesitates, then holds out her hand to the creature, which nuzzles and licks it.*]

4 This passage is written in the form of a ________.

A. short story

B. poem

C. script

D. prose

5 When Tarala says "Captain?" she is most likely expressing which emotion?

F. anger

G. disbelief

H. sadness

J. fear

6 What is Captain Aramus's opinion of this Cateravite?

A. It is gentler than described.

B. It is fierce.

C. It is dangerous.

D. It is helpless.

7 Compared to Captain Aramus, Tarala is ________.

F. more daring

G. younger

H. more cautious

J. more foolish

Timed Writing: Description

Directions Think about a conversation you had with someone else. Recreate the conversation in a script. Use dialogue and stage directions to make your dialogue realistic and easy to follow. **(20 minutes)**

5-7 Reading Skills
Compare and Contrast

In learning new reading skills, you will use special academic vocabulary. Knowing the right words will help you demonstrate your understanding.

Academic Vocabulary

Word	Meaning	Example Sentence
compare *v.* *Related words:* comparison, compares	to tell how two or more people, events, ideas, or things are alike	Guong's essay *compares* the histories of China and Japan.
convince *v.* *Related words:* convincing, convinced	to make someone believe in or do something	Jenna *convinced* her sister to go with her to the pool.
contrast *v.* *Related words:* contrasting, contrasts	to tell how two or more people, events, ideas, or things are different	The advertisement *contrasts* the nutritional value of bagel chips with that of tortilla chips.

When you **compare** two or more things, you tell how they are similar. When you **contrast** two or more things, you tell how they are different. As you read, you can use a Venn diagram to help you keep track of similarities and differences between characters, events, places, or ideas. This will help you better understand what you read.

Below, a student compares Mrs. Markham and the beggar from "What Do Fish Have to Do With Anything?" Similarities of the two characters are written in the section of the diagram common to both circles, and their differences are written in the two outer sections.

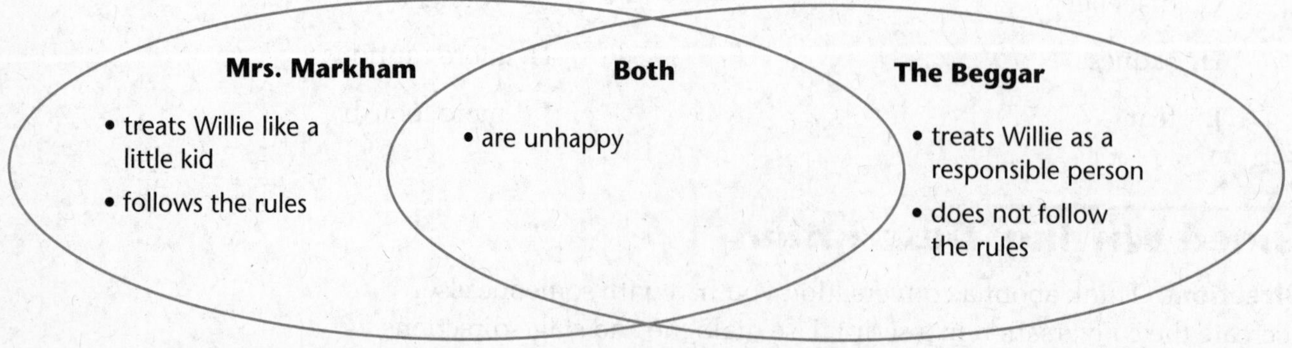

Mrs. Markham
• treats Willie like a little kid
• follows the rules
Both
• are unhappy
The Beggar
• treats Willie as a responsible person
• does not follow the rules

while reading your anchor book

Directions As you read the following passage, note in the margin how the students' opinions are alike and different. Then use your notes to complete the graphic organizer below.

In Their Own Words: Kids Talk About Popularity

Want to know what kids really think about cliques, geeks, and being cool? Read on for the innermost thoughts of two preteens, as shared on a website run by KidsPeace, a national charity.

BABYJOHN: "At my old school, I didn't have many friends. When I moved, I was suddenly accepted into the in crowd. But I have bad memories of being unpopular, and I sometimes worry that my closest friends will exclude me."

SHORTY11: "During the school year, I was rejected and not invited to parties, movies, etc. But once the summer began, I met new people who accepted me for who I was, not for the clothing I wore, or for my looks. So my advice to other kids is to hang on to the friends you've got and make an effort to meet new people. And now that I'm going into seventh grade, I think that the problem is a lot better."

1 **Compare and Contrast** Fill in the Venn diagram to show what is similar and different about Babyjohn's and Shorty11's experiences at school.

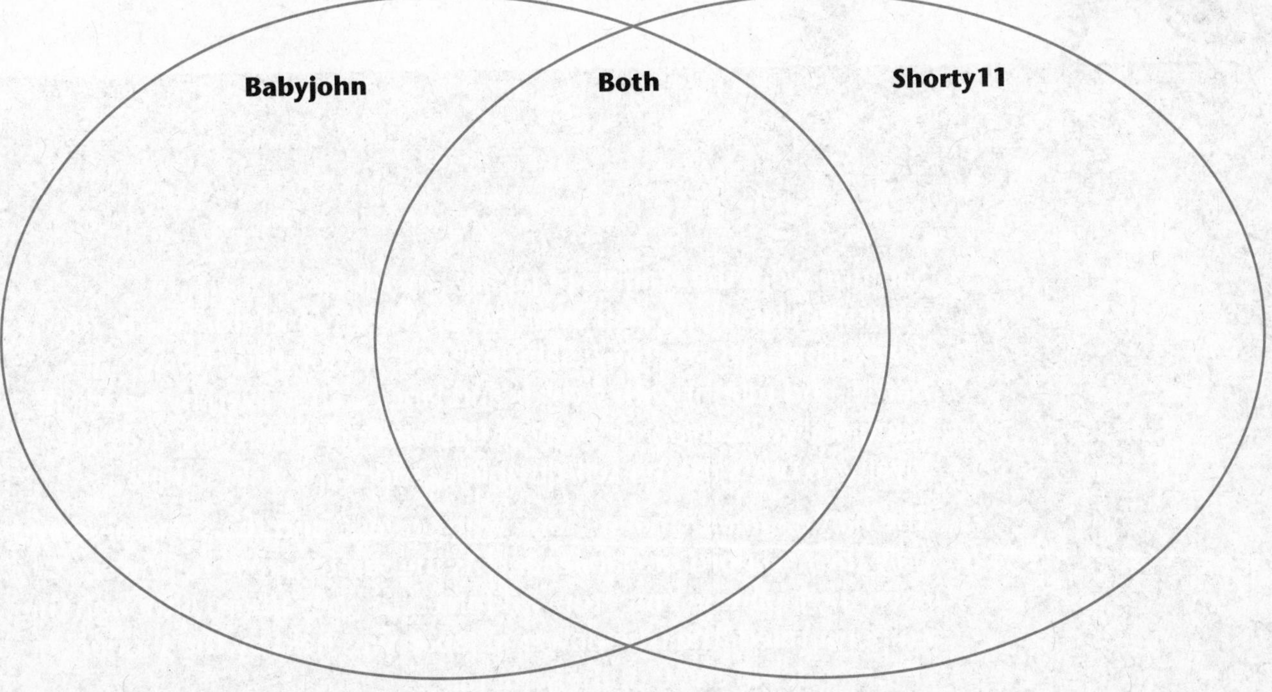

while reading your anchor book

In the following selection, the author compares and contrasts the lives of a boy and a girl born to a samurai family in Edo, Japan. *Guiding Question:* **How does the time and place of your birth affect who you are?**

If You Lived in Samurai Japan

by Virginia Schomp

"Soga Goro Gallops Bareback to Oiso" by Taiso Yoshitoshi c.1885

A Samurai's Life

Samurai were the knights of Japan—members of a warrior class that ruled over the Japanese islands for nearly 700 years, from 1185 to 1867. Samurai wore armor, rode horses into battle, and fought with swords and lances. They lived by a code of honor called *bushido*, or "way of the warrior." This code stressed loyalty to one's master,self-discipline, and respect for others.

The name *samurai* means "one who serves," and the samurai served only their warlord or clan leader. As the samurai rose to power, even the Japanese emperor was forced to obey them. Although the emperor ruled, the true power in Japan was held by the shogun, or commander in chief, of the samurai.

If you had been born during the days of the samurai, your way of life would have been determined by your social class and whether you were male or female. Follow along the course and trace what your life might have been like as a boy or girl living in a samurai family.

If you were born in Edo[1]...

Life as a Boy

Your birth is a cause for great celebration. When you are a month old, your mother takes you to the local Shinto[2] shrine to give thanks and ask for the *kami's*[3] continuing protection. Your parents love and pamper you but teach you to respect your elders and always behave properly.

Age 7 You dress in your first *hakama*, a pair of wide trousers worn over a *kimono*[4]. You visit the shrine to tell the kami that you have passed from babyhood to childhood. You learn how to ride horseback and use a small bow and wooden sword.

Age 10 You may go to a Buddhist monastery or samurai training school. You work hard learning to read and write, studying Chinese classics, and training with sword, spear, and bow.

Life as a Girl

Like that of a boy, your birth is a cause for great celebration. When you are a month old, your mother takes you to the local Shinto shrine to give thanks and ask for the kami's continuing protection. Your parents love and pamper you but teach you to respect your elders and always behave properly.

Age 7 You wear your first long kimono, tied around the waist with a colorful sash. You visit the shrine to tell the kami that you have passed from babyhood to childhood.

Ages 7–13 You help your mother at home, doing household chores and taking care of your younger brothers and sisters. Your mother teaches you a little reading and writing, proper behavior and dress, and the arts of *ikebana*[5] and the tea ceremony.

Edo (ē′ dō) *n.* prior to 1868, Tokyo (Japan's capital city) was known as Edo.
Shinto (shin′ tō) *n.* a religion of Japan dating from the early eighth century.
kami (kä′ mē) *n.* a divine being in the Shinto religion.
kimono (kə mō′ nō) *n.* a robe with wide sleeves and sash, part of the traditional costume of Japanese men and women.
ikebana (ē′ ke bä′ nä) *n.* the Japanese art of arranging flowers.

A young Japanese girl practicing calligraphy—the art of beautiful handwriting—in a traditional kimono

Life as a Boy

Age 14 The front part of your head is shaved as a sign that you have become a man. You are given a steel sword and a suit of armor. Now you are ready to fight in battle.

A Warrior You follow your lord into battle. In peacetime you work at his castle or in town and spend most evenings relaxing with samurai friends.

In Old Age Few warriors live a long life. If you manage to survive into old age, you retire from fighting but are still treated with great respect.

Life as a Girl

Age 12 or 13 Your eyebrows are plucked until only a thin arch remains. This ceremony marks your passage into womanhood. Soon your parents will cho a husband for you, and you will move int his family's home.

Wife and Mother You spend most of y time at home caring for the children anc managing the household. You also may train in the martial arts.[5]

In Old Age You live a quiet life. If your husband has died, you may live with you son's family or become a Buddhist nun a live in a convent.

When you die, your body is cremated. The ashes are buried at a Buddhist temple, and your spirit may be enshrined at the local Shinto shrine.

[5] **martial arts** (mär′ shəl ärts) *n.* skills, mainly of Japanese origin, that began as systems of self-defense.

The samurai believed their swords were the source of their warrior spirit. Out of respect, they named their swords.

Mother and son wear *geta*, wooden clogs made to prevent their kimonos from getting soiled.

Thinking About the Selection

If You Lived in Samurai Japan

1 **Compare and Contrast** Complete the Venn diagram to show similarities and differences in the lives of boys and girls in a samurai family.

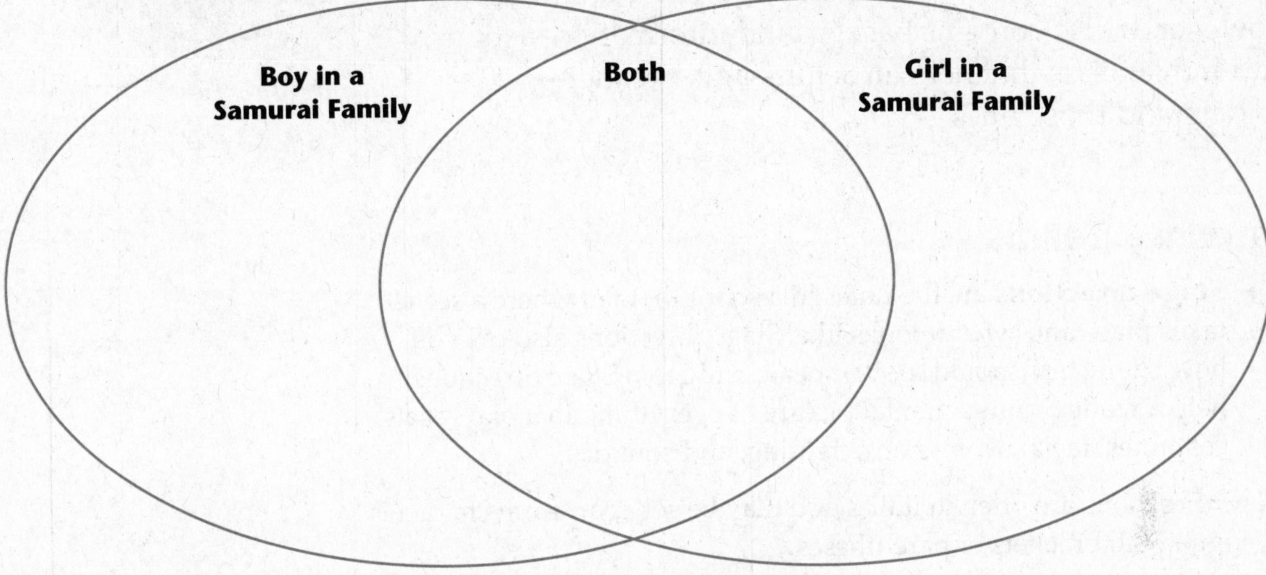

2 **Interpret** Do you think the author is trying to convince her readers that a boy born in Edo has a better life than a girl born in Edo? Explain your answer.

____

____

____

Write Answer the following questions in your Reader's Journal.

3 **Generalize** How does the time and place of your birth affect who you are?

4 **Compare and Contrast** Choose two people, places, events, or things in your Anchor Book. Use a Venn diagram to show how they are both alike and different.

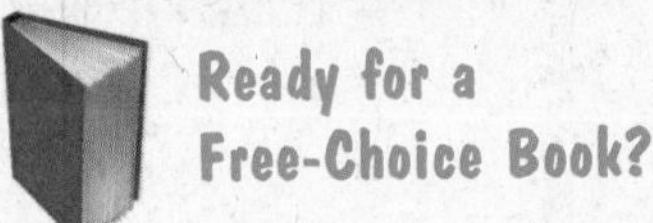

Ready for a Free-Choice Book?

Your teacher may ask if you would like to choose another book to read on your own. Select a book that fits your interest and that you'll enjoy. As you read, think about how your new book compares with your Anchor Book.

5-8 Literary Analysis
Stage Directions

You probably know that the lines an actor recites on stage come from a **script.** A script contains more than lines, however. It also contains background information, actions, and movements that help an actor—and a reader—better understand those lines.

Literary Terms

- **Stage directions** are the notes in a script that tell where a scene takes place and what it looks like. Stage directions also tell you how characters should move, speak, and look. Stage directions help a reader paint a mental picture of everything in a play—sets, costumes, facial expressions, lighting, and sound.

Stage directions are often in italics and may be set apart from character dialogue with brackets or parentheses.

> [*Carnival music can be heard in the distance. A Ferris wheel turns in the background. Two kids rummage frantically through the pile of junk behind the fence in the foreground. One girl paces back and forth continuously as if on the lookout for something.*]
>
> **HILLARY:** [*Head down*] Hurry up, you guys! Mr. Fletcher's gonna be here any second. Hurry up!

Stage directions can describe the following.

Costumes

- clothes the actors wear
- can help clarify the time period and place in which the play is set

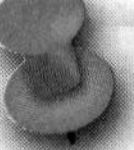

Sound

- sounds made by specific things or heard at specific events
- help make the play seem real

Scenery

- structures that make the stage look like the place where the scene happens
- may be a painted backdrop or a structure built just for the play

Props

- objects actors use, or that appear on the stage
- make the setting more believable

Lighting

- the effects made by lights shining on the stage
- helps to create atmosphere

while reading your anchor book

Directions The following excerpt is from a teleplay, a type of play that is performed on television. As you read, underline stage directions that indicate an actor's movements. Circle words or phrases that describe the characters.

About the Author
Visit: PHSchool.com
Web Code: exe-6503

from *The Monsters Are Due on Maple Street*

by Rod Serling

[*The group suddenly starts toward the house. In this brief fraction of a moment they take the first step toward performing a metamorphosis that changes people from a group into a mob. They begin to head purposefully across the street toward the house at the end. STEVE stands in front of them. For a moment their fear almost turns their walk into a wild stampede, but STEVE'S voice, loud, incisive, and commanding, makes them stop.*]

STEVE. Wait a minute . . . wait a minute! Let's not be a mob!

[*The people stop as a group, seem to pause for a moment, and then much more quietly and slowly start to walk across the street. GOODMAN stands alone facing the people.*]

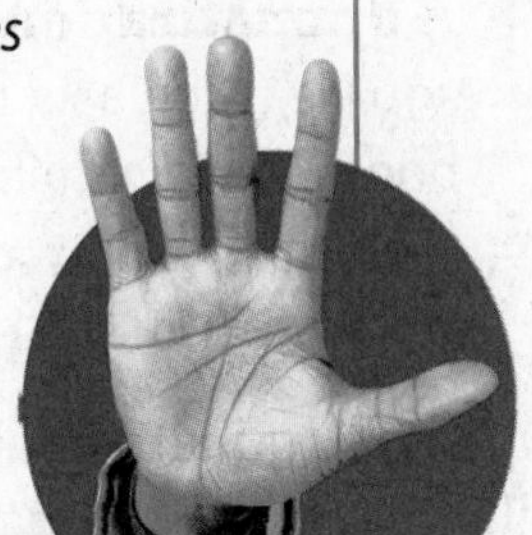

1 **Explain** What information do the stage directions give you about the scene?

2 **Analyze** How do the stage directions help to reveal Steve's character?

3 **Describe** Write stage directions that describe Steve's appearance based on what you know about Steve's character. Explain why you chose to describe him this way.

while reading your anchor book

Dramatization

Playwrights can find inspiration everywhere. More than 2,500 years ago, playwrights were so inspired by the world around them that they created plays for religious and agricultural festivals. Today, playwrights use novels, comic strips, and even paintings as sources for writing their scripts.

Literary Terms

- A **dramatization** is a play that has been adapted from another source, such as a novel. For example, Norton Juster wrote the book *The Phantom Tollbooth.* Susan Nanus wanted to make the story into a play, so she used the same characters, plot, and conflict from the story to write a script.

How is a dramatization different from the work it comes from? The following chart compares and contrasts a novel and a drama.

Novel	Drama
is written in prose	is written in script format
is meant to be read	is meant to be read or watched in a performance
is divided into chapters, which are then divided into paragraphs	is divided into acts, or units of actions, which are then divided into scenes, or smaller acts
words characters say are put inside quotation marks	words characters say are called lines or speeches
story is told by the narrator	story is told through the words and actions of characters and through stage directions
novels can take hours, days, or weeks to read	most plays take from ninety minutes to three hours to perform

Directions Read the dramatization on the following page. Then complete the chart and answer the question.

while reading your anchor book

from ***The Phantom Tollbooth*** *by Norton Juster*
adapted by Susan Nanus

Go Online
About the Author
Visit: PHSchool.com
Web Code: exe-6504

Scene ii The Road to Dictionopolis

[*ENTER* MILO *in his car*]

MILO. This is weird! I don't recognize any of this scenery at all. [A SIGN *is held up before* MILO, *startling him.*] Huh? [*Reads.*] WELCOME TO EXPECTATIONS. INFORMATION, PREDICTIONS AND ADVICE CHEERFULLY OFFERED. PARK HERE AND BLOW HORN. [MILO *blows horn.*]

WHETHER MAN. [*A little man wearing a long coat and carrying an umbrella pops up from behind the sign that he was holding. He speaks very fast and excitedly.*] My, my, my, my, my, welcome, welcome, welcome, welcome to the Land of Expectations, Expectations, Expectations! We don't get many travelers these days; we certainly don't get many travelers. Now what can I do for you? I'm the Whether Man.

MILO. [*Referring to map.*] Uh . . . is this the right road to Dictionopolis?

WHETHER MAN. Well now, well now, well now, I don't know of any wrong road to Dictionopolis, so if this road goes to Dictionopolis at all, it must be the right road, and if it doesn't, it must be the right road to somewhere else, because there are no wrong roads to anywhere. Do you think it will rain?

MILO. I thought you were the Weather Man.

WHETHER MAN. Oh, no, I'm the Whether Man, not the weather man.

1 **Apply** Use details from the script to describe the elements listed in the chart.

Scenery	
Characters	
Props	
Sound Effects	
Costumes	

2 **Distinguish** What homophones—words that sound the same but are spelled differently—did you find in this excerpt? Why do you think these homophones are used?

Use your new knowledge about stage directions and dramatization to help you understand the following selection. *Guiding Question:* **Can the results of a survey help us decide who we are? Why or why not?**

from

YOU'RE A GOOD MAN, CHARLIE BROWN
THE BROADWAY MUSICAL

by **Clark Gesner**

Based on the comic strip *Peanuts*
by **Charles M. Schulz**

while reading your anchor book

Background You're a Good Man, Charlie Brown *is a musical based on Charles Schulz's well-known comic strip* Peanuts. *The musical first opened in New York in 1967 and was performed nearly 1,600 times. All of the characters are children, except for Snoopy, who is a dog.*

Vocabulary Builder

Before you read, *you will discuss the following words. In the Vocabulary Builder box in the margin, use a vocabulary building strategy to make the words your own.*

offstage **rampage** **tentatively** **candor**

As you read, *draw a box around unfamiliar words you could add to your vocabulary. Use context clues to unlock their meaning.*

Marking the Text

Stage Directions and Dramatization

As you read, *underline the stage directions. After you read, note the purpose of each direction.*

SCHROEDER. I'm sorry to have to say it right to your face, Lucy, but it's true. You're a very crabby person. I know your crabbiness has probably become so natural to you now that you're not even aware when you're being crabby, but it's true just the same. You're a very crabby person and you're crabby to just about everyone you meet. (LUCY *remains silent—just barely*) Now I hope you don't mind my saying this, Lucy, and I hope you'll take it in the spirit that it's meant. I think we should all be open to any opportunity to learn more about ourselves. I think

Socrates[1] was very right when he said that one of the first rules for anyone in life is "Know thyself." (LUCY *has begun whistling quietly to herself*) Well, I guess I've said about enough. I hope I haven't offended you or anything. (*He makes an awkward exit*)

LUCY. (*Sits in silence, then shouts* **offstage** *at Schroeder*) Well, what's Socrates got to do with it anyway, huh? Who was he anyway? Did he ever get to be king, huh! Answer me that, did he ever get to be king! (*Suddenly to herself, a real question*) *Did* he ever get to be king? (*She shouts offstage, now a question*) Who was Socrates, anyway? (*She gives up the* **rampage** *and plunks herself down*) "Know thyself," hmph. (*She thinks for a moment, then makes a silent resolution to herself, exits and quickly returns with a clipboard and pencil.* CHARLIE BROWN *and* SNOOPY *have entered, still with baseball equipment*)

CHARLIE BROWN. Hey, Snoopy, you want to help me get my arm back in shape? Watch out for this one, it's a new fastball.

LUCY. Excuse me a moment, Charlie Brown, but I was wondering if you'd mind answering a few questions.

CHARLIE BROWN. Not at all, Lucy. What kind of questions are they?

LUCY. Well, I'm conducting a survey to enable me to know myself better, and first of all I'd like to ask: on a scale of zero to one hundred, using a standard of fifty as average, seventy-five as above average and ninety as exceptional, where would you rate me with regards to crabbiness?

CHARLIE BROWN. (*Stands in silence for a moment, hesitating*) Well, Lucy, I . . .

LUCY. Your ballots need not be signed and all answers will be held in strictest confidence.

CHARLIE BROWN. Well still, Lucy, that's a very hard question to answer.

LUCY. You may have a few moments to think it over if you want, or we can come back to that question later.

CHARLIE BROWN. I think I'd like to come back to it, if you don't mind.

LUCY. Certainly. This next question deals with certain character traits you may have observed. Regarding personality, would you say that mine is *A* forceful, *B* pleasing, or *C* objectionable? Would that be *A, B,* or *C*? What would your answer be to that, Charlie Brown, forceful, pleasing or objectionable, which one would you say, hmm? Charlie Brown, hmm?

CHARLIE BROWN. Well, I guess I'd have to say forceful, Lucy, but . . .

1 **Socrates** (säk′rə tēz′) *n.* ca. 470–399 B.C. Greek philosopher.

Vocabulary Builder

offstage
(ăf′stāj′) *adv.*

Meaning

rampage
(ram′pāj′) *n.*

Meaning

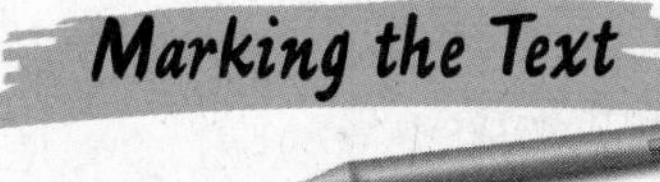

while reading your anchor book

LUCY. "Forceful." Well, we'll make a check mark at the letter *A* then. Now, would you rate my ability to get along with other people as poor, fair, good or excellent?

CHARLIE BROWN. I think that depends a lot on what you mean by "get along with other people."

LUCY. You know, make friends, sparkle in a crowd, that sort of thing.

CHARLIE BROWN. Do you have a place for abstention?

LUCY. Certainly, I'll just put a check mark at "None of the above." The next question deals with physical appearance. In referring to my beauty, would you say that I was "stunning," "mysterious," or "intoxicating"?

CHARLIE BROWN. (*Squirming*) Well, gee, I don't know, Lucy. You look just fine to me.

LUCY. (*Making a check on the page*) "Stunning." All right, Charlie Brown, I think we should get back to that first question. On a scale of zero to one hundred, using a standard of fifty as average, seventy-five as . . .

CHARLIE BROWN. (*Loud interruption*) I . . . (*quieter*) . . . remember the question, Lucy.

LUCY. Well?

CHARLIE BROWN. (**Tentatively**) Fifty-one?

LUCY. (*Noting it down*) Fifty-one is your crabbiness rating for me. Very well then, that about does it. Thank you very much for helping with this survey, Charlie Brown. Your cooperation has been greatly appreciated. (*She shakes hands with* CHARLIE BROWN)

CHARLIE BROWN. (*Flustered*) It was a pleasure, Lucy, any time. Come on, Snoopy.

LUCY. Oh, just a minute, there is one more question. Would you answer "Yes" or "No" to the question: "Is Lucy Van Pelt the sort of person that you would like to have as president of your club or civic organization?"

CHARLIE BROWN. Oh, yes, by all means, Lucy.

LUCY. (*Making note*) Yes. Well, thank you very much. That about does it, I think. (CHARLIE BROWN *exits, but* SNOOPY *pauses, turns, and strikes a dramatic "thumbs down" pose to* LUCY) WELL, WHO ASKED YOU! (SNOOPY *makes a hasty exit.* LUCY *stands center stage, figuring to herself on the clipboard and mumbling*) Now let's see. That's a fifty-one, "None of the above," and . . . (*She looks up*) Schroeder was right. I can already feel myself being filled with the glow of self-awareness. (PATTY *enters. She is heading for the other side of the stage, when* LUCY *stops her*) Oh, Patty, I'm conducting a survey and I wonder if . . .

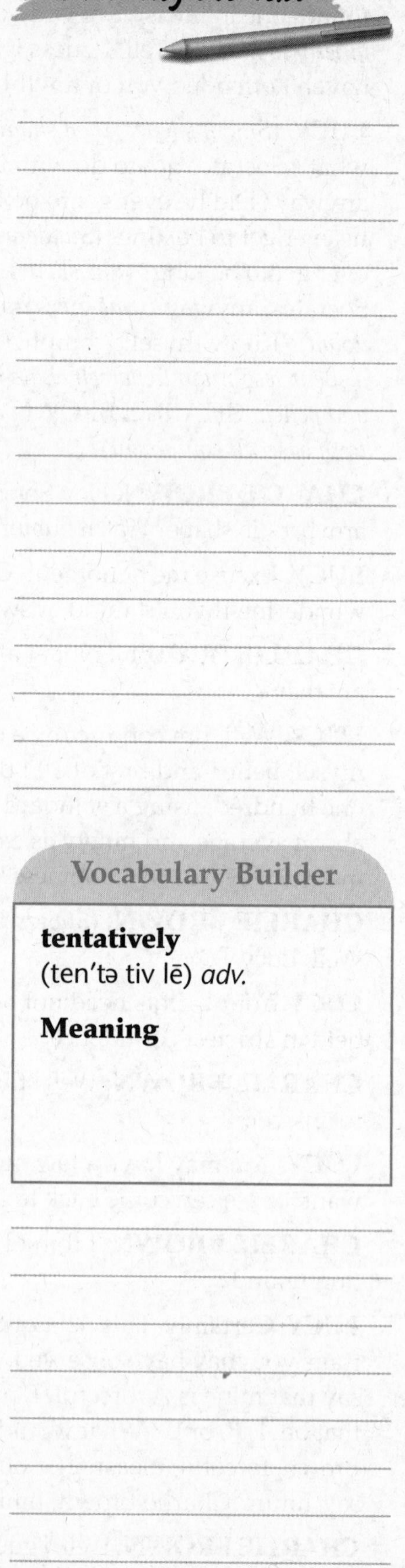

PATTY. A hundred and ten, C, "Poor," "None of the above," "No," and what are you going to do about the dent you made in my bicycle! (PATTY *storms off.* LUCY *watches her go, then looks at the audience*)

LUCY. It's amazing how fast word of these surveys gets around. (LINUS *wanders in and plunks himself down in front of the TV.* LUCY *crosses to him, still figuring.*)

LUCY. Oh, Linus, I'm glad you're here. I'm conducting a survey and there are a few questions I'd like to ask you.

LINUS. Sure, go ahead.

LUCY. The first question is: on a scale of zero to one hundred, with a standard of fifty as average, seventy-five as above average and ninety as exceptional, where would you rate me with regards to crabbiness?

LINUS. (*Slowly turns his head to look at her, then turns back to the TV*) You're my big sister.

LUCY. That's not the question.

LINUS. No, but that's the answer.

LUCY. Come on, Linus, answer the question.

LINUS. (*Getting up and facing* LUCY) Look, Lucy, I know very well that if I give any sort of honest answer to that question you're going to slug me.

Marking the Text

while reading your anchor book

Literature in Context
Comic Strips Through Time

Link to History

The first illustrated comic strips appeared in the seventeenth century. Around 1800, they began to take the shape we know today. Figures were drawn in outline, and very little background appeared. During the nineteenth century, cartoons began to appear in newspapers and magazines.

At the end of the nineteenth century, newspapers came out with full-color comics. A daily black-and-white strip appeared in a Chicago newspaper in 1904, and by 1915, the comics were a standard feature in most big newspapers.

In the following decades, adventure comic strips in newspapers became so popular that publishers introduced comic books. Since then, comic-book characters like Superman, Batman, and Spider-Man have made the leap from comic book to drama.

Good to Know!
In 1938, Superman made his first appearance in *Action Comics* #1. A copy cost ten cents. Today, a copy of this issue can be worth over $100,000!

LUCY. Linus. A survey that is not based on honest answers is like a house that is built on a foundation of sand. Would I be spending my time to conduct this survey if I didn't expect complete **candor** in all the responses? I promise not to slug you. Now what number would you give me as your crabbiness rating?

LINUS. (*After a few moments of interior struggle*) Ninety-five. (LUCY *sends a straight jab to his jaw which lays him out flat*)

LUCY. No decent person could be expected to keep her word with a rating over ninety. (*She stalks off, busily figuring away on her clipboard*) Now, I add these two columns and that gives me my answer. (*She figures energetically, then finally sits up with satisfaction*) There, it's all done. Now, let's see what we've got. (*She begins to scan the page. A look of trouble skims over her face. She rechecks the figures. Her eternal look of self-confidence wavers, then crumbles*) It's true. I'm a crabby person. I'm a very crabby person and everybody knows it. I've been spreading crabbiness wherever I go. I'm a supercrab. It's a wonder anyone will still talk to me. It's a wonder I have any friends at all—(*She looks at the figures on the paper*) or even associates. I've done nothing but make life miserable for everyone. I've done nothing but breed unhappiness and resentment. Where did I go wrong? How could I be so selfish? How could . . . (LINUS *has been listening. He comes and sits near her*)

LINUS. What's wrong, Lucy?

LUCY. Don't talk to me, Linus. I don't deserve to be spoken to. I don't deserve to breathe the air I breathe. I'm no good, Linus. I'm no good.

LINUS. That's not true, Lucy.

LUCY. Yes it is. I'm no good, and there's no reason at all why I should go on living on the face of this earth.

LINUS. Yes there is.

LUCY. Name one. Just tell me one single reason why I should still deserve to go on living on this planet.

LINUS. Well, for one thing, you have a little brother who loves you. (LUCY *looks at him. She is silent. Then she breaks into a great, sobbing "Wah!"*) Every now and then I say the right thing.

(LUCY *continues sobbing as she and* LINUS *exit. . .*).

Vocabulary Builder

candor
(kan′ dər) *n.*

Meaning

▲ **Critical Viewing**
How would you describe Lucy's mood in this picture?

Vocabulary Builder

After you read, *review the words you decided to add to your vocabulary. Write the meaning of words you have learned in context. Look up the other words in a dictionary, glossary, thesaurus, or electronic resource.*

Thinking About the Selection

from You're a Good Man, Charlie Brown

1 **Apply** Use what you know about drama and stage directions to describe these elements from *You're a Good Man, Charlie Brown.*

Scenery	
Characters	
Props	
Conflict	

2 **Analyze** Identify a passage you thought was funny. What made it so humorous?

3 **Infer** What message do you think the author was trying to express in the scene? How does humor help to reveal that message?

Write Answer the following questions in your Reader's Journal.

4 **Evaluate** Can the results of a survey help us decide who we are? Why or why not?

5 **Analyze** Choose a scene from your Anchor Book. Rewrite the scene as if it were written as a novel. What elements did you use that are not in the play?

while reading your anchor book

5-9 Literary Analysis
Conflict in Drama

Whether you are reading or watching a play, you should be aware of the different ways conflict is revealed. Because drama is written to be performed, it does not contain many descriptive details that hint at the conflict. Instead, drama relies on characters' words and actions to reveal conflict.

Literary Terms

- All types of fiction contain a **conflict,** or a struggle between opposing forces. Conflict makes the story interesting and moves the plot forward. Look at the example to see how the same conflict is expressed differently in a novel and in a drama.

Novel	Abby was so angry she couldn't look Lexa in the face. All she could do was hold her arms straight at her sides, clench her fists, and bite her lower lip to keep herself from yelling. To make matters worse, Lexa didn't even seem to care.
Drama	ABBY. [*Looks away, then says in an accusing tone.*] How could you, Lex? [ABBY *stands rigid, her hands curled into fists. She bites her lip to keep from yelling at* LEXA, *who stands facing her, calm and with a mocking smile on her face.*]

- When you read drama, the dialogue often reveals the conflict. Stage directions describing a character's facial expressions and movements also reveal conflict to a reader.
- When you watch drama, however, you *see* the characters experience conflict. Actors use facial expressions and body gestures and adjust the volume and tone of their voices to reveal conflict.

The chart below shows how novels and drama present conflict differently.

In a novel, conflict is revealed through...	In drama, conflict is revealed through . . .
• **author's descriptions** of characters' actions	• **stage directions,** which describe characters' actions
• **narrator's descriptions** of characters	• **characters' actions,** such as facial expressions, body movements, and volume of voice
• **characters' dialogue** and thoughts	• **dialogue** that characters speak

Directions Read the following passage from a short story. Underline details that provide clues about the conflict. Answer the questions.

from "The Circuit" *by Francisco Jiménez*

One Friday during lunch hour Mr. Lema asked me to take a walk with him to the music room. "Do you like music?" he asked me as we entered the building.

"Yes, I like *corridos,*" I answered. He then picked up a trumpet, blew on it and handed it to me. The sound gave me goose bumps. I knew that sound. I had heard it in many corridos. "How would you like to learn how to play it?" he asked. He must have read my face because before I could answer, he added: "I'll teach you how to play it during our lunch hours."

That day I could hardly wait to get home to tell Papá and Mamá the great news. As I got off the bus, my little brothers and sisters ran up to meet me. They were yelling and screaming. I thought they were happy to see me, but when I opened the door to our shack, I saw that everything we owned was neatly packed in cardboard boxes.

1 **Describe** What is the narrator's conflict?

2 **Apply** Rewrite the last paragraph to show how a playwright might have written it. What is the main difference in the way that this action would be described in a drama?

3 **Contrast** Suppose the passage was from a play instead of a short story. How would the conflict be presented differently?

In the following play, notice how the playwright uses dialogue and stage directions to develop the conflict. *Guiding Question:* **How do our conflicts with others help us to learn about ourselves and who we are?**

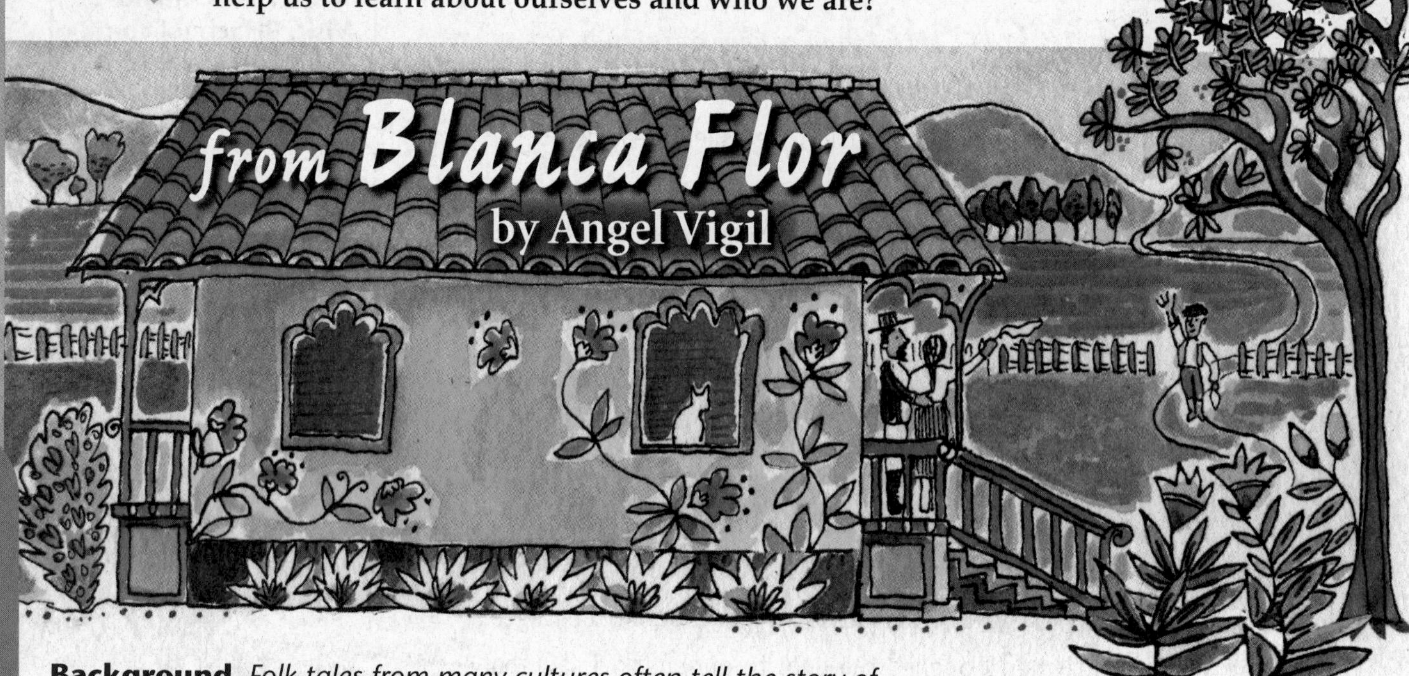

from Blanca Flor

by Angel Vigil

Background *Folk tales from many cultures often tell the story of a person seeking fortune in dangerous places. In this dramatization of a popular Spanish folk tale, Juanito sets out to seek his fortune, and soon finds trouble—and magic.*

Vocabulary Builder

Before you read, *you will discuss the following words. In the Vocabulary Builder box in the margin, use a vocabulary building strategy to make the words your own.*

fortune **valiant** **frantically** **barren**

As you read, *draw a box around unfamiliar words you could add to your vocabulary. Use context clues to unlock their meaning.*

Marking the Text

Conflict in Drama

As you read, *underline important details about the problem faced by the main character. In the margin, describe the conflict.*

Characters

(in order of appearance)

The Narrator

Juanito, a young man

The Duende, a gnomelike, mischievous creature who lives in the forest

Blanca Flor, a young woman

Don Ricardo, an evil man

Scene 1.

IN THE FOREST.

The Narrator. *Blanca Flor*, "White Flower." There never was a story with such a beautiful name as this story of Blanca Flor. At the beginning of our story, a young man named Juanito has left home to seek his fortune in the world. With the blessing of his parents to aid and protect him, he has begun what will be a fantastic adventure. At the beginning of his journey, he wanders into a forest and stops by a stream to rest and eat some of the tortillas his mother had packed for his journey.

[JUANITO *enters and walks around the stage as if looking for a comfortable place to rest. He finally decides upon a spot and sits down. He takes out a tortilla from his traveling bag and he begins to talk to himself.*]

Juanito. Whew! I'm hot. This river looks like a good spot to rest for a while. I'm so tired. Maybe this journey wasn't such a good idea. Right now I could be home with *la familia* eating a good supper that *mamacita* cooked for us. But no, I'm out in the world seeking my fortune. So far I haven't found very much, and all I have to show for my efforts are two worn-out feet and a tired body . . . oh, and don't forget (*holding up a dried tortilla*) a dried-out tortilla . . . (*He quickly looks around as if startled.*) What was that? (*He listens intently and hears a sound again.*) There it is again. I know I heard something . . .

[*As* JUANITO *is talking,* THE DUENDE *enters, sneaking up behind him.*]

Juanito. Must be my imagination. I've been out in the woods too long. You know, if you're alone too long, your mind starts to play tricks on you. Just look at me. I'm talking to my tortilla and hearing things . . .

The Duende (*in a crackly voice*). Hello.

Juanito. Yikes! Who said that! (*He turns around quickly and is startled to see* THE DUENDE *behind him.*) Who are you?

The Duende (*with a mischievous twinkle in his eye*). Hello.

Juanito. Hello . . . who, who are you? And where did you come from?

[THE DUENDE *grabs the tortilla out of* JUANITO's *hand and begins to eat it. During the rest of the scene* THE DUENDE *continues to eat tortillas.*]

Juanito. Hey, that's my tortilla.

The Duende (*in a playful manner*). Thank you very much. Thank you very much.

Juanito (*to the audience*). He must be a forest Duende. I've heard of them. They're spirits who live in the wood and play tricks on humans. I better go along with him or he might hurt me. (*He offers* THE DUENDE *another tortilla.* THE DUENDE *takes the tortilla and begins to eat it, too.*) I hope he's not too hungry. If he eats all my tortillas, I won't have any left, and it'll be days before I get food again. I'll have to eat wild berries like an animal. (*He reaches for the tortilla and* THE DUENDE *hits his hand.*) Ouch, that hurt!

The Duende. Looking for work, eh?

Juanito. Now I know he's a Duende. He can read minds.

The Duende. No work here. Lost in the forest. No work here.

Juanito. I know that. We're in the middle of the forest. But I know there'll be work in the next town.

The Duende. Maybe work right here. Maybe.

Juanito. Really. Where?

[THE DUENDE *points to a path in the forest.* JUANITO *stands up and looks down the path.*]

Juanito. There's nothing down that path. I've been down that path and there is nothing there.

The Duende. Look again. Look again. Be careful. Be careful. (*He begins to walk off, carrying the bag of tortillas with him.*)

Marking the Text

Juanito. Hey, don't leave yet. What type of work? And where? Who do I see? Hey, don't leave yet!

The Duende (THE DUENDE *stops and turns*). Be careful. Danger. Danger. (*He exits.*)

Juanito. Hey! That's my bag of tortillas. Oh, this is great. This is really going to sound good when I get back home. My tortillas? . . . Oh, they were stolen by a forest Duende. Not to worry . . . (*He yells in the direction of the departed* DUENDE.) And I'm not lost! . . . This is great. Lost and hungry and no work. I guess I'm never going to find my **fortune** in the world. But what did he mean about work . . . and be careful . . . and danger. I've been down that path and there was nothing there . . . I don't think there was anything there. Oh well, there is only one way to find out. It certainly can't get much worse than things are now, and maybe there is work there.

[JUANITO *exits, in the direction of the path* THE DUENDE *indicated.*]

Scene 2.

FARTHER IN THE FOREST.

The Narrator. In spite of the Duende's warning, Juanito continued on the path of danger. As he came into a clearing, he came to a house and saw a young woman coming out of it.

[JUANITO *enters,* BLANCA FLOR *enters from the opposite side of the stage and stops, remaining at the opposite side of the stage.*]

Juanito. Where did this house come from? I was here just yesterday and there was no house here. I must really be lost and turned around. (*He sees the young woman and waves to her.*) Hey! Come here. Over here! [BLANCA FLOR *runs to* JUANITO.]

Blanca Flor (*with fear in her voice*). How did you find this place? You must leave right away. The owner of this place is gone, but he will return soon. He leaves to do his work in the world, but he will return unexpectedly. If he finds you here, you'll never be able to leave. You must leave right away.

Juanito. Why? I haven't done anything.

Blanca Flor. Please, just leave. And hurry!

Juanito. Who are you? And why are you here?

Marking the Text

Vocabulary Builder

fortune
(fôr′ chən) *n.*

Meaning

Blanca Flor. I am Blanca Flor. My parents died long ago, and I am kept by this man to pay off their debts to him. I have to work day and night on his farm until I can be free. But he is mean, and he has kept prisoner others who have tried to free me. He makes them work until they die from exhaustion.

Juanito. Who would be so mean?

Blanca Flor. His name is Don Ricardo.

[DON RICARDO *enters, suddenly and with great force.*]

Don Ricardo (*addressing* JUANITO). Why are you here! Didn't she tell you to leave!

Blanca Flor (*scared*). Don't hurt him. He is lost in the forest and got here by mistake. He was just leaving.

Don Ricardo. Let him answer for himself. Then I will decide what to do with him.

Juanito. (*gathering all his courage*). Yes, she did tell me to leave. But . . . but I am in the world seeking my fortune and I am looking for work. Is there any work for me to do here?

Don Ricardo. Seeking your fortune! They always say that, don't they, Blanca Flor. Well, I will give you the same chance I have given others. For each of three days, I will give you a job. If in three days you have completed the jobs, then you may leave. If not, then you will work here with me until you are dead. What do you say, fortune-seeker?

Blanca Flor (*pulling* JUANITO *aside*). Do not say yes. You will never leave here alive. Run and try to escape.

Marking the Text

Juanito. But what about you? You are more trapped than anybody.

Blanca Flor. That is not your worry. Just run and try to escape.

Juanito (*suddenly turning back to* DON RICARDO). I will do the work you ask.

Don Ricardo (*laughing*). Blanca Flor, it is always your fault they stay. They all think they will be able to set you free. Well, let's give this one his "fair" chance. (*To* JUANITO) Here is your first job. See that lake over there? Take this thimble[1] (*he gives a thimble to* JUANITO) and use it to carry all the water in the lake to that field over there.

Juanito. You want me to move a lake with a thimble?!

Don Ricardo. You wanted work, fortune-seeker. Well, this is your job. Have it finished by morning or your fate will be the same as all the others who tried to save poor Blanca Flor. (*He exits.*)

Juanito. What type of man is he? I have heard legends of evil men who keep people captive, and in my travels I heard many stories of young men seeking their fortunes who were never seen again, but I always thought they were just stories.

Blanca Flor. You have had the misfortune to get lost in a terrible part of the forest. Didn't anyone warn you to stay away from here?

Juanito. Yes . . . one person did. But I thought he was a forest Duende, and I didn't really believe him.

Blanca Flor. It was a forest Duende. In this part of the forest there are many creatures with magic. But my keeper, his magic is stronger than any of ours.

Juanito. Ours? . . . What do you mean, ours? Are you part of the magic of this forest?

Blanca Flor. Do not ask so many questions. The day is passing by, and soon it will be morning.

Juanito. Morning. I'm supposed to have moved the lake by then. I know this job is impossible, but while God is in his heaven there is a way. I will do this job. And when I am done, I will help you escape from here.

[JUANITO *and* BLANCA FLOR *exit.*]

---

[1] **thimble** (thim′ bəl) *n.* a small cap worn to protect the finger that pushes a needle in sewing.

Marking the Text

while reading your anchor book

Scene 3.

THE NEXT MORNING.

[JUANITO *and* BLANCA FLOR *enter. As* THE NARRATOR *speaks,* JUANITO *and* BLANCA FLOR *act out the scene as it is described.*]

The Narrator. Juanito took the thimble and started to carry the water from the lake. He worked as hard as he could, but soon he began to realize that the job really was an impossible one, and he knew he was doomed[2]. He sat down and began to cry because his luck had abandoned him and because his parents' blessings offered no protection in that evil place. Blanca Flor watched Juanito's **valiant** effort to move the water. As she watched him crying, her heart was touched, and she decided to use her powers to help him. She knew that it was very dangerous to use her powers to help Juanito and to cross Don Ricardo, but she felt it was finally time to end her own torment[3]. As Juanito cried, Blanca Flor took out her brush and began to brush his hair. She cradled Juanito in her arms and her soothing comfort soon put him to sleep . . . .

Marking the Text

Vocabulary Builder

valiant
(val′ yənt) *adj.*

Meaning

---

[2] **doomed** (do͞om′ d) *adj.* condemned to a terrible fate.

[3] **torment** (tôr′ ment′) *n.* severe physical or mental suffering.

[*As soon as* JUANITO *is asleep,* BLANCA FLOR *gently puts his head down and leaves, taking the thimble with her.*]

The Narrator. When Juanito awoke, he **frantically** looked for the thimble and, not finding it, ran to the lake. When he reached the lake, he stood at its banks in amazement. All the water was gone. He looked over to the other part of the field, and there stood a lake where before there was nothing. He turned to look for Blanca Flor, but instead there was Don Ricardo.

[DON RICARDO *enters.*]

Don Ricardo (*in full force and very angry*). This must be the work of Blanca Flor, or else you have more power than I thought. I know Blanca Flor is too scared to ever use her powers against me, so as a test of your powers, tomorrow your next job will not be so easy. See that **barren** ground over on the side of the mountain? You are to clear that ground, plant seeds, grow wheat, harvest it, grind it, cook it, and have bread for me to eat before I return. You still have your life now, but I better have bread tomorrow. (*He exits, with a flourish.*)

[JUANITO *exits.*]

Scene 4.

THE NEXT MORNING.

[*As* THE NARRATOR *speaks,* JUANITO *and* BLANCA FLOR *enter and act out the scene as it is described.*]

The Narrator. Immediately upon waking the next morning, Juanito tried to move the rocks in the field, but they were impossible to move because of their great size. Once again, Juanito knew that his efforts were useless. He went over to the new lake and fell down in exhaustion. As he lay in the grass by the lake, Blanca Flor came to him once more and began to brush his hair. Soon, Juanito was asleep.

[BLANCA FLOR *exits.*]

The Narrator. As before, when he awoke, Juanito dashed to the field to make one last attempt to do his work. When he got there, he again stopped in amazement. The field was clear of rocks, and the land had been planted and harvested. As he turned around, there stood Blanca Flor. [BLANCA FLOR *enters.*]

Blanca Flor (*she hands a loaf of bread to* JUANITO). Give this to Don Ricardo.

Juanito. How did you do this?

[DON RICARDO *enters, quickly.*]

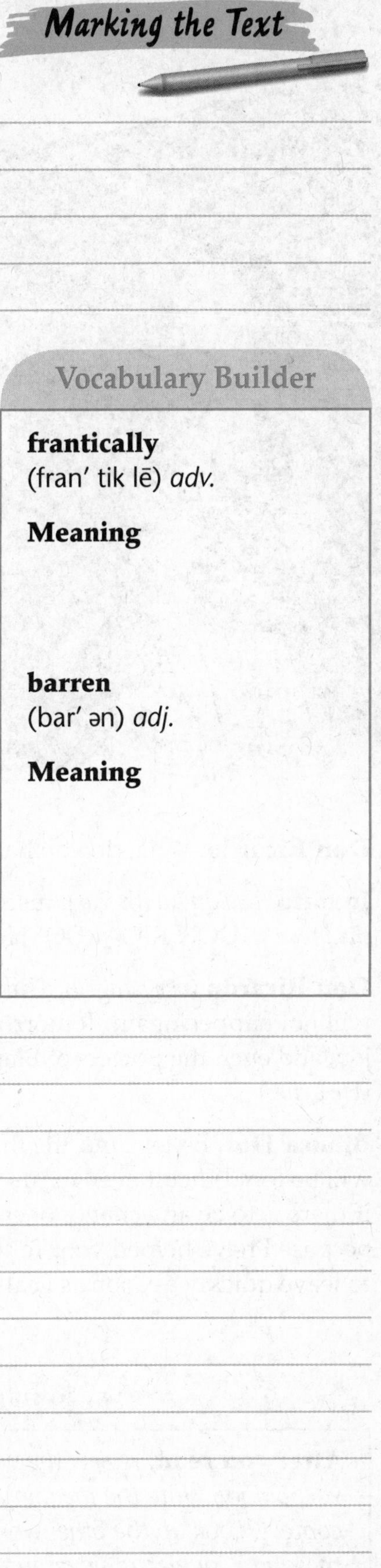

Marking the Text
Vocabulary Builder
frantically
(fran′ tik lē) adv.
Meaning
barren
(bar′ ən) adj.
Meaning

Don Ricardo. What do you have?

Juanito (*shaking with fear*). Just . . . just this loaf of bread. (*Giving the bread to* DON RICARDO) Here is the bread you asked for.

Don Ricardo (*very angry*). This is the work of Blanca Flor. This will not happen again. Tomorrow, your third job will be your final job, and even the powers of Blanca Flor will not help you this time! (*He exits.*)

Blanca Flor. Believe me, the third job will be impossible to do. It will be too difficult even for my powers. We must run from here if there is to be any chance of escaping his anger. He will kill you because I have helped you. Tonight I will come for you. Be ready to leave quickly as soon as I call for you . . ..

Marking the Text

Vocabulary Builder

After you read, *review the words you decided to add to your vocabulary. Write the meaning of words you have learned in context. Look up the other words in a dictionary, glossary, thesaurus, or electronic resource.*

Thinking About the Selection

from Blanca Flor

Go Online
About the Author
Visit: PHSchool.com
Web Code: exe-6507

1 **Analyze** What conflict does Juanito face? Use details from the play to support your response.

2 **Apply** Rewrite the selection from the play as if it were part of a novel.

Play	Novel
[DON RICARDO *enters, quickly.*] Don Ricardo. What do you have? Juanito (*shaking with fear*). Just . . . just this loaf of bread. (*Giving the bread to* DON RICARDO) Here is the bread you asked for.	

3 **Define** Choose a Spanish word from the play. Use clues from the text and what you know about word roots to determine its meaning. Write what you think the word means. Explain your answer.

Write Answer the following questions in your Reader's Journal.

4 **Discuss** How do our conflicts with others help us to learn about ourselves and who we are?

5 **Apply** What is the conflict in your Anchor Book? How does your Anchor Book reveal the conflict?

while reading your anchor book

5-10 Listening and Speaking Workshop
Reading Drama Aloud

In this workshop, you will use what you have learned about dialogue and stage directions to create a presentation that is clear and entertaining.

Your Tasks

- Work with your group to choose a scene from your Anchor Book. Analyze the scene so all members understand the conflict, emotions, and dialogue.
- Prepare and rehearse the scene with your group.
- Present your scene to the class.

Organize and Present Your Scene

1 **Plan the scene.** Choose a scene from your Anchor Book. In the chart, write down the characters, where the scene takes place, what the conflict is, and how each character experiences the conflict.

Characters	
Where the scene takes place	
Conflict	
How each character experiences the conflict	

Once you have analyzed your scene, decide on the best way to present it. Discuss how group members can convey the conflict through different body gestures, facial expressions, and volume of voice. Use your notes from the chart to help you.

2 **Prepare the scene.** Decide with your group members who will play each role. If there are not enough characters, stage the scene in two parts so that all group members get a chance to participate.

3 **Create a visual for your audience.** Discuss how you want the set to look. Work with group members to make it realistic. For example, if the scene takes place in the woods, bring branches and leaves in to class or create them to use as background.

4 **Rehearse your presentation.** Practice your scene. Use the stage directions to guide you. Make the characters come alive by wearing costumes, using different facial expressions and body gestures, and changing the volume of your voice. Be sure to make eye contact with your group members and with your audience to engage their interest.

SPEAK: Rubric for Oral Interpretation

Assess your performance. For each question, circle a rating.

CRITERIA	RATING SCALE
	NOT VERY VERY
CONTENT How well did the group's presentation reflect the prompt?	1 2 3 4 5
ORGANIZATION How organized was the group when presenting its scene?	1 2 3 4 5
DELIVERY How well did the group demonstrate appropriate eye contact, pacing, phrasing, and intonation?	1 2 3 4 5
COOPERATION How well did the group work together?	1 2 3 4 5

LISTEN: Rubric for Audience Self-Assessment

Assess your role as an audience. For each question, circle a rating.

CRITERIA	RATING SCALE
	NOT VERY VERY
ACTIVE LISTENING How well did you focus your attention on the performance?	1 2 3 4 5
ACTIVE LISTENING How well did you demonstrate active listening with appropriate silence and body language?	1 2 3 4 5

5-11 Language Coach
Grammar and Spelling

Gerunds and Gerund Phrases

Go Online
Learn More
Visit: PHSchool.com
Web Code: exp-6503

A **gerund** is a verb form ending in *-ing* that names an action or an event. It is used as a noun and is sometimes the subject of a sentence.

A **gerund phrase** contains a gerund and the words related to it, such as modifiers and objects. The phrase tells you more about the action or event.

Look at how Morgan, a character in a play, uses gerunds and gerund phrases in dialogue.

Gerund	**MORGAN:** Studying is always difficult to do when my friends are nearby.
Gerund Phrase	**MORGAN:** Studying for a test is always difficult to do when my friends are nearby.

- To decide which words are a part of the gerund phrase, ask yourself whether the words tell more about the activity or event named by the gerund. If they do, then they are a part of the gerund phrase.

Example: I enjoy hiking in the woods.
(*In the woods tells where the hiking is done*)

Author's Craft

Varying sentences makes writing more interesting. To practice revising with gerund phrases, examine the passage about Samurai Japan beginning on page 390. Choose a sentence, and rewrite it to include a gerund phrase.

Directions Write the gerund form of each verb. Then use the gerund and the phrase given to write a sentence. Underline the gerund phrase.

1 **guess:** the answers

Example: guessing; Guessing the answers on a test is sometimes better than not answering at all.

2 **decide:** when to eat lunch

____

____

3 **want:** a kitten

____

____

4 **ride:** a bike without a helmet

____

____

Participial Phrases

Learn More
Visit: PHSchool.com
Web Code: exp-6504

A **participle** is a form of verb that often acts as an adjective. There are two types of participles.

Type	Ending	Example Sentence
Present Participle	*-ing*	I reached out to catch the falling dish.
Past Participle	*-ed* or *-(e)n*	Stunned, I let out a gasp.

A **participial phrase** is a past or present participle combined with a group of words. The entire phrase acts as an adjective. Like a regular adjective, a participial phrase helps to describe something or someone.

Example
Avoiding the question, Cynthia changed the subject. *Avoiding the question* describes Cynthia.
The team, disappointed by the loss, walked back to the locker room in silence. *Disappointed by the loss* describes the team.

Author's Craft

Playwrights try to give actors the most specific stage directions possible. Scan page 401 of *You're a Good Man, Charlie Brown,* and find a stage direction that uses only participial phrases. Rewrite it so that it is no longer a participial phrase. Do you think an actor would interpret the new stage direction in the same way as the old one? Why do you think the playwright chose to use this participial phrase?

Directions In the chart below, two writers wrote about the same subject. One writer used participles and participial phrases, while the other did not. Circle the participles and underline the participial phrases you find. Then answer the question.

Writer 1	Writer 2
Filming a beautiful wedding like this one was Lorne's job. Lorne wasn't just a man with a video recorder. He was an artist. He captured smiles, memories, and happiness.	Standing off to the side of the aisle, Lorne filmed the beautiful wedding. Filming was his job, but Lorne, watching the ceremony through his lens, liked to think he was an artist, capturing smiles, memories, and happiness.

Which writer's writing is more interesting to read? Explain why.

____

____

Revising With Participial Phrases

Knowing how to use participial phrases to join two shorter sentences can improve your writing. Not only will your writing sound less choppy, but it will also be more interesting and exciting to read. Look at the examples in the chart below.

Choppy Sentence	Rewritten Sentence
The house was built in 1812. It was originally a general store.	Built in 1812, the house was originally a general store.
The tenor was singing with all his might. He was trying to be heard over the orchestra.	The tenor, singing with all his might, was trying to be heard over the orchestra.

Directions Read the passage below. Rewrite sentences using participial phrases so that the passage is easier and more interesting to read.

The giraffe was coming their way. Onlookers at the zoo were excited. They scrambled to find leaves to feed to the giraffe. Some of the onlookers pushed and yelled to get a good spot near the fence. They were so loud they seemed to scare the giraffe. The giraffe was still interested. It tiptoed on its long legs to the fence. It lowered its head to grab the leaves. Then it stuck out its long, dark tongue and curled it around one branch. The giraffe pulled the entire thing into its mouth. The onlookers cheered. They took pictures of the giraffe.

Combining Sentences for Variety

Good writers use different sentence lengths to add variety to their writing. They often combine short sentences to form a longer one to make their writing more interesting. One way to combine sentences is to use different phrases. Look below at the different types of phrases you can use in your writing.

Prepositional Phrase	▸ Use a prepositional phrase as an adjective or as an adverb. preposition + object of the preposition + related words **Example:** The chimp swung from the branches.
Participial Phrase	▸ Use a participial phrase to describe a person, place, or thing. *-ing* or *-ed* form of verb + related words **Example:** Calling to her chicks, the mother bird led her babies to safety.
Gerund Phrase	▸ Use a gerund phrase as a noun. *-ing* form of verb used as a noun + related words **Example:** Healing sick animals is something Hannah always wanted to do.

The examples below use phrases to combine choppy sentences.

Choppy: The shell was under the rock. The shell was very rare. **Combined:** The shell *under the rock* was very rare. (prepositional phrase)
Choppy: The waves crashed around the surfer. They upset her balance. **Combined:** *Crashing around her,* the waves upset the surfer's balance. (participial phrase)
Choppy: I don't like to go on roller coasters. They make me feel sick. **Combined:** *Going on roller coasters* makes me feel sick. (gerund phrase)

Directions On a separate sheet of paper, write a paragraph about a a family event you attended recently. Use all three types of phrases in your writing. When you have finished, reread your paragraph. Underline and then label the phrases you used as *prepositional*, *participial*, or *gerund*. Look for ways to combine your sentences.

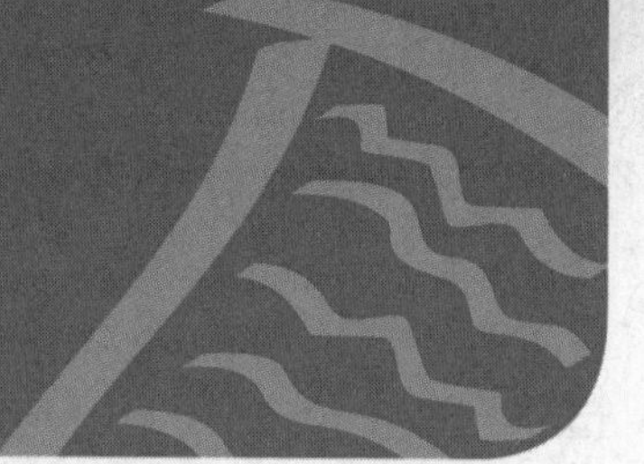

5-12 Writer's Workshop
Exposition: Cause-and-Effect Essay

Almost any event—no matter how simple or complex—involves causes and effects. A **cause-and-effect essay** is a short piece of expository writing that explains why something happens or what will happen as a result of the event. Follow the steps in the workshop to help you write a cause-and-effect essay about a topic that interests you.

Purpose To write a cause-and-effect essay about a topic that interests you

Audience You, your teacher, and your classmates

To be effective, your cause-and-effect essay should include the following elements.

- a specific topic that shows a clear cause-and-effect relationship
- details and facts that support your focus statement and topic sentences
- transition words or phrases that help you make connections between ideas
- error-free writing, paying specific attention to participial phrases and gerunds

Prewriting—Plan It Out

Choose your topic. Use one of the following prewriting strategies to help you choose the topic of your essay.

- **Brainstorming** In a group, discuss topics that have caused something to happen. You can begin by suggesting a broad topic such as "historical events" or by using a fill-in-the-blank exercise like, "Why did _______ happen?" Jot down all topic ideas. Then go over your list and choose the best idea for your essay.
- **Browsing** Look through magazines or local newspapers for subjects that interest you. Circle key words or ideas and think about their causes and effects. Choose a topic for your essay based on what you find.

Narrow your topic. Use a cause-and-effect web like the one shown at right to narrow the focus of your essay. Write the broad topic at the top. Then write causes in the circles below the broad topic. Label each circle *Cause*. Write at least one effect in circles stemming from each cause and label each one *Effect*. Use these causes and effects for your essay.

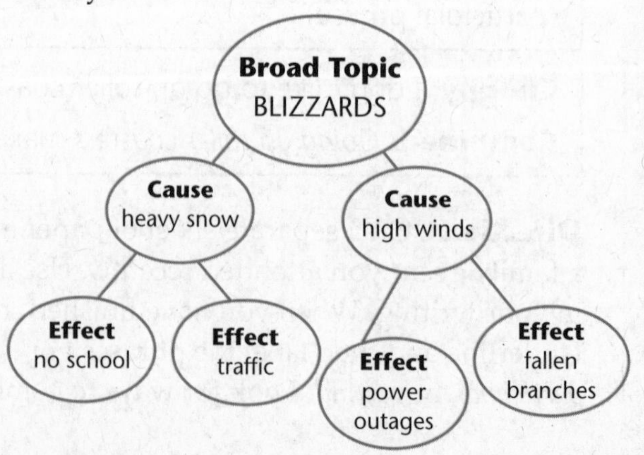

Gather details. To find details that support your topic, you may need to do some research. On a separate sheet of paper, create a two-column chart with the labels *Cause* and *Effect*, as shown on the right. Use the chart to organize your facts and ideas.

Cause	Effect

Drafting—Get It on Paper

Organize your writing. You might have identified one cause with many effects, or many causes with one effect. Use one of the organization plans below to help you organize your writing.

Many causes lead to one effect.	Write one paragraph about each cause.
One cause leads to many effects.	Write one paragraph about each effect.
Many causes lead to many effects.	Write paragraphs describing one cause and one effect, in chronological order.

Focus your ideas. One of the first things your audience reads is your focus statement, the main idea of your essay. Use your notes to create a focus statement that introduces the causes and effects you will be discussing in an interesting way.

Example If the town builds a new apartment complex, the traffic congestion and parking will become unbearable.

Make your writing clear. Make sure your essay shows strong relationships between causes and effects. Write a topic sentence for each paragraph so your audience knows exactly which cause and effect you will be discussing. Provide supporting details to avoid being vague, or nonspecific.

Use transitions. Use transition words and phrases such as *because, as a result,* or *since* to make your cause-and-effect connections clear.

Transition for a cause	Transition for an effect
Because the U.S. is dependent on gas-powered cars, carbon monoxide emissions are alarmingly high.	As a result, we are experiencing global warming.

Revising—Make It Better

Check your organization. Check that each paragraph focuses on one idea, such as a specific cause or effect.

Peer Review Have a partner read your essay and respond to how you've organized causes and effects. Revise it to achieve the reaction you had intended.

Directions Read this student cause-and-effect essay as a model for your own.

Go Online
Learn More
Visit: PHSchool.com
Web Code: exr-6502

Student Model: Writing

Bryson McCollum, Cummings, Georgia

Don't Get Burned

Sunscreen should always be worn when you are out in the sun because the sun can be very dangerous to your skin. If your skin is exposed to the sun's ultraviolet rays without sunscreen, it will turn red, burn, and hurt. Many people believe that burning their skin is one step closer to their desire of getting a tan. They do not realize that both burning and tanning your skin can damage it. Once you burn or tan and the redness or color begins to fade, the damaged skin may begin to peel, leaving a new, unhealthy, thin, and sensitive layer of skin.

> The student begins his cause-and-effect essay with a strong focus statement.

> Details about the sun's ability to cause skin damage help support the focus of the essay.

What you do to your skin as a child and as a young adult will affect your skin for your entire life. Sunscreen can help. Doctors recommend that children apply sunscreen often and at least 30 minutes before going out in the sun. Adults, children, and young adults will benefit from using sunscreens with sun protection factor (SPF) numbers of 15 or higher. The SPF numbers give some idea of how long you can stay out in the sun without burning. For example, an SPF of 15 should protect you for approximately 150 minutes—nearly two-and-a-half hours—in the sun. While some sunscreens say they are waterproof, they do not give you total protection from water and sweat. As a result, it is also recommended that sunscreen be applied often.

> Specific examples clarify doctor recommendations and sunscreen information.

Nobody's skin is immune to skin cancer. If your skin is damaged a lot by the sun during your childhood and adult years, your chances of getting skin cancer are greater than they are for people who have taken better steps toward protection. If you have been burned several times in a short period of time, you should be checked by a doctor because some forms of skin cancer cannot be detected.

> Each of the paragraphs deals with one cause or one effect that relates back to the writer's focus statement.

So, think twice the next time you are at the beach or the pool without sunscreen, hoping to absorb the sun. Be careful and apply sunscreen to protect yourself from skin damage. Remember that even though a tan may look nice for a few days, it may cause you health problems and unhealthy-looking skin in the future.

Editing—Be Your Own Language Coach

Before you hand in your cause-and-effect essay, review it for language convention errors. Pay special attention to your use of participial phrases and gerunds.

Publishing—Share It!

When you publish a work, you produce it for a specific audience. Consider one of the following ideas to share your writing.

- **Develop an oral presentation.** Read your cause-and-effect essay aloud to your family and peers. Then encourage a discussion by the group.
- **Make a movie proposal.** Turn your essay into a storyboard by showing which images you would choose to represent your focus statement and supporting evidence.

Rubric for Self-Assessment Assess your essay. For each question, circle a rating.

CRITERIA	RATING SCALE
	NOT VERY VERY
IDEAS Is your essay focused, with clear cause-and-effect relationships?	1 2 3 4 5
ORGANIZATION How well do you employ a clear and logical organization?	1 2 3 4 5
VOICE Is your writing lively and engaging, drawing the reader in?	1 2 3 4 5
WORD CHOICE How appropriate is the language for your audience?	1 2 3 4 5
CONVENTIONS How correct is your grammar, especially your use of participial phrases and gerunds?	1 2 3 4 5

5-13 Discussing Your Anchor Book

Literature Circles

Characterization Characters in a story spring to life through characterization. In short stories and novels, authors use details to develop a character. In drama, actors perform the characters, so a playwright has to rely on dialogue and stage directions to develop strong, realistic characters.

Characterization in Drama

Choose a character from your Anchor Book. With your group, follow the steps to analyze your character and to explain how the playwright reveals the character's personality.

1 **Identify** Characters in drama, like people, have character traits, or qualities that make them unique and interesting. Character traits include *happy, angry, nervous, funny,* and *silly.*

Think of the character you chose. Discuss your character's traits with your group. In the space below, list these traits.

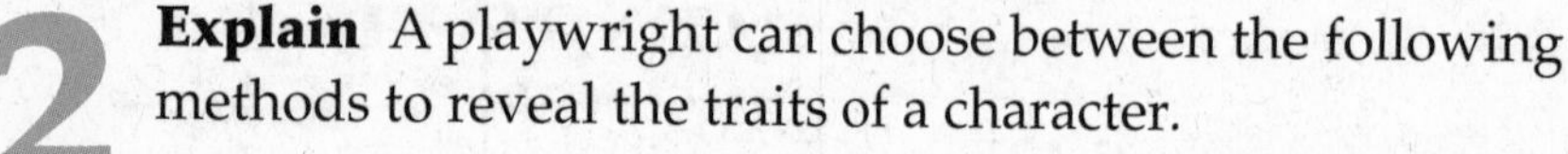

2 **Explain** A playwright can choose between the following methods to reveal the traits of a character.

- **Direct characterization** A playwright makes a straightforward statement about a character through the stage directions and the character's dialogue. In the example that follows, the playwright directly states Leroy's character trait in the stage directions.

> [LEROY *is a short, excitable man who gets frustrated very easily. He barges into the room.*]
> **LEROY:** Look at this! [LEROY *shoves a crumpled eggshell in front of* DENISE.] I knew this would happen!

- **Indirect characterization** A playwright uses the words and reactions of other characters to tell the reader what a specific character is like. The playwright uses stage directions and other characters' dialogue to reveal this character's personality in an indirect way. Through Denise's dialogue in the following example, the playwright indirectly tells the reader that Leroy gets upset often.

DENISE: [*As soon as* LEROY *enters the room,* DENISE *notices long dribbles of yolk on his shirt. She mutters to herself*] Now what? [*Says out loud*] Calm down, Leroy. There's no need to get upset again about one silly egg.

Directions In the following chart, write the character traits your group identified. Determine where in your Anchor Book each character trait is revealed. Tell whether the playwright used direct or indirect characterization to reveal each character trait, and explain how you know. Then answer the questions.

Character:			
Character Trait	**Where the Trait Is Revealed**		**Direct or Indirect Characterization?**
	Dialogue, Stage Directions, Details	**Page Number**	

1 **Describe** With your group, choose one of the character traits you described in the chart. Describe another way the playwright could have revealed this trait.

2 **Respond** Do you think a playwright has a more difficult job than a novelist when making a character seem realistic? Explain why or why not.

5-14 Connecting to Your Anchor Book

Anchor Book Projects

Now that you have finished reading your Anchor Book, get creative! Complete one of the following projects.

Plan a Musical

A

A musical is a type of drama that tells a story through song and dance. Like plays, musicals have sets, characters, and dialogue.

1. Choose a scene from your Anchor Book that you could turn into a musical. Think of the tone of the scene and decide what kind of music or songs you could add to it to create this tone. On a separate sheet of paper, list the music and explain why you chose it.
2. Dancing is a big part of any musical. Decide how you want your characters to move to the music. Reread the scene, specifically the stage directions, and make notes about the positions of the characters. Include details about how and when you want the characters to dance.

Your plan should include the following elements.

- music that is appropriate to the scene from your Anchor Book
- a thoughtful analysis of your music choices
- a detailed description about the characters' movements

Rewrite the Ending

B

Both comedies and tragedies can be about serious issues. One major difference between the two types of dramas is that a comedy has a happy ending and a tragedy does not. Decide whether your Anchor Book is a comedy or a tragedy. Then rewrite the ending to reflect the opposite type of drama.

1. To determine whether your Anchor Book is a comedy or tragedy, briefly describe the conflict and tell if it is presented in a funny or serious way. Tell how the conflict is resolved and which characters are involved.
2. Use your imagination and your notes about the conflict and characters to rewrite the ending of your Anchor Book so it reflects the opposite type of drama.

Your ending should include the following elements.

- a thoughtful representation of the conflict and the characters in your Anchor Book
- an imaginative, rewritten ending that reflects your analysis and the drama chosen
- writing that is clear and error-free

Design a Set

C

As you read a novel, you can picture the setting in your mind because the writer has described it in detail. In plays, the setting is meant to be seen. The stage, backdrops, furniture, and props make up the set. The set should give the audience an idea of the time and place of the action.

1. Choose an important scene from your Anchor Book. Reread the stage directions in that scene to help you visualize what the set should look like. Jot down notes about where and when the scene takes place.
2. Design a set for this scene. Using the stage directions and your notes, draw or use a computer to create a visual of the set.
3. Present your set to the class. Describe the scene your set shows and why you chose to design the set the way you did.

Your set should include the following elements.

- identifiable and familiar objects from your scene
- visual clues that tell the viewer when and where the scene takes place

Free-Choice Book Reflection

You have completed your free-choice book. Before you take your test, read the following instructions to write a brief reflection of your book.

My free-choice book is ______________________________.

The author is ______________________________.

1 Would you recommend this book to a friend? Yes _____ No _____

Briefly explain why.

____

____

Write Answer the following question in your Reader's Journal.

2 **Compare and Contrast** *How do we decide who we are?* Compare and contrast how your Anchor Book and free-choice book help to answer this question. Use specific details from both books to support your answer.

after reading your anchor book

Standardized Test Practice

Answer the questions below to check your understanding of this unit's skills.

Reading Skills: Summarizing

Read this selection. Then write a summary of it on the lines below.

Marcia was not pleased when she heard the news. Her mother had decided to move the family north. A new highway was being built there, companies were starting up, and there would be more work. Marcia felt helpless as she left her comfortable neighborhood, and dragged her feet behind her younger brother to board the plane that was bound for Chicago. She dreaded the thought of going to a new school, and she had heard bad things about Chicago winters.

Marcia began to feel better once she completed her first day at her new school. Her teacher introduced her to the other students, and some classmates invited her to sit with them at lunch. She thought, "Chicago may not be so bad after all!"

Summary: ______________________________

____

____

Reading Skills: Compare and Contrast

Read the selection. Then answer the questions that follow.

Would you rather read a novel or go to the movies? You can preview both by reading reviews on the Internet or asking your friends. Long books can take weeks to finish, but a blockbuster movie usually lasts only a few hours. With books, you must imagine what the setting and characters look like, whereas with movies, the director shows you what the characters and setting are like. Both books and movies tell a story, however. A thrilling movie score and sound effects can intensify your feelings about a movie plot and its characters. However, if the movie's special effects are outdated, you might find yourself distracted from the story. Both books and movies can be enjoyable and memorable forms of entertainment.

1 What do reading books and watching movies have in common?

A. You can preview both books and movies.

B. Both feature famous celebrities.

C. They always take the same amount of time to enjoy.

D. The setting and characters are shown in the same way.

2 According to the passage, how are books and movies different?

F. Reading can be an enjoyable way to spend your time.

G. Movies and books both tell a story.

H. The movie director shows you what the characters and setting are like.

J. Movies are memorable, but books are easy to forget.

Literary Analysis: Elements of Drama

Read the selection. Then answer the questions on the following page.

[DARIA *and* SHANE *are sitting in the tenth row so they have a good view of the screen. The lights in the theater dim. The movie begins, but two people in the row behind them are talking.*]

MOVIEGOER 1: [*To* MOVIEGOER 2 *in a loud voice*] This movie better be good, because if it isn't, I just wasted nine dollars.

[DARIA *looks at* SHANE *in annoyance.* SHANE *returns the look.*]

MOVIEGOER 2: Oh, did I tell you I talked to Cory last night?

MOVIEGOER 1: No way! What did she say?

[*Other people in the audience shift uneasily in their seats. These two people talking during the movie are beginning to irritate them.*]

DARIA: [*Whispers to* SHANE] I can't believe how rude these people are!

MOVIEGOER 2: She said it was over. No more chances.

[DARIA *has had enough. She stands up, turns around, and addresses the audience.*]

DARIA: [*Loudly*] Excuse me, everyone. [*She points to the two people.*] These two think the theater is a good place to talk about their personal lives. [*Turns to the two people*] Can you tell us more since you have our attention now?

[*The two moviegoers are first stunned, then embarrassed, by* DARIA's *speech. They both shake their heads.*]

DARIA: Thank you. [*Sits down. The audience claps.*]

3. What is the **conflict**?

   A. Daria is annoyed with the two moviegoers.

   B. Daria stands up and talks during the movie.

   C. The two moviegoers talk during the movie, which annoys the audience.

   D. The two moviegoers sit behind Daria and Shane.

4. How is the conflict revealed?

   F. through stage directions and dialogue

   G. through stage directions

   H. through dialogue

   J. through characters' dialogue and expressions

5. Which **stage direction** best reveals the resolution?

   A. [DARIA *looks at* SHANE *in annoyance.* SHANE *returns the look.*]

   B. [*Turns to the two people*]

   C. [*The two moviegoers are first stunned, then embarrassed, by* DARIA'S *speech. They both shake their heads.*]

   D. [*Sits down. The audience claps.*]

6. Which of the following describes a **dramatization**?

   F. a novel based on a play

   G. a play based on a novel

   H. a very dramatic play

   J. a book written about a movie

Language Skills: Vocabulary

Choose the best answer.

7. Which word originated from the Latin word for hand, *manus*?

   A. manual

   B. many

   C. mane

   D. make

8. Many English words come from which two languages?

   F. Spanish and Dutch

   G. Chinese and Greek

   H. Latin and Italian

   J. Greek and Latin

9. What is a **borrowed word?**

   A. a word that borrows another meaning

   B. a word borrowed from another language

   C. a word with borrowed letters

   D. a word with a borrowed prefix or suffix

10. What is the meaning of the word *brevity*?

   F. summary of text

   G. written letter

   H. shortness of time

   J. short note

Language Skills: Spelling

Choose the best answer.

11 Which of these statements is true?

A. All schwa sounds in English are spelled the same.

B. Schwa sounds are not common.

C. There are many ways to spell the schwa sound.

D. Schwa is a word root.

12 Choose the word that is spelled correctly.

F. teribull

G. terribul

H. terible

J. terrible

Language Skills: Grammar

Choose the best answer.

13 Which of the following is a **prepositional phrase**?

A. to the mall

B. climbing up

C. very slowly

D. softly singing

14 Which of the following words could begin a **prepositional phrase**?

F. pretty

G. slowly

H. from

J. making

15 In the following sentence, which word is the **object of the preposition?**

Pecking and digging, the wild turkeys walked among the fallen nuts.

A. pecking

B. walked

C. among

D. nuts

16 Which sentence has a **gerund phrase**?

F. Walking around the neighborhood keeps me fit.

G. Yelling at the players, the coach hurried the team off the field.

H. The baseball player is hitting the ball over the fence.

J. There is a fly flying in my room.

17 Which of these is a **participial phrase**?

A. laughing

B. tired of arguing

C. after dinner

D. wait for the light

18 Which of the following is the definition of a **gerund**?

F. a sentence containing a subject and a verb

G. a verb form ending in *-ing* that names an action or an event

H. an adverb or an adjective

J. a verb that begins with a prefix

How much should our *communities* shape us?

Unit 6 Genre focus: The Research Project

Unit Book Choices
With this unit you will read one book as an Anchor Book. There are many good books that would work well with this unit. The following pages offer six suggestions.

Free-Choice Reading
Later in this unit you will be given an opportunity to choose another book to read. This is called your Free-Choice Book.

You might read...

A Myths and Monsters

B The Emperor's Silent Army

C HIROSHIMA

D Paths to Peace

E The Story of Muhammad Ali

F Spies

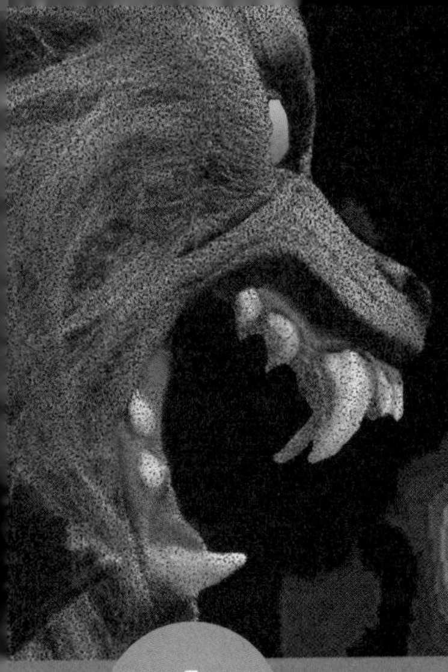

Myths and Monsters: From Dragons to Werewolves

by Laura Buller

A You might read Anchor Book A

Summary Monsters do exist—at least in the human mind. Monsters have been brought to life by the imagination of different cultures across the world since time began. From the gods and giants of ancient mythology to the werewolves and vampires of today, find out why people feel the need to invent these gruesome characters.

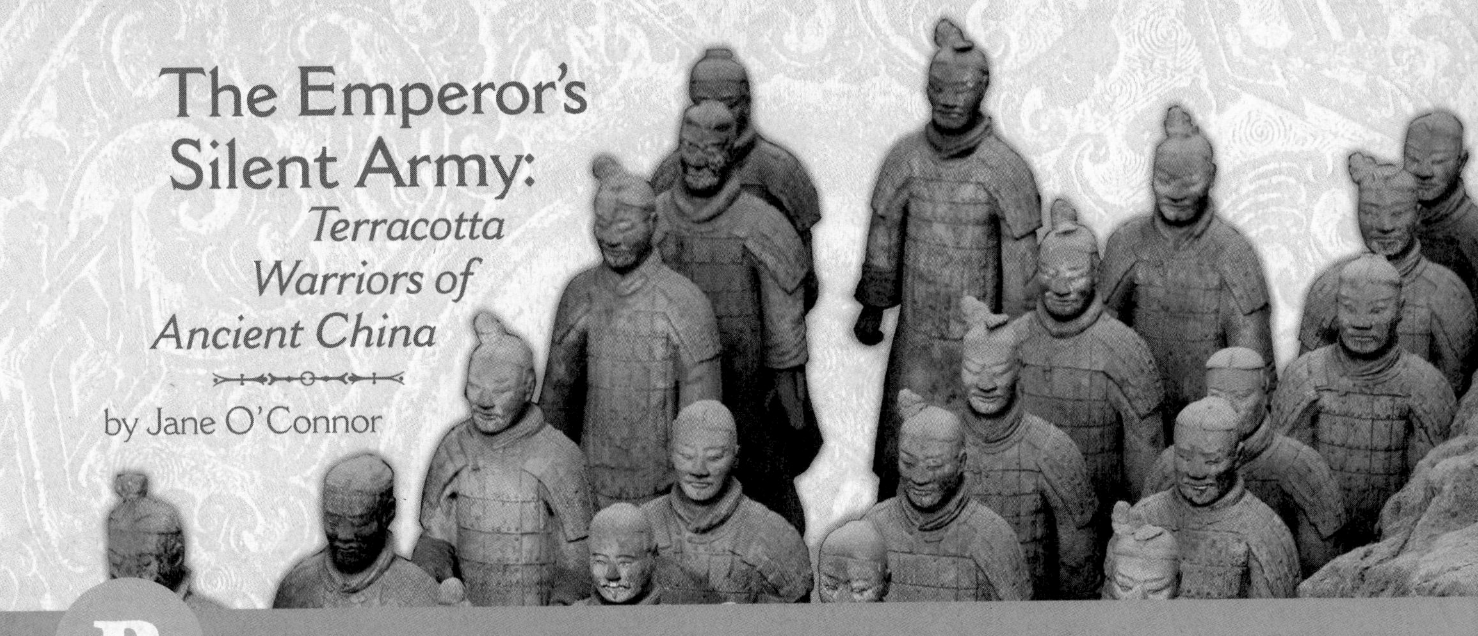

The Emperor's Silent Army: *Terracotta Warriors of Ancient China*

by Jane O'Connor

B You might read Anchor Book B

Summary In March 1974 in Lintong County, China, three farmers digging a well came across a world wonder: a buried army of 7,500 life-size terracotta soldiers and horses that had lain untouched for over 2,200 years. Who created this clay army, and why?

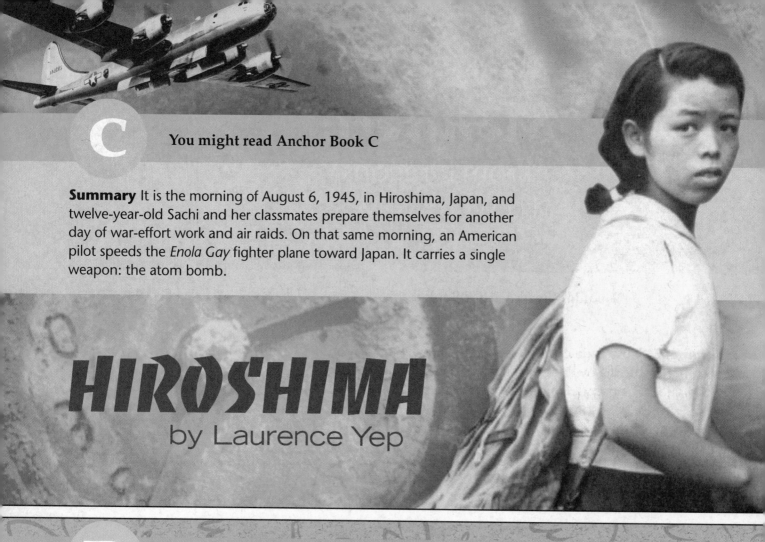

C You might read Anchor Book C

Summary It is the morning of August 6, 1945, in Hiroshima, Japan, and twelve-year-old Sachi and her classmates prepare themselves for another day of war-effort work and air raids. On that same morning, an American pilot speeds the *Enola Gay* fighter plane toward Japan. It carries a single weapon: the atom bomb.

HIROSHIMA

by Laurence Yep

D You might read Anchor Book D

Summary From Mahatma Gandhi and Eleanor Roosevelt to Martin Luther King, Jr. and Aung San Suu Kyi, these great leaders, who, with courage, determination, and sacrifice became peacemakers in the face of war and violence, are inspiration for a whole new generation of visionaries to come.

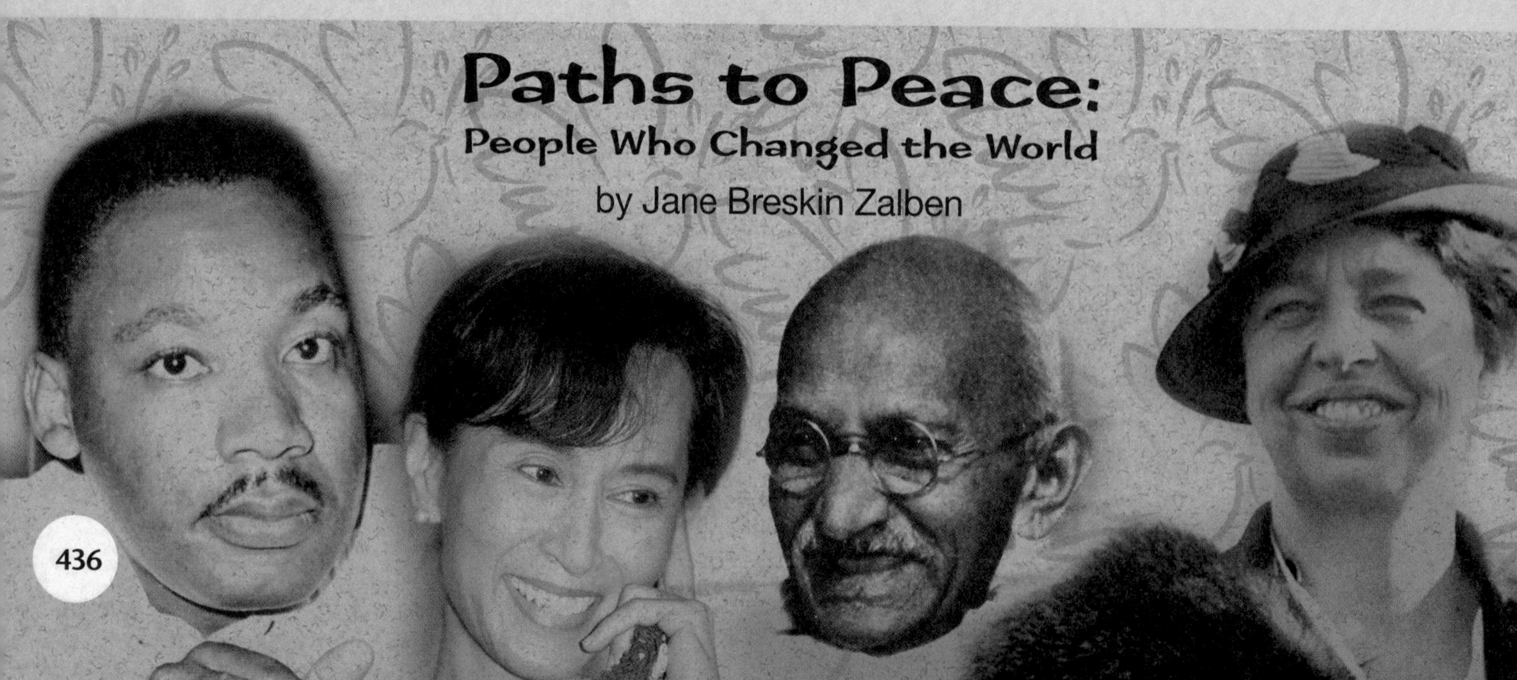

Paths to Peace: People Who Changed the World

by Jane Breskin Zalben

E You might read Anchor Book E

Summary Cassius Clay (later, Muhammad Ali) was not only a talented boxer who won six Golden Gloves tournaments and two national championships but also a powerful role model for all Americans. He was willing to stand up for what he believed, despite the penalties.

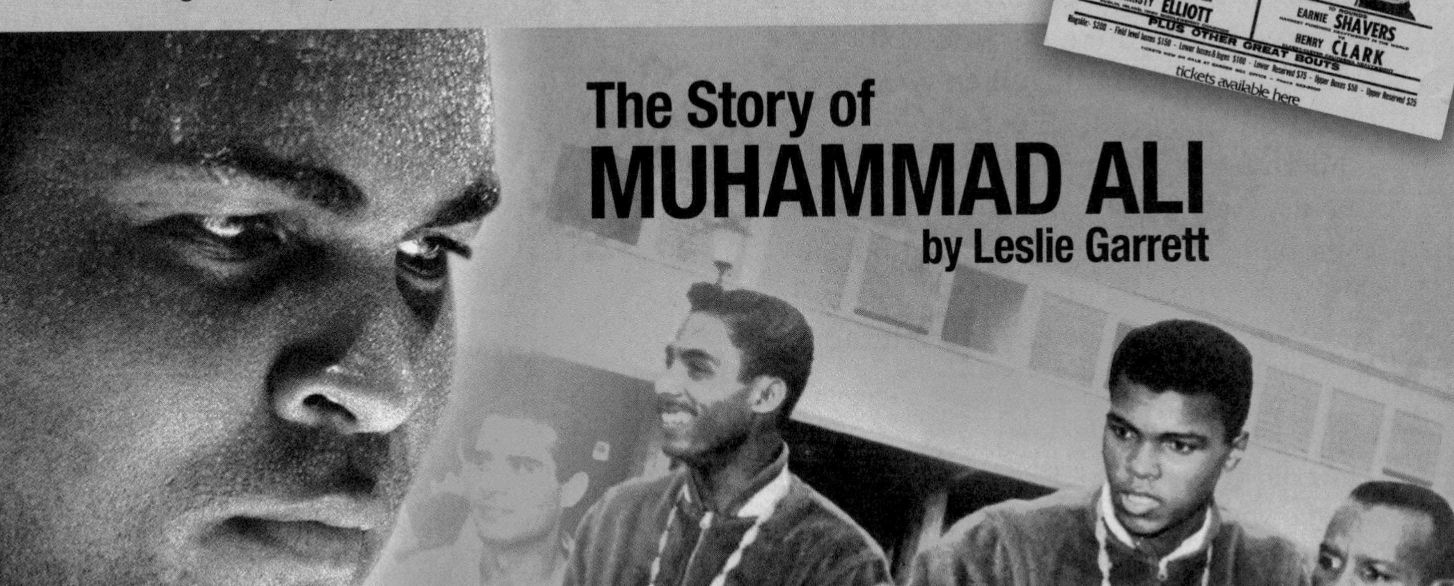

The Story of
MUHAMMAD ALI
by Leslie Garrett

F You might read Anchor Book F

Summary What do spies do, and how do they do it? The history of espionage includes men, women, and even children helping to protect—or betray—their own country, using all the possible tricks, cunning, and gadgetry at their disposal.

6-1 Understanding the Big Question

How much should our communities shape us?

Look around at the people in your school—your teachers, your classmates, other students, and staff members. Together, you form a community, a group of people who have something in common with one another. Teams, your family, your neighbors, even members of clubs and organizations are different types of communities. How much have you been shaped by the communities to which you belong?

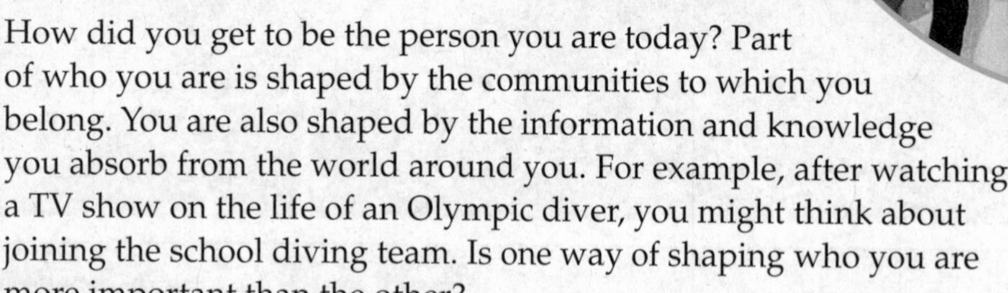

How did you get to be the person you are today? Part of who you are is shaped by the communities to which you belong. You are also shaped by the information and knowledge you absorb from the world around you. For example, after watching a TV show on the life of an Olympic diver, you might think about joining the school diving team. Is one way of shaping who you are more important than the other?

Directions Complete the graphic organizer. List the communities that have helped shape who you are. Then, list any sources of knowledge or information that have done the same.

Communities That Have Shaped Me	Sources of Knowledge and Information That Have Shaped Me
School	**Television**

Directions In the graphic organizer below, list five qualities or characteristics that define you as a person—such as traits about yourself (honest, good communicator), likes or dislikes (love horses, dislike peas), or personal beliefs (environmentally aware, vegetarian). Then, list how those qualities have been shaped by a community you belong to. Finally, list how the qualities have been shaped by knowledge or information you've taken in from the world around you.

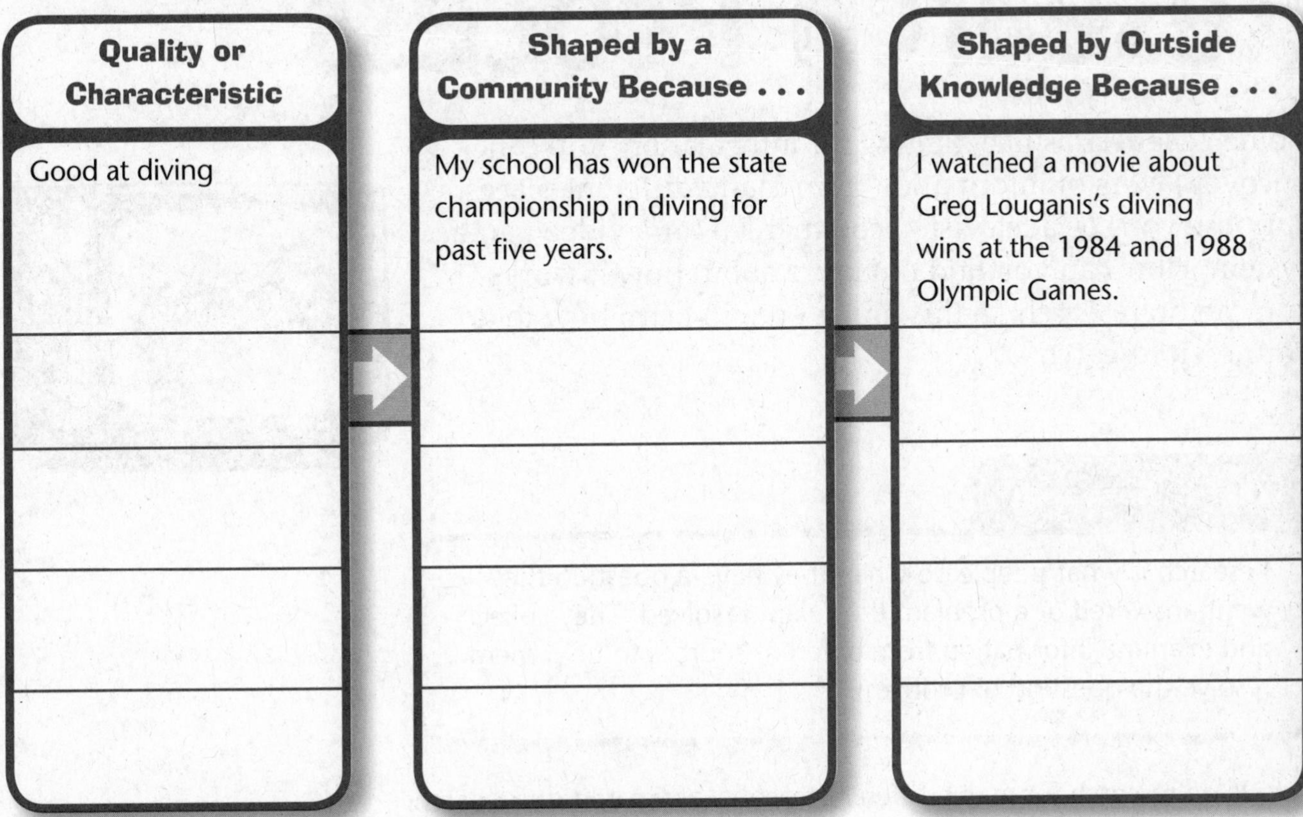

Quality or Characteristic	Shaped by a Community Because . . .	Shaped by Outside Knowledge Because . . .
Good at diving	My school has won the state championship in diving for past five years.	I watched a movie about Greg Louganis's diving wins at the 1984 and 1988 Olympic Games.

Sometimes communities shape a person too much and have a negative effect. For example, a student might become too serious about winning a contest. This might cause him or her to focus too much time preparing for the contest and not enough time doing homework and other activities. The student's grades might suffer, causing his or her parents to worry.

Apply What is another way a person could be shaped in a negative way by a community? Explain your answer.

As you read your Anchor Book, think about how communities shape the characters in the book. How is a character in your book shaped, positively or negatively, by a community? Why do you think so?

before reading your anchor book

You will start reading your Anchor Book soon. The next few pages in this book give you some background information plus a reading skill.

Introduction to the Research Process

Doing **research** is like digging for information. You can uncover layers of information from many different places. Suppose you see a television commercial for a video game system. How can you find out more about how it works? You can do research. In this unit, you will learn how to do your own research.

What Is Research?

Research is what people do when they have a question they want answered or a problem they want resolved. They collect and examine information from different sources to help them resolve the question or problem.

People do research for many different reasons. You could do research to find out more about the author of a book you just read. Scientists do research to find cures for diseases.

Why Do Research?

- To find ways to change or improve something
- To learn more about an unknown or interesting topic
- To prove something to be true or untrue
- To solve a problem or answer a question

What questions or topics interest you?

Getting Started

Get ready to write a research report. First, you'll choose a topic that you want to learn more about. Then, you'll write a four- to six-page report.

Your Research Process

Writing a research report requires a lot of organizing and planning. The following is a list of the main steps in researching. To help you complete each step on time, record the date that each step is due.

CHOOSING A TOPIC (LESSON 6–4)

1 Choose a topic and narrow it down so it is not too difficult to research.

Date Due ___________ Date Completed ___________

RESEARCHING (LESSON 6–5)

2
- Choose reliable sources.
- Take research notes.
- Avoid plagiarism.

Date Due ___________ Date Completed ___________

DRAFTING (LESSON 6–11)

3
- Write a focus statement.
- Write a first draft.
- Organize information into an outline.

Date Due ___________ Date Completed ___________

REVISING (LESSON 6–12)

4
- Check that your major points and details are organized.
- Revise your paragraphs.

Date Due ___________ Date Completed ___________

PUBLISHING (LESSON 6–13)

5
- Cite your sources.
- Proofread your draft.
- Write a works cited list.
- Publish and present your report.

Date Due ___________ Date Completed ___________

6-2 Reading Skills
Setting a Purpose for Reading

In learning new reading skills, you will use special academic vocabulary. Knowing the right words will help you demonstrate your understanding.

Academic Vocabulary

Word	Meaning	Example Sentence
establish *v.* *Related words:* established, establishment	to show to be certain by determining the facts	Mark looked at different books to *establish* which one would have the best information on bats.
scan *v.* *Related words:* scanned, scanning	to read through quickly	Before Marta started the test, she *scanned* the questions to make sure she knew what they asked.
skim *v.* *Related words:* skimmed, skimming	to glance through quickly	I *skimmed* the long list of names and dates to find out when it was my turn to present.

People read for many reasons. Before you begin to read a text, it is important to know your **purpose,** or reason, for reading. The purpose you **establish** for reading depends on the type of text you will read.

Purposes for Reading

- Sometimes your purpose for reading is clear from the start.
- Sometimes you need to set a purpose for reading before you begin reading a text. Doing this will help you focus your reading, because it allows you to understand exactly what you expect to get out of the experience.

How To Set a Purpose

- Preview a text before you begin reading. Look at the title, headings, graphics, and illustrations to help you determine what type of text it is. Record details in a details chart like the one on the right.
- **Skim** or **scan** some pages as a way to help establish your purpose.

Text details	What the details suggest
Title	
Headings	
Pictures	
Paragraph beginnings	

before reading your anchor book

After you have set a purpose for reading, follow these steps to help you achieve your purpose while you read and after you read.

While You Read	After You Read
Keep your purpose for reading in mind. Adjust your reading rate according to the purpose you set. For example, if your purpose is to look for information, you might want to read slowly.	Ask yourself, *Did I accomplish my purpose for reading this text?*

Directions Before you read the following passage, preview the text, headings, and graphics to set a purpose for your reading.

1 **Apply** What is your purpose for reading this selection?

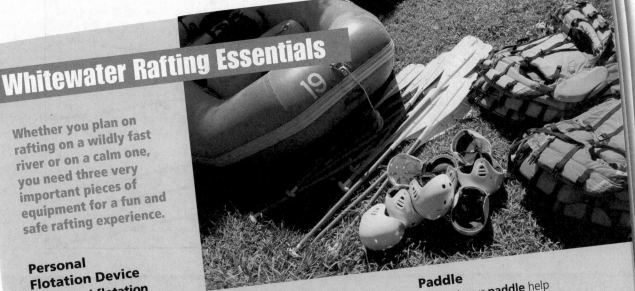

Whitewater Rafting Essentials

Whether you plan on rafting on a wildly fast river or on a calm one, you need three very important pieces of equipment for a fun and safe rafting experience.

Personal Flotation Device

A **personal flotation device,** or PFD, will keep you afloat should you fall out of your raft. Like a lifejacket, a PFD straps around your chest for a snug fit. A small pillow on the back of the device allows you to rest your head above water as you float on your back downstream to safety.

Helmet

Swift, churning water flows over rocks—lots of them. Your **helmet** protects you from seriously injuring your head if you fall out of your raft and strike a rock.

Paddle

You and your **paddle** help to push the raft along the river. In synchronized strokes with your group, you can comfortably and easily move the raft in any direction. The paddle is specific to whitewater rafting: at the end is a T-shaped handle so you can grip your paddle for the best hold when you pass through the rapids.

before reading your anchor book

The following map is from a Web site. Preview the page to set a purpose before reading. ***Guiding Question:*** **How do Internet communities help you get answers and information about the world?**

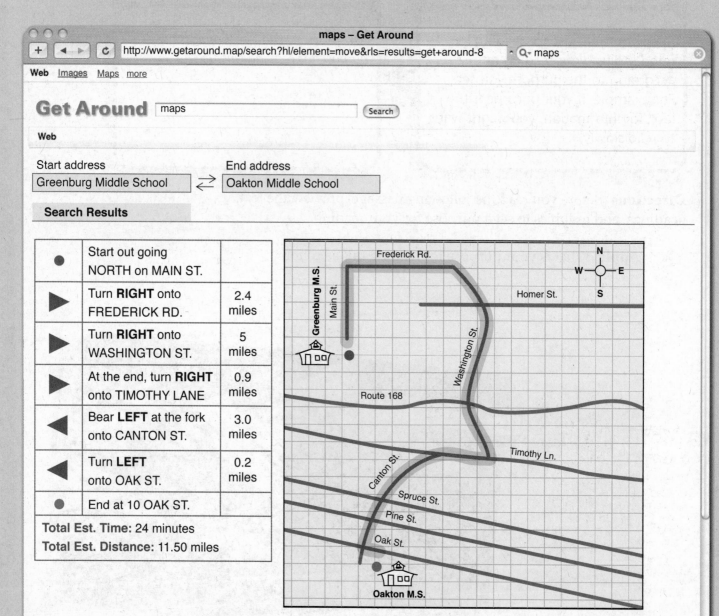

maps – Get Around

http://www.getaround.map/search?hl/element=move&rls=results=get+around-8

maps

Web Images Maps more

Get Around

maps

Search

Web

Start address: Greenburg Middle School

End address: Oakton Middle School

Search Results

●	Start out going NORTH on MAIN ST.	
▶	Turn **RIGHT** onto FREDERICK RD.	2.4 miles
▶	Turn **RIGHT** onto WASHINGTON ST.	5 miles
▶	At the end, turn **RIGHT** onto TIMOTHY LANE	0.9 miles
◀	Bear **LEFT** at the fork onto CANTON ST.	3.0 miles
◀	Turn **LEFT** onto OAK ST.	0.2 miles
●	End at 10 OAK ST.	

Total Est. Time: 24 minutes

Total Est. Distance: 11.50 miles

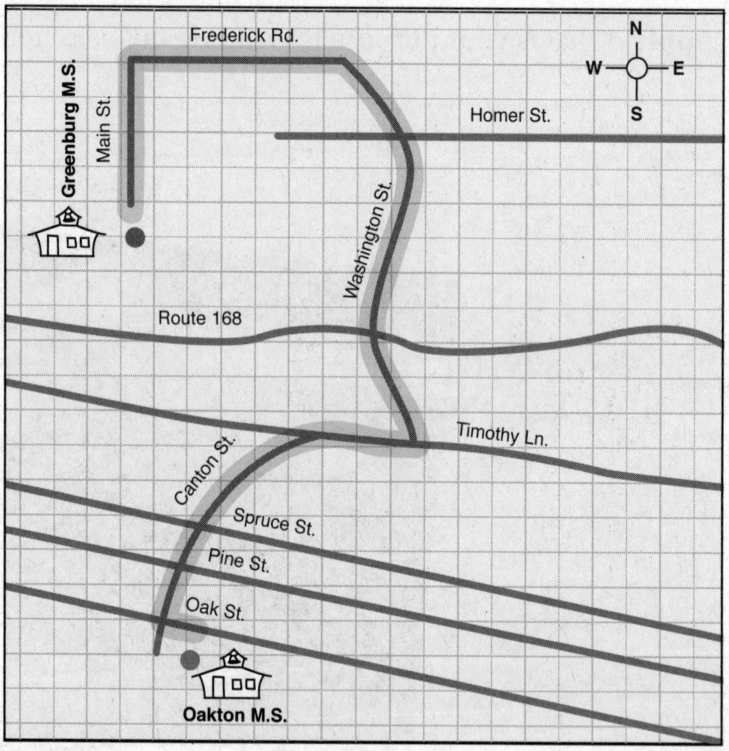

Frederick Rd.
N
W
E
S
Homer St.
Greenburg M.S.
Main St.
Washington St.
Route 168
Timothy Ln.
Canton St.
Spruce St.
Pine St.
Oak St.
Oakton M.S.

Thinking About the Selection

Map Directions

1 **Analyze** How did previewing the page help you to understand the directions as you read them?

2 **Distinguish** What features on the page helped you identify important information?

3 **Apply** Write directions telling someone how to travel from Oakton Middle School to Route 168 heading east.

4 **Analyze** What was your purpose for reading the map? What questions did you ask yourself about the map and directions to set your purpose for reading?

5 **Respond** If the map and directions did not help you accomplish your purpose for reading, how would you find the information you need? Explain.

Write Answer the following question in your Reader's Journal.

6 **Evaluate** How do Internet communities help you get answers and information about the world?

6-3 Vocabulary Building Strategies
Synonyms and Antonyms

Synonyms can help an author describe things that have something in common. A *huge* garden snake and a *gigantic* turtle are two ways of describing reptiles that are big. **Antonyms** describe opposite things—an *exciting* story is the opposite of a *boring* story.

Synonyms are words that have similar meanings. When two synonyms are used in the same sentence, one can help you unlock the meaning of the other. Look at the example below.

Example Sentence:	Mrs. Leary *compensated* Henry for shoveling her driveway, but Henry didn't wish to be paid.

Unfamiliar Word:	**Synonym:**	**Meaning of Unfamiliar Word:**
compensated	paid	paid for work

After unlocking the meaning of an unfamiliar word, check your answer in a dictionary or thesaurus. If the definition doesn't match your answer, restate the correct definition in your own words. That way, you are more likely to remember the synonym.

Directions Read the paragraph. Find the synonym for each underlined word and write it on the line. Then, write other words or phrases you know that are synonyms of the underlined words.

> Stephanie <u>opposed</u> the school board's idea of banning cell phones in school and planned to resist it at the next meeting. She created notecards and <u>produced</u> a presentation listing why cell phones should be allowed in school. She <u>arranged</u> all her materials carefully so she could present an organized presentation.

1. opposed: ______________________

2. produced: ______________________

3. arranged: ______________________

before reading your anchor book

Directions Read the sentences below. Find two words that are synonyms and write them and their shared meaning in the chart. Then, write another sentence using both words.

I loved going to the drive-in movies. It was a good remedy for the heat and three whiny children on a summer evening. The cure made us all happy.

First Synonym:	Second Synonym:	Meaning of Both Words:

Sentence:

An **antonym** is a word that means the opposite of another word. Knowing antonyms can give you clues that will help you to unlock the meaning of unfamiliar words.

Example: The *brief* meeting lasted only five minutes.
The *long* meeting lasted for an hour.

Brief is the opposite of *long*. If you know what the word *long* means, then you know that its opposite is *short*. So *brief* means "short."

Directions Read the paragraph and find the antonym for each underlined word. List each pair of words on the lines. Then, write the meaning of the antonym. Check your answers using a dictionary.

The Petrovich family <u>sent</u> more than 50 greeting cards to family and relatives during the holiday season, even though they only received 35 cards. The family decided it was better to maintain their friendships than to <u>abandon</u> them.

1 ______________________________

2 ______________________________

Ready? Start Reading Your Anchor Book *It's time to get started. As you learn from this worktext, your teacher will also give you reading assignments from your Anchor Book.*

6-4 The Research Process
Choosing Your Topic

A research report takes time and energy, so pick a topic that fascinates you. If you do this, you'll be sure to stay interested throughout the process!

Here are a few strategies that can help you choose a topic.

Self Interview	Ask yourself questions. *What do I like to do? What school subjects interest me?*
Category Lists	List people, places, things, and events. Choose one topic that interests you or relates to your life.
Brainstorm or Free-Write	Jot down ideas as they come to mind. Use a sentence starter, such as "I want to learn more about_____."
Clustering	Think of a subject that interests you. Make a web of the topics that relate to it. This can lead to new ideas.

Below is a student's cluster web on "Transportation."

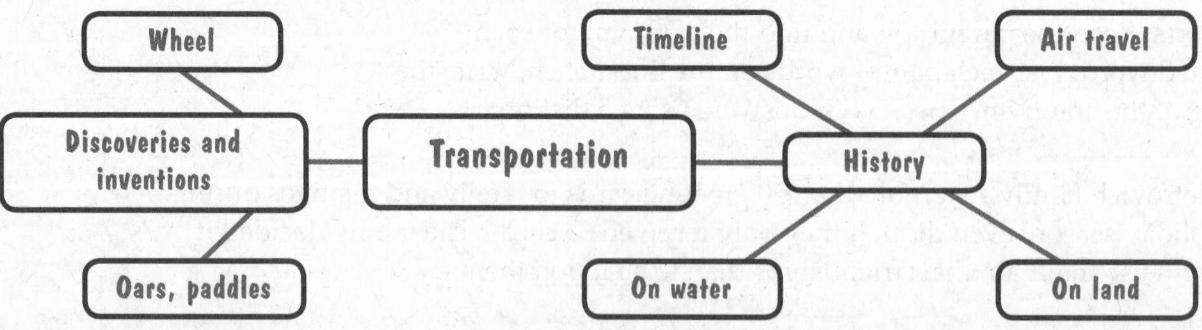

Apply Use one of the strategies above to help you choose your topic. Use a separate sheet of paper to take notes. Select one idea that you would like to research.

Narrowing Your Topic

Avoid choosing a topic that's too general or covers too much information. Narrowing your topic, or making it more specific, will make your research easier.

Ask questions about your topic. You can narrow your topic by asking yourself questions. Start with these two questions and write your answers on a separate sheet of paper.

- What do I already know about my topic?
- What do I want to learn about my topic?

The answer to each question might include **keywords,** or important words that will guide your search and help you narrow your topic.

Do research. A first round of research at the library or on the Internet can help you focus your idea. Use your keywords and these sources as a starting point for gathering ideas.

Type of Source	How It Helps
Research Texts	Scanning the **table of contents** and **index** of books about your topic can help you find specific ideas and more keywords for your search.
Library Sources	Looking through **encyclopedias** and **atlases** can help you quickly identify important ideas about a topic. Browsing lists of book titles in a library **index** or **catalog** can also stimulate ideas.
Internet Sources	Using a **search engine** to search with **keywords** can help narrow your topic. You can choose a few interesting **Web pages** to browse for more information on specific topics.

Research

Now think about your own research report.

Apply On a separate sheet of paper, write three questions you want to answer about your topic.

If you have trouble thinking of a question, a good way to begin is by using one of the five Ws: *Who, What, When, Where,* and *Why.*

Who took part in the rally?
What were the effects of the hurricane?
When did she become a politician?
Where did the festival take place?
Why was it an important issue fifty years ago?

Directions The table of contents below is from a book the student found while researching the history of transportation. Study the table of contents. Then, answer the questions that follow.

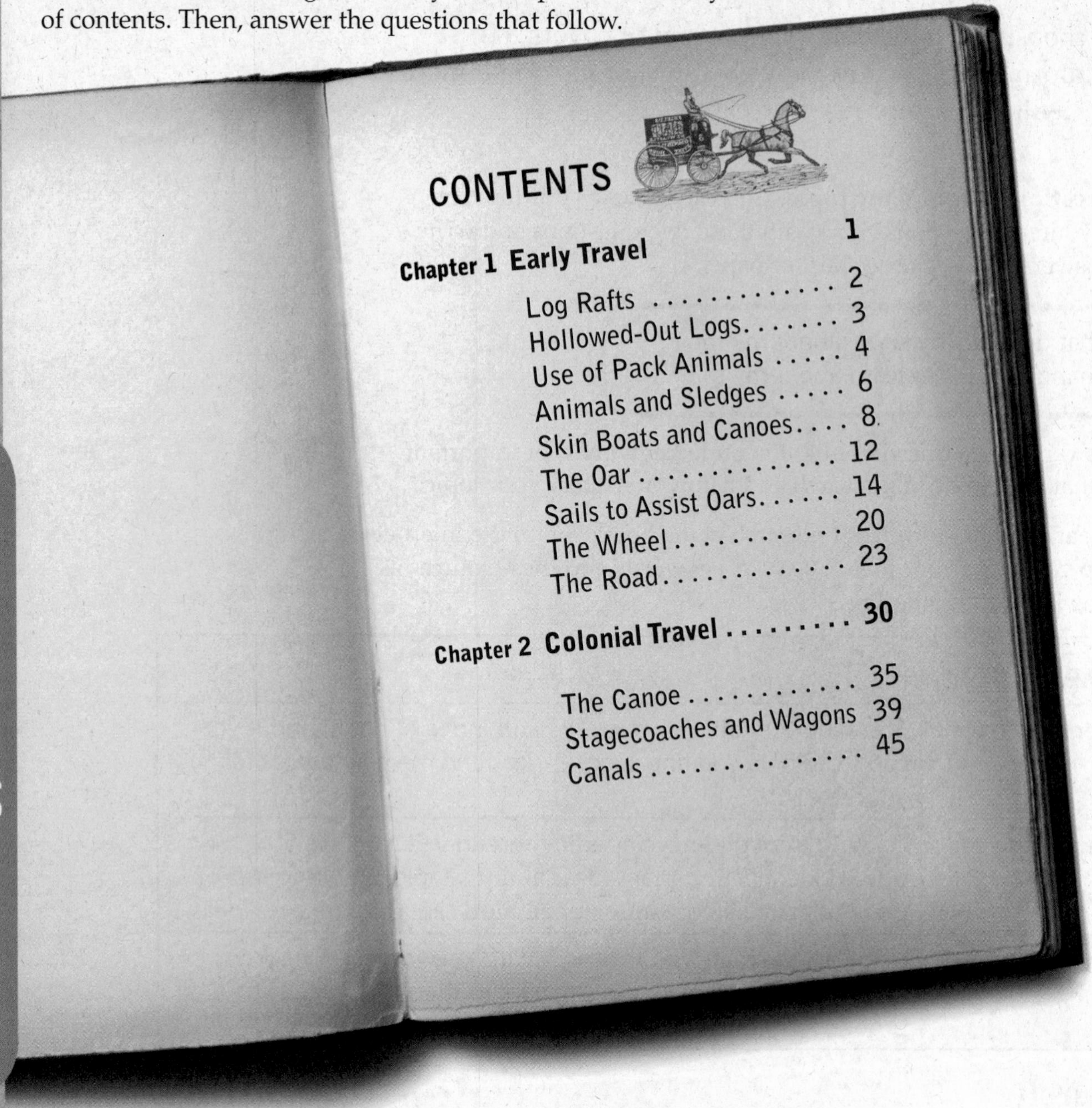

CONTENTS

1 **Apply** Read the subheadings in the table of contents. Find two topic ideas that narrow the focus of the student's original topic on the history of transportation. How do they narrow the student's focus?

2 **Synthesize** Write two questions the student might use to further narrow the focus of one topic identified above.

while reading your anchor book

Directions Reference books are used for many different reasons. Read the description of the three reference books. Then, answer the questions that follow.

Dictionary

A **dictionary** defines words and lists their parts of speech. It also shows how words are spelled, pronounced, and divided into syllables. Here is the dictionary entry for the word *gibbon*.

> **gib′ bon** (gib′ ən) *n.* a small ape of southeastern Asia with very long arms.

Encyclopedia

An **encyclopedia** contains articles and detailed information on many different subjects. An encyclopedia entry on gibbons would include information about the scientific name of the species, their physical characteristics, traits, habitat, and behavior.

Atlas

An **atlas** contains different types of maps of areas all over the world. An atlas can give you information about the areas where different species of gibbons live, the landforms found in the areas, and other types of animals that live there.

Almanac

An **almanac** is usually published every year. It contains statistical information including weather forecasts and astronomy.

1 **Apply** How would an atlas help you narrow your topic on gibbons?

____

____

2 **Deduce** Which reference source would be most useful for gathering information on the climate in which the gibbon lives? Why?

____

____

3 **Research** Use one of the above resources to identify more topic ideas for your project. List those topic ideas below. Circle the ones that are the most interesting to you.

____

____

Directions Internet searches can give you many ideas for narrowing your topic. By using keywords to search, you can find Web site summaries that describe more specific topics. Look at the page from an Internet search engine. Answer the questions that follow.

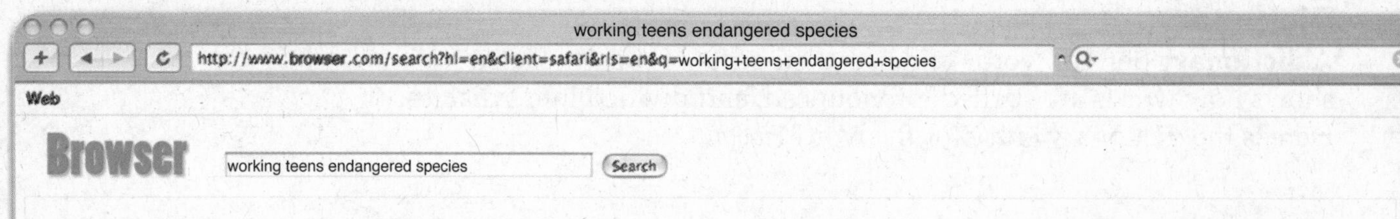

Wilmark Association **Teen** School Projects–**Endangered Species**
Please send the information on endangered species . . . of teenagers working together to save some of the world's most endangered and . . .
www.wilmark.edu/ya/teen/endangered.htm Cached - Similar pages

Kids and **Teens**: School Time Directory Our Environment: Living
Threatened and Endangered Species [Kids/Teens]-Illustrated . . . the animals that are at risk and the people who are working to help them. . . .
www.Especies.org/Kids_and_Teens/School_Time/Science/Living_Things/Animals/Endangered_Species Cached - Similar pages

Zoo News **Endangered species** in Washington State
Working with Sea animals Teens are an important part of that mission. ...
www.SeaTeens.org/janfeb2002/zoonews.htm - 16k- Cached - Similar pages

Environment Directory – Kids and **Teens** > Science > Living
Information related to endangered species. . . . Animals at risk and the people who work to help . . .
www.environment.gov/Kids_and_Teens/School_Time/Science/Living_Things/Animals/Endangered_Species/ Cached - Similar pages

Wise Science News I **Teens** dive for Science in the Caribbean Islands
Corals were listed as "threatened" under U.S. Endangered Species Act ...
www.wisesciencenews.com/articles/view/5111/ Cached - Similar pages

www.BooksOnScience.com
Endangered Species: Books: Alice Mooney, Dale Carney Customers who purchased Endangered Species . . . who manage to collect donations while working on their agenda. . . .
www.BooksOnScience.com/Endangered-Species-Alice-Mooney/dp/0567890 - 196k - Cached - Similar pages

Sponsored Links

Conservation
Hike through our 63-acre wildlife sanctuary. See birds of prey.
www.placesonearth.org

Take Action for Nature
Young people can make a difference
Read their stories & share your own
www.ActOnScience.com

Give to the Environment
Support Earthjustice
Fight toxic waste and pollution
www.earthpollution.com

1 **Evaluate** What keywords do you think the student used to find the sites on this search page? How do you know?

2 **Research** Create a list of keywords you could use to search for your topic on the Internet.

Thinking About the Research Process

Choosing and Narrowing Your Topic

1 **Apply** How could you use a book on the Civil War to narrow your topic of "The Civil War"?

2 **Evaluate** Think about the types of sources you have seen in this lesson. Which source do you think would be most helpful in your research? Why?

3 **Respond** Do you think using a cluster web would be a good strategy for narrowing a topic you don't know much about? Why or why not?

Research

Now think about your own research paper.

4 **Apply** Follow the steps you learned in this lesson to help you choose a topic to research. Identify your topic.

5 **Synthesize** Narrow your topic by conducting research and asking yourself questions. Write down three questions that will help you to find specific information about your topic.

6-5 The Research Process
Finding and Evaluating Sources

When you decide on a topic that *really* catches your interest, you'll want to do research to find more information. You can get information by researching newspapers, magazines, or the Internet. Once you find sources, you need to evaluate them and make sure the information they contain is true.

Information you find is not always accurate. Some sources may provide information that is out-of-date or contains factual errors. To make sure you can trust the information found in your sources, ask yourself these questions.

Is my source current?		Check **copyright** dates to see when the source was written and make sure the source is up-to-date.
Can I prove the information my source provides is true?		Check the **accuracy** of the source by using several different sources to verify a few facts. Make sure the author doesn't have a **bias**, or a strong opinion about a topic.
Are my Internet sources reliable?		Stay away from message boards, blogs, and most *.com* sites. Some *.com* sites, such as established news organizations, are reliable. Sites belonging to nonprofit organizations (*.org*), educational institutions (*.edu*), and government agencies (*.gov*) are usually good sources.

Directions Decide which source is more reliable for each research topic. Circle it. Then, explain your decision.

1 **Topic:** the types of trees found in Maine's forests

http://www.maineforests.gov **http://www.inmyforest.com**

2 **Topic:** how global warming has affected Australia's Great Barrier Reef

A travel article from 1998 **A scientific article from 2006**

Avoiding Plagiarism

How would you feel if your friend copied a story you wrote and then claimed that he wrote the entire thing himself? You might feel angry, or even cheated. Your friend **plagiarized,** or stole, your ideas and used them as his own.

When you research and write a report, you need to make sure you do not plagiarize, or copy the author's exact words and ideas. There are several ways you can avoid plagiarism.

1. **Take careful notes.** Jot down where you found each piece of information so you won't forget later.
2. **Use your own words.** Restate what you learn in your own words. If you want to use someone's exact words, put quotation marks around them in your notes. Be sure to identify who said them.
3. **Credit your sources.** When you use information from a source, you need to state in your report where you got that information. Giving credit to your sources is called **citing** your sources.

Directions Read the paragraphs. Then answer the question.

from the book *The Future of the Great Barrier Reef* by Lilith Shelley	Student's Notes
The ocean's rising temperatures are disastrous for coral reefs. Tiny organisms live in coral and provide necessary nutrients that allow coral to live. When the water grows too warm, these organisms die, which turns the coral white. This process is called bleaching, and can eventually cause the coral to die.	Coral reefs are in trouble. The organisms that live in coral reefs are victims of global warming. When the water grows too warm, these organisms die, which turns the coral white. This kills the coral.

Apply Explain how the student plagiarized Lilith Shelley's work. What should this student have done to avoid plagiarism?

____

____

____

Taking Research Notes

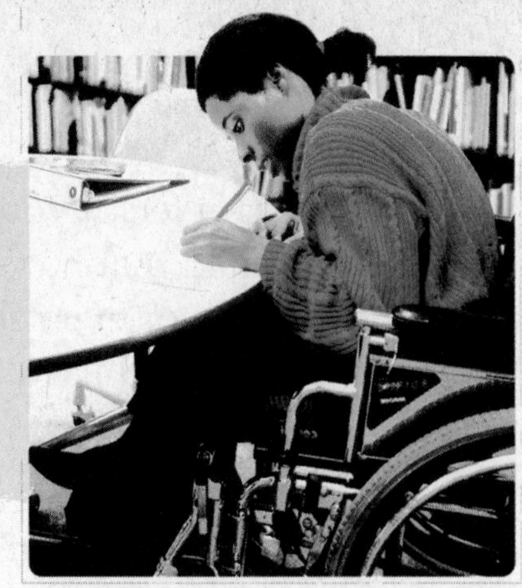

Taking notes as you gather information helps you to keep all your information organized. It also helps you to remember what you have learned and avoid plagiarizing another person's work. Choose the method that works best for you. Then get started!

Note Cards

Using note cards is a common method of note-taking. Note cards can be grouped together and organized easily. Plus, they are small enough to take to the library or to your house as you research your topic.

- **Create source cards.** Before you begin your note cards, you need to create **source cards** so you can keep track of all the sources you use. To do this, make one card for each source.

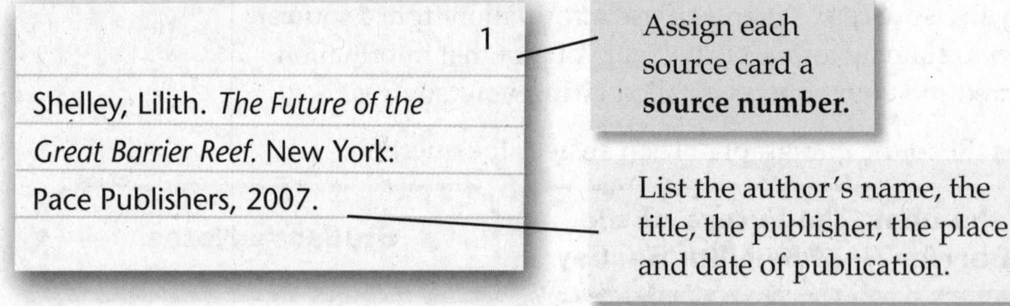

1
Shelley, Lilith. *The Future of the Great Barrier Reef.* New York: Pace Publishers, 2007.
Assign each source card a **source number.**
List the author's name, the title, the publisher, the place and date of publication.

- **Set up your note cards.** Follow these steps to keep all your information organized.

1. **Keyword** Write only one keyword on the top of each card.
2. **Source number** Write a source number on each card. This number matches the number on the corresponding source card.
3. **Page number** Write the page number from the source.
4. **Paraphrase** Restate information from a source in your own words.
5. **Quotations** Remember to use quotation marks when you copy exact words from a source.

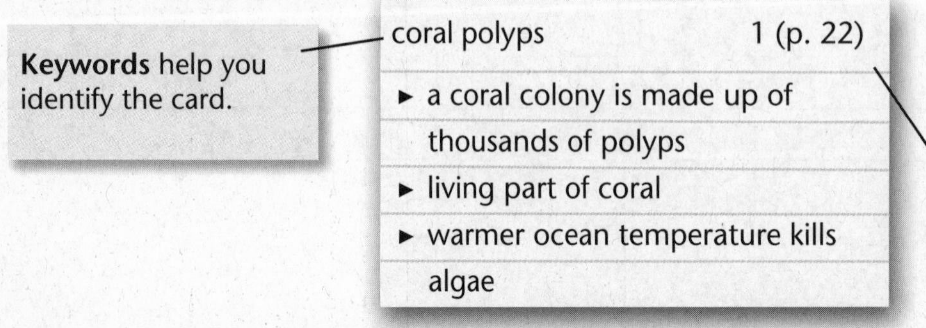

Keywords help you identify the card.
coral polyps
1 (p. 22)
▸ a coral colony is made up of thousands of polyps
▸ living part of coral
▸ warmer ocean temperature kills algae
The source number shows where the information comes from, and the page number shows where you found the information.

Idea Web

An **idea web** makes it easy to organize your notes and to see how information is related. Use the following steps to help you set up your web.

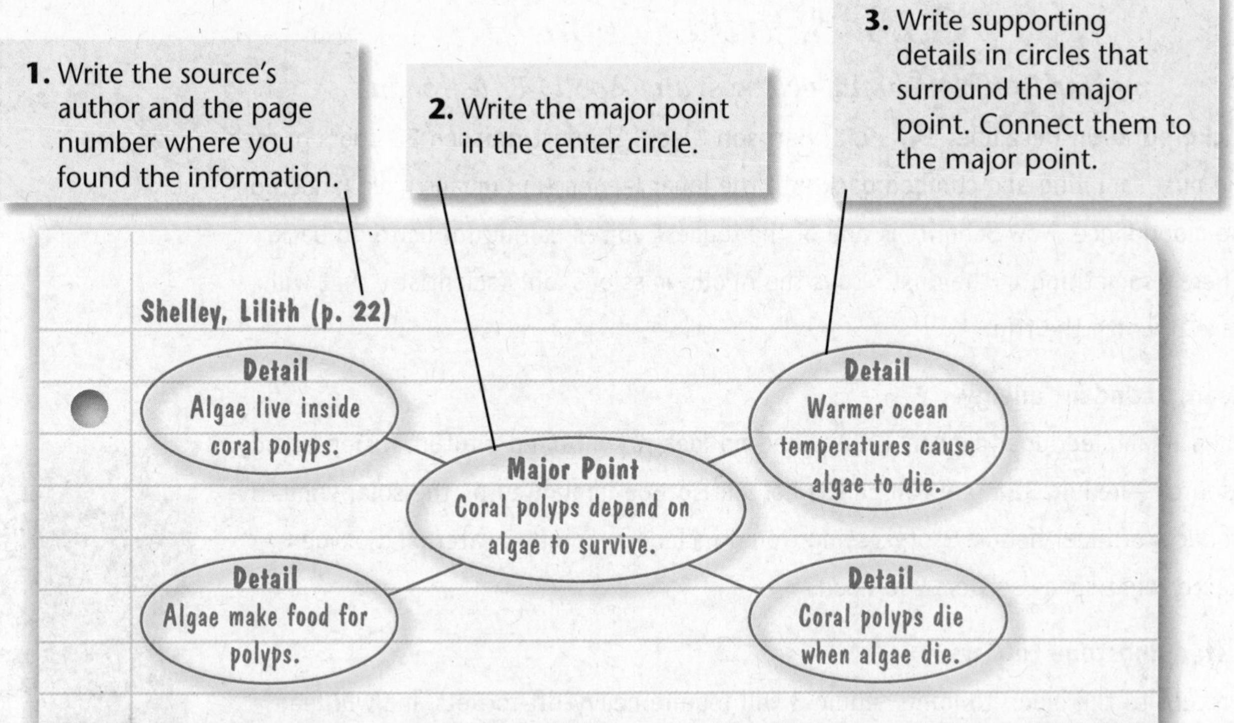

1. Write the source's author and the page number where you found the information.
2. Write the major point in the center circle.
3. Write supporting details in circles that surround the major point. Connect them to the major point.
Shelley, Lilith (p. 22)
Detail
Algae live inside coral polyps.
Detail
Warmer ocean temperatures cause algae to die.
Major Point
Coral polyps depend on algae to survive.
Detail
Algae make food for polyps.
Detail
Coral polyps die when algae die.

The Cornell Method

When you use the Cornell Method, you can use your notebook to keep all your notes in one place. This method works especially well when you are taking notes while listening to a speaker. The Cornell Method has three parts, which are explained below.

- **Questions** Write down questions you have about your notes, or questions that have not been answered yet.
- **Notes** Take detailed notes in the right-hand column.
- **Summary** Summarize the notes. When you look through your notes, these summaries will help you to remember the most important information to include in your report.

Shelley, Lilith (p. 22)	
Questions Why does coral die when the algae die? How does warmer water actually kill the algae?	**Notes** -a colony is made up of thousands of polyps -where algae live -algae make food for the coral polyp -warmer ocean temperature kills algae
Summary The life of a coral colony depends on the algae that live inside of it. When ocean temperatures rise, the algae die, which kills the coral polyps.	

You've just learned about three different ways to take notes. Now let's see how each method was used to research information on space exploration.

from *My Seven: Why We Must Go Back to the Moon*

by Harrison H. Schmitt, geologist and Apollo 17 astronaut

Background On December 14, 1972, Harrison "Jack" Schmitt finished 22 hours of rock and dust sampling and climbed back into the lunar lander. No humans have landed on the moon since. Now Schmitt is one of the loudest voices calling for us to go back. "There's something in the dust," says the Apollo missions' only scientist, "that will make it worth the trip."

Clean, abundant energy

When I sampled lunar dust in 1972, I had no idea it contained a future fusion-energy resource—helium 3, a rare (on Earth) helium isotope implanted by the solar wind. By-products of lunar helium 3 processing would include hydrogen, water, and oxygen—exactly what space settlers will need.

A steppingstone to Mars

A return to the moon to mine helium 3 will require heavy-lift rockets and will lead to fusion propulsion systems. I believe this combination ultimately will enable the exploration and settlement of Mars.

Note Card

Lunar Dust **3 (p. 1)**

Helium 3

- by-products would include hydrogen, water, and oxygen
- space settlers need these to survive
- will enable exploration and settlement of Mars

Cornell Method

Questions	Notes
Do many people think we should return to the moon? What do humans need to survive in space?	-no humans have been on the moon since December 14, 1972 -lunar dust implanted by solar wind -can be processed to create hydrogen, water, and oxygen -humans need these by-products to survive in space

Summary: No human being has been on the moon for almost 37 years. Not only is it time to return and explore the moon in order to see if it has changed, but it would also help to make it easier for humans to live in space.

Idea Web

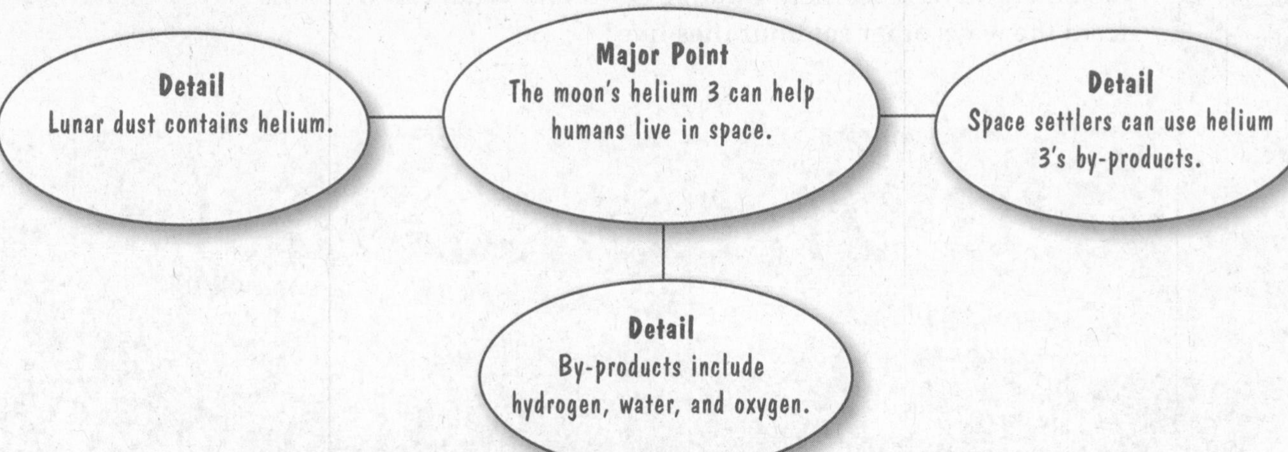
Detail
Lunar dust contains helium.
Major Point
The moon's helium 3 can help humans live in space.
Detail
Space settlers can use helium 3's by-products.
Detail
By-products include hydrogen, water, and oxygen.

1 **Evaluate** Which method of note-taking do you think is the best to use for this selection? Why?

2 **Apply** The note card contains the keyword "Harrison 'Jack' Schmitt." Fill in the card with notes about this keyword.

Harrison "Jack" Schmitt
3 (p. 1)

while reading your anchor book

As you read the following selection, you will take notes using the methods you have learned. *Guiding Question:* **What can we learn from the ways other communities live?**

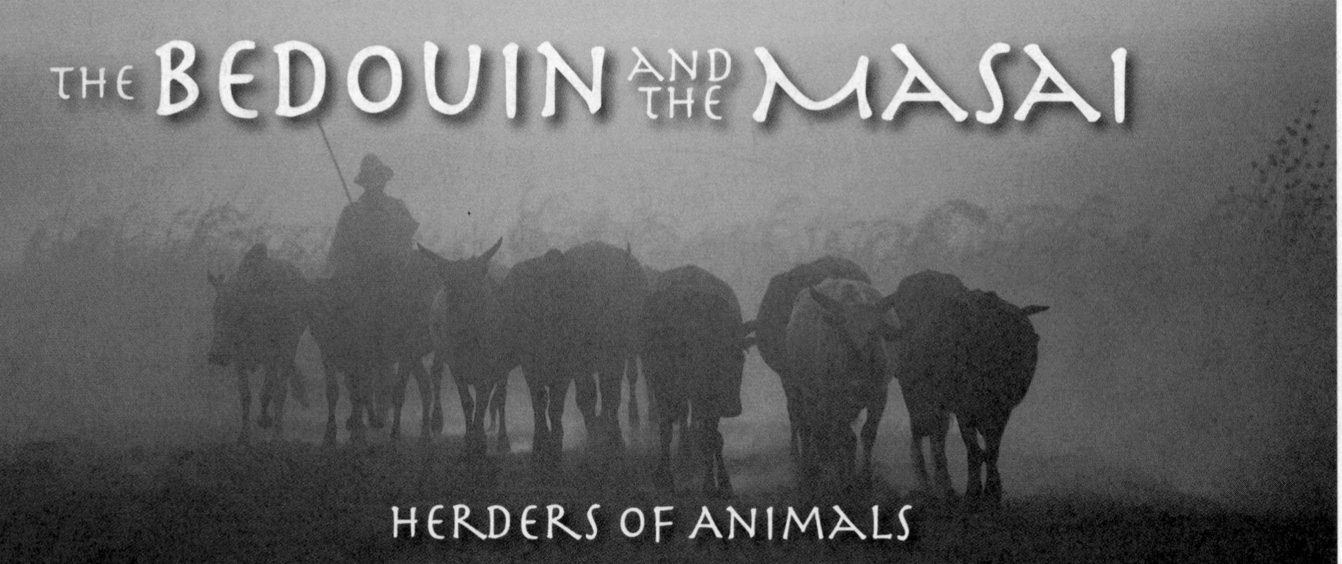

The Bedouin and the Masai

Herders of Animals

In some remote areas *of the world, there are groups of people whose lives are closely intertwined with the lives of their animals. Some of them are herders, who still live much as their ancestors did centuries ago.*

Animals are important in every aspect of the herder's life. The wealth of a herder is measured by the size of the herd. Everyday life revolves around the care of the animals. Many customs and rituals have been influenced by the animals that enable the herder to survive. From their animals, herders get most of what they need to survive. The animals supply them not only with food, drink, and clothing, but also with shelter and fuel. In return, the herders care for the animals. They take them to fresh pastures, care for the sick ones, and protect them from predators.

Unlike farmers, herders do not keep their animals in one place. Because the animals need more than one small area can provide, the people and their herds move frequently from one grazing place to another.

Constant movement is a major feature of the lives of herders. They do not have permanent homes. As a result, their easily built dwellings can be carried with them or left behind. Herders possess few material belongings. They own only as much as they can carry with them.

Of all the herders still existing in various parts of the world, two groups are especially interesting. One group is the Bedouin of the Middle East, and the other is the Masai of eastern Africa.

▲ **Good to Know!** Livestock, such as cattle and sheep, are the primary source of income for the Masai people. Livestock is traded for cash or other products. Today, as a result of global warming, droughts are becoming severe in East Africa and the Masai people are forced to find other means of livelihood.

Take notes using note cards on this first section about herders.

while reading your anchor book

THE BEDOUIN

In the dry, vast deserts of the Middle East, herders of camels, sheep, and goats live an ancient, nomadic life. These herders are the Bedouin, the Arab inhabitants of the desert. With little grass in the harsh desert, the Bedouin move often to find new pastures for their animals.

On a separate sheet of paper, take notes on the Bedouin using the Cornell method.

A Bedouin camp is both beautiful and practical. Long, low, tents, adapted to the needs of Bedouin life, are pitched together on the white sand. Each tent is made from long strands of goat, camel, and sheep hair. When wet, these fibers expand, making the tent waterproof. During the hot days, the sides of the tent are rolled up to provide shade and to let cool breezes through. At night, they are rolled down to keep out the cold wind. When the Bedouin decide to move their herds to new grazing land, they can lower their tents and pack their belongings within a few hours.

In the fall, winter, and spring, the Bedouin live and travel together in family groups of two to twenty tents. They move their herds across the desert, often following rain clouds. In the summer, the Bedouin gather together at wells, the only sources of water in the dry summer. Hundreds of tents are pitched together near the communal well and remain there for three or four months.

The Bedouin rely on their animals for most of their diet. Camel milk is the most important part of many meals. The people drink

▼ **Critical Viewing**
What do the details in this photo of a Bedouin woman reveal about the Bedouin's way of life?

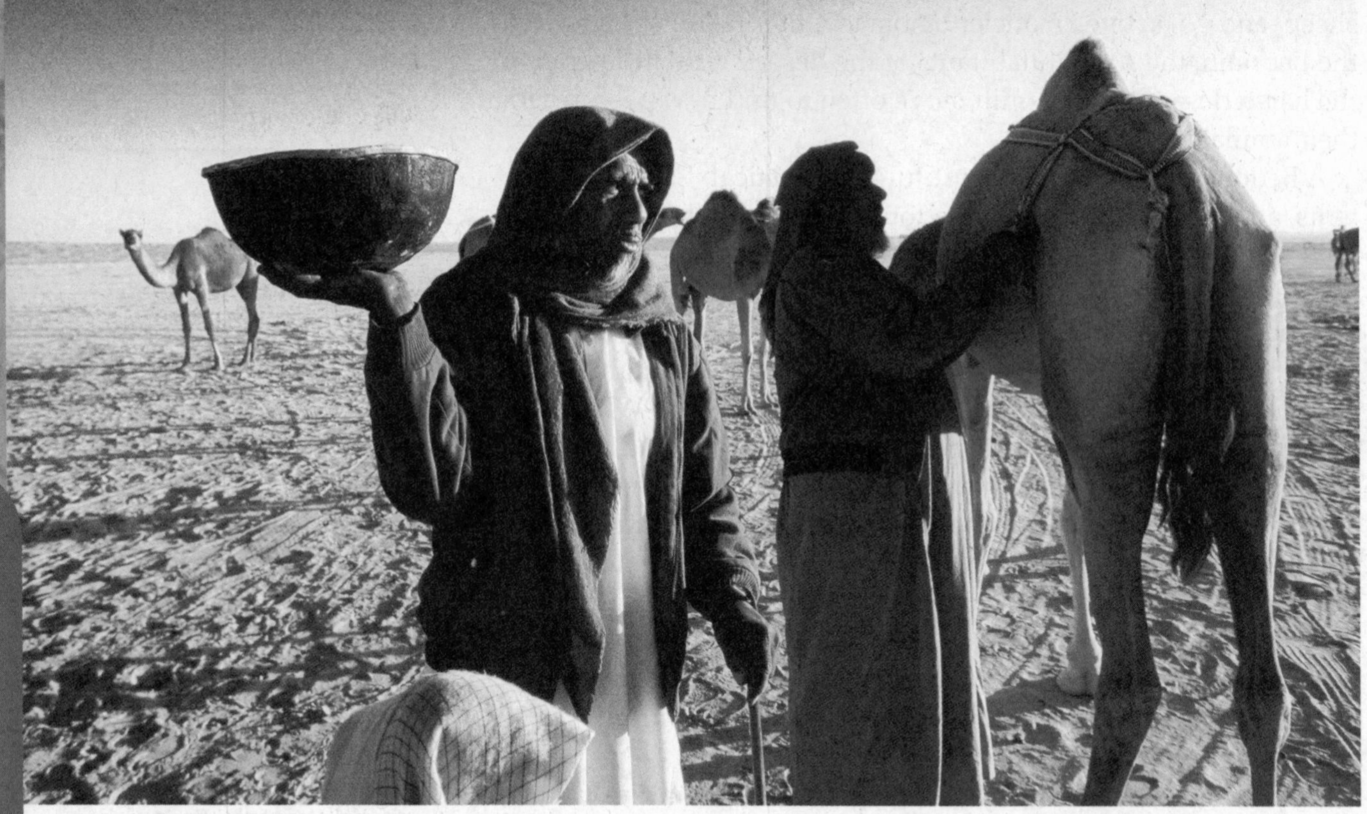

it fresh or make it into yogurt. Because the camels are so valuable, they are seldom killed to be eaten. On special occasions, however, the Bedouin enjoy camel meat as a festive treat.

The Bedouin cherish and respect the camel. Different Bedouin groups prize different camels of a particular color—white, black, or brown. The Arabic word for camel *(jamal)* comes from the same root as the Arabic word for beautiful (*jamil*).

In the past, the Bedouin herded only *dromedaries*. These single-humped camels were the most important animals in the desert, as well as the chief means of transportation for desert people. A camel can survive for long periods of time without water, it can tolerate extreme heat, and it possesses great endurance.

Until modern times, the wealth of a Bedouin family was measured only by the number of camels it owned. Today, sheep are becoming more and more important to the Bedouin economy. Because cars and trucks are now used as transportation in the desert, camels are no longer as valuable as they once were. Raising sheep is becoming more profitable than herding camels.

Much of Bedouin life, however, remains unchanged. The people still travel the desert, following their herds and keeping up old traditions.

▲ **Good to Know!**
The Bedouin still herd camels, moving their camps every three or four months to find different foraging grounds or areas that have food for their animals.

THE MASAI

The high, rolling, treeless plains in the African countries of Kenya and Tanzania are called savannas. On these plains live the Masai, herders of cattle, sheep, and goats. Masai people value their cattle most—no other possession is of equal worth to them. This attitude is the result of the important role cattle play in every aspect of Masai life.

A Masai village consists of a group of *bomas*. Built by the Masai women, bomas are dwellings made from a framework of twigs and covered by grass and leaves. To keep the structure warm and waterproof, it is plastered with a layer of cattle dung. Fences are put up around the boma village to protect the animals at night. Everyday life in the village revolves around the care of the cattle and other animals. Masai women and girls milk the cattle and prepare food using the milk. The men inspect the cattle for disease and treat any sick ones. During the day, the young boys take the cattle out to pasture and guard them from predators.

When their cattle need new grazing land, the Masai move on, leaving their bomas behind. If they come to a grazing place on the savanna where they have been before, the Masai patch up their old bomas. If the grazing place is new, the women and girls build new bomas. When staying in

Take notes on the Masai using an idea web. Write the major point in the center and the details around it.

▼ **Good to Know!**
Inset: Masai homesteads are arranged in a circular pattern. In this aerial view, herds of cattle are led out of a village in Amboseli National Park, Kenya.

Bottom: Children outside a Masai boma. These homesteads are traditionally shared by more than one family. Women construct the homes while men construct the fences that protect them.

a place for just a short while, the Masai live in simpler dwellings made of mud and animal hides.

From their cattle, the Masai get meat, milk, and blood for nourishment. After a cow is milked, the milk is divided into three parts. One part is used to drink fresh, the second part is stored and becomes a sour cheese. The third part is mixed with blood drawn from a cow to make a protein-rich drink. Cattle also provide the Masai with hides for clothing and bed covers.

Because cattle are so important to the Masai, a strong bond exists between the people and their animals. They know each animal's voice and markings, and they call the animals by name. The Masai have few material goods because all they need to own is their animals.

The Masai, a proud and noble people, have always been respected and feared by other African people. To become a warrior, a young man must prove himself by killing a lion with a spear. In the past, the Masai raided neighboring camps for cattle to make their own herds larger. According to Masai belief, all the cattle were given to the Masai at the beginning of the world. No one else had a right to possess any.

In recent years, the Masai have come to lead more peaceful lives. Still, modern civilization has not greatly affected them. The young people have the chance to go to the cities, but most Masai remain herders of cattle. They are close to their families and friends, and their love for their animals remains constant.

Herders live a life that is unique in today's world. Living in close contact with nature, they have no need for luxuries or conveniences. They remain in family groups, and they take pride in caring for the animals that ensure their survival.

▼ Good to Know!
Herding livestock used to be a job for the young boys in a Masai family. Today, with the arrival of formal education in the Masai region, this responsibility has been passed on to the parents. Now boys take over the responsibility on weekends or when there is no school.

Thinking About the Research Process

The Bedouin and the Masai: Herders of Animals

1 **Evaluate** Which method of note-taking did you find the easiest to use while reading the selection? Explain why.

2 **Discuss** Do you think the author favors one group of herders over the other? Use examples from the text to explain your answer.

3 **Analyze** Which note-taking method helped you understand how information was related? Explain your answer.

Research

Now, think about your own research report.

4 **Research** Locate a source for your research topic. Create a source card and, on a separate sheet of paper, take notes according to the format that works best for you.

Write Answer the following questions in your Reader's Journal.

5 **Draw Conclusions** What can we learn from the ways other communities live?

6 **Apply** Choose a short passage from your Anchor Book. Use one of the three note-taking methods to write down important information. Then explain why you chose this particular method.

while reading your anchor book

6-6 Analyzing an Informational Text
Web Page

Finding your way around a Web page can be confusing. When you use the Internet for research, you need to know how to find information quickly. Let's look at the various features of a Web page to learn how to navigate one easily.

Directions Read the following Web page. Examine the different features that can help you find information. Then answer the questions on the next page.

The **URL** (Uniform Resource Locator) at the top of the page is also known as the **Web address**. Remember to write down the URL and the date you viewed the site if you want to use it for research.

Many Web pages offer keyword searches, which help you find information. Type in a keyword to find articles related to your keyword.

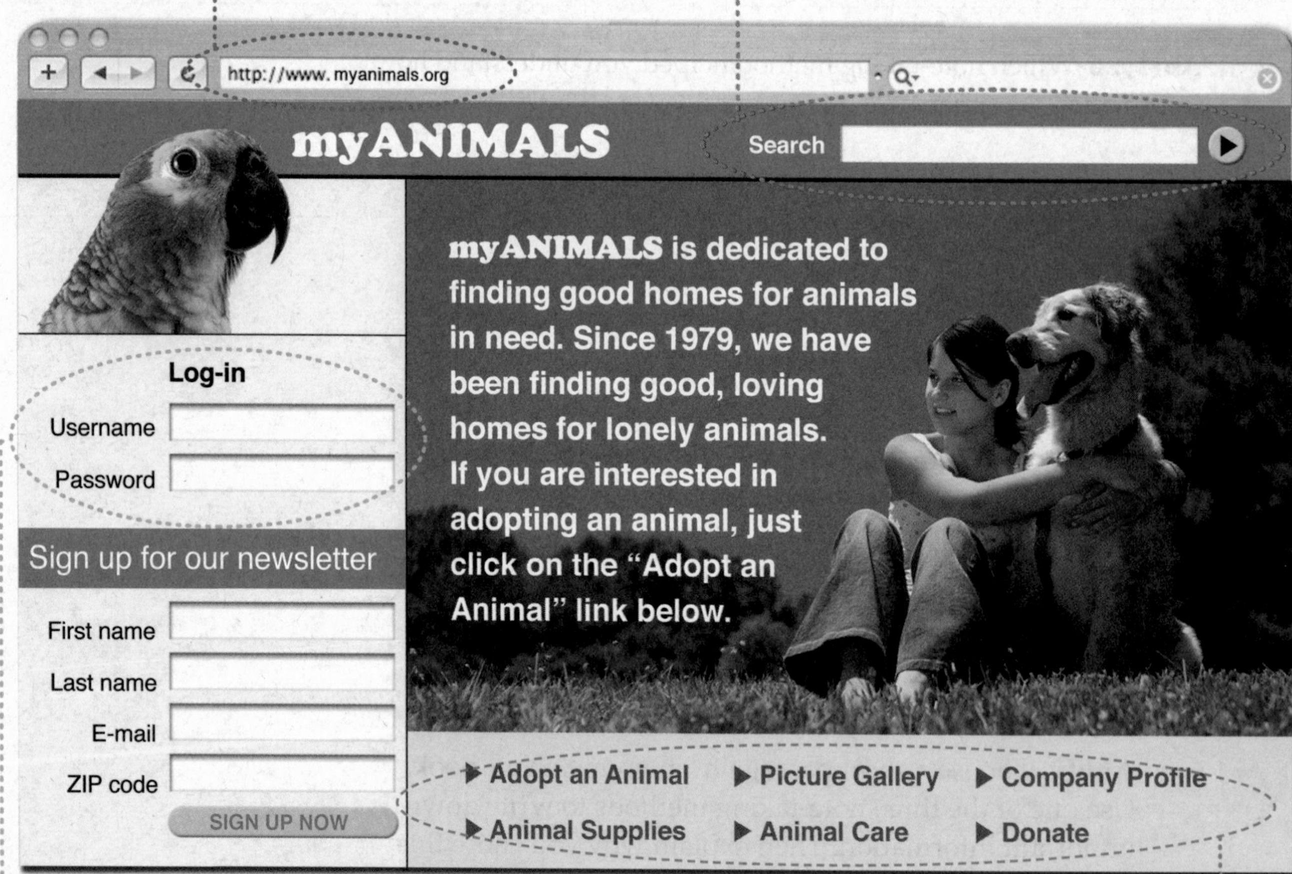

Many Web pages have log-in boxes where visitors can enter their name and password in order to access more information.

Most Web pages have a menu of options from which you can choose. Some sites have pull-down menus that appear only after you click on a heading.

1 **Explain** Why is it important to know a Web page's URL?

2 **Apply** Suppose you wanted to find information quickly on the Web page on page 466, but you were not sure how to find it. What would you do?

3 **Apply** How would you use the myANIMALS Web page to find out how to give money to the organization?

4 **Speculate** If you were doing a research project on how to care for a pet, do you think you would find appropriate articles on this Web site? Explain your answer.

5 **Evaluate** Do you think a Web site is the best way for an organization such as "myANIMALS" to share information and to promote its cause? Explain your answer.

6 **Speculate** Why do you think you need to use a password in a log-in box?

while reading your anchor book

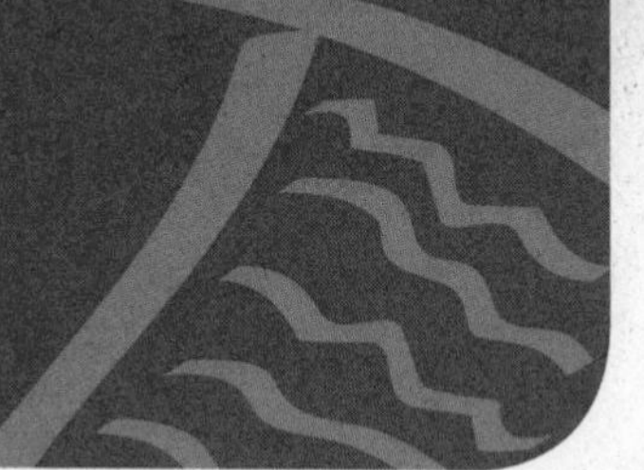

6-7 Language Coach
Grammar and Spelling

Independent and Subordinate Clauses

A **clause** is a group of words that has its own subject and verb. Writers use clauses to add information or to bring pieces of information together in a text. The types of clauses shown in the chart below will help make your sentences more interesting.

Go Online
Learn More
Visit: PHSchool.com
Web Code: exp-6601

Type of Clause	Definition	Example
Independent Clause	• has a subject and a verb • expresses a complete thought • can stand by itself as a sentence	The sun rises in the morning.
Subordinate Clause	• has a subject and a verb • does not express a complete thought • cannot stand by itself as a sentence	as soon as the sun rises

You can often identify a **subordinate clause** by the word that introduces it. These words often signal a subordinate clause: *after, as, because, before, if, since, that, until, where, which,* and *who.*

Example: ***after*** **we cleaned up the house**

A sentence can have both an **independent clause** and a subordinate clause. Use a comma or a semicolon (;) to connect the two clauses. In the examples, each subject is underlined, and each verb is circled.

Examples: After we cleaned up the house, the dog ran through it.

The cat refused to go outside, since the drizzling rain had become a downpour.

Directions Read the paragraph. On a separate sheet of paper, rewrite it using subordinate and independent clauses. Share your rewritten paragraph with a partner and discuss how the clauses make your writing more interesting.

I was nervous when the principal asked me to give a speech. I would have to write something to be read aloud at an assembly. The assembly was being held for Ms. Hagerty. She was a teacher who was leaving the school after many years. Many people would speak about how much they would miss her.

Author's Craft

Good writers use subordinate clauses to make their writing more interesting. Choose a memorable passage from this unit and look at it again. Does the author use many subordinate clauses? Find a place where the author could have used more subordinate clauses, and add them in yourself. How do subordinate clauses make the text more interesting?

Simple and Compound Sentences

A **simple sentence** is a common type of sentence structure used by writers. Simple sentences contain a single independent clause. They are used to express one complete thought. In the following examples, the subjects are underlined once and the verbs are underlined twice.

Simple subject and verb: My feet hurt.

Compound subject: My muscles and legs ache.

Compound verb: My fingers look and feel irritated.

Compound subject and compound verb: Kara and Scott trained hard and beat the school record.

A **compound sentence** is made up of more than one simple sentence. Two or more independent clauses are usually joined by a comma and a coordinating **conjunction,** such as *and, but, or,* and *so.* If the clauses are closely related in meaning, a writer might use a semicolon to join them. When a semicolon is used, conjunctions are not used.

Examples: Tyrone can practice guitar, or he can do his chores.
Ed is a good artist; he sketches almost anything well.

Directions Use the directions in parentheses to rewrite the sentences.

1 The team huddled. They talked about their strategy. (Rewrite as a simple sentence with a compound verb.)

___

2 The rain had gone on for three days. The wind lasted just as long. (Rewrite as a simple sentence with a compound subject.)

___

Read the paragraph below. On a separate sheet of paper, rewrite the paragraph. Insert a conjunction, a subject, or a verb where indicated. Then, share your paragraph with a partner.

3 Marina's end-of-school party was the highlight of the year. There was live music at the party, (*conjunction*) we (*verb*) all afternoon. Jenny and James (*verb*) on the trampoline (*conjunction*) (*verb*) in time with the music. Even though the (*subject*) was loud, the two (*subject*) named Jazzy and Pearl (*verb*) soundly right in the middle of the dance floor!

Complex Sentences

Writers can use **complex sentences** to combine two clauses that are not equal in importance. An independent clause contains the more important idea, and a subordinate clause contains the less important idea. Remember that an independent clause can stand alone as a simple sentence, but a subordinate clause cannot.

Go Online
Learn More
Visit: PHSchool.com
Web Code: exp-6603

Example: Because she studies, my sister gets good grades.

The independent clause is *my sister gets good grades.*

The subordinate clause is *because she studies.*

Directions Make each simple or compound sentence complex by adding a subordinate clause.

1 The rain and wind made driving impossible.

____

____

2 I did not like the taste of the dandelion greens, but I ate them.

____

____

Some clauses look like they are sentences, but when you look closely, you see that they are long and don't use correct punctuation. These sentences can't stand on their own. They are called **run-on** sentences.

Run-on sentence:	**Rewritten sentence:**
I found a shell it was broken so I put it back in the ocean.	I found a shell. It was broken, so I put it back in the ocean.

Directions On a separate sheet of paper, use correct punctuation to rewrite the paragraph. Underline simple sentences once and complex sentences twice.

3 You might think it's easy learning how to water ski but it's not as easy as it looks. After you manage to get the skis on your feet you have to figure out how to move around in them. It's best to have someone help you to the boat and hand you the line plan on dunking in the water a few times because getting up is the hard part. Hold on tight don't lean forward just let the boat lift you out of the water.

Author's Craft

Good writers are also good editors. They know how to revise their writing for sentence structure variety. Scan "The Bedouin and the Masai" on page 460. Choose a paragraph and identify the sentences as simple, compound, or complex. Then, revise the paragraph, changing most sentences into different types. How does your paragraph compare to the original?

Word Families

Words that have the same root are a part of the same **word family.** Some common English words originated from Greek roots, such as the ones shown below.

Go Online
Learn More
Visit: PHSchool.com
Web Code: exp-6604

Root	Meaning	Examples
-poli-	"city"	metropolis
-phon-	"sound"	telephone
-cyc-	"wheel" or "ring"	bicycle

Since the words in a word family all have the same root, you can use your knowledge of the root's meaning to help you unlock the meaning of unfamiliar words in that word family.

Directions Complete the webs below by listing words that are in the same family. You can use a dictionary.

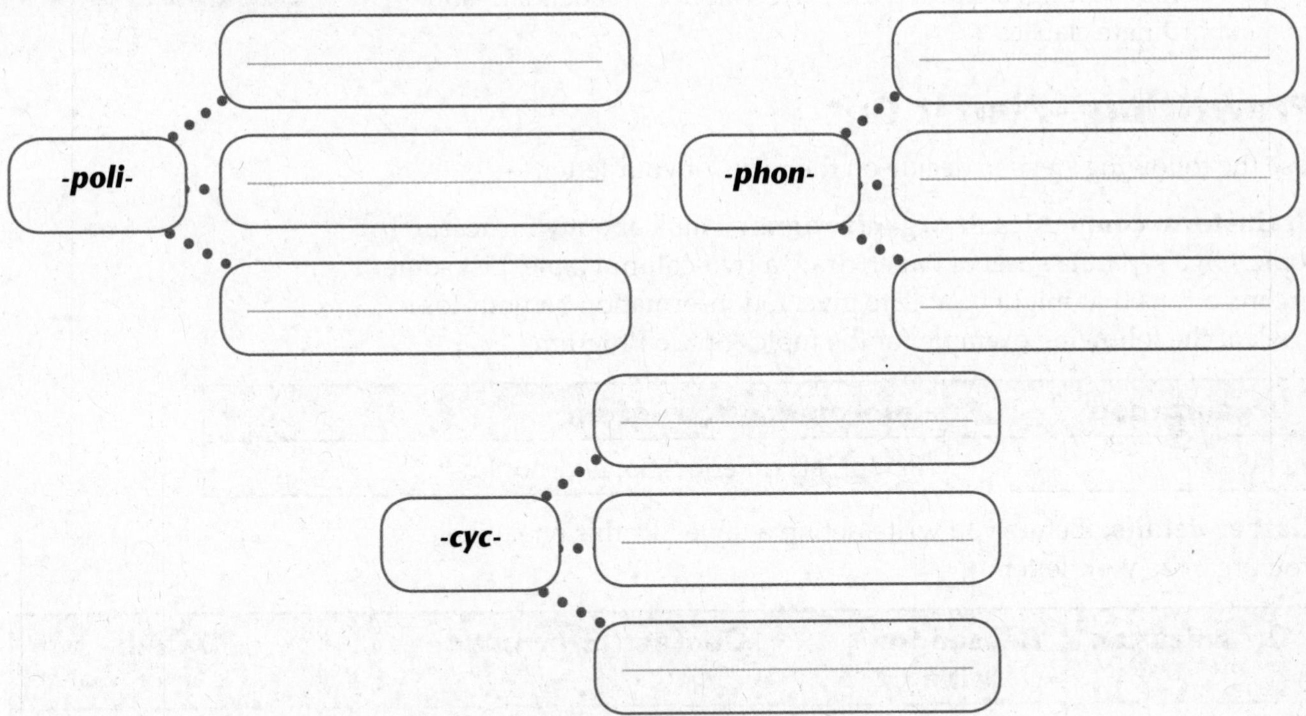

Directions Use the root from the chart above to spell each word correctly. Then use each word in a sentence.

1 polacy ____________________

____

2 sycle ____________________

____

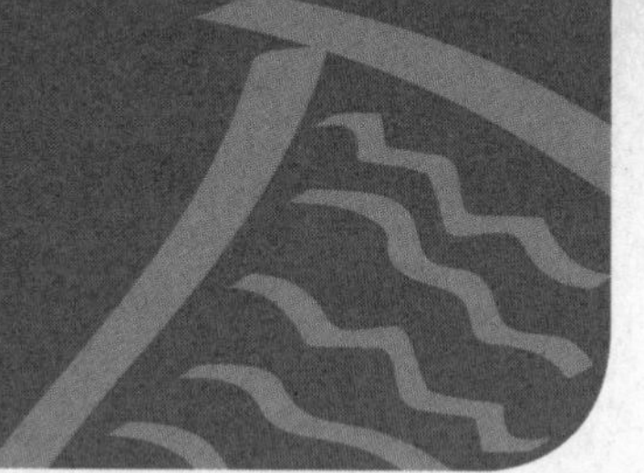

6-8 Writer's Workshop
Exposition: Business Letter

Letters are written for many reasons. We write letters to greet or to thank people, or to share news. Business letters are written to people you may not know, so the rules are different than they would be if your were writing a letter to your friend. In this writer's workshop, you will write a formal business-style letter to a company asking for information on your research topic.

Purpose To write a formal business letter requesting information for a research topic

Audience People in the organization

Your formal letter should include the following.

- clear demonstration of format and style for a business letter
- an introduction that clearly states what you're asking for
- formal and polite language throughout
- error-free writing, including the correct use of independent and subordinate clauses

Prewriting—Plan It Out

Use the following steps to decide on the focus of your letter.

Brainstorm companies or organizations. Think about your research topic. On a separate sheet of paper, draw a two-column table. List some organizations that might be able to give you information on your topic. Look at the following example for the topic "Space Programs."

Organization	Information to request
NASA	Pamphlets on educational programs

Gather details. Before you write, set up a table like this one to help you organize your letter.

Organization	Reason for Writing	Contact Information	Details
NASA	To request information on NASA's educational programs	NASA Educator Resource Center **NASA Langley Research Center** Virginia Air and Space Center 600 Settlers Landing Rd. Hampton, VA 23681-2199	I am passionate about science and space exploration and would like information on programs offered in my state.

Drafting—Get It on Paper

Use your completed table to help you draft your letter. The following steps will help you organize an effective letter.

Use the correct elements. Business letters include several specific elements. Look at the explanations of these, shown at right, and at the model letter on page 474.

Choose a letter format. The student model shows a letter in **block format**. It is the easiest format to remember because all parts of the letter start at the left margin. In the **modified block format,** the heading, closing, and signature are centered while the rest of the letter is in block format. See the examples that follow.

Block Format

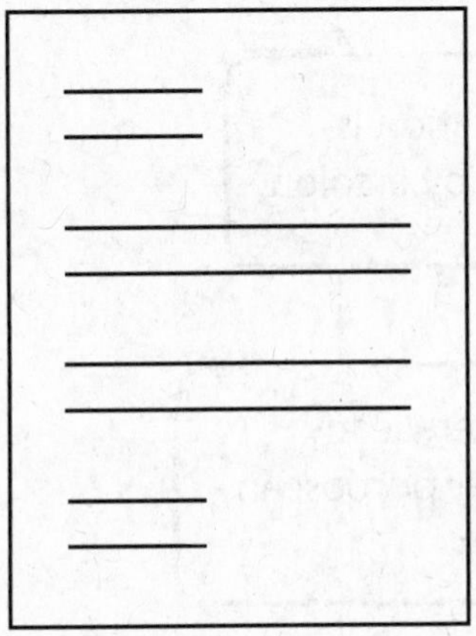

Modified Block Format

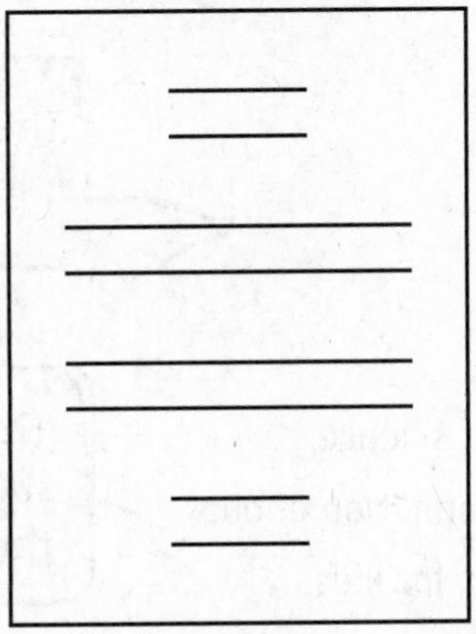

Parts of a Business Letter

Heading
Your name
Your address
Today's date

Inside address
Name of the recipient
Address of the recipient

Salutation
The greeting to the recipient, starting with *Dear,* followed by the recipient's name, and ending with a colon. If you do not know the recipient's name, use *Dear Sir or Madam.*

Body
The main part of letter that states your purpose and the information that supports it

Closing
A formal word or phrase such as *Sincerely* or *Respectfully,* followed by a comma

Signature
Your signed name
Your typed name

Shape your writing. In the first body paragraph, state your reason for writing the letter. In the following body paragraphs, include supporting details. Conclude with a short paragraph by saying thank you and restating your purpose. Use a polite tone.

Revising—Make It Better

Focus your letter. Use your knowledge of independent and subordinate clauses to keep your tone clear, focused, and formal.

Incorrect As soon as school is over. I want to go to a NASA space exploration program. I am interested in science.

Correct I am passionate about science. As soon as the school year ends, I hope to attend a NASA space exploration program.

Peer Review Ask for a partner's response to your letter. Revise it to achieve the reaction you had intended.

Directions Read a student letter, which is in block format. Use it as a model for your own business letter.

Student Model: Business Letter

Karen Long
1051 Any Street
Charlottesville, VA 22907

July 10, 2010

NASA Educator Resource Center
NASA Langley Research Center
Virginia Air and Space Center
600 Settlers Landing Rd.
Hampton, VA 23681-2199

Dear Sir or Madam:

I am in sixth grade, and I am passionate about science, especially geology. I am writing to request information about planetary geology programs in NASA's programs for kids.

I am asking for this information as part of a research project on the planets. Any information about the type of rock formations on other planets would be very helpful. I am also personally interested in this information, and one day would like to study outer space.

Thank you for your time. I look forward to hearing from you.

Sincerely,

Karen Long

Karen Long

Go Online
Student Model
Visit: PHSchool.com
Web Code: exr-6601

The heading and inside address are all the way to the left.

The salutation is followed by a colon.

The writer clearly states her purpose in the body.

By adding these details, the writer supports her request.

In the closing, the writer uses friendly but formal language.

The writer ends with her signature in the salutation.

Editing—Be Your Own Language Coach

Before you hand in your letter, review it for language convention errors. Pay special attention to your grammar, especially your use of independent and subordinate clauses.

Publishing—Share It!

When you publish a work, you produce it for a specific audience. Consider one of the following ideas to share your writing.

Swap your letter. Trade letters with a classmate and read the letter carefully. Write a response to the request for information.

Send your letter. Send your request to the organization you selected, using its contact information.

Reflecting on Your Writing

1 **Respond** Answer the following questions on a separate sheet of paper and hand it in with your final draft. What new insights did you gain about letter writing by learning to write a business letter? What did you do well? What do you need to work on?

2 **Rubric for Self-Assessment** Assess your letter. For each question, circle a rating.

CRITERIA	RATING SCALE
	NOT VERY — VERY
IDEAS Does your letter show a clear and focused request for information?	1 2 3 4 5
ORGANIZATION How well have you organized your letter according to the business letter format you chose?	1 2 3 4 5
VOICE Is your writing lively and engaging, yet formal and polite?	1 2 3 4 5
WORD CHOICE How appropriate is the language for your audience?	1 2 3 4 5
CONVENTIONS How correct is your grammar, especially your use of independent and subordinate clauses?	1 2 3 4 5

Standardized Test Practice

Reading Skill: Setting a Purpose for Reading

Read the passage. Then answer the questions.

Penguins live all over the world, and four species belong to a category called warm weather penguins. One of these species is the African penguin.

Traits

The African penguin lives in coastal South Africa and its offshore islands. Like other warm weather penguins, it grows to between 5 and 8 pounds—smaller than its more famous cousins, the king penguin, which weighs around 30 pounds and the emperor penguin, which can reach 90 pounds! African penguins are similar in coloring to these larger penguins.

A Threatened Species

African penguins once numbered in the millions. Today, only about 50,000 nesting pairs live in their native **habitat.** Several factors have contributed to this huge decline. During the nineteenth century, humans invaded this bird's habitat, depriving the African penguin of vital nesting sites. During the twentieth century, almost half of these penguins' eggs were harvested. Recently, oil spills have polluted their waters. Fortunately, the African penguin is now a protected species.

1 Which of the following can help you set a purpose for reading this passage?

A. boldfaced terms and headings

B. headings and dates

C. boldfaced terms and statistics

D. headings and descriptions

2 The most likely purpose for reading this selection is to ________.

F. learn what actions to take to protect the African penguin

G. compare penguin species

H. learn about warm weather penguins

J. learn about the African penguin

Analysis: Elements of Research

Read the passage. Then, answer the questions.

Do you believe that women talk more than men? If you do, you are not alone. According to an often-cited statistic, the average woman speaks 20,000 words per day, while the average man speaks 7,000. This statistic was first published in the 2006 book, *The Female Brain.*

When psychologists James Pennebaker and Matthias Mehl heard this statistic, they decided to investigate whether it was true. What they learned surprised them, because they, too, had accepted the popular myth that women are more talkative than men. Pennebaker, Mehl, and their colleagues equipped 396 college students with small voice recorders that measured the number of words the person spoke each day. The researchers found that men and women are equally talkative. Both averaged about 16,000 words a day. One difference Pennebaker and Mehl did find, however, is that women tend to talk about people, while men tend to talk about things. Their study was published in the journal *Science*.

3 This source is probably an excerpt from ___________.

A. an autobiography

B. a history book

C. a magazine article

D. a diary entry

4 If you wanted to take notes on this source by **paraphrasing,** you would ___________.

F. restate the information in your own words

G. use the Cornell method of note-taking

H. quote the author's exact words

J. check the information against another source

5 If you wanted to use this source for a research report, how could you avoid **plagiarism?**

A. Cite the source if you use the writer's words or ideas.

B. Use different types of sources.

C. Make sure the source is reliable.

D. Paraphrase instead of quoting.

6 Which **note-taking method** would you use to see how major points and supporting details are related to each other?

F. note cards

G. idea web

H. Cornell method

J. Internet method

Timed Writing: Finding and Evaluating Sources

Directions Write what your research topic is. Describe what you have done to find information in your research so far. Review the sources you have found. Which one do you think will be the most useful? Why? Which one do you think will not be useful at all? Why? **(20 minutes)**

6-9 Reading Skills
Cause and Effect

In learning new reading skills, you will use special academic vocabulary. Knowing the right words will help you demonstrate your understanding.

Academic Vocabulary

Word	Meaning	Example Sentence
cause *n.* *Related word:* caused, causes	a reason or source	Jin knew the cat was the *cause* of his allergies.
effect *n.* *Related words:* effected, effective	a result or outcome	My mother warned me about the *effect* of the sun's rays on my skin if I didn't wear sunscreen.
affect *v.* *Related words:* affected, affects	to influence	Getting only an hour of sleep can *affect* your performance in school.

A **cause** is an event, action, or feeling that makes something happen. An **effect** is the result of that cause—it's what happens. Identifying causes and effects as you read can help you better understand why events occur. Here are some steps for identifying causes and effects.

- Circle an important event that takes place in a passage. This is an effect.
- Ask yourself questions such as *Why did this event happen?* and *What led up to this event?*
- Look for signal words, such as *because, since,* and *due to,* that indicate a cause.
- Use a graphic organizer to see the relationship between the causes and the effect in a text. Look at the example below.

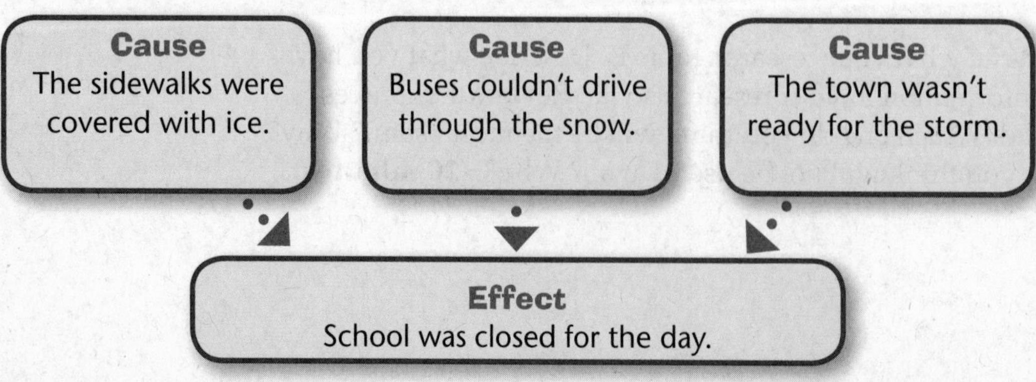

Cause
The sidewalks were covered with ice.
Cause
Buses couldn't drive through the snow.
Cause
The town wasn't ready for the storm.
Effect
School was closed for the day.

Directions Read the following passage. Notice how a student has identified the causes and effects of Japan's attack on Hawaii. Then, answer the questions.

from Hiroshima *by Laurence Yep*

. . . on December 7, 1941, Japanese planes attacked American ships in Hawaii without warning. Caught by surprise, many ships and planes were wrecked at the naval base, Pearl Harbor. The United States declared war on Japan and Japan's ally, Germany. With other countries, they fight a war called World War II.

By 1945, Germany has given up. Only Japan fights on. But the United States has a secret weapon—the atom bomb. Nothing is as powerful and as awful. The atom bomb is so terrible that the United States hopes it will make Japan stop fighting.

while reading your anchor book

1 **Cause and Effect** Complete the graphic organizer to show the effect of the Japanese attack on Hawaii.

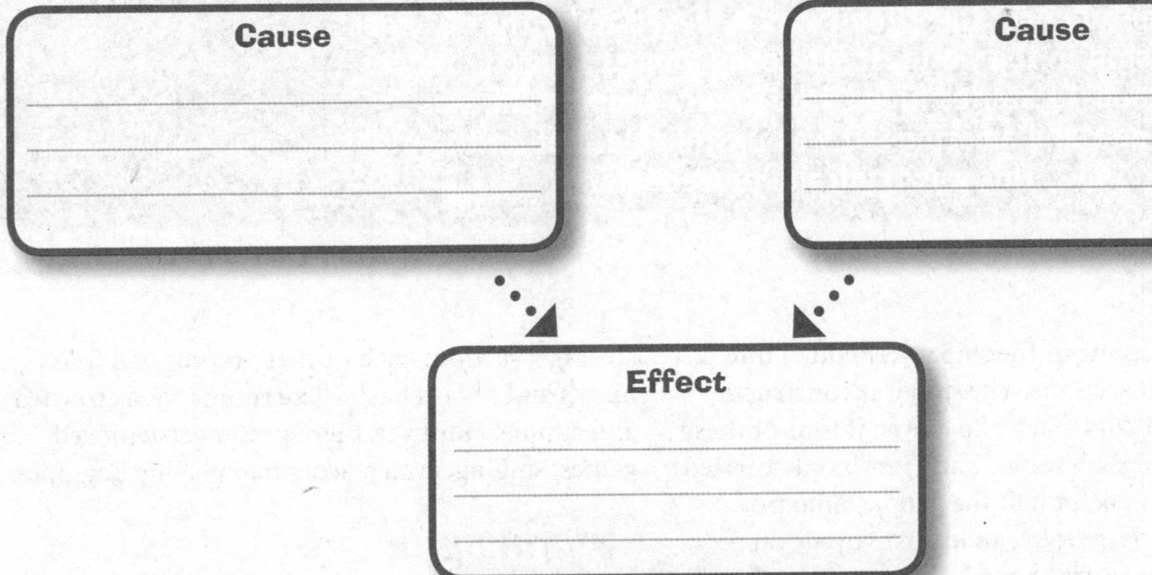

2 **Analyze** Why did the United States want to use the atom bomb against Japan?

Now analyze some other cause-and-effect relationships to determine why the *Titanic* sank. *Guiding Question:* How do you think the deaths of the people on the *Titanic* affected the communities they left behind?

The Titanic

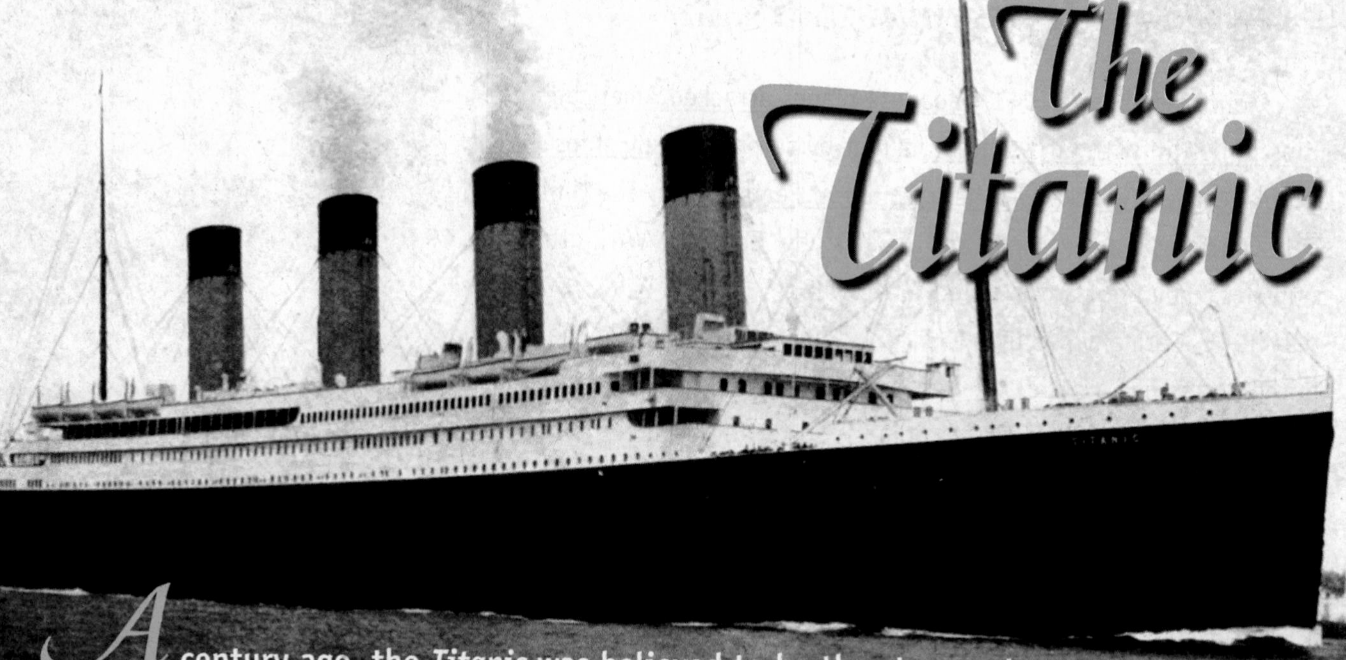

A century ago, the *Titanic* was believed to be the strongest and safest ship in the world. It stretched almost four city blocks long and stood 11 stories high. The *Titanic*, people said, was something new and amazing—it was unsinkable. But on the night of April 14, 1912, this was tragically proven wrong.

The *Titanic* was the length of four city blocks.

The hull, or frame of the ship, was divided into 16 watertight sections. The ship was constructed this way so it could stay afloat even if four of these sections filled with water. The *Titanic* only carried enough lifeboats for half the people onboard.

When the *Titanic* began its first voyage on April 10, there were about 2,200 men, women, and children aboard. Many of the passengers were rich and famous, like John Jacob Astor, one of the richest men in the world. He and other first-class passengers had rooms decorated like expensive hotel rooms. The second-class accommodations were not as grand, but they were still comfortable.

The *Titanic* also carried more than 700 emmigrants leaving their home countries to settle in a new land. Their rooms were located in the steerage[1] section. Each of these rooms had four bunks and a wash basin. The rooms were crowded and simple. However, these passengers enjoyed games, singing, even a Scotsman playing bagpipes.

Warnings at Sea

It was a clear, cool day on April 14, as the *Titanic* traveled full steam ahead in the North Atlantic. However, as early as 9:00 A.M., the wireless telegraph operator received warning messages regarding icebergs ahead. Over the next few hours, a total of six messages came from other ships.

[1] **steerage** (stir′ ij) *n.* a section in some ships with the poorest accommodations, occupied by the passengers paying the lowest fare.

The *Titanic's* captain, Edward J. Smith, received only some of these messages because the ship did not have a system set up for passing on messages from the operator to the crew to the captain. For this reason, no one person saw all of the messages. If the six warnings had been mapped out, they would have shown a wall of ice in the path of the *Titanic*. Captain Smith simply asked the men on lookout to watch for icebergs. The lookouts could only use their eyes, because they did not have binoculars with them on the lookout platform.

Disaster at Sea

Shortly before midnight, one of the men on lookout saw a large, white shape straight ahead. He rang bells, and a message was telephoned to the bridge where the captain commanded the ship. An iceberg was directly ahead of them—and the *Titanic* was headed straight for it!

The ship's officers gave orders to turn the *Titanic* so that it would miss the iceberg, but they were too late. The *Titanic* hit the iceberg and the ship slowly came to a stop. In one of the boiler rooms, where the engines were located, alarms went off, a wall gave way, and water began to rush in.

Just twenty-five minutes after midnight, the crew rushed to call other ships for help. Ships hearing the call began to change course to come to the aid of the *Titanic*. One ship, the *Californian*, was nearby but the radio operator did not get the message.

By 12:45 A.M., as water gushed into the *Titanic*, lifeboats were lowered. Women and children were instructed to get into the boats, but they did not realize how serious the danger was, so some saw no reason to take a ride in the icy sea. Some men laughed as they helped their wives into boats. They thought all would be well by breakfast.

The crew sent rockets into the sky, trying to attract the attention of other ships. The passengers began to realize that the *Titanic* was sinking.

At 2:20 A.M., the *Titanic* stood on end before sliding to its grave in the dark sea. The great, "unsinkable" ship sank in the cold waters of the North Atlantic. More than 1,500 people died in the disaster.

The Survivors

People were in the freezing water, struggling to reach the lifeboats. While most boats still had room in them, very little effort was made to pick up the swimmers.

The *Carpathia*, the first ship to come to the aid of the passengers, started taking people aboard by 4:10 A.M. There were about 700 survivors, including women, children, and men.

Other ships racing to the rescue learned that they were too late. The *Californian*, the one ship that had been nearby, had seen the rockets that the *Titanic* sent up. Yet, the crew was uncertain what they meant. At about 5:40 A.M., one crew member woke up the radio operator. The operator turned on his radio and contacted another ship. It was then that he learned that the *Titanic* had hit an iceberg and had sunk.

News of survivors was slow in reaching relatives. Newspaper stories were based on only a few facts, and many reports were false. On April 18, more than 30,000 eager people waited in New York as the *Carpathia* arrived.

Top: Purser Hugh Walter McElroy (left) and Captain Edward J. Smith worked on the *Titanic*.
Below: Passengers stroll along the deck of the *Titanic*.

The Investigations

In the weeks following the tragedy, the United States Senate and the Board of Trade in England held investigations. The reports stated that the *Titanic* had not been carrying enough lifeboats and their boats were not fully loaded. If the boats had been loaded to full capacity, at least 400 more lives could have been saved.

Investigators also found that the *Titanic* had been traveling too fast. As warnings about ice had reached the ship, the *Titanic* should have been moving at a slower speed.

Much of the blame for the lost lives went to the crew of the *Californian*. If they had helped the *Titanic* right away, many of the passengers might have been saved.

Exploring the Wreckage

The story of the *Titanic* has continued to unfold. In 1985, a team of scientists led by Robert E. Ballard of the United States and Jean-Louis Michel of France, found the wreckage of the ship. People had thought for years that the *Titanic* sank because of a gash—a long, deep cut—in its hull. However, one major flaw was that the steel used in the hull was too brittle for the cold waters. That meant that it broke easily when the ship hit the iceberg.

Many stories, articles, and films have described the greatest sea tragedy in history. In one nonfiction film, people can see the actual remains of the ship's railing and imagine what it was like to stand there almost one hundred years ago.

Exploring the *Titanic*

After finding the *Titanic,* Dr. Robert Ballard and Jean-Louis Michel and a team of researchers returned nine months later in 1986 to study the ship. Exploring two miles beneath the ocean's surface proved a unique challenge. The water pressure at that depth is so great that it would kill a person quickly. For this reason, the researchers had to prepare for the trip almost as they would for a trip into outer space. To reach the *Titanic,* the team used *Alvin,* a deep-ocean submersible that can carry three people at a time—two scientists and a pilot. *Alvin* can dive as deep as 4,500 meters (about three miles). Each dive lasts six to ten hours. The little sub has two robotic arms and a basket for collecting samples. Ballard's team also used a small undersea robot to explore and photograph the *Titanic's* many nooks and crannies. Over a period of several weeks, Ballard and his team took thousands of photos.

The 35,200-pound *Alvin* searches the ocean floor for the *Titanic* off the coast of Newfoundland.

Thinking About the Selection

The *Titanic*

1 **Cause and Effect** Complete the graphic organizer to show some of the reasons why the *Titanic* sank.

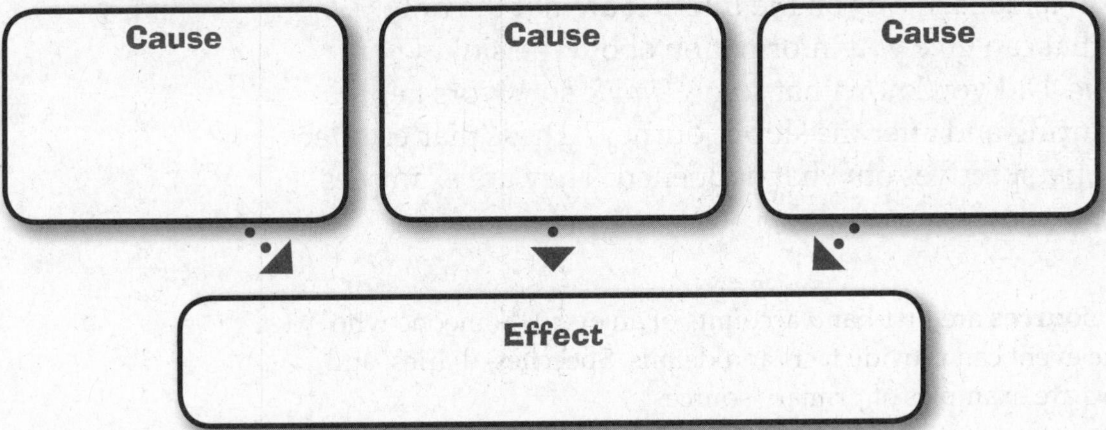

2 **Speculate** Had there been enough lifeboats onboard the *Titanic*, do you think all of the passengers could have been saved? Explain.

3 **Compare and Contrast** Compare the photograph of the *Titanic* on page 482 to the text of the feature "Exploring the *Titanic*." What sort of information does each offer? Why do you think a magazine article includes both words and photographs?

Write Answer the following questions in your Reader's Journal.

4 **Analyze** How do you think the deaths of the people on the *Titanic* affected the communities they left behind?

5 **Apply** Find an important event that happens in your Anchor Book. Then, using the cause-and-effect graphic organizer, identify and describe causes of this event.

Ready for a Free-Choice Book? *Your teacher may ask you if you would like to choose another book to read on your own. Select a book that fits your interest and that you'll enjoy. As you read, think about how your new book compares with your Anchor Book.*

6–10 Comparing Source Texts
Primary and Secondary Sources

Articles in a magazine or on the Internet are not the only sources that can give you information about the sinking of the *Titanic*. Did you know that some *Titanic* survivors kept diaries during and after the ship's journey? These diaries offer different perspectives on what happened. They are examples of primary sources.

Primary sources are first-hand accounts of an event. Someone who was at the event can provide facts and details. Speeches, diaries, and interviews are examples of primary sources.

Secondary sources are second-hand accounts of an event. These are an author's interpretation of information that he or she has gathered. Secondary sources can include quotations and ideas from primary sources.

Here are events and examples of the sources you could use to find information about each event.

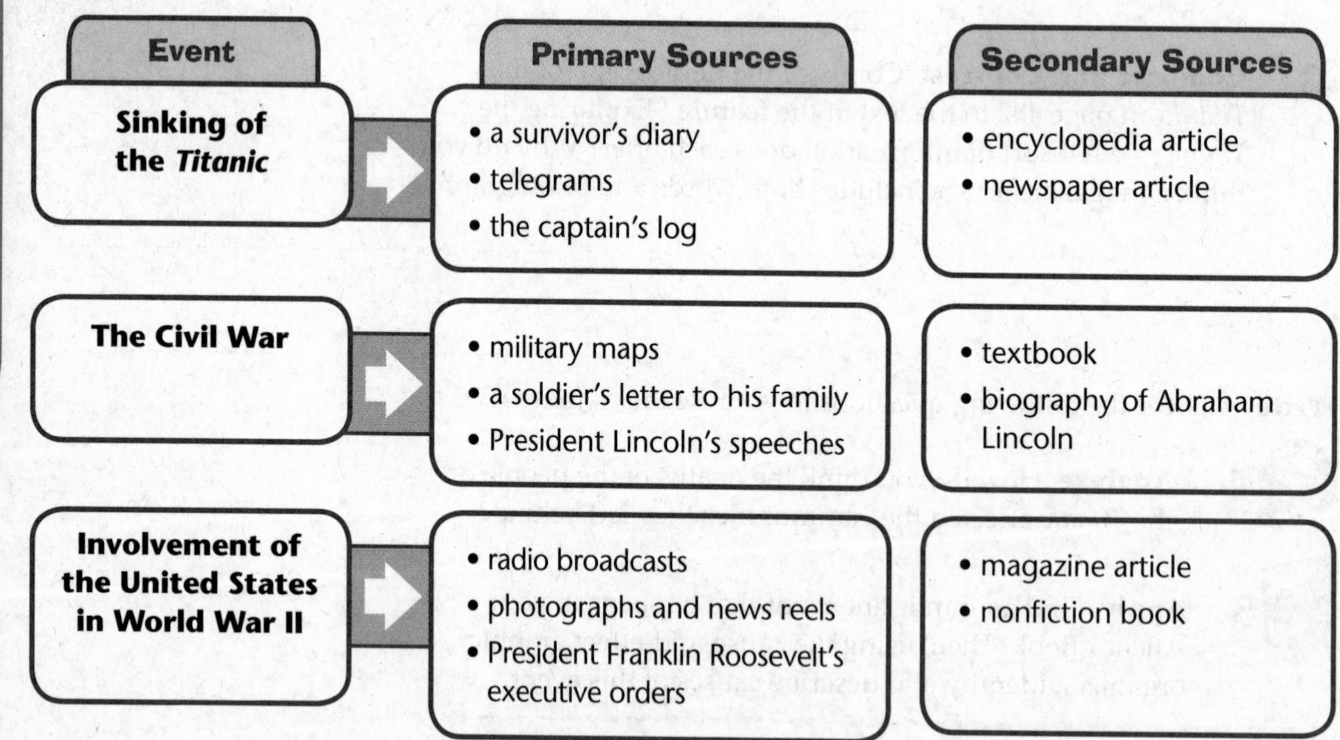

Event	Primary Sources	Secondary Sources
Sinking of the *Titanic*	• a survivor's diary • telegrams • the captain's log	• encyclopedia article • newspaper article
The Civil War	• military maps • a soldier's letter to his family • President Lincoln's speeches	• textbook • biography of Abraham Lincoln
Involvement of the United States in World War II	• radio broadcasts • photographs and news reels • President Franklin Roosevelt's executive orders	• magazine article • nonfiction book

Now it's time to read some primary and secondary sources. You can also go back to your own research from previous lessons and decide what primary sources or secondary sources you have used.

Directions Read the excerpts. Then, answer the questions.

Primary Source

The following speech was given by John F. Kennedy at his inauguration as President on January 20, 1961.

Go Online
About the Author
Visit: PHSchool.com
Web Code: exe-6601

from the Inaugural Address of John F. Kennedy

In the long history of the world, only a few generations have been granted the role of defending freedom in its hour of maximum danger . . . . The energy, the faith, the devotion which we bring to this endeavor will light our country and all who serve it—and the glow from that fire can truly light the world.

And so, my fellow Americans: ask not what your country can do for you—ask what you can do for your country.

My fellow citizens of the world: ask not what America will do for you, but what together we can do for the freedom of man.

Secondary Source

The following is an author's interpretation of Kennedy's speech. Notice how the writer uses a quotation from the primary source.

President John F. Kennedy's first speech to the nation was one of hope, optimism, and challenge. He charged his electorate,". . . my fellow Americans: ask not what your country can do for you—ask what you can do for your country." Not stopping with his fellow Americans, he even invited the "citizens of the world" to work together for the "freedom of man."

1 **Compare and Contrast** How is the information in the two excerpts similar? How is it different?

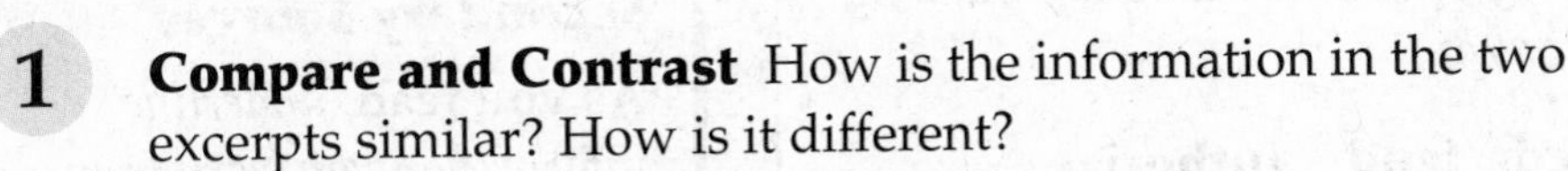

2 **Evaluate** What is the benefit of reading Kennedy's speech (primary source) rather than the interpretation (secondary source)? What is the benefit of reading the interpretation?

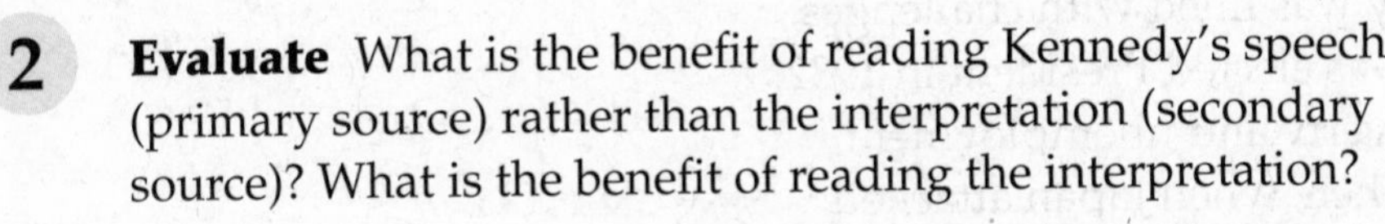

while reading your anchor book

Now use your knowledge of primary and secondary sources to distinguish between these two selections.
Guiding Question: **How were Japanese American communities in America shaped by the events of World War II?**

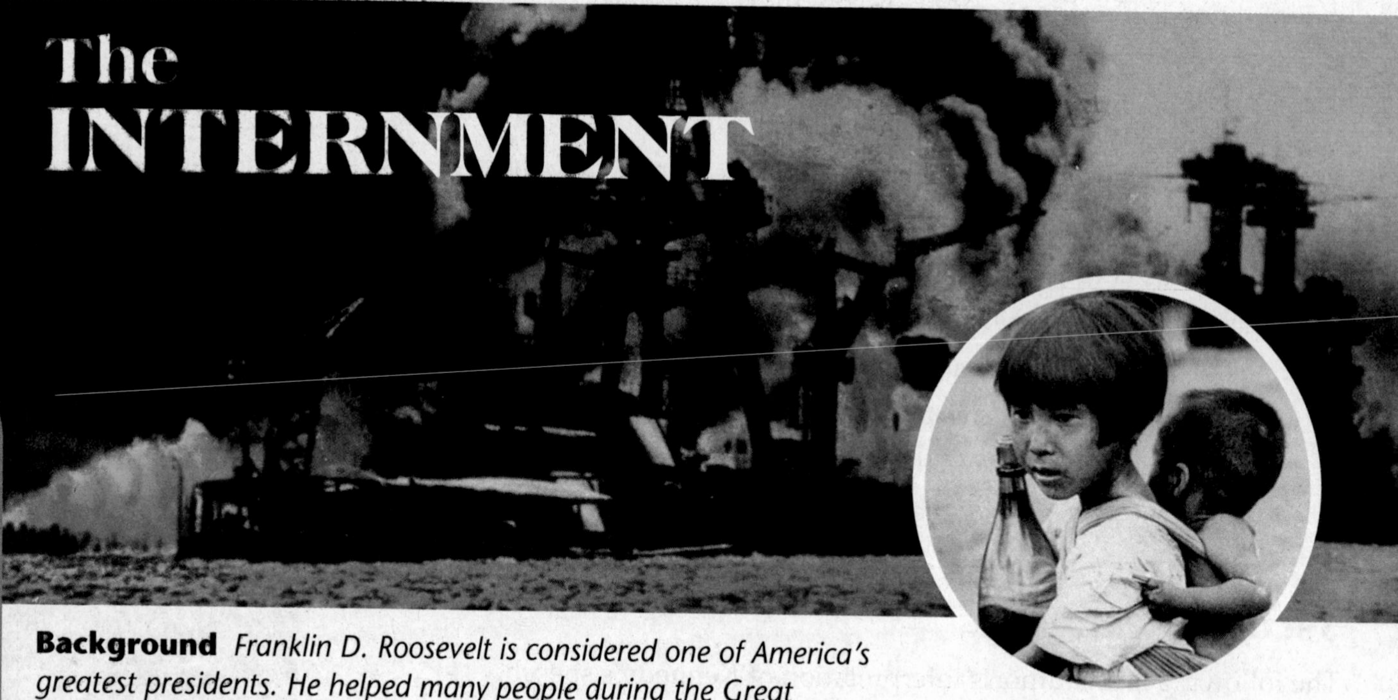

The INTERNMENT

▲ More than one half of the Japanese Americans moved into internment were children.

Background *Franklin D. Roosevelt is considered one of America's greatest presidents. He helped many people during the Great Depression and led the United States to victory in World War II. However, Roosevelt has been criticized for his actions in moving many Japanese Americans into* ***internment***[1] *during the war.*

Vocabulary Builder

Before you read, *you will discuss the following words. In the Vocabulary Builder box in the margin, use a vocabulary building strategy to make the words your own.*

neutrality deployed fend authorize

As you read, *draw a box around unfamiliar words you could add to your vocabulary. Use context clues to unlock their meaning.*

Marking the Text

Primary and Secondary Sources

As you read, *underline information you learn from the passages. Determine if each passage is a primary or secondary source.*

Franklin D. Roosevelt's presidency was filled with challenges and difficult decisions. When he was elected President in 1932, he faced the task of ending the poverty and unemployment caused by the Great Depression. Then, when Japan attacked Pearl Harbor in 1941, he took on what may have been his greatest challenge—guiding America through World War II. The war

[1] **internment** (in′ turn ′mənt) *n.* confinement

forced Roosevelt to make difficult decisions about how to achieve victory without compromising America's values.

Before Pearl Harbor, the United States gave assistance to other countries at war, but still considered itself neutral. With a surprise attack on the military base in Hawaii, however, this **neutrality** ended. America was officially at war with Japan, Germany, and Italy, who had formed an alliance.

With the onset of war, life in America changed. Thousands of soldiers were **deployed** to Europe and the Pacific. Many of those who stayed behind built machinery and other equipment for the war effort. Patriotism ran strong, and many people bought war bonds to support the war effort. Along with these feelings came suspicion toward anyone and anything associated with America's enemies in Germany and Japan.

It was in this atmosphere that Roosevelt made one of his most controversial decisions. He signed Executive Order 9066—an order that forced more than 120,000 Japanese Americans to leave their homes on the West Coast for internment in camps, where they were forced to live until near the end of the war. Roosevelt said that the internment was necessary to keep America safe. He was afraid that Japanese Americans who were still loyal to Japan might spy or otherwise secretly act against the United States.

After the order was given, many Japanese Americans on the West Coast were given ten days to relocate to the camps. They were allowed to bring three kinds of items: toiletries, clothing, and bed linens. Families faced difficult decisions: would they store their belongings or sell them? Pets were not allowed in the camps, so where would they go? Most chose to sell their belongings for low prices and leave their animals either with a neighbor, or on their own to **fend** for themselves.

Life in the camps was tough. Each room was furnished with an army cot, wood stove, and a single light bulb. Some of the rooms were former horse stalls and smelled of manure, and the walls were made of a flimsy black tar paper. Still, the residents of the camps were able to live their lives. Adults spent time planting gardens and forming clubs. Children attended schools taught by people who had been teachers before the war.

By the end of 1944, the United States government realized that the internees were not a threat. After nearly two years, the internment camps began closing on January 2, 1945. It took even longer for many people to acknowledge that Roosevelt's decision was a mistake. In 1988, President Ronald Reagan said that forcing American citizens into camps because of their nationality was wrong. This admission could not undo President Roosevelt's decision, but it acknowledged the sacrifice Japanese Americans made during the war—one that could have been avoided.

Vocabulary Builder

neutrality
(nyo͞o tral′ ə tē) *n.*

Meaning

deployed
(dē ploid′) *v.*

Meaning

fend
(fend) *v.*

Meaning

Marking the Text

EXECUTIVE ORDER 9066

By Franklin D. Roosevelt

Background *The following excerpt is from President Franklin D. Roosevelt's order that forced Americans of Japanese descent on the West Coast to relocate. Though the order does not specify where the people should go, camps were set up throughout the country to house more than 120,000 people.*

EXECUTIVE ORDER[1]
AUTHORIZING THE SECRETARY OF WAR TO PRESCRIBE MILITARY AREAS

WHEREAS the successful prosecution[2] of the war requires every possible protection against espionage[3] and against sabotage[4] to national-defense material, national-defense premises, and national-defense utilities. . . .

NOW, THEREFORE, by virtue of the authority vested in me as President of the United States, and Commander in Chief of the Army and Navy, I hereby **authorize** and direct the Secretary of War . . . to prescribe military areas in such places and of such extent as he or the appropriate Military Commander may determine, from which any or all persons may be excluded. . . .

I hereby further authorize and direct all Executive Departments, independent establishments and other Federal Agencies, to assist the Secretary of War or the said Military Commanders in carrying out this Executive Order, including the furnishing of medical aid, hospitalization, food, clothing, transportation, use of land, shelter, and other supplies, equipment, utilities, facilities, and services.

Vocabulary Builder

authorize
(ô'thər īz') *v.*

Meaning

1 **executive order** (eg zek' yo͞o tiv ôr'dər) *n.* an order or rule given by the president.

2 **prosecution** (präs'ə kyo͞o' shən) *n.* the continuation of something to its completion.

3 **espionage** (es'pē ə näzh') *n.* the act or practice of spying.

4 **sabotage** (sab'ə täzh') *v.* deliberate destruction by an enemy.

Vocabulary Builder

After you read, *review the words you decided to add to your vocabulary. Write the meaning of the words you have learned in context. Look up the other words in a dictionary, glossary, thesaurus, or electronic resource.*

Thinking About the Selection

The Internment *and* Executive Order 9066

Go Online
About the Author
Visit: PHSchool.com
Web Code: exe-6602

1 **Distinguish** What do you learn from "The Internment" that you don't learn from "Executive Order 9066"?

2 **Analyze** Is "The Internment" a primary or a secondary source? Explain why.

3 **Speculate** Why do you think President Roosevelt was afraid the Japanese people living in America would act secretly against the United States?

4 **Infer** Can you cite "Executive Order 9066" as a primary source? Why or why not?

5 **Respond** Do you think the executive order was fair? Why or why not?

Write Answer the following questions in your Reader's Journal.

6 **Discuss** How were Japanese American communities in America shaped by the events of World War II?

7 **Analyze** Determine whether or not your Anchor Book is a primary or secondary source. Explain how the information in your book helps you to know.

while reading your anchor book

6-11 The Research Process

Drafting Your Research Report

So far, you have chosen a topic, researched it, and taken notes. Now you are ready to write the first draft of your research report. What information will you include? You can begin with an outline to organize your notes in an understandable way.

The following tips can help you to write a strong and organized draft.

1. Know your focus Describe the main idea of your report in one or two sentences. This brief description is called a **focus statement.** Be sure to make your focus statement clear and specific.

2. Know your audience Keep in mind who will read your writing. For your science teacher, you would include more complex language and scientific terms. For a group of first graders, you would use simple vocabulary and short sentences.

3. Organization How will you present the information in your report? Look at the methods of organization shown below and the sample report title for each.

Chronological
describes events in the order in which they happened.

"The Life of Harriet Tubman" details the life of this famous woman.

Compare and Contrast
shows the ways in which two subjects are alike and different.

"A Better Power Source: Wind vs. Sun?" compares and contrasts these two energy sources.

Cause and Effect
explains how an event, action, or situation causes another event, action, or situation.

"How a Car Engine Works" explains a complex process that helps people to get where they need to go.

Think about your topic. Describe your audience and the organization method you will use. Then write a clear focus statement.

Audience: ______________________ **Organization Method:** ______________________

Focus Statement: ____

____

while reading your anchor book

Planning an Outline

An outline is like a map—it will help guide you through the writing of your first draft. Many writers use a graphic organizer like the one below to help them set up an outline. Fill out the chart to help you organize the information you will include in your outline.

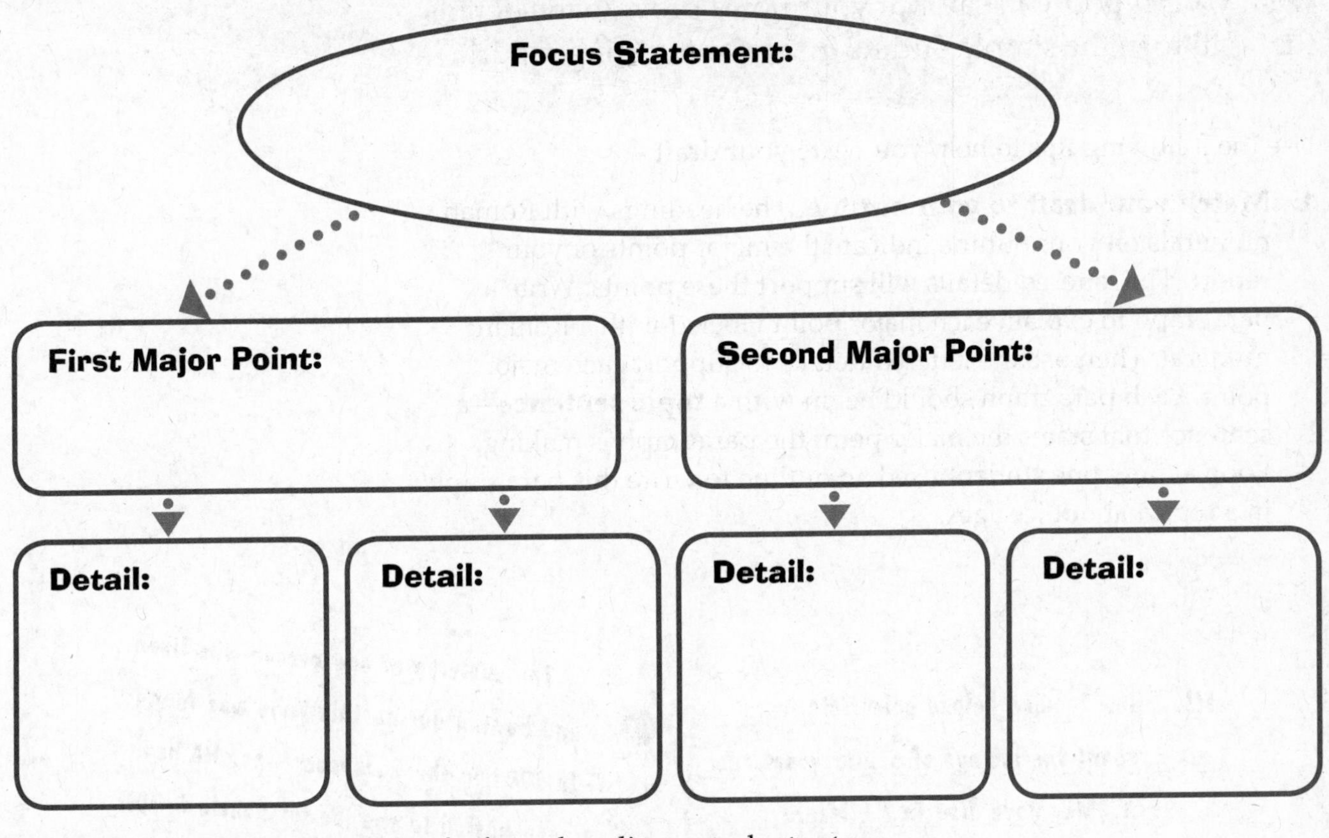

Look at the following example of a formal outline a student set up using an organizer. The student used a numbering format to structure the facts and details.

Formal Outline

- Use Roman numerals (I, II, III) for each major point.
- Use capital letters (A, B, C) to list supporting details under each Roman numeral.

The Ice Age

I. Introduction

II. What causes an ice age
   - A. Large amounts of water trapped under ice
   - B. Occurs every 200 million years or so
   - C. Climate changes

III. How Iceman helped scientists learn about the ice age of 5,000 years ago
   - A. May have died in a blizzard
   - B. His clothes and tools were studied

Use the graphic organizer you completed to write your outline on a separate sheet of paper.

while reading your anchor book

Writing Your Draft

Now that you have an outline, you're ready to write your draft. Remember, your outline gives you a broad idea of what your report will say, but your notes provide the details that will turn the simple outline into an interesting report.

Use the following tips to help you write your draft.

1. **Match your draft to your outline.** The headings with Roman numerals on your outline indicate the major points of your report. The lettered details will support these points. Write a paragraph to explain each major point labeled with a Roman numeral. Then use the lettered details to support each major point. Each paragraph should begin with a **topic sentence**—a sentence that states the major point the paragraph is making. Look at how one student used an outline to write this paragraph in a report about ice ages.

III. How Iceman helped scientists learn about the ice age of 5,000 years ago
   A. May have died in a blizzard
   B. His clothes and tools were studied

The skeleton of one person who lived and hunted during this time was found in 1901 in the European Alps. He had been buried in the ice for nearly 5,000 years. Nicknamed the "Iceman," scientists believed that perhaps he was caught in a blizzard or that he ran out of food, became weak, and died. Scientists were able to learn a lot about this ancient period from the leather clothes and animal skins he was wearing and the tools he was carrying.

2. **Support your major points with facts.** Make sure every piece of information you include supports the focus of your report. Using your outline, write sentences to express each major point in your report. Leave spaces between each major point to add the supporting facts, explanations, details, and examples that you included in your notes. Do more research if anything is unclear.

while reading your anchor book

3. **Connect your ideas.** Think about how to connect your facts, details, and explanations so they all work together. Use the words *however* and *as a result* to show connections between ideas and paragraphs.

Below is a student's report on ice ages. Notice how she supports her focus statement by including clear and detailed information.

Student Model: Drafting

Elizabeth Clearly, Maplewood, NJ

Ice Ages

Ice ages occur every two hundred million years or so. An ice age is defined as a long period of cold where large amounts of water are trapped under ice. Although ice ages happened long ago, studying their causes and effects helps contemporary scientists understand geological conditions of the world today.

The author gives a clear focus statement.

When an ice age does occur, ice covers much of the Earth. This ice forms when the climate changes. The polar regions become very cold and the temperatures drop everywhere else. The ice is trapped in enormous mountains of ice called glaciers. Glaciers can be as large as a continent in size. When the Earth's temperature warms up, the glaciers start to melt, forming rivers and lakes. Glaciers' tremendous weight and size can actually wear away mountains and valleys as the glaciers melt and move. The melting also raises ocean levels.

There are many different theories to explain why ice ages occur, but no one knows for sure. Many scientists agree that it is probably due to a combination of causes, including changes in the Sun's intensity, the distance of the Earth from the Sun, changes in ocean currents, the continental plates rubbing up against each other, and the varying amounts of carbon dioxide in the atmosphere.

Here the author uses a topic sentence to state a major point, which she then supports with factual information in this paragraph.

Good to Know!
Hubbard Glacier, Alaska, has been advancing towards the Gulf of Alaska since 1895. If it continues to advance, it will close off a deep inlet, Russell Fjord, creating the largest glacier-dammed lake in North America.

During the last ice age, or the Wisconsin Ice Age, people were living on the Earth. These people saw ice and snow all the time. It was never warm enough to melt, so it piled up. In summertime, women fished in chilly streams. The men hunted year-round.

The skeleton of one person who lived and hunted during this time was found in 1901 in the European Alps. He had been buried in the ice for nearly 5,000 years. Nicknamed the "Iceman," scientists believed that perhaps he was suddenly caught by a blizzard or that he possibly ran out of food, became weak, and died.Scientists were able to learn a lot about this ancient period from the leather clothes and animal skins he was wearing and the tools he was carrying.

Ice ages also affect life today. The ice sheets that formed weighed a huge amount. When the ice retreated, it left behind large rocks and other debris which otherwise would not be there. Also, without ice ages, large bodies of water like the Great Lakes simply wouldn't exist. We depend on these bodies of water every day for fresh drinking water, recreation, and shipping large quantities of materials.

Scientists discovered ice ages because of Louis Agassiz, a nineteenth-century scientist who is sometimes called the "Father of Glaciology." In Switzerland, he saw boulders or granite far from where any granite should be. He theorized that glaciers had caused these geologic features.

In each section, the author explores a different aspect of the ice ages. These are her major points. Here she is explaining a scientific discovery.

Baron Gerard De Geer, a Swedish geologist, estimated the end of the last ice age. In a similar way to the way we count tree rings to estimate a tree's age, De Geer used layers of sediment left by glaciers' summer melts to calculate the history of an ice age. He did much of his work in Sweden, but he also visited areas that had been affected by glaciers in New England.

Thanks to scientists like De Geer and Agassiz, we know about that remote age when glaciers roamed the Earth. We can now estimate the history of ice ages and determine what features—valleys, inland seas, mountains, lakes, rocks—were caused as you can see by the map displayed here of the Eastern United States. There is still a lot more to be discovered about ice ages, but one thing is clear: Glaciers had a powerful effect on the world as we know it today.

The author restates her focus statement and summarizes the major points that she presented in the introduction and supported in the body of the paper.

Thinking About the Research Process

Drafting

1 **Explain** How can an outline help you write a rough draft?

2 **Decide** Which organization would you choose for a research report on the topic "Football: The Beginnings"? Why?

3 **Evaluate** Would the following statement make a good focus statement for a research report? Explain why or why not.

> California has some very colorful people and intriguing events that have been written about throughout the history of the state.

4 **Speculate** Who do you think the audience was for the student who wrote the report on ice ages? Explain?

Research

Now think about your own research report.

5 **Apply** On a separate sheet of paper, use your outline to write your draft. For each Roman numeral topic in your outline, write the matching idea in your draft. Do the same for each capital-letter subtopic.

Write Answer the following question in your Reader's Journal.

6 **Apply** Identify the organization method, such as chronological, compare-and-contrast, or cause-and-effect, that is used in a passage in your Anchor Book. Explain why the author might have chosen this type of organization.

6-12 The Research Process
Revising Your Research Report

Good writers know that the process of writing a research report doesn't end with a draft. There's still revising to do! This step gives you a chance to improve vocabulary, change paragraph structure, and liven up your writing.

Analyzing Your Organization

This is the first step in revising your research report. After writing your first draft, you need to make sure your major points and details are organized and easy to understand. Here are some tips to help you through the process.

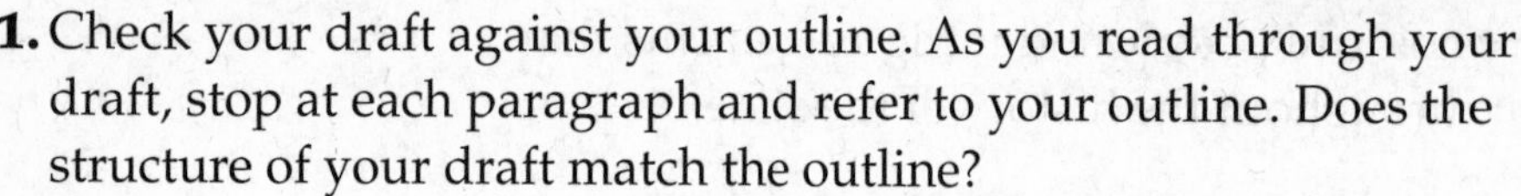

1. Check your draft against your outline. As you read through your draft, stop at each paragraph and refer to your outline. Does the structure of your draft match the outline?
2. Mark each paragraph and sentence with the Roman numeral and capital letter on your outline that matches the details in your paragraph. Look at the paragraph a student has marked and compare it to the student's outline.

I. Introduction
II. Horned Toads
   A. Habitat
   B. Diet

(II.A.) Horned toads live in hot, dry places throughout the southern United States. (II.B.) During the day, they look for food. (II.B.) Horned toads eat slow-moving creatures that live on the ground, like spiders, insects, and ticks. (II.B.) Their favorite food, however, seems to be ants.

Notice that the student used the same Roman numeral and capital letter (II.B) for details that support the same idea.

Apply Check the outline of your research report against your rough draft. Then describe what you learned about the organization of your draft.

Revising Your Paragraphs

Now that you have tightened up the organization of your report, it is time to take a look at each individual paragraph. You want to make sure your sentences work together to express the major point.

Use the checklist as you revise your paragraphs. Each paragraph should have the following elements.

- ❑ **A topic sentence (T)** that states the major point a paragraph is making
- ❑ **A restatement (R),** or more information about the major point in the topic sentence
- ❑ **Details (D)** that include facts and examples about the major point
- ❑ Information that is necessary and in agreement
- ❑ Smooth transitions between sentences

Look at the student model below. In the parentheses before each sentence write *T*, *R*, or *D* to identify each sentence as a topic sentence, restatement, or detail.

> (T) Horned toads lizards are built to live in the desert. ( ) When the temperature gets too warm, they use their bodies to burrow in the sand to cool off. ( ) With their noses, they dig head-first into the sand. ( ) Then, with their flattened heads, they wiggle forward, using their spiky sides to shovel dirt over themselves.

Writing Stronger Sentences

Your sentences should flow smoothly and express your ideas clearly.

After revising your paragraphs, be sure your sentence structure is strong and free of choppy, hard-to-follow sentences. Use the checklist as you revise your sentences.

- ❑ I have used a variety of simple, compound, and complex sentences.
- ❑ I have used clear, precise language and strengthened my writing with synonyms and antonyms.
- ❑ I have used consistent verb tenses.
- ❑ I have defined technical or difficult words.

Directions Read the following excerpt from a rough draft of a research report about ice ages. Notice the revision ideas on the right. Then, answer the questions that follow.

Student Model: Revising

Elizabeth Clearly, Maplewood, NJ

Large animals such as mammoths lived during cold periods called ice ages. An ice age is defined as a long period of cold. Large amounts of water are trapped under ice. Glaciers can be as large as a continent in size. Although ice ages happened long ago, studying their causes and effects helps contemporary scientists understand geological conditions of the world today.

When an ice age does occur, ice covers much of the Earth. This ice forms when the climate changes. The polar regions become very cold and the temperatures drop everywhere else. The ice is trapped in enormous mountains of ice called glaciers. When the Earth's temperature warms up, the glaciers start to melt. When the glaciers melt, they form rivers and lakes. Glaciers' tremendous weight and size can actually wear away mountains and valleys as the glaciers melt and move. The melting also raises ocean levels. There are many different theories to explain why the ice ages occur, but no one knows for sure.

Many scientists agree that it is probably due to a combination of causes, including changes in the sun's intensity, the distance of the Earth from the Sun, changes in ocean currents, the continental plates rubbing up against each other, and the varying amounts of carbon dioxide in the atmosphere.

This detail does not restate information in the first sentence—it simply repeats it.

The writer should combine these two choppy sentences

This paragraph contains many details, but the major point is not introduced in a topic sentence.

Good to Know! Glacier National Park in Montana was named for the more than fifty glaciers that formed its landscape millions of years ago.

while reading your anchor book

Thinking About the Research Process

Revising Your Research Report

1 **Evaluate** Look at the student model. How well did the student organize ideas in the first paragraph? Explain your answer.

2 **Apply** Combine the two highlighted sentences in the second paragraph to make them less choppy. Write your revision.

3 **Analyze** The third paragraph is missing a topic sentence that introduces the major point. Think about how you would describe the major point that the paragraph is making. Then write a topic sentence for the paragraph.

Research

Now think about your own research report.

4 **Revise** Exchange your draft with a partner. Then, on another sheet of paper, jot down some comments about how his or her report might be revised. Share your ideas with your partner. On the same sheet of paper, describe how you will change your own report based on your partner's suggestions.

Write Answer the following question in your Reader's Journal.

5 **Apply** Find a paragraph in your Anchor Book that includes short sentences. Revise the sentence by changing them into compound and complex sentences. Write your new paragraph.

6-13 The Research Process
Proofreading and Publishing

You are almost done with your report! There are two important things left to do: cite your sources and proofread. When you **cite** your sources, you give credit to other people's work. **Proofreading** means checking your spelling, punctuation, and word choice.

Cite Your Sources

Citing your sources helps you to avoid plagiarism. It also lets your reader know where to find more information if he or she wants to research the topic further. Follow these guidelines to cite your sources.

What to Cite

- Cite ideas that are not your own.
- Cite facts that are not commonly known.

  Commonly known fact: The Great Barrier Reef is off the coast of Australia.

  Fact that must be cited: Scientists at the Institute for Climate Studies predict that the Great Barrier Reef will be dead by 2050.

- Cite a **direct quotation.** When you use the exact words that another person wrote or said, put quotation marks around the words or sentence in addition to citing.

> Marine biologist Harvey Weinger states, "The Great Barrier Reef will become a giant skeleton, not a tourist attraction, if we do not work together to save it" (Shelley, p. 25).

Internal citations are enclosed in parentheses.

1. Put the author's last name, followed by a comma.
2. Include the page number from which the information was taken.

How to Cite

- Sentences containing a direct quote or a fact from a source need an **internal citation.** An internal citation comes at the end of the sentence, but always before the sentence's ending punctuation, as in the example above.
- Every report has a **works cited list.** This is an alphabetized list of your sources that comes at the end of your report. There are certain rules about punctuation to follow when you list each source. Refer to the works cited list on page 502 for additional examples.

To cite a book or play:

Author's last name, author's first name. *Title.* City of publication: Publisher, date of publication.

Example: Shelley, Lilith. *The Future of the Great Barrier Reef.* New York: Pace Publishers, 2007.

To cite a magazine or newspaper article, short story, or poem:

Author's last name, author's first name. "Title." *Title of magazine or newspaper, story collection,* or *poetry anthology.* Date of publication: page number.

Example: Poisson, Gene. "Great Barrier Reef Sees Worst Bleaching in 4 Years." *The Marine Environment* January 3, 2004: 13.

To cite a Web site:

Author (if given). "Title of Web page." Sponsor of Web site. Date of article <Web site address>

Example: Forte, Diane. "Coral Bleaching." International Conservation of Reefs. November 20, 2005. <http://www.icreefs.org/bleaching.html>

Proofread Your Report

You don't want a spelling mistake or other small error to distract your reader from the content of your report. Use the checklist to proofread your report.

Proofreading Checklist

- ❑ Identify and fix grammatical, spelling, or punctuation mistakes.
- ❑ Are the names of the authors you've quoted in your report spelled correctly?
- ❑ Did you confirm the titles of the books, articles, or other sources?
- ❑ When in doubt, go back to the source to check the information.
- ❑ Check that all sources are cited and included in the works cited list.

Publishing and Presenting Your Work

Try one of these ways of sharing your work with others.

Share your report with a large audience. Find an organization that would be interested in your report. Send it for publication.

Deliver a speech. Give a speech to another class. Use your focus statement as a guide and include only the most important details.

Directions Read the following portion of a student's final draft.

Student Model: Writing

Elizabeth Cleary, Maplewood, NJ

Ice Ages

Ice ages occur every two hundred million years or so. An ice age is defined as a long period of cold where large amounts of water are trapped under ice. Although ice ages happened long ago, studying their causes and effects helps contemporary scientists understand geological conditions of the world today.

When an ice age does occur, ice covers much of the Earth. This ice forms when the climate changes. The polar regions become very cold and the temperatures drop everywhere else. The ice is trapped in enormous mountains of ice called glaciers. Glaciers can be as large as a continent in size. When the Earth's temperature warms up, the glaciers start to melt, forming rivers and lakes. Glaciers' tremendous weight and size can actually wear away mountains and valleys as the glaciers melt and move. The melting also raises ocean levels.

What causes an ice age? According to different scientists, there could be a number of causes. For example, some scientists have theorized that the Earth's change in tilt affects global temperatures. The farther away the Earth is to the Sun, the less heat it gets; the closer it is, the more heat it gets. Others believe that changes on the Earth are responsible: shifts in ocean currents, movement of continental plates, and carbon dioxide in the atmosphere (Institute for Climate Studies Web site).

The skeleton of one person who lived and hunted during this time was found in 1991 in the European Alps. He had been buried in the ice for nearly 5,000 years. Nicknamed the "Iceman," scientists believed that perhaps he was caught in a blizzard or that he ran out of food, became weak, and died (Roberts, p. 38).

The writer defines her topic clearly in the focus statement.

Here the author presents factual information related to the possible causes of ice ages. The author follows this information with an internal citation to show where she got her fact.

The "Iceman" is uncovered.

Works Cited

"Ice Ages: Causes." Institute for Climate Studies. November 10, 2007. <http://www.ics.org/info/iceages/causes.html>

Roberts, David. "The Iceman." *National Geographic Magazine*. June 1993: 37–49.

Vail, Stephen. *An Icy Land*. Baltimore: Weymouth Publishing, 2006.

while reading your anchor book

Thinking About the Research Process

Final Draft: Ice Ages

1 **Analyze** Read the sentence below from the student's report. Why did the student include an internal citation?

Nicknamed the "Iceman," scientists believed that perhaps he was caught in a blizzard or that he ran out of food, became weak, and died (Roberts, p. 38).

2 **Explain** Why is it important to put quotation marks around direct quotes that you include in your paper?

Research

Now think about your own research report.

3 **Apply** Cite two of your sources and write them as they would appear in your works cited list.

4 **Evaluate** List three changes you made to your final draft. Explain how these changes resulted in a stronger final draft.

Write Answer the following question in your Reader's Journal.

5 **Analyze** Your Anchor Book might or might not cite other sources. If it does, what clues in the text might help you to know? If it does not, explain why you think the author did not cite sources. Explain.

6-14 Language Coach

Grammar and Spelling

Commas

A **comma** (,) is a punctuation mark used to separate words or groups of words. Commas signal the reader to pause. They can help prevent confusion about the meaning of a sentence.

Go Online
Learn More
Visit: PHSchool.com
Web Code: exp-6605

These examples show how to use commas to separate three or more words or phrases in a series.

Words in a Series	Snow monkeys are found in **Africa**, **India**, and **Asia.**
Phrases in a Series	Police officers **patrol the streets**, **make arrests**, and **book suspects.**

Commas help to make sentences more engaging. Compound sentences, introductory phrases and clauses, and words that name a person being addressed all use commas.

Compound Sentence	Male baboons are larger, but the females carry the young.
Direct Address	Well, Ella, have you cleaned the room?
Introductory Phrase	After all, I'm the one who knows where the key is.

Directions Revise the following paragraph by adding commas where appropriate.

You may know that beetles are insects but did you know that there are more kinds of beetles than any other kind of insect? The many kinds of beetles include fireflies ladybugs and weevils. All beetles have a few things in common: a hard exoskeleton two antennae and two compound eyes. In addition all beetles hatch from eggs and breathe through holes called spiracles.

____

____

____

____

____

____

____

Author's Craft

Writers use commas to help readers know where to pause in a sentence. Turn to the student model on page 493 and rewrite a paragraph without commas. Trade paragraphs with a partner and read your partner's paragraph aloud. Could you tell where to pause?

Semicolons and Colons

Sometimes two independent clauses are so closely connected in meaning that you can combine them into a single sentence. There is a special types of punctuation you can use to connect two related clauses.

A **semicolon** (;) connects two independent clauses that are closely related in meaning. A semicolon is also used to separate items in a series if those items contain commas.

Two Independent Clauses	Some cats have short hair; other cats have long hair.
Items in a Series	Austin, Texas; Boston, Massachusetts; and Atlanta, Georgia are all large cities.

A **colon** (:) is used after an independent clause to introduce a list of items. Colons are also used with numbers that tell the time in hours and minutes, in the salutation of business letters, and after a short command that is followed by a statement.

List of Items	The guide pointed out the following animals: a fox, a beaver, and a ram.
Time	6:10 P.M.
Salutation	Dear Mr. Ferguson:
Command	Beware: Guard dog is on duty.

Directions Follow the directions given to write a sentence.

Example: Join two independent clauses. Use (;).
I love butterscotch ice cream; I like bubble gum ice cream better.

1 List items. Use (:).

____

2 List items in a series. Use (;).

____

3 Write a command. Use (:).

____

6-15 Writer's Workshop
Research: Multimedia Presentation

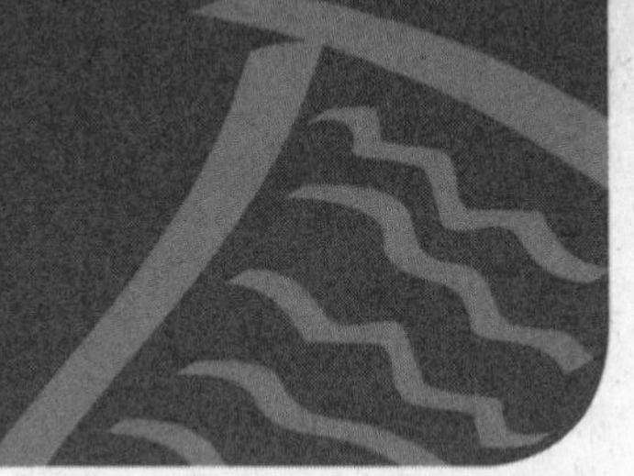

In a **multimedia presentation,** materials such as text, slides, photographs, music, video, and art are used to share information on a topic. With a partner, follow the steps outlined in this workshop to create a 15-minute multimedia presentation.

Your multimedia presentation should include the following elements.

- a topic that can be thoroughly covered in the time given
- a clear and specific focus statement
- supporting facts, details, examples, and explanations
- effective use of media elements
- error-free writing, including correct use of commas, colons, and semicolons

Purpose To create a 15-minute multimedia presentation on a topic that interests you

Audience Your teacher and your classmates

Prewriting—Plan It Out

Choose your topic. Work with your partner to answer questions, like the ones in the chart, about your interests. Then select the most interesting topic. Be sure that you can present it with various media.

Which sports do we like to play?	
What places do we want to visit?	
What period in history do we find interesting?	

Narrow your topic. A topic that is too broad will be hard to cover in the time you are given. Work with your partner to create a list of subtopics on a separate sheet of paper. Review your list and choose a subtopic you both agree on as the focus of your presentation.

Gather details. Research your topic and identify different interactive ways of presenting the information you find. Search the Internet and visit your local library for videos and audio clips of speeches or interviews, documentaries, photographs, art, and music relating to your topic. Think about your content, audience, and purpose as you make your selections.

Drafting—Get It on Paper

Make an outline. Like your research report, your presentation should have a clear focus statement supported by details and examples. Plan your presentation by creating an outline that organizes your ideas in an effective and clear way. All of the information you present should support your focus statement. End your presentation with a summary that restates your main idea and ends with a catchy phrase. Write your focus statement, two major points, and supporting details here.

Focus Statement
I. Major Point 1
A. Detail
B. Detail
C. Detail
D. Detail
II. Major Point 2
A. Detail
B. Detail
C. Detail
D. Detail

Write a script. Your script will include all your important ideas and details, plus dialogue, speeches, or quotes you want to add. Your script will also have cues that tell you when to use certain media during your presentation.

Use your outline as the basis for your script. Write each major point on one page, and include supporting details. Then, with your partner, decide who will speak at what time and who will control the media. Be sure to take turns.

Support your points with media. Once you know what you want to discuss in your presentation, think about the media you can use to enhance your presentation.

- Audio and video, such as music and interview clips, can make your most important points "pop" for your audience.
- Visual aids, such as photographs, maps, spreadsheets, drawings, slides, and charts, can help your audience better understand your presentation. Also, visual aids help to organize your information.
- Passing out handouts with interesting information can encourage your audience to get involved. You might even play a quick game to assess your audience's understanding of your topic.

Add media. Next, identify where in your presentation you can fit in the media elements you've gathered. Look for the ideas in your script that are related to the media elements and add them where they fit best. Include directions you will need to guide the media during your presentation. Take advantage of technology, such as animation or presentation software and digital or video cameras.

Student Model: Adding Media

Visual: Snow-covered mountains with an airplane flying near it.
Sound: Airplane flying
David: The picture says it all. If you have a pilot who can't read graphs or make course calculations, the plane might fly way off course.

The writers added media where appropriate and noted in the script when the media would be presented.

Revising—Make It Better

Once you have created your script and organized your presentation, use the following steps to help you revise and clarify your presentation.

1. **Revise to connect media.** Make sure that the media that you have chosen connects to the information you are presenting so your audience can follow your ideas. Review your script and locate areas where you can add more audio and visual aids to help strengthen your presentation. Are there ideas that are better illustrated through a photo or a sound effect than through a description?

Student Model: Revising to Connect Media

A word of advice: Never go to a concert where the musicians can't add the fractions of the notes to get the correct beat counts. If you do, though, you'd better have earplugs!

Sound: Music played off tempo

The writers realized that sound effects would illustrate their point better than a description could.

2 **Revise your word choice.** Read over your script while you think about your audience. Are there terms you need to define better? Is there an idea that is not explained clearly enough? Look for ways to engage your audience with vivid and detailed language.

3 **Rehearse your presentation.** Rehearse your script until you are comfortable with the presentation. Make sure you and your partner know when to speak and when to use your media. Also, be sure you can easily identify the controls on the audio and video players.

Peer Review Have a classmate read your script. Revise to achieve the reaction you had intended.

Directions Read this student presentation and use it as a model for your own.

Student Model: Writing

Go Online
Student Model
Visit: PHSchool.com
Web Code: exr-6602

David Papineau and Chris Casey, Indianapolis, IN

The Power of Numbers

Slide 1

Visual: Blank screen (blues and greens). As the presentation begins, the following words appear letter by letter:

The Power of Numbers

Sound: Typewriter

David: In this presentation, you will be shown the various uses of mathematics in a wide range of careers. You will also see some prime examples of what would happen if people did not know the fundamentals of mathematics in a real-life situation.

Math would be too broad a topic, but the writers have narrowed it to focus on how math is used in a variety of careers. Each slide will provide an example.

Slide 2
Visual: Violinist
Sound: Music played off-tempo
Chris: A word of advice: Never go to a concert where the musicians can't add the fractions of the notes to get the correct beat counts. If you do, though, you'd better have earplugs!

The writers chose to include music that is played out of rhythm to support their point.

Slide 3
Visual: Snow-covered mountaintop with an airplane flying near it.
Sound: Airplane flying
David: The picture says it all. If you have a pilot who can't read graphs or make course calculations, the plane might fly way off course.

The use of a visual emphasizes the disastrous effects of a pilot's not knowing math.

[Slides 4–10 provide examples developing the presentation's main idea.]

Slide 11
Visual: Blank screen (reds and yellows). As the presentation closes, the following words appear letter by letter: The Power of Numbers.
Sound: Explosion
Chris: So, now you've seen and heard a little bit about the power of numbers. A good grasp of math can help you in almost anything you choose to do!

Editing—Be Your Own Language Coach

Before you give your multimedia presentation, review it for language convention errors. Pay attention to correct usage of commas, colons, and semicolons.

Publishing—Share It!

When you publish a work, you produce it for a specific audience. Consider one of the following ideas to share your writing.

Present to a small audience. With a small group, take turns presenting your multimedia reports and offering feedback.

Take it on the road. Contact a local library, club, or retirement community that might be interested in your presentation.

Reflecting on Your Writing

1 **Respond** On a separate sheet of paper, answer the following questions and hand them in with your final draft. What new things did you learn about your topic after putting together this multimedia presentation? What did you do well? What do you need to work on?

2 **Rubric for Self-Assessment** Assess your presentation. For each question, circle a rating.

PLANNING

CRITERIA	RATING SCALE
IDEAS How clearly do you and your partner identify your topic?	NOT VERY — VERY 1 2 3 4 5
ORGANIZATION How well do you and your partner use a clear and logical organization?	1 2 3 4 5
VOICE Is your writing lively and engaging, drawing the audience in?	1 2 3 4 5
WORD CHOICE How appropriate is the language for your audience?	1 2 3 4 5
SENTENCE FLUENCY How varied is your sentence structure?	1 2 3 4 5
CONVENTIONS How correct is your grammar, including your use of commas, colons, and semicolons?	1 2 3 4 5

PRESENTATION

CRITERIA	RATING SCALE
VISUALS How well do you display information using graphic aids, such as posters, photographs, and illustrations?	NOT VERY — VERY 1 2 3 4 5
OTHER MEDIA How well do you use media elements, including audio and video?	1 2 3 4 5
PRESENTATION How clearly do you and your partner deliver your presentation?	1 2 3 4 5

6-16 Connecting to Your Anchor Book

Anchor Book Projects

Now that you have completed reading your Anchor Book, get creative! Choose one of the following projects.

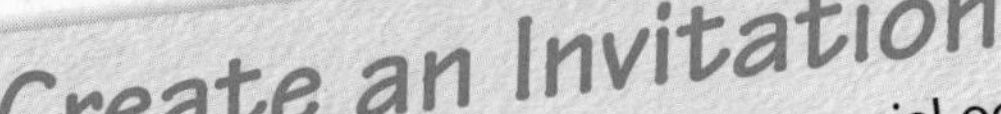

Create an Invitation

A

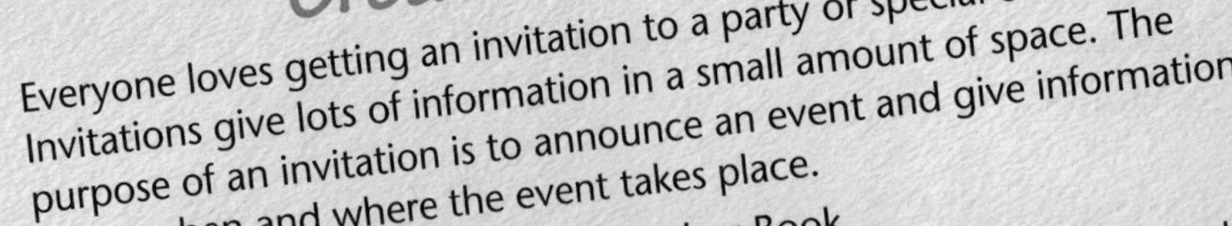

Everyone loves getting an invitation to a party or special occasion. Invitations give lots of information in a small amount of space. The purpose of an invitation is to announce an event and give information about when and where the event takes place.

1. Choose an event from your Anchor Book.
2. Design an invitation for the event on the computer or by hand. Include the date, time, location, RSVP information, and a short message about the event.
3. Share your invitation with a group. Discuss whether the invitation would make them want to come to your party.

Your invitation should include the following.

- an event from your Anchor Book
- colorful, friendly, and creative design
- information about where and when the event takes place and a detailed description of the event
- the name, phone number, and deadline for replying to the invitation

Start a Message Board

Discussing an issue is a great way to learn more about it. Some Web sites contain message boards—places where people discuss topics. One message, or post, can spark a huge debate, and there might be as many as fifty people responding to that one post!

1. Choose an issue from your Anchor Book. Describe the issue and then write your thoughts on an index card. Post your index card to a "message board" wall for your classmates to read and respond to.
2. Read other posts on the board. Respond to two of them. Write your responses on an index card and put them below the posts you're responding to.
3. Read your classmates' responses to your post. Do you agree with what they said? Why or why not? Post a response.

Your message board should include the following.

- your post that discusses an issue from your Anchor Book
- a well-thought out response to two classmates' posts
- at least one post that states whether you agree or disagree to a classmate's response to your own post and why

Play a Card Game

C

Card games are a fun way to challenge yourself and your classmates on how well you know the details of your Anchor Book.

1. Think of three questions about your Anchor Book. Write each question on one side of an index card. On the other side, write the answer.
2. Meet with classmates who have read the same Anchor Book. Have a volunteer collect the completed index cards from the students in your group. Have the volunteer shuffle the cards. Give an equal number of cards to each group member, making sure that the question on each card is facing up.
3. Take turns reading and answering each question. Group members can challenge each member's response. To check the answer, flip the card over.

Your card game should include the following.

- three questions that relate to your Anchor Book
- three responses that thoroughly answer each of your questions

Free-Choice Book Reflection

You have completed your free-choice book. Before you take your test, read the following instructions to write a brief reflection of your book.

My free-choice book is ______________________.

The author is ______________________.

1 Would you recommend this book to a friend? Why or why not?

____

____

Write Answer the following question in your Reader's Journal.

2 **Compare and Contrast** *How much should our communities shape us?* Compare and contrast how your Anchor Book and free-choice book help to answer this question. Use specific details from both books to support your answer.

after reading your anchor book

Standardized Test Practice

Answer the questions below to check your understanding of this unit's skills.

Reading Skills: Purpose for Reading

Read this selection. Then answer the questions that follow.

Hold the Hype

First, I was simply unexcited. Then my disinterest turned to annoyance. Now I'm absolutely fed up—with the buzz, the buildup, the plugs, and the promotion. I don't know about you, but I definitely don't need a cell phone that does everything but clean my bedroom. Sure, I'm all in favor of technological innovation. Solar panels and wind turbines generate environmentally-friendly electricity, and GPS chips can find lost hikers in a snowstorm. But I can't summon the same enthusiasm for how an all-in-one phone will eliminate the need for extra pockets. I'm fine with carrying my phone in one place and my music player in another. And e-mail? It can wait until I get home. So, spare me the hype. I'd rather spend my money on eliminating world hunger.

1 How do the first three sentences help you set a **purpose for reading?**

- **A.** They tell readers the passage is about a famous person.
- **B.** They let readers know they will be learning important facts.
- **C.** They indicate the author is annoyed, and make readers curious.
- **D.** They tell exactly what the topic is.

2 How does **skimming** this passage help you set a purpose for reading it?

- **F.** It helps you form an opinion about an unnamed subject.
- **G.** It gives you an idea of what the passage is about.
- **H.** It gives you facts about the topic.
- **J.** It helps you locate specific details.

Reading Skills: Cause and Effect

Read this passage. Then, answer the questions that follow.

Tori hefted her equipment bag onto her shoulder as she angrily slammed the door. "Wait!" called her little sister Jenny. "I think I put my mitt in your bag by mistake." By the time Tori had unpacked her stuff and found Jenny's glove, she was running late for tryouts. This didn't help her mood, which had already been ruined this morning by an argument with her older brother. "Who cares if you make the team?" Sam had sneered. "Softball isn't real baseball anyway." Finally, Tori arrived at the field and unzipped her bag. "Oh, no!" she exclaimed. Her bat was missing. She must have left it in her yard when she'd hurriedly repacked her things. It seemed that everything was conspiring to ruin her day. Tori shook her head. "No," she thought. "*I'm* the only one who can ruin my chance to make this team."

3 What was the original **cause** of Tori's bad mood?

A. Her sister Jenny's mitt was in her bag.

B. She was running late for tryouts.

C. She forgot to pack her bat.

D. She had an argument with her brother Sam.

4 What was the **effect** of Jenny's leaving her mitt in Tori's bag?

F. Tori's mood turned from good to bad.

G. Tori was running late for tryouts.

H. Tori decided she would let everything ruin her day.

J. Tori's brother criticized the game of softball.

Analysis: Elements of Research

A student wants to write a research report about dogs. Read this table of contents from a book the student found. Then, answer the questions that follow on page 516.

All About the Dog **by Warren Shepherd**

Contents

5 Using the table of contents on page 515, which **self-interview** question would best help you to narrow a topic on dogs?

A What is the history of the dog?

B. What are all the types of dogs?

C. Why did humans first tame dogs?

D. How many breeds of dogs are there?

6 Which of the following is a **primary source?**

F. a magazine arcticle

G. a speech

H. a textbook

J. an encyclopedia

7 Which of the following is the correct form of an **internal citation** for this book?

A *All About the Dog*, by Warren Shepherd, p. 9

B. (*All About the Dog*, by Warren Shepherd, p. 9)

C. Shepherd, p. 9

D. (Shepherd, p. 9)

8 Suppose you are writing a report on different types of sporting dogs. What kind of language would you use if your **audience** was a group of 8-year-olds? Explain.

____

____

____

____

9 Which of the following can help you **narrow** a broad research topic?

A. a first draft

B. an outline

C. a secondary source

D. a focus statement

10 What **method of organization** would you MOST likely use to write a report titled "All About Terriers and Hounds"?

F. height-and-weight

G. cause-and-effect

H. compare-and-contrast

J. chronological

Language Skills: Vocabulary

Choose the best answer.

11 What is the **synonym** for the underlined word in the following sentence?

Watching the horror movie put Kenny in a jumpy mood.

A. happy

B. watchful

C. jittery

D. restful

12 Fill in the blank with the **antonym** for the underlined word.

Don was enthusiastic about the book, but I was ________.

F. passionate

G. uninterested

H. unskilled

J. excited

Language Skills: Grammar

Choose the best answer.

13 Choose the correct revision of the following sentence.

Broccoli is not my favorite vegetable cauliflower appeals to me more.

A. Broccoli is not my favorite vegetable, cauliflower appeals to me more.

B. Broccoli is not my favorite vegetable; cauliflower appeals to me more.

C. Broccoli is not my favorite vegetable: cauliflower appeals to me more.

D. Broccoli is not my favorite, vegetable, cauliflower appeals to me more.

14 In which sentence is the **subordinate clause** underlined correctly?

F. Before she arrived, Gia bought milk.

G. Before she arrived, Gia bought milk.

H. Before she arrived, Gia bought milk.

J. Before she arrived, Gia bought milk.

15 Which of the following sentences is a **complex sentence?**

A. I love to go swimming. I go whenever I can.

B. I know how to swim, but Jenna needs lessons.

C. During the summer, I want to go swimming.

D. The ocean is my favorite place to swim.

16 Choose the sentence in which the **comma**(s) is/are placed correctly.

F. Kyle, a talented shortstop is an All Star.

G. Kyle a talented shortstop is an All Star.

H. Kyle, a talented shortstop, is an All Star.

J. Kyle, a talented, shortstop is an All Star.

English and Spanish Glossary

A

abode (TK) *n.* house or home
domicilio casa u hogar

acquired (ə kwīr′ed) *v.* gained through experience
adquirido obtenido por medio de experiencia

affect (ə fekt′) *v.* to influence
afectar influir en

all-enveloping (än′va lōp i[ng]) *adj.* enclosing completely, as if with a covering
envolvente que rodea completamente, como con una cobertura

analyze (an′ə līz′) *v.* to examine something very carefully
analizar examinar algo cuidadosamente

apply (ə plī′) *v.* to put something to practical or specific use
aplicar poner en práctica o para un uso específico

assess (ə ses′) *v.* to judge, measure
estimar juzgar, medir

assist (ə sist′) *v.* to give help or support
ayudar dar ayuda o apoyo

authorize (ô′thər īz′) *v.* to give permission for
autorizar dar permiso

B

barren (bar′ən) *adj.* lacking vegetation
baldío que carece de vegetación

beset (bē set′) *v.* to trouble persistently
acosar molestar persistentemente

bestow (bē stō′) *v.* to give
otorgar dar

brandishing (bran′ dish i[ng]) *v.* waving or shaking something in a challenging way
blandiendo moviendo o agitando algo de manera amenazante

C

candor (kan′ dər) *n.* frankness or sincerity of expression
candor franqueza o sinceridad en la expresión

captivity (kap tiv′itē) *n.* state (or condition) of being held as a prisoner
cautiverio estado de detención como un prisionero

cause (kôz) *n.* a reason or source
causa motivo o fuente

claim (klām) *v.* to state that something is true, often without evidence
afirmar establecer que algo es cierto, muchas veces sin evidencia

clarify (klar′ ə fī) *v.* to make or become clear
clarificar aclarar o esclarecer

classify (klas′ ə fī) *v.* to arrange or group according to some system
clasificar arreglar o agrupar de acuerdo a un sistema

communal (kə myōōn′ əl) *adj.* public
comunal público

compare (kəm per′) *v.* to tell how two or more people, events, ideas, or things are alike
comparar establecer cómo dos o más personas, eventos, ideas o cosas son parecidas

conclude (kən klōōd) *v.* to make a final decision
concluir tomar una decisión final

condemn (kən dem′) *v.* criticize
condenar criticar

confirm (kən fʉrm′) *v.* to prove to be true; to verify
confirmar probar la veracidad de algo; verificar

connect (kə nekt′) *v.* to bring two or more things together to make a different or new whole
conectar vincular dos o más cosas para completar o formar algo nuevo

consolation (kän′sə lā′shən) *n.* content; solace
consolación satisfacción; consuelo

contemplated (kän′təm plāt′ed) *v.* considered or pondered thoughtfully
contempló consideró o pensó atentamente

contrast (kən trast′) *v.* to tell how two or more people, events, ideas, or things are different
contrastar notar cómo dos o más personas, eventos, ideas o cosas son diferentes

contribute (kən trib′ yōōt) *v.* to give or supply to others
contribuir dar o suministrar a otros

convey (kən vā′) *v.* to communicate or make known
transmitir comunicar o hacer saber

convince (kən vins′) *v.* to bring to belief by argument or evidence
convencer hacer creer por medio de argumento o evidencia

covetousness (kuv'ət əs nes) *n.* envy; wanting what another person has
codicia envidia; el querer lo de otra persona

create (krēāt') *v.* to make, design
crear hacer, diseñar

crude (krōōd) *adj.* in an unrefined or natural state
crudo en un estado natural o sin refinar

cumbersome (kum'bər səm) *adj.* bulky
voluminoso corpulento

D

decreed (dē krēd') *v.* made into a law
decretó hizo ley

deduce (dē dōōs') *v.* to use reasoning to draw something out
deducir razonar para llegar a una conclusión

defend (dē fend') *v.* to support or maintain; justify
esquivar apoyar o mantener; justificar

define (dē fīn') *v.* to identify the meaning of something
definir identificar el significado de algo

deployed (dē ploi'd) *v.* distributed systematically or strategically
desplegó distribuyó sistemáticamente o estratégicamente

describe (di skrīb') *v.* to explain or depict
describir explicar o delinear

determine (dē tʉr' man) *v.* to decide or conclude
determinar decidir o concluir

discuss (di skus') *v.* to consider and talk about something
discutir considerar y hablar sobre un tema

distinguish (di sti[ng]' gwish) *v.* to recognize a difference in something or someone
distinguir reconocer en qué se diferencia algo o alguien

distract (di strak') *v.* to sidetrack; divert
distraer apartar; desviar

E

edgy (ej'ē) *adj.* irritable, tense
susceptible irritable, tenso

edicts (ē'dikts') *n.* commands
edictos órdenes

effect (efekt') *n.* a result or outcome
efecto resultado o consecuencia

emphasize (em' fə siz) *v.* to stress or bring out
enfatizar estresar o resaltar

establish (ə stab' lish) *v.* to show to be true by determining the facts
establecer demostrar que es cierto por medio de hechos determinantes

etching (ech' i[ng]) *n.* the technique of cutting images on glass or metal with acid
aguafuerte proceso de crear imágenes en vidrio o metal con ácido

evaluate (ē val' yōō āt') *v.* to judge, determine the worth or strength of something
evaluar juzgar, determinar el valor o la fortaleza de algo

examine (eg zam' ən) *v.* to give close or special attention
examinar prestar fija atención

explain (ek splān') *v.* to make clear or understandable
explicar aclarar o elucidar

extinction (ek stink'shən) *n.* disappearence
extinción desaparición

F

fate (fāt) *n.* something unavoidable that happens to someone
destino algo inevitable que le ocurre a alguien

fend (fend) *v.* to ward off; repel
defender ahuyentar; repeler

fortune (fôr' chən) *n.* success, prosperity
fortuna éxito, prosperidad

frantically (fran' tik lē) *adv.* in a distraught manner, as from fear or worry
frenéticamente de manera desesperada, a causa de temor o preocupación

G

generalize (jen' ər əl īz) *v.* to draw inferences or a general conclusion (from)
generalizar sacar conclusiones de manera general

grace (grās) *n.* favor, gift
gracia favor, regalo

grappling (grap'əl i[ng]) *v.* struggling
peleando luchando

H

haughtily (hôt'ēlī) *adv.* proudly, disdainfully
arrogantemente orgullosamente, despectivamente

hostile (häs'təl) *adj.* harsh, unpleasant
hostil arduo, desagradable

hovered (huv'ərd) *v.* lingered in place
merodeó rondó por un sitio

humanity (hyōō man'ə tē) *n.* human beings, mankind
humanidad seres humanos

I

identify (ī den' tə fī) *v.* to recognize as being, or to show to be the very person or thing known, described, or claimed
identificar reconocer o dar a conocer a la persona o cosa conocida, descrita o alegada

immortal (i môrt'l) *adj.* living forever
inmortal viviendo para siempre

impact (im pakt') *n.* violent contact
impacto contacto violento

incompetence (in käm'pə tənt z) *n.* inadequate ability
incompetencia habilidad deficiente

induce (in dōōs') *v.* persuade
inducir persuadir

infer (in fur') *v.* to draw conclusions based on facts
inferir sacar conclusiones basadas en hechos

influence (in' flōō əns) *v.* to cause a change in thought or action
influir en causar un cambio en pensamiento o acción

inhabitants (in hab' i tant z) *n.* permanent residents
habitantes residentes permanentes

intent (in tent') *n.* purpose
intención propósito

interpret (in tur' prət) *v.* to explain the meaning of something
interpretar explicar el significado de algo

interval (in'tər vəl) *n.* a period of time between two events
intervalo un período de tiempo entre dos eventos

investigate (in ves' tə gāt') *v.* to observe or inquire in detail
investigar observar o averiguar en detalle

L

lofty (lôf'tē) *adj.* very high
elevado bastante alto

M

macabre (mə käb'rə) *adj.* ghastly, grizzly
macabro espantoso, horroroso

monitors (män'i tərz) *v.* checks, watches, or keeps track of
monitorea chequea, vigila o rastrea

N

neutrality (nōō tral' ə tē) *n.* belonging to neither kind or side
neutralidad sin pertenecer a ningún lado o bando en específico

nonconformity (nän-kən fôrm ə tē) *n.* refusal or failure to act in accordance with accepted standards, rules, or laws
inconformidad el rechazo de o el no cumplir con los estándares aceptados, reglas o leyes

notion (nō'shen) *n.* idea
noción idea

nourishment (nur' ish mənt) *n.* something that provides nutrition
alimento algo que provee nutrición

O

offstage (ăf'stāj') *adv.* away from the area of a stage visible to the audience
entre bastidores fuera del área del escenario visible a la audiencia

P

paraphrase (par' ə frāz') *v.* to restate or reword a text or passage using different words
parafrasear expresar o redactar un texto o pasaje en otras palabras

pleasurable (plezh'ər ə bəl) *adj.* agreeable; gratifying
placentero agradable; gratificante

pompous (päm'pəs) *adj.* self-important
presuntuoso engreído

predict (prē dikt') *v.* to make a logical guess about future events
predecir hacer una conjetura sobre eventos que ocurrirán en el futuro

preview (prē′ vyōō) *v.* to look at or show beforehand
adelanto ver o mostrar de antemano

profound (prō found′) *adj.* extending to or coming from a great depth; deep
profundo proveniente de gran hondura; ondo

pumice (pum′is) *n.* an extremely porous, lightweight rock
piedra pómez roca extremadamente porosa y liviana

Q

quavered (kwā′ verd) *v.* trembled
tiritó tembló

R

rage (rāj) *n.* violent, explosive anger
furia ira explosiva, violenta

rampage (ram′ paj′) *n.* a course of violent, frenzied action or behavior
alboroto comportamiento violento o frenético

recall (ri kôl′) *v.* to remember
recordar acordarse

refer (ri fur′) *v.* to direct attention to
referir dirigir la atención hacia algo en específico

repentance (ri pen′təns) *n.* sorrow for past action
arrepentimiento pesar por una acción del pasado

represent (rep′ri zent′) *v.* to stand for or describe
representar simbolizar o describir

research (rē′surch′) *v.* to investigate carefully
buscar investigar detenidamente

respond (ri spänd′) *v.* to say or do something in reply or reaction
responder decir o hacer algo al contestar o reaccionar

restate (rē stāt′) *v.* to state again or in another way
reafirmar afirmar de nuevo o de manera distinta

retort (ri tôrt′) *n.* a quick, sharp, or witty reply
réplica una respuesta rápida, astuta o ingeniosa

review (ri vyōō′) *v.* to look at or view again
repasar mirar o ver de nuevo

revise (ri vīz′) *v.* to change something based on new ideas and information
revisar cambiar algo de acuerdo a nuevas ideas o información

rituals (rich′ōō əl) *n.* ceremonial acts
rituales actos ceremoniales

S

sanctuary (sa[ng]k′chōō er′ē) *n.* a safe place
santuario un lugar seguro

scan (skan) *v.* to look over quickly
hojear revisar rápidamente

scarcely (skers′lē) *adv.* barely
apenas escasamente

scarred (skärd) *adj.* showing a lingering sign of damage or injury
cicatrizado que demuestra una seña permanente de daño o herida

scholar (skäl′ er) *n.* person of learning
erudito persona culta

serenaded (ser′ə nād′ ed) *v.* performed a song to honor someone
dió una serenata interpretó una canción en honor de alguien

shrapnel (shrap′nəl) *n.* broken piece of an artillery shell
esquirla fragmento de artillería

shriveled (shriv′əld) *adj.* shrunken and wrinkled
marchita doencogido y arrugado

skim (skim) *v.* to read quickly, noting only important information
hojear leer apresuradamente, notando solo información importante

speculate (spek′ ya lāt′) *v.* to make an educated guess
especular conjeturar

stagnant (stag′ nənt) *adj.* not flowing or moving
estancado sin flujo o movimiento

stature (stach′ər) *n.* a person's natural height
estatura la altura natural de una persona

stealth (stelth) *n.* sneakiness
cautela manera furtiva

strained (strānd) *v.* made a great effort, force, or tension
se esforzó hizo un esfuerzo

sublimate (sub lə′ mat) *v.* to pass directly from one state to another, as from the solid to the vapor state
sublimar que pasa directamente de un estado a otro, como pasar del estado físico del sólido al vapor

submitted (səb mit′d) *v.* yielded or surrendered to the will or authority of another
sometió cedió o se rindió ante la voluntad o autoridad de otro

summarize (sum′ə riz′) *v.* to make a brief statement of the most important events in a story
resumir hacer una breve declaración de los eventos más importantes en una historia

support (sə pôrt′) *v.* to take the side of, uphold, or help; to help prove
apoyar favorecer, defender o ayudar; ayudar a probar

surged (surj d) *v.* moved suddenly, powerfully forward
surgió que se ha movido hacia delante de manera poderosa y repentina

synthesize (sin′ thə siz) *v.* put together elements to form a whole
sintetizar juntar elementos para completar algo

T

tendril (ten′ drəl) *n.* twisting stem of a climbing tree
zarcillo tallo enroscado de un árbol

tentatively (ten′tə tiv lē) *adv.* uncertainly; hesitantly
tentativamente inciertamente; dudosamente

threshold (thresh′ ōld) *n.* the point of entry, as into a structure or a new experience
umbral entrada, sea a una estructura o a una nueva experiencia

U

unbidden (un′bid″n) *adj.* not asked for
inesperado no solicitado

V

vanity case (van′tē kās) *n.* container designed for holding makeup
neceser estuche diseñado para guardar cosméticos faciales

verify (ver′ ə fī) *v.* to confirm
verificar confirmar

Index of Skills

Literary Analysis

Index of Skills

Reading Skills and Strategies

Vocabulary

Writing

Index of Skills

Grammar, Usage, Mechanics

Critical Thinking

Research Skills

Speaking, Listening, and Media Skills

Index of Features

Informational Texts

Literature Circles

Reader's Journal

Writer's Workshops

Assessment

Index of Features

Author Biographies

Author's Craft

Index of Authors and Titles

Index of Authors and Titles

W

Y

Z

Staff Credits

The people who made up *The Reader's Journey* team—representing design, editorial, education technology, manufacturing and inventory planning, market research, marketing services, planning and budgeting, product planning, production services, project office, publishing processes, the business office, and rights and permissions—are listed below. Boldface type denotes the core team members.

Rosalyn Arcilla, **Daniel Bairos,** Suzanne Biron, **Elizabeth Comeau,** Mark Cirillo, Jason Cuoco, Harold Delmonte, Kerry Dunn, **Leslie Feierstone Barna, Shelby Gragg,** Meredith Glassman, Cassandra Heliczer, **Rebecca Higgins,** Sharon Inglis, **Linda Johnson, Angela Kral,** Monisha Kumar, **Margaret LaRaia, Ellen Levinger, Cynthia Levinson, Cheryl Mahan, Elise Miley,** Linda Punskovsky, **Tracey Randinelli,** John Rosta, **Bryan Salacki,** Laura Smyth, Ana Sofia Villaveces, **Heather Wright**

Additional Credits

Editorial: Chrysalis Publishing Group, Inc.
Page layout, photo research, art acquisition, production: AARTPACK, Inc.

Text Credits

Ricardo E. Alegria
"The Three Wishes" by Ricardo E. Alegría from *The Three Wishes: A Collection of Puerto Rican Folktales.* Copyright © 1969 by Ricardo E. Alegría. Reprinted by permission of Ricardo E. Alegria.

Atheneum Books for Young Readers, an imprint of Simon & Schuster Children's Publishing Division
"Bunnicula" by Deborah and James Howe from *Bunnicula: A Rabbit-Tale of Mystery.* Reprinted with the permission of Atheneum Books for Young Readers, an imprint of Simon & Schuster Children's Publishing Division. Copyright © 1979 by James Howe.

Estate of Toni Cade Bambara
"Geraldine Moore the Poet" by Toni Cade Bambara from *Geraldine Moore the Poet.* Copyright © 1970, 1978, 1980 & 1981.

Bilingual Press/ Editorial Bilingue
"The Sand Castle" by Alma Luz Villanueva from *Weeping Woman: La Llorona and Other Stories.* Copyright © Bilingual Press/Editorial Bilingue from Bilingual Review, 1994 (Arizona State University, Tempe, AZ). Copyright © 1994 by Alma Luz Villanueva.

Boyds Mills Press
"The Case of the Monkeys that Fell From the Trees" from *The Case of the Monkeys That Fell from the Trees and Other Mysteries in Tropical Nature* by Susan E. Quinlan. Reprinted with the permission of Boyd Mills Press, Inc. Text copyright © 2003 by Susan E. Quinlan.

Candlewick Press
"What Do Fish Have to Do With Anything?" from *What Do Fish Have to Do With Anything?* by Avi, Copyright © 1997 by Avi.

ComplyRight
"Application for Employment" Copyright © 2007 by EDI. Reprint with permission, 2007 by EDI, Sunrise, FL (800) 999-9111.

Dorling Kindersley Limited, London
"The Roswell Incident" text from *Invaders From Outer Space: Real-Life Stories of UFOs* by Philip Brooks (Dorling Kindersley 1999). Text copyright © 1999 Phillip Brooks. Copyright © 1999 by Dorling Kindersley Limited, London.

Tamara Eberlein
"Question of Popularity" by Tamara Eberlein from Family Life, August 2001.

Samuel French, Inc.
From "The Phantom Tollbooth, Scene ii" by Susan Nanus and Norton Juster from *The Phantom Tollbooth.* Copyright © 1977 by Susan Nanus and Norton Juster. All rights reserved. CAUTION: Professionals and amateurs are hereby warned that "The Phantom Tollbooth," being fully protected under the copyright laws of the United States of America, the British Commonwealth countries, including Canada, and the other countries of the Copyright Union, is subject to royalty. All rights, including professional, amateur, motion picture, recitation, lecturing, public reading, radio, television and cable broadcasting, and the rights of translation into foreign languages, are strictly reserved. In its present form the play is dedicated to the reading public only. The amateur live performance rights are controlled exclusively by Samuel French, Inc. Any inquiry regarding the availability of performance rights, or the purchase of individual copies of the authorized acting edition, must be directed to Samuel French, Inc., 45 West 25th Street, NY NY 10010 with other locations in Hollywood and Toronto, Canada.

Greenwood Publishing Group
"Blanca Flor" by Angel Vigil from *Teatro! Hispanic Plays for Young People.* Copyright © 1996 by Teacher Ideas Press. Reproduced with permission of Greenwood Publishing Group, Inc., Westport, CT.

Grosset & Dunlap, Inc.
"Who Am I" by Felice Holman from *At the Top of My Voice and Other Poems.*

Acknowledgments

Harcourt, Inc.
"Born Worker" by Gary Soto from *Petty Crimes,* Copyright © 1998 by Gary Soto, reprinted by permission of Harcourt, Inc. "La Bamba" from *Baseball in April and Other Stories* by Gary Soto. Copyright © 1990 by Gary Soto. From *Tangerine* by Edward Bloor, Copyright © 1997 by Edward Bloor. All rights reserved.

HarperCollins Publishers, Inc.
"The Talking Skull" by Donna L. Washington from *A Pride of African Tales.* Copyright © 2004 by Donna Washington. Used by permission of HarperCollins Publishers.

Harper's Magazine
"Preserving a Great American Symbol" by Richard Durbin from *Harper's Magazine, October 1989* p.32. Copyright © 1989 by Harper's Magazine. All rights reserved. Reproduced from the October issue by special permission.

Houghton Mifflin Company, Inc.
"Blackberry Eating" by Galway Kinnell from *Mortal Acts, Mortal Words.* Copyright © 1980 by Galway Kinnell. "Ghost Crab" by Rachel Carson from *The Edge of the Sea.* Copyright © 1955 by Rachel L. Carson, renewed 1983 by Roger Christie. "The Origin of the Seasons" from *Greek Myths* by Olivia Coolidge. Copyright © 1949, and renewed 1977 by Olivia E. Coolidge. Reprinted by permission of Houghton Mifflin Company. All rights reserved.

Japan Publications
"Temple bells die out" by Matsuo Basho; and "Dragonfly catcher" and "Bearing no flowers" by Chiyojo, reprinted by permission from *One Hundred Famous Haiku* by Daniel C. Buchanan, Copyright © 1973 by Japan Publications.

Dr. Francisco Jiménez
"The Circuit" by Francisco Jiménez from *America Street: A Multicultural Anthology of Stories.* Copyright © 1993 by Anne Mazer. Reprinted with permission of the author Francisco Jiménez.

Alfred A. Knopf, an imprint of Random House Children's Books, a division of Random House, Inc.
"April Rain Song" from *The Collected Poems of Langston Hughes* by Langston Hughes, edited by Arnold Rampersad with David Roessel, Associate Editor, copyright © 1994 by The Estate of Langston Hughes. From *Stargirl* by Jerry Spinelli, copyright © 2000 by Jerry Spinelli. Jacket art © 2000 by Alfred Knopf. Used by permission of Alfred A. Knopf, an imprint of Random House Children's Books, a division of Random House, Inc.

Lanker Inc.
"I Was Not Alone: An Interview with Rosa Parks" by Brian Lanker from *I Dream A World: Portraits of Black Women Who Changed America.* Copyright © 1998 by Brian Lanker. Reprinted by permission.

Naomi Long Madgett
"Life" by Naomi Long Madgett from *One and the Many,* copyright © 1956; *Remembrances of Spring: Collected Early Poems,* copyright © 1993. Used by permission.

Margaret K. McElderry Books, an imprint of Simon & Schuster Children's Publishing Division
"Face It," reprinted with the permission of Margaret K. McElderry Books, an imprint of Simon & Schuster Children's Publishing Division from *A Suitcase of Seaweed and Other Poems* by Janet S. Wong. Copyright © 1996 Janet S. Wong.

Marshall Cavendish/Benchmark Books
"If You Lived In Samurai Japan" by Virginia Schomp reprinted from *Japan in the Days of the Samurai* by Virginia Schoma with permission of Marshall Cavendish.

Eve Merriam
"Simile: Willow and Gingko" by Eve Merriam from *A Sky Full of Poems.* Copyright © 1964, 1970, 1973, 1986 by Eve Merriam. All rights reserved. Used by permission of Marian Reiner.

National Geographic / NationalGeographic.com
"Ice Dogs Explorer on Siberia-to-U.S. Dogsled Attempt" by Brian Handwerk from *National Geographic News http://news.nationalgeographic.com/news/2003/11/1106_031107_icedogs.html.* Copyright © 2003 National Geographic Society. "Naming Tropical Storms" by Whitney Dangerfield from *National Geographic, October 2005.* Copyright © 2005 National Geographic Society "Showdown at Victoria Falls" by Karen E. Lange from *National Geographic, January 2007.* Copyright © 2007 National Geographic Society. "Space Trash and Treasure" by Michael Klesius from *National Geographic, January 2007.* Copyright © 2007 National Geographic Society. "Why We Must Go Back to the Moon" by Harrison H. Schmitt from *National Geographic, July 2004.* Copyright © 2004 National Geographic Society. Used by permission.

Naomi Shihab Nye
"Daily" by Naomi Shihab Nye from *Hugging the Jukebox.* Copyright © 1982 by Naomi Shihab Nye All rights reserved. By permission of the author, 2004.

Diana Nightingale
"Sparky" by Earl Nightingale from *Earl Nightingale's Greatest Discovery.* Copyright © 1987 by Earl C. Nightingale. Reprinted with permission of his widow, Diana Nightingale.

W.W. Norton & Company, Inc.
"The First Book" from *On the Bus With Rosa Parks* by Rita Dove. Copyright © 1999 by Rita Rove. Used by permission of W.W. Norton & Company.

Oxford University Press, Inc.
From "The Snake Chief" from *Tales from Africa* retold by Kathleen Arnott (OUP, 2000), copyright © Kathleen Arnott 1962, used by permission of Oxford University Press.

Pearson Education Inc.
"Antelopes" by Nila Banton Smith from *Be a Better Reader Eighth Edition A.* "The Alien Invaders", "Conflict Between the North and South", "Skill: Reading a Recipe", "The Titanic", and "Wiping Out Yellow Fever" by Nila Banton Smith from *Be a Better Reader Eighth Edition B.* "Remember the Maine" by Nila Banton Smith from Be a *Better Reader Eighth Edition C.* "Main Idea–Stated or Unstated: The War of the Worlds", "Using a Table of Contents", and "The Bedoin and the Masai: Herders of Animals" by Nila Banton Smith from *Be a Better Reader Eighth Edition D.* Copyright © 2003 by Pearson Education, Inc. or its affiliates. "Environmental Issues" by Staff from *PH Science Explorer: Environmental Science.* Copyright © 2005 by Pearson Education, Inc., or its affiliates. All rights reserved. "Keeping It Quiet" by Staff from *PH Science Explorer: Sound and Light.* From Prentice Hall Science Explorer Sound and Light. Copyright © 2005 by Pearson Education, Inc., or its affiliates. Used by permission. All rights reserved.

PFD Literary Agency
"One" by James Berry from *When I Dance.* (Copyright © James Berry, 1990) is reproduced by permission of PFD (www.pfd.co.uk) on behalf of James Berry.

G.P. Putnam's Sons
"How I Got My Name" from *Locomotion* by Jacqueline Woodson, copyright © 2003 by Jacqueline Woodson. Used by permission of G.P. Putnam's Sons, A Division of Penguin Young Readers Group, a member of Penguin Group (USA) Inc., 345 Hudson Street, New York, NY 10014. All rights reserved.

Random House, Inc.
From "The Diary of Anne Frank"(PLAY) by Frances Goodrich and Albert Hackett from *The Diary of Anne Frank.* Copyright © 1956 by Albert Hackett, Frances Goodrich Hackett and Otto Frank. CAUTION: Professionals and amateurs are hereby warned that *The Diary of Anne Frank,* being fully protected under the copyright laws of the United States of America, the British Empire, including the Dominion of Canada, and all other countries of the Universal Copyright and Berne Conventions, are subject to royalty. All rights, including professional, amateur, motion picture, recitation, lecturing, public reading, radio and television broadcasting, and the rights of translation into foreign languages, are strictly reserved. Particular emphasis is laid on the question of readings, permission for which must be secured in writing. All inquiries for *The Diary of Anne Frank* should be addressed to Random House, Inc., 1745 Broadway, New York, NY 10019. "Why Leaves Turn Color in the Fall" from *A Natural History Of The Senses* by Diane Ackerman. Copyright © 1990 by Diane Ackerman. From "You're a Good Man Charlie Brown" by Clark Gesner, copyright © 1967 by Clark Gesner. Copyright © 1965, 1966, 1967 by Jeremy Music, Inc. Used by permission of Random House, Inc.

Scholastic Inc.
From "Hiroshima" by Laurence Yep from *Hiroshima: A Novella* by Laurence Yep. Copyright © 1995 by Laurence Yep. From "Madame C.J. Walker" by James Haskins from *One More River to Cross: The Stories of Twelve Black Americans* by Jim Haskins. Copyright © 1992 by James Haskins. Reprinted by permission of Scholastic, Inc.

Scholastic Press, a division of Scholastic, Inc.
From "Esperanza Rising" by Pam Munoz Ryan. Published by Scholastic Press, a division of Scholastic, Inc. Copyright © 2000 by Pam Munoz Ryan. Reprinted by permission.

Neil Simon & Albert I. Da Silva
From "The Governess" by Neil Simon from *The Collected Plays of Neil Simon, Volume 2.* Caution: Professionals and amateurs are hereby warned that THE GOVERNESS, being fully protected under the copyright laws of the United States of America, The British Empire, including the Dominion of Canada, and all other countries of the universal copyright and Berne Conventions, are subject to royalty. All rights, including professional, amateur, motion picture, recitation, lecturing, public reading, radio and television broadcasting, and the rights of translation into foreign languages, are strictly reserved. Particular emphasis is laid on the question of readings, permission for which must be secured in writing. All inquiries for *The Governess* should be addressed to Neil Simon & Albert I. Da Silva, 111 N. Sepulveda Blvd., Suite 250, Manhattan Beach, CA 90266-6850.

Spoon River Poetry Press
"Cleaning the Well" by Ruffin Paul from *Lighting the Furnace Light.* Copyright © Paul Ruffin. Published by Spoon River Poetry Press. Used by permission.

Scott Treimel NY
"The Question" from *Dog & Dragons, Trees & Dreams.* Originally appeared In the Middle of the Trees. Copyright © 1959, renewed 1986 by Karla Kuskin. Used by permission of Scott Treimel NY.

University of North Texas Press
"Vulture's Flight" by Lynn Marie Cuny, from *Through Animals' Eyes: True Stories From A Wildlife Sanctuary* University of North Texas Press, 1998. Copyright © 1998 Lynn Marie Cuny. Used by permission.

University Press of New England
From "The Drive-In Movies" by Gary Soto from *A Summer Life.* Copyright © 1990 by University Press of New England, Hanover, NH. Reprinted with permission.

Acknowledgments

Viking Penguin, a division of Penguin Group (USA) Inc.
"De Huisache a Cedro: From Huisache to Cedar" from *Places Left Unfinished at the Time of Creation* by John Phillip Santos. Retitled "La Lena Buena", copyright © 1999 by John Phillip Santos. All rights reserved. From "Zlata's Diary" by Zlata Filipovic translated by Christina Pribichevich-Zoric from *Zlata's Life: A Child's Life in Sarajevo.* Translation copyright © Fixot et editions Robert Laffont, 1994. Used by permission of Viking Penguin, a division of Penguin Group (USA) Inc.

Viking Penguin, A division of Penguin Young Readers Group, a Member of Penguin Group (USA) Inc.
"To Whom It May Concern" from *Won't Know Till I Get There* by Walter Dean Myers, copyright © 1982 by Walter Dean Myers. Used by permission of Viking Penguin, A division of Penguin Young Readers Group, a Member of Penguin Group (USA) Inc. 345 Hudson Street, New York, NY 10014.

Writers & Artists Agency
From "Monsters are Due on Maple Street" by Rod Serling. Copyright © 1960 by Rod Serling; Copyright © 1988 by Carolyn Serling, Jodi Serling, and Anne Serling.

Note: Every effort has been made to locate the copyright owner of material reproduced on this component. Omissions brought to our attention will be corrected in subsequent editions.

Photo and Art Credits

Cover Design

Judith Krimski

Art Credits

Page 2: Elise Miley; **9:** Brian Zick; **11:** John Sanderson; **14:** Selçuk Demirel; **22-23:** Roy Germon; **85:** Ted Smykal; **106, 109-111, 114:** Jon Cannell; **118:** Dave Sullivan; **120-121:** Amy Wasserman; **142, 144-148, 150:** Carole Henaff; **174, 184:** Selçuk Demirel; **218:** John Sanderson; **222, 224-225, 227-228:** Christine Beauregard; **238, 240, 242:** Tomasz Walenta; **263:** Ted Smykal; **264:** Vassia Alaykova **287:** Wendy Wahman; **296, 298, 300:** Katelyn Foisey; **324-325:** Wendy Wahman; **364:** Selçuk Demirel; **367-368, 371-372, 374, 376:** Alex Williamson; **406, 408-410, 412, 414:** Micha Archer.

Photo Credits

UNIT 1

Page 4: ©Judith Collins/Alamy; **10:** (right) ©Momatluk-Eastcott/Corbis; **10:** (top left) ©Don Farrall/Getty Images; **10-11:** (bottom left) ©Goebel/zefa/Corbis; **12:** ©Worldspec/NASA/Alamy; **12:** (top) ©Kevin Schafer/zefa/Corbis; **12:** (bottom) ©Lowell Georgia/Corbis; **16:** (top) ©Gary Godby/iStockphoto; **16:** (bottom) ©Justina Sevostjanova/iStockphoto; **18:** ©photo by Warren Lehrer & Tom Wedell from the book *Brother Blue: A Narrative Portrait of Brother Blue*, a.k.a Dr. Hugh Morgan Hill by Warren Lehrer, Bay Press; **20:** ©Phil Talbot/Alamy; **21:** (right) ©Digital Art/Corbis; **21:** (bottom) ©Zimmytus; **24:** ©Photographer: Hector Mendez-Caratini, 2003. From the Smithsonian exhibition "Our Journeys/Our Stories: Portraits of Latino Achievement," sponsored by Ford Motor Company Fund; **27:** ©Food Collection/Stockfood; **28:** ©Phil Degginger/Alamy; **30:** (top) ©Tim Davis/Corbis; **30:** (middle) ©Jan Tadeusz/Alamy; **30-31:** (bottom) ©Atlantide Phototravel/Corbis; **31:** (left) ©Jake Hellbach/Fotolia; **31:** (right) ©Adrian Burke/Corbis; **32:** (top) ©Dave G. Houser/Corbis; **32:** (bottom) ©Leon Caneroi; **44:** ©Image Source/Corbis; **49:** (inset) ©Elena Kalistratova/iStockphoto; **49:** (left) ©Alice Edward; **50:** (top) ©Rykoff Collection/Corbis; **50:** (bottom) ©Bettmann/Corbis; **51:** (bottom) ©Bettmann/Corbis; **52:** (right) ©David J. & Janice L. Frent Collection/Corbis; **52:** (left) ©Corbis; **55:** ©sn4ke/shutterstock; **57:** ©Graca Victoria/Shutterstock; **57:** ©Loretta Hostettler/iStockphoto; **59:** ©Chris Rainier/Corbis; **60:** ©Reuters/Corbis; **62:** ©Antoine Gyori/Sygma/Corbis; **64:** The Face/Group Self Portrait ©Children's Movement for Creative Education (Photo displayed at the UN Exhibit AFTERSHOCKS, Artwork and memoirs by young people growing up after war and terror.); **65:** ©Brauchili David/Corbis Sygma; **66:** (inset) ©Tobias Munthe; **66:** ©Loretta Hostettler/iStockphoto; **76:** ©Eric Limon/Shutterstock.

UNIT 2

Page 88: ©PBNJ Productions/Getty Images; **90:** ©Penny Tweedie/Corbis; **93:** ©Annie Belt/Corbis; **95:** (top) ©Beverly Joubert/Getty Images; **95:** (bottom) ©Alan Crawford/iStockphoto; **95:** (left) ©Yva Momatiuk/John Eastcott/Minden Pictures; **95:** (right) ©Arthur Morris/Corbis; **96:** ©jonathan & angela/Getty Images; **98:** ©Brand X Pictures/Alamy; **100:** ©iStockphoto; **102:** ©Photodisc/Getty Images; **105:** ©Douglas Kirkland/Corbis; **113:** ©Morton Beebe/Corbis; **116:** ©used by permission of Gary Soto; **122:** Jerry Spinelli Papers, Class of 1963, Special Collections/Musselman Library, Gettysburg College.; **130:** ©Kevin Hill/iStockphoto; **135:** ©National Air and Space Museum, Smithsonian Institution (SI 95-8268); **136:** ©John Springer Collection/Corbis; **137:** (top) ©The Granger Collection, New York; **137:** (bottom) ©The Granger Collection, New York; **138:** (top) ©The Granger Collection, New York; **138:** (bottom) ©Corbis; **140:** ©Keith Johnson/iStockphoto; **141:** ©New York City Parks & Recreation; **146:** Courtesy of Veterans History Project, American Folklife Center, Library of Congress, 1980.; **152:** (left) ©Linda Bucklin/Shutterstock; **152:** (right) ©Linda Bucklin/Shutterstock; **152:** (bottom) ©Josh Gosfield/Corbis.

UNIT 3

Page 162: ©iStockphoto; **176:** ©Stockfolio/Alamy; **179:** ©Vince Mo/Fotolia; **180:** (bottom) ©Bettmann/Corbis; **180:** (top) ©Associated Press; **181:** ©Associated Press; **182:** ©Associated Press; **187:** ©David Tipling/Alamy; **188:** (left) ©Mike Grandmaison/Corbis; **188:** (right) ©Nature Display/iStockphoto; **189:** ©Wildlife Rescue & Rehabilitation, Kendalia, TX; **190:** ©Bill Schmoker; **191:** Photo by Angela Grimes. Courtesy of Wildlife Rescue & Rehabilitation, Kendalia, TX; **192:** ©Wildlife Rescue & Rehabilitation, Kendalia, TX; **195:** ©Eric O'Connell/Getty; **196:** ©Comstock disc; **198:** (left) ©Andrzej Tokarski; **198:** (right) ©Tihis/Shutterstock; **199:** (left) ©Lori Handelman/Fotolia.com; **199:** (right) ©Monika Adamczyk/Fotolia; **200:** (top) ©Yu-Feng Chan/Fotolia; **200:** (bottom) ©Toshi Hatsuki; **210:** ©Cappi Thompson/Fotolia; **215:** ©Jason Hosking/Getty Images; **216-217:** ©Hoa Qui/Jupiterimages; **217:** (top) ©Benedict Allen; **218:** ©Steve Watkins/Vividplanet; **220:** ©Izabela Habur/iStockphoto; **221:** ©Yong Hian Lim/iStockphoto; **226:** ©Bettmann/Corbis; **231:** ©Christian Pound/iStockphoto; **232:** ©Joseph Sohm/Visions of America/Corbis; **233:** ©Hillerich & Bradsby; **234:** ©Matthew Cavanaugh/epa/Corbis; **237:** ©Jurate Lasiene/iStockphoto; **244:** (bottom) ©Khz's portfolio here/Shutterstock; **244:** (inset) ©Pawel Strykowski/Shutterstock; **244:** (top) ©iStockphoto; **254:** ©BananaStock/Jupiter Images.

UNIT 4

Page 266: ©Nicole Weiss/Shutterstock; **268:** ©Inti St. Clair/Getty Images; **270:** (bottom) ©Susan Trigg/iStockphoto; **270:** (top) ©Justin Horrocks/iStockphoto; **272:** ©Silvia Otte/Getty Images; **273:** (top) ©DLILLC/Corbis; **273:** (bottom) ©Rob Jung/Juipter Images; **274:** (bottom) ©Arco Images/Alamy; **274:** (top) ©Rab Harling/Alamy; **276:** ©Roberta Casaliggi/iStockphoto; **278:** ©Gravicapa/Shutterstock; **280:** ©Dariusz Sankanski/Fotolia.com; **281:** (bottom) ©Johanna Mühlbauer/Fotolia.com; **281:** (middle) ©Larry Ye/Fotolia.com; **281:** (top) ©Designpics/Inmagine.com; **282:** (bottom) ©Theo Allofs/zefa/Corbis; **282:** (top) ©Cosi/Fotolia; **283:** ©Elena Elisseeva/Fotolia.com; **284:** Photo ©Sean Masterson/Scholastic Inc.; **288:** (top) ©Heinrich van den Berg/Getty; **289:** (bottom) National Oceanic & Atmospheric Administration; **289:** ©Purestock/Getty Images; **290:** ©Creative Archetype/iStockphoto; **292:** (bottom) ©Tad Denson/Shutterstock; **292:** (top) ©Katrina Brown/iStockphoto; **294:** ©Andrey Gvinyov/iStockphoto; **295:** ©iStockphoto; **308:** ©iStockphoto; **313:** ©Khafizov Ivan Harisovisch/Shutterstock; **314:** ©Scott Smith/Corbis; **315:** (bottom) ©Alexander Hofemann/iStockphoto; **315:** (top) ©CDC/Phil/Corbis; **315:** (middle) ©CDC/Science Source; **316:** (top) ©iStockphoto;

Photo and Art Credits

316: (bottom) ©Scott Bauer/US Department of Agriculture/Science Photo Library; **319:** ©Mike Kemp/Getty Images; **320:** ©LiquidLibrary/Jupiterimages; **321:** ©Carl De Keyzer/Magnum Photos; **322:** (bottom) ©Yurok/Shutterstock; **322:** (top) ©Yuri Arcurs/Shutterstock; **326:** ©Karl Thaller/iStockphoto; **327:** ©Lisa M. Robinson/Getty; **328:** (right) ©JG Photography/Alamy; **328:** (left) ©Sunnyfrog/Shutterstock; **330:** ©iStockphoto; **336:** ©iStockphoto; **338:** ©Philip Brittan/Alamy; **340:** ©Oleg Fedorenko/iStockphoto.

UNIT 5

Page 352: ©Jupiterimages/Brand X/Alamy; **354:** ©Associated Press; **358:** ©Bettmann/Corbis; **359:** ©Bettmann/Corbis; **360:** (left) ©Bettmann/Corbis; **360:** (right) ©Charles Rex Arbogast/Associated Press; **362:** ©Cathleen Clapper/iStockphoto; **378:** ©Gary Isaacs; **388:** ©Christopher Poliquin/Shutterstock; **389:** ©Tom Stewart/Corbis; **390:** (bottom) ©Historical Picture Archive/Corbis; **390:** (top) ©Asian Art & Archaeology, Inc./Corbis; **391:** ©The Art Archive; **392:** (left) ©Michael Masian Historic Photographs/Corbis; **392:** (right) www.histclo.com; **395:** ©Bonnie Schupp/iStockphoto; **396:** Handbook of Early Advertising Art by Clarence P. Hornung, Dover; **398:** PEANUTS ©United Feature Syndicate, Inc.; **401:** (top) ©Hulton Archive/Handout/Getty Images; **401:** (bottom) ©Hulton Archive/Handout/Getty Images; **402:** PEANUTS ©United Feature Syndicate, Inc.; **405:** (top) ©Marguerite Voisey; **405:** (bottom) ©iStockphoto; **416:** ©Robbie Jack/Corbis; **426:** ©James Steidl/iStockphoto.

UNIT 6

Page 438: ©Dirk Anschutz/Getty Images; **440:** (inset) ©Michal Rozanski/iStockphoto; **440:** ©Winston Davidian/iStockphoto; **443:** ©Jupiterimages; **446:** ©Matthew Cole/iStockphoto; **447:** ©Russell Tate/iStockphoto; **448:** ©Brian Sullivan/iStockphoto; **450:** (top) 1800 Woodcuts by Thomas Bewick and His School, Dover; **450:** (bottom) ©Christine Balderas/iStockphoto; **452:** ©Nik Wheeler/Corbis; **454:** ©Chip Simons/Getty; **456:** ©Bob Daemmrich/Photo Edit, Inc.; **458:** ©Detlev van Ravenswaay/Photo Researchers, Inc.; **459:** ©BloomImage/Corbis; **460:** ©Stockbyte/Getty Images; **461:** ©George Steinmetz/Corbis; **462:** ©James L. Stanfield; **463:** (top) ©Gavriel Jecan/Corbis; **463:** (bottom) ©DLILLC/Corbis; **464:** ©Nik Wheeler/Corbis; **466:** (left) ©Paul Kline/iStockphoto; **466:** (right) ©Serdar Yagci/iStockphoto; **479:** ©Roger Ressmeyer/Corbis; **480:** ©POPPERFOTO/Alamy; **481:** (top) ©Ralph White/Corbis; **481:** (bottom) ©Ralph White/Corbis; **482:** (left) ©Rod Catanach/Woods Hole Oceanographic Institution; **482:** (right) ©Ralph White/Corbis; **485:** ©Bettmann/Corbis; **486:** (top) ©Getty Images; **486:** (bottom) ©Getty Images; **488:** (left) ©Time & Life Pictures/Getty Images; **488:** (right) ©Time & Life Pictures/Getty Images; **490:** ©Petre Dazeley/The Image Bank/Getty; **493:** ©Richard Wainscoat/Alamy; **496:** (top) ©Arthur Morris/Corbis; **496:** (bottom) ©Alexander Potapov/iStockphoto; **498:** ©Robert Glusic/Getty Images; **500:** ©Thinkstock/Jupiterimages; **502:** ©TLC/BBC World Wide; **502:** BBC horizon programme; **510:** ©Daniel H. Bailey/Alamy.